Scottish Borders Council
Ranger Service
Harestanes
Ancrum
Jedburgh TD8 6UQ
Tel: (01835) 830281

THE BREEDING BIRDS OF SOUTH-EAST SCOTLAND

The Breeding Birds of South-east Scotland

A Tetrad Atlas 1988-1994

R.D. Murray
M. Holling
H.E.M. Dott
P. Vandome

PUBLISHED BY

THE SCOTTISH ORNITHOLOGISTS' CLUB

ATLAS WORKING GROUP

AREA ORGANISERS

M.R. Leven, *Lothian* 1988-1989
M. Holling, *Lothian* 1990-1994
R. Robertson, *Berwickshire and Roxburghshire* 1988-1990
R.D. Murray, *Tweeddale and Ettrick & Lauderdale* 1988-1990, *Borders* 1991-1994

SPECIES ACCOUNTS EDITORS

H.E.M. Dott
M. Holling
R.D. Murray

DATA MANAGEMENT AND ANALYSIS

P. Vandome

BUSINESS MANAGER

J.G. Mattocks

ILLUSTRATIONS

C. Rose (Cover)
S. Brown
B.J. Hurley
F. J. Watson

Contents

Maps in the text

Graphs in the text

Colour plates between pages 6 and 7

Foreword

THE SCOTTISH ORNITHOLOGISTS' CLUB

21 Regent Terrace, Edinburgh EH7 5BT, Scotland Telephone: 0131-556 6042

In 1976 the *Atlas of Breeding Birds in Britain and Ireland* was published by the BTO. The Scottish Ornithologists' Club worked closely with the BTO and co-ordinated much of the field-work throughout Scotland. That was followed in 1986 by the *Atlas of Wintering Birds in Britain and Ireland*, again with a significant contribution to the field-work by SOC members. In 1993, the *New Atlas of Breeding Birds in Britain and Ireland* was produced with the SOC participating as both co-organiser and co-publisher.

These National Atlases utilise the 10 Km grid which inevitably gives little in the way of detail at the regional level. Some time ago a number of English counties started using tetrads, a much finer grid of two kilometre squares, which enabled much more detailed information to be generated.

This level of detail requires an immense amount of fieldwork by a capable and well organised team of enthusiasts, often in areas rarely visited by bird watchers. The south-east of Scotland is the first area in Scotland to complete this considerable task with the support of the Lothian and Borders branches of the SOC, and we look forward in the future to other regional tetrad atlases for which work is currently underway.

Atlasing provides much pleasure to those carrying out the field-work; but the more demanding and onerous task is correlating and assembling the mass of information that is generated from the field observations and using this to produce informative maps and species accounts. The result in this case is an authoritative work showing the status of breeding birds in South-east Scotland, including, for the first time, population estimates, and how the current distributions relate to the present habitat and to past knowledge.

The SOC seeks to encourage and assist such atlases and the Club hopes that this first regional tetrad atlas will provide an inspiration for all other Scottish regions to follow. It is an excellent example of the valuable contribution that volunteers can make in providing the essential base from which all conservation work can in future be carried forward in our ever-changing environment.

Ian Darling - President

Scottish Charity No. CR 38075   VAT Reg. No. 268 9065 15

Abbreviations used in the text and appendices

the *Atlas*, this *Atlas*	The present book.
Old Atlas	Sharrock, J.T.R. 1976. *The Atlas of Breeding Birds in Britain and Ireland.* BTO, Tring.
New Atlas	Gibbons, D.W., Reid, J.B. and Chapman, R.A. 1993. *The New Atlas of Breeding Birds in Britain and Ireland: 1988-1991.* Poyser, London.
Winter Atlas	*Lack, P. 1986. The Atlas of Wintering Birds in Britain and Ireland.* Poyser, Calton.
AON, AOS	Apparently occupied nests, apparently occupied sites.
Andrews	Andrews, I.J. 1986. *The Birds of the Lothians.* SOC, Edinburgh.
BBR	Borders Bird Reports (began 1979).
BBS	Breeding Bird Survey. National annual survey organised by BTO.
B&R	Baxter, E.V. and Rintoul, L.J. 1953. *The Birds of Scotland.* Oliver and Boyd, Edinburgh. 2 vols.
BTO	British Trust for Ornithology.
BWP	Cramp, S. (ed.) 1977-94. *Handbook of the Birds of Europe, the Middle East, and North Africa. The Birds of the Western Palearctic.* Oxford University Press, Oxford. 9 vols.
Bird Reports	The local bird reports: BBR, LBR.
CBC	Common Birds Census. National annual survey organised by BTO.
EBB	Edinburgh Bird Bulletins (issued 1950 to 1957).
ENHS	Edinburgh Natural History Society journals (began 1972).
FIBR	Forth Islands Bird Reports (began 1994).
IMBOR	Isle of May Bird Observatory Reports.
JNCC	Joint Nature Conservation Committee.
LBR	Lothian Bird Reports (began 1979).
Murray	Murray, R.D. 1986. *The Birds of the Borders.* SOC, Edinburgh.
NCC	Nature Conservation Council.
NNR	National Nature Reserve
R&B	Rintoul L.J. and Baxter, E.V. 1935. *A Vertebrate Fauna of Forth.* Oliver and Boyd, Edinburgh.
RSPB	Royal Society for the Protection of Birds.
SAHSR	St. Abb's Head Seabird Reports.
SNH	Scottish Natural Heritage.
SOC	Scottish Ornithologists' Club.
Thom	Thom, V.M. 1986. *Birds in Scotland.* Poyser, Calton.
WBS	Waterways Bird Survey. National survey organised by BTO.

The most frequently referred to works with abbreviations shown in italics above are abbreviated thus in the texts.

Tetrad locations of place-names frequently referred to in text

Main hills, rivers and towns are shown on the end-paper maps.

Aberlady	NT48K,L,Q	Hule Moss	NT74E
Bass Rock	NT68D	Inchmickery	NT28A
Bavelaw/Threipmuir Reservoir	NT16R,S	Inchkeith	NT28W
Bemersyde	NT63B	Lamb	NT58I
Craigleith	NT58N	Linlithgow Loch	NT07D
Cramond Island	NT17Z	Musselburgh	NT37L
Duddingston Loch	NT27W	Portmore Loch	NT25K,Q
Eyebroughy	NT48Y	St. Abb's (Head)	NT96E
Fidra	NT58D	St. Mary's Loch	NT22L
Fruid Reservoir	NT01Z,NT11E	Talla Reservoir	NT12A,F
Gladhouse Reservoir	NT25W,35B,C	Threipmuir Reservoir/Bavelaw	NT16R,S
Harperrig Reservoir	NT06V	Tyninghame	NT67J,P,68F
Hirsel	NT84F	Whiteadder Reservoir	NT66L
Hoselaw Loch	NT83A	Yetholm Loch	NT82D,E

The Tetrad Atlas Project

The Breeding Birds of South-east Scotland is published by the Scottish Ornithologists' Club, and is sponsored by the SOC, East of Scotland Water and the Royal Society for the Protection of Birds. It has been produced by a small team of individuals on behalf of the SOC. It stands as a monument to and an advertisement for the Club, which is the Scottish body that leads the investigation and recording of birds in Scotland.

This *Atlas* reports the results of a survey of breeding birds in SE Scotland in 1988-94, SE Scotland comprising the former Lothian and Borders Regions. The geographical unit on which recording was based is the tetrad, an area 2km square, based on even-numbered kilometre grid lines in the National Grid. A fuller explanation is given under Definitions, Methodology and Fieldwork but this unit was chosen in order to give the finest detail compatible with the fieldworker resources available. There are 1,756 tetrads in SE Scotland.

In 1987, the British Trust for Ornithology's *New Atlas* project was being launched, ready for fieldwork to begin in April 1988. Fieldwork was already underway for a Scottish tetrad Atlas project, covering the Clyde recording area. At that time, inspired by that project, Ray Murray with Mike and Liz Leven began to discuss the idea of a tetrad Atlas for Lothian and Borders, to run in parallel with the BTO Atlas. Very quickly recording forms and instructions were produced and volunteers from the local branches of the SOC were recruited to go out and survey tetrads of their choice in the area. Mike co-ordinated work in Lothian, and the organisation in Borders was split between Ray and the then BTO Regional Representative, Rob Robertson. In 1989, Peter Vandome took it upon himself to begin the design of a database to store data collected for a local Atlas project, and Mark Holling moved to the area fresh from a year's experience of BTO Atlas work in England. A meeting between the five individuals later that year to discuss the computerisation of data and the future of the project ensured the long-term involvement of both Peter and Mark. Mike and Liz, however, were soon tempted abroad to work (and birdwatch) in Hong Kong, and the mantle of Lothian Organiser was handed to Mark. Harry Dott then volunteered to help out with organisation, planning and, ultimately, the writing of the book that was inevitably to be produced to document the project. Sadly, Rob Robertson met an untimely death in 1990, and Ray took on organisation for all of Borders. The core team of writers and editors thus evolved, and in 1996 the team was relieved and strengthened by the addition of Jim Mattocks who covered the business side of dealing with sponsors, printers and advertising. This allowed the authors to concentrate on the ornithology and the technical challenge of compiling texts, maps, graphs and illustrations onto one computer.

The task was mammoth. During the project time, two of the production team retired from careers, another changed jobs, three coped with moving house, and at least two had to become more computer literate, but none gave up! It is impossible to estimate the effort expended but a conservative guess would be 4,000 days across the team, excluding fieldwork. This is equivalent to nearly 11 years continuous effort by one person! It is hoped that the product justifies the work involved. We decided to attempt to emulate what must be the best tetrad atlas published in Britain, the *Tetrad Atlas of the Breeding Birds of Devon*. This fine publication has set the standard that all later atlases should strive to reach. Any similarities in style and presentation are quite deliberate! We are certainly proud of the resulting publication and the vast database of bird and habitat data now available for posterity.

The Breeding Birds of South-east Scotland provides the first record of the precise distribution of all breeding species in the region. It details where the birds and habitats are, points to any increases or declines in the bird populations, and can be used to highlight any threats to birds and their habitats. The book is therefore essential to local land-use planners, organisations concerned with agriculture, water and forestry, and all conservation organisations and researchers. It will be of informative and absorbing interest to birdwatchers, countryside enthusiasts and the public in general. Any profits the book may generate will be used, through the SOC, for local bird conservation work.

The book breaks entirely new ground. In recent decades, books on the birds of Lothian and of the Borders were produced in 1986 by Ian Andrews and Ray Murray respectively, summarising the status of birds in the two regions. A wealth of records are also published each year in the annual local bird reports. Two national surveys, organised by the BTO and SOC, have in the past mapped the distribution of all birds on a 10km x 10km square basis. Only the present survey has mapped all species at the tetrad level, a scale twenty-five times more detailed than the national atlases provide. This book interprets the mapped distributions and documents any changes by comparison with all previous information. It has not been afraid to challenge existing literature where appropriate. Population estimates for all breeding species are also provided, with details of how they are calculated included to allow comparison with future surveys and estimates.

Acknowledgements

Many people have contributed to the book in different ways. Although the editors have revised all the text and are responsible for its accuracy, a quarter of the species articles have been written by invited authors, including a number by David Kelly and Ian Poxton. All authors' names appear with their contributions. Ian Andrews wrote the major part of Additional Species Accounts, detailing breeding records not covered in Main Species Accounts. We are indebted to these people for their efforts. A large and unmeasureable part of the book's appeal is due to the artists' illustrations: Chris Rose (cover), Steven Brown, Brent Hurley and Derick Watson. In addition to our sponsors, Scottish Natural Heritage provided help with a grant towards data handling and kindly allowed us to view and compile habitat data from their complete set of aerial photographs of South-east Scotland. We would especially like to thank Chris Badenoch of SNH for this interest and encouragement. In addition, Pip Tabor of SNH scoured ornithological journals to provide a list of useful references to assist with the writing of species accounts.

The Lothian Bird Recorder, Ian Andrews, gave advice and access to the Lothian bird data base, and the Scottish Wildlife Trust allowed their local Reserves files to be searched. Local ornithologist 'stalwarts' G.L. (Gerry) Sandeman and R.W.J. (Bob) Smith helped with opinions and allowed use of their diaries of unpublished notes. The long-running series of annual Forth island bird counts is due to Bob Smith more than any one other person, from his braving the seas in a two-man canoe at the start, to the subsequent boat trips with many helpers. At a near final stage of the book Ian Andrews, Iain Gibson, John Hamilton, David Thorne and Alan Wood helped with proof-reading and checking sections of the book.

Shane Voss re-introduced Peter Vandome to the art of computer programming with great skill and patience. Alan Morton, the author of the Dmap mapping progam which was used to produce the maps, provided valuable support and encouragement. Keith Chapman and

Sylvia Laing helped at short notice in resolving the problems of using both Macintosh and PC computer systems and Alan Walker gave assistance concerning computing generally.

The staff at our printers, Burns Harris & Findlay, and especially Robert Burns, Fraser Duncan, Albert Finnegan and Bill Milne, were patient with our delays and generous with friendly advice and assistance in preparing our material. Expert proof-reading enabled us to avoid numerous errors and production of the book was handled with great efficiency.

With such a time-consuming project, our families deserve our gratitude for their forbearance during the last ten years. Thanks therefore to Lorna Cheyne, Wilma Dott, Fleur Mattocks, Oonagh McGarry and Sheila Murray who also helped in various direct ways.

The very substance of the book is of course due to the many people (over 230) who recorded the birds during the seven years. They are listed below with other sources of records, and without them this book would never have been possible. Thank you all.

Fieldworkers

It has not been possible to compile an entirely accurate list of fieldworkers as some record sheets were submitted without a name, or one difficult to read. We apologise to anyone whose name has been omitted or mis-spelt.

I. Abernethy	T. Cadwallender	A.M. Forrest	P. Hood	B.A. Martin	C. Rose
K. Adam	C. Cairney	M.M. Forsyth	I. Horn	C. Martin	E. Rose
R. Anderson	H.A. Calasca	D. Garratt	S. Horsburgh	R.K. Martin	M.B. Ross
S. W. Anderson	M. Calasca	H.J. Giegerich	B. Hurley	A. Maule	J.R.S. Ryden
I.J. Andrews	C. Cameron	P. Gill	E. Hurley	D.J. Methven	S. Sankey
J. Andrews	R. Campbell	S. Gillies	A.O. Inglis	A. Middleton	A. Scott
B. Appleyard	K. Chapman	T.J. Gillies	H. Jackson	W.E. Middleton	D. Simpson
C.O. Badenoch	K. Cherry	E.J Glass	G. Jamieson	A.D. Millar	R. Singleton
I. Bainbridge	P. Clapham	N.J. Gordon	J. Jamieson	R. Milne	F. Slack
I.P. Baird	G. Clark	P.R. Gordon	D.C. Jardine	M. Moss	A.J. Smith
J.H. Ballantyne	B. Conway	A. Graham	D. Kellett	A. Mossup	A.P. Smith
A. Barclay	B. Cowan	D.K. Graham	D.J. Kelly	M. Mowat	E.M. Smith
T. Barclay	W. Cowan	W. Graierson	A. Kerr	R.D. Murray	G.D. Smith
A. Barker	J. Craig	G.D. Grieve	H. Kerrod	C.K. Mylne	M.C. Smith
D. J. Bates	M. Craig	J.B. Halliday	L.A. Lamont	D. Napier	R.W.J. Smith
M. Bates	R.S. Craig	S. Halliday	E.R. Landells	A. O'Connor	T. Smith
W. Baxter	E.S. da Prato	D. Hamilton	B. Lennox	M. Osler	L. Souter
M. Bell	S. da Prato	F.D. Hamilton	M. Lennox	H. Ouston	E. Speak
R. Bell	G. Dalby	I.R. Hamilton	M.R. Leven	J. Palfery	P.W. Speak
J.G. Bennie	A. Davison	J. Hamilton	E. Lewis	A.J. Panter	D. Sprange
G. Bevan	C.N. Davison	M. Hamilton	M. Lindsay	D. Parkinson	J. Steele
M.J. Bickmore	T. D. Dobson	S. Hamilton	G. Linklater	G. Paterson	J. Strowger
H.B. Bird	H.E.M. Dott	H.L. Harper	M. Little	J.L. Paterson	B.E.H. Sumner
P. Black	T.W. Dougall	J.F. Harper	J.D. Lough	D. Patterson	P. Taylor
M.E. Braithwaite	K. Duffy	W.G. Harper	C. McBain	R.D. Payne	M.Thornborough
A.T. Bramhall	R. Durman	A. Hart	R. McBeath	M. Porteous	D. Thorne
A. Brown	J. Easton	T. Hartland	F. McConnell	I.R. Poxton	M. Thornton
A.W. Brown	A. Edwards	E. Hastings	S. MacDonald	G. Prest	P. Vandome
D. Brown	R.R. Elliot	S. Haugh	O.C. McGarry	C. Pringle	L.L.J. Vick
H.S. Brown	D. Ellis	T. Heard	M. McGrady	D.G. Pyatt	M. Wardhaugh
J.S. Brown	F. Evans	A. Heavisides	E.J. MacGregor	J. Randall	W. Waugh
L.M. Brown	D. Fairlamb	J. Helliwell	C.C. McGuigan	J. Rennie	J. Wilcox
W. Brown	H. Falconer	R. Helliwell	D. McInnes	A. Richards	B. Wiley
M. Bryce	W. Fawkes	E. Henderson	C. McKay	S. Riddell	M. Wills
W.J. Bryce	S. Ferguson	F. Henderson	D. McKeen	K. Rideout	J. Wilson
G. Buchanan	A. Fisher	G. Henderson	D. McKenna	J. Rielly	A. Winter
A. Buckham	J. Fisher	M. Henderson	I. Mackie	D. Ritchie	E.J. Wise
F.J. Buckland	G.J. Fitchett	M.J. Henderson	J. Maclachlan	Barry Robertson	R. Wynde
C. Buist	V.J. Flanders	K. Heron	D.A. MacLeman	Brian Robertson	
J. Busby	K. Forbes	C. Hill	B. McNulty	R. Robertson	
M. Cadwallender	P.J. Ford	M. Holling	J. Manson	C.K. Robeson	

Other Sources of Records

Bawsinch SWT Reserve hide log	*Livingston Bird Report*	St. Abb's Head NNR Log
Borders Bird Report	Lothian and Borders Raptor Study Group	Scottish Natural Heritage
British Trust for Ornithology	*Lothian Bird Report*	Scottish Ornithologists' Club
East Scotland Tern Conservation Group	Mute Swan Census 1990	Scottish Wildlife Trust
Heron Survey 1988	Nature Conservancy Council	*Southern Reporter*
Hule Moss hide log	Ring Ouzel Survey 1994	Tweed Commissioners
	Rook Survey 1994	Wildfowl and Wetlands Trust

South-east Scotland and its Habitats for Breeding Birds

Lothian and Borders occupy the most south-easterly part of Scotland, forming a major part of the border with England. This unique position gives the area the warmest and driest summer climate in Scotland. Together with a varied topography, which extends from a complex coastline along the Firth of Forth to over 800m in the Tweedsmuir Hills, these conditions have produced a diversity of habitat that allows no fewer than 157 species of bird to breed in the area.

The habitats are dominated by agriculture, ranging from arable cultivation on the rich soils of the warm lowlands that specialise in cereals to extensive stock-rearing areas with poorer soils in the more extreme climatic conditions of the hills. With a history of farming that stretches back at least 4,000 years, the natural woodland cover has long since vanished or been consigned to areas unsuited to most forms of farming and this means that SE Scotland has less than one tenth of one percent of its natural woodland cover left, one of the lowest percentages anywhere in Britain. Some retreat from the bareness of the last few hundred years has taken place, initially with the planting of policy woodlands in the ground of large estates, and later by commercial forestry, to give SE Scotland just over ten percent of woodland cover. The removal of the natural forests allowed the development of extensive areas of grass and heather moorland in the uplands, mostly heather in the northern hills and grass in the southern and western hills.

The horseshoe of hills is drained by one great system, that of the Tweed which flows eastwards into the North Sea, and a number of smaller rivers that flow northwards into the Firth of Forth. The coasts are varied, from soft muds and sands in the inner Forth, to low rocky shores and then cliffs on the outer Forth. A number of small islands lie offshore. Finally, urban environments, dominated by the conurbation of Edinburgh, but also scattered across the area in a string of small towns and villages, provide another varied habitat for the birds of SE Scotland.

Structure and Topography

The topography of SE Scotland is illustrated on the end-paper maps. The rocks that form the area were based on events that started some 500 million years ago in the Palaeozoic when the rocks that underlie northern and southern Britain were located on different continents, separated by the Iapetus Ocean. The sediments that formed at some distance from the shore in the deepest water were mostly fine muds that would gradually turn into sedimentary rock shale, and form the underlying strata of SE Scotland. These Ordovician and Silurian rocks, which are exposed in much of the western Borders, were raised up from the ocean depths by the collision of the Laurentian continent (modern North America) and proto-Europe 300-400 million years ago in the Devonian and Carboniferous. This mountain-building process, through pressure and heating, altered much of the bedrock to greywacke, a metamorphosed shale locally known as whinstone.

This collision between the continental masses not only laid down the bedrock of the area but formed many of its major features. As the Iapetus Ocean gradually closed up, arcs of volcanic islands formed offshore where oceanic crust was dragged down, producing considerable volumes of lavas. These islands were later welded onto one of the approaching continents as a belt of tough volcanic rocks and today, after erosion, form the prominent Pentland Hills.

The closure of the Iapetus Ocean produced a variety of sedimentation basins that allowed different types of rocks to form at different times. Near the continental margin, the streams that flowed from the mountainous leading edges of the continents washed progressively coarser sediments into the shallowing seas that separated them. Sands replaced muds and the Old Red Sandstones of the eastern Borders were deposited as river deltas and lake beds in the Devonian. Further offshore in the tropical seas, conditions in the Devonian and Carboniferous allowed limestone to be formed from reef communities and the skeletal remains of pelagic planktonic animals.

The Southern Upland Fault, the major demarcation between Lothian and Borders, was created during the Carboniferous, as crustal flexing produced major rifting and saw the whole of what would become the Central Lowlands sink downwards at the same time as the Highlands and the Southern Uplands were thrust upwards. This event meant that the tougher, more homogeneous, greywackes of the Borders were situated in the same level of the crust as the softer, more mixed rocks of the Central Valley. After millions of years of erosion, it was the softer sandstones and limestones of the Central Lowlands and the eastern Borders that were more easily eroded,

leaving the more resistant greywackes to form the Borders hills, divided from each other by the scarp of the Southern Upland Fault that forms such a prominent landmark along the northern edge of the Moorfoots and Lammermuirs.

In the Carboniferous the low-lying trough of the Central Lowlands and the eastern Borders was covered by a shallow equatorial sea that periodically inundated the land in response to further crustal movements. Limestones were laid down in these waters but when the land later rose these deposits were replaced with sandstones and then muds as marshy river deltas covered over the shallow marine basins. Lush rainforests grew on these deltas that later rotted under layers of mud and sand as the land sank once more. These later formed the coal and oil-shale deposits of Midlothian and West Lothian that were to be extensively mined in the 19th and 20th centuries.

As might be expected there was large-scale volcanic activity associated with this continental pile-up. Two main types of rocks and hence landscapes were produced. Large scale faulting allowed huge amounts of lava to spill out on or near the surface, building up

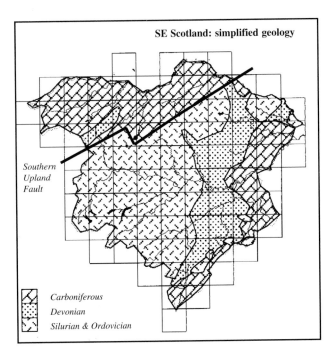

SE Scotland: simplified geology

Southern Upland Fault

Carboniferous
Devonian
Silurian & Ordovician

to form lavas of considerable depths in some areas. Today these form the large low hills that dot the landscape of Central Scotland and can be seen in the Bathgate Hills, Craiglockhart Hill in Edinburgh, the Garleton Hills in East Lothian and St. Abb's Head in Berwickshire. Where volcanoes occurred, the plugs that solidified in their vents formed, after erosion, the more localised but usually prominent hills that are best typified by Edinburgh Castle Rock, Arthur's Seat, North Berwick Law, the Bass Rock, Eildon Hills and Rubers Law.

There were few later influences on the bedrock of SE Scotland until the Tertiary period when Britain was uplifted and tilted by the collision of Africa with Europe. The eastwards tilt to the crust had a great influence on drainage patterns, with long eastward flowing rivers that would once have been tributaries of the Rhine before the flooding of the North Sea basin. Locally this formed the eastwards-facing horseshoe drainage system of the Tweed basin and what would have been a similarly shaped basin prior to the inundation of the Firth of Forth. This truncation of the Forth drainage left Lothian with a number of short northwards-flowing rivers.

The finishing touches to the landscape were produced by the Pleistocene ice sheets that generally flattened off the relief producing, through erosion, the rounded hills of much of the area. It also was responsible for the undulating lowland topography by moulding the bedrock and subglacial tills into a fluted terrain of bumps and hollows, or through the dumping of vast deposits of fluvioglacial sands and gravels as the ice sheets melted at the start of the current interglacial period. Hard resistant rocks such as the volcanic plugs were eroded to produce mostly westward-facing cliffs, while around their bases deep troughs were scoured, later to be filled with lochs and marshes.

The influence of geology on the local avifauna mostly comes indirectly through the mediation of other landscape factors such as vegetation or land-use. The geological history is responsible for the distribution of high and low ground and rock type. These in turn affect the climatic regime which then has an impact on the plant cover, both natural and man-influenced. However, geology does directly affect birds in the range and distribution of shoreline types, which is discussed later, and in the presence or absence of cliffs.

Hills and Cliffs
SE Scotland has a 'soft' geology of readily-eroded sedimentary rocks and a landscape that shows signs of intense long-term erosion. This is manifested in the erosion surfaces created as weathering gradually wore down the landscape to a flat plain. When later uplifted by the crustal movements this flat, worn landscape was attacked afresh by the forces of erosion. The remains of this ancient erosion surface are visible in the summit plateaux of the hills in SE Scotland where, between 600-800m, the hill summits form a flat featureless landscape that has been deeply dissected by the drainage system. On the readily-eroded sandstones, whinstones and shales that form these hills, erosion has created steep-sided valleys, but rarely cliffs. Many cliffs on the valleys' flanks that were created by valley glaciation have been subsequently buried by centuries of frost-shattering to form steep screes.

Based on the highest and lowest point in each tetrad, the range of altitude map shows the arrangement of steep and shallow slopes in the area. Much of the lowland is predictably flattish with less than 125m between the highest and lowest point of the tetrads. Isolated groups of tetrads mark the volcanic hills that stick up above the generally rolling landscape. The horseshoe shape of the hills of the Tweed basin is visible, as are the Pentlands, as being of mostly low gradient with 125-300m between the highest and lowest points in each tetrad. Note, however, the relatively straight scarp face along the Southern Upland Fault that marks the northern limit of the Moorfoot and Lammermuir Hills. The tetrads with the steepest slopes are

mostly confined to the highest parts of the Moorfoot and Tweedsmuir Hills where the forces of erosion have been most marked. The heavier rainfall and scouring by the last glaciers 10,000 years ago create a landscape of steep-sided valleys with occasional low crags that stick through the screes that often litter these valley sides.

Cliffs are therefore often small and rarely vertical. This has a limiting factor on the range of cliff-nesting birds, such as **Golden Eagle**, **Peregrine** and **Raven**, with some birds nesting instead in quarries, trees, large boulder screes or even on the ground where no alternatives exist.

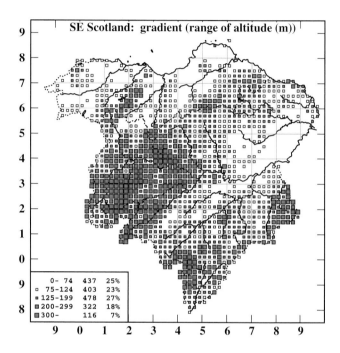

The cliff map, taken from cliff symbols on Ordnance Survey maps, shows some correspondence with the gradient map in that most cliffs are located in the steep hills. Note, however, the lack of cliffs on the flatter Lammermuirs. The highest cliffs occur along the Berwickshire coast, on some of the islands and on the steep volcanic plugs. The small cliffs scattered in low-lying areas are mostly on these volcanic crags or in quarries, especially near Edinburgh.

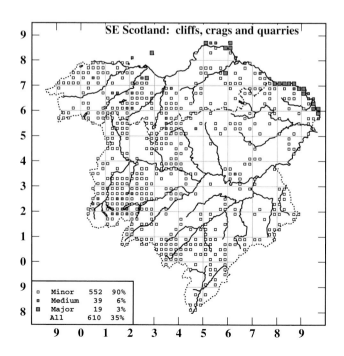

Shore

As far as birds are concerned there are primarily three types of shore that influence the distribution of breeding species: mud, sand and rock. The occurrence of these shoreline types is controlled to a great extent by the geography of erosion and deposition and a tripartite pattern has developed in SE Scotland with muds in the inner Forth west of Queensferry and in sheltered bays, sands in the middle Forth between Queensferry and Dunbar and rocks in the outer Forth, mostly east of North Berwick.

Muddy Shores

Mud is mostly deposited in sheltered bays where the tiny particles that form mud are able to settle to the seabed in the quiet water at high tide. As mud mostly originates from rivers, it is frequently found in sheltered estuaries associated with the deltaic deposits dumped at river mouths.

Muddy estuarine shores are rather uncommon in SE Scotland but can be found at the mouth of the rivers that flow into the Forth: west of the mouth of the Almond at Dalmeny; west of the mouth of the Esk at Musselburgh, in Aberlady Bay and at the mouth of the Tyne in the enclosed bay at Tyninghame. There may have been a similar area of mud west of the Water of Leith at Newhaven and Granton, but this has long since vanished through reclamation as Edinburgh expanded. The construction of locks at Leith docks has also meant that the supply of mud to this area has been substantially lost.

The only large stretch of muddy shore occurs west of the Forth Bridges between Queensferry and Blackness, where currents are slow in the sheltered inner Firth. While the distribution of mud is important for passage and wintering ducks and waders, few breeding species are affected by the distribution of mud shores. Only the **Shelduck** shows some correlation with these estuaries, there being appreciable concentrations of birds along the Blackness shore and at Dalmeny, Musselburgh, Aberlady and Tyninghame.

Sandy Shores

Sand is prevalent in more dynamic shores where currents and wave action carry away the light mud particles but deposit the larger sand grains. Like mud, sand often originates from rivers, and it is around river mouths that sand most accumulates.

Drum Sands around the mouth of the Almond extend from Hound Point to Silverknowes while the sands of Portobello and Joppa probably originated from the Water of Leith and partly from the Esk. The Esk also sends sand along the shore to Seton, Longniddry, Aberlady and Gullane where the Peffer Burn also makes contributions. The long beaches from Seacliff south to Dunbar have their origins in the Tyne. Sands are rare in Berwickshire but small beaches are present at Pease Bay, Coldingham and Eyemouth. The much larger volumes of sand deposited by the Tweed are carried away southwards at Berwick to line the shores of Northumberland and have created Holy Island.

While sand beaches offer little by way of food, they are attractive to some species as nesting habitat with feeding in the nearby estuaries. **Arctic**, **Common**, but most particularly **Little Terns**, are especially associated with sandy shores although **Ringed Plover** and **Oystercatcher** also find these areas suitable for nesting.

Rocky and Cliff Shores

In contrast to the sand and mud shores where deposition is the main agent responsible for the formation of the shoreline, erosion operates to create rocky shores. The actions of waves and currents are the main influences and it is mostly on the open shores of the outer Forth facing the North Sea that the rocky shores of SE Scotland are to be found.

These start east of the Esk at Prestonpans forming the low headlands that intersperse the mostly sandy shoreline along the coast to North Berwick. The first steep rocky shores and low cliffs occur near Tantallon but the mouth of Tyne means that much of the next section of shore is sandy. East of Dunbar, however, the supply of sand shrinks and rocks are dominant. Shores are mostly low until the Southern Upland Fault is crossed around Dunglass and the cliff section of coast begins. Other than in the small bays where a few streams make their way to the sea, the remainder of the shore is dominated by cliffs. They reach over 150m in the stretch between Fast Castle and St.Abbs and over 100m between Eyemouth and Burnmouth. The shores of the Forth islands are also mostly dominated by rocky shores or cliffs. The Bass Rock is the most precipitous, the remainder being lower with cliffs only reaching to 30m.

About 190,000 pairs of seabirds breed in the Firth of Forth (including the Fife islands). The principal mainland breeding colonies are along the high Berwickshire cliffs where about 50,000 pairs nest, mostly around St. Abb's Head. The species are, in order of abundance, **Kittiwake**, **Guillemot**, **Fulmar**, **Herring Gull**, **Razorbill**, **Shag**, **Cormorant** and **Puffin**. **Fulmars** breed along the Lothian cliffs at Tantallon and Bilsdean but some of these cliffs are too low to stop ground predators. The Forth islands (including those that are in Fife) have a different balance of species. Burrow nesting **Puffins** are predictably scarce on the mainland, most breeding on the Isle of May, Inchkeith and Craigleith. 40,000 pairs of **Gannets** nest on the Bass Rock. Other than those that breed on roofs, most **Lesser Black-backed Gulls** are island specialists.

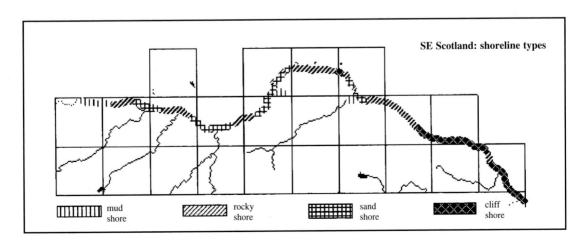

SE Scotland: shoreline types

mud shore   rocky shore   sand shore   cliff shore

Photo captions

The aerial photographs shown here are presented to display the diversity of habitats available for birds in SE Scotland. They were taken in June 1995 by members of the editorial team, Mark Holling, Harry Dott and Ray Murray. Each picture is accompanied by a four-figure grid reference to help locate the position of the aircraft, as well as the direction in which the scene is being viewed. This should help with the interpretation of the view. Captions for each picture are presented on this page and on the text page immediately following the photographs.

The Hirsel, Coldstream
Talla Reservoir

1

Ettrick Forest lochs
South Esk valley at Moorfoot
Torphichen, West Lothian

2

Philipstoun, West Lothian
Garleton Hills at Ballencrieff
The Merse at Kimmerghame

3

Cramond	Barns Ness
Gosford & Aberlady	
Aberlady & Gullane	

4

Photo 1

Top: The Hirsel from NT8329 looking S above Dunglass Wood.
The Hirsel is typical of many large estates in SE Scotland, with considerable acreages of high-quality woodland and an artificial lake constructed for amenity value. The woodland here holds several specialities: Nuthatch, Hawfinch, Marsh Tit and Willow Tit, as well as excellent numbers of Blackcaps and Garden Warblers. The Hirsel Lake is an important winter wildfowl roost and holds small numbers of breeding Pochards and Shovelers. The Lees Farm bend of the Tweed is visible in the middle distance. The river haughs between Coldstream and Kelso have large numbers of breeding Sand Martins, Mute Swans, Mallards and the majority of Scotland's Yellow Wagtails. The Cheviot (815m) is visible in the extreme distance.

Bottom: Talla Reservoir from NT0925 looking S above Tweedsmuir.
The reservoir is partly surrounded by the Tweedsmuir Forest which was planted in the 1970s and now covers considerable areas of the upper Tweed catchment. Planted before the Forestry Commission's guidelines for forest planning, the straight lines of the forest-edge and rides march across hillsides with little recognition of the terrain. The forest is at the closed-canopy stage and bird-poor. The small area of older woodland below the dam, however, holds some Wood Warblers, Redpolls and Siskins. The reservoir is steep-sided, stony and deep and holds few birds. Red-breasted Mergansers bred here in the 1980s. The summits of the Tweedsmuir Hills can be seen in the background with Broad Law (840m) to the left.

Photo 2

Top: Ettrick Forest Lochs from NT3923 looking SW above Hutlerburn Hill.
Three of the Ettrick Forest lochs, Akermoor on the left and the two Shaws Lochs to the right, until recently stood in the splendid isolation of grass and heather moor. These lochs hold nationally important populations of Wigeons as well as good numbers of other waterfowl. The spruce forests are about 30 years old and are reaching their first cycle of cropping. Excellent numbers of Crossbills and Siskins can be present. With felling in the near future species like Tree Pipit should benefit.

Middle: South Esk valley from NT3260 looking SW above Carrington.
The well-wooded valley of the South Esk holds some of the best semi-natural woodland in Lothian, the steep sides offering trees a refuge from farming activities. The water-supply reservoirs at Rosebery and Gladhouse can be seen in the middle distance with the steep scarp of the Moorfoots running along the Southern Upland Fault beyond. At 250m the farming is a mix of arable and stock-rearing farms, the fields dominated by grass. The village of Temple is visible in the middle foreground.

Bottom: Torphichen from NS9471 looking E above Couston.
The varied nature of the West Lothian landscape, with an extensive network of good hedges, scrub, small woods and hill-top plantations is readily apparent. Other features such as small lochs near Beecraigs in the distant left and marshes, as in the mineral workings at Couston in the foreground, mean this area contains some of the best species diversity in SE Scotland.

Photo 3

Top: Philipstoun from NT0678 looking S above Philipstoun House.
Unlike the other arable areas of SE Scotland, the fields in West Lothian are typically much smaller and more interrupted by small woods and shelterbelts. This appears to offer a better habitat for farmland birds. West Lothian is littered by the remains of the oil-shale industry in the form of bings, two of which can be seen. The area is crossed by the M9 motorway and by the Union Canal which runs next to the large bing but is totally hidden by a line of trees. This canal holds good numbers of Mute Swans, Coots and Moorhens.

Middle: Central East Lothian from NT4877 looking SE above Ballencrieff.
The huge fields of barley, wheat and oil seed rape are characteristic of much of East Lothian between Dunbar and Musselburgh. The farming is intensive and other than along the thin hedges, woodland is not especially common. The volcanic intrusion of the Garleton Hills, rising high above the low rolling terrain forms an island of old pasture and woodland, where soils are too thin for ploughing. Haddington is visible in the right background. This area used to be a stronghold of Corn Buntings, Tree Sparrows and other farmland passerines but the recent loss of winter stubbles and the increased use of agricultural chemicals have led to birds becoming scarce.

Bottom: The Merse from NT7852 looking SE above Gavinton.
The rolling plain of the Merse is intensively farmed with huge fields of barley, wheat, oil seed rape and silage grass stretching off to the North Sea coast in the extreme distance. Woodland is mostly confined to the grounds of large estates, the wooded policies of Kimmerghame occupying the middle distance. Bird-rich hedges are scarce, the photo showing evidence of hedges grown out into isolated trees along the main roads. The area is not especially rich for birds but does hold considerable numbers of Yellowhammers and Whitethroats. Quails and Little Owls are scarce and local here but the woods can hold Marsh Tits.

Photo 4

Top Left: Almond Estuary at NT2077 looking W above Silverknowes.
The mud and sand shores of the inner Forth were deposited in the sea from rivers. The River Almond enters the sea in the middle distance at Cramond. Most mud is deposited immediately on entering the sea, so that the muddiest area is around the mouth of the Almond and the concrete-clad sewage pipe that extends off to the right towards Cramond island (out of shot). The shores beyond the immediate river mouth are mostly sandy beaches extending to Silverknowes at the bottom of the picture and Dalmeny at the top. The Forth Bridges are visible above the low haar in the distance.

Top Right: East Lothian coast at NT7178 looking E off Barns Ness.
The mostly rocky shore of the outer Forth starts about Barns Ness and extends away to the English border. Sand shore becomes restricted to small beaches such as that below the lighthouse at Barns Ness in the foreground or at Skateraw immediately in front of Torness nuclear power station. Most of the foreshore here is a raised beach, marking former sea levels. The shoreline height steadily increases to the east, merging into the Berwickshire cliffs in the extreme distance where the Lammermuir Hills meet the sea.

Middle: East Lothian coast at NT4177 looking E above Gosford Bay.
East Lothian has a mixed coast of sandy beaches separated by small rocky headlands such as those at Ferny Ness to the right, Craigielaw Point in the middle distance and Gullane Point in the extreme distance. Further away from wave disturbance and sheltered by the sands is the muddy estuary of the Peffer Burn at Aberlady Bay in the middle distance.

Bottom: Aberlady Bay at NT4683 looking S off Gullane Point.
In addition to the sands of the outer bay and the muds of the inner bay, Aberlady Bay Nature Reserve covers an extensive area of rough grassland between the golf course to the left and the shore to the right. This is one of the few areas of semi-natural grassland remaining at low altitude in SE Scotland. These grasslands hold large populations of Meadow Pipits, Skylarks and other species of open country. Good numbers of waders breed in the saltings behind the shore or along the open beach. While there are good woodlands at Luffness to the rear of the bay, the open nature of the East Lothian cereal belt is apparent in the distance.

Photo captions

The aerial photographs shown here are presented to display the diversity of habitats available for birds in SE Scotland. They were taken in June 1995 by members of the editorial team, Mark Holling, Harry Dott and Ray Murray. Each picture is accompanied by a four-figure grid reference to help locate the position of the aircraft, as well as the direction in which the scene is being viewed. This should help with the interpretation of the view. Captions for each picture are presented on this page and on the text page immediately before the photographic plates.

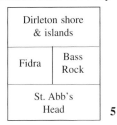

Dirleton shore & islands		
Fidra	Bass Rock	
St. Abb's Head		**5**

South Edinburgh & Pentlands
South Esk valley at Moorfoot
Moorfoots at Garvald   **6**

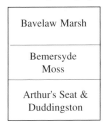

Lammermuir Hills at Cranshaws
Tweedsmuir Hills at Stanhope
Bowmont Water in Cheviot Hills   **7**

Bavelaw Marsh
Bemersyde Moss
Arthur's Seat & Duddingston   **8**

Photo 5

Top: Yellowcraigs shore at NT4786 looking E above over Gullane Bay.
The chain of islands off North Berwick is visible here. The nearest, Eyebroughy, is connected to the shore at low tide and of little importance for breeding birds. In order of distance, the islands are Fidra, Lamb, Craigleith and Bass Rock. The sandy soil of the raised beaches on the shore to the right are extensively planted with pines at Yellowcraig and Archerfield.

Middle Left: Fidra at NT5188 looking S.
The rocky island of Fidra, owned by the RSPB, was bought to protect the terns that bred there in the 1950s and 1960s. While they no longer breed the island supports a small but mixed population of seabirds. The Yellowcraig plantations dominate the mainland shore.

Middle Right: Bass Rock at NT6086 looking N.
The volcanic plug of the Bass Rock, festooned with Gannets, is a prominent beacon at the entry of the Forth. The Isle of May and Fife Ness can be seen in the extreme distance. Nearly 40,000 pairs of Gannets breed on the Bass, in addition to substantial populations of other seabirds such as Shags, Lesser Black-backed Gulls, Guillemots, Razorbills, and a few Puffins.

Bottom: St. Abb's Head at NT8971 looking SE.
The rugged deeply indented cliffs at St. Abb's Head offer safe nest-sites for some 50,000 pairs of birds which breed on the 100m cliffs. These are mostly Kittiwakes and Guillemots, but many Razorbills, Herring Gulls, Shags and Fulmars also breed as well as a few Puffins. Eyemouth, the main fishing port of SE Scotland, can be seen towards the distant left with the coast disappearing beyond towards the English border. St. Abb's Head is also a noted site for passage migrants.

Photo 6

Top: Southern Edinburgh looking SW from NT2570 above Morningside.
The open nature of suburban Edinburgh is evident with the Braid Hills to the lower left and Braidburn Park and the grassy areas around the Oxgangs housing scheme to the lower right. The margin of the city is sharply delimited by the city bypass, separating the housing from the green belt around Hillend, Swanston and Bonaly. The steep scarp of the Pentland Hills dominates the middle distance from Hillend on the left to the southern edge of the hills on the extreme top right. The water-storage reservoirs of Bonaly and Threipmuir are just visible.

Middle: Moorfoot Hills from NT2853 looking S from Gladhouse Reservoir.
The steep-sided but flat-topped Moorfoot Hills, deeply dissected by the headwaters of the South Esk, dominate this view. The hills are mostly grass and heather covered although the most distant hills around Glentress are forest-clad. Note the improved pastures extending to the foot of the slope around the 300m contour. The valley is an important site for Ring Ouzels and Wheatears while the hill summits hold Golden Plovers, Dunlins and this is one of the few sites where Twites have bred in recent years.

Bottom: Moorfoot Hills from NT3652 looking S from Garvald Farm.
The summit plateau of the Moorfoot Hills with the Dewar Water (in deep shadow) extending to the rear right and the Ladyside Burn to the rear left, both tributaries of the Gala Water. Nationally important populations of Merlins and Golden Plovers inhabit the open heathery moors with Ring Ouzels and Black Grouse in the steep-sided valleys.

Photo 7

Top: Lammermuir Hills from NT6660 looking N above Cranshaws Hill.
The low rounded Lammermuir Hills are widely managed for Red Grouse. The evidence of burning to encourage the growth of heather of different ages is evident on Cranshaws Hill. In the background The Bell oak and birch wood marks one of the few patches of semi-natural woodland that has survived on steep terrain, unsuited to other forms of agriculture. Red Grouse, Buzzards, Merlins and occasionally Hen Harriers occur on the moors. The Bell holds Redstarts, Redpolls and occasional Wood Warblers.

Middle: Tweedsmuir Hills from NT1030 looking SE above Stanhope glen.
The flat-topped plateau of the Tweedsmuir Hills is dominated by the whale-back of Broad Law (840m) in the middle left and Hart Fell (808m) on the far right. Deep, steep-sided valleys radiate in all directions carrying streams into the headwaters of the Tweed and Yarrow. The encroachment of commercial forestry is visible on the valley flanks to the right. The summit plateau holds good numbers of Golden Plovers, a few Dunlins and occasionally Dotterel. The area is a stronghold for Peregrine and Raven.

Bottom: Cheviot Hills from NT8024 looking SE above Cliftoncote.
The ridge of the Cheviot Hills, visible on the horizon, gives rise to the Bowmont Water, a north-flowing tributary of the Tweed. The open, grassy nature of the Cheviot valleys with gentle slopes is evident in the photo as are the relatively recently planted conifer plantations. While holding few rare birds, these hills hold vast numbers of Curlews, Meadow Pipits and Skylarks while the glens have good numbers of Wheatears and Whinchats.

Photo 8

Top: Bavelaw Marsh from NT1563 looking SW above Marchbank Hotel.
Despite being a part of Threipmuir water-supply reservoir, the control of water levels has allowed Bavelaw to develop as perhaps the single most important area of wetland in Lothian for breeding waterfowl. Great Crested and Little Grebes, several species of duck, Black-headed Gulls and good numbers of waders breed in and around the marsh. The adjacent SWT reserve at Red Moss, marked by the white walkway, holds large numbers of Willow Warblers in the birches and Meadow Pipits on the heather.

Middle: Bemersyde Moss from NT6032 looking NW above Clinthill.
Scoured out by Pleistocene glaciers, Bemersyde is one of the few remnants of the basin mires that occurred across Berwickshire prior to the era of agricultural 'improvements'. Bemersyde has one of the largest Black-headed Gull colonies in Britain and holds breeding Pochards, Shovelers, Teal, Tufted Ducks, Ruddy Ducks, Mallards, Coots and Moorhens. It is also an important winter roost for Greylag Geese, Goosanders and Whooper Swans. The remnant of the former eastwards extension of the moss, Whitrig Pond, is visible in the middle distance.

Bottom: Holyrood Park from NT2871 looking N above Prestonfield.
The volcanic peak of Arthur's Seat dominates the three glacially-scoured lochs of Holyrood Park in central Edinburgh. Dunsapie Loch is visible high on the hill in the middle rear while Duddingston Loch occupies the foreground. A breeding site for Greylag Geese, Mute Swans, Tufted Ducks, Mallards and sometimes Great Crested Grebes, the loch also has a Heronry in the trees and a large reed bed to the right. The scrub between the loch and golf course in the right foreground is the SWT Bawsinch reserve which has good numbers of breeding warblers, tits and other woodland birds.

Rivers and streams

The pattern of the river system is readily apparent on the map which shows all of the main channels as large and medium-sized streams forming the network that drains the area, northwards into the Forth and eastwards into the North Sea. The bar-chart shows that below 400m the proportions of the different sizes of streams is fairly constant across the altitude intervals, other than a larger number of tetrads on the flatter ground at the lowest level with no streams at all. Large rivers are predictably rare above 400m.

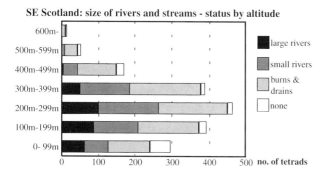

SE Scotland: size of rivers and streams - status by altitude

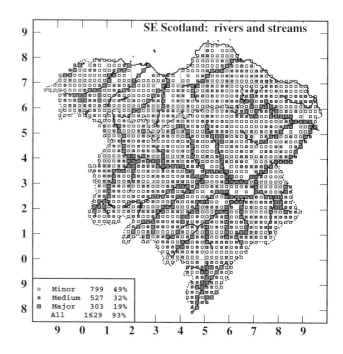

SE Scotland: rivers and streams

Minor	799	49%
Medium	527	32%
Major	303	19%
All	1629	93%

The structure of the river basin and the distribution of areas where erosion or deposition is dominant can also influence bird distributions. Species that breed along the rivers such as **Grey Wagtail** and **Dipper** prefer steeper gradients where erosion has cut narrow steep-sided valleys typically near the break of slope at the foot of the hills. **Kingfisher and Sand Martin,** which nest in sand cliffs, are much more likely to be found on the low-lying haughs where the river slows as it spreads out across the flood-plain and deposits its load of sand and gravel. **Goosanders**, on the other hand, are more catholic in their preferences and can occupy either type of river substrate, the presence of their prey probably controlling the details of their distribution.

Waterbodies and Wetlands

Lochs, ponds and marshes mostly occupy holes in the ground. As water flows downhill it has to fill these depressions before it can continue its journey to the sea, and so forms a pond or loch, depending on the size, and later a marsh if the hole becomes filled with decaying vegetation or is infilled with mud and sand deposits.

The bar-chart shows that waterbodies are uncommon in the landscape of SE Scotland with most tetrads lacking either feature and the same applies to wetlands (chart not shown). Small waters, many man-made, are most common below 300m on farmland or near human habitation. The large waters that tend to occur at higher levels between 200-400m are mostly water storage reservoirs. Wetlands are rare near sea-level where human use of the land is most intense and marshes presumably long since drained, filled in or built over. They are most widespread between 100-300m, (where 73% occur) on the flattish damp ground at the edges of the hills where they form basin mires or blanket bog.

The principal natural process by which these holes were created in SE Scotland was the scouring of the landscape by glacial erosion during the Pleistocene which created hollows large and small. The largest is undoubtedly St.Mary's Loch (NT22), part of which has been infilled by alluvial fans from streams to separate off the neighbouring Loch of the Lowes (NT21). Most lochs are smaller, typically between 50-300ha, and are most frequent in the Ettrick Forest (NT30,31,41,42,51,52&53) where there are are over 40 waters, mostly above 200m. Elsewhere large lochs are rare, the largest and most interesting being at Linlithgow (NT07D), Duddingston (NT27W), Portmore (NT25K&Q), Hule Moss (NT74E), Yetholm (NT82D&E), Hoselaw (NT83A) and Coldingham (NT86Z).

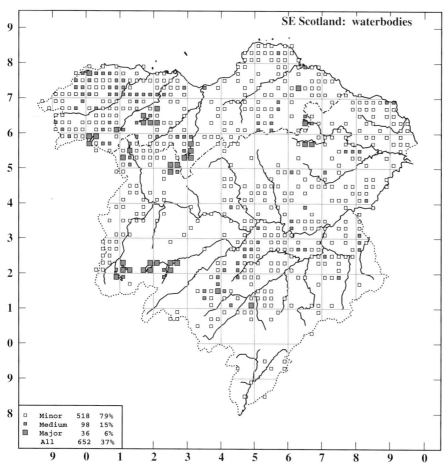

SE Scotland: waterbodies

Minor	518	79%
Medium	98	15%
Major	36	6%
All	652	37%

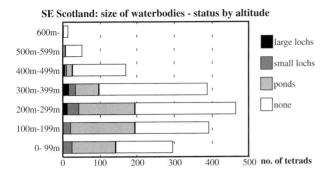

SE Scotland: size of waterbodies - status by altitude

Smaller natural ponds are not especially common as most have been infilled since the end of the glaciation to form marshes. The extension of the Ettrick Forest lochs between Galashiels, Hawick and Kelso holds a large number of these basin mires, as does the area north of the Tweed between Earlston and Greenlaw. The best of these is undoubtedly Bemersyde (NT63B&C) but this is a sad remnant of the former glories of Berwickshire which extended in a broad sweep towards the coast, and apparently once held breeding **Bittern**. Sadly most have been drained. On poorly drained flatter ground in the hills many glacially-sculpted hollows have been infilled by blanket bog, particularly in the extreme west of West Lothian (NS96) and in NT15&25 between Penicuik and West Linton. While many of these have been drained or plundered for peat, a few such as Red Moss (NT16R), Tailend Moss (NT06D) and Easter Inch Moss (NS96Y) are of ornithological interest.

Man-made waters are widespread, varying from the giant water storage reservoirs that serve our local population to the small ponds found on many farms. Farm ponds were commonplace in earlier centuries, serving as drinking water for farm animals, as curling ponds, and as a power source for farm watermills. Sadly many of these were infilled earlier this century, through dumping farm rubbish, by deliberately breaking the dams or naturally through growth of willows, coarse grasses and sedges. Having lost or destroyed these ponds, landowners to their credit are now busy creating a multitude of ponds and small lochs for amenity, shooting, recreation and conservation purposes. Many were unknown to *Atlas* workers until they were stumbled upon, not being on the most recent maps. A number of lochs were created on large estates as decorative amenity waters during the last century and those at Gosford (NT47P), Bara (NT56U), Presmennan (NT67G), the Hen Poo (NT75S) and the Hirsel (NT84F) are especially good for waterfowl.

Water storage reservoirs vary in their attractiveness for birds, depending on their altitude, depth, the nature of their substrate and the degree to which the levels fluctuate when water is drawn down. The large, deep and rocky reservoirs in the high hills such as Fruid (NT11Z), Talla (NT12A&F), Baddinsgill (NT15H&I), Alemoor East (NT31X), Watch Water (NT65N&T) and Whiteadder (NT66L) are not particularly good for breeding birds. Others, such as Cobbinshaw (NT05D,E&J), Harperrig (NT06V) West Water (NT15B), Bavelaw (NT16L&R), Gladhouse (NT25W&NT35B) and Alemoor West (NT31S) with softer substrate can hold substantial populations of ducks, waders and gulls.

Climate

Such a varied topography means there are considerable differences in the climate across the area ranging from the cold wet uplands in the west to the warm dry lowlands in the east.

Prevailing winds bring wet Atlantic air masses, unobstructed by the low relief of the Clyde and Dumfries area, directly onto the southwestern hills and deliver over 1,000mm of rain annually to most of the area south of the Tweed above 200m and the summits of the Pentlands and Moorfoots further north. The higher parts of the Tweedsmuir Hills and the western Cheviots get even more precipitation, in excess of 1,500mm (see map). In contrast the Lammermuirs are comparatively dry. These differences in the amount of rain partially explain the variation between the vegetation cover of the various hill ranges, the wetter western and southern hills being more grass-clad while the northern and eastern hills have a greater coverage of heather, a species better able to cope with drier conditions.

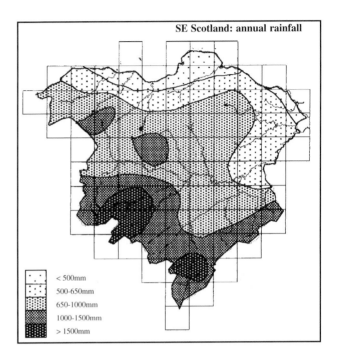

The Lothian and Berwickshire coastal lowlands and the Merse, on the lee slope of the hills under the prevailing south-westerly wind, are in the rain shadow of the western and southern hills and receive less than 650mm of rain annually. The small areas of coast between Musselburgh and Dunbar and around Eyemouth are indeed the driest parts of Scotland, with less than 500mm of rain each year. This dryness is enhanced by the föhn effect where the descending air that has passed over the western hills warms as it descends. This warming air evaporates water vapour in the clouds to cause the rain shadow. In addition, the warmth boosts evaporation rates from land and water surfaces and from plants and hence increases potential water deficits.

The pattern of temperature variation across SE Scotland faithfully reflects that of precipitation, the higher hills being the coldest areas while the dry lowlands are the warmest. Again this pattern can be seen in most climatic indicators, the high tops of the Tweedsmuir and Moorfoot Hills forming a zone of cold and wet climate; the general hill area above 300m being cool and wet; that between 100-300m fairly warm and dry; and the area below 100m warmest and dryest. Thus the first and last frosts and maximum days of snow lie along the Tweedsmuir and Moorfoot summits, while the highest numbers of sunshine hours and the greatest water deficit is most marked in pockets along the coast in East Lothian and Berwickshire.

The topography and climate therefore show a close correspondence and accordingly most species maps in the main text are accompanied with a contour map that has been selected, wherever possible, to help elucidate the environmental factors that most influence that species' range within SE Scotland. While birds are rarely directly responsive to climate or topography, their ranges are influenced by the vegetation cover, which in turn is a reflection of these factors, be it natural or changed by human usage.

Agriculture

Farming is the dominant form of land-use in SE Scotland. The nature of the particular form of agriculture in any location is controlled to a great extent by climate and soils, and given the climatic and topographical variation across the area, there can be no surprise that great differences in the form of farming can be seen across SE Scotland. The first farmers in SE Scotland probably arrived about 4,000-5,000 years ago and immediately started to modify the forested landscape through direct forest clearance for fields or indirectly through their stock animals preventing forest regeneration. The removal of woodland was probably piecemeal up to about 3,000 years ago when pollen analysis indicates a widespread removal of forest cover, doubtless in the face of population increase and newer farming techniques. The arrival of Christianity and the monasteries over 1,000 years ago accelerated the process with the establishment of a thriving wool export market and the consequent spread of sheep. While large landowners were able to grow rich on this cash crop, the majority of the area was doubtless devoted to subsistence farming until the 18th century. The arrival of new techniques, new breeds, farm machinery and the Enclosures, which together formed the Agricultural Revolution, must have changed the old patterns considerably and created the landscape we see today. The old strip fields of runrig and open common land vanished, being replaced by hedges and dykes that divided up the landscape, and the large country estates with their wooded policies made their appearance.

The broad pattern for agriculture in SE Scotland today reflects the opportunities for the growth of different crops in climates and soils best suited to their growth and the resultant development of more specialist farming than ever before. The time of subsistence farming, when a farm grew everything it needed, is well past. Farms now grow what they are best at growing and buy in what they need from other farms. The days of the mixed farm are passing. Farm units now tend to be specialists at cereals, factory-farming, market-gardening or stock-rearing. Even those that deal with stock specialise into those where stock is born and reared and those that only bring animals on, buying lambs or calves and fattening them on the cereals or fodder crops before sending them to market. As a general rule the farms above 200-300m tend to specialise in growing grass and rearing stock while cultivation, typically cereal growing, is most important below these altitudes.

Cultivated Ground

While there are clear differences between fields of root crops, cereals, and silage grass, both to the farmer and to birds that inhabit these fields, in the longer term the crops are interchangeable. Indeed one field may contain all these three crops in successive years. When the habitat analysis of the area started it was hoped that it might be possible to make a more detailed subdivision between the types of cultivated ground outlined above. However, study of the aerial photographs quickly indicated that there would be no consistent way of distinguishing between cultivated arable fields put over to cereals and fields of improved grass sown for silage and grazing. The seven years extent of fieldwork for the *Atlas* also militated against a finer gradation of arable cultivation as fields could easily pass between categories over the seven year interval.

This was also true when the birds that inhabit these fields were examined, as many farmland species are equally at home in both cultivated arable fields and fields put over to grass, some using the various fields throughout the year but more often using different fields at different times of the year. **Lapwings**, for instance, might nest in fields newly ploughed in spring but once their young hatch the parents usually move them into adjacent grass fields to feed. Other species such as **Rook**, **Grey Partridge**, **Oystercatcher** and **Yellowhammer** also utilise both types of field at various times in the year, as well as the hedges that divide them.

The map and altitude bar chart for arable and improved grassland shows it to be the principal form of land management below 300m in SE Scotland. In the analysis of the land use at tetrad level, 96% of tetrads below 200m have arable farming recorded as common or abundant, dropping only slightly to 83% between 200-300m. Only above 300m does the share of land devoted to arable farming really fall, dropping to 38% up to 400m and just 8% above 400m.

The map of arable and improved grassland in SE Scotland, shows arable land to be abundant in a broad, fairly continuous distribution across most of the low-lying ground of the area below 300m. The only notable exception is the urbanised area of Edinburgh, extending between the Firth of Forth and the Pentland Hills, where arable fields are scarce but not altogether absent. The upper limit of cultivation is generally the 300m contour but improved grasslands, rather than arable fields, occur above 300m across the passes between the northern hills in the Middleton-Soutra area (NT35&45) and in the West Linton-Leadburn area (NT14,15,24&25). In the southern and western hills, including Liddesdale, the limit of cultivation is slightly below the 300m contour and although improved grassland is

SE Scotland: arable and improved grassland

□	Scarce	198	14%
▪	Common	196	14%
■	Abundant	1006	72%
	All	1400	80%

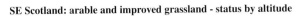

SE Scotland: arable and improved grassland - status by altitude

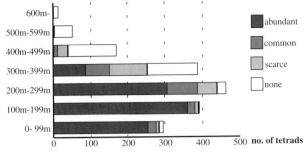

Legend:
- abundant
- common
- scarce
- none

(bar categories: 600m-, 500m-599m, 400m-499m, 300m-399m, 200m-299m, 100m-199m, 0-99m; x-axis: 0 to 500 no. of tetrads)

species, the probability of nest destruction increasing with the frequency of the operations.

While the farmland birds of much of southern Britain have been drastically affected by the intensification of farming in recent decades, the numbers of birds in the farmland of SE Scotland have generally been maintained. Some like the **Lesser Whitethroat** have been increasing of late and even **Buzzards** are moving into areas of mainly cultivated ground. However, the scarcer species such as **Tree Sparrow** and **Corn Bunting** are in trouble, particularly the latter species which is in imminent danger of becoming locally extinct.

found almost to the head of most valleys, it is usually rather scarce. An anomalous area below 300m in the SE Lammermuirs in NT65&75, which shows reduced cover of arable ground, is mostly the land around Hule Moss given over to grouse moor.

At lower levels, especially below 200m, arable cultivation is dominant. Cereals are most widely grown, barley being more important than wheat, and while oats are uncommon they have made a slight comeback in recent years. Oil seed rape is a widespread alternative to cereals. Rotations are becoming less common, weed control and nutrients being dealt with by chemical means. Where they are grown, grass crops are almost always short rotation sowings for silage, and very rarely for hay, and typically grown for fattening stock that has been reared elsewhere. Farms with the best soils often grow some market vegetables, such as potatoes, cabbage, cauliflower, carrots and leeks, especially around Edinburgh and in parts of East Lothian.

Improved grass dominates between 200-300m in stock-rearing areas. For the first two to four years after sowing, fields are usually used purely for silage during the growing season, grazing occurring only after the last cut of grass. If not immediately re-sown, the field will then be grazed for several years until weeds such as Nettle, Docks and Buttercup encroach at which point it will be weed-killed and ploughed ready for sowing.

The intensity of management of cultivated ground has increased enormously in recent decades and this is suspected to be the prime reason for the decline in the populations of some farmland birds in Britain. Cereal production is especially intensive with crops being sprayed regularly with herbicides and pesticides which remove most of the weed plants and the insects that once fed numerous hedgerow birds. Autumn sown cereals also mean a fast turnover between crops and the disappearance of winter stubble, once a major source of food for seed-eating birds which enhanced their winter survival. Stocking rates on grassland have also increased to such an extent that many fields of improved grass offer as much cover as a lawn. The almost universal use of sown grass for silage creates a grass monoculture whose lack of diversity means a total lack of food plants for invertebrates. Regular farm operations, whether ploughing, harrowing, sowing, spraying or cutting, have reduced the attractiveness of grass and cereal fields as breeding habitat for a number of

Unimproved Grassland

Unimproved grassland, or rough grazing, typically occurs in areas that are uncultivatable for a number of reasons. It is dominant at higher altitudes above 250m where climates are cold and wet, soils are thin, stony, peaty or ill-drained and the terrain too steep or too dangerous to plough. In the lowland rough grazing is scarce and often restricted to river flood plains, rocky knolls, reclaimed ground and bings. Along the coast rough grazing or permanent pasture can be common in a narrow zone on the coastal slope above cliffs and in sand dunes and coastal saltings.

The bar-chart overleaf confirms the scarcity of rough grazing below 200m, being common and abundant in less than a fifth of the tetrads. Above 200m it becomes steadily more important, being common and abundant in 70% of tetrads between 200-300m and in over 85% of tetrads above 300m. Above 500m it is absolutely dominant, rough grazing being about the only form of land-use possible at these altitudes, well above the levels that commercial forestry might be planted.

The map shows that unimproved grassland is mostly associated with the hill areas, the lower limit of where it is abundant falling at about 250m. The only significant areas of rough grazing below 200m occur in Liddesdale, along the coast at Aberlady where there

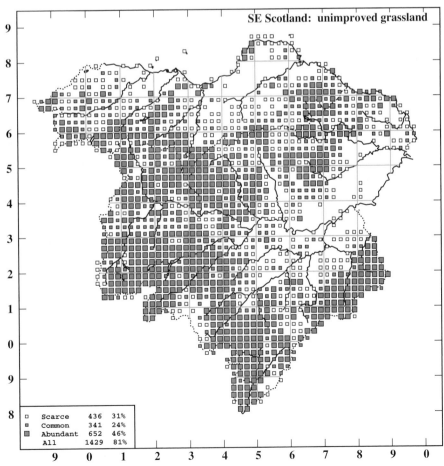

SE Scotland: unimproved grassland

□	Scarce	436	31%
▪	Common	341	24%
▣	Abundant	652	46%
	All	1429	81%

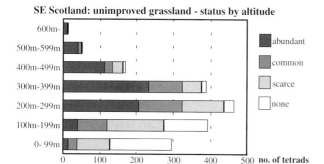

SE Scotland: unimproved grassland - status by altitude

are dunes, along the steep coastal slope above the Berwickshire cliffs, and around Edinburgh where parks at Arthur's Seat, the Braids and Craiglockhart are evident. Reclaimed or derelict ground can also be seen on the outskirts of Edinburgh at Musselburgh, the Gyle and Old Craighall. The isolated tetrads in West Lothian mark coal and oil-shale bings and other 'waste' ground.

The rough grazings of higher level farms are typically in their hill pastures, any cultivated ground mostly being silage fields for winter feed on the better ground on the valley bottoms. At lower levels, further away from the high hills, farms will be mostly silage except for fields of winter fodder, mostly turnips, kale and rape. Although barley is still grown on some farms, this crop seems to be disappearing. Sheep are the most important animal on most upland farms, cattle becoming more widespread at lower levels.

The rough grazing areas of the northern hills hold a significant community of breeding waders, with many **Curlews**, **Redshanks**, **Lapwings**, **Snipe** and **Golden Plovers**, and nationally important numbers of **Ring Ouzels** and **Black Grouse**. The commonest and most widespread of birds are undoubtedly **Meadow Pipits** and **Skylarks** but more localised populations of **Wheatears**, **Stonechats** and **Whinchats** can also be found.

Heather Moors

Heather moors can be regarded as a specialised form of farming, the principal crops being sheep and Red Grouse. Heather has a number of xerophytic adaptations and consequently grows best in drier areas where there is a greater likelihood of water deficit during part of the year. Accordingly heather moor is mostly found in the drier northern hills, especially further east in the Lammermuirs. The wetter southern and western hills, where grass grows best, are mostly sheepwalk. Large areas are still managed for grouse, being regularly burned and showing the characteristic patches of different age that demarcate extent of the burning in different years. Other moors are less well tended and are now so heavily grazed by sheep that **Red Grouse** are becoming scarce and in some cases almost extinct. Many areas of heather have also been lost to forestry in recent decades.

The bar-chart shows that heather moor is an upland habitat, mostly found above 200m. It is most widespread in SE Scotland between 300-500m, where just under half of the tetrads are rated as having a common or abundant cover of heather. Heather extends to the highest hill summits over

800m in the Tweedsmuir Hills where it occurs on the summit ridges as a short sward, closely nibbled by sheep and sculpted by the wind.

The map confirms the altitudinal distribution of heather moor, the majority of the habitat being limited to areas above the 300m contour. Five major blocks of heather are seen that match most of the areas of highest ground in SE Scotland: the Pentland, Moorfoot, Lammermuir and Tweedsmuir Hills plus the high ground at Roan Fell and Cooms Fell (NY48&49) in Liddesdale. While the Cheviots have a good cover of heather further south in Northumberland, the Scottish side is mostly grass-dominated as are the southern part of the Tweedsmuir Hills and the Ettrick Forest. Below 300m the area at Coldingham Moor (NT86) is obvious and the significant area of the eastern Lammermuirs at Hule Moss and Dirrington (NT74&75) should also be noted. These lower areas of heather moor are completely surrounded by improved ground and it is almost certain that only the whims of their owners in the past have saved them from conversion to cultivation.

These heather moors, in addition to being the stronghold of **Red Grouse**, hold a tiny population of **Hen Harriers**, a larger number of **Merlins** and are strongly associated with **Golden Plovers** above the 400m level. **Dunlins** breed on more restricted wetter areas either on summit ridges or boggy moors.

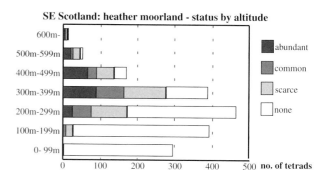

SE Scotland: heather moorland - status by altitude

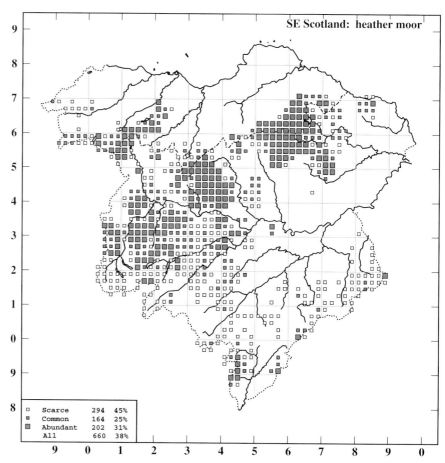

SE Scotland: heather moor

□	Scarce	294	45%
▨	Common	164	25%
■	Abundant	202	31%
	All	660	38%

Woodlands

Environmental historians assure us that in the post-glacial period, when the climate was a little warmer than it is at present, all of SE Scotland was covered with woodland. Recent findings, at sites like Rotten Bottom high in the Tweedsmuir Hills at nearly 700m (NT11M), show fragments of trees that grew *in situ* there 6,000-7,000 years ago. This climax forest was thought to be entirely deciduous, being dominated by Ash, Elm and the two oak species. Only in a few extremely dry areas, such as screes or sand dunes, might conifers such as the Scots Pine or Juniper be dominant, more moisture-demanding trees failing to flourish without the considerable drought adaptations that conifers possess.

This forest cover was steadily removed by man and his animals over the course of the last 5,000 years until little or nothing remained of the original cover. Within Britain the county of Peeblesshire is said to be the worst example of this environmental degradation, with just 0.06% of its area having what is thought to be a remnant of its original forest cover.

The nadir for woodland cover in SE Scotland was probably reached at the start of the 20th century. Wildwood had largely been removed or reduced to tiny fragments that clung to steep ground along valley sides basically unsuited to any kind of farming. These gallery woodlands survive in relatively remote or inaccessible locations such as Roslin Glen (NT26S), Crichton (NT36V), Woodhall Dean (NT67R), and in the Monynut (NT76G&L), Whiteadder (NT76Q), Jed (NT61N&P), Yarrow (NT32Z) and Rule (NT61C) oakwoods, as well as the flood-plain woods at Ettrick (NT21X).

This dire situation was partially redeemed by the wooded policies of large estates that were planted for visual amenity and for sporting interests in the 19th century. Today the estates at Dawyck (NT13S), Dalmeny (NT17P), Penicuik House (NT25E&J), Dalkeith House (NT36I&J), Bowhill (NT42D&I), Gosford (NT47P), Monteviot (NT62H), Floors Castle (NT63B), the Hirsel (NT84A&F), Duns Castle (NT75S&X) and many others, some with woodlands open to the public, are amongst the best areas of woodland in SE Scotland.

The felling of timber during the First World War, because of the blockade of shipping by the Germans, forced government to invest in forestry. The Forestry Commission started extensive plantings mostly of conifers between the wars and as commercial companies entered the market after the 1960s parts of the Borders started to be covered in unrelenting plantations of pine and spruce. The forests of the middle Tweed between Peebles and Selkirk were planted a little earlier than the massive plantings at Craik (NT30&31), Wauchope (NT50&51) and Newcastleton (NY58&59). Plantings have been more modest in recent years, with forests in the upper Tweed at Tweedsmuir (NT01&02), the Yarrow valley (NT22), Monynut and Spartleton (NT66&76) being established by commercial growers.

As the map shows, mixed and deciduous woodlands are best established in lowland areas, with concentrations along the river valleys. This is supported by the bar-chart that shows the tetrads where such woods are common and abundant are

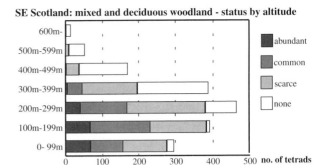

mostly found below 300m. Indeed when small woodlands are included, a substantial proportion, some 95% of all lowland tetrads, hold some mixed and deciduous woodland habitat. Above 300m this proportion falls rapidly with altitude but the presence of some deciduous woodland can be traced almost to the headwaters of each major valley in the highest hills, albeit just a scatter of Rowans or birches in the high cleughs.

The presence of abundant woodland on the map is particularly marked along the valleys of the North and South Esk (NT26&27), the Leader (NT53&54) and the Jed (NT61). Large estates are evident at Dalmeny (NT17), Portmore (NT24), Tyninghame (NT67&68) and the Hirsel (NT84) amongst many others.

These remnant semi-natural woods and wooded estate policies can hold excellent woodland bird faunas. The ranges of some woodland species, such as the **Marsh Tit** and **Nuthatch**, just extend into Scotland in the eastern Borders, and are mostly found on large estates, as is the **Hawfinch**, which although also very scarce in Scotland is a little more widespread. The old oakwoods, which are more generally distributed, often hold good numbers of **Green Woodpeckers**, **Pied Flycatchers**, **Redstarts** and **Wood Warblers.** Species preferring scrubbier woods, such as **Chiffchaff**, **Blackcap** and **Garden Warbler**, are more general still.

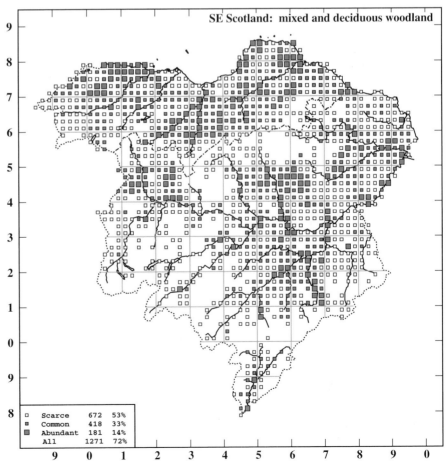

SE Scotland: mixed and deciduous woodland

□	Scarce	672	53%
▪	Common	418	33%
▨	Abundant	181	14%
	All	1271	72%

Coniferous woodland is generally planted at higher altitudes. The bar-chart shows the 200-400m level to be most important with 90% of all tetrads at these altitudes holding some coniferous forest and such woods being common and abundant in over half of them. The proportion is much lower below 100m where less than 15% of tetrads hold much conifer woodland. Plantations or shelterbelts occur at very high levels with about half of all tetrads between 500-600m showing some plantings, mostly shelterbelts. Whether such trees will ever produce worthwhile timber is to be doubted and questions should be asked concerning grant-aid for the destruction of potentially good moorland habitat in some areas for little gain.

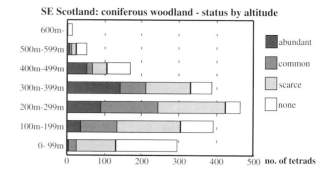

While a variety of trees were planted in earlier years such as Lodgepole Pine, Douglas Fir, Western Hemlock and Norway Spruce, modern plantations tend to be dominated by the species that grow best in SE Scotland, the Sitka Spruce, Scots Pine and hybrid Larch.

Conifers attract different suites of birds at different stages in the development of the forest. The fencing of new plantings allows a great flush of ground vegetation once grazing stops. The extra food for small herbivorous mammals, mostly voles, starts population explosions that can attract large numbers of predators, including **Short-eared Owl**, **Barn Owl**, **Hen Harrier**, **Kestrel** and **Buzzard**. The shrubby habitat can also provide suitable habitat for **Whinchat, Willow Warbler** and **Grasshopper Warbler**. As the trees get larger, their developing canopy starts to shade out the ground cover and tree specialists start to arrive to take advantage of the seed production, especially where birches manage to seed themselves. **Sparrowhawk**, **Redpoll**, **Willow Warbler**, **Goldcrest** and **Coal Tit** find such woods attractive. After about 20 years, true woodland specialists such as **Goshawk**, **Woodcock**,

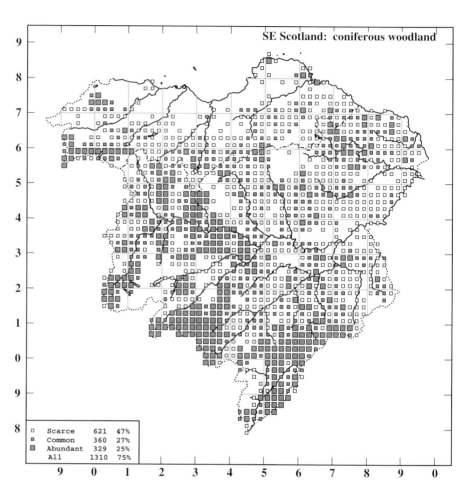

Siskin, and **Crossbill** arrive. The opening up of the forest on felling also provides opportunities. **Tree Pipits** in particular like the new openings and in recent years **Grey Wagtails** seem to favour clear-fell with steep drains running through them. Although **Nightjars** can be found in such areas in England, none has yet been found in SE Scotland, despite searching.

Seed-eating species, particularly **Crossbill**, **Redpoll** and **Siskin,** can exhibit huge changes in their numbers in coniferous plantations,

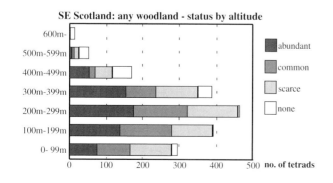

depending on the success of the cone crop. That in its turn depends on the spring weather when the flowers yield pollen. In good years there can be thousands, even tens of thousands, of birds in each forest, in poor years almost none.

Some woodland birds are not limited to either deciduous or coniferous woodland. The graph for 'any woodland' shows the extent to which woodland of any type is present across SE Scotland. From sea-level up to 300m virtually all tetrads hold some woodland and so generalist species such as **Blackbird**, **Robin**, **Wren**, **Chaffinch** and **Woodpigeon** could potentially be ubiquitous. Indeed many of these species with catholic habitat preferences are extremely widespread. Note that the huge extent of conifer forest above 200m means that woodland is especially common and abundant between 200-400m.

Human Settlement

Archaeologists maintain that there has been human occupation in SE Scotland since the end of the Pleistocene, hunters moving through the area within a few thousand years or so after the retreat of the last ice caps. These pioneer hunter-gatherer bands would have had little impact on the avian environment and probably little on individual birds unless they were perhaps the **Great Auk** or **Capercaillie** that were being hunted. Larger changes occurred when the first farmers arrived 4,000-5,000 years ago as fields were cut out of the forest and grazing animals started their destruction of seedlings that would eventually result in the area being deforested.

While human settlement may have had little initial impact on the landscape, the successive innovations in farming and a steady build-up of human population probably started to profoundly change the overall appearance of the countryside around 1,000 years ago, when the development of the wool trade with England and Europe sealed the fate of the forests. However, even then the extensive nature of the farming doubtless created opportunities for many birds to expand their ranges into the newly created open environments. Open country species such as **Curlew** or **Lapwing** must have been exceedingly rare when SE Scotland was covered with the climax forest.

Today there is nowhere in our area that has not been profoundly altered by the hand of man, and nowhere is this impact most felt than in and around human settlements. The urban environment appears to affect birds in three main ways, all dependent on their particular habitat needs. They are attracted to it, they avoid it or it is of no relevance to them. In general it is the open country species that avoid urban environments, the essential need for open space, suitable food, clear sight-lines and low disturbance being absolutely missing. Accordingly human settlements, particularly towns and cities, appear as vacant spaces on the maps of species such as **Lapwing**, **Oystercatcher**, **Swallow**, and **Yellowhammer**.

Woodland and scrub species vary in the rigidity of their habitat needs as to whether urban environments are avoided or not. Widespread and so presumably adaptable species such as **Robin**, **Wren**, **Carrion Crow** and **Great Tit** find the gardens and parks of urban areas just as congenial as the surrounding countryside, although densities differ. Others such as **Treecreeper**, **Jackdaw**, **Whitethroat** and **Mistle Thrush** are able to cope with villages and small towns but are only able to penetrate large towns and cities where pockets of less altered habitats are available such as in large parks and woodlands.

Some species that have very exacting habitat requirements can be positively attracted to housing. **House Martins** still breed on cliffs and in sea-caves in SE Scotland but their local range would be very different if they had not been adaptable and started to use human buildings for their nests, the vertical walls and overhanging eaves replicating the essential requirements of caves and cliffs. Similarly **Swifts** would be almost extinct in the area as the tree-holes that are used in those parts of the range where human settlement is absent are very scarce in SE Scotland. **Magpies** also show an affinity with settlements as in these environments they are protected from zealous gamekeepers that have removed them from considerable areas of the landscape of SE Scotland.

In the open countryside farms and gardens act as havens for woodland birds in otherwise unsuitable terrain. Many a shepherd's steading with a screen of trees to protect it from the wind has its population of **Robins**, **Blackbirds** or **Song Thrushes** that would

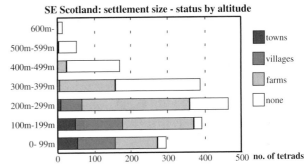

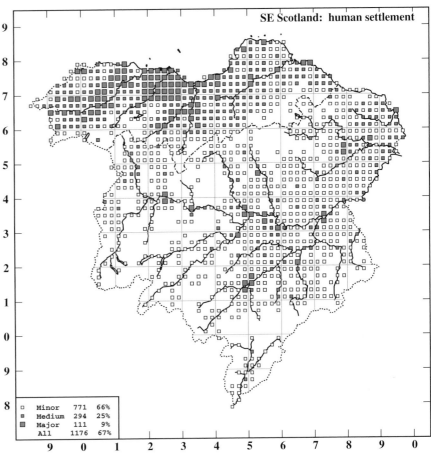

not otherwise be present but for the garden. Similarly the extent that the **Swallow** is able to penetrate the hills is entirely dependent on human settlement. Indeed even the lowliest ramshackle wooden shed is able to provide shelter for a nest in an otherwise uncongenial environment.

The map above shows that the pattern of human settlement in SE Scotland bears an overall resemblance to that of farmland. As farms are included in the analysis, forming the least intensively settled part of the human environment, this similarity is not surprising. Thus farms are visible across much of the low ground and penetrate well into the hill valleys, marking the extent of hill sheep steadings. The bar chart shows few farms occur above 400m but they form the most widespread type of settlement in tetrads above 100m. Villages are most widespread at lower elevations, the map showing the Lothian lowlands to be well populated with few low-lying tetrads lacking at least a small settlement. The contrast between Lothian and Borders in this respect is striking, villages being the norm in lowland Lothian and the exception in the Tweed valley. Large settlements show a similar pattern with the Edinburgh conurbation extending outwards across the low ground into West Lothian and the Esk valley. Away from the city, larger population centres are more isolated but are arranged along the river valleys which act as communication corridors between settlements.

The Avifauna of South-east Scotland: a discussion of the *Atlas* results

The first part of this chapter discusses some features of the overall picture of SE Scotland's birds that became apparent during the compilation of the *Atlas*. The establishment of a local baseline for bird distribution has allowed the whole avifauna to be examined as a unit and a number of interesting observations are made concerning species ubiquity, species numbers and avifaunal changes over the last two to three decades. The chapter examines what can be learned from the completion of the *Atlas*. The potential of the *Atlas* as a conservation tool is examined, before finishing with what lessons we have learned about the accuracy of the national atlases within the area.

The avifaunal baseline

The prime aim of publishing *The Breeding Birds of South-east Scotland* is to establish a snapshot of the status of breeding birds in the area between 1988 and 1994. For the first time ever, all species have been systematically surveyed over the same period of time and at tetrad level using a uniform methodology.

The *Atlas* and its database can now serve as a baseline against which to compare all future work on breeding bird populations within the area. It is hoped that future workers will use the data presented here with some confidence, whether in a new atlas 20 years from now or in single-species surveys in the more immediate future. Possessing data on the number of tetrads where species were recorded in 1988-94 will allow direct comparisons to be made in future years.

Just as useful will be the possibility to make accurate estimates of numbers through population sampling. For instance, a survey of Whitethroats might count all the birds in a 5% sample of the tetrads where the species was found in 1988-94. Counts in just 31 tetrads, chosen at random from the 616 in this *Atlas*, could be achievable in a single breeding season. Such a survey would tell whether Whitethroats were still as widespread, and allow estimation of the likely breeding population. A number of tetrads where the birds were absent in 1988-94 might be included in the analysis to indicate whether there had been any additional spread since. The habitat database will allow selection of these vacant tetrads as a stratified sample, based on the Whitethroat's habitat preferences, so as to select tetrads where the species is likely to find suitable breeding habitat. Searching randomly-selected squares for a species you strongly suspect does not breed there, because the habitat appears clearly unsuitable, is not conducive to fieldworker satisfaction!

The *Atlas* is a huge advance on the guesses that were necessary to interpret the often casual and unsystematic collection of records and anecdotal comments that have hitherto been available through the *Bird Reports*. Other than where specific surveys had been done, the authors of previous attempts to summarise the breeding populations of birds in SE Scotland had to rely mostly on subjective impressions, perhaps based on years of experience, but subjective nonetheless. An accurate and objective picture of all species' status has now been achieved which we hope will stand up to scrutiny in the future. As part of this picture, Tables 1 and 2 present the most widespread, and most numerous species.

Compared with the British ordering in the *New Atlas*, Woodpigeon and Coal Tit are substantially higher in both tables (ten or more places higher), Curlew and Oystercatcher are each over 30 places higher on ubiquity and Carrion Crow and Rook are substantially higher. Goldcrest and Siskin are substantially higher in terms of abundance. Mallard and House Sparrow are substantially lower on ubiquity and Great Tit on abundance. Apart from the rather surprising position of Mallard, these results are consistent with what might be

Table 1. Top 30 Most Widespread Species in SE Scotland

		% of tetrads	No. of tetrads
1	Wren	95	1,672
=2	Carrion Crow	92	1,620
=2	Chaffinch	92	1,620
4	Willow Warbler	88	1,554
5	Woodpigeon	87	1,534
6	Robin	87	1,527
7	Skylark	86	1,510
=8	Blackbird	83	1,456
=8	Song Thrush	83	1,456
10	Swallow	81	1,419
11	Pied Wagtail	80	1,401
12	Pheasant	77	1,352
13	Meadow Pipit	75	1,313
14	Starling	73	1,287
15	Dunnock	73	1,282
16	Rook	71	1,246
17	Coal Tit	69	1,208
18	Curlew	69	1,203
19	Jackdaw	67	1,181
20	Blue Tit	67	1,174
21	Goldcrest	67	1,173
22	Kestrel	66	1,156
23	Lapwing	66	1,154
24	Mallard	64	1,119
25	Black-headed Gull	61	1,075
26	Mistle Thrush	60	1,059
27	Oystercatcher	59	1,044
28	Yellowhammer	59	1,043
29	Linnet	57	1,004
30	House Sparrow	55	968

Table 2. Top 30 Most Abundant Species in SE Scotland

		Estimated population (pairs)
1	Chaffinch	200,000
2	Wren	134,000-167,000
3	Goldcrest	105,000-150,000
4	Meadow Pipit	127,000
5	Willow Warbler	112,000
6	Coal Tit	98,000
7	Robin	92,000
8	House Sparrow	80,000-90,000
9	Blue Tit	75,000
10	Pheasant	65,000-70,000
11	Blackbird	64,000
12	Dunnock	63,000
13	Starling	51,000-62,000
14	Woodpigeon	61,500
15	Rook	55,000
16	Skylark	54,400
17	Guillemot	46,600
18	Siskin	45,500
19	Kittiwake	35,000-40,000
20	Gannet	39,751
21	Yellowhammer	32,400
22	Great Tit	30,000
23	Song Thrush	29,000
24	Puffin	26,100
25	Linnet	20,000
26	Black-headed Gull	19,713
27	Jackdaw	19,000
28	Red Grouse	18,400
29	Herring Gull	15,650
30	Pied Wagtail	14,000

The species above are presented in order of maximum population estimated for SE Scotland in 1988-94. For seabirds the Forth population is given and the counts relate to a specific year. See Appendix for details.

expected for an area with a large amount of coniferous woodland and rough grassland, and relatively little urbanisation.

Text authors were asked to bear in mind future scrutiny when they were assessing population size. Unless there had been a census that allowed authors to make authoritative statements about numbers, most other totals could only be informed, subjective estimates. Text authors were asked to explain explicitly their thinking as to how they arrived at the final totals. This will allow future workers to know precisely how estimates were made so that any new data can be incorporated into the analysis when amendments may be made to the totals published here. The authors are only too willing to be shot down in flames for their figures, but only if the challengers of our conclusions come up with better data, producing a better result!

Changes in the avifauna of SE Scotland

A glance through this *Atlas* will reveal that bird distributions are rarely stable. Birds respond to changes in food and climate, and changes in human activities, such as persecution, can either have an immediate impact on a particular species or a delayed impact through human-inspired changes to the landscape. While a major reason for writing this *Atlas* is to provide a baseline for any future local changes, we are lucky that we can use the BTO *Old Atlas* for monitoring regional changes since 1968-72. Although 25 times less detailed than this publication, it does allow some discussion of changes to the local avifauna since then. On a 10-km square basis it is unreasonable to expect to see any change in the most widespread species. As they occupy all squares in both surveys, no change is discernible. The tables below were compiled by comparing the *Old Atlas* 10-km square distribution with that found in the tetrad survey.

Table 3. New colonists
Species not recorded in SE Scotland in the *Old Atlas*.

	Occupied 10-km squares
Red-necked Grebe	5
Black-necked Grebe	4
Slavonian Grebe [1]	4
Mandarin	7
Garganey [1]	7
Goldeneye [1]	22
Ruddy Duck	10
Osprey [1]	7
Little Ringed Plover [2]	-
Dotterel	7
Nuthatch	8
Reed Warbler [2]	-

All species exclude observed records, [1] = not proved to breed
[2] = has bred or attempted to breed since 1994

Colonising and spreading species
In the table of recent colonists (Table 3) a number of birds are associated with water features, only the Dotterel and Nuthatch occurring in other types of habitat. This may be simply fortuitous. A number of wetland species are known to have expanded their ranges across much of northern Europe during the course of the 20th century, and the expansion into Scotland may be part of this greater range change. The exotic Mandarin and Ruddy Duck, species originating from escaped stock, and the Nuthatch, are the only species that show a substantial spread since colonising. The remainder, despite the large number of squares in the case of the Goldeneye, will probably remain occasional or infrequent breeding species in the area for the foreseeable future. The Reed Warbler, which only bred in Borders for the first time in 1997, is the only wetland species that may have considerable scope for future spread.

For species in Tables 4 & 5, better population monitoring of waterfowl and raptors, and the establishment of the *Bird Reports* as depositories for records, may be partly responsible for the observed

Table 4. Species showing major spread
Species that show over 100% increase in 10-km squares since *Old Atlas*.

	Old Atlas	Tetrad Atlas	increase
Greylag Goose	1	23	x 23.0
Canada Goose	4	10	x 2.5
Gadwall	3	15	x 5.0
Pintail	3	8	x 2.7
Hen Harrier	11	25	x 2.3
Goshawk	3	38	x 12.7
Buzzard	23	63	x 2.7
Golden Eagle	2	5	x 2.5
Peregrine	8	48	x 6.0
Red-legged Partridge	2	38	x 19.0
Quail	5	43	x 8.6
Water Rail	6	17	x 2.8
Great Black-backed Gull [1]	1	3	x 3.0
Little Owl	5	12	x 2.4
Kingfisher	16	38	x 2.4
Fieldfare	1	25	x 25.0
Lesser Whitethroat	5	28	x 5.6
Jay	13	34	x 2.6
Siskin	27	75	x 2.8
Crossbill [1]	5	54	x 10.8

All species exclude observed records , [1] = probable and confirmed records only

Table 5. Increasing species
Species that show over 10% increase in 10-km squares since the *Old Atlas*.

	Old Atlas	Tetrad Atlas	% change
Little Grebe	41	46	12
Fulmar	11	13	18
Grey Heron [1]	30	40	33
Shelduck	10	18	80
Wigeon	13	16	23
Shoveler	17	22	29
Pochard	18	21	17
Red-breasted Merganser	4	6	50
Goosander	29	54	86
Sparrowhawk	67	79	18
Oystercatcher	68	78	15
Ringed Plover	30	37	23
Lesser Black-backed Gull [1]	5	9	80
Herring Gull [1]	9	15	67
Feral Pigeon	44	71	61
Collared Dove	50	67	34
Long-eared Owl	29	44	52
Green Woodpecker	37	53	43
Great Spotted Woodpecker	59	66	12
Tree Pipit	52	63	21
Yellow Wagtail	15	21	40
Garden Warbler	55	67	22
Blackcap	62	70	13
Wood Warbler	29	46	59
Chiffchaff	47	65	38
Pied Flycatcher	21	36	71
Marsh Tit	17	22	29
Magpie	31	57	84
Goldfinch [1]	62	74	19
Twite	4	6	50
Hawfinch	9	15	67

All species exclude observed records , [1] = probable and confirmed records only

changes. This is especially true of the scarce species such as Water Rail, Quail, Little Owl, Kingfisher and Hawfinch, records of which might have remained unpublished in diaries in the past. The apparent increase in Feral Pigeon may be a result of some observers not recording it in 1968-72 .

The recovery of the raptor populations in 25 years is dramatic. The changes due to the banning of use of some organochlorine poisons in the environment, a consequent reduction in the impact of persecution due to population recovery, changes in keepering practices, protection measures and better monitoring, can be seen in Hen Harrier, Sparrowhawk, Buzzard, Golden Eagle and Peregrine. Jay and Magpie have also benefited from reduced persecution, while the Goldfinch no longer suffers from the bird trappers as it did earlier in the 20th century. Goosander populations are also doing well in the face of continued persecution from the angling industry in the Tweed.

Introduced species such as the geese, Goshawk and Red-legged Partridge show large changes but it is the birds of conifer woodlands that show some of the most dramatic increases, given that many were already widespread at the time of the *Old Atlas*. Goshawk, Long-eared Owl, Tree Pipit, Jay, Siskin and Crossbill have prospered with the spread of commercial forestry. Although not in the table the *Atlas* fieldwork noted spread of Bullfinch and Grey Wagtail into commercial conifer woodlands, species that have hitherto not been associated in the literature with such habitats.

There is also a substantial number of species that prefer mixed and deciduous woodland that show smaller, less dramatic increases. The bases of the increases in Great Spotted and Green Woodpeckers, Blackcap, Garden Warbler and Chiffchaff differ between species. The woodpeckers may have benefited from Dutch Elm Disease providing extra food, while the warblers may have had low populations in the late 1960s due to climatic change in their winter quarters which has since ameliorated. The increase in Marsh Tit and Hawfinch is more apparent than real, better monitoring probably being the key to their presence in the tables.

Species such as the Goosander, Oystercatcher, Ringed Plover, Collared Dove, Little Owl, Yellow Wagtail and Lesser Whitethroat that colonised SE Scotland earlier in the 20th century, clearly made substantial ground in the 25 year interval since the *Old Atlas*. Some like the Oystercatcher and Collared Dove must now be reaching full occupation while Goosander, Lesser Whitethroat and Yellow Wagtail still have substantial scope for further colonisation. The spread of the Little Owl has probably ceased, although good information on this enigmatic species is difficult to obtain.

The presence of the gulls in the tables masks a more general increase amongst seabirds whose populations have boomed since the 1960s. However, such are the breeding site requirements that few are able to expand far from areas where they bred previously. In species such as the Gannet, Shag and the auks, the populations have trebled but show little sign of this increase on the maps. The gulls are more flexible in this respect and have taken to roof nesting, thus avoiding competition or disturbance on the increasingly crowded islands and cliffs.

Declining species

It is gratifying to state that there have been no total losses of breeding birds in SE Scotland since 1968-72, although Corncrake and Nightjar may only be represented by the occasional migrant that calls in the forlorn hope of attracting a mate. The species in the biggest danger of local extinction (Table 6) is undoubtedly the Corn Bunting, which could disappear in the next five years. The terns are also in trouble, the Little, Roseate, and Sandwich Terns rearing hardly any young in the Forth in recent years and all showing evidence of decline.

Other water-based birds, the Common Tern, Kittiwake, Common Gull and Black-headed Gull have all shown a shrinkage in the number of breeding 10-km squares. Only in the Common Tern is this a problem, Common Gulls having recently established a very large colony compared to former times, and Black-headed Gulls concentrating their efforts at one 'mega-colony' and several other large sites. Great Crested Grebe shows a small contraction, warning of the need to maintain suitable breeding conditions and lack of disturbance for vulnerable water-based birds.

Species such as Redshank, Ring Ouzel and Raven reflect the difficulties some upland birds have suffered in recent years. The 'improvements' to upland farms through drainage of damp fields and the conversion of former rough grazing to improved grassland have removed valuable habitat for not only Redshanks but also for Curlew, Lapwing and Snipe. Afforestation of the uplands may have had an adverse effect on the range of Golden Plover, Ring Ouzel and perhaps Raven, through moorland breeding or feeding grounds being taken over by forest. Swifts may have been affected by loss of breeding sites in the south and west from afforestation, and they show some gains in other areas.

Treecreeper is the only woodland species to show a contraction, against the trend of increase in several woodland species. This may reflect losses after the hard winter of 1990-91 in areas where the species is always scarce.

Migrant species may suffer problems in their wintering grounds. This certainly caused reductions in Sand Martins and Whitethroats and may underlie low numbers of Ring Ouzels. Fortunately both the Whitethroat and Sand Martin are showing signs of recovery, as is the Stonechat population which was devastated by cold winters in the 1970s and 1980s.

Arable farmland

Much has been written in recent years about the problems that farmland birds are experiencing in Britain due to the general intensification of farming. This has come about due to a number of changes in farming practice: herbicides and insecticides are more efficient and used on a more widespread basis; stocking rates of sheep on hill farms have increased; silage has largely replaced hay as a major winter feed; and autumn sown cereals have replaced most winter stubbles.

The *Atlas* has been able to identify another change that is not as widely reported – the increasing specialisation of hill-farming units. In recent times most hill farms had in-bye land to grow cereals to provide additional winter food for their stock. This seems to have largely disappeared, farmers presumably buying in hay, silage and grain from lowland farms or pelleted feed from manufacturers. As a result, the availability of food for seed-eating birds and other farmland birds in such areas has vanished. The planting of commercial forestry on what were formerly hill sheep farms has accentuated this change in some areas.

While this may be a general feature on the upland edges of SE Scotland, the pattern of this withdrawal of arable crops in higher

Table 6. Declining species
Species that show significant decrease of 10% or more in 10-km squares.

	Old Atlas	Tetrad Atlas	% change
Great Crested Grebe	21	18	-14
Kittiwake [1]	9	7	-22
Grey Partridge	79	71	-10
Corncrake	21	8	-62
Woodcock	75	65	-13
Redshank	71	62	-13
Black-headed Gull [1]	40	33	-18
Common Gull [1]	10	7	-30
Common Tern [1]	11	9	-18
Swift	64	55	-14
Sand Martin [1]	70	58	-17
Stonechat	28	22	-21
Ring Ouzel	46	35	-24
Whitethroat	72	64	-11
Treecreeper	75	67	-11
Rook [1]	73	62	-15
Raven	25	20	-20
Tree Sparrow	62	53	-15
Reed Bunting [1]	77	66	-14
Corn Bunting	36	16	-56

All species exclude observed records , [1] = probable and confirmed records only altitude farms is most visible in the southern and western parts of Peeblesshire at the head of the Tweed (NT01,02,03,11&12), Selkirkshire around St.Mary's Loch (NT21,22&31) and southern Roxburghshire in Teviotdale (NT30,40&50) and Liddesdale (NY48,49,58&59). This pattern can be most easily seen in the 10-km maps as vacant squares in the 1988-94 map that were fully occupied during the *Old Atlas* in 1968-72 ,while in the main maps these farmland birds are often now only found in a few tetrads in the upland valleys where remnants of the older form of agriculture still persist. The withdrawal is best seen in the maps of Grey Partridge, Stock Dove, Barn Owl, Whitethroat, Rook, House Sparrow, Tree Sparrow, Greenfinch, Linnet, Reed Bunting and Yellowhammer. Similar changes to farming techniques must have effectively removed Corncrake and Corn Bunting from much of SE Scotland in earlier eras.

The Atlas: a conservation tool
The hard work of the ten years between 1988-98 does not finish with the publication of *The South-east Scotland Breeding Bird Atlas*. The database created will be a valuable tool for handling a variety of tasks that will hopefully help to tease out the more subtle influences that affect the distribution of individual species, groups of species and perhaps the entire avifauna of the area.

Some preliminary analyses here on habitat associations provide a glimpse of how the *Atlas* data might be used as a tool for conservation purposes. Although these possibilities were recognised early on, limited space in the *Atlas* has meant that these potentially interesting aspects have not been tackled fully for the time being.

The TATLAS and DMAP software allow any group of species to be selected and portrayed in a composite map (coincident species analysis). Specimen maps of 18 deciduous woodland specialists are shown here. The first map shows all tetrads where some combination of the selected species occurs. The symbols are graded according to the number of the selected species occurring in individual tetrads. In effect therefore, this map displays the broadest range that a deciduous woodland specialist might have, ranging from tetrads where only a single species occurs to tetrads that hold most of the species selected. The pattern of the river systems is picked out by the tetrads with the most diverse avifauna, indicating that birds select the semi-natural woodlands that still survive on the steep slopes of rivers, particularly along the Tweed, Whiteadder and Esk.

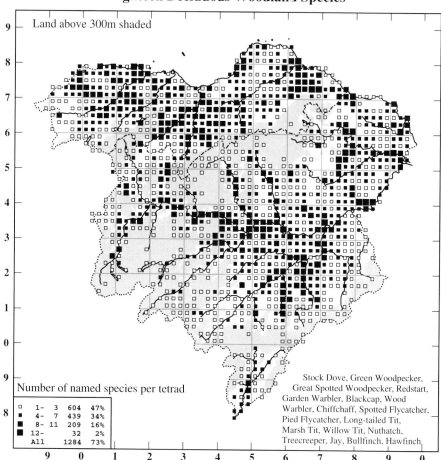

Eighteen Deciduous Woodland Species

Land above 300m shaded

Number of named species per tetrad

□	1- 3	604	47%
▪	4- 7	439	34%
■	8- 11	209	16%
■	12-	32	2%
	All	1284	73%

Stock Dove, Green Woodpecker, Great Spotted Woodpecker, Redstart, Garden Warbler, Blackcap, Wood Warbler, Chiffchaff, Spotted Flycatcher, Pied Flycatcher, Long-tailed Tit, Marsh Tit, Willow Tit, Nuthatch, Treecreeper, Jay, Bullfinch, Hawfinch

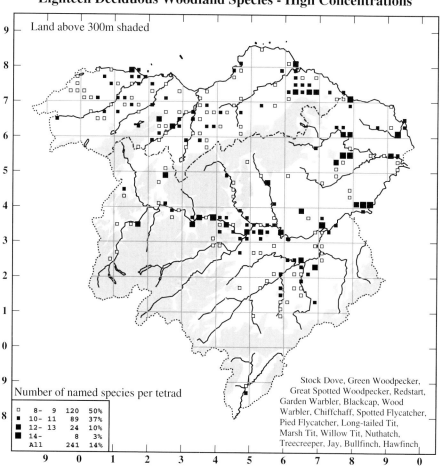

Eighteen Deciduous Woodland Species - High Concentrations

Land above 300m shaded

Number of named species per tetrad

□	8- 9	120	50%
▪	10- 11	89	37%
■	12- 13	24	10%
■	14-	8	3%
	All	241	14%

Stock Dove, Green Woodpecker, Great Spotted Woodpecker, Redstart, Garden Warbler, Blackcap, Wood Warbler, Chiffchaff, Spotted Flycatcher, Pied Flycatcher, Long-tailed Tit, Marsh Tit, Willow Tit, Nuthatch, Treecreeper, Jay, Bullfinch, Hawfinch

The second map, using the same data, highlights tetrads that hold a high percentage of these deciduous woodland specialists. In removing the species-poor tetrads this map depicts the best deciduous woodlands for bird diversity in SE Scotland.

The largest dots identify the wooded policies of large estates such as the Hirsel, Duns Castle (NT75S&X), Floors Castle (NT73C), Ayton Castle (NT96F), Holylee (NT33Y) and Pease Dean (NT77V). The best sites, with 17 of the 18 species, are the Hirsel (lacking only Wood Warbler) and Duns Castle (lacking only Nuthatch). The remainder of the larger dots show the importance of valley woodlands, especially along the middle Tweed and Whiteadder.

The third map shows a similar analysis for the waders, a group of species whose fortunes in recent years have given rise to some concern. Farm 'improvements', whether through drainage or the conversion of rough pasture and old permanent grassland to 'improved' grassland for intensive grazing and silage cropping, has led to a decline in the numbers of waders breeding in farmland across much of Britain. All common wader species have been mapped, other than the Woodcock whose habitat lies outwith the type of farmland under threat from agricultural changes.

The map shows tetrads where four or more of the nine species occur and demonstrates the upland nature of tetrads with good wader diversity in SE Scotland, *c*.85% of all dots lying above 300m. Within the uplands the squares with the best diversity lie in three main types of area, the valley haughs, the upland lochs and reservoirs and more generally across the northern hills. The latter, with open rolling moorland and damp rough grazing is particularly obvious in the row of 10-km squares between NT05 and NT75. The best tetrads, each holding all nine species, were at Harperrig Reservoir (NT06V&16A).

This preliminary method for identification of the best sites for woodland birds, waders or any other group of species, represents a valuable tool for conservation. It identifies species-rich tetrads, possibly indicative of high biodiversity. Further analysis of the habitat characteristics of the tetrads with high species diversity could show what they have in common. It might then be possible to identify precisely the site features that promote diversity and perhaps develop a model of an ideal tetrad for woodland birds or waders. As the habitat analysis presented here is rather coarse, a more refined set of criteria would be needed to do this with assurance. Conservation bodies could then identify and target their efforts to conserve the species or groups of species involved, whether it be in recording more precise habitat parameters, monitoring populations levels or focusing financial aid to retain the current diversity. Any future changes can also be monitored through repeat surveys.

Nine Wader Species - High Concentrations

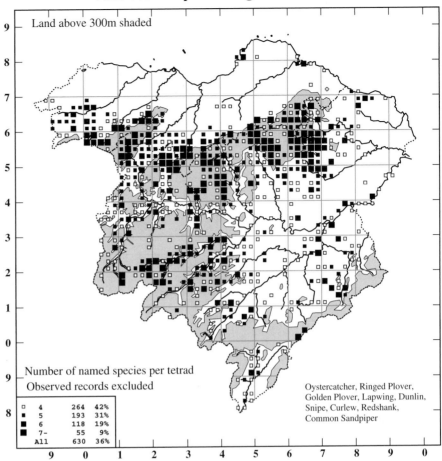

Land above 300m shaded

Number of named species per tetrad
Observed records excluded

□	4	264	42%
■	5	193	31%
■	6	118	19%
■	7-	55	9%
	All	630	36%

Oystercatcher, Ringed Plover, Golden Plover, Lapwing, Dunlin, Snipe, Curlew, Redshank, Common Sandpiper

The BTO Atlases
The Old Atlas

In the 1968-72 BTO Atlas it is now clear that a number of 10-km squares in SE Scotland must have been poorly surveyed. This is apparent in some species where 10-km squares were shown as vacant in the *Old Atlas* but in the current *Atlas* have a high percentage of occupied tetrads. While some population change might have occurred in the 20 years or so between the surveys, it would require a spectacular change to account for an increase from no occupied tetrads in 1968-72 to 12 or more in 1988-94. This might not be so noticeable were it not for the fact that certain 10-km squares show up in this way in many different species accounts, namely NT31 (Craik), NT44 (Stow), NT86 (Coldingham Moor) and NT87 (Fast Castle).

Amongst some scarcer breeding species, the *Old Atlas* shows a number of records of probable or confirmed breeding for which there appears to be no other documentation. Authors have queried a number of dots on the *Old Atlas* maps, such as breeding of Pintail in NT84, inland breeding of the large gulls, a possible breeding record of Spotted Crake in NT84, confirmed breeding of Marsh Tit in NT13 and others. While the recorded breeding of Lesser Black-backed Gulls in squares such as NT21 might be ascribed to over-enthusiastic interpretation of a pair of non-breeding gulls in summer along the shores of the Loch of the Lowes, records such as the Spotted Crake and Marsh Tit, species that have always required a description for submission to the ornithological authorities, are less acceptable.

The *Old Atlas* states that all records were scrutinised to check for anomalies and transcription errors by the local organisers, before being checked again by the national organisers. It is noticeable that the above anomalies are all in Borders, which had no fewer than three organisers during the course of the five-year survey, including the Scottish national organiser who clearly had to take on areas where there were problems in finding local organisers. In Lothian where Bob Smith and Keith Macgregor were the local organisers, the authors of the current *Atlas* have had little cause to query the *Old Atlas* dots. There is definitely no substitute for local knowledge by an enthusiastic and expert organiser.

The New Atlas

The *New Atlas* abundance maps presented some difficulty where the pattern shown of local bird numbers differed considerably from our experience, our expectations and, more especially, from our maps. This was evident for woodland species in the large conifer plantations of southern Roxburghshire, the *New Atlas* showing that area to hold low numbers of Wren, Goldcrest, Coal Tit, Siskin, Redpoll and Common Crossbill. As the adjacent parts of Kielder, in essentially identical forest habitats, had high numbers, some anomaly is suggested. The explanation is perhaps to be found in the *New Atlas* effort map (p.8) which shows a marked difference in the fieldwork on either side of the border, Northumberland having the highest category, Southern Roxburghshire the lowest. Although fieldworker effort is not supposed to have had a significant impact on the maps (*New Atlas* p.2), this may be an example where it did. It is also possible that the particular year when the fieldwork that produced the data for the *New Atlas* abundance maps was carried out may have affected the results. Species such as Crossbill and Siskin may have had markedly different population levels due to differences in the seed supply, while Goldcrest and Coal Tit can suffer high winter mortality due to widespread rime on tree branches in hard winters. Such variation did indeed occur between survey years for these reasons, and so differences in the timing of fieldwork may possibly have carried over into the final maps. No human boundary in areas of similar habitat should have been visible on the abundance map.

The *New Atlas* methodology involved a two hour visit to tetrads, the BTO calculating that the majority (*c.*70%) of common species would be found within that period. However, as the detection rate of species increases with the time spent surveying, this meant that many 10-km squares in the parts of the British Isles that received fewest visits suffered from low detection rates amongst scarce, localised, nocturnal and generally difficult-to-locate species. This in turn had an impact on the *New Atlas* change maps which show the changes in the 10-km squares where species were found. In large parts of northern and western Britain and much of Ireland, areas which received relatively fewer visits, the change maps for many species show widespread losses. If the present book had used the *New Atlas* 10-km maps, rather than our own, a similar effect might have pertained to the upland areas of southern and western SE Scotland. Accordingly there is little reference to the *New Atlas* change maps in the species texts.

The *New Atlas* national population estimates are queried in a number of accounts. This might be due to local surveys that allow us precise knowledge of the local population, or where our knowledge of local densities clashed with what was presented in the *New Atlas*. The species include several waders, Feral Pigeon, Tawny Owl, Grey Wagtail, Dipper, Wheatear, Ring Ouzel, Redstart, Chiffchaff and Goldcrest. Note that several species here are more common in northern Britain than they are further south, where much of the data for the BTO's population indices were derived. As the *New Atlas* estimates were often based on CBC or WBS figures, the bias towards southern Britain is only to be expected. Hopefully the more widespread BBS survey will help to rectify this regional bias in future.

Arctic Terns

Definitions, Methodology and Fieldwork

The survey area, time period and survey unit

The geographical extent of the survey corresponds to the area of the two regional local authorities in SE Scotland at the time of the survey, Lothian Region and Borders Region, plus the island of Inchkeith which lies in Fife Region. This is the area referred to as SE Scotland throughout this book. The external boundary of the two regions, and the boundary between the two regions, which is shown as a dot-dash line on the maps, are those pertaining at the end of the survey period.

There were two changes in the regional boundaries during the period of the survey. One was a small adjustment to the external boundary between Lothian Region and Strathclyde Region just south of Blackridge, West Lothian District, which added a small area to Lothian Region affecting tetrads NS86Y, NS96D and NS96I. It is unlikely that the additional area was surveyed since observers were unlikely to have had maps showing the revised boundary. The other change was in the boundary between Lothian and Borders Regions near Gilston and Soutra Hill, where an area was transferred from Lothian to Borders Region on 1 April 1989. This affects tetrads NT45C, D, H, I, M, N, P, and U. Recording was not affected, as no distinction was made between the two regions in field work.

Islands in the Forth which are included are: Cramond Island, Inchmickery, Inchkeith, Eyebroughy, Fidra, the Lamb, Craigleith and the Bass Rock. The Forth bridges are included. Inchkeith is included, despite lying in Fife, since seabird counts there are normally carried out from Lothian. In respect of seabirds a wider population, the Firth of Forth population, is also discussed, including those birds that breed on the Fife islands other than Inchkeith, and using the extensive records from seabird counts as well as *Atlas* records. In this way all birds that breed between Fife Ness and the English border are treated as a single population unit and are referred to as the Forth or Firth of Forth populaton. This area is sub-divided into Inner Forth: all islands and shore west of Gullane Point; and Outer Forth to the east of Gullane Point, except where the Berwickshire coast and the Isle of May are dealt with separately.

The survey period for the fieldwork is the seven year period 1988-94 inclusive. Originally it was intended to complete the survey in five years, 1988-92, and it was during this period that birdwatchers throughout the area were involved. The survey was extended by two years in order to fill in gaps, and the fieldwork was performed mainly by the organisers and a small number of colleagues.

The survey unit, the basis on which all observations were recorded, is the tetrad, or 2km grid square based on even-numbered kilometre lines of the national grid. Each tetrad is referenced by a five character code in the standard form used by the BTO and other local atlases. First are the two letters designating the 100km square; then two digits designating the 10-km square within it; and finally one letter designating the tetrad within the 10-km square. There are 25 tetrads and all letters of the alphabet except O are used thus:

E	J	P	U	Z
D	I	N	T	Y
C	H	M	S	X
B	G	L	R	W
A	F	K	Q	V

For example, Arthur's Seat, Edinburgh lies in tetrad NT27R.

All tetrads with a part within the survey area which could be distinguished in the field were included, but where a tetrad spanned an external boundary, only the area within SE Scotland was surveyed. This means there are a number of boundary tetrads, such as NT01H or NT11R, where only a very small area was surveyed. Every tetrad was visited, and at least one species was recorded in every tetrad. In all 1,756 tetrads are included, in 1,475 of which the entire tetrad lies within SE Scotland. Of these, 349 lie in Lothian, 1,059 in Borders, and 67 on the border between the two regions. Seven tetrads contain islands only and 69 are coastal (i.e. contain the High Tide line), of which one, NT58D, also contains the island of Fidra. The external boundary with another Scottish region or England passes through 203 tetrads (38 in Lothian, 164 in Borders and one in both) and two further tetrads are both coastal and on the external boundary. This gives a total of 447 tetrads for Lothian only, 1,240 for Borders only and 69 for both. Of the 205 tetrads on the external boundary, approximately 43 contain less than 0.5km^2 within SE Scotland, of which approximately 21 contain less than 0.25km^2, with a correspondingly restricted list of species.

Taxonomy and names; hybrids

The systematic order and scientific names are as in the British Birds *List of Birds of the Western Palearctic*, 1997. English names are as in the British Birds *List of Birds of the Western Palearctic*, 1984, except that *Loxia curvirostra* is called Common Crossbill. Feral Pigeon is regarded as a species (there are no pure Rock Doves *Columba livia* in SE Scotland). Sub-species are not distinguished with the exception of Hooded Crow *Corvus corone cornix* and Carrion Crow *C. c. corone* x Hooded Crow hybrids. Observers were asked to distinguish Red-legged Partridge x Chukar hybrids but this was not done comprehensively and the two species and their hybrids are treated together.

Species recorded which are not in Category A of the British Ornithologists' Union list are, in Category C (in addition to Feral Pigeon): Mandarin, Ruddy Duck, Red-legged Partridge, Pheasant, Golden Pheasant and Little Owl; and in Category D: Wood Duck and Chukar. Further, the Greylag Geese and Canada Geese recorded were feral originated birds.

Definition of breeding season

For most species the breeding season during which records could be obtained was 1 April to 31 July. Exceptions were: Grey Heron, Dipper and Mistle Thrush, March-June; pigeons and doves, April-August; owls (except Short-eared), January-July; Raven, December-July; Siskin, May-July with some April records of song included; and Crossbill, December-May plus observed records in June-July.

Observers were warned to take care later in the breeding season over fledged young of species which can disperse widely, such as waterfowl, gulls, Lapwing, Wheatear, Mistle Thrush and Rook.

Recording categories

The recording categories used are based on those established by the BTO and the European Ornithological Atlas Committee (EOAC) and explained in full in the *Old Atlas* and *New Atlas*. They are based on three levels of evidence of breeding, possible, probable and confirmed, with a number of observational guides associated with each. In addition, the EOAC introduced an Observed category for birds present with no evidence of breeding behaviour and a similar category was subsumed in the *New Atlas* 'present, no breeding evidence' category. We used an Observed category as well as the well-established categories of Possible, Probable and Confirmed Breeding in order to obtain the fullest possible picture of the birds present during the breeding season in SE Scotland, and its definition was framed to include non-breeding birds present, including winter visitors lingering after their normal departure time (but not normally birds on passage), and post-breeding flocks away from the breeding place (e.g. Rooks) and families which probably bred elsewhere (e.g. Wheatears).

The recording categories used and their codes are as follows for observations within the breeding season for the species concerned:

O	OBSERVED and using the tetrad (not flying over), not on passage, and not otherwise classifiable
M	Possible (may be) breeding
H	In possible breeding HABITAT
S	SINGING bird present
L	Probable (likely) breeding
P	PAIR in breeding habitat
T	TERRITORY, i.e. repeated territorial behaviour
D	DISPLAY and courtship
N	Visiting probable NEST site
A	AGITATED behaviour or ANXIETY calls from adults
I	Brood patch indicating INCUBATION
B	BUILDING nest or excavating nest-hole
CB	Confirmed breeding
DD	DISTRACTION DISPLAY or injury feigning
UN	USED NEST or egg shells from survey period
ON	Adults entering or leaving a nest site indicating an OCCUPIED NEST or sitting on a nest
FL	Recently FLEDGED YOUNG (nidicolous birds) or downy young (nidifugous birds)
FY	Adults carrying FOOD for YOUNG or faecal sacs
NE	NEST containing EGGS
NY	NEST containing YOUNG

The use of Observed led to some problems. For species such as Grey Heron, gulls, feeding Swifts and hirundines, and Rook, it yielded valuable information on the presence of non-breeding birds and birds away from breeding sites. However, observers found it a difficult category to use which involved an element of subjective judgement. Some erred on the side of caution, especially in the early years, and used Observed where Habitat would have been appropriate. Others virtually ignored it. Difficulty was also experienced over separating out birds on passage and records were retained if there was doubt, and more generally for scarce species. Another difficulty was identifying late-staying winter visitors. Unless records were submitted as supplementaries, with date and numbers, the organisers could not edit these records appropriately.

As experience was gained from the fieldwork, observers were advised not normally to use the Observed category for many species, especially passerines. Records in the category Observed obviously have to be interpreted with caution as the authors have done individually for each species in the texts but we believe its use has provided valuable information and experience which could be drawn upon to refine its use in future surveys.

Another category which requires comment is Territory, where we modified the interpretation. The instructions initially issued to observers stated that this requires at least two observations of territorial behaviour at the same site, within the same season, and separated by at least a week. Unfortunately, many tetrads in SE Scotland are difficult of access and some require walks of over an hour or longer to reach. It was therefore just not possible to revisit some tetrads to check that possibly common or abundant birds were still behaving territorially. Accordingly, the requirement for recording Territory was widened for common birds in the later years of the survey. A male singing against another male was taken as evidence of Territory, as was two instances of territorial behaviour in different parts of the tetrad or in different years.

Organisation of fieldwork

The area was divided into the same recording areas used by BTO for the *New Atlas,* and based on 10-km squares. An organiser in each area was responsible for organising fieldwork in that area. A steering group, consisting of the area organisers plus a few others closely connected with the survey, prepared fieldwork instructions, recording sheets, newsletters reporting back to observers, and organised the processing of records as they came in.

Initially there were three recording areas which, with their 10-km squares, were:
Lothian   NS86-87,95-97, NT05-07,15-17,25-28,34-37,44-48. NT56-58,66-68,77.
Borders - Berwickshire and Roxburghshire
NT30-31,40-41,50-52,60-65,70-76,81-87,94-96. NY39, NY48-49,58-59,69.
Borders - Tweeddale and Ettrick & Lauderdale
NT01-04,10-14,20-24,32-33,42-43,53-55.

For 1988-89 the area organisers were: Lothian: Mike Leven; Berwickshire and Roxburghshire: Rob Robertson; Tweeddale and Ettrick & Lauderdale: Ray Murray. In 1990 Mark Holling took over as Lothian area organiser after Mike Leven left the area. In 1991, after the regrettable death of Rob Robertson, the two Borders areas were merged with Ray Murray as the organiser.

Observers were recruited mainly through local branches of the SOC, the local BTO network and volunteers for the *New Atlas* fieldwork. A major problem for the organisers was to get adequate and uniform coverage in a large area much of which is sparsely populated, and where birdwatchers tended to concentrate on a relatively small number of areas, particularly along the coast. Observers were sent a list of tetrads they were asked to survey, recording sheets, and a set of instructions which explained the project and its relationship with the *New Atlas,* how they could help, hopefully taking on a distant site as well as a local one, necessary definitions, a code of conduct, advice on rare birds, unusual and interesting records, nocturnal and difficult species, and instuctions on completing the recording sheets.

There were two types of recording sheet for full and supplementary records. Full records were those from a tetrad to which an observer had been assigned, while supplementary records were the result of casual observations. The recording sheet for full records was for a single tetrad and had a list of about 100 of the commonest birds (initially two versions were produced, one with and one without seabirds, but the former was discontinued). There were four columns, one for each category of occurrence or breeding, and observers were asked to enter the correct code in the correct column. There were spare lines for species not in the standard list, and boxes for the tetrad designation, observer's name and address, the year, and the name of the main feature of the tetrad. Both the four columns and the name as well as the tetrad reference were intended to give some checks on the validity of the data.

Supplementary record sheets asked for the observer's name and address and had columns for species, date, locality, comments, tetrad reference and four columns for the record.

The tetrads for which each observer submitted records were recorded, and whether the records were full or supplementary. The distinction is of limited usefulness, however, since it became blurred, particularly in the later years when everyone was filling in gaps.

As the survey progressed, and the results were computerised, it became possible to issue tetrad recording sheets on which the records received to date were shown. This enabled the observer to concentrate on new species records or on upgrading records. An example is shown below for NT33T as it might have been issued for the 1991 season, showing records for 1988-90.

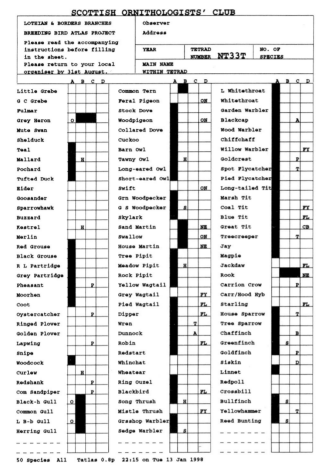

In the last few years, summary sheets showing the records received to date for a whole 10-km square were issued to observers for their guidance in filling in gaps over a wide area. These had a column for species, and 25 columns for the tetrads with symbols showing the highest category of record received to date.

Other sources of records than direct fieldwork were drawn on. Some were the results of species surveys, such as the Mute Swan census of 1990 or the Ring Ouzel survey of 1994, others came from miscellaneous sources such as logs in hides, but the bulk came from the local *Bird Reports*. These were scanned systematically for the less common species and over 850 useable records obtained. The major problem in doing this was identifying the tetrad concerned since most records appear under the name of a locality. Where the locality could be found on the map (not always possible!) a judgement was made on whether the record lay unambiguously in a particular tetrad. If not, it was sometimes possible to check with the original observer and some readers may recall being rung up with an enquiry about a long-past observation. These enquiries were always dealt with courteously and with patience. Otherwise, the pattern of existing records was examined. If the record could have come from a tetrad with a record, it was ignored. If not, it was assigned to the tetrad judged most likely. Thus a conservative approach was adopted in using *Bird Report* records but it is likely some records appear in a tetrad adjacent to the correct one.

By 1990 to some extent, and certainly by 1991, the pattern of results received could be used to plan the fieldwork. Initially it was a matter of identifying large gaps, particularly in southern Borders, and special weekends in May and June based on Borders Regional Council Outdoor Centres were organised in 1990 and 1991 at which groups of around half-a-dozen spent all hours of daylight (and some of the night) over a weekend in concentrated fieldwork, covering 30-40 tetrads. In 1990 these took place at Towford (NT71L) and Craikhope (NT30H), and in 1991 at Scotch Kershope (NY58H), Pyatshaw (NT54Z) and Craikhope. In subsequent years similar day trips were organised. These trips made a major contribution to coverage of the remoter areas as well as being memorable social occasions. By 1991, finer targeting was possible. Gaps on the interim maps for common species, such as Song Thrush, suggested areas where more work was needed. Comparison of the map of species per tetrad with habitat did the same though the comparison had to be a crude one.

Thus the data collected were used in various ways to enhance the effectiveness of the survey in the remaining years. It was used in feedback to observers to inform and enthuse them and to show them where work could most usefully be done in the next season. The instruction leaflet for 1991 had a map showing coverage to date, and a newsletter for 1991 included maps for Sand Martin, Willow Warbler, Golden Plover and Redstart as well as a map showing tetrads with no coverage and low coverage, and histograms showing the distribution of tetrads according to the number of species recorded for 1988-89 and 1988-90. By then over 55,000 records had been collected, about 40 per cent of tetrads had at least 31 species recorded, and some 350 tetrads had low or no coverage.

In the final two years, the targeting was more precise. The information available was greater, the gaps smaller, and the fieldworkers were small in number but experienced. For example, one day trip was organised, successfully, to fill in suspected gaps in the Pied Flycatcher distribution.

Confidentiality

It was recognised from the outset that full information on some species could not be published. The instructions to observers included a paragraph advising that records of rare or sensitive species which the observer thought should be confidential should be submitted separately to the Local Recorder and would not be mapped without permission. This paragraph also stated that in any case local rarities and vulnerable species would not be mapped without appropriate consultation, and that species such as Merlin and Peregrine would not be mapped on a tetrad basis.

Data processing and record checking

Initially, records were stored manually, using a simple, but highly effective method. Record sheets were grouped according to 10-km square. For each square an envelope held the record sheets and there was a master recording sheet usually covering two sheets of paper. This had a column on the left giving the standard list of species with some spare lines for further species, and 25 narrow columns, one for each tetrad. The highest category of breeding was recorded for each species in each tetrad in the boxes. Since records could be upgraded, possible breeding was represented by a diagonal stroke, this was raised to probable breeding by adding the opposite diagonal stroke, giving an X, and when breeding was confirmed the box was blacked in, indicating that record was as complete as it could be.

This system worked well for three to four years, and many interim maps were produced using these records, but it would have been difficult to operate accurately as the volume of records increased. In 1989 Peter Vandome joined the project and undertook to put the records on computer, writing a program called TATLAS for the purpose. Input of records to the computer began in February 1991, and as the computer system developed and was shown to be reliable the manual records were gradually superseded.

All records were submitted to the area organiser who checked, particularly, that the named site corresponded to the tetrad, and for obvious anomalies amongst the records. The records were then logged. In the early years this was done manually as explained above, but from 1991 all records, retrospectively from the start of the project, were entered on a computer. A print-out of the record entries, together with the original record, was returned to the area organiser for checking, and any corrections were made. Where supplementary records were submitted, the location was checked on the map to ensure it lay in the correct tetrad. For records extracted from bird reports, a tetrad had to be assigned, as described above.

Towards the end of the project, other checks and corrections were carried out. Some were queries about particular species arising from the writing of the species accounts. Some arose from reviews of the Observed category and of the interpretation of the Territory category. In addition, the database was scanned tetrad by tetrad for anomalies; a few were found and corrected.

All analyses and the data needed for the maps were produced by the TATLAS program. The mapping data were fed into the DMAP program written by Alan Morton which produced the maps.

Accuracy and errors
Errors could occur on the recording sheet, or at some later stage of processing. These possibilities will be considered in turn.

A species may not be recorded when it is present; a species may be recorded when it is not present; a species may be correctly recorded but in the wrong category; a record may be submitted for the wrong tetrad; and, less significantly, a record may be attributed to the wrong year or wrong observer. Another way of looking at these errors is in terms of errors of observation and errors of record keeping.

That species were missed is obvious, and this probably constitutes the largest error. It is an error which will be greater for nocturnal, skulking and less vocal species. A less extreme form of this error is where a species was recorded at a lower category than it could have been. Indeed, it is likely that many records of possible breeding, and most of probable breeding, were of birds which actually bred. The opposite error can, and no doubt did, occur where a higher than justified category was recorded, particularly of fledged birds which had moved from their breeding site such as Wheatears. Some records were downgraded for this reason. To reduce the danger of incorrect categories being recorded, from 1989 onwards certain categories deemed not to be applicable were blacked out on the recording sheet. These included Possible and Probable for Grey Heron, Possible for gulls and hirundines and Observed for a large number of species including some ducks, game birds, pigeons, owls and most passerines. For Rook only Observed or nest records were accepted, FL and FY being downgraded.

No doubt there was some misidentification of species but we have no reason to believe this was more than a trivial problem as checks on anomalies were continued during writing of the species accounts.

Under-recording will have varied with observer, since some were able to put in more time, some had more acute hearing, some were familiar with a greater range of birds and their habits. This is unlikely to have led to significant biases, however, since for 82% of tetrads at least two observers submitted records. The inevitable under-recording is therefore likely to be the main form of error by observers and further consideration of its extent is given below.

Observers completed a tetrad recording sheet for the appropriate tetrad by placing the category code in the correct column on the line for the species concerned. Whether done directly, in the field, or subsequently from a field notebook, recording or transcription errors could have occurred. The category code could be checked against the column, and some records were queried for this reason. In some cases a tick rather than a specific code was entered. In such cases one of the codes M, L, or CB was recorded according to the column ticked. The most likely (and serious) recording error is an entry against the wrong species or tetrad.

A wrong species is likely to have been one adjacent to the correct one on the sheet and some such errors were easier to detect than others. For example, Tree Pipit, Meadow Pipit and Rock Pipit appear consecutively on the recording sheet. An inland record of a Rock Pipit was investigated and found to refer to Meadow Pipit. A similarly erroneous record of Tree Pipit would have been less likely to have been discovered, however, since there are 209 tetrads in which both species occurred.

A subjective judgement is that the most likely form of record keeping error is ascribing records to the wrong tetrad. Observers were given detailed instructions on identifying tetrads and entering both the tetrad reference and the central location within it. When recording forms were issued they sometimes had both these details blank, and sometimes one or both were completed by the organiser, except that forms produced by computer with current records included obviously had the tetrad reference. Despite the instructions, there was clearly potential for using the wrong form when an observer was carrying several, especially when several were working together and passing the forms between each other. A few forms were discarded where it appeared an error had been made because of an inappropriate species list or lack of correspondence between the tetrad reference and the named locality. Thus some 'wrong tetrad' errors were detected but it is impossible to say how many slipped past the checking process, though any remaining are unlikely to affect the rarer species, since these distributions were scrutinised and any dubious records checked.

Entry of records into the computer did not start until 1991, so there was a backlog. Some record forms did not have a date on them and it is possible some records for 1988 and 1989 were entered for the wrong year. There are few analyses in this book which distinguish year, but this point is relevant to further analyses which may be performed. Some forms did not state the observer, and 89 records had to be attributed to 'Anon'.

Coverage and number of records
Records were stored according to tetrad, species, year and breeding code (including Observed). If more than one record for a particular tetrad, species and year was received, only that with the highest category code was stored. It is therefore possible to measure the

Number of records

	1988	1988-89	1988-90	1988-91	1988-92	1988-93	1988-94
Species recorded	163	173	175	181	184	186	189
Tetrads	880	1,228	1,525	1,682	1,725	1,751	1,756
Species-Tetrads records	19,592	32,068	45,314	55,426	63,623	68,282	70,934
Species-Tetrads-Years records	19,592	35,398	50,872	65,793	79,017	87,099	92,730
Average Species/Tetrad	22	26	30	33	36	39	40
Average Records/Tetrad	22	29	33	39	45	50	53

total number of species-tetrads records, i.e. the total of species per tetrad across all tetrads, regardless of year; and the total number of species-tetrads-years records, where records are summed across years as well. From each of these measures, averages per tetrad can be calculated. The table at the foot of the previous page shows how the number of records built up during the period of the survey.

During the main part of the survey to 1992, nearly 20,000 records were submitted in 1988, with about 15,000 in following years, falling to 13,000 in 1992.

The distribution of records between Lothian and Borders regions cannot be measured precisely since records in tetrads along their boundary are counted twice as they have parts in each region. The two recording areas (defined above) are exclusive, however, and these two approximate breakdowns between the two regions are shown in the table below.

Number of records by Region

	All	Lothian region	area	Borders region	area
Species recorded	189	174	178	170	168
Tetrads	1,756	516	604	1,309	1,152
Species-Tetrads records	70,934	23,830	27,777	49,673	43,157
Species-Tetrads-Years records	92,730	32,098	37,648	64,015	55,082
Mean Species/Tetrad	40	46	46	38	37
Mean Records/Tetrad	53	62	62	49	48

On average, there were about eight more species per tetrad in Lothian than in Borders. There is a greater proportion of diverse and favourable habitat in Lothian, as well as a greater concentration of birdwatchers there, particularly in Edinburgh, and the difference no doubt reflects both factors. The average number of records per species per tetrad was also higher (1.35) in Lothian than in Borders (1.29) reflecting greater observer coverage which yielded more multi-year records for species in a given tetrad. A way of making some allowance for habitat differences is to analyse by altitude, since species diversity decreases with altitude and there is more high altitude land in Borders. The following table shows this for the (slightly overlapping) Lothian/Borders breakdown.

Average Species per Tetrad by Region and Average Altitude

Average Altitude (m)	All	Lothian	Borders
0- 99	48	49	47
100-199	47	49	45
200-299	44	47	43
300-399	35	39	34
400-499	25	30	24
500-599	17	19	17
600-	9	-	9
All	40	46	38

From this table it appears that roughly half the difference of eight species is accounted for by differences in altitude profile, and the rest by differences in intensity of coverage.

An alternative way of representing the coverage is the map of species per tetrad in the next column showing the highest numbers in West Lothian, Midlothian, the coastal belt of East Lothian, and along the river valleys of the Borders.

The median number of species per tetrad is 41. The extremes of the distribution are one tetrad with just one species recorded (NT11R), and four with 90 and over (NT16R, NT25W, NT48Q, and NT96E).

Excluding Observed, there are 16 tetrads with 70 and over species and three (NT16R, NT48Q and NT84F) with 80 and over.

An obvious question is: how does the coverage compare with other local tetrad atlases? The following table shows the average number of species per tetrad in a selection of other atlases. Bearing in mind that species diversity is greater in the south of England than in Scotland, and that for comparability of altitude a figure nearer to the Lothian average of 46 might be more appropriate in comparing this *Atlas* with others, these figures suggest that coverage in the *Atlas* is well within the scatter of results for other atlases. The table also shows this Atlas to cover one of the largest areas.

Species per Tetrad in Local Atlases

County	Fieldwork Period	Number of Tetrads	Mean Species per Tetrad
SE Scotland Murray *et al.* 1998	1988-94	1,756	40
Bedfordshire Harding 1979	1968-77	371	48
Cheshire & Wirral Guest *et al.* 1992	1978-84	670	51
Devon Sitters 1988	1977-85	1,834	46
Gwent Tyler *et al.* 1987	1981-85	388	55
Hampshire Clark and Eyre 1993	1986-91	1,031	56
Hertfordshire Smith *et al.* 1993	1988-92	491	58
Kent Taylor *et al.* 1981	1967-73	1,000	40
London Montier *et al.* 1977	1968-72	856	45
Norfolk Kelly 1986	1980-85	1,455	42
Northumberland Day *et al.* 1995	1988-93	1,410	29
Sheffield Hornbuckle *et al.* 1985	1975-80	300	52
Sussex James 1996	1988-92	1,014	45

Number of Species Recorded

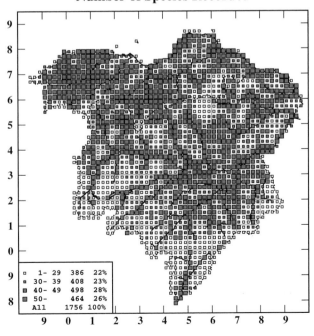

□	1- 29	386	22%
▪	30- 39	408	23%
▩	40- 49	498	28%
■	50-	464	26%
	All	1756	100%

It is also of interest how complete the coverage was. That is, in what proportion of tetrads where a species occurs was it actually recorded? There cannot be a definitive answer to this but for two species there is some information. In the last two years of fieldwork (and in 1995) a special effort was made to find Wrens and Chaffinches in tetrads where they had not previously been recorded. The effort in respect of Chaffinches was rather less than for Wrens. The number of tetrads where the species were recorded in the different periods was:

	1988-92	1988-94	1988-95
Wren	1,490	1,672	1,693
Chaffinch	1,563	1,620	1,620

The period 1988-92 was that of 'normal' fieldwork for these species, when fieldworkers were seeking records for as wide a range of species as possible and not looking for particular species, and Wrens were recorded in 84.9% of tetrads, Chaffinches in 89.0%. By 1995 the corresponding figues were 96.4% and 92.3%. It appears that Wrens were under-recorded by at least 11%, and Chaffinches by at least 3%. Since the search for Wrens was thorough, it is unlikely the under-recording was greater than 12%, while for Chaffinches it might have been up to 6%.

Chaffinches are very easily detected at most stages of the breeding cycle and these results suggest under-recording of the order of 5% in 'normal' fieldwork. Wrens are very easily detected when singing or with fledged young but can be elusive at other times, and where they are at low densities song can be infrequent. A corresponding under-recording rate of the order of 10-12% is suggested for such a species. These figures are not presented as actual under-recording rates, but as suggestive of the extent of under-recording after a period of 'normal' or generalised fieldwork. In the *Atlas* we believe under-recording is below a 'normal' rate for species other than Wren and Chaffinch because of the specially directed fieldwork in the last two years.

Observer coverage

There was a core group of about a dozen observers who formed the backbone for the project, contributing records for 80 or more tetrads. There were others who took responsibility for a group of tetrads, and there were others who contributed records for a few tetrads, perhaps their local patch or around their home. Many were active members of their SOC branch, others were unknown to the organisers, being visitors or friends of observers giving them some assistance. The distribution of individual observers according to the number of tetrads they submitted records for is below.

Distribution of individual observers by number of tetrads for which records were contributed

Number of Tetrads	Number of Observers
1	37
2-4	56
5-9	43
10-19	39
20-29	26
30-49	13
50-79	9
80-89	2
90+	10

The 'top ten' observers were: Ray Murray (847), Harry Dott (557), Mark Holling (471), Peter Vandome (400), Tom Gillies (263), Tom Barclay (215), John Ballantyne (199), Peter Gordon (142), Oonagh McGarry (110) and David Thorne (110).

Number of Observers

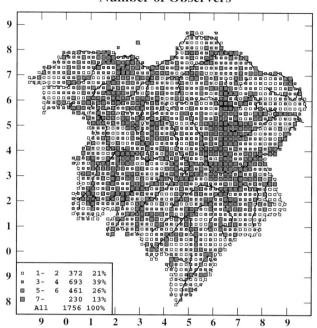

□	1- 2	372	21%
▪	3- 4	693	39%
▪	5- 6	461	26%
▪	7-	230	13%
	All	1756	100%

Another way of considering observer coverage is in terms of the number of observers contributing records for each tetrad. The distribution is below.

Number of Observers	Number of Tetrads
1	97
2	275
3	347
4	346
5	277
6	184
7	105
8-9	101
10+	24

The map above shows the pattern of observer coverage. The surprising feature is the concentration of multi-observer tetrads in the area of NT63,64&65. The explanation is that much of this area was the subject of special 'blitzes' by organised groups particularly in the last two years to deal with under-coverage. On these occasions several observers might submit records for a tetrad in one day.

Effects of weather

The effects of weather are two-fold. Firstly, there is variation in how cold or mild, or how wet or dry, a spring is, and this can influence the frequency of bird song and display, and also determine how visible some species are. Wind in particular is a major problem in assessing the species present in an area, as song is reduced and in any case hard to hear, and birds keep to cover. This variation, however, is levelled out in a survey which covers seven years.

Secondly, there is the effect on fieldworkers. Observers are less likely to go out on inclement days and a series of poor weekends could mean that less fieldwork could be done than might have been planned. This is likely to have had only a marginal effect, because of the long survey period. However, more remote areas which were surveyed largely by teams working together over one or two days would have been less productive if the weather turned out to be wet or windy. This was the case in the Liddesdale and Newcastleton Forest areas in June 1991, but return visits were organised thus reducing this effect. The use of interim maps to point out areas with low species totals in the last two years of the survey helped focus efforts to counteract some of these effects.

General, somewhat subjective, summaries of the weather in the April-July period for 1988-94 are noted below:

1988   dry cool May, average later
1989   dry and sunny for much of the period
1990   early spring, largely dry and sunny
1991   cold winter with prolonged snow in hill areas, resulting in a late spring and low passerine numbers; then cool and cloudy, with a wet June; much less passerine song than usual
1992   cold and wet into late April, trees very late into leaf, but then very dry until end of June and a good breeding season from May onwards
1993   wet and cool April and May with some flooding, cloudy but drier later
1994   average becoming dry in June.

Lessons learnt from fieldwork

With a seven year project it is inevitable that, if repeated, some things would be treated differently. A major point of note is that, as every tetrad was visited to survey birds, some elementary habitat data could have been collected at the time. This would have ensured that habitat information was current, at the time the birds were surveyed.

The organisation and collection of data proved to be very effective, but additional space on the forms to collect the dates when visits were made would have helped plan repeat visits. The length of time spent in an area may have been useful in some circumstances, and would have helped ensure that future censuses receive similar effort. Some observers found gaining proof of breeding easier than others and more help in the instructions or through brief workshops at meetings might have helped spread this knowledge to maximise the quality of data submitted. Similarly, fieldcraft techniques help maximise the number of species found in a tetrad.

Habitat classification

Habitat	Minor/Scarce	Medium/Common	Major/Abundant	Source and Notes
Coniferous Woodland	Less than 8 hectares	Between Minor and Major	$1/2$km^2 in one block or 1km^2 + scattered	Maps and photos. Base level on largest block in tetrad with area indicated.
Mixed and Deciduous Woodland	Less than 4 hectares	Between Minor and Major	At least $1/4$km^2	Maps and photos. Base level on largest block in tetrad, but if total area is twice that for next level, upgrade.
Any Woodland				See note below.
Arable or Improved Grassland	Less than $1/4$km^2	$1/4$ - $1/2$km^2	At least $1/2$km^2	Aerial photos.
Unimproved Grassland	Less than $1/4$km^2	$1/4$ - $1/2$km^2	At least $1/2$km^2	Aerial photos and 1:25,000 map rough grassland symbol.
Heather Moorland	Less than $1/4$km^2	$1/4$ - $1/2$km^2	At least $1/2$km^2 (less if high quality)	Aerial photos.
Waterbodies	1-2 <250m across	Between Minor and Major	> 800m across or 3 or more 250-800m across	Maps. Measurements are greatest dimension, assuming width at least half this. Downgrade (subjectively) otherwise.
Rivers	1-2km thin. Only upper reaches but not counting top of burns above top fork. Or < $1/2$km thick	2km + thin or $1/2$ - $1 1/2$km thick	$1 1/2$km + thick	1:50,000 maps. Thick means rivers with double lines
Wetland	1-5 marsh symbols on map	6 - 9 marsh symbols together or 10 - 19 in all	10 + marsh symbols together or 20 + in all	1:25,000 maps (plus local knowledge).
Cliffs, Crags and Quarries	Quarries or small crags and scars	Large quarry or medium crags	Major crags and cliffs	Maps. Subjective estimate.
Human Settlements	1 - 3 farms with cottages	4 + farms with cottages or villages/small towns < $1/2$km^2	$1/2$km^2 + built up area	Maps.

Note: The Any Woodland habitat was set as the maximum level of Coniferous Woodland and Deciduous/Mixed Woodland, except that if each of these was at level 2 (Common), Any Woodland was set at level 3 (Abundant)

More diligence about confirming and checking the tetrad being visited would have helped clarify the few cases of uncertainty, although all sheets submitted were checked against the range of habitats present in the tetrad. More *Bird Report* records could have been used if birdwatchers had suppled grid references for breeding records of scarce or localised species.

Finally, as the fieldwork meant that observers visited a wide variety of habitats, some recording of densities of common species in typical habitats would have been possible, and very helpful in later analysis. Examples might be counts of the number of Song Thrushes heard singing in a village or a stretch of spruce plantation, or the number of Swifts screaming around a nest site. These could have been noted and such examples collected for future use. There is great potential for such basic sample measurements in the future.

Collection of habitat data

Observers were not asked to collect habitat data, it being expected that simply getting a good coverage of breeding records would be a daunting enough task. Instead, habitat and altitude data were compiled from two sources: Ordnance Survey maps (both 1:50,000 and 1:25,000) and aerial photographs held by SNH.

The maximum and minimum altitude in each tetrad was measured on maps. This was not as easy as it may sound, and despite checks, in some cases a maximum less, and minimum greater, than the true value was probably recorded. These values were added to the tetrad records in the database and the computer calculated two other variables: Average Altitude and Range of Altitude for each tetrad. Average Altitude is the average of maximum and minimum altitude (ie the median altitude), while Range of Altitude is Maximum Altitude minus Minimum Altitude.

The habitat variables were recorded at three levels plus nil. In the analyses these levels are described as Minor, Medium and Major, or Scarce, Common and Abundant depending on the nature of the habitat feature.

Three woodland habitats were distinguished: Coniferous, Mixed and Deciduous and Any Woodland. The Mixed and Deciduous Woodland habitats could not be split into separate mixed and deciduous categories as neither the maps nor the aerial photographs facilitated this.

The habitats based on ground cover other than woodland which we wished to use were: Arable Farmland, Improved Grassland, Unimproved Grassland, Heather Moorland and Scrub. Unfortunately, using the maps and aerial photographs there was no reliable means of identifying Scrub and this had to be dropped. Neither was it possible to distinguish Arable Farmland from Improved Grassland, and these two habitats had to be merged.

Three habitats involving water are used: Waterbodies, Rivers and Wetland. Two further habitats used are Cliffs, Crags and Quarries, and Human Settlements.

Details of the way in which the habitat variables were compiled, and in particular, the definition of the different levels, are given in the table on the previous page. Definitions of the levels were arrived at after a good deal of discussion and experimentation. The guiding principles were that they should be easily implemented and should, so far as we could judge, yield levels which differed in their bird populations. For example, it was not thought appropriate to distinguish between coniferous woodland of 2-3km^2 and 3-4km^2 since the bird populations would be similar, and in this case the highest level was taken as $^1/_2$km^2 in one block or 1km^2 scattered or more. There is a subjective element both in interpreting the definitions and in making measurements from the maps and aerial

photographs, but we hope that reasonable consistency has been achieved because the scanning of the aerial photographs was carried out as a team, and difficulties were discussed as the work progressed.

Writing of species accounts

Most of the species accounts have been written by three of the authors (RDM, HEMD and MH). Volunteers were sought from the local branches of the SOC to select species and to write texts, and a further 14 authors came forward. The texts have been written to a tight framework and each author was supplied with details about the required structure, together with the species map, habitat data, extracts from local *Bird Reports* and some potential references. An important part of the process was analysis of the habitat data, changes in distribution since the *Old Atlas* and the *New Atlas* Abundance maps. All completed texts were then reviewed and edited by the editorial team of HEMD, MH and RDM, and texts circulated several times until a near-final version was ready for proof-reading by another individual.

Each species text has five main sections: a general introduction, notes about recording and fieldwork, interpretation of the map, discussion about changes, and calculation of a population estimate. For some species, ideas for possible future surveys are also given. Each section is presented in the same order to make reference by the reader easier. Further information on the format is provided in the introduction to the Main Species Accounts.

Estimation of populations

The population estimate is an important part of the species account, adding a different dimension to the distribution displayed in the species maps. Population estimates were derived for all species breeding in SE Scotland at the time of the survey. These estimates were calculated from a variety of sources, depending on the available information. The figures presented in the species texts and summarised in the Appendix are quoted as a single figure where possible to show the actual or approximate number of breeding pairs in a year, but a range is given where either the population varies between the two limits across several years, or where we have been unable to calculate figures more accurately because of limited information. In a few species, where we know that there has been a significant population change since the 1988-94 period, a figure applying to a more recent year is given, but this is stated.

Where possible, the results of recent actual counts of the whole local population were used. These were available for many seabirds using locally gathered information from the Forth Seabird Group and the East of Scotland Tern Conservation Group. Scarcer raptors are similarly monitored annually by the Lothian and Borders Raptor Study Group, providing reliable figures for species such as Hen Harrier, Merlin and Peregrine. Some other scarce breeding species in SE Scotland, or colonial breeders, are also counted regularly by birders, allowing confidence in the estimates for the rarer grebes and ducks, and Grey Heron.

Now that the *Atlas* is complete, sufficient is known about most species with populations of less than 100 pairs to be able to calculate a good estimate. Such species include localised ones like Marsh Tit, Pied Flycatcher, Dunlin and Water Rail, and species with much reduced ranges like Corn Bunting. Even now, however, we do not have enough information to be very accurate about scarce yet elusive species like Mandarin and Little Owl.

For commoner and more widespread species, where the population is less than 2,000 pairs, the *Atlas* and evidence in recent local *Bird Reports* provide good data to allow reasonable totals to be calculated. Sometimes these are based on recent surveys, like those for Shelduck, Ringed Plover and Sand Martin. For many others where the number of pairs in a tetrad is typically low (1-5 pairs), an estimate based on the number of tetrads holding the species can be calculated. Supplemented by data from the *Bird Reports*, this is helpful for the woodpeckers, and localised passerines such as Tree Pipit, Redstart and Wood Warbler. Using habitat and altitude data it has been possible to refine some estimates based on actual or subjective estimates of density in differing habitats. Thus for Siskin, different densities are assumed for birds in tetrads with a large area of coniferous woodland than for other habitats.

Common and widespread species pose more of a problem. One significant piece of information is lacking for many species, that is real density figures at a tetrad level. Most published density figures relate to densities measured in small patches of good quality habitat extrapolated up to provide a number of pairs per square kilometre. With fragmented habitats typical of much of the modern landscape, these densities are rarely (if ever) achieved on the ground across a whole square kilometre. More realistic figures are rarely available and there is a useful piece of work here to be followed up in the future. Accordingly it has been necessary to work on subjective figures based on what little information is available. Much of this was derived from the authors' field experience through the fieldwork for this *Atlas*.

Ongoing, national, annual, censuses organised by the BTO do, however, provide some data on the numbers of species occurring in local plots. The Waterways Bird Survey has been especially useful in providing figures for the density of species such as Dipper and Common Sandpiper which have linear territories along rivers and burns. The Common Birds Census also provides density figures but the derived densities are typically higher than for SE Scotland generally, as the small plots are usually chosen in productive areas. The newer Breeding Bird Survey uses randomly chosen 1km squares ('plots') as its recording unit and, at least for the widespread species, produces more representative density figures. In 1996 there were 32 plots in Lothian and Borders, covering a wide range of habitats. The BBS uses two 1km transects across the plot, measuring the numbers of contacts with birds. The BTO provides the annual results in tabular form listing the proportion of plots with records of each species, the mean number of birds contacted in occupied plots and the maximum numbers encountered in any plot.

For the purpose of estimating densities of birds in our *Atlas* area, we used the BBS results for all plots lying within SE Scotland for the available years 1994-1996. The mean number of contacts was used in estimating a density figure. Species were assessed according to their visual and audible conspicuousness over distance. Thus Wrens may only be detectable over 50m on either side of the transect, while for Redshanks the distance is judged to be 200m. Thus the mean number of contacts applied to different proportions of the 1km square for different species. While the Wren figure would be multiplied by five to produce a density for the whole plot, the Redshank figure would be multiplied by 1.25. Some adjustment was then made to convert the number of contacts to pairs, usually taken at two-thirds of the estimated contact figure.

Another approach was to use the most recent British estimate. The simplest calculation was based on the BTO estimate of the national population, where the total is divided by the number of 10-km squares where the species was recorded in the *New Atlas*. Thus the British Wren population of 7,100,000 pairs in 2,747 10-km squares produces a figure of 2,584 pairs per 10-km square, or 26prs/km^2. Occurring in 1,672 tetrads (6,688km^2), this gives a local population of 173,888. Alternatively, as SE Scotland comprises about 2.6% of the land area of Britain, it might be expected that the local population would be 2.6% of the British total (184,600 in the case of Wren). Comparison with the *New Atlas* Abundance maps shows whether we can expect a species to be more or less abundant in SE Scotland compared with other areas of Britain.

The derived totals make fascinating reading and invite speculation. It is hoped that someone will take up the challenge of questioning and refining these totals by additional fieldwork measuring real densities at 1km^2 or tetrad level in different areas of SE Scotland, and by sample or complete surveys of selected species.

Main Species Accounts

Layout and Content of Species Accounts

This section includes accounts of all species for which there was evidence of breeding, defined as at least two records in the probable or confirmed breeding categories. For convenience, the scope of the chapter is extended slightly by including all the grebes.

For most species there is a two-page spread with text on one page facing maps and graphs on the other. The main map shows the tetrad distribution, while two small maps show the distribution at 10-km square level for 1968-72 (from the *Old Atlas*) and 1988-94. The graphs normally show the records according to altitude and/or habitat features. In a few cases, two or more species are covered in one spread, and for some sensitive species there are no maps. Species appear in systematic order except where it is convenient to take species which are doubled up slightly out of order.

The normal structure of the text begins with a brief introduction to the species, including habitat requirements and nest sites in a British context. Next are comments on fieldwork and recording; how easy the species was to find; the balance of the breeding categories and relative frequency of specific categories such as fledged birds or occupied nests; and any lessons from the fieldwork relevant to the completeness, reliability and interpretation of the results. The most important parts of an *Atlas* such as this are the species maps, so these are described and interpreted in detail. In some cases, actual sites are referred to, with tetrad references for less well known sites. These references are to enable the reader to locate the area referred to, and not to delimit the site. The site itself may be a small part of the tetrad or may extend into other tetrads. The most frequently referred to sites, plus the location of towns and other familiar places are listed elsewhere. After the distribution is described, any points of interest are discussed and comparisons over time and space are made. An estimate of the population in the *Atlas* area is made and possible future work considered. The text ends with the name(s) of the author(s).

The main map shows the coast as a solid line and the land boundary dotted. The boundary between Lothian Region and Borders Region is a dot-dash line. Major rivers (broadly those shown on 1:25,000 Ordnance Survey maps with two banks in dark blue and light blue between, rather than a single blue line) and lochs and reservoirs are shown with solid lines. Grid lines are at 10-km intervals in grey and the digit of the 10-km square grid reference appears on the axes. On most maps (not those with a purely coastal distribution) there is grey shading for land above 200m, 300m or 400m, as considered appropriate for the species concerned and indicated by a legend in the top left-hand corner. A box in the top right-hand corner gives a summary of the distribution. A small open square indicates where the species was observed only, while red squares of increasing size indicate possible, probable and confirmed breeding. Below these is a line for the total. Against each category is the number of tetrads in which the species was recorded in that category, and a percentage. For individual categories, the latter gives the records in that category as a percentage of all records of the species. That against the total category gives the percentage of all 1,756 tetrads in which the species was recorded.

The small maps similarly show three sizes of filled square, with the addition of open squares for observed records in the map for 1988-94. Because the *Old Atlas* incorporated records from outside SE Scotland, squares on the land boundary (and NT28 which includes part of Fife) are not directly comparable in the two maps. To mitigate this problem, records from certain 10-km squares having little area in SE Scotland have been excluded from both maps. This affects NS86 & 87, NT04, 10, 28 and 94, and NY39, 47, and 69.

For certain species some squares in the 1968-72 maps may be displaced from their correct position by up to two 10-km squares or may have been omitted. This was done in the *Old Atlas* to preserve confidentiality for some sensitive species. The species which could be affected in the *Atlas* area are: Goosander, Hen Harrier, Goshawk, Buzzard, Peregrine, Common Tern and Fieldfare. The *Old Atlas* should be consulted in order to make a judgement of the likelihood that records in the *Atlas* area are affected.

Careful consideration was given to the confidentiality of records of sensitive species, and Dave Dick, RSPB Senior Investigations Officer, Scotland, Peter Gordon, RSPB Conservation Officer for SE Scotland, the Lothian and Borders Raptor Study Group and the East Scotland Tern Conservation Group were all consulted. With their agreement, the treatment is as follows: no maps are given for Red-necked Grebe, Slavonian Grebe, Black-necked Grebe, Golden Eagle, Osprey, Dotterel and all terns except Common Tern; while for Hen Harrier, Goshawk, Merlin, Peregrine and Raven the map is at the 10-km square level. In these maps the dots represent the number of tetrads within the square in which the species was recorded, regardless of the category of breeding, except that squares in which the species was recorded only at the observed level are identified. The key in the bottom right-hand corner gives details of the grouping. There is no small 10-km square map for 1988-94 for the latter group of species and it should be noted that the main map and the 1968-72 map are not directly comparable since the dots represent different things. Apart from these sensitive species, only one confidential record was received via the Local Recorder. This was for a Little Owl, and it has been mapped effectively at 10-km square level; i.e. the record has been placed at the centre of the square in which it occurred, so that it appears at tetrad M.

Most of the graphs give the species' distribution according to altitude (average, or median, altitude within each tetrad) or habitat categories, as indicated by the heading. They normally relate to records of apparently breeding birds, so observed records are excluded. For the two combined species, Carrion and Hybrid Crow and Red-legged Partridge and Chukar, the graphs are based on records of the main species only. The categories appear on the vertical axis and percentages on the horizontal axis. There are two ways in which the percentages representing the distribution can be calculated and both are normally shown. Take for instance the altitude category of 200-299m. The number of tetrads at this altitude in which the species was recorded expressed as a percentage of the total number of tetrads at this altitude indicates how attractive or important this altitude is to the species. Alternatively, the number of tetrads at this altitude in which the species was recorded can be expressed as a percentage of all records of the species, indicating roughly what proportion of the population nests at this altitude. Roughly, because no allowance is made for variations in the number of pairs nesting per tetrad. Most attention is focused on the former representation, which is described as "% of tetrads occupied" in the legend but in some cases the latter, "% of records of species", is of significance.

For some species such as Grey Heron where the observed category is of interest, observed and records indicative of breeding for the "% of tetrads occupied" graph are shown separately. Some graphs which require two scales have one on the left vertical axis, the other on the right, with the appropriate legend below each scale. Other forms of graphs are presented for special cases which should be self-explanatory, and further data for some species, especially historical data for seabirds, are given in Appendices.

Little Grebe
Tachybaptus ruficollis

The Little Grebe is the most numerous and widespread grebe in SE Scotland, probably due to its relatively undemanding habitat preferences. Medium sized shallow waters with a dense growth of both submerged and emergent vegetation, and an abundance of small fish and aquatic invertebrates are preferred. Dense vegetation promotes a good population of prey animals and provides a nest-site for this rather shy and retiring species.

Whilst by no means difficult to record, Little Grebes can be difficult to see on thickly-vegetated ponds. The trilling song is therefore an important indicator and was the sole evidence at some sites. Probable breeding records were typically sightings of pairs that were not followed up later in the season. Breeding was confirmed in over half of the tetrads, mostly of adults feeding young on the water. Only eleven nests were actually ever seen by observers.

Whilst the range is governed by the presence of waterbodies, the habitat analysis shows a marked preference for medium to large-sized waters, approximately 40-45% of all such water bodies of these sizes in SE Scotland being occupied. The remaining 60% of unoccupied waters hints that there is considerable scope for population expansion in the area.

The map shows two main concentrations: around Edinburgh and in the Ettrick Forest. Although there are some natural lochs in and around Edinburgh, the majority are man-made, built to service the water demands of the city in the 19th century. Most sites in the Ettrick Forest are natural. The two areas differ in altitude, most of the Lothian sites being below 100m compared to above 200m further south. East Lothian sites have much in common with those around Edinburgh, most being amenity ponds or water-supply reservoirs. Breeding has occurred on the Union Canal near Linlithgow and Woodcockdale (NS97Y) in 1986, 1988 and 1993. On the rivers, birds may have bred on a cut-off of the Tweed that resembles a pond at Bellspool (NT13S) and on the main river between Norham and Ladykirk (NT84Y). These records could represent a move on to moving water and may reflect a national trend of expansion onto rivers and canals noted since the 1970s (Marchant & Hyde 1980).

The *Bird Report* records show breeding season reports on 134 waters, 60 in Lothian and 74 in Borders. This matches the 131 tetrad registrations, despite some waters covering more than one tetrad. Most sites (71%) have held just one pair, but larger waters typically hold 2-5 pairs. Only Gladhouse with seven pairs and Bavelaw with a massive 17 pairs hold more. It is unlikely that all of these waters simultaneously hold breeding Little Grebes. The

Bird Report data suggest min-max figures of 146-215 pairs breeding in the area: Lothian, 70-113 pairs and Borders, 76-102 pairs. An annual figure of around 170 pairs seems likely.

The *New Atlas* uses a figure of 4-8 pairs per occupied 10-km square to calculate the British population, which would suggest 180-360 pairs for SE Scotland. This is rather high compared to the local estimate of 170 pairs and may mean there is a lower density here than elsewhere in Britain.

The population figure is a big increase over former estimates and almost certainly represents a real increase in numbers. In the 19th century the species was scarce locally and mostly a winter visitor. It then increased greatly, becoming a common breeder by the 1930s (*B&R*). No significant Scottish trends have been evident since (*Thom*). However, the 60 Lothian sites mentioned above is a huge increase over the 27 sites known between 1979 and 1984 (*Andrews*) and it is almost certain that this is a real population increase (R.W.J. Smith *pers. comm.*), although better knowledge of the Little Grebe as a result of the *Atlas* survey doubtless plays its part. There is little known of the history of the Borders population.

Reports of double broods are not uncommon despite the statement in the *New Atlas* that there is little firm evidence that they occur. The *Lothian Bird Report* quotes examples of double broods at Milkhall Pond in 1984 and 1988, the Royal Botanic Gardens and Markle Loch in 1985, Marl Loch at Aberlady from 1985-1987, Tailend Moss and Penicuik House in 1987 and 1988, Straiton Pond in 1988 and Bara Loch in 1990. Breeding success has been casually monitored in Borders and this varies between 1.5-2.7 young per observed brood, averaging 2.05 young per brood between 1985 & 1995. This is lower than the British average of 3.0 young per brood reported by Moss & Moss (1993).

Flocks form on a few waters in the autumn. The record counts were 40 at Hoselaw and 66 at Linlithgow in October 1980. Recent counts are lower with 22 at Gladhouse in August 1988 and 16 at Portmore Loch in October 1990. More birds now winter on ponds and even more recently on the rivers, recalling the 30 birds that typically overwinter on the neighbouring upper Clyde. The recent run of mild winters may have influenced this trend.

The Little Grebe, with a small population occurring at well-defined sites, would be easy to monitor in future by a single-season survey to see if the hinted population increase is genuine. **R.D.Murray**

Little Grebe

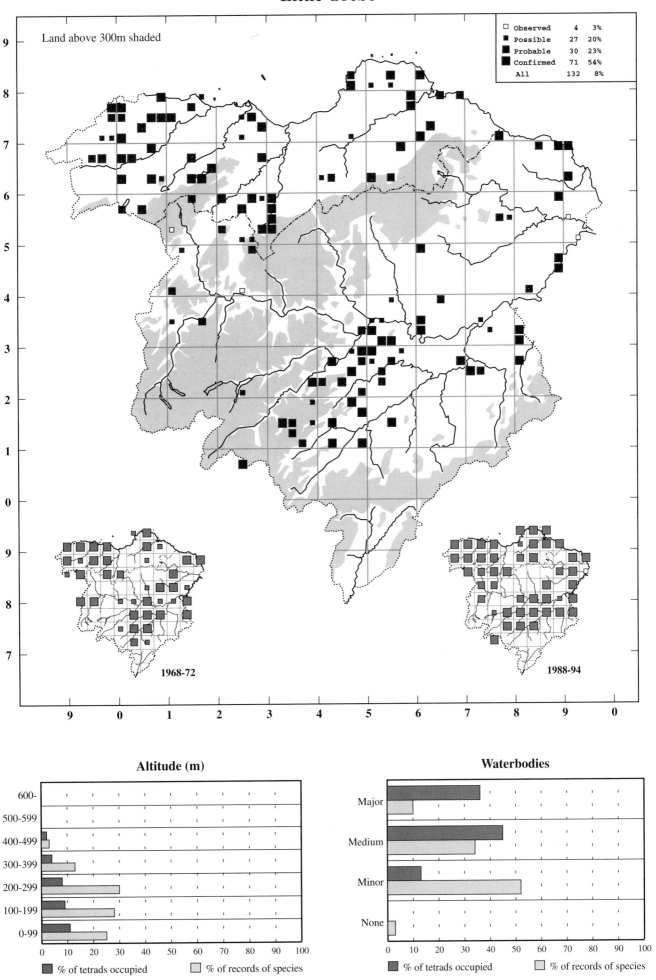

Land above 300m shaded

□ Observed	4	3%
■ Possible	27	20%
■ Probable	30	23%
■ Confirmed	71	54%
All	132	8%

1968-72

1988-94

Altitude (m)

600-	
500-599	
400-499	
300-399	
200-299	
100-199	
0-99	

0 10 20 30 40 50 60 70 80 90 100

■ % of tetrads occupied   ☐ % of records of species

Waterbodies

Major	
Medium	
Minor	
None	

0 10 20 30 40 50 60 70 80 90 100

■ % of tetrads occupied   ☐ % of records of species

Great Crested Grebe
Podiceps cristatus

Shallow eutrophic waters, with a fringe of emergent plants for the nest site, open water for feeding opportunities and room for a running take-off, are the main habitat needs of the Great Crested Grebe. Deep waters are avoided. Fish are the main food with aquatic invertebrates forming a small part of the diet.

Birds arrive on breeding waters from late February or early March. Prospecting occurs in March and April with birds breeding from April onwards. Young are usually not evident until late May, especially on the higher waters where breeding occurs a little later. Being obvious on open water, this species was easy to record. Breeding was proved in 43% of the tetrads where birds were present, shared between occupied nests and records of young.

The range comprises the Edinburgh reservoirs on the fringes of the Pentlands and Moorfoots, the Ettrick Forest lochs and the isolated Hoselaw and Yetholm Lochs to the east. There are fewer sites than is apparent as several waters, e.g. Linlithgow, Gladhouse, Alemoor and Yetholm, register in more than one tetrad. The absence of birds from the Lammermuirs and parts of the Merse is puzzling.

Breeding is sufficiently rare for most birds to be reported annually in the *Bird Reports*. Since 1979 breeding has been attempted on 15 waters in Lothian and 26 in Borders. Most sites are only sporadically used, especially in Borders where half the lochs held birds for just 1-2 years in the 1979-1995 period. Only Linlithgow, Bavelaw, Gladhouse and Duddingston in Lothian, and Portmore, Hoselaw, Lindean and Shielswood (NT41P) in Borders, were used for more than half the period. Just Linlithgow (5-24 pairs), Gladhouse (2-8), Duddingston (1-4) and Bavelaw/Threipmuir (1-6) hold reasonable numbers. Elsewhere 1-2 pairs is the norm. The second graph shows the varying levels of occupation (not all pairs breeding), the mid-1980s having higher numbers than much of the *Atlas* period. Success is generally poor with only about a third of sites achieving any success in a single year. Only the main Lothian sites have consistent success. The best-ever reported year was in 1989 when 30 pairs reared 28 young, while 19 pairs managed just a single young in 1991. Success is extremely poor in the Borders.

Altitude may be a factor in determining success and thus the frequency of occupation. Almost all Borders sites are above 200m and while many Lothian sites are lower, both Gladhouse (270m) and Bavelaw (250m) are high up in the hills. Compared to Linlithgow and Duddingston at lower levels where up to 15-22 young have been reported in the best years, success on these higher waters is patchy. *Thom* states that "nesting has been recorded up to 250m", thus it is hardly surprising that success is variable and often poor on the Borders lochs which are amongst the highest breeding sites in Scotland, the waters at Hellmoor, Kingside and the Shaws lochs all being just under 350m above sea level.

A stable water level is very important in any species with a floating nest and constant fluctuations at reservoirs lead to failure. Birds have only been consistently successful at Bavelaw since the 1970s and at Gladhouse since the 1980s, when water levels were better regulated. Fluctuating levels at Crosswood, Alemoor and Whiteadder Reservoirs probably rule these waters out as regular sites.

Commercial angling at Portmore and Roslynlee (NT25U) have led to these sites being abandoned through disturbance, despite birds prospecting in the spring. Like sites elsewhere in Scotland (*Thom*) the reduction in the numbers at Linlithgow, from 12-24 pairs in the early 1980s to about 3-8 pairs at present, may also be connected with disturbance from high levels of both angling and sailing activity. Smith (1974) regarded Linlithgow as a key site in the area, the regular production of large numbers of young there maintaining population levels elsewhere. The recent reduction in numbers there is disturbing although more regular breeding at Gladhouse and Bavelaw due to the stabilisation of water levels may offset this loss.

Great Crested Grebes were close to extinction in Britain in the late 19th century, mainly due to the demand for their plumage by the fashion trade. They were first known to breed in Lothian in 1907 at Cobbinshaw, and in Borders in 1912 at Portmore Loch, spreading to approximately the current range by the the 1940s and 1950s. The 10-km square maps show a slight contraction of range between the *Old Atlas* period and the present, despite the *Old Atlas* survey lasting only five years compared to seven for the current project.

Local Great Crested Grebes were surveyed as part of a national survey in 1965 when 19 waters held 19-27 pairs (Prest & Mills 1966). By 1973 this total had dropped to just 13 waters with 15-20 pairs (Smith 1974). Birds have been recorded in the *Bird Reports* on a total of 41 waters since 1979, 27 of them between 1988-94. The maximum number of pairs in any year since 1979 was 40 pairs in 1987, when numbers were boosted by counts during the Wigeon census on the Ettrick Forest lochs that year, and 33 pairs in 1988 during the *Atlas* period. These figures contradict any idea of a decline in numbers although the relative importance of different lochs has changed. The current population is about 25-35 pairs at about 16 sites in any single year.

Great Crested Grebes breed on a limited number of sites, so could be easily monitored more regularly and while there is no current concern about the population level, the continuing poor breeding success may be a cause of concern in the future.   **R.D.Murray**

Great Crested Grebe

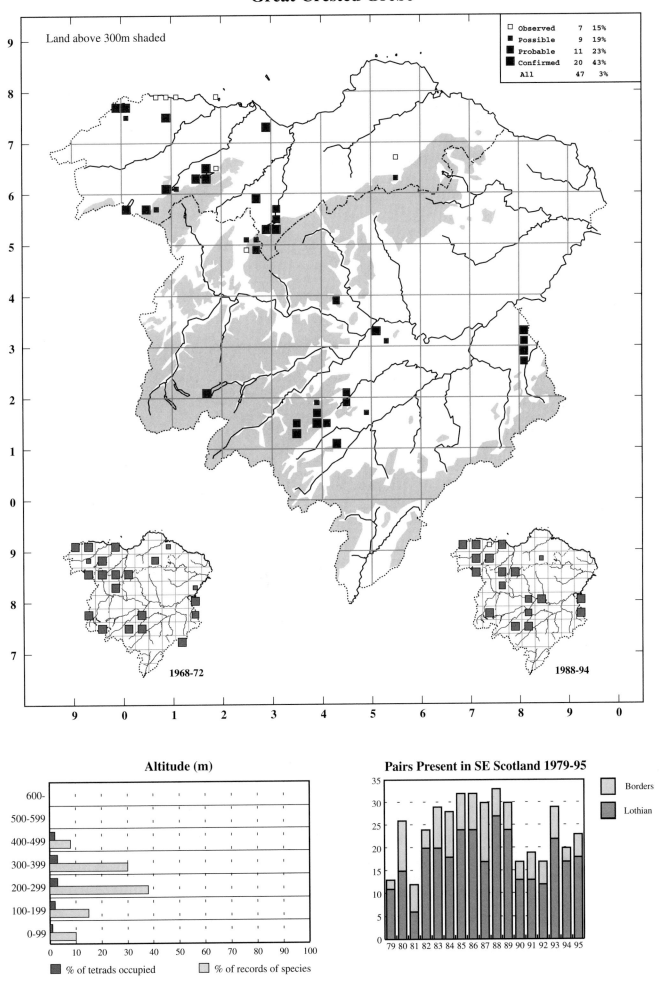

Land above 300m shaded

	Observed	7	15%
	Possible	9	19%
	Probable	11	23%
	Confirmed	20	43%
	All	47	3%

1968-72

1988-94

Altitude (m)

□ % of tetrads occupied   □ % of records of species

Pairs Present in SE Scotland 1979-95

Borders
Lothian

Red-necked Grebe

Podiceps grisegena

The Red-necked Grebe is the only Palearctic species of grebe that does not breed regularly in Britain. On the continent this species nests on medium-sized waters with a good fringe of emergent vegetation and often surrounded by woodland. Like the Black-necked Grebe, breeding sites can be associated with Black-headed Gull colonies.

Since the 1970s individuals and occasionally pairs have summered in parts of Scotland. Birds first appeared at an undisclosed Lothian water in 1980 and while not present in every year, possible nests were built without any further evidence of breeding being obtained. In 1988, however, an egg was seen at this site in Lothian, and although it later disappeared, this constitutes the first and only definite attempt of breeding in Britain (Anon 1989).

While an occasional bird was seen at two Lothian sites since 1988, attention has moved to a Borders water where a pair has been present in each summer from 1989 to 1997. Frustratingly,

while this pair copulate frequently and build nest-platforms, there has been no definite success and indeed it is not certain whether an egg has ever been laid in the years that the birds have been present up to 1997. Incubation has been suspected but never proven. Single birds have also been seen at another Borders site on occasions, about 20km away from the regular site and, while one of the resident pair could have been involved, it is more likely that these records refer to transient birds.   *R.D.Murray*

No map is shown here in order to protect the confidentiality of the sites involved.

No. of 10-km squares: 5   No. of Tetrads: 6

Observed	0	0%
Possible	3	50%
Probable	2	33%
Confirmed	1	17%

Slavonian Grebe

Podiceps auritus

The Slavonian Grebe is a rare breeding bird in Britain. The species first colonised the Scottish Highlands in 1908 and to date has established a small population of about 60 pairs, almost wholly in the Highlands around the Great Glen near the area of the initial colonisation. Slavonian Grebes prefer to breed on mesotrophic lochs, typically nesting in beds of Bottle Sedge *Carex rostrata*. Such habitat is very rare in southern Scotland but does exist in some of the Ettrick Forest lochs. Thus it is not beyond possibility that this species may breed at some time in the future at one of these sites.

As the Firth of Forth is one of the main wintering sites for Slavonian Grebes in Britain, with up to 150 present in late winter and spring (*Andrews*), it is hardly surprising that occasional birds turn up on fresh waters in the spring and occasionally linger into the summer.

Slavonian Grebes were present in five tetrads between 1988-1994. The most significant record was of a single bird that summered at Branxholme Wester Loch (NT41F) between 1985 and 1989 but

with no indication of ever having attracted a mate. It was last seen returning in April 1989 but was not subsequently relocated. Another single bird was seen at Bavelaw-Threipmuir in April and May 1988, before moving to Gladhouse in June. Birds were also present at Gladhouse Reservoir in 1991 when a pair appeared in late April. Although one of these birds lingered into early May there were no subsequent sightings. Yet another was at Bavelaw-Threipmuir in April and May 1993.   *R.D.Murray*

No map is shown here.

No. of 10-km squares: 4   No. of Tetrads: 5

Observed	0	0%
Possible	4	80%
Probable	1	20%
Confirmed	0	0%

Black-necked Grebe
Podiceps nigricollis

This rare species of grebe breeds on shallow eutrophic waters, often associated with Black-headed Gull colonies. It is likely that the grebes derive a measure of protection from predators of both gull and grebe eggs and young through the watchfulness and mobbing behaviour of the gulls. Some emergent vegetation is necessary for the nest site, and although floating mats of water plants can be important these are not a necessity for breeding and certainly not present at the two local sites.

The first British breeding record was in Wales in 1904 and Black-necked Grebes probably first bred in Scotland at Cobbinshaw Reservoir in 1929 (NT15D). Up to five pairs bred there between 1930-34 with another pair at Bavelaw in 1934. This focus of breeding records then vanished and since then Black-necked Grebes have become very scarce in SE Scotland, even as wintering birds along the coast (*Andrews*). It seems possible that the focus of colonisation for this species moved north of the Firth of Forth, shifting from Lothian to Fife, Perthshire and later Angus (*Thom*).

Between 1979 and 1991 the *Bird Reports* show that spring records on inland waters remained scarce with just six reports of singles: at West Water in 1983; Hoselaw in 1987; the Hirsel in 1989; and at Portmore, Gladhouse and Bemersyde in 1991.

A pair bred successfully for the first time in Borders in 1992, and may have attempted to breed in 1993 at the same site. Although no birds were reported in 1994, breeding has since occurred successfully at two Borders waters between 1995 and 1997. In 1997 a minimum of seven adults were present in spring although only two pairs bred.

It is unclear whether the source of these birds was from the Fife/Angus populations to the north or from more recently established colonies to the south in Northumberland. The most recent report of the Rare Breeding Birds Panel (Ogilvie 1996) shows that the British breeding population has effectively doubled between 1989 and 1994 from *c*.40 to *c*.80 pairs. This seems to be part of a more general increase seen across NW Europe (*New Atlas*). Scotland no longer holds the majority of British Black-necked Grebes with much of the recent expansion occurring in the English Midlands.

R.D.Murray

No map is shown here in order to protect the confidentiality of the sites involved.

No. of 10-km squares: 4	No. of Tetrads: 4	
Observed	0	0%
Possible	3	75%
Probable	0	0%
Confirmed	1	25%

Fulmar

Fulmarus glacialis

The Fulmar was long confined in Britain to just one site, St.Kilda. It started a relentless spread, colonising northern Scotland in the late 19th century and most of the remainder of the British coastline during the 20th century, except for the flat coastlines of southern and eastern Britain. The cause of this spread is uncertain but may be related to the increase in offal provided by the whaling and fishing industries. The spread has now slowed but not stopped.

Prime Fulmar breeding habitat has steep, slightly vegetated, rocky or earthy cliffs with recesses tucked away from the elements. Although colonial, the nest sites are loosely scattered as dictated by the distribution of suitable recesses. Pairs are intolerant of close proximity, rarely nesting within squabbling distance. While primarily a bird of steep coastal cliffs, pressure caused by the enormous population increase has resulted in small numbers inhabiting cliffs and quarries at some distance from the sea, ruined and inhabited buildings and even sand dunes in less disturbed mainland sites and islands. Fulmars feed only at sea and spread ocean-wide in winter.

Fulmars are long-lived. First breeding in males is most often at eight years and in females at 12 years of age. Birds surviving to adulthood can live for several decades, the oldest ringed adult being over 40 years old (Dunnet 1992). Sub-adults prospect likely ledges for some years before breeding. As incubating adults are indistinguishable from sitting non-breeding sub-adults or others, Fulmars are normally censused by counting apparently occupied sites (AOS), that is ledges bearing one or two birds and apparently capable of holding an egg (Lloyd *et al.* 1991). Only a single chick is reared annually.

Atlas registrations were either of observed records, mostly birds soaring on the coast near nest sites, or of confirmed breeding, all occupied nests. It was decided that the *Atlas* criteria should match current seabird census methodology and where observers were unsure whether sitting birds were incubating or not the record was considered as confirmed, matching the apparently occupied site criteria used by seabird nest counters.

The coastal tetrads on the map with confirmed breeding faithfully reflect the distribution of steep-gradient coast in SE Scotland. Almost the entire Berwickshire coast is eminently suitable for Fulmars, being mainly cliffs or steep ground and often difficult of access for both humans and mammalian predators. Lothian has little such coast except at Bilsdean (NT77), near Dunbar (NT67), Seacliff to Tantallon (NT58&68) and Hanging Rocks, near Eyebroughy (NT48). All of the Forth islands now hold colonies of breeding Fulmars other than Cramond Island (NT17Z) and a few minor islets and stacks. Inland sites are relatively recent additions to the local range, with colonies at Arthur's Seat (NT27), Torphin Quarry (NT16&26) and Traprain Law (NT57). These inland colonies and the tiny coastal colony at Hanging Rocks (NT48) near Gullane cause the only differences between the 10-km maps of the *Old Atlas* and the present one.

Observed records are mostly in East Lothian and Berwickshire where there are coastal breeding colonies. However, there are a number of records to the west of Leith (NT27) indicating that numbers of Fulmars regularly fly further up the Forth foraging for food, even as far as Blackness (NT07) the most westerly shoreline in SE Scotland. While the occasional bird (NT27K) might be expected to be seen flying near the existing colonies in Edinburgh or near the coast as at Reston (NT86Q), the records from Gladhouse and the Eildon Hills (NT53L) are less expected but fit a pattern of vagrancy that sees odd inland records between April and July every year or so.

The tables in the Appendix show the development of all Forth Fulmar colonies. The first phase of prospecting was wholly in the outer Firth of Forth at St. Abb's Head, the Isle of May and Bass Rock from 1914 onwards, with proof of breeding coming about a decade later. Steady increase followed, most rapidly at St. Abb's Head including spread westwards to Fast Castle by the 1950s. More colonies soon arose further into the Forth, attaining large numbers at Tantallon and Inchkeith by the 1960s. All of the island colonies were established by the 1960s, other than Inchmickery which was colonised in 1975. Numbers at individual colonies fluctuate, but overall the Forth population is still inexorably rising, as the first graph shows. Examples of two individual colonies are shown in the second graph. Only on parts of the Berwickshire coast, where the Fox is more common than previously, and on Inchkeith, which has had more disturbance by humans and domestic animals than any other island, have numbers apparently already peaked. New counts along the Berwickshire coast to determine trends there are badly needed, the last complete counts having been in 1987.

The inland colonies (see Appendix) were established in a late phase of colonisation, presumably due to population pressure at the main coastal and island sites. Fulmar chicks were first recorded at Torphin Quarry, Arthur's Seat and Traprain in 1978, 1981 and 1993 respectively. Records suggest that numbers at these sites levelled off quickly after the initial build-up and may not be rising further (Dott *in prep.*). No other inland colonies have become established, although a pair hatched young south of Cockburnspath in 1955 and in the Garleton Hills in 1980. Birds have visited crags at North Berwick Law (NT58M), Edinburgh Castle Rock (NT27L), Blackford Hill (NT27K) and parts of the Pentlands but never stayed to nest.

From the arrival of the first birds early this century, the Fulmar population of the Forth in 1995 stands at about 4,165 AOS, comprising *c.*2,200 on the mainland coast, *c.*1,900 on the islands and *c.*65 inland. This population is still increasing slowly at 3.3% per annum through the 1980s and 1990s (Thompson *et al.* 1997), similar to national trends. The British population increase (excluding St.Kilda) was 13-19% per annum up to 1939, but reduced to 4% per annum from 1939-1987 (Lloyd *et al.* 1991). With an estimated 540,500 pairs in Britain (*New Atlas*), the Forth holds only 0.8% of the British population. **H.E.M.Dott**

Fulmar

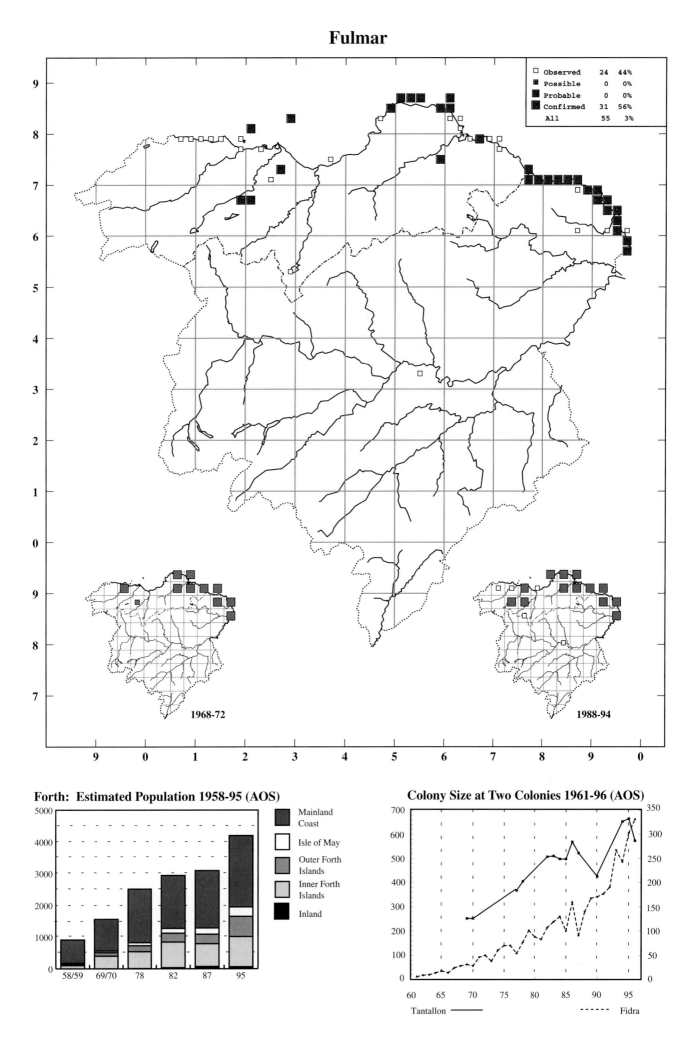

	Observed	24	44%
Possible	0	0%
Probable	0	0%
Confirmed	31	56%
All	55	3%

1968-72

1988-94

Forth: Estimated Population 1958-95 (AOS)

Mainland Coast
Isle of May
Outer Forth Islands
Inner Forth Islands
Inland

58/59 69/70 78 82 87 95

Colony Size at Two Colonies 1961-96 (AOS)

60 65 70 75 80 85 90 95

Tantallon ——   Fidra - - - - -

41

Frederick J Watson 98

Gannet

Morus bassanus

The Gannet is confined to the North Atlantic and breeds colonially on cliffs and the upper slopes of rocky islands. SE Scotland holds one of its largest and longest established colonies at the Bass Rock in the Firth of Forth. For most of the year Gannets are commonly seen offshore from the coasts of Lothian and Borders. Seeing the Gannet dive steeply into the water to catch fish is one of the most dramatic sights to be seen around our coasts and enlivens many a day's birding along the Forth.

Gannets only breed at one site in SE Scotland, the Bass Rock off the East Lothian coast near North Berwick (NT68D). In addition, singles and apparent pairs have occupied part of a cliff to the north of the lighthouse at St. Abb's Head (NT96E) in 1979, 1982, 1990, 1992 and since, and birds have occasionally been seen on Craigleith (*Bird Reports*). Elsewhere, other gannetries have been started by birds staying ashore in summer so it is possible that St. Abb's Head could become a new colony in the future.

Although for most of the year Gannets can be seen at sea throughout the Forth below the Forth Bridges and off the Berwickshire coast, Gannets were recorded close inshore during *Atlas* fieldwork only in a handful of tetrads east of the Bass Rock. Note, however, that fishing birds are frequently present off the Berwickshire coast but clearly went unrecorded in *Atlas* fieldwork. Not surprisingly, these records are clearly related to the position of the Bass Rock at the mouth of the Forth and the favoured fishing grounds further east in the North Sea. Work on the distributions of seabirds in the North Sea showed that most high concentrations of Gannets are within 100km of breeding colonies (Tasker *et al.* 1985).

It is not known when the Bass Rock was first colonised by Gannets, but it is noted as a gannetry by a 15th-century author (in Nelson 1978). Early accounts indicate that the whole surface of the island was covered with nests and that they were most numerous towards the summit of the rock. A decline occurred in the 19th century due to exploitation by man. In the middle of that century, about 1,800 juveniles were taken annually for food, but the greatest slaughter must have been the wanton shooting of birds flying around the

rock. These birds seemed simply to be used as targets for "sportsmen". Estimates of the population on the Bass Rock at that time are not thought to be reliable, but indications are that less than 4,000 pairs nested at the turn of the century. Culling ceased in 1885 and with protection and favourable feeding conditions, the population has been able to increase (Nelson 1978).

Since the start of the 20th century, the population has been counted regularly (see table below and graph). Nowadays, counts are normally completed in June or July, to coincide with the time when pairs are in the late stages of incubation or have small chicks. The latest count of almost 40,000 AOS was made at the end of the *Atlas* period, in July 1994. Clearly the population has increased steadily since the beginning of the century, making good the losses of the Victorian era. Surprisingly the rate of increase is showing no signs of slowing down and has effectively doubled in the nine years between 1985 and 1994. The increased size of the colony is clearly evident when old photographs of the Bass Rock are compared with contemporary pictures. Whether this rate of increase will continue at the Bass Rock is open to speculation. The colour plate of the Bass Rock in the introductory chapters makes it evident that room for expansion is decreasing rapidly as nests are built on the remaining vacant parts of the island. It may well be at that point that one of the neighbouring islands, St. Abb's Head or the Isle of May might be colonised. The growth of the Gannet colony on the Bass Rock has had an impact on other species that breed there. The decline in the Rock Pipit may have been caused by this expansion and it is possible that the growth of colonies of other species, such as gulls, may have been limited by the presence of Gannets.

Year	Count (occupied sites unless stated)
1904	7,000-8,000 individuals
1913	3,250 pairs
1929	4,147 nests
1936	4,140 nests
1939	4,374 nests
1949	4,820 nests
1962	6,690-7,126
1968	8,977
1974	9,500-11,500
1977	*c.*13,500
1984	18,162
1985	21,589
1994	39,751 (34,397 nests)

Sources: Nelson (1978) except for counts in 1984 & 1985 (Murray & Wanless 1986) and 1994 (Murray & Wanless 1997).

Until the 1920s, the Bass Rock was the only gannetry on the British east coast, and Nelson's calculations based on the above population estimates indicate that the increase on the Bass Rock probably came about through recruitment of Bass Rock birds, rather than via immigration from elsewhere. The recent increase from 1985 to 1994 represents a spectacular rise of up to 84%, an average annual rate of 7.0%. In addition, other colonies on the east coast may have been colonised by birds from the Bass Rock.

In 1994, the total Scottish population of the Gannet was estimated to be 167,407 apparently occupied sites and the total world population in 1994-95 was believed to be 201,000 (Murray & Wanless 1997). The SE Scotland population on the Bass Rock therefore represents nearly 24% of the Scottish population of the species, and, incredibly, almost 20% of the world total (see graph).

Not only is the Bass Rock of global significance for the Gannet, the species occurs at a higher density here than any other species anywhere in SE Scotland. Multiplying the density up from the actual area of the Bass Rock gives an equivalent of about a quarter of a million nests per square kilometre!   ***M.Holling***

Gannet

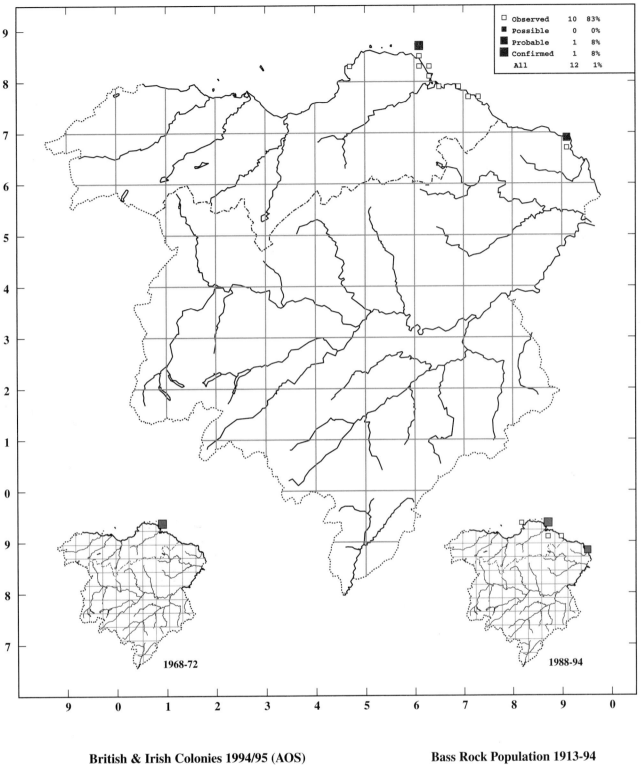

1968-72

1988-94

British & Irish Colonies 1994/95 (AOS)

Ireland (5)
England & Wales (4)
Scar Rocks
Ailsa Craig
Bass Rock
Troup Head
Flannans
St Kilda
Sula Sgeir
Sule Stack
Shetland (4)

0   10000 20000 30000 40000 50000 60000 70000 80000

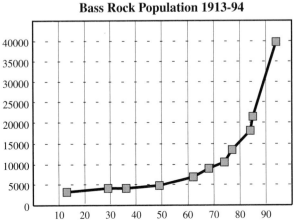

Bass Rock Population 1913-94

40000
35000
30000
25000
20000
15000
10000
5000
0

10   20   30   40   50   60   70   80   90

Frederick J Watson 98

Cormorant
Phalacrocorax carbo

The Cormorant is a large and conspicuous seabird that builds a bulky nest of twigs and seaweed. Cormorants tend to nest colonially on broad coastal cliff ledges and on the tops of stacks. There are, however, some inland tree-nesting colonies, for instance at Mochrun Loch in Dumfries and Galloway. Cormorants also occur widely inland on rivers, lochs and reservoirs where they do not breed.

During the breeding season Cormorants were found along much of the coast and also in a significant number of inland tetrads. In the *Atlas* period breeding was confirmed on four islands in the Forth and in two coastal tetrads in Berwickshire. These records were all of nests with eggs or young. The remaining sightings were all categorised in the observed category.

The observed records make it apparent that Cormorants can be seen along most stretches of the coast right up the Forth as far as Blackness. Records come from both rocky and sandy stretches of the coast, and, not surprisingly, concentrations occur closest to the breeding colonies. Although a few Cormorants were reported at inland waters in West and Midlothian, they are really only regular during the breeding season along the Tweed up as far as Mertoun in NT63. There seems to have been an increase in this habit over the last decade, but it is not well documented in the *Bird Reports*. The largest numbers have been at the roost on Dreeper Island (NT84X) in April, e.g. 30 there on 7 April 1991. Birds occur as far inland as Talla and Megget reservoirs in NT12.

During 1988-94 breeding occurred near North Berwick on Craigleith, the Lamb and Eyebroughy, on Inchkeith higher up the Forth, and on the Berwickshire coast at Fast Castle (NT87K) and Fancove Head (NT96L). Cormorants first colonised Lothian in 1957 when five pairs were found on the Lamb (Smith 1969). The first recorded breeding in Borders was in 1969 at Fast Castle Head where three pairs were counted during the Operation Seafarer survey (*Murray*). The small colony at Fancove Head was only occupied in 1989; the site is almost wave-washed and this may explain its abandonment. These, the only mainland colonies, are both on stacks.

The main colonies on the south side of the Forth are on the Lamb and Craigleith. In addition, on the northern (Fife) side of the Forth two islets, Haystack and Car Craig, held in the order of 180 breeding pairs during the survey period. These colonies have been included in the tables in the Appendix since nearby Cormorant colonies tend to fluctuate widely in size between successive years (Smith 1969, Lloyd *et al.* 1991); during 1988-94 Eyebroughy was deserted and Haystack was colonised. Inchkeith was recolonised in 1992 after four pairs had nested there in 1984. Full details are given in the Appendix. The totals for the whole Forth area fluctuate wildly but continue to increase, with a peak at over 500 in 1991-2 (see first graph).

Earlier in the 20th century Cormorants were certainly present as a non-breeding species in the Forth, but earlier accounts of "Skarts" make it impossible to sort out the status of Cormorants and Shags individually (*B&R*). Since 1972, the most consistently counted colonies are the Lamb and Craigleith which had average populations of 135 and 62 nests respectively during the 25-year period 1972-1996 inclusive (see second graph). Fast Castle was occupied throughout but nests were not always counted. The average between 1976 and 1996 was 39 nests.

Despite the increase in inland breeding elsewhere in Britain (*New Atlas*), there have been no records of this habit in Lothian and Borders, probably because of persecution, due to the Cormorant's liking of fish coveted by anglers. Although there is no evidence of damage to fish stocks, there have been significant culls of Cormorants in Scotland: 3,832 birds were culled under licence in 1982-92 (Scottish Office figures) and this scale of destruction must have an impact on the breeding numbers and status of Cormorants.

During the survey period the SE Scotland population, including the Fife islands, averaged 320 pairs, representing approximately 9% of the Scottish population and 4.5 % of the British population, surprisingly large proportions especially in view of the fairly recent arrival of the Cormorant as a breeding species in the Forth area.

Although most colonies are monitored annually, efforts should be made to count all colonies each year, and to count young produced to help determine the annual breeding success. To help document the spread of inland birds, more frequent and regular counts of concentrations away from the coast should also be made.

M.Holling & M.Moss

Cormorant

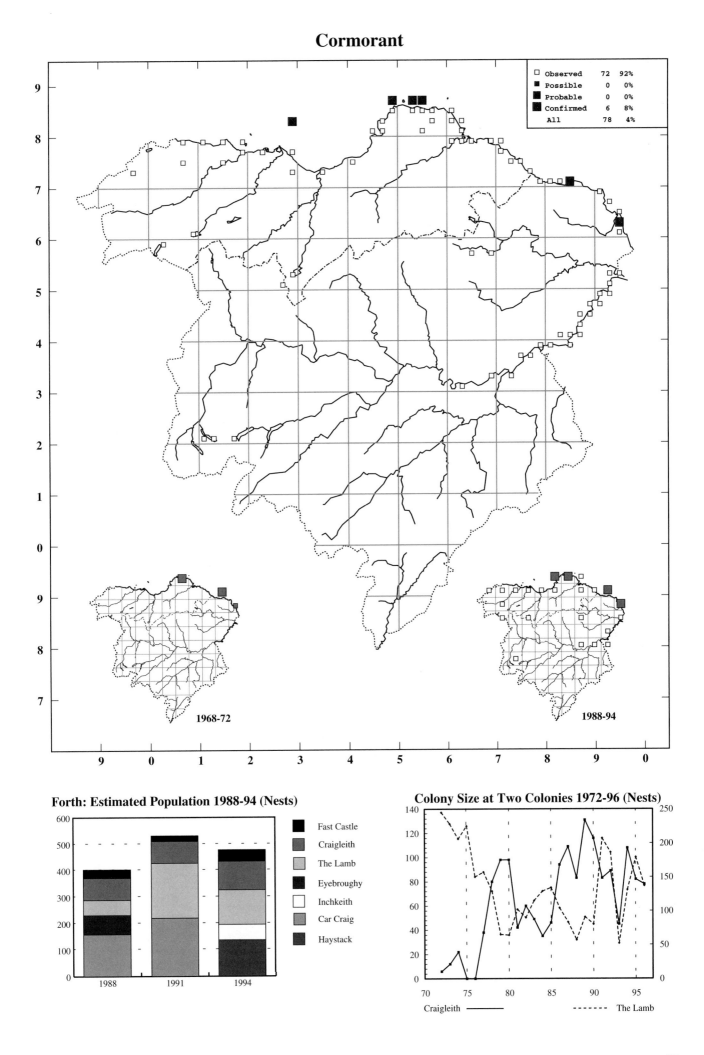

□ Observed	72	92%
■ Possible	0	0%
■ Probable	0	0%
▨ Confirmed	6	8%
All	78	4%

1968-72

1988-94

Forth: Estimated Population 1988-94 (Nests)

Fast Castle
Craigleith
The Lamb
Eyebroughy
Inchkeith
Car Craig
Haystack

Colony Size at Two Colonies 1972-96 (Nests)

Craigleith ———   The Lamb - - - - -

Shag

Phalacrocorax aristotelis

The old name "sea-craw" summarises the appearance of the Shag. Sitting upright on offshore rocks, wings hanging out to dry, Shags are a familiar sight along the rocky shorelines of Britain. As their food is caught on the sea-bed, Shags are birds of shallow coastal waters (<40m depth), rarely found more than 15km from the shore (Wanless *et al.* 1991). Breeding is confined to "hard" shorelines although birds feed on "soft" shores and are regular there in winter. The limitation to "hard" shores is associated with the need to nest on cliffs and islands which are more common on rocky coasts.

Conspicuous nesters, mostly breeding at known sites that are fairly regularly censused, Shags were easy to record. Records were dominated by confirmed breeding registrations at the colonies and by observed records elsewhere, with only single reports of possible or probable breeding.

Birds were observed along much of the rocky coastline of SE Scotland, almost continuously from Gullane to the border. Further west where rocky shores are uncommon and Shags nest on islands fairly distant from the coast, birds were rarely recorded at the shore. While feeding is possible along much of the coastline, colonies require cliffs or islands where birds are free from ground predators. West of Dunbar such sites are wholly limited to islands while to the east of Dunbar breeding occurs on mainland cliffs.

Almost all of the Forth islands hold breeding Shags. Only the tidal islands at Cramond Island and Eyebroughy, and Inchgarvie, which supports part of the Forth Bridge, are shunned by Shags, probably due to the presence of ground predators such as rats.

With the exception of the odd nests at Dunbar harbour, mainland breeding is unknown in Lothian. There are few cliffs in Lothian but the lack of birds at Tantallon (NT58X&68C) is a little puzzling but may be due to the attraction of the Bass Rock just offshore. No such choice exists in Berwickshire and the map shows that most birds are found between Fast Castle (NT87K) and St. Abb's Head with an outlier at Fancove Head (NT96L) where the cliffs are highest, steepest and where stacks are most frequent. Cliffs do extend between St. Abbs and Fancove, and towards Bilsdean (NT77R) to the west and the English border to the south, but these are mostly lower and presumably less attractive for breeding.

Comparison with the *Old Atlas* shows a gain in NT67 corresponding to the Dunbar colony which became established since 1972. Seabird monitoring now provides a much fuller picture of Shag population trends than is possible from comparisons between the 10-km maps.

While Shags have a long history of breeding in the Forth, breeding was formerly confined to the Isle of May, Bass Rock and St. Abb's Head (*B&R*). While breeding was noted at Brander (NT87Q) and on Craigleith (NT58N) by the 1930s and the Lamb (NT58I) by 1955, the great expansion has been since the 1960s. Inchkeith (NT28W) was colonised in 1965, Fidra in 1971, Car Craig (NT18W) in 1973, Cow & Calves and Inchmickery (NT28A) in 1976, Dunbar (NT67U) in 1983 and Inchcolm in 1992. Shags bred on Cow & Calves (Fife) in the 1970s until they were dispossessed by Cormorants. Recent colonisation has therefore been mostly in the inner Forth presumably originating from the older-established colonies in the outer Forth.

There has been a great increase in numbers to accompany the range expansion. Less than ten pairs bred between the Tay and the Humber during the early 1900s (*New Atlas*), but the Forth population increased to *c.*1,500 in 1970 and *c.*3,500 pairs by 1990 (see first graph and Appendix). The population increase has been shared by

both long-established colonies and those more recently founded. Protection from persecution is considered to be the main explanation for the improved success (Potts 1969).

The increase in Shag numbers has not been constant since the 1950s and has been subject to several reversals although none as spectacular as that of the 1990s (see graph). Numbers in the Forth peaked in 1992 when *c.*4,020 pairs bred (including estimates for sites with no counts) but this had dropped to *c.*800 pairs by 1994 (-80%). The marked decline in the Forth and NE England populations in 1993 was thought to have been birds opting out from breeding due to being in poor condition after the stormy winter and spring of 1992-93, but another bad winter in 1993-94 caused widespread mortality with large numbers wrecked along North Sea coasts (Walsh *et al.* 1995). Poor breeding success has been typical since 1993, and by 1996 numbers had only recovered to *c.*1,200 pairs, 30% of the pre-crash totals (Thompson *et al.* 1996). Recovery appears to have been more rapid at the inner Forth colonies than those further east (D. Fairlamb *pers. comm.*) A crash of a similar magnitude occurred in the Isle of May population in 1975-76 due to "red tides", a shellfish poisoning, when 65% of the population vanished over three seasons. Numbers typically recover in less than five years (Armstrong *et al.* 1978) although Harris & Wanless (1996) conclude that recovery from the recent crash may take ten years. See the second graph for fluctuations at two colonies.

In 1996 *c.*1,277 pairs probably bred in the Forth (1,095 counted and 182 estimated for unsurveyed Berwickshire) although *c.*4,017 pairs bred as recently as 1992 (3,429 counted and 588 estimated for the unsurveyed Bass Rock and Berwickshire). About 56% of all Forth Shags bred in SE Scotland. In total the Forth population represented about 6% of the 1992 British population.   ***R.D.Murray***

Shag

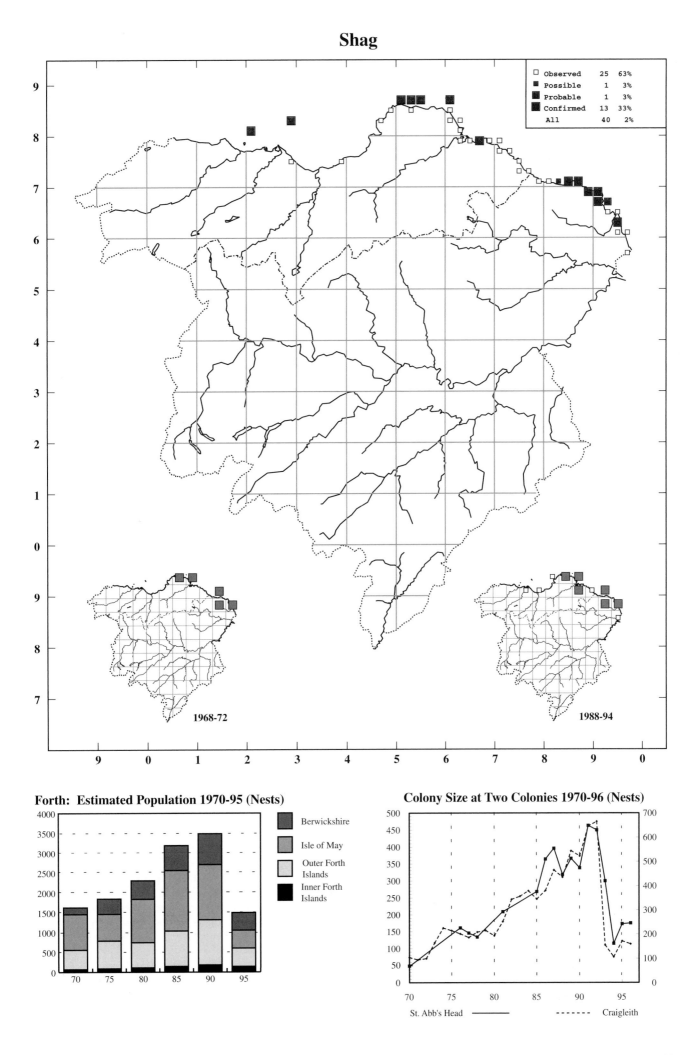

☐ Observed	25	63%
■ Possible	1	3%
▦ Probable	1	3%
■ Confirmed	13	33%
All	40	2%

1968-72

1988-94

Forth: Estimated Population 1970-95 (Nests)

- Berwickshire
- Isle of May
- Outer Forth Islands
- Inner Forth Islands

Colony Size at Two Colonies 1970-96 (Nests)

St. Abb's Head ⎯⎯⎯ Craigleith ------

Grey Heron
Ardea cinerea

The Grey Heron is widespread over much of Britain, missing only from mountains, occurring wherever there are bodies of open and running water, as well as in coastal areas, eating whatever fish and other aquatic animals are available. Herons construct large stick nests high in the woodland canopy.

Observers were asked to restrict records of Grey Herons to observed for flying or foraging birds and confirmed when a nest-site was recorded. 93% of the registrations involved observed birds, while only 7% were of breeding sites.

Herons were reported from a third of the area, a remarkable total for a bird dependent on water. Birds were really only missing from the highest hills and areas with little open drainage. There are some gaps along the river systems: the Water of Leith in Edinburgh, the North Esk between Penicuik and Dalkeith, and the Yarrow around St. Mary's Loch. While the absence in Edinburgh is not surprising, the absence from the North Esk and Yarrow is odd. Both sites have apparently good habitat and there is no obvious reason why Herons should not be present.

Marquiss (1989) found that densities in Scotland varied with altitude, larger numbers of birds living at lower levels that offered more feeding opportunities. This effect is not very noticeable in the altitude graph where there is no great drop-off until 400m. However, the graph only measures ubiquity, not density.

Heronries in dense, thicket-stage spruce plantations, the most widespread site type, can be very difficult to find. It is even hard to see the nests in such plantations, the best evidence of occupation being moulted feathers, egg shells, foreign twigs and droppings. The calls of large young in mid-May were often the only way some colonies were discovered. Nest counting is fraught with difficulty in such sites as it is hard to distinguish between old and occupied nests. Discarded egg-shells can be the only reasonable proof of breeding in such cases, without resorting to climbing.

In Scotland generally, 84% of Herons chose Scots Pine or spruce in 1954 (Garden 1958). This finding is reiterated in colonies in SE Scotland where 79% of heronries where the tree type is known were in conifers, 10% were in mixed trees and just 10% in deciduous trees (see graph). While choice may sometimes be dictated by availability, birds may choose to nest in conifers which offer both shelter and seclusion.

A comparison with the *Old Atlas* shows considerable differences have occurred since 1972, although little is known of the precise location and size of colonies in 1968-72. While confirmed breeding has increased from 24 to 40 squares, their distribution is rather different with only 16 common to both periods. Even adding the

probable squares from the *Old Atlas* only raises the figure to 30. There is every likelihood that Heron numbers have increased since 1972. The redistribution reflects Marquiss's (1989) findings that Grey Herons frequently change breeding sites.

The BTO Heronries Census data helped in locating colonies but unfortunately there has been a lack of continuity of counts over the years. Some old sites known to the BTO could not be located while others received only a single visit between 1988-94. Some new sites were discovered during *Atlas* work (12 in Borders, 7 in Lothian). Others vanished, mostly due to tree felling or thinning. Continuity of counts is generally better in Lothian, especially in recent years (see Appendix).

There have been counts at 61 sites in SE Scotland since 1982, 40 in Borders and 21 in Lothian. Not all sites are extant, at least four having been felled. The counts used here are mostly averaged over the 1988-94 period, but at eleven sites a mean was taken from the 1982-87 period as more recent counts were not available. This produced a total of 336 nests at 59 sites (two sites having no useful figures). Marquiss (1989) found that casual counts at heronries in Scotland were inclined to underestimate the actual numbers breeding, only counting 68% of the actual nests. This factor would raise the local population figure to 494 nests at 59 sites. However, as some sites have been abandoned within the period of the survey, this estimate has been modified downwards to 450 pairs.

Marquiss calculated breeding densities of 4.4 pairs/10km^2 for the higher parts of the Southern Uplands and 4.9 pairs/10km^2 for the Lothians and Merse, based on 22 colonies in the area. A calculation based on the 59 colonies mentioned above over the area of SE Scotland (6,500km^2) suggests a higher figure of 6.9 pairs/10km^2 overall for high and low areas. As Scottish densities varied between 1.6 in parts of the Highlands to 9.2 on Tayside coasts, the overall figure of 6.9 pairs/10km^2 may reflect the rich feeding opportunities in the area.

It is certain that a good number of colonies were missed. Observed records show a fairly even coverage of birds along the river system that is not reflected by the distribution of colonies, with heronries "missing" from parts of the Lyne, Almond, North Esk, Tyne, Leader, Rule, Jed, middle Tweed, middle Teviot, Blackadder and Whiteadder. Perhaps searches could be directed to these areas in future. These gaps might raise the local population estimate of 450 pairs to somewhere in the region of 500-550 pairs, forming about 14% of the likely Scottish population of 4,100 pairs.

The lack of regular colony counts in the area is lamentable, all the more so as so many sites are known. This could easily be resolved with just a little will and organisation.   *R.D.Murray*

Grey Heron

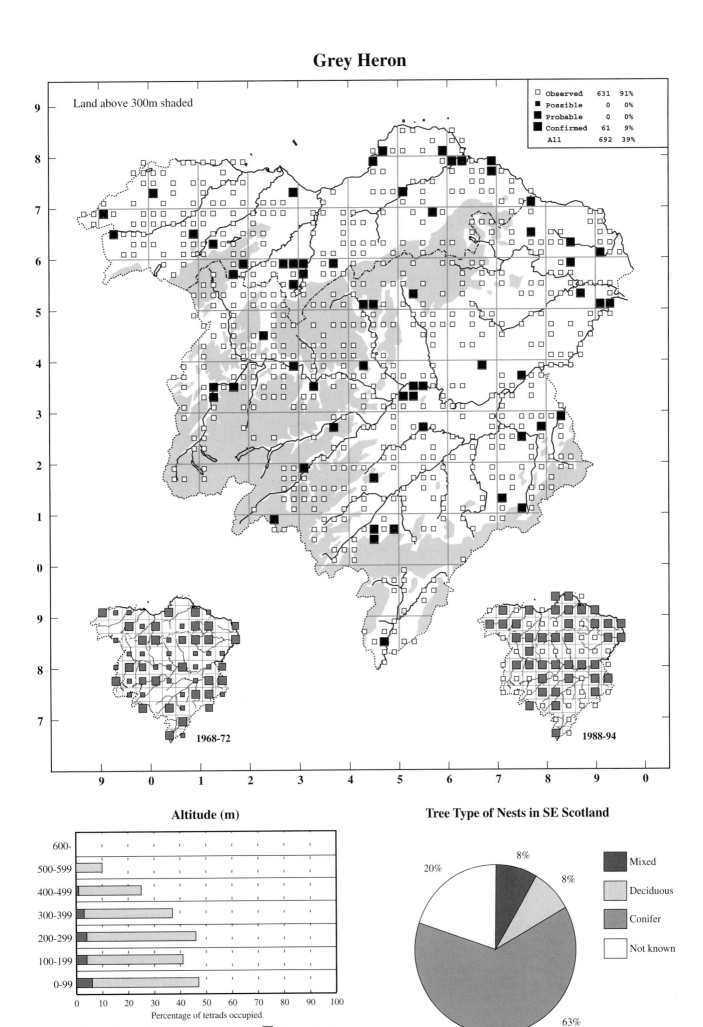

Land above 300m shaded

	Observed	631	91%
	Possible	0	0%
	Probable	0	0%
	Confirmed	61	9%
	All	692	39%

1968-72

1988-94

Altitude (m)

Percentage of tetrads occupied

Breeding evidence   Observed only

Tree Type of Nests in SE Scotland

8%
8%
20%
63%

Mixed
Deciduous
Conifer
Not known

Mute Swan
Cygnus olor

The large size and striking plumage of the Mute Swan make it one of the most readily identifiable birds. As a result of its aggressive nature while defending a territory, nest or young, it is widely believed to be capable of inflicting serious injuries and is thus treated with great respect by the general public. Mute Swans breed on most types of fresh water, ranging from ponds to reservoirs, lochs, canals and slow-flowing rivers, feeding on aquatic plants. Sheltered coastal areas are also used, mostly by sub-adult non-territorial birds and only occasionally by nesting pairs.

The large nest built close to water makes this species relatively easy to census. Probable or confirmed breeding was recorded in 86% of occupied tetrads. Four-fifths of probable records were of pairs, while confirmed records were split between occupied nests and broods. The Lothian population has been the subject of a long-term census which started in 1978 and all likely sites are scrutinised annually. As a whole, however, the area only achieved good coverage during the national counts in 1986 and 1990. The principal fieldwork problem relates to the great length of rivers in the Borders, where finding pairs and confirming breeding was time-consuming and difficult. Pairs can be overlooked, leading to census data being incomplete. Full coverage has only become regular since 1995.

The map indicates a contrast between the Lothians and Borders with most Lothian pairs breeding at standing freshwater while in Borders there is a greater reliance on rivers. Despite this obvious difference on the map, three-quarters of all records came from tetrads with standing water bodies. Medium-sized waters appear to be in greatest demand with almost half of all tetrads with such waters holding birds, in contrast to only a sixth of tetrads with small-sized waters. Tetrads with pond-sized waters are much more numerous and held 42% of all records, compared to 22% for medium-sized waters and only 5% for the largest waters. Large, deep waters rarely have feeding opportunities for Mute Swans. The map shows occupied tetrads in: the parks of eastern Edinburgh (Duddingston, Dunsapie, Lochend, Craiglockhart and Blackford in NT27); the grounds of large country houses in East Lothian (Donnelly & Bara in NT56, Newbyth & Balgone in NT57&58, Pressmennan & Broxmouth in NT67), Midlothian (Penicuik House in NT25) and Berwickshire (Mellerstain & Nenthorn House in NT63, Spottiswoode in NT64, Duns Castle in NT75, Manderston in NT85); reservoirs at Hopes (NT56) and the Whiteadder (NT66); and in the natural Ettrick Forest lochs between the middle Tweed and Teviot (about 20 waters in NT41,42,51,52&53). Although not standing water, the Union Canal in West Lothian also stands out as a favoured habitat (NS97&NT07).

The use of rivers is most obvious along the Tweed and its tributaries the Teviot and Whiteadder, but occupied tetrads are also apparent along the Almond (NS96,NT06&17), the Esk (NT37) and the Tyne (NT57&67). The density of occupation along the lower Tweed, Whiteadder and Teviot is genuine and not an artifact of repeated censusing of shifting nest sites or broods along the river in different months and different years (*q.v.*Goosander). Detailed census work in 1995 revealed that the map is representative of the distribution of swans in that area (Murray *et al.* 1996) with territories all along the river system below Kelso and Denholm.

While the Mute Swans of SE Scotland breed at some of the highest altitude sites in Great Britain (Rawcliffe 1958), some Ettrick Forest lochs being above 300m, two-thirds of all occupied tetrads were below 200m and about half below 100m. The sweep of near coastal sites in Lothian and along the Tweed suggests a real preference for low-level breeding sites. Ringing of broods over many years shows upland broods may be several weeks later in reaching a similar state of growth compared to low level broods and this may affect winter survival and be the basis for the preference for low-lying sites.

Comparison with the *Old Atlas* shows similar numbers of 10-km squares were occupied in both periods, seven squares showing gains and eight showing losses. As only eleven sites were used in the seven additional squares, the losses over the period may have been similarly marginal. The losses all occur in 10-km squares with, at best, only single sites that could be suitable for breeding.

The *New Atlas* abundance map shows high numbers along the Union Canal, around Edinburgh, on the lower Tyne and in the middle Tweed and Teviot. The lower Tweed is shown as having moderate, rather than high, abundance despite the good numbers that breed there. This area can suffer from nests being destroyed in spring floods and if the *New Atlas* counts occurred in such a year, this may account for the lower abundance indicated.

Due to a series of censuses there is detailed knowledge of Mute Swan numbers in SE Scotland. A count in 1961 found 59 territorial pairs in Lothian but this was reduced to just 20 pairs by the 1978 national census. A specific reason for this decline has not been identified. During the 1983 national census 28 territorial pairs were recorded and by 1988 the figure had increased to 39 pairs with further increases since producing a record 67 territories in 1995 (Brown & Brown 1984b, Brown & Brown 1997, Ogilvie 1986). In addition a change has occurred in Lothian in the percentage of the different types of habitat used by territorial pairs with 44% and 45% of pairs on rivers in 1961 and 1978 respectively, compared to 23% in 1988 and only 13% in 1994. There are fewer complete counts in Borders. In 1978 39 pairs bred, rising to 49 pairs in 1983 before jumping substantially to 86 pairs by 1990. The total has since increased to 97 pairs by 1995 and over 105 pairs in 1996.

The increases locally mirror the upward trend in numbers in Scotland as a whole (Brown & Brown 1993), in Britain (Delany *et al.* 1992) and across Europe (Earnst 1991). The territorial population of SE Scotland numbered 141 pairs in 1990 (see graph). This had risen to 165 pairs by 1995, of which 86% of pairs breed annually (Brown & Brown *in prep.*). SE Scotland holds 13% of the Scottish territorial population.

Non-territorial flocks occur at Linlithgow Loch, Cramond, St. Margaret's Loch, Musselburgh and Tyninghame in Lothian and along the Tweed and Teviot Haughs in Borders. These each regularly hold 30 birds and exceptionally more than 70, and altogether total another 150-200 resident in SE Scotland in summer. This number is small compared to the Berwick flock which usually has in excess of 200 birds and exceptionally as many as 700.   ***A.W.Brown***

Mute Swan

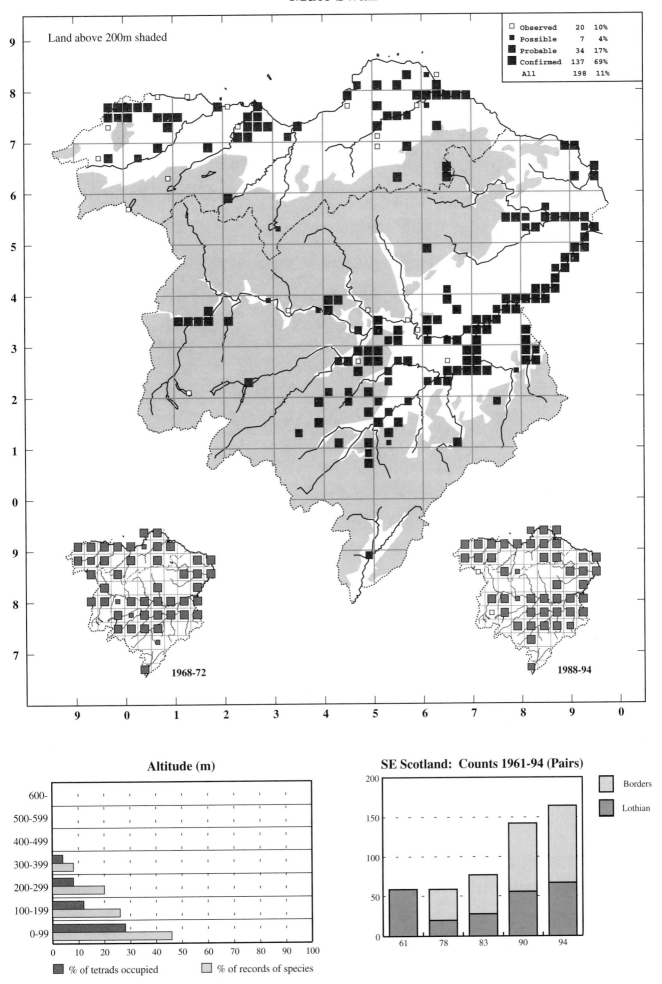

Land above 200m shaded

☐	Observed	20	10%
■	Possible	7	4%
■	Probable	34	17%
■	Confirmed	137	69%
	All	198	11%

1968-72

1988-94

Altitude (m)

■ % of tetrads occupied   ☐ % of records of species

SE Scotland: Counts 1961-94 (Pairs)

☐ Borders
■ Lothian

51

Greylag Goose
Anser anser

The wild Greylag Goose breeds throughout much of Europe and Asia. In Britain drainage and hunting led to its extermination from most of the country, and since the 19th century wild-stock birds breed only in the Hebrides and the far north and west mainland. There are now wild feral populations stemming from releases of goslings by wildfowling clubs and landowners since the mid 20th century, notably in SW Scotland, Perthshire, the Lake District, Kent, Norfolk and elsewhere. Natural spread has since occurred from some of these. In SE Scotland the spread has become dramatic. Greylags nest at wet sites, moors, rough pasture, and particularly like the safety of islands. Wild geese are migratory, most of the Greylags wintering in Scotland being from Iceland.

The map reveals only a few observed and possible records. Confirmed and probable breeding form 64% of all occupied tetrads. This is remarkable in a large, mobile species where part of the population consists of immature birds, and shows that in SE Scotland most Greylags, breeders and pre-breeders alike, spend much of their time in summer close to the nesting localities. Three quarters of confirmed records were of parents with small young and a fifth were of birds on nests. The breeding sites on the map are on the margins of reservoirs in the Pentlands Hills and below the Moorfoot Hills, scattered ponds mostly on private estates, public amenity lochs in Edinburgh, and two on the Forth islands Inchkeith and Fidra. The altitude graph shows 80% of Greylag breeding tetrads are below 300m, with two peaks of occurrence at 0-100m and 200-300m, the latter being due to upland reservoirs.

The 10-km square maps reveal just how recently Greylags have colonised SE Scotland. The present map shows no less than 16 squares with confirmed and probable breeding and ten more with possible breeding and observed birds, compared with just one square in 1968-72. The main spread has been in Lothian, but recently Greylags have appeared at a scatter of sites in Borders. The graph shows the increase as indicated by numbers of broods sighted, and the Appendix details all sites with nests or small young during 1988-94. Further spread has taken place since the *Atlas* fieldwork and Greylag Geese have nested at Morton Loch (NT06R), Kierhill Pond (NT16P) and Dundas Loch (NT17D) in 1995, Balgone Small Loch (NT58L), Waughton Reservoir (NT58Q) and Newbyth Pond (NT57Z) in 1996, and Blackford Pond (NT27K) in 1986 (failed), 1995 and 1996 where Mute Swans last nested in 1994.

SE Scotland's Greylags originate from two sources. The first is at Duddingston Loch in Edinburgh where 13 birds were introduced in 1961 (Anderson & Waterston 1961). Five of these disappeared but the remaining birds bred in 1963, and five more yearlings were released in 1987 (C. McLean *pers.comm.*). By the 1970s up to 15 pairs per year bred at Duddingston (*Andrews*), but this decreased

to only a few pairs in the 1980s-90s at the same time as birds dispersed to nest at other sites, and there is no doubt that most of the SE Scotland Greylags have descended from the Duddingston birds. In the west of the area a separate introduction occurred about 1988 when six or eight goslings were released at Harburnhead (NT06K) in an estate with ponds and rough ground, and these had increased to about 130 birds by autumn 1994 (H.J. Spurway *pers.comm.*). This source is too recent to be the origin of most of the Lothian and Borders Greylag Geese, but Harburnhead birds do regularly fly to and from Harperrig Reservoir (NT06V), and there may well be some mixing of Duddingston and Harburnhead stock in parts of West Lothian. The recent breeders at Baddinsgill (NT15H) and West Water (NT15B) Reservoirs in Borders may have crossed the Pentlands from West Lothian.

While numbers fluctuate at some sites, the population overall continues to rise, with East Lothian being an area of most recent colonisation. Greylags are now regular at most of the sites shown with probable and possible symbols on the map, and may soon nest at Cobbinshaw (NT05D&E) and Crosswood (NT05N) Reservoirs, Inchcolm island, Linlithgow Loch, Bemersyde, Millar's Moss (NT96E), and other places. There have been occasional releases at Duddingston Loch of tame Canada, Barnacle, White-fronted and domestic geese, most of which produced no offspring except Canada Geese. There have been some Greylag x Canada or Greylag x Barnacle hybrids but fortunately their progeny do not seem to persist.

The Greylag population always contains many non-breeding birds, presumably immatures. In 1994, *Bird Reports* indicate that in May-June there were at least 360 Greylags at Duddingston and Edinburgh ponds, 40-50 at Gladhouse, *c*.180 in the Pentlands at Harburnhead, Threipmuir, Harperrig, Cobbinshaw and Glencorse, *c*.40 in East Lothian, and 20 in Borders. This suggests a total May-June population of *c*.650 birds. In the same year in July-September when young become similar to adults, counts suggest 360 in Edinburgh, 90-100 around Gladhouse, *c*.250 in the Pentlands, up to 100 at Linlithgow Loch, and 90-100 in East Lothian and Borders, indicating *c*.900 adults and young altogether. The number of breeding pairs in 1994 must have been near 76 (see Appendix), but as some pairs undoubtedly nest unsuccessfully and go undetected, the true figure may be at least 100 pairs.

In 1994 SE Scotland had *c*.650 feral Greylag Geese in early summer including *c*.100 breeding pairs, and by late summer *c*.900 birds including juveniles. 650 birds represent a sizeable increase from a few birds in 1961, and form 3% of the British population (*New Atlas*). In other parts of Scotland some introduced populations have died out (Brown & Dick 1992).   **H.E.M.Dott**

Greylag Goose

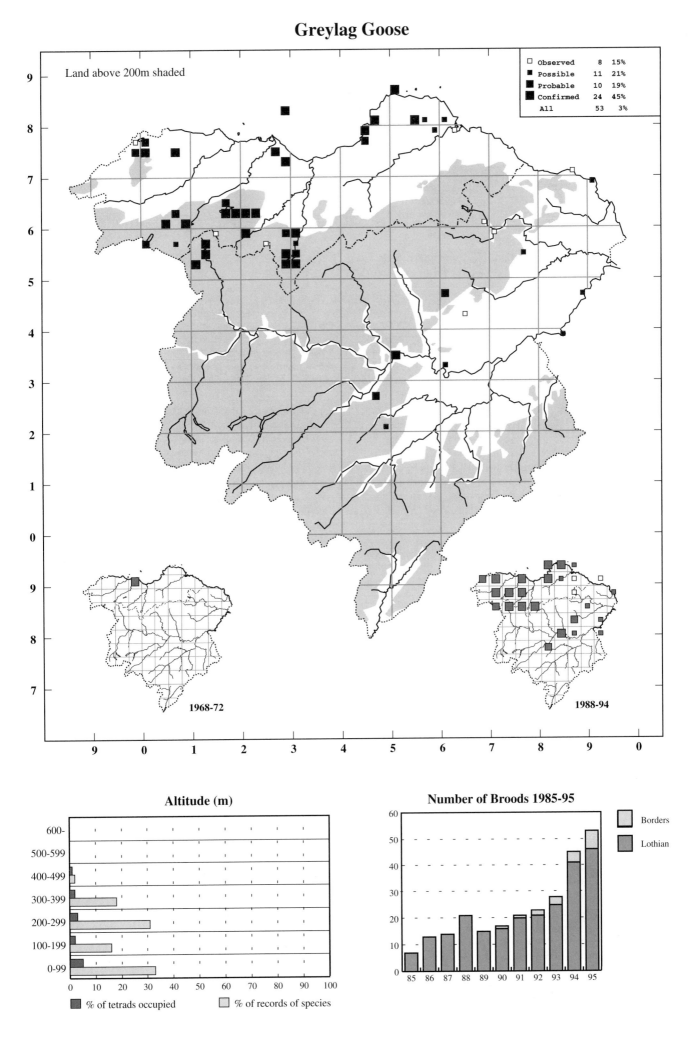

Land above 200m shaded

	Observed	8	15%
	Possible	11	21%
	Probable	10	19%
	Confirmed	24	45%
	All	53	3%

1968-72

1988-94

Altitude (m)

- 600-
- 500-599
- 400-499
- 300-399
- 200-299
- 100-199
- 0-99

■ % of tetrads occupied   □ % of records of species

Number of Broods 1985-95

Borders
Lothian

85 86 87 88 89 90 91 92 93 94 95

Canada Goose
Branta canadensis

Canada Geese were brought to Britain from North America in the 17th century. The first reports of feral birds came from Middlesex in 1731. Numbers increased throughout the 19th century, often aided by deliberate introductions by wildfowlers. Today the Canada Goose is a familiar and widespread species in England but remains only locally common in Scotland. The Scottish population of the Canada Goose currently has two main centres, in Dumfriesshire and in Strathmore, with small numbers scattered widely elsewhere.

In its native North America the Canada Goose is very adaptable, and combined with its readiness to tolerate the presence of people this has enabled it to colonise all types of habitat. Canada Geese favour natural and ornamental waters where the margins are open and have emergent vegetation that is not too dense. They shun enclosed waters with tall vegetation that can provide cover for ground predators. They also avoid upland waters.

The Canada Goose is a large, obvious species and was relatively easy to record during fieldwork. Most probable records were of pairs, while confirmed records were mostly of broods with a few nests. While it is an uncommon and rather local breeding species in SE Scotland, its relative conspicuousness means that most birds in the area were probably recorded.

The main concentration of tetrads was in the middle Tweed where breeding was confirmed in five tetrads and probable in a further seven. This focus had its origins in a release of birds at Mellerstain (NT63P) in the 1960s. Although this flock appears to have dispersed from Mellerstain since then, a few of its descendants are presumably responsible for the breeding witnessed in the *Atlas*. Breeding, however, is very erratic and the birds, always single pairs, rarely bred in successive years in any one site. In the *Atlas* period birds successfully bred at Bemersyde and Bassendean (NT64D) in 1991 and at Bemersyde and Whitrig (NT63H) in 1992 and probably at Gordon Quarry (NT64L) in 1988. A pair also bred at Folly Loch (NT62N) in 1995. Other sites have had pairs reported but no further evidence of breeding. The cluster of records in this area are therefore a cumulative impression of breeding between 1988-94, rather than what occurs in every year. The records from St. Abbs (NT96) are based on a pair dispersing from a local waterfowl collection in 1993.

In Lothian breeding has occurred at Duddingston since 1989, a single pair producing a brood annually there up to 1995 at least. These birds may have arrived at Duddingston of their own volition, possibly from Yorkshire-Beauly Firth moult migrants stopping off on their passage during the summer months. Birds at Folly Loch bore Beauly rings and may have had similar origins. Other Canada Geese have been released at Duddingston, notably single birds in 1967 and 1971. These bred with Greylags and the hybrids seen

there, and at Threipmuir and Gladhouse, may date from these introductions. The probable breeding record at Gladhouse may indeed involve these Canadas or their apparently sterile hybrid offspring moving with feral Greylags. The only other recent breeding record from Lothian dates from 1978-79 at Balgone Loch (NT58R) in East Lothian.

During the 19th century Canada Geese were released on a number of sites in East Lothian and at Duddingston. The Duddingston birds disappeared by 1920 but a flock at Gosford survived until the war when they almost certainly supplemented the rations of troops based in the area. In the *Old Atlas* the Canada Goose was recorded at just four 10-km squares with confirmed breeding in NT62 and NT63, presumably the Mellerstain introduction. Although there is little information on the history of this flock it is thought to have been established in the late 1950s or early 1960s and at one time numbered as many as 50-60 birds. This had fallen to about 20-30 birds in the early 1980s but these seem to have largely dispersed by the period of the *Atlas* and breeding was not actually reported there between 1988-94 (C.O. Badenoch *pers.comm.*). It is likely that such breeding is not self-sustaining in our area, even from such a large introduction, and that without recruitment from elsewhere it will eventually die out.

During the *Atlas* period the total population in any single year in SE Scotland was probably only between two and five pairs. After several introductions earlier in the century the presence of breeding birds in the area seems to be fading and without the occasional recruitment of passing moult migrants it might have already disappeared. This is in marked contrast with the British population which the *New Atlas* records as increasing by 8% per annum. The range is also spreading and the *New Atlas* showed a 75% increase in the number of occupied 10-km squares. The majority of these were in England where the Canada Goose may have been consolidating its range mostly by infilling gaps within the former range in southern and central England rather than any huge expansion to the north, other than in the Solway and Strathmore.

With the British population of 59,500 birds expanding by 8% per annum, natural colonisation of SE Scotland seems inevitable. On their own, however, introductions do not appear to be self-sustaining. The Canada Goose will remain a very scarce and erratic breeder until the intervening area is colonised. Even in Northumberland, very much closer to the main English population, there were less than 50 pairs recorded in their Atlas survey between 1988-92, only a slight increase on previous counts (*Day*). Natural population increase and spread are such that Canada Geese may not properly colonise our area until the 2020s. **D.Kelly**

Canada Goose

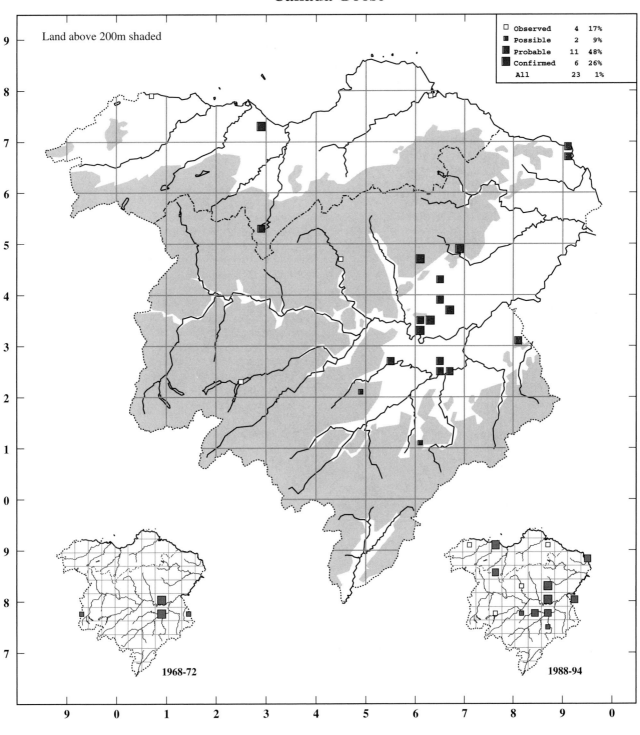

Land above 200m shaded

☐	Observed	4	17%
◼	Possible	2	9%
◼	Probable	11	48%
◼	Confirmed	6	26%
	All	23	1%

1968-72

1988-94

Altitude (m)

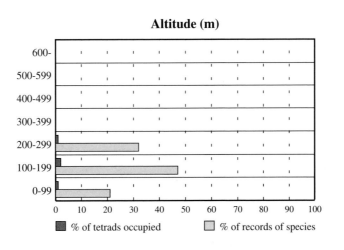

◼ % of tetrads occupied   ☐ % of records of species

Shelduck
Tadorna tadorna

The Shelduck is essentially a coastal species, favouring muddy and sandy coastlines with adjacent sand dunes. It feeds mainly on invertebrates, especially the snail *Hydrobia*, by wading in shallow water or wet mud. It nests in holes, typically old rabbit burrows in coastal dunes. Nest-boxes can be substituted. A small minority nest inland, and some pairs have used haystacks and deserted barns away from the coast.

In the *Atlas* fieldwork, more than half of all records were of probable status, mostly of pairs. Despite creches of young birds being very easy to record, only a quarter of records were of confirmed breeding, possibly indicative of low success rates.

Shelducks nest at several localities along the Forth coastline which are dominated by sand and mud deposition from the Almond, Esk and Tyne. These provide suitable tidal substrates for the invertebrates eaten by Shelducks and shorelines with suitable soils and cover for pairs to nest. Gaps occur along the urbanised stretch between Silverknowes (NT27D) and Longniddry (NT47N) where disturbance and a lack of nest-sites probably restrict the presence of birds, and in Berwickshire to the east of Redheugh (NT87F) where the cliff habitats are unsuitable. The coastal population has two distinct components: colonial breeding near the Almond estuary (24 pairs in 1992), Aberlady Bay (25 pairs) and the Tyne estuary (27 pairs); and isolated pairs on non-estuarine coast away from these sites such as between Blackness and Queensferry, Gosford Bay to Pefferside and between Dunbar and Redheugh. Confirmed breeding records are scarce but were reported at the estuarine sites at Cramond, Aberlady and Tyninghame and along the more open shore at White Sands (NT77D). It is likely that some records of probable breeding along the open shore do represent genuine attempts to breed, as pairs are seen actively displaying, while others may represent adults from the breeding concentrations that may be feeding further along the shore.

On the Forth islands, only Inchmickery, Inchcolm and the Isle of May have had breeding records, typically just one or two pairs. Near-coastal sites, near the River Tyne at Traprain (NT57X) and Knowes (NT67E) and the ponds at Greenside (NT86E), Dowlaw (NT86P) and Millar's Moss (NT96E), occasionally have visiting pairs but no confirmed breeding. In the past breeding at near-coastal sites occurred regularly at Drem (NT58A), 4 km inland of Aberlady, which held between 15-19 pairs in the 1970s. Further inland, where

breeding has been almost unknown in SE Scotland, the scatter of confirmed breeding records represents a new trend of inland nesting that has occurred during the course of the *Atlas* fieldwork. Birds bred at Whitton Loch (NT71P) in 1990-92, Shiphorns Sandpit (NT25K) in 1992-97 and Leadburn Sandpit (NT25G) in 1993-97 while Hoselaw Loch, the Hirsel and Crosswood Reservoir (NT05T) were visited by pairs between 1988-94. Since 1994 pairs have bred at Hoselaw in 1995 and the Folly Loch (NT62N) in 1996 while pairs have been seen at Bemersyde and Wooden Loch (NT72C).

Other than the inland breeding, there has been little change in the overall distribution of Shelducks in the area since the *Old Atlas*, although there have been considerable fluctuations in the details of the local range. At Tyninghame, spring maxima, presumably representing the breeding stock, have remained fairly constant since 1957, unlike Aberlady Bay where distinct variations have been documented. In the 1950s about five pairs bred at Aberlady but by the 1960s numbers increased, perhaps due to an increase in the area of muddy shore, until there were 43-46 nests in the 1970-73 period (Hamilton & Macgregor 1960, Jenkins *et al.* 1975). Numbers have fallen since 1986 with only 25 pairs in 1992. Changes in sedimentation may again be responsible with saltmarsh encroachment reducing feeding opportunities although a reduction in sewage output into the bay may also be important. Increased use of beaches for recreational activities has also led to local declines along the coast. Eight pairs nested in the dunes and fields between Gosford Bay (NT47N) and Yellowcraigs (NT58D) in the early 1970s in an area where only one recent record of breeding is known. Birds nested at Musselburgh Lagoons between 1973-83 but have since ceased due to habitat changes there as the lagoons were infilled.

Breeding productivity varies from year to year with chick mortality often high, especially at the colonial sites. In some years the Aberlady population of 25 pairs struggles to fledge ten young in total. 1992 was moderately successful with 180 young counted throughout the Lothians, of which half were between Dunbar and Skateraw (Andrews 1993). A detailed study in the 1970s showed that survival of ducklings was higher where breeding densities were low, e.g. at Dalmeny, Gosford, the Peffer Burn at Aberlady, Drem and Barns Ness (Jenkins *et al.* 1975). Losses at colonies are mostly because of nest failures and high duckling mortality due to predation by Herring Gulls when parents are distracted by territorial disputes. Egg-dumping can be a problem with at least a third of clutches at Aberlady laid by more than one female. These nests have a significantly higher level of failure due to desertion than clutches laid by a single female (Pienkowski & Evans 1982).

The number of adults present in SE Scotland declines by mid-July as birds leave to moult in the Kinneil-Grangemouth area of the upper Forth where 2,500-3,000 Shelduck annually moult (Bryant 1978, *Scottish Bird Reports*) although a few adults with late broods can remain at Dalmeny, Aberlady and Tyninghame (Andrews 1993).

In the early 1980s the Lothian population was estimated to be between 80-120 pairs (*Andrews*). The 1992 national survey found a total of 129 breeding pairs and 45 non-breeders in Lothian and a single pair in Borders (Andrews 1993, *Scottish Bird Report*). A slight increase to three or four pairs has now taken place in Borders. A total of 150 potential pairs is thus indicated, representing 16% of the birds in Scotland but just 1.5% of the British population.

I.J.Andrews

Shelduck

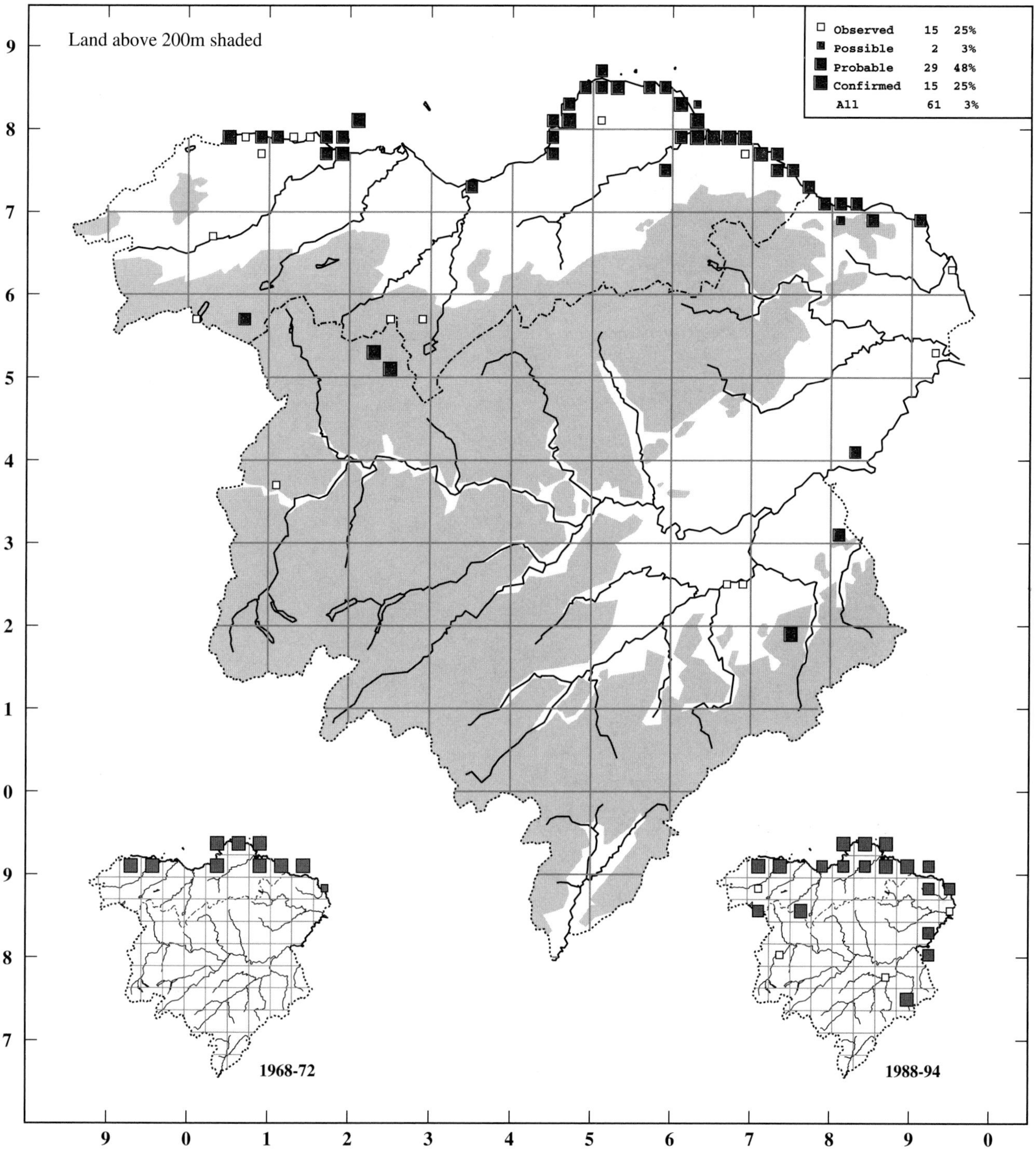

Land above 200m shaded

□ Observed	15	25%
▪ Possible	2	3%
◼ Probable	29	48%
◼ Confirmed	15	25%
All	61	3%

1968-72

1988-94

Mandarin
Aix galericulata

The exotically-plumaged Mandarin, one of the most colourful ducks, originates from China, Korea and the Russian Far East. It has managed to establish itself in various parts of Britain through escapes from wildfowl collections and through deliberate introductions.

In the field the bird is unexpectedly drab at a distance and easily overlooked. It was also difficult to record in SE Scotland due to a combination of its reclusive habits and the densely-wooded stream habitats that it prefers for breeding. Accordingly most of the small number of records are of single birds or pairs. Only two records of broods are known.

Mandarins habitually nest in tree-holes and so require trees with fairly large holes in reasonable proximity to water. This puts them into competition with other large-hole nesters like Goosanders, Jackdaws, Tawny Owls and Stock Doves, not to mention Grey Squirrels. Another requirement is their peculiar diet (for a duck) of beechmast, acorns and other seeds in the autumn.

Mandarins established themselves in our area when a small number of free-flying birds in a waterfowl collection at Brockholes Farm near Grantshouse (NT86G) took to flying out to the nearby Eye Water to feed in 1980. It is not certain when breeding first took place in the wild but it almost certainly occurred before the first confirmed record in 1988 when the Eye Water between Grantshouse and Houndwood was deliberately searched for breeding birds and broods were found at Renton (NT86H) and Houndwood (NT86L), both near Brockholes. Since then birds have been seen further down the Eye Water towards Reston and Eyemouth, and also in the neighbouring Whiteadder drainage both at Abbey St. Bathans and further upstream at Monynut.

All of these sites have the necessary cover along parts of the river, and both tree holes and autumn food in the oakwood remnants that occur in the tiny deans off the Eye Water and along much of the upper Whiteadder and Monynut Waters. The more extensive oakwoods in the Whiteadder drainage may indeed be a more suitable habitat in the longer term for Mandarins compared to the Eye drainage.

In 1989 a male Mandarin was apparently paired to a female Mallard at the Hen Poo, or Duns Castle Loch as it is also known (NT75S). A brood of 12 young was later seen but it is not clear whether the Mandarin was their biological father. Such pairings are not atypical on the margins of a species range where prospective mates are in short supply.

The outlying *Atlas* records suggest movements are limited with some dispersal away from the Eye area in autumn and winter, mostly into neighbouring watersheds. There are odd breeding season records from Gosford (NT47P), near Peebles (NT24A) and Lochend Loch in Edinburgh (NT27S) on the map. Whether these birds originated from the Eye is not known but in the face of the probable collapse of the Tay population (*Scottish Bird Reports*), many of the records of Mandarins in eastern Scotland may now originate from the Berwickshire birds. Fortunately a new feral population established itself in Argyll during the early 1990s, mostly breeding in Tawny Owl nest boxes (*Argyll Bird Reports* 1993-95), so a continued presence in Scotland seems hopeful.

The Berwickshire population is still tiny and may number fewer than ten pairs. Nevertheless this is probably slightly larger than that in Argyll and much larger than the Tay remnant. The *New Atlas* mentions up to 50 birds being present on the Eye Water. This is definitely erroneous and may be a number generated by the BTO's abundance calculations that were taken from the timed visits.

While the Berwickshire birds form an important element of the Scottish population, the Scottish numbers are dwarfed by those in England, estimated to be around 3,500 pairs (*New Atlas*, Davies 1988). In world terms the Mandarin Duck is an endangered species with a world population of just 7,000 pairs in the wild in what is almost certainly a shrinking habitat base in China and Korea (Madge & Burn 1988). The British feral birds now form a large proportion of the world population of Mandarins that live in the wild. While the numbers of our local birds are fairly small they are certainly worth monitoring and, having a fairly small range mostly confined to two small river systems, relatively easy to survey. ***R.D.Murray***

Mandarin

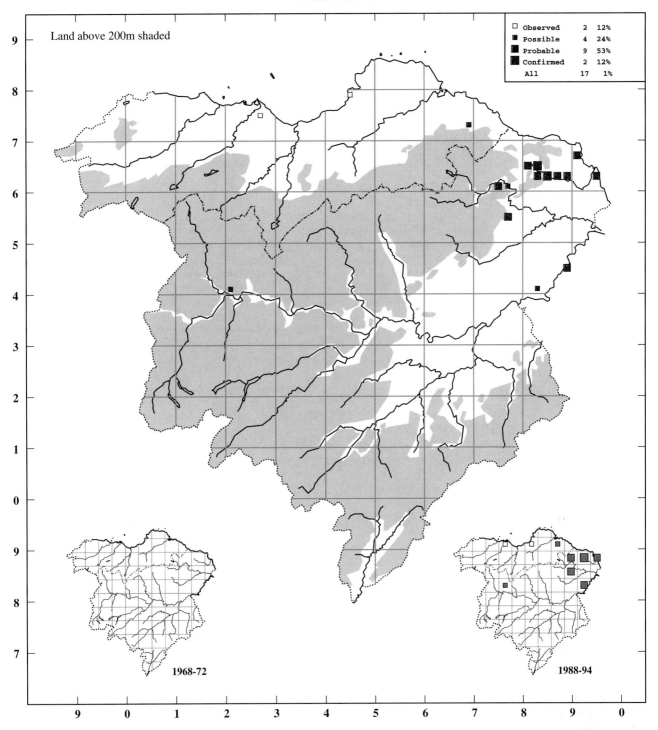

Land above 200m shaded

	Observed	2	12%
	Possible	4	24%
	Probable	9	53%
	Confirmed	2	12%
	All	17	1%

1968-72

1988-94

Wigeon
Anas penelope

The Wigeon is one of a group of ducks which colonised Britain during the 19th century, the first breeding in Britain being in Sutherland in 1834. In SE Scotland the earliest breeding came from the Ettrick Forest area in 1893, although summering birds had been recorded there since the mid-1880s. The Wigeon remains a northerly species in the British Isles, the bulk of the population being in northern Scotland with southern outliers in the Southern Uplands and Pennines. The birds that occasionally breed in East Anglia may be injured birds rather than part of the main population. Breeding Wigeon prefer shallow, open lochs and pools with plentiful submerged or floating vegetation but without well developed emergent or marginal growth. They are grazing ducks and breeding lochs must be within a reasonable distance of suitable grass but also provide a good supply of insect food for ducklings.

Wigeon prefer upland waters, three-quarters of all sites being between 200-400m. Many upland lochs and reservoirs in SE Scotland may be suited to Wigeon but birds are rarely seen in summer away from a small number of traditional breeding sites where they associate in loose, scattered colonies. Wigeon can be secretive and their nests may be some distance from water. Even when hatched the young do not necessarily always associate with one another or with their mother. Adults may also graze at some distance from the breeding loch. Only a third of reports were of probable or confirmed records. The eleven probable records were dominated by sightings of pairs, while the five confirmed records were of broods. A similar number of tetrads hold observed or possible records, all sightings of single birds. Coastal records have been classed as observed as breeding here is unlikely. Inland sightings away from the Ettrick Forest area such as the reservoirs at Whiteadder (NT66L), West Water (NT15B) and Gladhouse and the lochs at Whitton (NT71P) and Hule Moss may, however, represent a real interest in breeding.

The core area on the map is clearly in the Ettrick Forest, between the Ettrick and the Teviot, where birds were present in 17 tetrads between 1988-94. The Ettrick Forest Wigeon population was most recently surveyed by Thomson & Dougall (1988) in 1987 when some 17 waters held 39 pairs, of which 15 pairs were confirmed to have bred. The principal site was Alemoor Reservoir (NT31X) which held eight pairs, although breeding was not confirmed at that site. Girnwood Loch (NT31R) held five pairs, while Broadlee (NT41A), Clearburn (NT31M), Sheilswood (NT41P) and the Branxholme Lochs (NT41F) all held three pairs each. The population was similar to that found in 1978 when 25-37 pairs were estimated by Dougall (1978). Not all these sites were recorded as holding birds in 1988-94. The nearby St. Mary's Loch and the Megget Reservoir (NT12W) have recent offshoots of this population. The first breeding was reported at St. Mary's Loch in 1984 when a brood was seen. Another was recorded in the *Atlas* period in 1993.

Away from this core area there are scattered records in the east at Whitton (NT71P) and Yetholm Lochs, the Hirsel Lake, Hule Moss and the Whiteadder Reservoir, and in the west on the flanks of the

Pentlands at West Water and Gladhouse Reservoirs, Tailend Moss (NT06D) and Bathgate Bog (NT96T). While no suspicion of breeding occurred during the *Atlas* period, Wigeon have bred in the past at Harperrig (NT06V), Threipmuir and Linlithgow, all before 1948. Since 1950 pairs attempted to breed at Gladhouse in 1968, 1974-75 and in 1980 (*Andrews*). In most years a few Wigeon are seen in summer in Lothian, most frequently at Tyninghame, Cramond, Musselburgh or Aberlady. It is this summering at Tyninghame that has produced the probable record, despite the habitat there being unlike the hill lochs. Pricked birds, injured by wildfowlers, may have been involved.

Comparisons between the *Old Atlas* and *New Atlas* show a slight alteration in the breeding range since 1968-72. While birds were reported from many more 10-km squares in 1988-94, the majority of these 'gains' refer to the isolated records of single birds. In terms of 10-km squares with probable or confirmed breeding the *Old Atlas* found evidence in seven squares compared to only six in the present survey (discounting NT67). Dougall (1978) pointed out that probable breeding occurred at Buckstruther Moss (NT51K) in 1971 that was not included in the *Old Atlas* map. The *Old Atlas* shows confirmed records in NT21 and NT23 that are not known to either the present or the former Local Recorders and were not known to Dougall (1978) who thoroughly reviewed all past records. As there are only three ponds or lochs in the two squares concerned, Loch of the Lowes, Loch Eddy and Hallmanor Pond, these records must be regarded as being dubious. Despite suggestions to the contrary the Wigeon appears to be maintaining a small but stable population in SE Scotland, losses from sites such as Buckstruther Moss being balanced by new sites at St. Mary's Loch and Megget Reservoir.

The Thomson & Dougall (1988) survey produced 30-39 pairs and this remains the best estimate of our local population. The *New Atlas* suggested a British population of 300-500 pairs and therefore SE Scotland holds 9-13% of the British population, a significant proportion of the whole.

The local population is found on lochs which are either slightly acid or of neutral pH status. Lochs of this type are vulnerable to acidification which could destroy the insect food supply that ducklings are dependent upon. Upland lochs in Dumfries & Galloway have already been adversely affected by acid precipitation, and it is possible that this could have some impact on the Ettrick Forest area. Acidification is exacerbated by afforestation of upland areas by conifers and these forests can cover the vital grazing areas used by Wigeon and therefore reduce the attractiveness of nearby lochs. Forest Enterprise has recognised this problem and have recently altered the proximity of the forest edge to some of the lochs in Craik Forest. Considering the relative importance of the Ettrick Forest population it is important that some monitoring is carried out on a periodic basis. The previous counts will act as an important baseline for repeated surveys and add to the rather scant casual information that is supplied to the local bird reports each year. **D.Kelly**

Wigeon

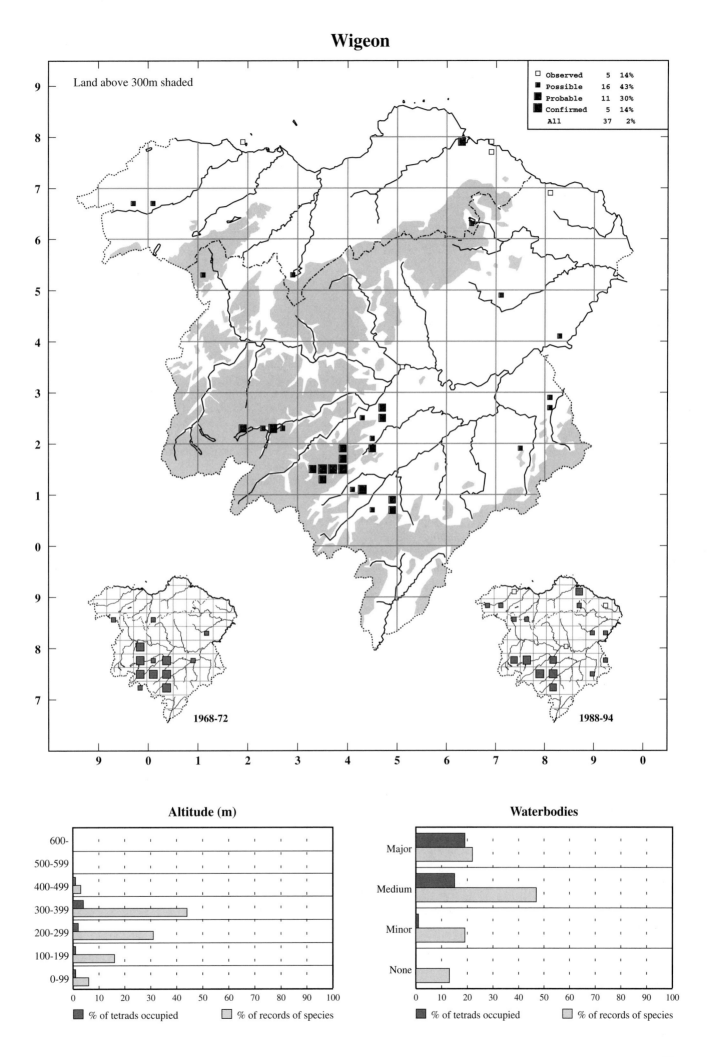

Land above 300m shaded

☐ Observed	5	14%
■ Possible	16	43%
◪ Probable	11	30%
■ Confirmed	5	14%
All	37	2%

1968-72

1988-94

Altitude (m)

■ % of tetrads occupied   ☐ % of records of species

Waterbodies

■ % of tetrads occupied   ☐ % of records of species

Gadwall
Anas strepera

The Gadwall is a widespread but irregular breeding species across much of central and northern Europe that shows a scattered breeding distribution in the British Isles. In Scotland it mostly occurs as an uncommon passage migrant and scarce winter visitor. The Gadwall may have been more numerous in the last century as there is evidence of a decline between the end of the 19th century and the 1940s. The Scottish breeding population is mostly found in Fife and Tayside where the main concentration is at Loch Leven. A few breed in Orkney, the Uists and in the northern Highlands. Extensive eutrophic lowland waters with dense cover on the banks are required for breeding. The nest is usually under thick shrubs or in long grass, typically close to open water for security, although it can be further from the waters edge when on islands. The Gadwall is said to be particularly sensitive to shooting and other disturbance and this coupled with the shortage of suitable extensive low-lying waters may account for the relative lack of success in colonising SE Scotland.

The drabness of Gadwall plumage and the similarity of female Gadwall and Mallard certainly contributes to this species being overlooked. As the male abandons the female during incubation, lone female Gadwalls can be difficult to locate. This difficulty, allied with the scarcity of Gadwall, increases problems with interpreting the map in that the identification factor will lead to underestimation of their presence, while the cumulative effect of a few records each year for a seven-year period, can lead to overestimation. Treat the map with caution!

The map shows the scarcity and dispersed nature of Gadwall in SE Scotland. Birds show up regularly in very small numbers, typically 1-3 birds, in winter and spring, especially along the Lothian coast. Some remain at these wintering or passage sites well into April and birds can occasionally drop in for a day or so between May and July. Such records probably account for the tetrad registrations at all of the coastal or near-coastal sites in the Lothians and Berwickshire. These are all well-watched birding sites where Gadwall would be more likely to be picked out from other duck species. While these sites may fulfil immediate needs, most are not suitable for breeding. Inland sites are more promising and the records may indicate genuine attempts at breeding, although some were undoubtedly passage birds dropping in for a few days en route to Fife or more distant parts. Only a single confirmed breeding attempt occurred between 1988-94, when a female was seen with young at Hule Moss in 1992. Breeding may have been attempted at Bavelaw and Whitton (NT71P) in 1992. The remaining sites at Alemoor (NT31X), Bemersyde, Seafield Pond (NT67P) and the Hirsel had pairs present for part of the breeding season. The best attended site was Bavelaw

where pairs were present in four of the seven years of the *Atlas* survey. Elsewhere birds were rarely present in more than two of the seven years. In the post-*Atlas* period breeding probably occurred at the Hirsel in 1995 and young were seen at Bavelaw in 1996, the first successful Lothian record.

Comparison with the *Old Atlas* shows a definite increase in breeding attempts although data for both periods are so meagre that firm conclusions are difficult to draw. The *Old Atlas* does, however, indicate a confirmed breeding attempt in NT56 along the Lammermuir Edge. There are a number of potentially suitable waters in this square but there is no documentation supporting this record anywhere in the literature. In such circumstances the provenance of this record must be doubted.

The picture of the 1988-95 period accords well with what is known of the history of breeding Gadwall in SE Scotland. Historically there were breeding attempts at Biel (NT67I) in 1924, Threipmuir Reservoir in 1933-34, Gladhouse Reservoir in 1960-61 and Branxholme Wester Loch (NT41F) in 1984. Earlier breeding at Rachan Pond (NT13C) in 1906 involved pinioned birds. Success seems elusive as no young have been seen other than in the most recent attempts in 1984, 1992 and 1996 (*Andrews*, *Murray*).

While the old records occur at a frequency of less than one attempt per decade, it is noticeable that three or four successful attempts have occurred in the last 12 years. There has been an increasing number of birds reported as wintering or on passage in recent years, particularly in Lothian, and records from the *Bird Reports* show a steady, if fluctuating, increase in April-July records in SE Scotland since 1979 (see graph). Whether this is due to the Scottish population being buoyant over the same period is not known but an increase in breeding attempts might be expected if this is the case. Such a trend has been taking place amongst the English population with considerable expansion since 1970 (Fox 1988). The British population increase in recent years has been calculated at 4% per annum.

In conclusion the Gadwall appears to be an extremely scarce breeding species in SE Scotland with perhaps only 1-2 pairs present in any year. It nevertheless appears to be increasing in terms of both numbers of birds present and in the numbers of breeding attempts. Suitable waters seem to exist and a small population may become established in future years.

J.G.Mattocks

Gadwall

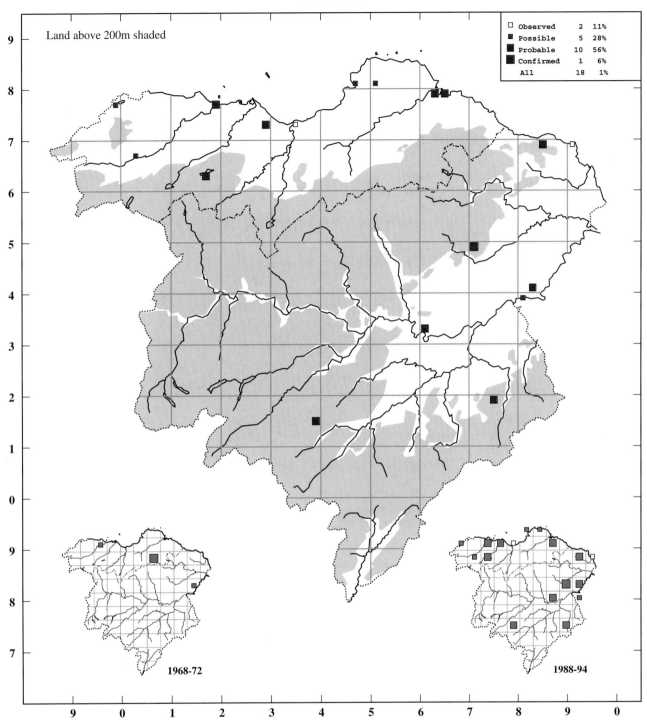

Land above 200m shaded

	Observed	2	11%
	Possible	5	28%
	Probable	10	56%
	Confirmed	1	6%
	All	18	1%

1968-72

1988-94

SE Scotland: Records and Birds from Bird Reports 1979-95

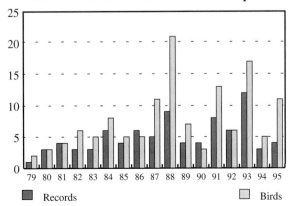

Records   Birds

63

Teal

Anas crecca

The typical breeding habitat of Teal is upland pools and marshes. This preference is reflected in the distribution, the Teal being most abundant in northern Scotland from Orkney south to Strathspey, encompassing the largest area of upland vegetation in Britain. Teal also nest in low-lying wetlands, the main habitat in southern Britain. Whether nesting in lowland or upland, Teal choose the same type of pools, avoiding large, open waters for smaller, more enclosed, pools with dense marginal vegetation. On larger waters, Teal use the more sheltered and enclosed areas. They often nest along hill burns where standing water is absent and occasionally will lead their young to deep, stony lochs and reservoirs. Teal are shy and will not normally nest in areas subject to disturbance.

Small and relatively inconspicuous ducks, that often linger close to or within dense marginal growth, Teal can be difficult to record. Almost all possible and probable records were of single birds or pairs on suitable habitat. Confirmed breeding is more difficult to record. The nest is usually placed in dense vegetation and is exceedingly difficult to locate. Additionally, ducklings are brooded under cover during the day, only being led to water to feed after dusk. Considering the secretive habits and nocturnal feeding behaviour of the Teal, it is likely that they bred in many more tetrads than in those where breeding was confirmed. Most confirmed records were of broods with a few involving females performing distraction display or injury-feigning.

Teal are widespread, if rather localised in SE Scotland. The map shows they are found mostly away from low-lying areas near the coast. There are loose concentrations in the Pentlands, Moorfoots and Lammermuirs. Further south Teal are more scattered but numbers of occupied tetrads are loosely grouped in the Tweedsmuir Hills and Ettrick Forest lochs. As ponds and lochs are generally scarce in all of these hills, many birds must use the hill burns. Good numbers are found on the deeper lochs and reservoirs such as Harperrig (NT06V), West Water (NT15B), North Esk (NT15P), Fruid, Megget (NT12W) and St. Mary's Loch. Teal are mostly absent in the Cheviots and in the Newcastleton Hills. On the lower ground of the Tweed basin and along parts of the East Lothian and Berwickshire coast, Teal are very localised and confined mostly to the ponds and lochs that occupy glacier-formed hollows in the flatter landscape where complete drainage has been impossible. These sites imply that despite the unpromising landscape of arable farmland, Teal can exist in such areas if suitable sites are present and that the generalised limitation of Teal to hill areas may be an artifact of the destruction of suitable habitat on the lower ground through agricultural 'improvements' over the last few centuries. The greater frequency of sites in the middle Tweed suggests that there has been less habitat degradation there compared to the Lothian lowlands. In the latter area only three sites, Cousland (NT36U), Balgone (NT58R) and Broxmouth (NT67Y&Z) held probable or confirmed records of Teal outwith the protected areas of Tailend Moss (NT06D) and the Almond Pools (NT06I), Aberlady Bay and Linlithgow and Duddingston Lochs. The reasons for the absence of Teal from the hills of southern Roxburghshire is not immediately apparent. Ponds are definitely rare, but the hill burns look identical to those further north. The heavily grazed grass-covered hills with very short swards may be a factor as this 'grass-desert' certainly contrasts with the taller vegetation of the wetter and more heather-clad northern hills.

The altitude graph shows Teal as being most abundant between 200-400m and relatively rare below 100m. The sparser distribution of birds in the Tweedsmuir Hills may well be a function of the higher altitude as birds appear to avoid the highest levels.

The status of the Teal in SE Scotland has changed little since 1968-72. Comparisons with the *Old Atlas* 10-km map show an almost identical number of occupied 10-km squares despite a third of squares showing gains or losses. One obvious change is the disappearance of birds from the Newcastleton area. Those 10-km squares with extensive forestry show no losses and indeed three show minor gains, although only a handful of tetrads are involved. There would appear to have been some redistribution in the lowlands where six 10-km squares show gains as against just four losses, although again only a handful of tetrads are involved.

The *New Atlas* abundance map shows SE Scotland holds moderate numbers of Teal with areas of highest abundance in the Pentlands, the Ettrick Forest, Bemersyde, Hule Moss, Dowlaw (NT86P) and Hoselaw. The importance of the latter four sites seems to have been inflated somewhat. While they do hold good numbers of birds, spot counts early in the season before all winter birds have left might have unduly influenced the numbers used in the analysis. Nevertheless SE Scotland does seem to hold appreciable numbers of Teal.

The breeding habits of Teal are such that they are usually under-recorded in local bird reports, the upland sites where they breed being seldom visited by casual birders. The *Borders Bird Report* details records from 87 sites between 1979-95. Applying minimum-maximum figures to the numbers of birds recorded at these sites, approximately 120-150 pairs were recorded. As 24% of all *Atlas* records came from Lothian, a *pro-rata* adjustment of this figure would raise the local estimate to somewhere in the region of 150-190 pairs. As Teal are almost certainly under-recorded in the *Bird Reports*, raising the figure by another 20%, to 180-230 pairs, may hint at the real population present, using bird records as a basis.

Although the *New Atlas* says it uses a density of 3-5 pairs per 10-km square to calculate the British population, the quoted figure for the national total actually uses a figure of 1.3-2.3 pairs per occupied 10-km square. This would give 78-138 pairs in SE Scotland, about half of the local estimates based on this *Atlas*. Taking our figures, SE Scotland apparently holds 5-9% of the British breeding population. This suggests that the *New Atlas* numbers are pessimistic and should be revised upward by a factor of at least two.

While the Teal population might not be as low as the *New Atlas* calculates, there is little doubt that the range has suffered a major contraction across Britain with a loss of 16% of occupied 10-km squares since 1968-72. While our local population appears to have been largely unaffected, there should be no complacency about the potential of Teal suffering in the future. While the fears concerning the spread of forestry have been mitigated by more enlightened forestry practices, fears about acidification of upland waters are still present. Some monitoring of our relatively healthy population may be in order to provide a benchmark for measuring future changes.

D.Kelly

Teal

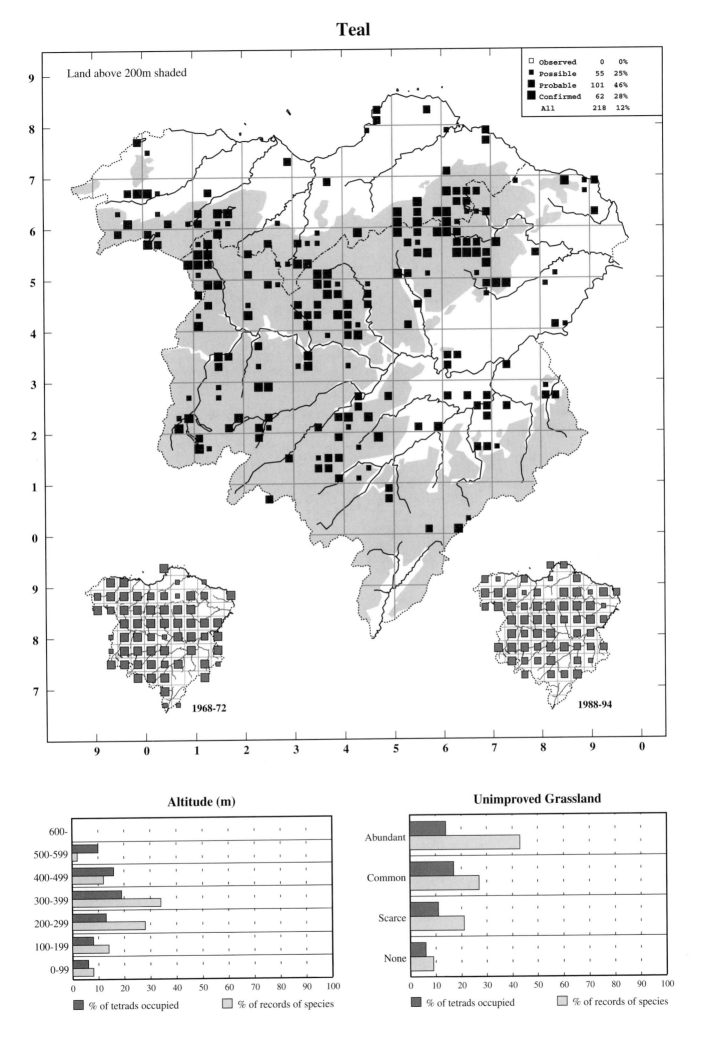

☐ Observed		0	0%
▪ Possible		55	25%
◼ Probable		101	46%
◼ Confirmed		62	28%
All		218	12%

Land above 200m shaded

1968-72

1988-94

Altitude (m)

■ % of tetrads occupied   ☐ % of records of species

Unimproved Grassland

Abundant

Common

Scarce

None

■ % of tetrads occupied   ☐ % of records of species

Mallard

Anas platyrhynchos

The commonest and most familiar duck in Britain, the Mallard has the least demanding habitat requirements of any waterfowl. This has allowed it to occupy most freshwater and some brackish aquatic habitats from marshes, tiny streams and drains to large rivers, ponds and lochs. Their tolerance of man has allowed them to move into our towns, provided they are not molested. The width of their habitat spectrum is partly the result of their ability to utilise various methods of feeding (grazing, dabbling, diving) and through their very catholic food requirements.

The survey found Mallards over most of SE Scotland, making them the most ubiquitous of the waterfowl. Being bold and conspicuous birds, they were not difficult to find, even in dense vegetation. The proportion of confirmed breeding was quite high, with over 80% of the confirmed records being of females with young. Probable breeding was also dominated by one category, over 90% of records being of pairs.

The map shows just how widespread a bird that requires the presence of water can become, with two-thirds of the area having records of Mallards. The next most widespread waterfowl, the Moorhen, could only manage 33% of the area while the next most widespread duck, the Goosander, was only found in 14% of tetrads. Even amongst the aquatic passerines, Dipper rates at 37% and Grey Wagtail at 46%. While Mallard, in 64% of the tetrads, is by no means universal, the widespread nature of the species is nevertheless remarkable.

The gaps in the distribution were mostly in hill areas (for example, NT11, NT23 & NT55), in commercial forestry (NT30, NT33 & NT60) and farmland with intensive cereal production where patches of open water, drains and streams are scarce (NT47 & NT84). There are some tetrads along the coast where Mallards breed and successful breeding was recorded for several of the Forth islands on Inchmickery and Inchkeith and Craigleith. Mallards also breed on Inchcolm (Fife) and are regularly reported on Fidra. The absence of fresh water on these islands shows the remarkable width of habitat tolerance in the Mallard.

As might be expected, Mallards are more widespread below 300m where water bodies and rivers are most abundant. Nevertheless even at higher levels above 400m, up to 40% of all tetrads held Mallards during the survey. While most tetrads with a pond or loch had breeding Mallards, over half of the tetrads where they occurred had no pond or loch. Most of these tetrads undoubtedly had rivers and streams and again this demonstrates the Mallard's ability to prosper in less than optimal habitat.

There were no changes in the 10-km square maps of SE Scotland since the *Old Atlas*. This is hardly surprising in a species that already occupied 100% of the 10-km squares in the *Old Atlas* and whose national population has increased considerably since then (*Trends*).

Paradoxically, but not untypically, there is less information on local Mallard numbers than there is for many scarcer species. Reports submitted to the *Bird Reports* often focus on numbers of broods rather than the number of pairs. Thus the best sites for breeding Mallards in Lothian appear to be Bavelaw, Gladhouse, Linlithgow and Musselburgh, all of which can produce 10+ broods annually. Only Bemersyde and the Hirsel match this in Borders, although the Teviot and Tweed Haughs can be very productive with counts of 40+ broods along less than eight kilometres of river.

Organised counts in the past give some guidance to the likely numbers. A survey in Lothian for other waterfowl in 1986 counted Mallard broods (Brown 1987), while the Tweed Goosander survey in 1987 also included counts of Mallard (Murray 1988). The 1987 Borders count produced totals of about 1,000 pairs (plus 250 singles) from part of the Tweed basin in March and April, followed by a count of about 220 broods in July. As only part of the river was counted, an estimate of 1,450 pairs was made for the 400km of river surveyed, based on the 3.0-3.5 prs/km of river found in the main survey. 300 river broods were also estimated for July. Counts of birds based on still waters in Borders indicate that around 300 broods are raised annually, possibly reflecting about 1,000 pairs at the start of the breeding season. A possible breeding population of *c*.2,450 pairs for Borders seems appropriate. Counts for Lothian are sketchier but the 1986 Wildfowl Census (Brown 1987) found about 150 broods on mostly still waters, perhaps from about 450 pairs. As Mallards also breed on the Lothian rivers, islands and some waters that were not counted, a possible figure of around 650 pairs is more realistic. This rough estimate of 3,100 pairs in SE Scotland, with 75% occurring in Borders, quite neatly fits the fact that about 73% of the tetrads with Mallard records were also in Borders.

The BTO estimated the British population to average about 20 pairs per 10-km square in the *Old Atlas* but this had increased to 38 pairs in the *New Atlas*. The latter figure would indicate a local population of 2,470 pairs, somewhat less than the estimated 3,100 pairs based on actual counts.

Some 1,028 broods were counted casually in Borders between 1985 and 1995. A total of 5,991 young were seen, averaging 5.8 young per brood, within a range of 3.7 to 6.6 (see second graph).

R.D.Murray

Mallard

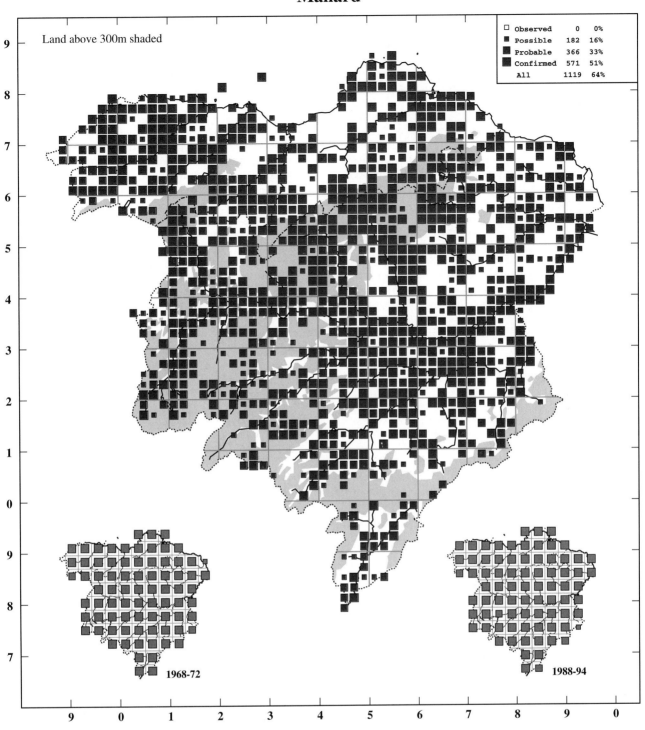

Land above 300m shaded

☐ Observed	0	0%
◼ Possible	182	16%
◼ Probable	366	33%
◼ Confirmed	571	51%
All	1119	64%

1968-72

1988-94

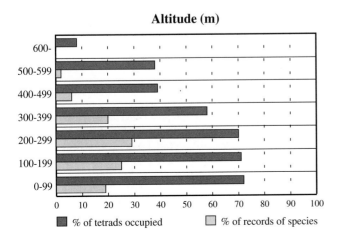

Altitude (m)

◼ % of tetrads occupied ☐ % of records of species

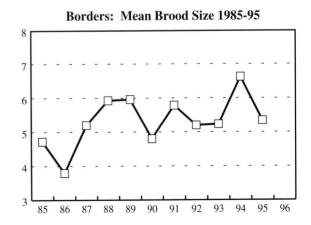

Borders: Mean Brood Size 1985-95

Pintail
Anas acuta

In Britain the graceful Pintail is mostly an uncommon and localised winter visitor to favoured estuaries such as Solway Firth. It is one of Britain's rarest breeding ducks. Elsewhere in the Holarctic it is a very common breeding duck in drier continental interiors, becoming less common towards the wetter maritime fringe of western Europe. It has a wide choice of nesting habitat, the only constant need being that the waters must be shallow and free of dense shoreline vegetation. It first bred in Inverness-shire in 1869, one of a group of ducks which colonised Britain in the 19th century. Pintails now breed regularly only in Orkney and the the remnant marshes of East Anglia and Kent. The traditional site at Loch Leven has been largely deserted since 1962, although a pair bred there in 1993.

They have bred twice in SE Scotland, at an undisclosed site in Selkirkshire in 1901 and between Bavelaw and Harperrig in 1912. Thus Pintails are mostly a scarce passage migrant and uncommon winter visitor to the area, mostly recorded in the Lothians where numbers may have declined of late, judging from *Bird Report* records. The nearest regular wintering flock is in the upper Forth estuary near Grangemouth and most reports come from similar habitats at Aberlady and Musselburgh. Despite the greater numbers of birds in Lothian there has been no hint of breeding. In Borders Pintail numbers increased in the 1980s and isolated individuals and pairs have lingered on at some sites in late spring.

The map shows a few records that almost all involve wintering and passage birds that have lingered after March and so were encountered during *Atlas* fieldwork. Pintail reports from Musselburgh, Aberlady, Tyninghame and St. Abb's Head have all been allocated as observed records, as they probably involved passage birds moving through in April and May. A pair appeared at Dowlaw Dam (NT86P) in successive springs in 1989-90, remaining for up to a month up to late April. Other than the length of their stay these records were probably little different from other coastal records. Single birds seen at Rosslynlee (NT25U) and Roxburgh (NT73A) may also have been birds moving through. Records that perhaps held more potential for breeding occurred at Hoselaw in 1990 and 1991 and at Tailend Moss (NT06D) in 1994. In each case a pair was seen in April with only a single male later in May thus providing a prospect that the females may have been incubating. No further proof of breeding was obtained in these cases. The record of a pair near Shaws Lochs (NT32V) in June 1991 is thought to have involved escaped birds.

The *Old Atlas* map shows breeding from three 10-km squares. The NT05 record is not known and may lie in Clydesdale outwith SE Scotland. Similarly, there is no knowledge of a record in NT62. In NT84 confirmed breeding is shown, perhaps at the Hirsel, but there is no trace of any confirmed breeding in the literature. Like some other *Old Atlas* records these must be treated with caution.

The distribution shown on the map shows a wide scatter which is to be expected from a bird which is an uncommon passage migrant with no nearby nesting concentrations. The breeding population of Pintail in Britain is around 50 pairs, an insignificant number compared to the millions that breed across northern Eurasia and North America. If Pintails breed at all in SE Scotland it is likely to be sporadic and involve only isolated pairs. It is doubtful that Pintails will ever produce a regular breeding presence in the area. As breeding Pintails are so rare, any breeding sites discovered should be kept as confidential as possible to prevent disturbance. **D. Kelly**

Garganey
Anas querquedula

The Garganey has a wide range in the warmer climatic zones of Europe and Asia, from Britain to the Russian Far East, becoming scarcer in the damper, cooler climate of maritime Europe. In winter the whole population migrates to sub-Saharan Africa and southern Asia. The preferred breeding habitat is densely-vegetated shallow freshwater wetlands with a patchwork of emergent vegetation and open water. In Britain Garganeys are birds of southern and central England, being intermittent and scattered nesters towards the north and west. In Scotland it is mostly an overshooting spring migrant, appearing between April and July, with a light autumn passage. Garganey numbers in Scotland are determined by the size of the immigration into Britain, which in turn fluctuates according to the spring weather. Only 12 birds managed to reach Scotland in 1987, compared to a probable record count of 84 in 1990.

They have bred three times in Scotland, at Aberlady Bay in 1923, Ayrshire in 1979 and Aberdeenshire in 1990. These few records may underestimate the situation as breeding Garganeys are very secretive, nesting in dense, grassy vegetation. This behaviour may lead to breeding attempts being overlooked in areas of low observer coverage, such underwatched areas being typical of most of Scotland. The map shows these spring migrants, usually briefly seen in late April and May. Records of single birds appear as possible records, while pairs are shown as probable records. At no time was breeding suspected but the map does show where birds can appear. Since the *Bird Reports* were first published in 1979, Garganeys have been seen in spring at just 14 sites in SE Scotland, eight of them in the *Atlas* period (see Appendix). Aberlady is, by far, the best site to see Garganeys, with birds present in half of the 17 springs. Indeed only the Mire Loch at St. Abbs and Musselburgh also have multiple ecords and these in just two years. The scatter of records is precisely what might be expected of an overshooting migrant.

It is possible that Garganeys may breed in SE Scotland in future but it is unlikely that they will ever be regular breeders unless there is a profound climatic change. Our climate is too cool and rainy for this continental species. Even in southern Britain Garganeys have never been numerous and may have declined, possibly through habitat loss as a result of drainage. The *New Atlas* estimated a British population of 40-60 pairs, insignificant when compared to the estimated European population of two million birds. **D.Kelly**

Pintail

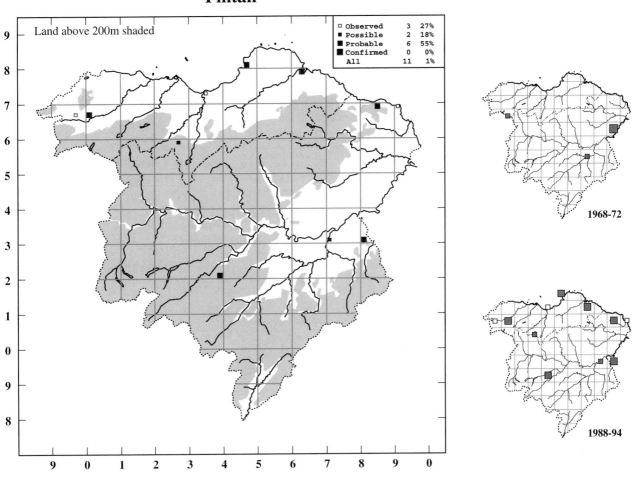

☐ Observed		3	27%
▪ Possible		2	18%
◼ Probable		6	55%
◼ Confirmed		0	0%
All		11	1%

Land above 200m shaded

1968-72

1988-94

Garganey

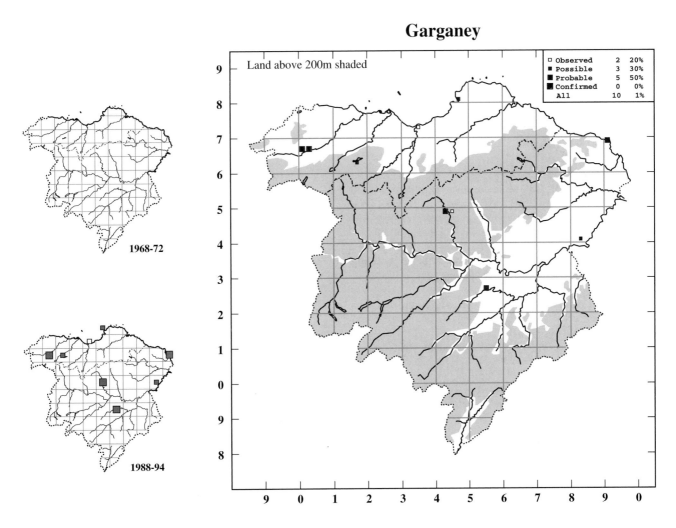

☐ Observed		2	20%
▪ Possible		3	30%
◼ Probable		5	50%
◼ Confirmed		0	0%
All		10	1%

Land above 200m shaded

1968-72

1988-94

Shoveler
Anas clypeata

A colourful drake Shoveler should be relatively easy for an observer to find but in late spring, when the duck is on eggs, the drakes begin their moult into eclipse and become rather retiring. The Shoveler is a predominantly continental species, although tolerant of the cooler and more moist maritime climate of western Europe, and found exclusively on freshwater. Over the last 150 years Shovelers have spread into western Europe, colonising as far west as Iceland. Breeding Shovelers invariably choose shallow eutrophic lochs and pools, showing a preference for areas where rank uncut vegetation surrounds the water. The drakes are territorial and will defend an area of shoreline and water while ducks may place their nests as close as five metres to one another. The preference for lowland eutrophic water is highlighted by the *New Atlas* where the highest numbers of birds are found in the coastal marshes of Kent, East Anglia and the Humber, as well as on the washlands of Norfolk and Cambridgeshire. In Scotland the centre of abundance is in Strathmore and around Loch Leven, with outlying populations in Orkney and the Outer Hebrides. Shovelers are absent from much of northern and western Britain, where the climate is less clement and the freshwater less fertile.

The Shoveler is an uncommon and highly localised breeding species found in just 2% of the tetrads. The presence of birds is not difficult to prove and as Shovelers are scarce, almost all records are passed on to the local recorders. All probable records concerned pairs, while all confirmed records dealt with the relatively rarer sighting of ducklings.

The map shows a species that is mostly limited to eutrophic waters in the low-lying coastal parts of the Lothians and the middle and lower Tweed basin. In Lothian the main site is around Bavelaw Marsh and Threipmuir Reservoir where up to four pairs have been reported and breeding occurred in four of the seven years between 1988-94. A single pair also bred at East Fortune Ponds (NT58K) in 1993. Birds may have bred at Tailend Moss (NT06D) between 1988-90 but, like the remainder of sites in West Lothian, breeding was never confirmed. Elsewhere pairs were seen in spring at Aberlady Bay, Duddingston, Linlithgow, Musselburgh, Dalmahoy (NT16I) and near Broxburn (NT07W), while singles appeared at the Almond Pools (NT06I), Cobbinshaw (NT05D), Gladhouse, Drem (NT58A) and Belhaven (NT67P). In the Borders the most regular site is the Hirsel Lake with up to three pairs and at least as many surplus males present in most summers, and breeding confirmed in 1988-89 and 1992. Breeding also occurred at Hule Moss in 1992-93. Pairs were present at Bemersyde, the Hen Poo (NT75S), Millar's Moss (NT96E), Ploughlands (NT62Y) and Whitrig (NT63H) in the *Atlas* years, while single birds were seen at Dowlaw (NT86P), Hoselaw, South Slipperfield (NT15F) and Yetholm Loch. While many of these records, especially the single birds and a few of the pairs, may represent late wintering birds or passage migrants, there is undoubtedly a small population regularly breeding in the area, centred on the Hirsel and Bavelaw. Elsewhere breeding is more

temporary and rarely sustained. Why this should be is uncertain but Shovelers have never been common in SE Scotland. Perhaps the numbers are dependent on the strength of immigration in the autumn from Europe, with breeding occurring in years after especially high numbers. There certainly seems some relationship between waters that regularly get good numbers of birds between September and December and the frequency that breeding takes place.

The earliest record of breeding in SE Scotland is from Aberlady on some date "prior to 1843" (*B&R*). The traditional sites in Lothian were Threipmuir and Gladhouse but breeding ceased at both by 1978, the blame being put on Mink. Breeding has also been reported in Lothian at Biel (1909), Cobbinshaw (1956), Drem (1975-76) and Aberlady (1986) (*Andrews*). In Borders, the Merse has always held the majority of nesting Shovelers and although old confirmed records are rare, breeding mostly occurred at the Hirsel and Hoselaw. Outwith the *Atlas* period Shovelers also bred at Bemersyde in 1986-87, Yetholm Loch in 1986 and at the Hirsel and Folly Loch (NT62I) in 1995 (*Bird Reports*).

Comparison between the *Old Atlas* and *New Atlas* shows considerable change, perhaps not surprising in a species that shows as little site fidelity as the Shoveler. While 17 squares were occupied in 1968-72 and 22 in 1988-94, 12 are registered as gains, with seven showing as losses. In Lothian the gains are at Aberlady, Duddingston, Musselburgh, Linlithgow, the Almond Pools and Tyninghame while in Borders the new 10-km squares are at St. Abbs, the Hen Poo, Hule Moss, Faldonside (NT53B) and Greenlaw (NT64X). In each area the losses are more difficult to name as there are no records of the precise locations of the records in 1968-72. However, records from NT21 and NT42 are unexpected in view of the current distribution of Shoveler. As with many *Old Atlas* records of scarce birds, these *Old Atlas* records, with no other supporting evidence, should be treated with some caution. Some contraction of range towards the margins can be seen to be the main change to have taken place since the *Old Atlas*. The local situation may reflect the national picture in that the best sites are all in protected areas and this has allowed Shovelers to be relatively successful at these sites. Nationally Shovelers have declined in unprotected marginal areas such as ponds and marshes that have been drained and neighbouring rough grassland tidied up or heavily grazed. In SE Scotland Shovelers are more successful now than at any other period in the 20th century. From a low point in the late 1970s, the species seems to have recovered and re-established itself as a scarce but regular breeding bird.

SE Scotland is on the margins of the British range, and local birds may be an outlier of the Perthshire population. In the best years, as in 1987 and 1994, there may have been as many as 15 pairs in the area, with at least ten other males present. This might fall to less than ten pairs in the poorest years. As the production of young is still a fairly rare event, the local population is probably reliant on immigration to sustain itself.   *D.Kelly*

Shoveler

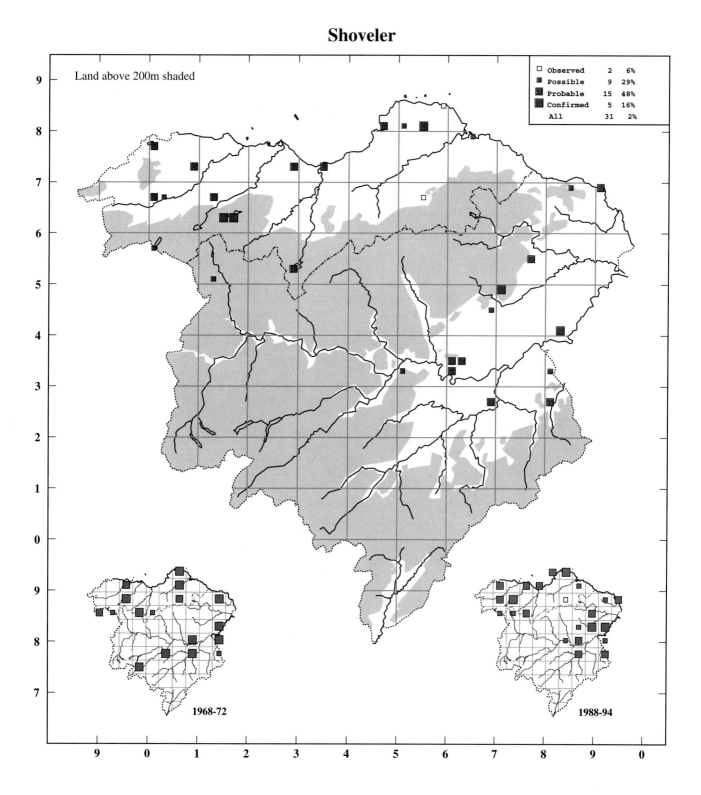

Land above 200m shaded

□	Observed	2	6%
▪	Possible	9	29%
▪	Probable	15	48%
■	Confirmed	5	16%
	All	31	2%

1968-72

1988-94

Pochard
Aythya ferina

Pochards like low-lying shallow eutrophic waters that have an extensive open water surface and an abundance of emergent and submerged vegetation. Dense vegetation is required for the nest site which is usually situated close to the water's edge, often on a thick platform of aquatic vegetation in a reed-bed. Pochards are omnivorous, dabbling and diving for various aquatic plants and invertebrates.

Being distinctive waterfowl Pochards were not difficult to find for the *Atlas* survey when present. Probable records were mostly of pairs while confirmed records were wholly of broods.

The map shows the scattered nature of Pochard distribution in summer, suggestive of a species with exacting habitat demands. Of the sites where breeding has been confirmed, only Bara Loch (NT56U) fits all of the habitat criteria mentioned above as being preferred across Britain. The Hirsel Lake and Yetholm Loch lack submergent vegetation while Bemersyde and Yetholm Marsh (NT82D&I) lack extensive open water. In tetrads with only probable breeding, Gladhouse, Scoughall (NT68B), Threipmuir, Harelaw (NT52G), Hoselaw and Millar's Moss (NT96E) held pairs in 1988-94 but mostly only in a single year (see Appendix).

Pochard numbers have been monitored annually in Britain since 1986 by the Rare Breeding Birds Panel and the species is sufficiently rare for most summer records to have been reported to local recorders. It is from the *Bird Reports* that the most valuable data for discussing Pochards are derived. Few waters hold birds with any regularity: just Bara Loch, Duddingston, Threipmuir, Hirsel, Yetholm Loch, Yetholm Marsh, Hoselaw and Bemersyde. Elsewhere birds occasionally show up, but typically only males are present and attempts at breeding are very rare and are rarely repeated in later seasons. Males always outnumber females. Some sites seem to only attract males while at any site with females present, the females are always outnumbered, sometimes as much as 8:1. Care should be taken here not to include the post-breeding moult flocks, which are predominantly male, that gather between late June and August. Females in these flocks can be outnumbered as much as 40:1. The lack of females in SE Scotland is a feature in Pochard counts throughout the year and may be a reason why the species is not particularly successful and has never really consolidated the colonisation.

The Pochard is one of a group of duck species that colonised Britain in the 19th century, reaching Britain about 1815 but colonising slowly. It first bred in Scotland in 1871, arriving in SE Scotland around 1878-79. It has remained a scarce breeding species with a small population both nationally and locally (Fox 1991). SE Scotland is on the edge of the Scottish range, the Pochard being most numerous in the Fife/Angus area where there are thought to be about 25-35 pairs nesting.

The recent history of the Pochard in the area was centred on Duddingston where 8-10 pairs bred annually in the 1950s, peaking at c.15 pairs in the 1960s with a few pairs breeding at nearby St. Margaret's and Dunsapie Lochs. This dropped to five pairs by 1978. Single pairs bred at Bavelaw-Threipmuir in 1968 and 1974-75. Nesting at Duddingston may have been related to the flocks that wintered there and on the sea at nearby Seafield. The 5,000-8,000-strong Seafield flock loafed at Duddingston during the day and some may have stayed to breed. The flocks were associated with grain-rich sewage that was discharged at Seafield. The decline of the flock and the subsequent fall away in the breeding population dates from when sewage was treated before being discharged. The last breeding record at Duddingston was in 1979, a year after the Seafield treatment works came fully into operation.

Breeding now only occurs at the regular sites. Since 1979, nesting has only been proved in Lothian on five occasions: at Duddingston in 1979, Bavelaw in 1980, Tailend Moss (NT06D) in 1986 and Bara Loch in 1993-94. Breeding has been more regular in Borders with broods present at the Hirsel in 1983, 1985-89, 1991-92 & 1994, at Bemersyde in 1989, 1991-92 and 1994-96, at Yetholm Marsh in 1989-91 and 1994-96 and at Yetholm Loch in 1994 &1996. A newly-created water at Folly Loch (NT62I) produced a brood in 1995 (Appendix). There is typically only a single pair in Lothian although five pairs were present in 1989. Borders usually has 4-13 pairs, averaging some eight pairs in each summer between 1985-96 (see graph). The current population of SE Scotland is between 5-13 pairs in any year with an additional 10-12 males present.

Success is variable, with total failure in some years, to 11 broods and 43 young from 13 pairs in 1991. The mean size of some 32 broods mentioned in the *Bird Reports* was 3.9. *BWP* quotes average brood sizes (at fledging) of successful pairs as 4.4 in Germany. As productivity here is slightly lower, it seems likely that the local population is not self-sustaining and depends on recruitment from elsewhere.

There is an influx of Pochards into the area in mid-June. It is likely that they come to moult. Numbers decline somewhat after August, well before the arrival of wintering birds in September-October. Although numbers vary from year to year the moulters favour a limited number of waters and in recent years the June-August peak counts have been as follows: 110 Hirsel (1993), 76 Duddingston (1989), 74 Hoselaw (1987) and 69 Yetholm Loch (1995). The origins of these birds is not known.   ***R.D.Murray***

Pochard

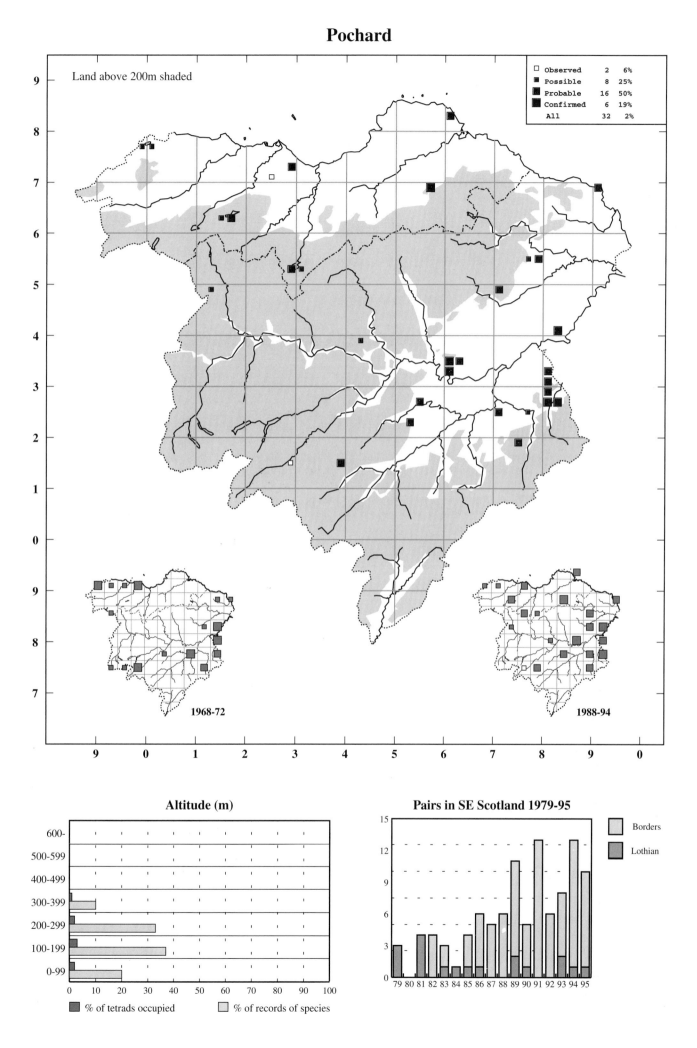

Land above 200m shaded

□ Observed	2	6%
▪ Possible	8	25%
◪ Probable	16	50%
■ Confirmed	6	19%
All	32	2%

1968-72

1988-94

Altitude (m)

■ % of tetrads occupied   ▫ % of records of species

Pairs in SE Scotland 1979-95

Borders

Lothian

Tufted Duck
Aythya fuligula

The Tufted Duck is such a familiar species in SE Scotland that it may come as a surprise to many that the area was only colonised 100 years ago. It is now widespread on inland waters of all sorts, only shunning the large, deep and stony reservoirs and fast-flowing rivers. Tufted Ducks are mostly carnivorous, diving for aquatic molluscs, crustaceans and insects, so there is every likelihood that these deep, stony waters are too deep to provide sufficient food.

Tufted Ducks were found in 12% of the area, suggesting that all but the smallest ponds are occupied. Diving ducks are usually easy to locate as they frequent the open water areas of lochs and ponds. The pair formed most of the 45% of records of probable breeding and confirmed breeding was found in another 38% of the tetrads, almost wholly being broods. Tufted Ducks breed later than other ducks and broods can be seen between mid-June and mid-August. As *Atlas* fieldwork finished in July some will have been missed in the survey although all August records of broods from the *Bird Reports* were included.

The map shows the band of ponds and reservoirs to the west and south of Edinburgh and the cluster of waters in the Ettrick Forest. These areas hold the majority of Tufted Ducks in SE Scotland, there being only a thin scatter of tetrads to the east where ponds are less numerous. The Teviot below Nisbet and the Tweed below Kelso show almost continuous occupation along their lengths. Although the amalgamation of records from different years will doubtless exaggerate this, Tufted Ducks are present along much of these parts of the river system. Elsewhere rivers are rarely used. The Union Canal is harder to trace but is responsible for registrations in NS97, NT07, NT17 & NT27. Throughout Britain the Tufted Duck is essentially a bird of lowland eutrophic waters, being less abundant on higher oligotrophic waters. In SE Scotland the altitude graph shows that Tufted Ducks were present on most of the Ettrick Forest lochs, between 250-350m above sea-level. Only on the deep waters at Talla, Fruid and Megget (NT12W) Reservoirs and at St. Mary's Loch are birds absent. Chironomid midge larvae form a major part of the Tufted duckling diet and there is evidence (Giles 1990) that suggests that waters of more than 5 metres depth present problems for foraging ducklings. It is likely that the depth of these waters preclude breeding although birds show up there occasionally.

Counts of 341 broods at all stages in Borders between 1984-1995 provide a mean brood size of 4.7 within a range of 3.4 - 6.3. *BWP* gives no yardstick against which to compare this range with others elsewhere in Europe.

Tufted Ducks first bred in SE Scotland at Gladhouse in 1889. Although most suitable waters are said to have been occupied by 1910, it is likely that there has been steady infilling of the local distribution since, with birds moving on to less suitable waters as the prime sites became occupied. Comparison with the *Old Atlas* map supports this view with a 10% increase in occupied 10-km squares since 1972, and a steeper rise in the level of probable and confirmed breeding.

The move to rivers is a relatively recent phenomenon dating from about 1986 on the Tweed when a brood was seen at Norham (NT84Y) (*Bird Reports*). The river-breeding habit has since spread along much of the middle and lower Tweed and Teviot and these rivers now hold a considerable number of birds, possibly as many as 50-60 pairs in a good year. The first reports of breeding on the Union Canal also date from 1986. It is possible that the two events may be related, perhaps due to population pressure on the existing waters. Many waters created in the recent spate of new pond construction for both conservation and shooting are often immediately occupied by Tufted Ducks.

The *Bird Reports* record 133 waters (53 in Lothian and 80 in Borders) as having held Tufted Ducks between 1979-1994, not including the birds that are present along the Union Canal and the Tweed and Teviot. This does not match the 210 tetrads where birds were reported but several waters occupy more than one tetrad (15 tetrads) and the river birds account for about 50 tetrads. Several sites consistently hold good numbers (6-18 pairs): Bavelaw and Gladhouse in Lothian, and Bemersyde, Hirsel, Hoselaw, Hule Moss and Williestruther (NT41V) in Borders. Gladhouse alone held 30-45 pairs until the 1970s when numbers dropped (*Andrews*).

The imbalance in the sex ratio creates difficulties in calculating the local population. There is normally a preponderance of males, especially on larger waters. In some cases males may outnumber females by a ratio of 2:1 or even 3:1. A local population of 120 pairs in Lothian and 260 pairs in Borders plus an extra 150 males throughout the area can be calculated from the mean numbers of birds reported in the *Bird Reports* since 1979, but as not all sites will be occupied in a single year the likely population of the area will be a little less at about 350 pairs with 100-120 surplus males. The Lothian figure is supported by a census of Tufted Ducks in 1986 (Brown 1987) which found 96-118 pairs at 36 sites.

Local densities run about 1.5 pairs per occupied tetrad or seven pairs per occupied 10-km square. This figure is in excess of the *New Atlas* estimate of 4.7-5.4 pairs per occupied 10-km square for Britain as a whole but the *New Atlas* does show high population abundance in West Lothian and eastern Roxburghshire. The calculation of a British population of 7,000-8,000 pairs (Owen *et al.* 1986) means that the local population contributes an excellent 5% of the national figure.

R.D.Murray

Tufted Duck

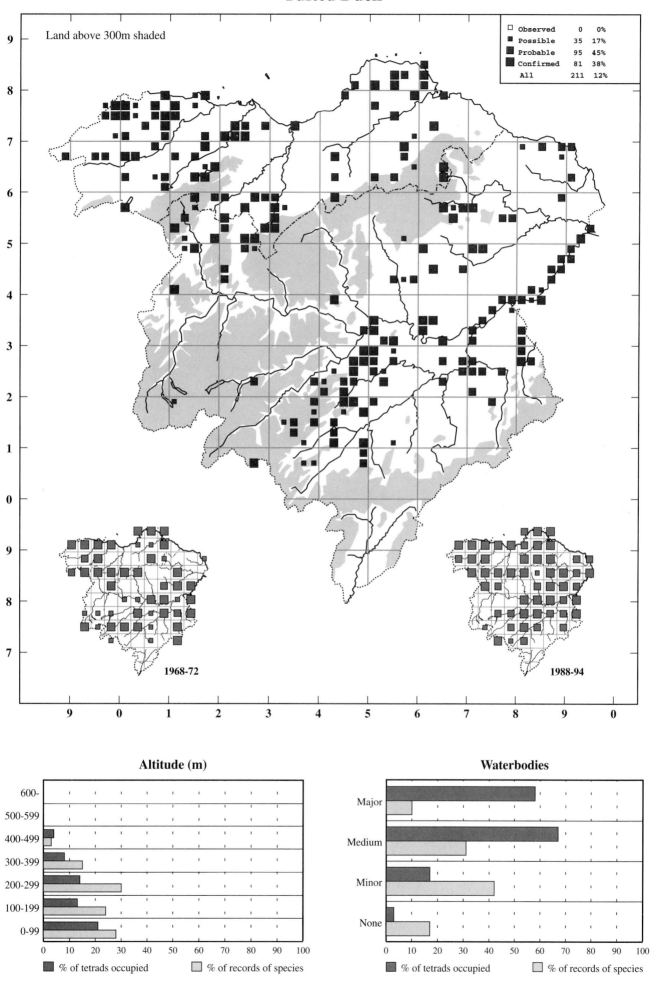

Land above 300m shaded

☐ Observed	0	0%
■ Possible	35	17%
■ Probable	95	45%
■ Confirmed	81	38%
All	211	12%

1968-72

1988-94

Altitude (m)

■ % of tetrads occupied   ▢ % of records of species

Waterbodies

■ % of tetrads occupied   ▢ % of records of species

Eider
Somateria mollissima

The Eider, one of our largest ducks, is perhaps more famous with the general public through the product eiderdown than through familiarity with the birds themselves, despite the fact that the boldly marked males and the brown females are common along the coasts of much of northern Britain. Consuming shellfish, especially mussels, and other marine invertebrates, Eiders are often seen in rafts offshore or in small groups lounging on rocks at low tide.

Although Eiders are easily seen along the shoreline, sightings do not necessarily indicate that breeding occurs. Large numbers of Eiders that breed along the North Sea coasts between Aberdeenshire and Northumberland move into the sheltered waters of the Firth of Forth to moult and overwinter. Non-breeders also summer. Birds from either source may have been recorded in the *Atlas*. Almost all the probable records were sightings of pairs. Confirmed records were widespread, about half were of broods, the remainder birds on nests. Observed records mostly came from shores where observers thought there was little chance of birds actually breeding. A major problem with relying on sightings of broods as proof of breeding is that in recent years Eiders have mostly nested on the Forth islands and then ferried the small ducklings to the mainland coast where there are better feeding opportunities and more shelter (Calladine *et al.* 1995). Hence the sighting of a creche of Eider ducklings is not necessarily positive proof of breeding within, or even near, the tetrad concerned.

The map shows Eiders along all of the coast, from Blackness in the west to Lamberton in the east. Observed records dominate west of Queensferry and on much of the coast between Cramond and Port Seton. However, as the nest from Leith Docks and broods at Musselburgh show, some of these observed records could have belonged to higher categories. East of Port Seton, probable and confirmed records dominate.

Eiders are described as breeding in the Forth at Inchkeith and the Isle of May from at least the 17th century. Other sites are mentioned including the Bass Rock, Inchmickery, Eyebroughy and Fidra, (*B&R*), but it is clear that, while common, Eiders suffered a great deal of disturbance and persecution through egg-collecting and shooting for food, especially in the 19th century when the population declined considerably. Indeed counts from the early 20th century suggest numbers were at a very low ebb with many of the breeding islands deserted or with just a handful of ducks nesting. Only at keepered sites such as Tyninghame, where as many as 80 ducks nested along the shore, were there appreciable numbers breeding. Birds were even shot for food in the 1939-45 war.

Numbers have increased rapidly since the 1960s, probably after the Protection of Birds Act of 1954 started to take effect. Calladine *et al.* (1995) calculated that an 8.5% per annum population increase has occurred on the Isle of May, Inchkeith, Inchmickery, Inchgarvie and Inchcolm in the last decade or so. Numbers on Fidra and Craigleith are more stable although Fidra too shows a substantial increase. Islands with no great tradition of breeding, the Lamb, Bass Rock, Car Craig and Haystack, now have small numbers breeding regularly. The Forth islands population in the 1960s is estimated at *c*.300 nests, compared to *c*.2,340 nests in 1994 (see table).

There seems to have been a major switch in the location of the Forth breeding population. Between 1910-1940 large numbers bred at coastal sites like Tyninghame and Archerfield (*B&R*) when very few bred on the islands. Since then, through protection, the island nesters have increased and while nesting still occurs on the mainland, the majority of the Forth Eiders now nest on the islands (see pie-chart).

Nests were found in just seven mainland tetrads: two at Aberlady, two at Seacliff-Scoughall (NT68B&C) and singles at Leith Docks (NT27T), Tyninghame and near Thorntonloch (NT77L). All other records of confirmed breeding on the mainland were sightings of broods. It therefore has to be concluded that many broods on the map between Aberlady and Barns Ness (NT77I) and around Dalmeny (NT17) could in fact have originated from nests elsewhere. Calladine *et al.* (1995) showed with studies of marked birds that most broods on the Fife coast originated from the Isle of May, some broods travelling as much as 24km within 7-10 days of hatching. They speculate that, with the Lothian shore only 15km distant, some broods seen there may also originate from the May. However, the East Lothian islands have a sufficiently large breeding population to account for most coastal broods without resorting to such a marathon journey by very tiny ducklings. With a lack of evidence for widespread mainland nesting, these Eiders may act like those on the Isle of May and move their broods to nursery areas with better feeding and shelter, accounting for most broods between Aberlady and Barns Ness. Dalmeny and Musselburgh may act as a nursery areas to the birds originating from the inner Forth islands as no nests have been found there.

The only coastal site with any numbers breeding is Aberlady where there can be great problems with predation of eggs and young by mammalian predators, gulls and corvids (*Andrews*). Aberlady has had as many as 120 breeding females in recent years but these regularly only manage to fledge a small number of young. While 88 young were seen there in 1988 and 56 in 1997, the average between 1990-96 was just eight ducklings fledging (*Bird Reports,* I.M. Thomson *pers. comm.*). Tyninghame holds about 30 females. Broods are rare in Berwickshire, most records being of probable rather than confirmed breeding. The cliff shoreline may not be conducive to the rearing of Eider ducklings.

Breeding on the mainland is becoming more uncommon in the face of predation and disturbance and most birds now breed on the islands where they are free from ground predators and where public access is limited. An alternative strategy was tried in the 1970s when a few pairs bred successfully at West Fenton, 6km inland up the Peffer Burn from Aberlady (Jenkins *et al.* 1971). This habit may still persist as there is a registration of a pair in the same area (NT58A). A recent decline in coastal breeding has also been documented in Fife where shore nesting has almost ceased (Smout 1986, Calladine *et al.* 1995). It seems likely that more than 95% of the current breeding population in the Firth of Forth now nests on the islands. About 2,500 females breed in the Forth, approximately 8% of the British population, 850 pairs of this total being in Lothian and Borders, some 3% of the British population.
R.D.Murray

Eider

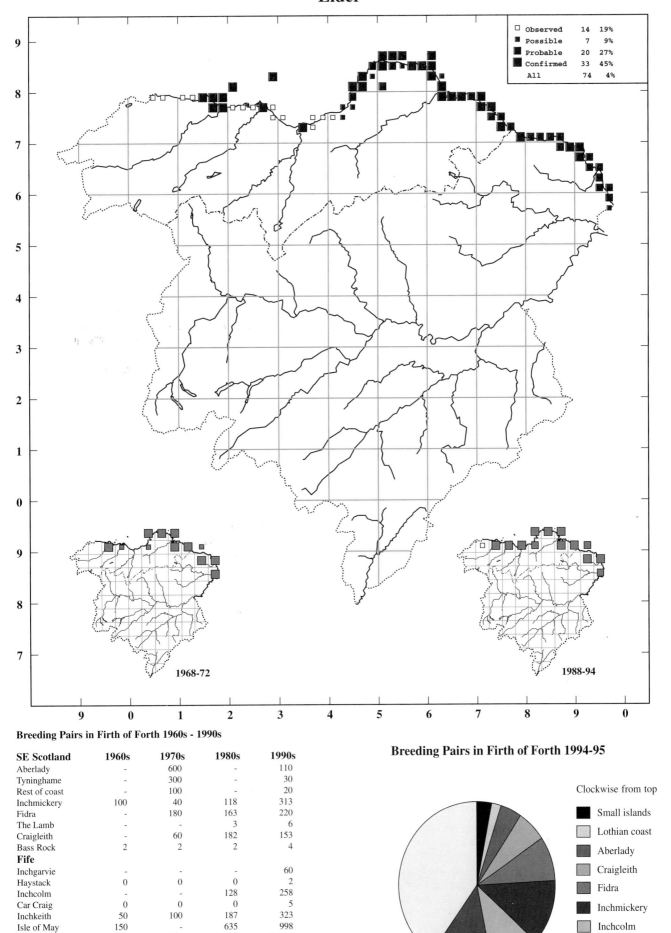

	Observed	14	19%
	Possible	7	9%
	Probable	20	27%
	Confirmed	33	45%
	All	74	4%

1968-72

1988-94

Breeding Pairs in Firth of Forth 1960s - 1990s

SE Scotland	1960s	1970s	1980s	1990s
Aberlady	-	600	-	110
Tyninghame	-	300	-	30
Rest of coast	-	100	-	20
Inchmickery	100	40	118	313
Fidra	-	180	163	220
The Lamb	-	-	3	6
Craigleith	-	60	182	153
Bass Rock	2	2	2	4
Fife				
Inchgarvie	-	-	-	60
Haystack	0	0	0	2
Inchcolm	-	-	128	258
Car Craig	0	0	0	5
Inchkeith	50	100	187	323
Isle of May	150	-	635	998
Forth - Total	302	1,382	1,418	2,502

Source: *Bird Reports*, Andrews 1986 & Calladine 1995.
Numbers approximate for 1960s & 1970s. Those for 1980s mostly refer to 1987, those for 1990s mostly refer to 1994.

Breeding Pairs in Firth of Forth 1994-95

Clockwise from top

- Small islands
- Lothian coast
- Aberlady
- Craigleith
- Fidra
- Inchmickery
- Inchcolm
- Inchkeith
- Isle of May

Total: 2,502 pairs

Goldeneye
Bucephala clangula

Until the 1970s Goldeneyes in Britain were normally thought of simply as common wintering waterfowl from Scandinavia and Russia. While small numbers of birds, typically only singles, might stay behind late in the spring or even over-summer, there was little expectation that breeding would occur in Britain until nest-boxes were erected in various sites around Speyside which successfully encouraged birds to nest there in the 1970s. Despite nest-boxes being put up for them in other parts of Scotland most instances of breeding remain confined to the Highlands.

In SE Scotland small numbers of Goldeneyes commonly stay into May and occasionally into June. The majority of May records doubtless refer to late wintering and passage birds from or through our area en route to Scandinavia. Odd birds are seen in June and July, however, averaging 2-3 birds each year (see table). Some years, such as 1987, 1990 and 1991, have had many more than the average. Whether the birds that over-summer are injured, ill or genuinely attempting to breed is not known but display has been recorded on occasions.

As the map shows, summering birds occurred at a considerable number of sites in SE Scotland between 1988-94. Records from coastal sites have been arbitrarily assigned observed symbols, it being less likely that birds might nest in such sites. On freshwater sites, single birds seen on single occasions account for all of the possible records, while probable records are evenly divided between records of two or more birds, equating to pairs, or single birds seen on more than one occasion, equating to territory. Most of the records, however, refer to single sites in single years and only a handful of localities are consistently favoured by late and summering birds: Cobbinshaw (NT05D), Gladhouse, Portmore and the Hirsel. Gladhouse is perhaps the site that holds birds most frequently in summer with June and July records in nine of the 17 years between 1979 and 1995 and two or more birds in four of these summers with as many as five birds in 1987 and four in 1990.

Nest-boxes have been set up at several sites in SE Scotland over the years in the hope that they may be used by Goldeneyes, with no success. There is evidence from both Scotland and Scandinavia that Goldeneyes may prefer boxes in the vicinity of rivers rather than still-waters, and with most females in the Strathspey nest-box scheme taking their broods immediately to the Spey on hatching (Dennis 1987) it may be that the rivers in SE Scotland could be better candidates for nest-boxes than still-water sites like Alemoor (NT31X) and Gladhouse. This also means that the birds that sometimes stay late on the lower Tweed may be of greater interest

than has been hitherto supposed. It is likely that breeding occurred at just such a site in 1991 when a brood of Goldeneyes was seen near the mouth of the Tweed in Northumberland. The site where the female nested was not known but the wooded parts of the Tweed below Norham seem the most likely possibility, on either the Scottish or English bank of the river. Goldeneyes have been successful on another occasion in Northumberland (*Day*) although details of the area where breeding occurred have been withheld.

Several hundreds of birds overwinter and move through the lower Tweed in spring and so a nest-box scheme might well encourage more breeding attempts in the area. However, such a scheme might fall foul of the angling interests in the area as Goosanders would also use the boxes. It is suspected that many natural Goosander nests are routinely destroyed by anglers each year and so any nest-box scheme could result in part of the Goosander breeding population being set up as sacrificial lambs. This is unfortunate as Goldeneyes have been slow to spread from Speyside and while they have nested both on the Tweed and Tay in recent years (Ogilvie 1996) such records are sporadic. The Tweed could be an ideal candidate for a further scheme to help consolidate the presence of this beautiful duck as a breeding species in Britain. **R.D.Murray**

SE Scotland Goldeneye: summer records: 1979-95.

	May 15-31	Jun 1-30	Jul 1-31	Aug 1-31	Sep 1-15
1979	1	1	-	-	-
1980	2	-	-	-	1
1981	1	1	2	1	-
1982	4	4	-	1	2
1983	7	2	-	-	5
1984	8	2	2	1	2
1985	19	3	1	4	1
1986	2	-	-	1	3
1987	1	10	3	1	1
1988	6	2	4	2	1
1989	1	3	1	2	1
1990	2	7	5	5	5
1991	12	11	2	1	4
1992	2	5	1	3	1
1993	6	3	1	-	-
1994	3	-	1	1	2
1995	5	3	2	3	6
Total	82	57	25	25	35
Mean	**4.8**	**3.2**	**1.5**	**1.5**	**2.1**

Source: *Bird Reports* - only records from freshwater sites included.

Goldeneye

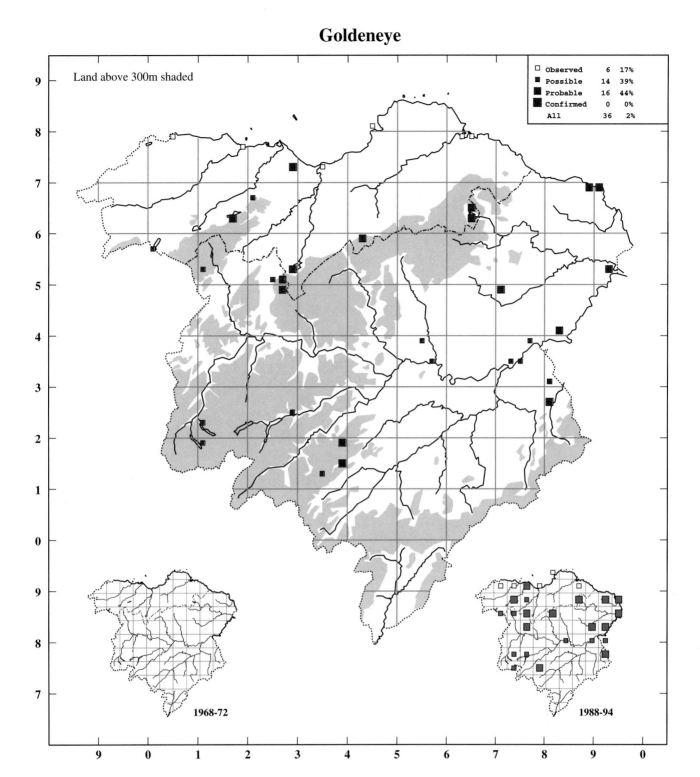

Land above 300m shaded

	Observed	6	17%
	Possible	14	39%
	Probable	16	44%
	Confirmed	0	0%
	All	36	2%

1968-72

1988-94

79

Red-breasted Merganser
Mergus serrator

The Red-breasted Merganser is mainly a species of northern and western Britain. It breeds on fast-flowing rivers, estuaries, freshwater lochs and along the shores of western sea-lochs, mostly nesting in dense vegetation, tree-roots and down rabbit burrows. Mergansers feed on small fish and marine invertebrates. Red-breasted Merganser diet has much in common with that of the Goosander but the prey items are typically much smaller, almost everything being less than eight cm long.

In SE Scotland the Red-breasted Merganser is perhaps most familiar as a coastal wintering species being present along the shores of the Firth of Forth from August to March in considerable numbers, although numbers have fallen since the early 1980s when the counts peaked at almost 1,000 birds. In recent years *c.*500 birds are present during September-October. It is possible that the late summer flocks are moult assemblies. Red-breasted Mergansers are most numerous along the muddier shores to the west of Gullane, numbers diminishing as the coastline becomes increasingly rocky further east towards Berwickshire. Small numbers also gather at the Tweed Estuary in winter and have occasionally been reported further upstream within Borders during Goosander censuses.

The coastal *Atlas* records wholly refer to these wintering birds, some of which linger into April and May. As expected these observed records are limited to the muddier Edinburgh and West Lothian shoreline and around Aberlady.

Red-breasted Mergansers are extremely rare as a breeding species in SE Scotland. Indeed breeding has only ever been proven on two occasions, both previous to the *Atlas* period. Inland *Atlas* records only came from five sites: Gladhouse, Talla and Fruid Reservoirs, St. Mary's Loch and the Tweed at Tweedsmuir (NT02X). Three registrations were reports of pairs, one was of an anxious redhead, the other, at Tweedsmuir, was simply a bird in suitable habitat.

Breeding was first proved in the area in 1979 when a brood was seen on Fruid Reservoir after two pairs had frequented neighbouring Talla Reservoir that spring. The birds may have originated from just over the watershed to the west of Tweedsmuir where a small population had become established at the head of the Clyde, Ae and Nith drainage at the Camps (NT02B) and Daer (NX91Z) Reservoirs during the 1970s and 1980s. Numbers increased in the Tweedsmuir Hills in the early 1980s, peaking at five females in 1982, before falling back to about 2-3 females for some seasons afterwards. Birds were seen downriver at Stanhope (NT12E), at St. Mary's Loch and the upper Manor valley (NT23A) in 1984, the widest-ever spread of records in SE Scotland.

In Lothian there have been summer records of Mergansers on Harperrig Reservoir (NT06V) in June 1979 and at Gladhouse in May 1983 (one male) and April 1991 (a pair). There has been no reason to suspect breeding in any of these cases.

This local colonisation was part of a larger scale trend of southwards expansion of Red-breasted Mergansers across Britain. After a rapid expansion elsewhere in Scotland in the early 20th century, a more gradual expansion is still continuing with breeding in northern England and Wales (Gregory *et al.* 1997). The move into the Clydesdale reservoirs and the Tweedsmuir Hills may be localised colonisations within this southwards expansion. However, declines have also occurred in Scotland since the *Old Atlas*, including parts of Dumfries and Galloway to the southwest of the Tweedsmuir Hills (*New Atlas*), possibly in response to licensed culling by angling interests.

There is no doubt that there have been fewer records in recent years (see table below) and that the colonisation may be failing for the time being. Whatever the current trend, the Tweedsmuir Hills population is certainly tiny and perhaps only numbers just 1-2 pairs.

R.D.Murray

Inland summer records in SE Scotland 1979-95

	79	80	81	82	83	84	85	86	87	88	89	90	91	92	93	94	95
Borders (m/f)	3/2	2/2	4/3	?/5	-	3/3	?/2	-	3/2	1/2	-	-	1/1	0/1	1/1	1/1	-
broods	br5	-	-	-	-	br6	-	-	-	-	-	-	-	-	-	-	-
Lothian (m/f)	1	-	-	-	1/0	-	-	-	-	-	-	-	1/1	-	-	1/1	-

Red-breasted Merganser

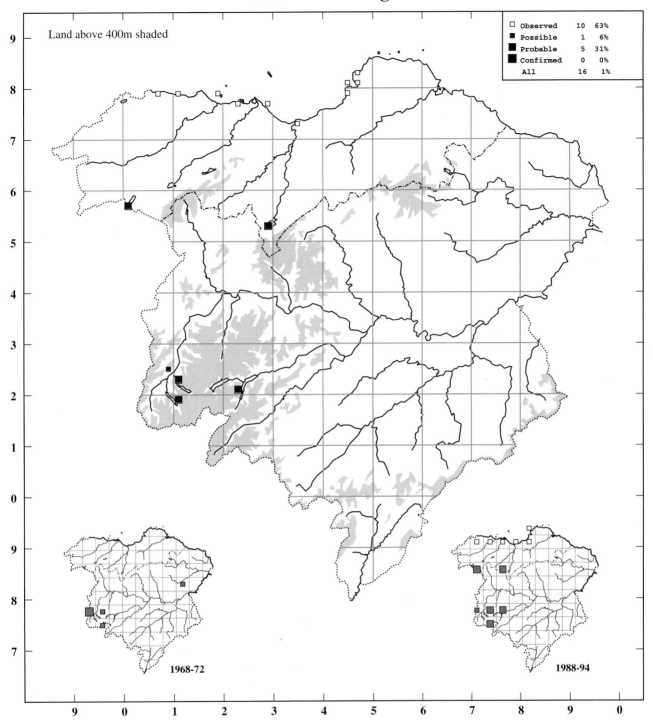

Land above 400m shaded

☐	Observed	10	63%
◼	Possible	1	6%
◼	Probable	5	31%
◼	Confirmed	0	0%
	All	16	1%

1968-72

1988-94

Goosander
Mergus merganser

The Goosander is a bird of rivers, feeding and breeding along the watercourses and mostly using still waters as roost sites. It is a fish-eater, using its 'toothed' bill to catch whatever food is most easily available. However, the Goosander has come into conflict with man and is widely, and unfortunately legally, persecuted because it predates young Salmon and Trout. Studies (Marquiss *et al.* 1991) on the stomach contents of birds culled by Tweed bailiffs, show that mostly Eels are eaten and salmonids are a minor, seasonal part of the diet. The Salmon smolt eaten are often smaller fish that are unlikely to return from the sea as breeding adults and so there is no evidence to show that Goosander predation has any significant impact on fish stocks (see also Murray 1992).

Probable records were dominated by sightings of pairs while confirmed records were mostly of redheads with broods, nests being difficult to find. Broods can be mobile (Marquiss & Duncan 1994) and initially observers were asked only to record young broods. However, even such broods can move distances (13-21 km) and as there was no way to know which broods had moved and which had not, all broods were subsequently recorded. The map therefore shows a combination of natal and nursery areas for young Goosanders.

The map shows a species tied to rivers, mostly in the Tweed basin. The absence from Lothian rivers is stark and may relate to the history of colonisation. Birds can be found along all parts of a river from the headwaters right down to the sea. However, the altitude diagram shows that 95% of Goosander records were from areas below 400m, occupying 15-18% of each altitude band below that level. Their preference for large rivers, more frequent at lower altitudes, is indicated by the fact that 60% of records came from tetrads with wide rivers, presumably because the greater area of substrate offers better fishing. There are gaps, some due to a genuine absence of birds, as on the Tweed near Innerleithen (NT33) where disturbance is considerable, or along well-wooded narrow tributaries such as the Ale (NT42&52) where birds are hard to detect. The map exaggerates the distribution of Goosanders because Goosanders tend to use different parts of the river throughout the year (Marquiss & Duncan 1994), nesting in the upper reaches but rearing their young further downstream. The distribution will also be exaggerated as birds will also have been on different stretches of the river in both the same and in different years. It nevertheless shows the relative importance of the upper and lower Tweed, Yarrow, lower Teviot and Whiteadder.

The Tweed has had a recent history of census work on Goosanders, initially for national surveys, but later to counter arguments for culls (*Bird Reports*). January counts indicate 700-800 birds overwinter, dropping to 450-500 by late March. Counts of spring males suggest that 200-220 pairs may attempt to breed. However, summer counts have found *c.*60 redheads with 25-35 broods over about half of the river system. Doubling these figures gives an estimate of 120 redheads and *c.*60 broods for the Tweed basin. The redheads without young may be failed breeders. While 120 breeding attempts is half of what might be expected from spring counts, the results are not dissimilar to what Marquiss & Duncan (1994) found on the Dee in NE Scotland where 61 pairs in spring managed only 32 broods by summer.

Large pre-moult assemblies of up to 150 birds gather in May on the lower Tweed, roosting at the Hirsel. The flocks were once thought to be wholly male but recent counts have shown that up to 55% are redheads and may include many of the redheads that are missing from summer counts. The males mostly travel to northern Norway to moult (Little & Furness 1985), the redheads apparently moulting just off the main estuaries of eastern Scotland (Marquiss & Duncan 1994). Since the 1980s a moult flock has grown at Tyninghame, reaching 143 birds in 1994. Other flocks may be growing off Berwick and Musselburgh. Birds disperse in late September just as the Hirsel roost re-establishes itself, rapidly building up as birds return to the Tweed. The record Hirsel count used to be 360 in October 1993, mostly redheads, with *c.*40% of them juveniles hatched in that year, but this has been exceeded with over 700 birds in autumn 1997 (*Bird Reports*).

Counts since 1984 show such a consistency in numbers that they cast considerable doubt on the justification of culling Goosanders. Despite hundreds of birds being shot in the late 1980s and early 1990s, numbers seem to remain the same.

Britain was first colonised in Perthshire in 1871. There has been a steady expansion in range and numbers ever since, the distribution now reaching Wales (1960s) and Devon (1980s) (*New Atlas*). Goosanders first bred at St. Mary's Loch in 1930 and slowly spread down the Yarrow and Ettrick valleys by the 1950s (*B&R*) and along the upper Tweed, Teviot and in Liddesdale by the period of the *Old Atlas* in the late 1960s. The spread since then has been dramatic and is easily seen by comparing the 10-km square maps where the number of occupied squares has doubled since 1972. Much of the main river was colonised by the 1980s with the northern hills being more slowly occupied into the 1990s. The first Lothian broods were seen on the Esk near Dalkeith in 1985 and 1990 (*Bird Reports*).

About 50 pairs were estimated for the Borders in the 1970s (Meek & Little 1977). Today the Tweed basin holds about 220 pairs although only 120 females may attempt to nest, these raising 50-60 broods each year. Broods are large and 136 brood counts show an average size of 7.6 which hints that as many as 400 young may be produced annually in the area. Such numbers make it seem likely that the spread will continue and that Goosanders should occupy all rivers in the area in future years.

The *New Atlas* abundance map shows the Tweed to be an area of the highest abundance. Carter (in the *New Atlas*) treats counts of males in spring as being equivalent to the number of pairs, estimating the British population to be 2,700 pairs on such a basis. As local spring counts indicate about 220 males are present, the Tweed therefore holds about 8% of the British total.   **R.D.Murray**

Goosander

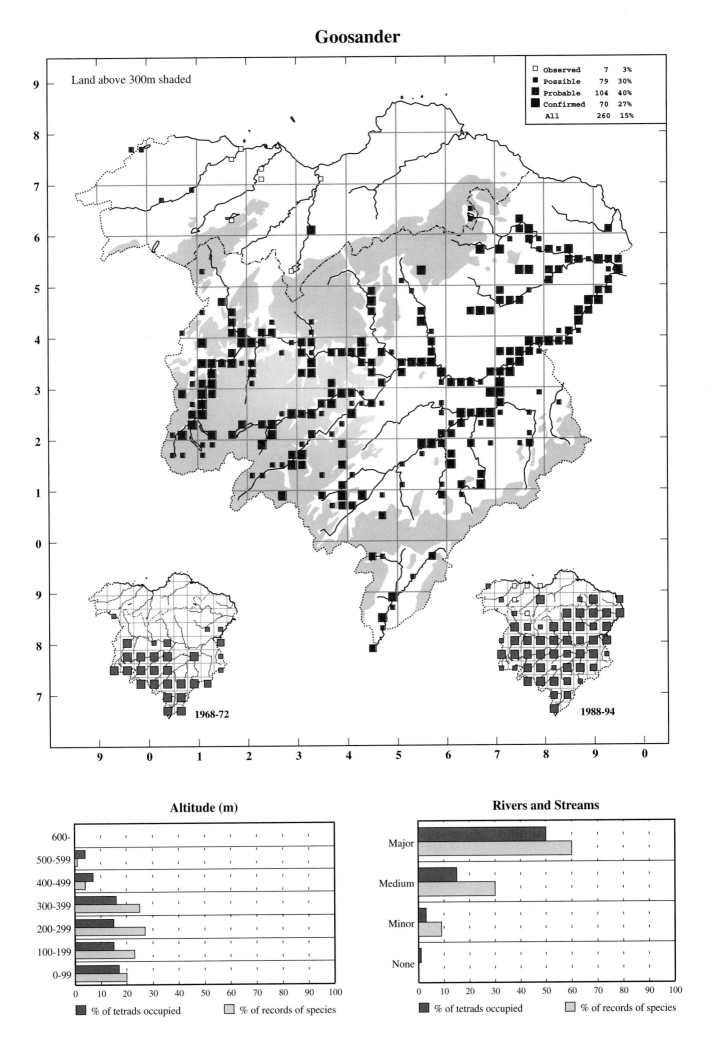

□ Observed	7	3%
■ Possible	79	30%
▨ Probable	104	40%
■ Confirmed	70	27%
All	260	15%

Land above 300m shaded

1968-72

1988-94

Altitude (m)

600-	
500-599	
400-499	
300-399	
200-299	
100-199	
0-99	

■ % of tetrads occupied   □ % of records of species

Rivers and Streams

Major	
Medium	
Minor	
None	

■ % of tetrads occupied   □ % of records of species

83

Ruddy Duck
Oxyura jamaicensis

In 1947 three pairs of this North American duck escaped from the Wildfowl Trust at Slimbridge and started breeding there, in a feral state, the following year. Numbers have steadily increased and the Ruddy Duck has since spread across a large area of Britain and is now threatening to colonise continental Europe. While it may fill a vacant niche in Britain, this is not the case in southern Europe where the globally-rare White-headed Duck resides. Hybridisation has taken place and the offspring appear to be fertile and this has raised fears that the small White-headed Duck population might be swamped by Ruddy Duck genes and so vanish as a distinct species (Gantlett 1993).

Ruddy Ducks show a preference for small, shallow waters that are mostly surrounded by emergent vegetation. Their success in Britain has been attributed to high levels of hatching and chick survival and their ability to produce double broods although there is no evidence so far that any such broods have been reared in SE Scotland.

The population is currently well monitored, being rather scarce but easily seen on most waters and hence reported to the local recorders.

The first-ever Ruddy Duck records in Scotland date from 1979 when breeding occurred at Loch Kinnordy in Angus (*Scott. Bird Report*). They first showed up in SE Scotland in 1983 when single males arrived at the Hirsel and Linlithgow Loch. Six males appeared the following year in the central Borders but did not linger. In spite of a few birds appearing each spring over the next few years nothing was to happen until 1989 when a pair attempted to breed at Bemersyde Moss.

An influx of *c.*15 birds in 1990 failed to produce any breeding attempts but it is possible that some sites were prospected in the autumn of that year as pairs were more widespread in the following spring on waters that had held Ruddy Ducks in the autumn. In 1991 broods were seen at Bemersyde and Wooden Loch (NT72C). Breeding has occurred annually since with broods at Hule Moss (NT74E), Bemersyde and Wooden Loch. In 1996 there was a dramatic doubling in the number of breeding sites with broods at the Folly Loch (NT62I), Hoselaw Loch and Yetholm Marsh (NT82D&I). Pairs have also been seen on the Hirsel Lake and Yetholm Loch between 1995-97 (See graph and Appendix for details).

Most of the activity has been focused in the middle Tweed area where the various waters already used by Ruddy Ducks are in relatively close proximity to one another. In Lothian birds are more scattered. They have been fairly regular at Duddingston since 1984 and at Bavelaw since 1988, with a few singles at Gladhouse and elsewhere. However, there have been only two years during the *Atlas* period when pairs were reported. Display was seen at Bavelaw in 1988 but, in mid-July, was probably too late in the season for a serious attempt at breeding, although Ruddy Ducks do breed late, as witnessed by the newly hatched brood at Wooden Loch on 21st August 1991. Pairs remain rare in Lothian but were seen on Bavelaw (NT16L/R) in 1990 and 1994, Gladhouse (NT25W) in 1994, Cobbinshaw Reservoir (NT05D&E) in 1996 and on Linlithgow Loch (NT07W) in 1997.

Productivity seems good despite the predation of the first brood at Bemersyde in 1989. The eleven broods produced at Bemersyde, Hule Moss and Wooden Loch in the seasons 1991-1995 fledged no fewer than 37 young. The large numbers of birds present in the autumn of 1997, including no fewer than 41 birds at Hule Moss and 14 at Hoselaw Loch, hints of even better success more recently (*Bird Reports*). Allied with the success of Ruddy Duck elsewhere in Scotland (*Scott. Bird Report*) it seems likely that this species may increase and spread in much the same way as the Tufted Duck must have done 100 years ago when it colonised Scotland.

All of the sites favoured by the Ruddy Duck in SE Scotland appear to match the stated preferences in the *New Atlas* for small and shallow ponds lined with emergent vegetation. Indeed it may be the lack of the vegetated surroundings that could be limiting birds in Lothian where such waters are less frequent than in the middle Tweed area. Nevertheless while the middle Tweed area is currently leading the way, the colonisation of Lothian seems inevitable and likely to occur before 2000.

The population of SE Scotland in 1997 was approximately 26 pairs with an additional 10-15 males. Judging from the rate of increase, there will be a considerable population in a few years time. With a British population of about 600 pairs, the proportion living in SE Scotland is close to the national average at about 3%.

R.D.Murray

Ruddy Duck

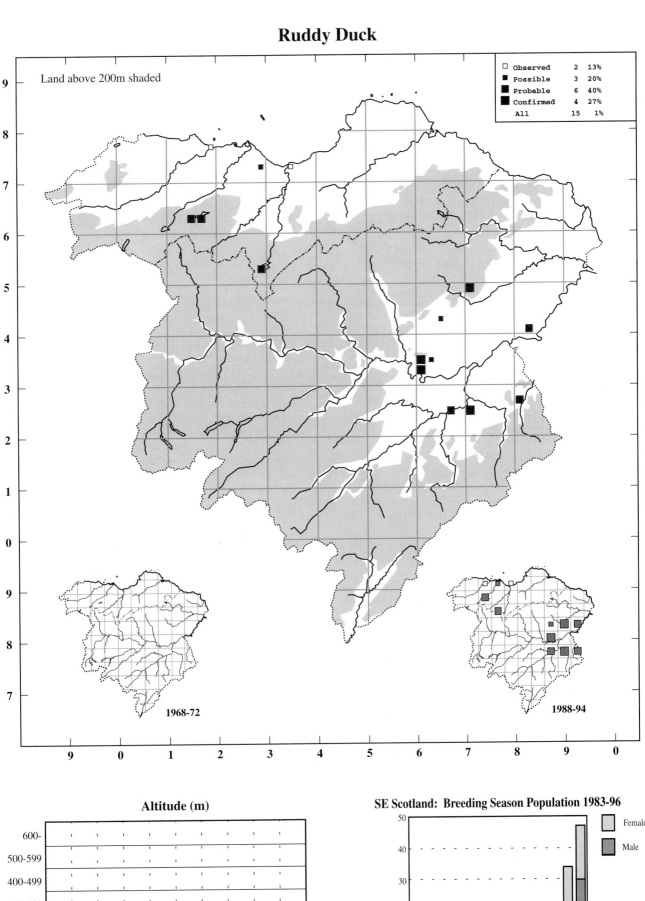

Land above 200m shaded

☐ Observed	2	13%
■ Possible	3	20%
■ Probable	6	40%
■ Confirmed	4	27%
All	15	1%

1968-72

1988-94

Altitude (m)

% of tetrads occupied   % of records of species

SE Scotland: Breeding Season Population 1983-96

Female
Male

Hen Harrier
Circus cyaneus

The Hen Harrier is potentially a widespread breeding bird over moorlands of Britain. It inhabits open, gently sloping or undulating country, especially moors with heather or rough grassy or rushy vegetation, suitable for Meadow Pipits and field voles which are favoured prey species. Young open-stage conifer plantation is also a preferred, though transient, habitat.

Such habitat includes grouse moor, and Hen Harriers do take some young Red Grouse. However, any effect they may have on Red Grouse numbers, beyond the natural surplus which would disappear in any case before the following breeding season, is small compared with the effect of moor management on Red Grouse numbers. Nonetheless, the Hen Harrier has been one of the most persistently shot, poisoned or destroyed species of bird, driven to near extinction on mainland Britain by the early 20th century. The great afforestation programme of the post-war years provided new nesting opportunities with less persecution, and allowed a widespread but patchy comeback over the upland parts of Britain. However, illegal persecution still strongly controls the Hen Harrier's distribution today. Harrier breeding success on grouse moors is held far below that on other heather moors and young plantation by illegal killing (Bibby & Etheridge 1993). Annually, 11-15% of Scottish female Hen Harriers (excluding Orkney) are killed on grouse moors, so that these moors act as a "sink habitat", roughly absorbing the surplus raised each year from other habitats (Etheridge *et al.*1997). The species is among the 20 to have suffered the worst declines of all British birds from 1800-1995 (Gibbons *et al.*1996).

Although Hen Harriers are not hard to discover due to their slow, deliberate hunting method, *Atlas* survey workers were not always able to spend many hours in potential Harrier terrain, and the records mapped here also incorporate data from the Raptor Study Group. For security reasons the map shows distribution by 10-km squares, with dot sizes based on possible, probable and confirmed breeding records amalgamated, and as they are also seven years' accumulated records they give an impression of greater distribution than that of any single year.

The tetrads in which Hen Harriers were sighted form just 9% of the area of the 26 occupied 10-km squares shown on the map, a pitiful scatter compared with what the distribution could be. A glance at the heather moor distribution map shows how much greater the Hen Harrier's distribution could be. The total area of good heather moor, along with some rough grass areas and young forestry, suggests that about 40 10-km squares could be suitable for breeding Hen Harriers with some of these squares potentially holding several

pairs each. Instead, only 13 10-km squares have confirmed or probable records, the majority of these containing very few birds.

Most records are in the Moorfoot Hills where heather moor, grass moor and forestry all occur, and in the Lammermuirs where there are large expanses of heather and grass moor. Altogether there were more tetrads with possible records than with confirmed and probable together, and these may be due to younger unmated birds or to potential breeders whose partners had been shot. It is well known to local ornithologists that some pairs establish territories each season and "disappear" soon afterwards due to illegal, rather than natural, causes. The altitude graph shows that although 85% of tetrads with Hen Harriers were at 300-500m, only 9% of land at this level of altitude had Hen Harriers even over the seven-year period. Almost none were below 200m. The second graph shows a strong association with large areas of heather, though 14% of Harriers were where heather was insignificant, presumably on grass moor or first-stage forestry.

In any single year during the survey the number of breeding attempts is much smaller than the seven-year map suggests: about 1-2 in Lothian and 2-5 in Borders. However, although so undeservedly repressed, the distribution may have improved a little in recent years. While the *Old Atlas* shows only three 10-km squares with confirmed or probable breeding, the *New Atlas* shows nine, and the present *Atlas* 12. Although the increase to 12 may be an artefact due to the longer survey period, there is little doubt that more birds are present in the 1990s than in the 1980s. This could be due to increased immigration from elsewhere or to some more favourable keepering attitudes here.

In Lothian the Hen Harrier was only an occasional visitor or sporadic breeder through all of the 20th century until the early 1980s, though common previously (*Andrews*). In Borders its status was similar, with no known breeding between 1924 and 1982 (*Murray*). In Lothian in the 1980s and 1990s, summer reports come from 2-3 localities per year with successful breeding by one pair in a few years only, while in Borders 2-4 breeding attempts occurred in most years with birds seen at additional sites during some summers (*Bird Reports*). There has been a marginal increase in winter sightings from the 1980s to 1990s. Thus the total numbers in SE Scotland are about 3-7 breeding pairs, only *c.*0.8% of the Scottish and British population of 1988-89 (Bibby & Etheridge 1993) which may have since decreased (*Scott. Bird News* 48). Let us hope future attitudes will allow this beautiful bird to be seen in better numbers here alongside other land-use interests. **H.E.M.Dott**

Hen Harrier

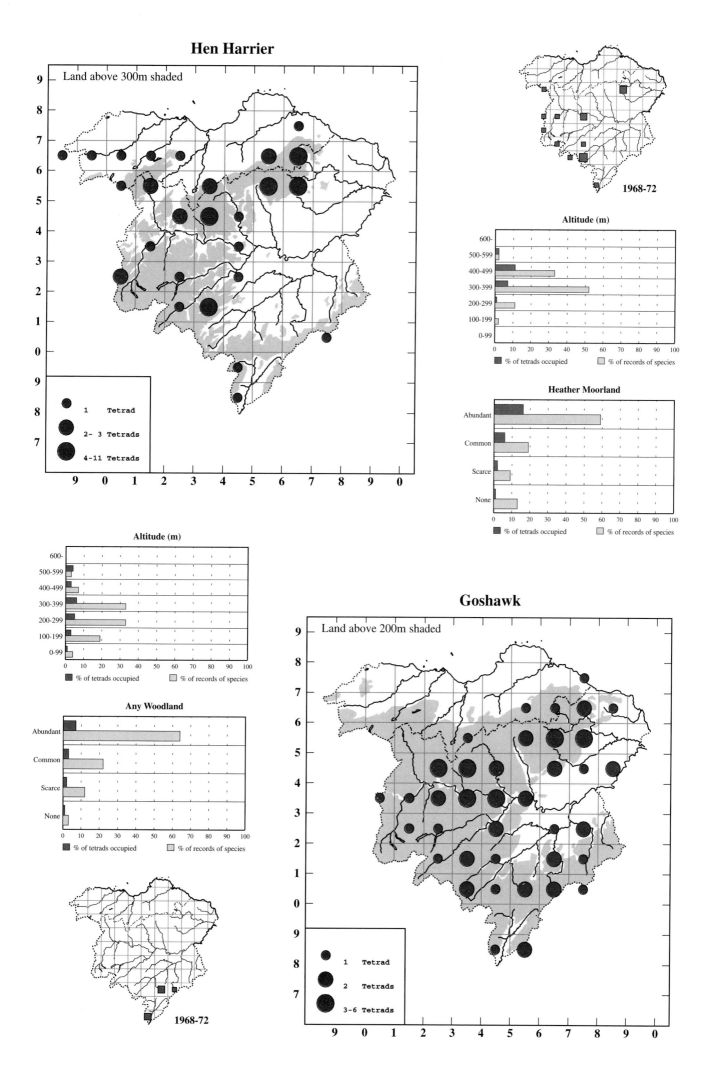

Land above 300m shaded

1 Tetrad
2- 3 Tetrads
4-11 Tetrads

Altitude (m)

600-
500-599
400-499
300-399
200-299
100-199
0-99

0 10 20 30 40 50 60 70 80 90 100

■ % of tetrads occupied   □ % of records of species

Heather Moorland

Abundant
Common
Scarce
None

0 10 20 30 40 50 60 70 80 90 100

■ % of tetrads occupied   □ % of records of species

1968-72

Altitude (m)

600-
500-599
400-499
300-399
200-299
100-199
0-99

0 10 20 30 40 50 60 70 80 90 100

■ % of tetrads occupied   □ % of records of species

Any Woodland

Abundant
Common
Scarce
None

0 10 20 30 40 50 60 70 80 90 100

■ % of tetrads occupied   □ % of records of species

1968-72

Goshawk

Land above 200m shaded

1 Tetrad
2 Tetrads
3-6 Tetrads

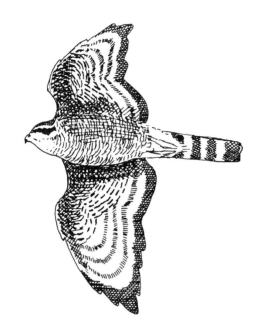

Brown

Goshawk

Accipiter gentilis

Goshawks are remarkably elusive for such big birds, and often go unrecorded in areas for many years. They nest in tall trees, especially conifers, and are usually associated with large mature coniferous plantations. Much of their hunting is done in more open country and even small woods can hold nesting pairs if the birds are not disturbed. The species has a long history of persecution due to the occasional predation of game birds. Regular breeding in Britain ceased in the 1880s after numbers had initially been diminished by large scale deforestation followed by intense persecution in the 19th century. Breeding became regular again in the 1960s and the population has slowly increased and expanded its range since then. The origin of these "recolonists" was birds which escaped from or were deliberately released by falconers. Egg collecting and the taking of young by hawk keepers held population levels at a low level, but while these threats have declined over the last twenty years, there is still much persecution by game rearing interests, especially of young birds killed in the nest or soon after fledging. As a result of these concerns there is much secrecy about the numbers and distribution of the species throughout Britain, and SE Scotland is no exception.

The discovery of a Goshawk during *Atlas* fieldwork was rare and consequently a highlight of the few days in the field when it occurred. Most reports were of single birds, occasionally of displaying individuals or pairs. A very small number of current or used nests were found; in other instances recently fledged birds were found or adults were seen carrying food. The records collected by *Atlas* fieldworkers have been supplemented with records from the Lothian & Borders Raptor Study Group and Forest Enterprise workers to provide a fuller picture. These are mostly records of nests or territorial pairs which are closely monitored during the breeding season.

The map (see previous page) shows distribution at 10-km square level only, to provide some protection for the breeding pairs. Even then it does not by any means give the full picture as many nesting records are kept secret and not reported to either the local Bird Recorders or the Raptor Study Groups. This applies particularly to Lothian where the *Atlas* provides little evidence of Goshawks being present at all. Circumstantial evidence since the *Atlas* period indicates that the species may now breed, but there is as yet no documentary evidence. There are too few records to show any relationship with altitude, although most records occur between 150 and 400m, with some up to 550m. The distribution is limited mainly by the availability of suitable undisturbed nesting habitat such as extensive plantation forests.

The evidence presented nevertheless suggests a wide distribution in Borders, with records in over half of all 10-km squares. Most occupied areas are along the edges of hill ranges and in afforested valleys, including the large forests in the Tweed valley, Craik Forest (NT30) and the northern flanks of the Cheviots. There has been a major expansion in range since the *Old Atlas*, when Goshawks were seen in only three 10-km squares, and no breeding was confirmed. Goshawks first attempted to breed in the border forests in 1972 following releases in Northumberland and Roxburghshire in the late 1960s and early 1970s but successful breeding was not recorded until 1977. Monitoring of the population of the Forest Enterprise Border Forest area (which includes parts of Northumberland and Dumfries & Galloway) by the Forestry Commission and the Border Goshawk Study Group revealed a population of 40 pairs in 1987 rising to 71 in 1994 (Northumberland Wildlife Trust 1995). There has been a corresponding increase in the number of casual records reported to local Bird Recorders.

In 1994, 11 nests were monitored by the Lothian & Borders Raptor Study Group in Borders, all on privately owned sites. Since then, there has been a steady increase in the number of monitored sites, to 19 in 1997. This increase is partially due to increased efforts by ornithologists, but also reflects the steady increase in numbers of Goshawks. Similar numbers are censused annually on Forest Enterprise land where 15-20 pairs are known to nest, and circumstantial evidence suggests a further 5-10 pairs elsewhere. This indicates a population for SE Scotland of 45-60 pairs in 1997. Although higher than previously published totals, this number is much lower than the potential number which could be supported in the habitats available in the area. Without persecution and given time a population of at least 200 pairs seems quite possible.

The *New Atlas* suggested a British population of around 200 pairs in 1988, but since then this has been revised to around 400 (1994 figures) with 80 pairs in Scotland (Northumberland Wildlife Trust 1995). In 1994 there were 71 known occupied home ranges in the English/Scottish border forests, with 33 of these in Scotland.

Up to a third of nests on private land fail each year, often due to deliberate interference. There continues to be evidence of persecution of Goshawks, especially of juveniles frequenting the vicinity of Pheasant release pens in the autumn. Despite this apparent conflict with game-rearing interests, no effort has been put into quantifying any loss of gamebirds or into investigating methods to reduce any impact. The Goshawk is a fully legally protected species with a limited range. It is important to continue the monitoring of the local population and the Lothian & Borders Raptor Study Group has appointed a Goshawk co-ordinator to further this aim. Birdwatchers should report all sightings to local Bird Recorders. Only then can an accurate picture of the Goshawk's local status be maintained.   ***M.Holling***

Golden Eagle
Aquila chrysaetos

Golden Eagles apparently bred in the Borders in historical times with nests in the Tweedsmuir and Cheviot Hills. No more precise details are available from the old literature. Whatever the exact status, Golden Eagles were definitely wiped out as a breeding species during the 19th century with the advent of Victorian sporting estates and freely available firearms.

For much of the 20th century Golden Eagles were a rare visitor to the area, mostly in Borders, although there was a Lothian record in 1951. The birds presumably mostly originated from the tiny population in the SW Scotland.

Since the 1970s the numbers of reports started to increase slowly, leading to a pair breeding in 1979. Despite nest-site changes, a pair have continued to inhabit the same general area since and these were joined by another pair in a different area in 1994. Both pairs have produced fledged young.

Away from the nest-sites Golden Eagles were recorded on at least 15 occasions during the *Atlas* period, including six times actually during *Atlas* fieldwork. These records and other reports outwith the breeding season reveal a picture of a number of juveniles, immatures and even adults in the hill ranges across the whole area, most frquently seen in the better-watched northern hills. Some are probably wandering juveniles but others appear to set up temporary hunting ranges for a few months. Descriptions of individuals suggest just a few birds are involved, perhaps 3-4 birds in addition to the breeding adults.

There appears to be considerable goodwill on the part of estate-owners and keepers nowadays towards Golden Eagles. There has been no hint of birds being persecuted and given that nest-sites remain free from disturbance, including that from over-enthusiatic birders, it is hoped that numbers will gradually increase.

R.D.Murray

Osprey
Pandion haliaetus

There is no historical evidence that Ospreys have ever bred in SE Scotland although old accounts mention them nesting at Loch Skene, above the Grey Mare's Tail, just over the boundary in Dumfriesshire. It is likely, however, that a local population did exist in the "ornithological prehistory" but became extinct due to a combination of habitat destruction, persecution and egg collecting. Through much of the 20th century the Osprey became a rare vagrant in SE Scotland and it was not until the recolonisation of the Highlands in the 1950s and 1960s that numbers increased to the state where it could be considered a rare but annual passage migrant.

As the Highland population grew in the 1970s and 1980s, the numbers of passage birds steadily increased and individuals even started to linger for a few weeks in May and in July and August, probably Scottish or Scandinavian non-breeders. However, even by the mid-1980s (*Andrews, Murray*) records averaged just 4-5 birds

per year. This increased to an average of 18 records per year during the *Atlas* period, with a few cases of pairs and trios lingering at sites for a few weeks, and several instances of individuals summering. While colonisation has been eagerly anticipated for many years and artificial nest-platforms built to encourage potential breeding pairs, there is no evidence that birds have done more than prospect thus far. Birds have most frequently lingered at a relatively limited number of sites that appear to offer a good choice of nesting and feeding areas. With one of Scotland's major river systems and a coast with a number of productive bays, SE Scotland definitely has the potential to support a considerable number of Ospreys.

With the Scottish population topping 110 pairs in 1997 (R.H.Dennis *pers.comm*), and in the same year the first sighting of a displaying pair in spring in SE Scotland, one or both of which then summered, there is a hint that colonisation may be very close.   *R.D.Murray*

Sparrowhawk
Accipiter nisus

The Sparrowhawk is the archetypal predator of small woodland birds, also feeding in the surrounding fields and hedges. In winter some birds also move into coastal areas where shorebirds can form much of the diet. It is more secretive than the better-known Kestrel but is one of our most widespread and abundant raptors second only in Britain to the Kestrel. Throughout this century it has been heavily persecuted by pheasant-rearing gamekeepers. Also, like many of our raptors, it was very sensitive to organochlorine pesticides which were increasingly used in the 1950s and 1960s. Since the use of these chemicals was banned in the late 1960s and early 1970s, it has recovered to such an extent that in some areas, notably the City of Edinburgh, it is seen more regularly than the Kestrel.

Finding Sparrowhawks is largely a matter of luck although birds can be searched for in March and April when they display. More than half of all records were of possible status, mostly sightings of single birds in suitable habitats. Probable records were shared between pairs, territorial behaviour and display. Confirmed records were shared between adults carrying food for the young, occupied and used nests and fledged young. In mature closed-canopy conifer woods it was worthwhile searching for Sparrowhawk nests, the large, loosely-built nests typically built right up against the trunk.

While Sparrowhawks were recorded up to 550m, some 75% of occupied tetrads were actually below 300m. The map shows a scattered range across SE Scotland that reflects the distribution of the woodland habitats it breeds in. The density of occupied tetrads is greater in areas with wooded valleys such as the middle Tweed (NT23,33&43), Gala Water (NT44), Esk (NT36) and Rule (NT51) and where wooded estates are common such as in West Lothian (NS97), around Dunbar (NT67) and the middle Teviot (NT62). Its abundance in and near Edinburgh is well demonstrated (NT26&27). Conversely occupied tetrads are more scarce where there are few trees, such as in the cereal-growing areas of East Lothian (NT47&57) and the Merse (NT74&84) and in open hill areas. Few birds penetrate the uplands but pairs can nest in the more mature plantations or old shelterbelts in the hills. There is a high proportion of vacant tetrads in the forested areas of Craik, Wauchope and Newcastleton

where Sparrowhawks are almost certainly present in considerable numbers. However, these remote areas were less well surveyed and, given the problems of locating Sparrowhawks, it is highly likely that the map underestimates the presence of birds in these areas.

Habitat data show that Sparrowhawks occur in between a third and a half of all tetrads that hold woodland, there being a distinct preference for tetrads where woods of any sort are common or abundant. Indeed 75% of all records came from tetrads where woods are widespread. Sparrowhawks favour woods with trees spaced in a particular way, not too dense, nor too open. Newton (1986) found a spacing of 2-4m to be the optimum, the precise value varying according to the tree species. Conifers are favoured over deciduous trees for nest building and birds return to the same area each year. In SW Scotland, woods less than one hectare rarely held birds, while those greater than 20ha always had a nest (Newton 1986). This may be the reason why there are few Sparrowhawks in the hills and glens of SE Scotland, many of the numerous shelterbelts being below the favoured size. Conversely the large plantations such as Craik may have trees spaced too closely together to allow birds to hunt and may account for some of the difficulty in locating birds there. The Sparrowhawk is not surveyed by the local raptor study group and with the exception of a study in Edinburgh there has been no systematic work on breeding Sparrowhawks in the area.

The colonisation of Edinburgh probably began about 1980 and the increase has continued. In 1986-90 a study of breeding Sparrowhawks was undertaken within Edinburgh by Mike McGrady. He noted that the particular structure of Edinburgh favours the Sparrowhawk with woodland accounting for 12% of the city and grassland occupying another 17%. The former is important to the bird as it is here, even in the city centre, that it nests and hunts. More than 20 pairs regularly nest in the city, usually one pair per small wooded area, with more than half the pairs nesting in woods of 2-4ha size. This is different from rural Sparrowhawks that favour much larger woods. In the larger Edinburgh woodlands, such as Corstorphine Hill, three nests sites have been located although only a single pair succeeded in breeding in any year (McGrady 1990).

There was a 20% increase in Sparrowhawk numbers in Britain between the *Old Atlas* in 1968-72 and the *New Atlas* in 1988-91. During the *Atlas* period Sparrowhawks were only absent from a single marginal square, compared to 13 in the *Old Atlas*. The standard of proof of breeding is very much higher with 72 squares with probable and confirmed breeding between 1988-94 compared to only 39 in the *Old Atlas*. This difference in the standard of evidence probably reflects the much greater difficulty in finding Sparrowhawks in 1968-72.

The breeding population is difficult to estimate because of the different sizes and structures of woods that hold breeding birds. Based on the fact that birds were recorded in 650 tetrads it is possible to use two methods to estimate the local population based on figures given by Newton (1986). If all woods of 20ha hold at least a single nest, and each tetrad had a maximum of two such woods, the local population would be around 1,300 pairs. Newton's figure of 14-96 nests per 10-km square for all his study areas (0.6-4.0 nests per tetrad) would produce a maximum of 2,600 pairs. This latter figure may have to be reduced as SW Scotland is generally more wooded than our area. A compromise figure can be based on the approximate sizes of woodland in the habitat analysis of SE Scotland; with tetrads where woods are scarce holding a single pair, tetrads where woods are common having two pairs, and three pairs where woods are abundant. This would give around 1,400 pairs or 4.3% of the British population.   *I.R.Poxton & R.D.Murray*

Sparrowhawk

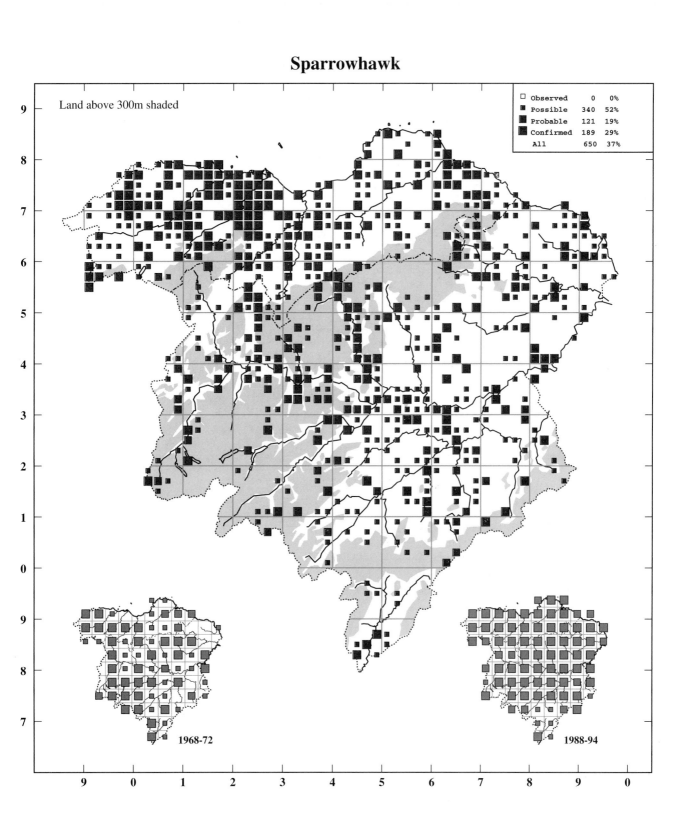

Land above 300m shaded

☐ Observed	0	0%
▪ Possible	340	52%
▪ Probable	121	19%
▪ Confirmed	189	29%
All	650	37%

1968-72

1988-94

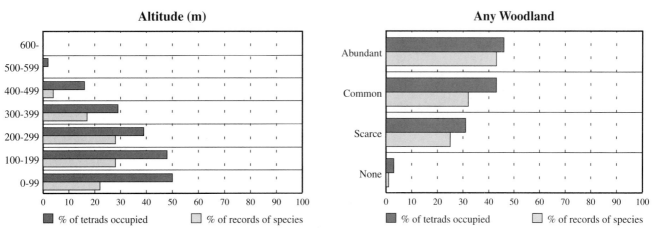

Altitude (m)

Any Woodland

% of tetrads occupied   % of records of species

% of tetrads occupied   % of records of species

Buzzard
Buteo buteo

The sight of a Buzzard soaring over a sunny hillside is a pleasure that can now be enjoyed by many in SE Scotland. This impressive bird of prey is associated with open partly-wooded landscapes where it feeds mainly on Rabbits and voles, taken live or as carrion. In SE Scotland it nests almost exclusively in trees, although elsewhere it also nests on crags, which are not common locally. Until recently it has been most common in wilder western landscapes where rough grazing dominates, but now it also finds a home in the more productive lowlands of the east of Scotland.

The *Atlas* period coincided with a major expansion of the range of this species in SE Scotland. Buzzards are reasonably conspicuous early and late in the season, and fieldworkers found Buzzards in areas where they were not previously known. Some pairs may have been missed during the incubation period (mainly in May) when Buzzards tend to be elusive, but the range expansion encouraged more diligent recording of this species so the distribution map is a good record of the distribution in 1988-94. Over half of all records received were of probable breeding with reports of pairs dominating. Confirmed records were mainly of nests with young, with fledged young, adults carrying food for young and occupied or used nests sharing the remainder. All other records were assigned to the habitat category as anywhere with at least a small clump of trees can offer potential nesting habitat for this species.

By 1994 Buzzards had been recorded in a quarter of all tetrads. The map shows that the bulk of the population occurred in a broad band from the heads of the valleys of the Ettrick, Yarrow and Tweed in the Tweedsmuir Hills, across north-east to the Moorfoots and Lammermuirs. There were also a few Buzzards in upper Teviotdale and Liddesdale. Although the majority of Buzzards are still in Borders, there were scattered pockets in northern West Lothian, in southern Midlothian and along the northern flanks of the Lammermuirs in East Lothian. The hill territories follow the valleys, with the upper Tweed, Eddleston Water (NT24), Gala Water (NT44) and Whiteadder (NT66&76) standing out clearly. Elsewhere the slopes of the edges of the hill ranges seem to be favoured, such as the northern edge of the Moorfoots and the southern flanks of the Lammermuirs. These areas are all characterised by mixed grazing land with shelterbelts, and all have very high populations of Rabbits. Extensive conifer plantations are occupied if there are large enough clearings to offer hunting opportunities. In 1988-94 Buzzards were absent from much of the Cheviots and most low ground below 200m. Lowland tetrads tend to be associated with larger woodland policies and plantations, such as at Dalmeny (NT17T), Tyninghame, Mellerstain (NT63P&U) and Rutherford (NT62N,P&U). Habitat analysis shows no clear correlation with any major habitat feature, typical of a species which prefers varied, mainly open, landscapes. Almost half of the tetrads were where woodland is abundant, perhaps indicating the dependence on trees for nesting.

There has been a 150% increase in the number of occupied 10-km squares since the *Old Atlas*, with a major range expansion from a core in western Borders, centred on Broughton (NT13).

This situation has already changed since the *Atlas* fieldwork finished. Work on the history of the local populations in both Borders (Holling & McGarry 1994) and Lothian (Smith 1994) has shown that the numerical increase is even more spectacular (see graph). In Borders, the Buzzard was extinct as a breeding species in the 1920s *(B&R)*, following many decades of intense persecution by gamekeepers. Breeding was only noted again in the late 1960s. By 1988 there were only six territorial pairs reported, although other records originated from a total of 33 tetrads. Five years later, the population was estimated to be 120 pairs (Holling & McGarry 1994), later refined to 161 following the receipt of additional information. By 1994, the Borders population was thought to be at least 250 pairs (*Bird Reports*). Since then, analysis suggests a total in 1997 of around 500 pairs, due to considerable in-filling in the range documented in this *Atlas*, and also expansion into the lower Tweed and Teviot and valleys and slopes in the Cheviots (Holling *in prep.*). Many tetrads now contain more than one pair, and in some areas of Borders Buzzards occur at around 1.0prs/km^2.

The Buzzard was lost from Lothian in the early 19th century. In 1968-72, one or two pairs attempted to breed in Midlothian and East Lothian, yet by 1988 there were still only two pairs. By 1994 the situation had dramatically changed with 38 territorial pairs recorded, increasing to 60 by 1997 (G.D. Smith *pers. comm.*). Although some of this increase may have been due to some under-recording in the late 1980s, immigration from the expanding Borders and Clyde populations seems to be the most likely cause.

This expansion is not restricted to SE Scotland: Buzzards are now much more frequently seen in Ayrshire and the Clyde areas, plus all of eastern Scotland, including Fife, Angus, NE Scotland and Caithness (*Scottish Bird Reports*), and also in parts of eastern and central England. This spread has been attributed to a change in attitude by gamekeepers resulting in much reduced illegal persecution. Buzzards are still the most frequently poisoned species of raptor (RSPB) but the incidence of poisoning (both deliberate and accidental) has declined. The change in attitude has coincided with the introduction of the Larsen trap which is a very successful method used to catch Carrion Crows without the need for laying poisoned bait. Once Buzzards are tolerated in an area, high Rabbit populations allow them to breed successfully. Broods of three are common in the area and if young are hatched most pairs raise the whole brood successfully (G.D. Smith *pers. comm.*).

The last national survey of Buzzards was in 1983 (Taylor *et al.*1988), but the status of the species in many areas of the country has changed considerably since then. With around 560 pairs in SE Scotland, and increases elsewhere in Britain, the most recent published British population estimate of 12,000-17,000 pairs based on the 1983 census (*New Atlas*) seems to be far too low and urgently needs revisiting. According to the *New Atlas* abundance map, much higher densities are achieved in Argyll, Wales and SW England than locally. To contribute to the national picture, monitoring of Buzzards in sample areas of SE Scotland should continue. **M.Holling**

Buzzard

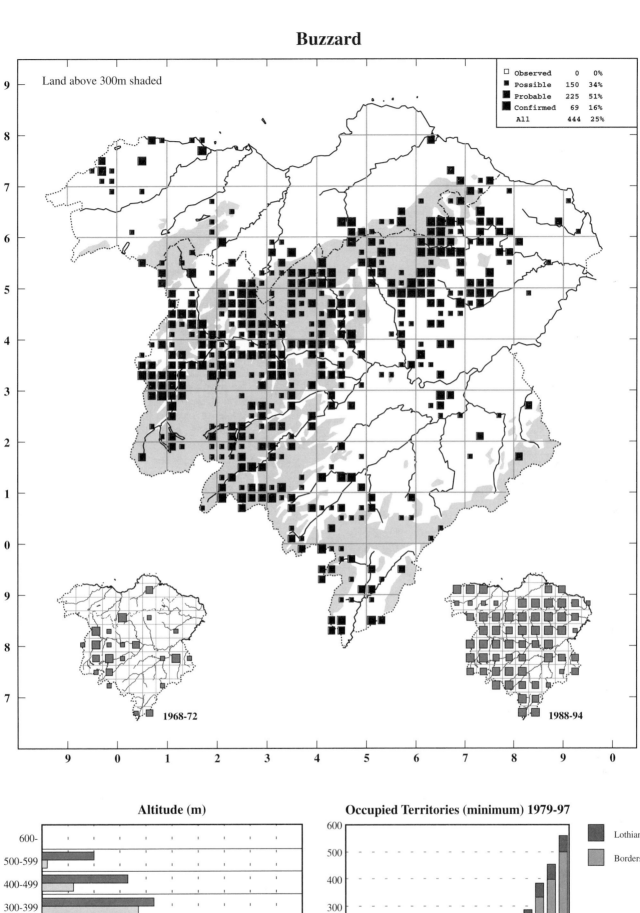

Land above 300m shaded

	Observed	0	0%
	Possible	150	34%
	Probable	225	51%
	Confirmed	69	16%
	All	444	25%

1968-72

1988-94

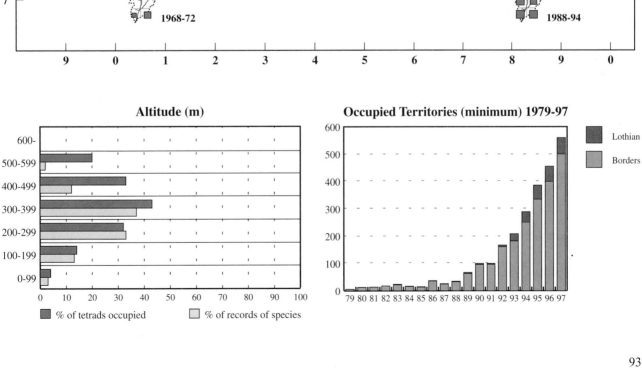

Altitude (m)

% of tetrads occupied   % of records of species

Occupied Territories (minimum) 1979-97

Lothian

Borders

Kestrel
Falco tinnunculus

The Kestrel is predominantly an open country bird, favouring a diet of small mammals, especially voles, worms and insects, but it is adaptable and so can be found in many different kinds of environment. Grass verges of new roads and young forestry have provided good hunting habitat in recent years. Many types of nest site are used, favourites being ledges on cliffs or buildings, holes in trees, or the disused stick nests of other birds, especially corvids. Kestrels are most abundant and breed most successfully in good vole years.

One of the easier species to record, the Kestrel was recorded in 66% of all tetrads, making it the most widespread of SE Scotland's raptors. It was easier to prove breeding later in the season when young were large and calling in the nest, or recently fledged. About a third of confirmed records were of adults carrying food, and a similar proportion were of fledged young. Over 40% of all tetrads with Kestrels show only possible breeding, indicating a single record over the *Atlas* period. Many of these will, however, relate to pairs as during May and June female Kestrels are rarely seen, spending much of the time on the nest. Nearly half of probable records were of territory. The long survey period of seven years also helped to counteract any effect of population change due to changes in vole abundance.

The map shows a general decrease in the number of occupied tetrads from west to east. The Kestrel is more sparsely distributed in parts of East Lothian and the Merse (for example in parts of NT47,57,74&84). This corresponds to lower-lying, high-grade farmland with large fields dominated by grain growing, where voles may well be scarce. The altitude graph shows that up to 500m Kestrels occur in over 60% of all tetrads, but that there is a significant fall-off above that height. This lower density at higher altitude can be seen for example in the Tweedsmuirs (NT12), parts of the Lammermuirs (NT55) and in the Cheviots (NT81&82). Kestrels are also only local where extensive blanket forestry occurs as at Craik (NT30) and Wauchope forests (NT50&51) where it is likely that the occupied tetrads correspond with open areas of clear-fell or grassland. There is an unexplained gap in the Lyne valley (NT14) which may correspond with an actual lack of Kestrels (R.D.Murray *pers. comm.*).

The areas showing the highest concentration of tetrads with confirmed breeding are where there is mixed land use of stock and arable farming, hedges, woodland strips, boundary trees and farmsteads, as in much of West Lothian and Midlothian, from the lower Tyne to the Lammermuirs (NT67), and where such land or unimproved grassland dominates in the middle to upper valleys of the Tweed and its tributaries, including the Blackadder and Whiteadder.

The data show some correlation with the amount of unimproved grassland below 500m except in West Lothian where the rich diversity of habitat provides the feeding and nesting conditions required. At all altitudes up to 500m the Kestrel shows an affinity for unimproved land, occupying over 70% of all tetrads where unimproved grassland is abundant or common, but only about half of all tetrads where this habitat is scarce or absent. This indicates that the Kestrel can extend into arable areas where there is no unimproved land. Above 500m, most land is unimproved, but as noted above, Kestrels are scarcer here. Village (1990) found densities to be higher on Scottish grassland than on arable farmland in England, where there were fewer voles and less suitable nest sites. This might explain the sparsity in parts of East Lothian and the Merse, although densities have since risen on fenland, and East Anglia is now a stronghold (*New Atlas*). Village's studies in Eskdalemuir, close to the south-western edge of the Atlas area (NS29&NT20) found that breeding mainly occurred in the valleys in odd mature trees by abandoned steadings and sheepfolds, with pairs on the open hillsides limited by the lack of suitable nest sites. Many of the gaps in the map for SE Scotland may therefore reflect such a shortage.

At 10-km square level the distribution has changed little since the *Old Atlas* although there is a suggestion of some increase by consolidation in several 10-km squares which recorded only possible breeding in the earlier survey (see maps). By the time of that survey the Kestrel had recovered from losses due to organochlorine pesticides, persecution and the harsh winter of 1962-63. In 1991, the British population was generally thought to be increasing (Carter 1995) but more recently the species has been added to the Amber list of Birds of Conservation Concern because of a moderate decline over the last 25 years.

Village (1990) found breeding densities ranged from 32prs/10-km square in Scottish grassland to 12prs/10-km square in arable farmland. Riddle (1979) found around 29prs/10-km square overall for Ayrshire, with highest densities in the lowlands and fewer in urban and upland habitats with fewer nest sites. Some local 10-km squares will hold in excess of 30 pairs, for example NT24 (Peebles) and NT17 (west of Edinburgh), while NT63 (Smailholm area) and NT82 (Yetholm) have only one tetrad each with confirmed or probable breeding. Local BBS data suggest one contact per 1.0km² over 25% of plots, equating to 1.0prs/km² where Kestrels occur.

The *New Atlas* uses a mean density of 20prs/10-km square which would suggest around 1,400 pairs in SE Scotland. The equivalent density of 0.2prs/km², if extrapolated up by the total number of occupied tetrads, gives a lower figure of 925 pairs. Alternatively, allowing for 30prs/10-km square in the 16 most populated 10-km squares, and one pair per tetrad in all other occupied tetrads, a figure between these two extremes of 1,200 is attained. This equates to more than 2% of the British population.

O.C.McGarry

Kestrel

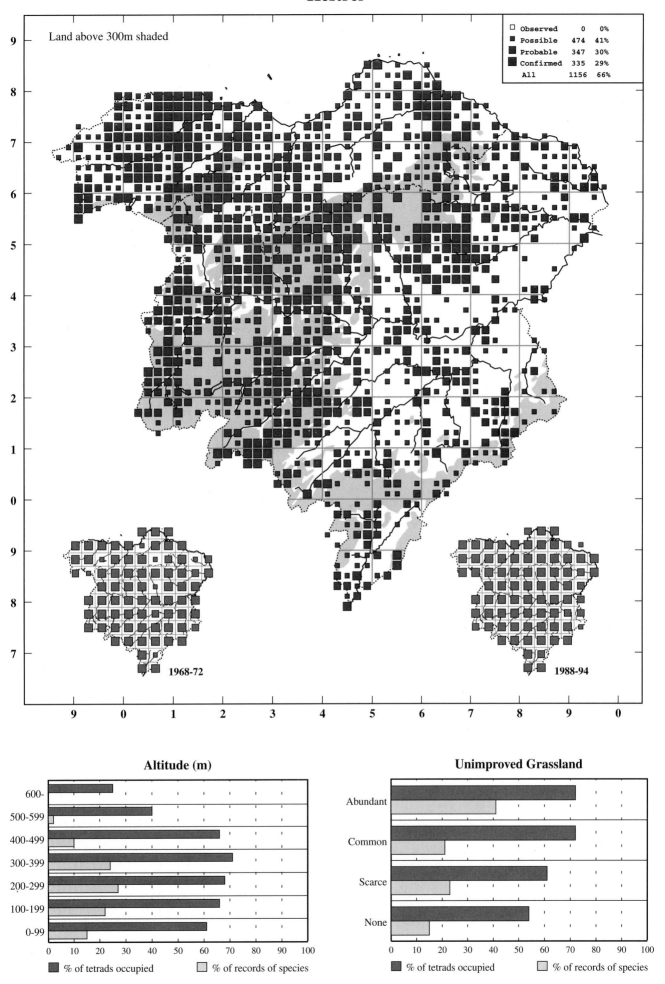

Land above 300m shaded

	Observed	0	0%
	Possible	474	41%
	Probable	347	30%
	Confirmed	335	29%
	All	1156	66%

1968-72

1988-94

Altitude (m)

■ % of tetrads occupied ■ % of records of species

Unimproved Grassland

■ % of tetrads occupied ■ % of records of species

Merlin
Falco columbarius

Our smallest falcon is one of the least common breeding raptors. It is a bird of undisturbed heather moorland, where its spirited flight is rarely seen by casual observers. In the breeding season it is reported infrequently and its presence is usually missed unless searched for. The Merlin is perhaps more familiar when seen away from its breeding grounds on the coast in winter. The British breeding distribution is restricted to Scotland, northern England and Wales. Numbers are considered to be declining, or at best stable, due to the loss of habitat to forestry, to overgrazing of heather moor by sheep and deer and to inadequate management of grouse moors.

The Merlin is a difficult species to survey and its Schedule 1 status has meant that most records were collected by experienced, licensed fieldworkers. Its rarity and aesthetic appeal has meant that an active group of enthusiasts began a long-term study in 1984 that has since monitored the populations of the Lammermuirs and Moorfoots, and to a lesser extent the Pentlands and parts of the Tweedsmuir Hills. Coverage of the other upland areas of the region has been increased in recent years, partly as a result of this *Atlas*, but more particularly due to the national Merlin Survey of 1993-94 organised by the RSPB.

The site fidelity of the Merlin has meant that occupation of traditional sites can be confirmed by experienced observers from tell-tale signs such as "kills" or pellets on plucking posts and long streaks of "whitewash" on fence posts and boulders, even if the birds themselves are not seen. In the *Atlas,* confirmed and probable records together accounted for over half of the occupied tetrads, a remarkably high percentage that would be unlikely to have been attained unless there had been intensive fieldwork by the Raptor Study Group. Possible and observed tetrads were mostly in the vicinity of those with probable and confirmed breeding and are thus likely to represent birds from these breeding sites on hunting forays. The scatter of eight possible records in the Ettrick Forest area doubtless represents nests currently unknown to the Raptor Study Group. Confirmed records were mostly of occupied nests, most of the remainder being of fledged young from nests that were not located. Most probable records were of pairs.

The map emphasises the Merlin's predilection for upland moors, especially those managed for Red Grouse. Almost all confirmed nests were found between 300-600m. The Lammermuirs, and to a lesser extent the Moorfoots, are the major strongholds of the Merlin in SE Scotland, reflecting the well-managed grouse moors in these hills. The southern edge of the Pentlands, the area around Broad Law (NT12&13), the hills between Manor Water and the Traquair-Yarrow valley road (NT23), and those south of Megget Reservoir (NT11&21) are also areas of good heather that is managed for grouse and hold numbers of breeding Merlin. The hills bordering

Northumberland and Dumfriesshire (NT60&NY49) have some local concentrations but the extensive forestry and heavy grazing must have reduced the land previously available to Merlins. Similar reasons may account for there being less Merlins in the uplands near Cheviot (NT71&81), the upper Ettrick, Borthwick and Teviot (NT21,31&41) and the source of the Tweed (NT01,02,03&11). The distribution in SE Scotland is tied to that of good quality heather and thus shows similarities to the ranges of Red Grouse, Golden Plover and Ring Ouzel although the Merlin is more restricted than any of these.

The habitat analysis supports this view with 85% of all tetrads where heather moorland was abundant holding Merlins. Similarly, over half of all records came from these large moors while all but 10% of Merlin records, excepting the observed records, were from tetrads where heather moor was either abundant or common. In altitudinal terms Merlins were found mostly between 250-500m, the median altitude being about 350m.

Comparison with the *Old Atlas*, which probably received poor coverage for this species, indicates that there may have been a marginal increase in the range of Merlins in areas such as the southern Pentlands and around Kielder. However, since 1984 the local monitoring, particularly in the Lammermuirs where the effort has been intensive and uniform, shows that the population has been relatively stable.

Most Merlins in SE Scotland nest in scrapes on the ground in heather. Much less frequently some nest in old Carrion Crow nests in single trees or shelter belts on moorland. Elsewhere in Britain, Merlins have now adapted to crow nests within the edge of large conifer plantations as in Northumberland at Kielder (Little and Davison 1992), NW Scotland (Rebecca 1992), SW Scotland (Orchel 1994) and in Wales (Parr 1994). In SE Scotland Carrion Crows have not yet begun to nest in such plantations in a major way, although the habit may be about to start (Dott 1994b). If this happens it could provide Merlins with new nesting opportunities, particularly in Borders where there are large tracts of upland plantation.

The Merlin population in the Lammermuirs has been measured since 1984 and has ranged between 9-19 pairs, with a mean of about 14 pairs. More recent surveys in the Moorfoots show that up to 12 pairs may be present there. Together with the small numbers in the less studied hills to the south and west, SE Scotland probably has a total population of breeding adults in the order of 50-60 pairs. There is little information on non-breeders. The most recent estimate of the British population (Rebecca & Bainbridge 1998) is *c.*1,300 pairs. SE Scotland's numbers represent 4% of this total.

I.R.Poxton

Merlin

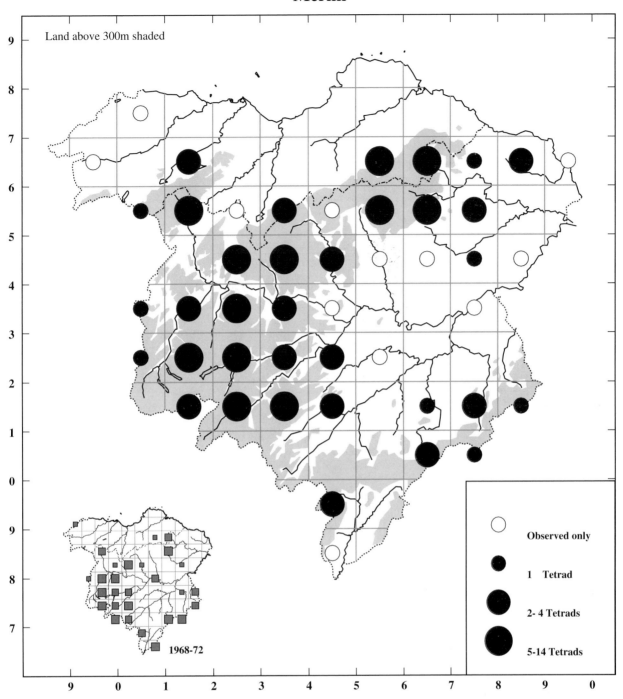

Land above 300m shaded

Legend:
○ Observed only
● 1 Tetrad
● 2- 4 Tetrads
● 5-14 Tetrads

1968-72

Altitude (m)

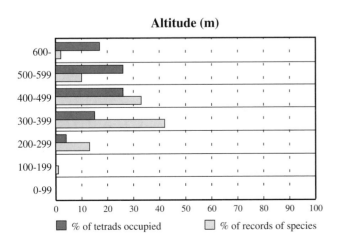

600-	
500-599	
400-499	
300-399	
200-299	
100-199	
0-99	

0 10 20 30 40 50 60 70 80 90 100

■ % of tetrads occupied   □ % of records of species

Heather Moorland

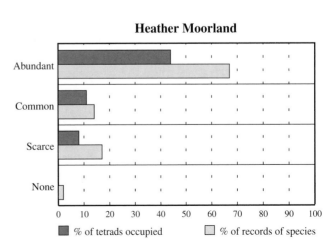

Abundant	
Common	
Scarce	
None	

0 10 20 30 40 50 60 70 80 90 100

■ % of tetrads occupied   □ % of records of species

Brown

Peregrine
Falco peregrinus

This magnificent hunter occurs world-wide in all continents but Antarctica, yet is still considered threatened and to see one is a privilege. Peregrines require open country for hunting, rock faces for nesting, and breed mainly in the mountainous parts of Britain and around steep coasts. Their fortunes have varied. Prized by falconers and egg collectors and slaughtered by game-bird protectors, they were also hit by harmful agricultural pesticides in Britain in the 1950s-1960s which drastically reduced their numbers. Over much of Britain the Peregrine population has now recovered and reached a higher population than ever documented, though in earlier times it could have been higher. However, in NW Scotland and the Northern Isles numbers are still in decline, possibly due to pollution accumulating in their seabird prey.

The population in SE Scotland has been monitored by dedicated observers in the region's Raptor Study Group since the early 1960s, and almost all breeding sites were known prior to the *Atlas* fieldwork commencing. It would be safe to say that the majority of sites with breeding Peregrines during the *Atlas* period were found. The number of tetrads on the map with probable and confirmed records (absorbed into single symbols per 10-km square) is higher than the number of Peregrine sites known in any one year. This is because some Peregrine pairs use alternative nest sites in different years and seven years' records are shown, and accordingly the map exaggerates the breeding distribution for any one year. Observed records are likely to represent birds prospecting new sites or hunting in the extremes of their territories.

The map shows a wide scatter of tetrads with breeding. The majority are clearly associated with higher ground, with a small group along the coast and some on low ground. The latter are almost all where rock is exposed either as natural cliffs or as quarry faces, particularly on the Berwickshire coastal cliffs, and one each on a Forth island and the Forth Rail Bridge. In the high ground the map shows the greatest concentration to be in SE Scotland's highest hills amongst the headwaters of the Tweed drainage system, with a good presence in the northern hills and a few in the south. The altitude graph confirms the map interpretation with nearly 70% of Peregrines breeding at 300-500m, while two fifths of all tetrads at 500-600m hold Peregrines. Few Peregrines breed at 100-200m between the coastal and high ground birds. The lack of correlation between the Peregrine map and that of cliff features other than along the coast, reflects the poor quality of many small crags, quarries and outcrops.

Until the mid 1980s, Peregrine nests in SE Scotland were virtually all on steep natural rock faces of considerable height. Nesting in quarries (mainly disused) began in the last ten years, and is now practised by 22% of the breeding population. Still more recently, ground-nesting on sloping banks with little or no rock began and now occurs in 10% of pairs, while among rock-face nesters many are using small rocks, almost ground-nesting. Quarry nesting has increased recently in other parts of Britain and involves 13% of UK pairs (Crick & Ratcliffe 1995) and over 20% of pairs in Ireland (Moore *et al.* 1997). Ground nesting is still less common than quarry nesting (Crick & Ratcliffe 1995) and in SE Scotland may be above the national mean. Peregrines have now nested successfully on the Forth Rail Bridge, and a pair laid in a former Carrion Crow's nest in a larch tree in SE Scotland, though failed to hatch young probably due to bad weather. Nesting on trees or structures such as buildings, bridges or pylons is rare in Britain (Ratcliffe 1984, Crick & Ratcliffe 1995).

The now wider types of nest-site locations may result from both increase in Peregrines and from persecution. The second graph shows the rapidity of recent increase of SE Scotland Peregrines, and the proportions of pairs which reared young successfully or failed due to natural cause or to human interference. Sadly, in every year but one, failures by human interference greatly outnumber those with natural causes (see second graph), and the majority of these interferences were on or adjacent to keepered ground (Scottish Raptor Study Groups 1997, & local RSG information).

In previous centuries Peregrines may have been widespread in the mountainous parts of SE Scotland, and up to the 1930s were known on the Berwickshire cliffs, the Bass Rock, Craigleith and Isle of May (*R&B*). In Lothian throughout the 20th century until the 1980s they were rare as breeders (*Andrews*), though some were present mainly in Borders in the 1930s (Crick & Ratcliffe 1995). Due to the pesticide years, there were only 1-5 pairs per year from 1965-1980 (Raptor Study Groups), their approximate distribution showing on the small map opposite. The main map and second graph show the great expansion since then.

During the *Atlas* period the SE Scotland Peregrine population rose from 14 to 35 breeding pairs, and reached 40 pairs in 1997, 3.4% of the latest British population estimate (Stone *et al.* 1997). There is an additional number of non-breeding birds sufficient to usually replace loss of a breeding bird within the same season. Ringing shows that immigration from outwith SE Scotland has occurred.

G.D.Smith & H.E.M.Dott

Peregrine

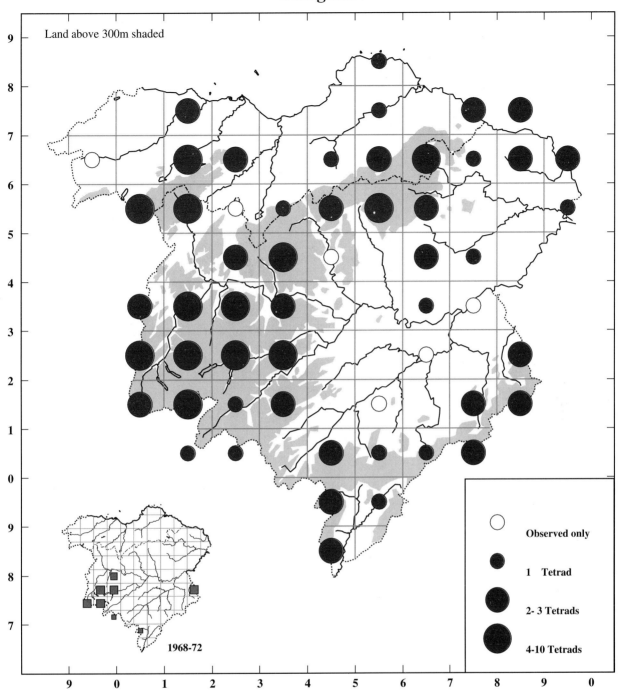

Land above 300m shaded

1968-72

Observed only

1 Tetrad

2- 3 Tetrads

4-10 Tetrads

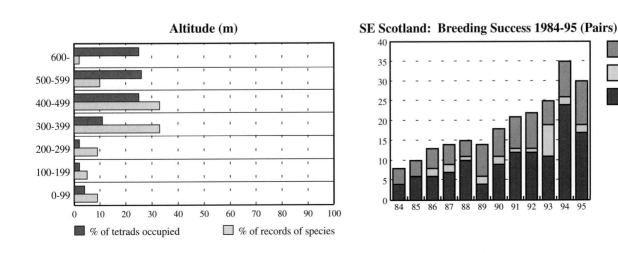

Altitude (m)

600-	
500-599	
400-499	
300-399	
200-299	
100-199	
0-99	

0   10   20   30   40   50   60   70   80   90   100

■ % of tetrads occupied   □ % of records of species

SE Scotland: Breeding Success 1984-95 (Pairs)

Failed, human interference

Failed, natural causes

Successful

84 85 86 87 88 89 90 91 92 93 94 95

Red Grouse
Lagopus lagopus

No day spent in heather moorland should be without the sound of cackling grouse, or the sight of this plump and robust gamebird whirring across the hillside. The Red Grouse sub-species (*L. l. scoticus*) is confined to the UK and to heather moorland, as the adults almost exclusively eat heather. It occurs at high densities on moors which are specially managed for this species through burning and gamekeeping. In the past, large numbers have been shot in August and September, whereas more recently some grouse shooting estates have not been able to shoot due to the low numbers of birds present at the end of the summer. Red Grouse populations in Scotland fluctuate on a six or seven year cycle that is thought to be linked, at least in part, to the delayed density-dependent effects of a nematode parasite. The national longer-term decline in the species is believed to be caused by habitat degradation, as many grouse moors have been heavily grazed by sheep which has encouraged grasses rather than heather to dominate the vegetation, although many estate-owners would also like to blame the presence of raptors such as Hen Harrier and Peregrine.

Nearly half of all occupied tetrads are of confirmed breeding, mostly records of broods. Pairs, territorial behaviour and display provided most probable breeding records. Noisy cock birds are conspicuous early in the season, but grouse can be less easy to find on wet and windy days, and are in any case much quieter once females are sitting on nests or with young broods. Where heather is sparse in mainly grassy moors, Red Grouse occur at lower densities, or not at all. Evidence of Red Grouse was also sometimes obtained by the presence of moulted feathers and droppings, helping complete the picture in areas where the species is scarce.

The Red Grouse provides one of the clearest associations between a habitat type and a bird species in SE Scotland. There is an almost perfect match between the Red Grouse map and that of heather moorland. Red Grouse occur in over 90% of tetrads where heather is extensive. The more extensive areas of heather, such as the Lammermuirs and Moorfoots, also show the most confirmed breeding records, reflecting the high densities of Red Grouse in these areas which are managed for grouse. South of the Yarrow, the species is more localised, with much of the hill land here now blanketed with coniferous plantations or short sheep-grazed grass. Gaps in the distribution are evident at Craik (NT30) and Wauchope (NT50) forests.

The graph of occurrence against altitude shows that most Red Grouse occur at over 300m, linked to the distribution of heather. Indeed, 43% of occupied tetrads lie between 300-400m. Nevertheless, 50% of all tetrads above 600m hold Red Grouse, so if the hills in SE Scotland were higher more birds might live at this level. Some exceptions, where grouse occur below 300m, can be seen on the map. The most significant is the area around Hule Moss (NT74&75) where heather moor is maintained for grouse but which is largely surrounded by arable land. In West Lothian, there are records of Red Grouse at Blawhorn Moss (NS87U&Z) and Polkemmet Moor (NS96) although only singles were seen in each tetrad and this must be peripheral habitat for the species. Red Grouse also occur close to the coast where heather survives on Coldingham

Moor (NT86) although numbers are declining here (R.D. Murray, *pers. comm.*). There is an isolated population on the Eildon Hills (NT53K&L) which are topped with heather. Although there is a high rate of use of heather moor, the habitat graph shows that a significant number of records (38%) came from tetrads where heather is scarce or even absent. Perhaps less dominant males occupy these sub-optimal habitats and may not breed.

Looking back to the period of the *Old Atlas*, the Red Grouse was more widely distributed at 10-km level. Losses have since occurred in the Cheviots. The likely culprits for these losses are a combination of tree planting and heavy sheep stocking levels. There is now very little heather in these hills. The remaining strongholds in the Cheviots now are the hills around Roan Fell (NY48&NT49) and along the border between Peel Fell and Carter Bar (NT60). The loss of birds from the south is probably much greater than is apparent at the 10-km square scale, as the number of occupied tetrads in each 10-km square in this area is now low. The gains in NT67 & NT77 involve just three tetrads, two of which refer to possible breeding only.

The *New Atlas* abundance map for Red Grouse shows that most of the range in SE Scotland holds moderate densities with large numbers in the Lammermuirs and Moorfoots. However, there are very few useful data on Red Grouse published in the *Bird Reports*: most counts refer to winter flocks and totals are usually of individuals in unspecified areas. Exceptions include counts in the Lammermuirs in 1984, 60 birds in 1.6km in March and 46 territories in a 12km transect in April, and 37 in 7km^2 of the Moorfoots in May 1993. In May 1994, 49 were counted in four tetrads in the Moorfoots. An average density varying between 3.20-6.25 birds per km^2 was recorded in the area between West Cairns plantation and East Cairn Hill (NT05E) and Temple Hill (NT06A) in the Pentlands (Henderson 1996). Wader study work on Culter Fell (NT03), on the boundary of our area, found a density of 2.5prs/km^2 (SNH unpublished). These casual reports probably underestimate the numbers actually present. A more intensive survey of grouse moors found an average of *c.*15 birds in 0.5km^2 in April counts over four seasons (Redpath & Thirgood 1997), equating to *c.*30 birds/km^2. The *Old Atlas* states that the highest densities achieved on artificially managed moors can be 50-60 prs/km^2, but this is for moors developed over base-rich rocks, which is not the case for most of SE Scotland. Base-rich substrates increase soil fertility and consequently the nutritional value of the heather.

To estimate the population of Red Grouse in SE Scotland, a conservative 20prs/km^2 for tetrads with abundant heather moor is assumed, with 5.0prs/km^2 for tetrads where heather is common, 2.0prs/km^2 where it is scarce and only 1.0prs/km^2 in tetrads with no heather. This gives a figure for SE Scotland of 18,400 pairs and equates to 7.3% of the British population, which seems reasonable as the northern hills of SE Scotland have Red Grouse densities as high as any other in Britain according to the *New Atlas*. Clearly to monitor the future numbers and density of this commercially important species, regular counts of territorial birds in defined areas is required.   *M.Holling*

Red Grouse

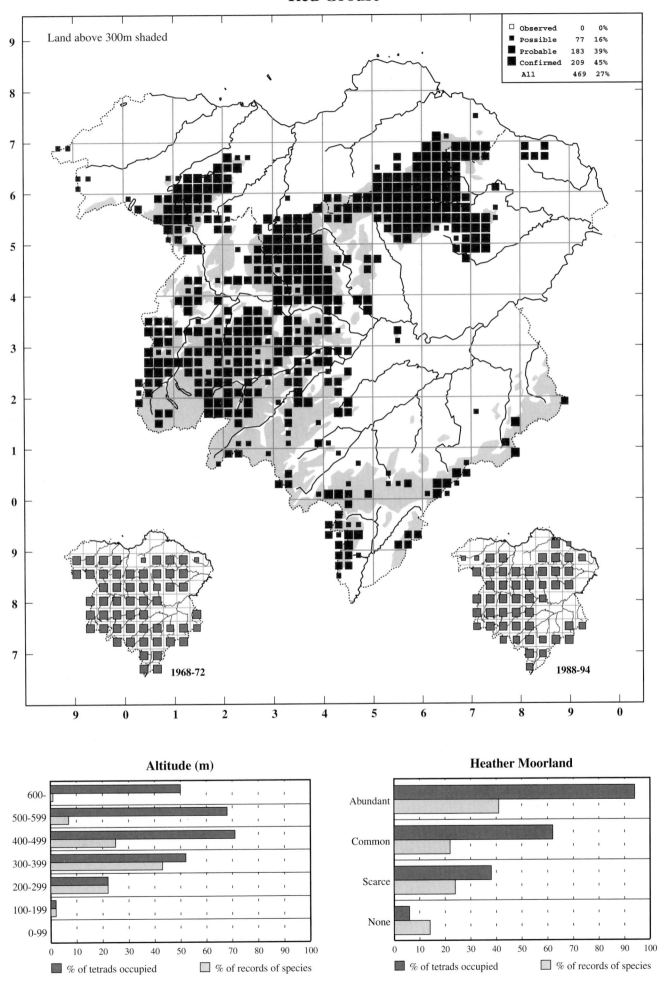

Land above 300m shaded

☐ Observed	0	0%
■ Possible	77	16%
■ Probable	183	39%
■ Confirmed	209	45%
All	469	27%

1968-72

1988-94

Altitude (m)

- 600-
- 500-599
- 400-499
- 300-399
- 200-299
- 100-199
- 0-99

■ % of tetrads occupied   ☐ % of records of species

Heather Moorland

- Abundant
- Common
- Scarce
- None

■ % of tetrads occupied   ☐ % of records of species

Black Grouse
Tetrao tetrix

For many birdwatchers the Black Grouse is a sought after species which can be surprisingly difficult to find in some areas. However, the reward of finding a lek on a bright, still and frosty spring morning is one that is not forgotten. Black Grouse are associated with moorland and forest edge habitats which support both a diverse range of food plants such as blaeberry and heather and also trees such as birch and Rowan. In summer, tall ground vegetation to provide invertebrate food for the chicks is important for breeding success. During the 20th century this species has declined markedly and the distribution has shrunk to the north and west to such an extent that Scotland now contains the majority of Black Grouse in Britain.

Thorough searching of suitable tetrads during fieldwork for the *Atlas* would usually reveal Black Grouse if present. Early in the season, displaying males are conspicuous at leks and the bubbling calls carry far on still days. Accordingly, over half of all registrations were of probable breeding records, mostly due to displaying males. The remainder of probable records were of males and females seen close together, or singles seen again on repeat visits. Most other reports were of single birds, often flushed during hill walks. Only a small number of confirmed records were received, mainly of family parties with a few nests and females trying to distract observers away from nests. A few additional records were extracted from the *Bird Reports*.

The map shows the close association of the species with the hills. Most records are from land over 300m, although this apparent altitudinal relationship is probably because most rough grass and heather moorland generally occurs only above this height. Where rough moor is present at lower levels, such as at Greenlaw Moor around the north-eastern part of NT64, Black Grouse were found to be present. Detailed analysis of the data shows that 80% of records come from altitudes between 250-450m, occupying just under half of all land at these levels. The densest pattern of occupied tetrads is in the Moorfoots and southern hills in a block southwards from the Moorfoot edge (NT35) to the Ettrick valley (NT21&31). Elsewhere, Black Grouse are clearly more localised, as in the Pentlands, upper Tweed and Cheviots. They are absent from most of the Lammermuirs, except on some of the fringes with forestry plantations, such as between Soutra (NT45Z) and Hopes Reservoir (NT56L), around the Monynut Edge (NT66Y,76I&M) and the southern edge including Greenlaw Moor. They were formerly plentiful here (*Andrews*). Although the species is generally sedentary, a wandering adult male was seen on two dates in April 1990 at Aberlady.

Habitat analysis indicates relationships between distribution and unimproved grassland, heather moor and coniferous woodland. The strongest relationship is with rough grazing, as 70% of birds occur where rough grazing is abundant. However, it appears that the more diverse the habitat in a tetrad, with rough grazing, heather and some conifer, the more likely are Black Grouse to be present (see graph). The national decline is attributed to habitat degradation in the uplands, especially overgrazing by sheep. There is now much less birch woodland and unimproved grass-heather habitat, especially with a range of vegetation heights and diversity of plant species.

Much unimproved grassland habitat has been lost due to reseeding and afforestation. Afforestation initially improves the diversity and structure, providing new sites for Black Grouse, but suitability declines as the trees mature. Last century flocks of up to 100 were recorded in hill oat-stubble fields (Chapman 1889) - these fields have long gone and numbers like this are no longer recorded. This loss of winter feeding, as upland farms no longer grow cereal crops for fodder, may well have increased winter mortality rates.

Comparison with the *Old Atlas* reveals conflicting conclusions. The number of occupied 10-km squares is unchanged. There seems to have been range extension into the eastern Lammermuirs, probably associated with the Monynut and Crystal Forests planted in the 1970s and 1980s. However, these gains are marginal, affecting only a few tetrads. Conversely, there has been some contraction from the south, with loss from NT30 (Craik Forest) and parts of Liddesdale. This is probably associated with the maturation of the blanket forests there. This picture of a population holding its own may be changing, however, as recent detailed surveys by the RSPB indicate a major slump in numbers across Scotland.

The number of records submitted to the *Bird Reports* varies annually dependent on observer effort, and it is unusual for the same sites to be counted in subsequent years. The maximum number of sites reported was 57 in Borders (1992 & 1994) and 12 in Lothian (1993). The highest annual total was 274 birds in Borders in 1994 and 65 in Lothian in 1993. Many of the records referred to lekking males and give an indication of the minimum population during this period. The largest leks reported in Lothian were 18 at Fala Moor (NT45I) in 1993; and 16 males and seven females near Gladhouse in December 1992. In Borders, the largest counts at one site were 24 males at Williamslee in the Moorfoots (NT34B) in 1986 and 25 males at Syart, near Megget Water (NT22B) in 1991.

During the *Atlas* period, records were received from 227 tetrads. Some of these will have contained more than one lek. In the *Bird Reports* for the period, 44% of leks were of only one male, 33% of 2-5 males, and 24% six or more males. Assuming one, four and six males in each of these sub-divisions, a minimum population of 730 lekking males would be indicated. As some leks were considerably larger, the population could have been over 800.

Following the national decline documented in Baines & Hudson (1995), the RSPB and Game Conservacy Trust initiated a national survey in 1995-96. In SE Scotland, sample 5-km squares and other areas surveyed in 1995-97 covered a total of $c.785km^2$ and 229 lekking males were found. Additional accurate counts produced another 130 males. A further 152 males were identified from tetrads in this *Atlas* which were not covered by the above work, assuming one male per tetrad. This produces a more accurate and recent estimate for SE Scotland of over 500 lekking males, with a maximum of around 600. This comprises a substantial and therefore important 10% of the re-estimated national population of 6,300 males (Hancock *et al.* in press.). With a declining national population, and a significant proportion in SE Scotland, it is essential that local monitoring of leks continues. Local birders can contribute by making counts at the same sites over a number of years. *M.Holling*

Black Grouse

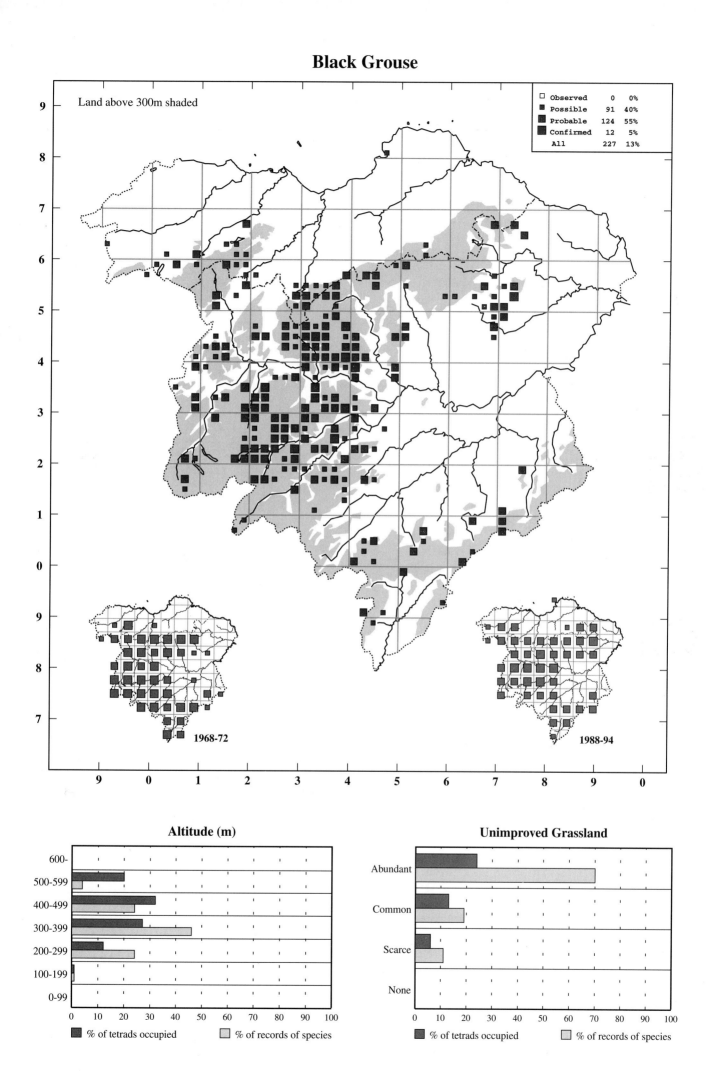

Land above 300m shaded

☐ Observed	0	0%
◼ Possible	91	40%
◼ Probable	124	55%
◼ Confirmed	12	5%
All	227	13%

1968-72

1988-94

Altitude (m)

◼ % of tetrads occupied ◻ % of records of species

Unimproved Grassland

◼ % of tetrads occupied ◻ % of records of species

Red-legged Partridge
Alectoris rufa
and **Chukar** *Alectoris chukar*

Populations of these two gamebirds were introduced to Britain in the 18th and 19th centuries, well north of their natural range, to supplement the numbers of birds available for shooting each autumn. They are part of a predominantly southern Palearctic superspecies whose range extends from Spain (Red-legged Partridge) and North Africa (Barbary Partridge *A.barbara*), across southern Europe (Rock Partridge *A.graeca*) to the Middle East and China (Chukar) and into southern Arabia (Philby's Rock Partridge *A.philbyi* and Arabian Red-legged Partridge *A. melanocephala*). The Red-legged Partridge is a bird of arable farmland in the drier parts of Britain that most resemble the warm temperate areas of Europe where they originate, especially in having dry summers as low rainfall appears conducive to successful breeding. Light sandy soils, even heaths and sand-dunes, are favoured while lightly wooded areas are also used, much more so than by Grey Partridges.

Red-legged Partridges can be easy to find due to their relative docility, many birds being very approachable. Whether this is innate behaviour, or that they are tame because they have been captive-bred, is not known, but many birds could be approached within ten metres and were often found in and around farms and small villages as well as in open countryside. Locally birds do not appear to be particularly vocal, possibly due to the low density of the population, so the majority of observations were of birds seen rather than heard. Probable records were dominated by pairs while the few confirmed records were mostly of adults with young.

Despite laying more than twice as many eggs as the Grey Partridge and both the male and female incubating the eggs, Red-legged Partridges are very susceptible to predation of clutches, necessitating rigid protection from predators to ensure good numbers for shooting. A large number of separate introductions were necessary to establish the population in Britain to a point where it was self-sustaining in southern and eastern England. Although this was achieved towards the end of the 19th century, constant replenishment of the feral populations by releasing captive-bred stock has been necessary to maintain local populations at levels that can tolerate the extent of shooting that exists. This is especially true further north and west in Britain where the colder, wetter conditions may be less favourable for breeding, hardly surprising in a southern European species. Large-scale and continual introductions seem necessary to produce a viable population here, as small-scale releases outside the main part of the British range have always eventually failed (*Old Atlas*) perhaps partly due to the species' habit of dispersing away from the point of release.

In SE Scotland all Red-legged Partridges have originated from such releases. Birds were only present in two 10-km squares during the *Old Atlas* survey, Scottish releases apparently dating from the last year of that survey in 1972. Comparisons with the *Old Atlas* show a very much wider distribution now. However, with records from 78 tetrads spread over 38 of the 10-km squares and averaging just two tetrads per occupied 10-km square, the density of records is very low. Indeed only five 10-km squares have more than three occupied tetrads during 1988-94, probably all near points where birds were introduced, chiefly in West Lothian in the Livingston area (NS96, NT06&16), in Midlothian around Temple (NT35) and in the Merse around Duns and Coldstream (NT73,74,75&84). Some other individual tetrads such as those in Dalmeny estate (NT17) and at Tyninghame (NT68), probably refer to even smaller-scale releases, as were 12 released at Bowhill (NT42D) in 1986, 40 at Longformacus (NT65Y) in 1988 and 50 at Dalmeny (NT17T) in 1989 (*Bird Reports*). With birds being released in areas with such little arable land it is hardly surprising that they often disperse widely after release. Many of the possible records, often in hilly areas (10% of the records occur above 250m), may concern such birds searching for suitable habitat. Red-legged Partridge remains have even been reported from Peregrine eyries in hill areas.

In the late 1960s and early 1970s releases across Britain included pure captive-bred Chukars as well as Red-leg x Chukar hybrids, apparently from game-farm stocks that were selectively bred for their egg-laying capabilities. These hybrids bred even less successfully in the wild than pure Red-legs (*New Atlas*). Releases of hybrids stopped in 1992 when licenses for releases were discontinued. Chukars and their hybrids were seen in eight tetrads in SE Scotland during the 1988-94 period. Other than at St. Abbs (NT96E), where Chukars bred over several years, no other site has had birds reported in more than a single year. It seems probable that others were overlooked, particularly hybrid birds, being misidentified amongst the other records of Red-legged Partridge.

Red-legged Partridges will continue to exist in the area only as long as birds are released. It is clear from the most recent *Lothian Bird Reports* that the species is rapidly approaching extinction in Lothian, the number of records dropping to single figures. In Borders the fashion for releasing birds also seems to be on the wane. Certainly it is clear that none of the releases are self-sustaining and that birds are either shot or have such poor breeding success as to be non-viable without recruitment from captive-bred birds.

Any local population estimate is clearly compromised by these releases but it is unlikely that any more than a hundred or so pairs were present at any time in the *Atlas* period. At the time of publication, with extinction perhaps approaching in Lothian and a probable reduction in Borders, the 1997 population may be around 40 pairs. **R.D.Murray**

Red-legged Partridge or Chukar

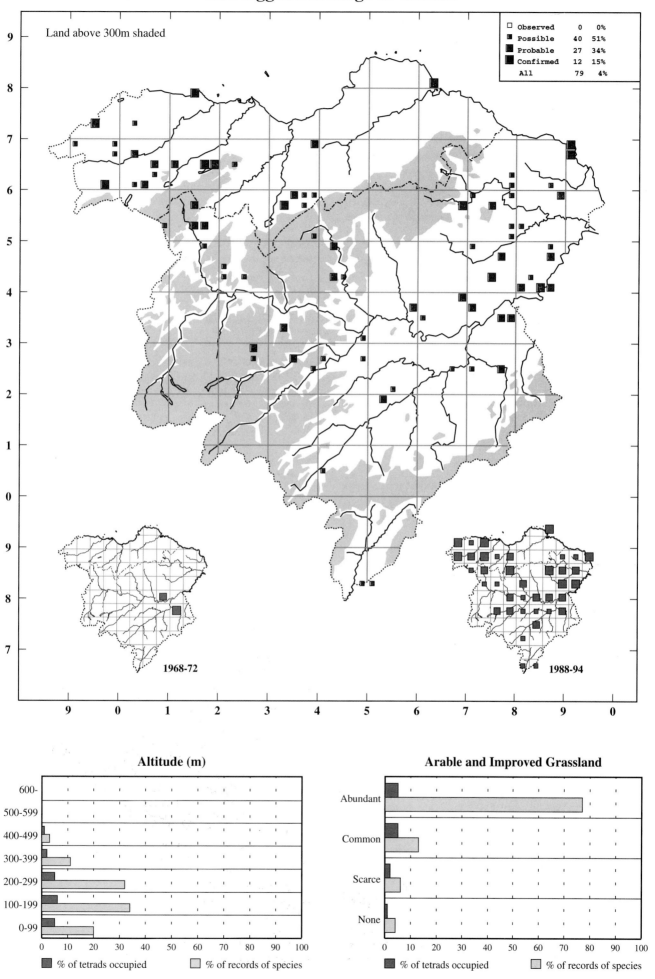

Land above 300m shaded

	Observed	0	0%
	Possible	40	51%
	Probable	27	34%
	Confirmed	12	15%
	All	79	4%

1968-72

1988-94

Altitude (m)

600-
500-599
400-499
300-399
200-299
100-199
0-99

0 10 20 30 40 50 60 70 80 90 100

■ % of tetrads occupied   ☐ % of records of species

Arable and Improved Grassland

Abundant
Common
Scarce
None

0 10 20 30 40 50 60 70 80 90 100

■ % of tetrads occupied   ☐ % of records of species

Grey Partridge
Perdix perdix

A fast-moving but tight flock of dumpy birds with whirring wings and distinctive chestnut tails glimpsed as they sweep out of sight over a rise or around a hedge is the usual indication that a flock of Grey Partridges are present. Primarily thought of as birds of arable farmland, Grey Partridges are actually at home in several open habitats where there is sufficient cover for a nest and a reasonable supply of seed and insect food. It is a bird whose population has undergone a serious decline in recent decades that could be on the verge of going down the same route as the Corncrake and other birds that depend on more traditional forms of agriculture.

As befits a species that inhabits the open fields of arable farmland, recording can be somewhat hit-or-miss. Birds that sit tight within cereals are virtually undetectable during recording visits but conversely the croaking calls of territorial males allowed otherwise hidden birds to be recorded, day or night. Grey Partridges were typically seen in pairs or family parties, providing most of the probable and confirmed records. Sweeps of arable areas of the Merse for Quail on summer nights added a number of reports that might not otherwise have been recorded.

The map shows a species with a predilection for arable farmland, being found mostly in the low ground of both Lothian and Borders in a pattern similar to other arable species such as Yellowhammer, Linnet and House Sparrow. Habitat data show a very positive correlation between Grey Partridge and tetrads where arable and improved grassland is widespread, 80% of the bird records occurring in two thirds of all tetrads where such habitats are abundant. The altitude data support this conclusion with over 80% of records of birds coming from tetrads between sea-level and 300m, the altitude zone in which arable farming is dominant. However, it should also be noticed that 20% of Grey Partridges occur above 300m in areas where arable farmland is uncommon and highlights this species' ability to live in areas of rough grazing at higher levels. Indeed analysis of habitat data (not graphed) indicates that a quarter of all Grey Partridge records are from tetrads with abundant rough grazing. Presumably most were at higher altitudes although areas like Aberlady Bay and Musselburgh at low levels also have good areas of unimproved grassland. A small number of birds were reported in tetrads whose mean altitude was above 500m, some of the highest breeding records in Britain.

In detail the map shows Grey Partridges across most of the low ground of Lothian other than the heavily urbanised parts of Edinburgh and the surrounding conurbation. This low-level range extends along the coast into Berwickshire and widely into the Tweed basin, and far up the river valleys into the high hills at the headwaters of the Tweed, Yarrow, Ettrick and Teviot. Again, typical of many arable and woodland species, the density of occupied tetrads seems to be less in the Merse than in corresponding parts of the Lothian lowlands. This may be an artifact of the intense recording effort in Lothian or possibly more intensive use of chemicals in Borders fields. The extent to which birds penetrate higher ground above 300m is interesting as it is mostly in the Middleton-Soutra gap between the Moorfoot and Lammermuir Hills along the Gala and Leader, where improved grassland extends along the A7 and A68 roads. Penetration is also visible in the Moorfoots along the Dewar-

Leithen Water valleys (NT34) and across the Lammermuirs along Spartleton Edge (NT66). Habitats here are anomalous as these areas are dominated by heather moorland and rough grazing. It is possible that these records represent releases of captive-bred birds by shooting interests. The relative lack of birds in the large stock-rearing area below 300m between Hawick, Selkirk and Kelso may indicate either a certain amount of under-recording there or that some other factor such as the heavier rainfall here may be important in limiting numbers. The total lack of birds in Liddesdale, where conditions are even wetter, is notable and may support this latter view.

In the *Old Atlas* Grey Partridges were recorded in eight squares more than in the present survey. There are also reductions in the level of proof in another 12 squares, typically from confirmed to probable or possible breeding. Both the losses and the squares where proof of breeding was hard to obtain seem to be mostly in the western and southern margins of the area where the density of occupied tetrads per 10-km square is low, averaging less than four tetrads per square. This suggests that birds have disappeared from these marginal areas due to an accentuation of the factors that already make these areas marginal. It is suggested elsewhere in this *Atlas* that the change from the traditional farming in the hills, where many upland farms had small areas of arable land to provide winter cereal feed, to more specialised livestock units that buy in their cereal feeds, may be responsible for the marginal shrinkage of range in these upland areas. This is also seen in Yellowhammer, Linnet, House Sparrow and Rook. This slight retreat from the upland has also been seen in Northumberland (*Day*) and Grampian (Buckland *et al.* 1990) and is hinted at in the *New Atlas* change map.

The *New Atlas* abundance map shows large areas of the highest abundance across much of lowland West and East Lothian, the Berwickshire coast, the Merse and the area of higher ground across the Moorfoot-Lammermuir gap, with much of the remaining occupied area on the map opposite showing moderate-to-good numbers. Indeed our area has a high proportion of good abundance, as high as in most parts of Britain, which suggests that SE Scotland holds more than average numbers of birds.

Grey Partridges do not hold great interest to birders and consequently details of breeding numbers rarely figure in the *Bird Reports*. da Prato (1985) found overall densities of 6prs/km^2 around Tranent in an area of the highest abundance according to the *New Atlas* while BBS returns suggest around 3-4prs/km^2 across the whole area. *Thom* mentions that densities in East Lothian have crashed from 25prs/km^2 in the early 20th century to around 5prs/km^2 at present, mostly due to intensification of farming. Densities of 5-15prs/km^2 are also mentioned in Aberdeenshire. The Game Conservancy estimates the British population as 150,000 pairs in spring 1992 (*New Atlas*) which equates to an overall density of 0.9prs/km^2 across all of Britain. Local figures suggest much higher numbers with perhaps 5prs/km^2 in the best areas. As densities probably fall with rising altitude, a value of 5prs/km^2 is used for occupied tetrads up to 150m, 3prs/km^2 up to 300m and 1pr/km^2 above that level. This produces a figure of 10,750 pairs, 7% of the British population, a figure that fits the picture of relative abundance shown in the *New Atlas* abundance map. **T.D. Smith & R.D.Murray**

Grey Partridge

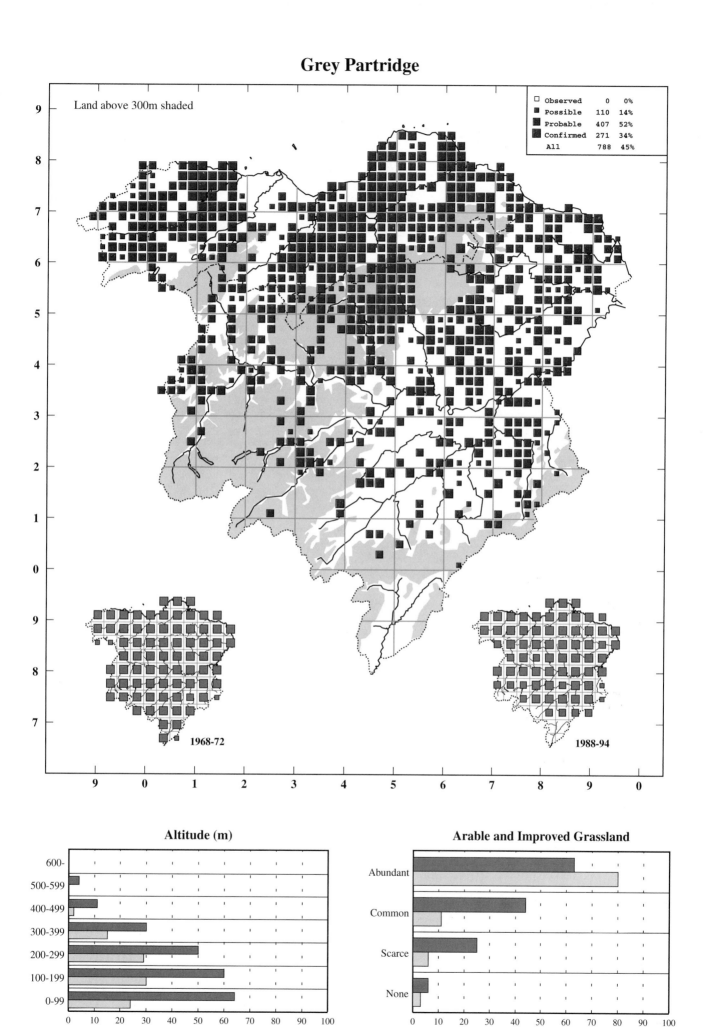

Land above 300m shaded

☐ Observed	0	0%
■ Possible	110	14%
■ Probable	407	52%
■ Confirmed	271	34%
All	788	45%

1968-72

1988-94

Altitude (m)

% of tetrads occupied   % of records of species

Arable and Improved Grassland

% of tetrads occupied   % of records of species

107

Quail
Coturnix coturnix

Quails are very seldom seen. The main clue to their presence, the so-called 'wet-my-lips' call, usually from the middle of a cereal field, forms the basis of most records. They summer in cereal fields, especially spring-sown barley, first arriving in mid-May although many appear between mid-June and mid-July. The last summering birds disappear in mid-August with passage birds moving through into October on their way to Africa.

In most years it is usually one of the scarcest summer visitors to Lothian and Borders with fewer than ten reports in a typical year. Larger numbers are reported occasionally, perhaps 20-30 in a year, but very rarely, as happened in 1989, a large-scale influx occurs which puts all other occurrences in the shade. The erratic nature of Quail numbers can be easily seen in the second graph where Quail numbers were low for most of the period between 1979-1988, usually 1-15 birds reported annually. The sudden jump to about 150 birds in 1989 was extraordinary. Numbers have been better than average since 1989 but this may be due to better observer awareness and birds being actively searched for during the summer months, rather than any great increase in the numbers appearing each summer. In general, however, the numbers of Quails seen and heard locally reflect the fluctuating numbers present across Britain each summer.

Calling birds, mostly the trisyllabic call of males but occasionally the low grunting call of the female, form the bulk of *Atlas* records. While Quails do call during the day the period when they are most vocal is around dusk and dawn. Perhaps half of all local records have come from observers making overnight visits in June and July specifically to record Quails and other nocturnal birds. This was especially true in 1989, the peak year. In most cases single birds were heard on single occasions and registered as possible breeders. Where a number of males were calling simultaneously or a single male was heard at the same site in different years, this was registered as a territory and these formed 90% of the probable records, the remainder being on the rare occasions when females were also heard. There were just four confirmed records during the *Atlas* period, all in 1989, when egg shells were found near Ballencrieff Mains (NT47Z), family parties were seen near Gladhouse (NT35C) and Reston (NT86Q) and a dead juvenile was found near Skirling (NT03U).

With 56% of all Quail records occurring in a single year there was some concern that the pattern of records in 1989 might be materially different from that obtained in the other years of the *Atlas* survey. Fortunately the distributional pattern is very similar, the primary difference being in the actual number of records. The map shown opposite therefore represents the composite picture for Quails over all seven of the years of the survey between 1988-94. While it clearly exaggerates the apparent presence of Quails in SE Scotland, the distribution itself is a fairly true representation of areas in which Quails are often present in SE Scotland.

The map shows that Quails were mostly recorded in clusters in areas where arable farming was dominant, despite there being large areas surrounding these clusters where conditions were apparently identical. Gill (1993) found a similar distribution of Quails in the Gowanwhill area of NE Scotland in 1992 where birds clustered in one small part of an area covering several hundred square kilometres. This clustering was attributed to the males strategy of attracting females. Clusters would be formed within a few evenings of arrival, a cluster of calling males being better able to attract females to their vicinity than more scattered birds. Once pairs were formed, the birds dispersed within the general area. However, being polygynous the males continue to call hoping to attract additional females. It is interesting to note that the Gowanhill birds all occurred between 110m-155m altitude, the same altitude range that held the modal peak for birds in SE Scotland, comprising 25% of all records.

There are clusters in typically arable-dominated areas at Aberlady-Drem (NT48&58), south of Dunbar (NT67), Rosebery (NT35), Reston-St. Abbs (NT86&96) and in the Tweed and Teviot drainage around Smailholm-Coldstream (NT63-83) and Morebattle (NT72). The small group of tetrads in the west near Biggar (NT03&04) is an extension of a larger area in Clydesdale comparable in area to that of the middle Tweed (Murray 1991b). While isolated tetrads may seem unimportant, sites such as Clarilaw (NT51J) and west of Broughton (NT03Y) have histories of occupation over several years during the *Atlas* period, usually because the observer reporting the birds lived within the tetrad. In less typical habitat birds were found in rough grazing in the Pentlands in NT16&26.

Comparisons with the *Old Atlas* show a huge increase in the number of occupied squares since then. While much of this increase was undoubtedly due to the events in 1989, numbers have increased in recent years. Just five 10-km squares held Quails in 1968-72. This compares to 37 squares in 1989 and 29 squares in the other years between 1988-94. The wide spread of records outwith the bumper year suggests that Quails either occur more frequently or that they are now better recorded than ever before. While some combination of these explanations is likely, much of the increase is probably attributable to better observer awareness and reporting.

An estimate of the local population is clearly beset by the wild fluctuations in the numbers of Quails reaching Britain each summer. In addition it is almost certain that an appreciable fraction of the number that do arrive are not recorded, the majority of birds reported being found during overnight searches for Quails. The 'normal' numbers of birds reported each year (see graph) has varied between six in 1991 and 40 in 1992. Even if that represents just half of the actual birds actually present in SE Scotland, the population at best will only be in the area 10-60 singing males. How many pairs this represents is not known. In 'Quail-years' such as 1989, this figure may increase to perhaps 250 singing males. **R.D.Murray**

Quail

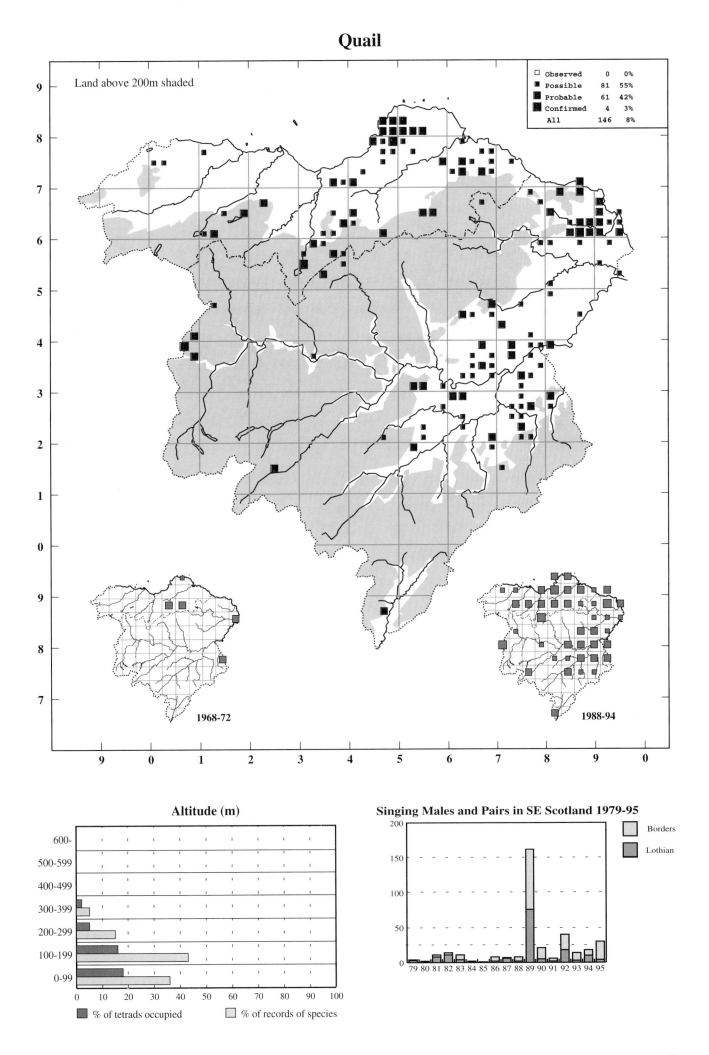

☐ Observed	0	0%
■ Possible	81	55%
■ Probable	61	42%
■ Confirmed	4	3%
All	146	8%

Land above 200m shaded

1968-72

1988-94

Altitude (m)

■ % of tetrads occupied   ☐ % of records of species

Singing Males and Pairs in SE Scotland 1979-95

☐ Borders
■ Lothian

Pheasant
Phasianus colchicus

Introduced to the British countryside at least 1,000 years ago, the Pheasant is so much a part of the British countryside that some find it difficult to believe that Pheasants have their origin in the forests of the Middle East, India and China. Today Britain is populated by a mixture of wild birds that act like their ancestors, feral birds whose population is cosseted by artificial feeding and protection, and gun-fodder, released from breeding pens and about as wild as domestic chickens. Like many gamebirds, Pheasants are polygynous, males attracting and defending a harem of females within the territory, which will include open fields for feeding, and woodland for nesting and sheltering during the day and roosting during the night. Shoots, growing plants and seeds, of both arable crops and woodland plants, along with invertebrates, form the main part of the diet.

Pheasants are amongst the easiest of birds to record, the observers attention being attracted by the loud crowing of displaying males, and the racket made by disturbed birds alarm-calling and wing-whirring as they crash through the trees to make their escape. Probable records were equally shared by registrations of pairs, territorial behaviour and display, while two-thirds of confirmed records were of fledged young. Hen Pheasants, or perhaps their predators, have a habit of dropping intact eggs. Whether intact or eaten, eggs provided about a fifth of confirmed records.

The map shows a very widespread species that occupies most parts of SE Scotland other than the high hills and urban areas. The large gaps in the range correspond to open treeless uplands in the Pentlands (NT15,25&26), Moorfoots (NT34), Lammermuirs (NT55&66), Tweedsmuir Hills (NT01,11,12,13,22&23) and the Cheviots (NT60,70&81), and in the urbanised Edinburgh-Musselburgh area (NT26,27&37). Pheasants penetrate the hills along the valleys where cultivation offers limited feeding opportunites and where plantations and shelterbelts offer cover. The absolute upper limit is around 600m. Below 400m about four-fifths of all tetrads hold Pheasants. At the lowest level the vacant areas are mainly around urbanised regions. Excepting the gap for Edinburgh (NT27), the Pheasant distribution closely resembles that of arable and improved grassland and this impression is supported by the strong correlation seen in the habitat graph where 92% of all tetrads where these habitats are abundant were occupied.

As with other ubiquitous species that breed in virtually every 10-km square, comparison with the *Old Atlas* map yields little information other than the fact there has been insignificant change in the gross features of the Pheasant's local range. Even CBC data on population changes are unhelpful in a species whose numbers may be dominated as much by releases as by any natural factors. However, the CBC has found that numbers have doubled in recent years in areas where releases are important, while 'wild' populations are in decline (*Trends*). Releases are certainly common in SE Scotland, and many plantations on large estates and even small estates operate release pens.

The *New Atlas* abundance map shows that Pheasants are extremely numerous in SE Scotland with a huge area of the highest abundance extending in a broad band from Lauderdale south to Hawick and east down the Tweed and Teviot to Coldstream, with smaller areas on the Berwickshire coast and between Tranent and Dunbar. Other than the gaps indicated on the *Atlas* map opposite the only area with less than moderate numbers is West Lothian where estates are smaller and releases possibly less frequent.

The *New Atlas* quotes average densities of 3.9 territorial males and 7.3 females per km^2 excluding high hills and moors away from poor habitats with 10.3 territorial males per km^2 in areas managed for Pheasants. The number of females and non-territorial males in such areas is determined by the numbers maintained and released, rather than by 'natural' factors. While the numbers released in our area are not known, the shooting interests being reluctant to release figures to the general public, the fact that 3,253 birds were shot on just one Borders estate in 1984 (*Bird Reports*) implies that Bowhill released over 7,000 birds that autumn, the average total being shot each winter running at 45% of the autumn release. With a number of equally big estates and numerous rough shoots it seems likely that as many as 50,000 birds may be released each autumn throughout SE Scotland to supplement the existing numbers.

With little data on the size of releases it is clearly difficult to make even an informed estimate of Pheasant numbers. da Prato (1985) found just 1pr/km^2 in the Tranent cereal growing area while local BBS data from 1994/95 give about 5-7prs/km^2 in 60% of returns. The BBS value would give a local population of 27,000-38,000 pairs, far too low in view of the numbers probably released but possibly close to the numbers of wild and feral birds in the area. The *New Atlas* estimate of the British population, 1,650,000 'pairs', suggests an overall density of 725 pairs/10-km square, or 7.25prs/km^2. However, as a considerable part of the local area has the highest value on the *New Atlas* abundance map, a higher figure of 10prs/km^2 might be more realistic, producing a figure of 65,000-70,000 pairs with substantially bigger numbers each autumn when birds are released. Numbers could then be nearer 200,000 birds, such is the scale of mortality through shooting.   ***R.D.Murray***

Pheasant

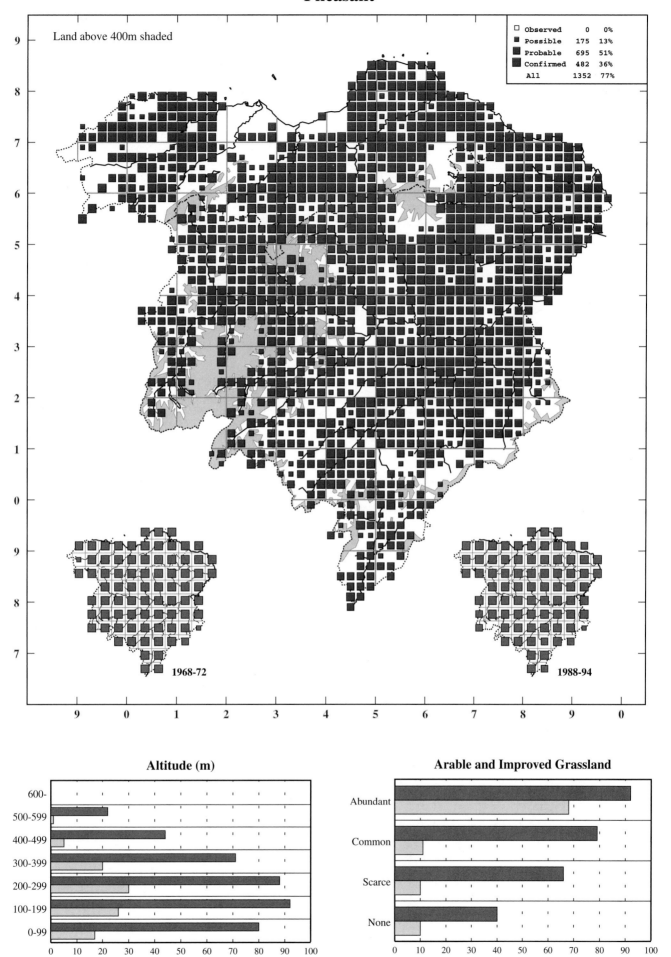

Land above 400m shaded

□ Observed	0	0%
■ Possible	175	13%
■ Probable	695	51%
■ Confirmed	482	36%
All	1352	77%

1968-72

1988-94

Altitude (m)

■ % of tetrads occupied   ■ % of records of species

Arable and Improved Grassland

■ % of tetrads occupied   ■ % of records of species

111

Water Rail
Rallus aquaticus

A denizen of densely-vegetated marshes and reed-beds, the Water Rail is seldom detected as it moves around concealed from casual observation both by the thick cover it lives in and by restricting its main territorial calling to around dusk and dawn. Elongated toes allow it to walk confidently across mud while its slender camouflaged body lets it slip between reed and rush stems with minimal disturbance. The Water Rail is omnivorous eating greenery, seeds, fish, insects and carrion.

Most Water Rails are detected through their calling but, as it is not a familiar bird in SE Scotland, many must have passed unrecorded through observers not recognising the full range of vocalisations; the squeals and grunts, the ticks and trills. However, most possible and probable records were of calling birds, with sightings of birds very rare. Sightings of young are rarer still and occurred in just 15% of Water Rail tetrads, a very low percentage for confirmed records, but hardly surprising in such a furtive species. It is almost certain that Water Rails are very much under-recorded although it is likely that the skeleton of the local range in SE Scotland has been established on the map.

The map shows the scattered nature of the distribution with a definite cluster of sites between Hawick and Selkirk and looser aggregations to the south-west of Edinburgh and east of Kelso. It is immediately apparent that the Lothian sites have a higher rate of confirmed records than elsewhere. This is probably because the Lothian sites are mostly at well-watched localities, while the Selkirk-Hawick sites are rarely visited by anyone, including birders.

The main cluster of Water Rail sites consists of a series of basin mosses situated in grooves carved out by the moving ice sheets during the glaciations. These hollows filled up with water when the ice melted and small lochs were created. Most have since become mosses through vegetation succession. Some retain amounts of open water, such as those at Whitmuirhill Loch (NT42Y) and Branxholme Wester Loch (NT41F), while others, like those at Blackpool Moss and Beanrig Moss (NT52E) and Lilliesleaf Moss (NT52M), are dominated by willows. These mosses are small, most being less than 10 hectares, but most are safe from 'improvements' as drainage would be difficult and in many cases uneconomic. Several have become National Nature Reserves. The four sites east of Kelso are around the lochs at the Hirsel and Hoselaw and in marshy valley bottoms at Linton Bog (NT72X) and Yetholm Marsh (NT82D). In Lothian the sites at Tailend Moss (NT06D), Duddingston, North Berwick Law (NT58M) and Danskine Loch (NT56T) are all situated in basin mosses similar to those in Borders. Bavelaw and Gladhouse are in low-lying areas artificially inundated by reservoirs, the Almond Pools (NT06I) are flooded industrial workings while the Marl Loch at Aberlady is a series of pools dug for conservation purposes.

Water Rails occupy just a fraction of the wetland sites shown on the Ordnance Survey 1:25,000 map. While many of these wetlands might be unsuitable for various reasons, it seems likely that Water Rails could be more widespread than the distribution map shows. *Bird Report* records since 1979 add just another four more sites to the *Atlas* map (See Appendix).

Comparisons with the *Old Atlas* show an apparently huge increase in the number of occupied 10-km squares, rising from six in 1968-72 to 17 in 1988-94. Part of this increase may be related to the length of the survey periods and partly to better knowledge of both the bird and its local distribution since the advent of the *Bird Reports*. Birders know of Water Rail sites and often actively search for the

species. There is also little doubt that previously unknown sites were found by *Atlas* workers, so the extent to which Water Rail numbers have actually increased since 1972 is uncertain. Water Rails bred at least once at Bavelaw and Duddingston prior to the 1960s (*Andrews*) and it seems likely that they may have bred there occasionally more regularly than the records suggest, but have been overlooked. In Borders there is no reason to believe that Water Rails have not bred on the mosses from time immemorial and that the extent of their distribution has only come to light in recent years, rather than there having been any great population explosion. In the face of an apparent decline in the British population (*New Atlas*), the local increase in records is probably almost wholly due to better knowledge of the actual status of Water Rails in SE Scotland.

The Appendix indicates that most records involved just single birds calling. However, survey work when the National Nature Reserve was established in NT52E at Nether Whitlaw, Murder Moss, Beanrig and Blackpool Moss during the 1970s indicated that 10-12 pairs were present across the four sites (C.O. Badenoch *pers. comm.*). Elsewhere Lindean Reservoir (NT42Z) held 3 birds in 1991, while Bavelaw-Threipmuir had 6 pairs in 1995. If all sites held the maximum number of birds recorded in the *Bird Reports* between 1979-96 simultaneously, there might be as many as 50 'pairs' in SE Scotland. This is, however, unlikely and the true number may only be half that total, 25 pairs. It is very likely that many more Water Rails are present and that only a systematic survey could reveal the true picture. As the number of sites is limited, such a survey, equipped with tape lures to reveal the presence of birds, is not too difficult to contemplate.
R.D.Murray

Water Rail

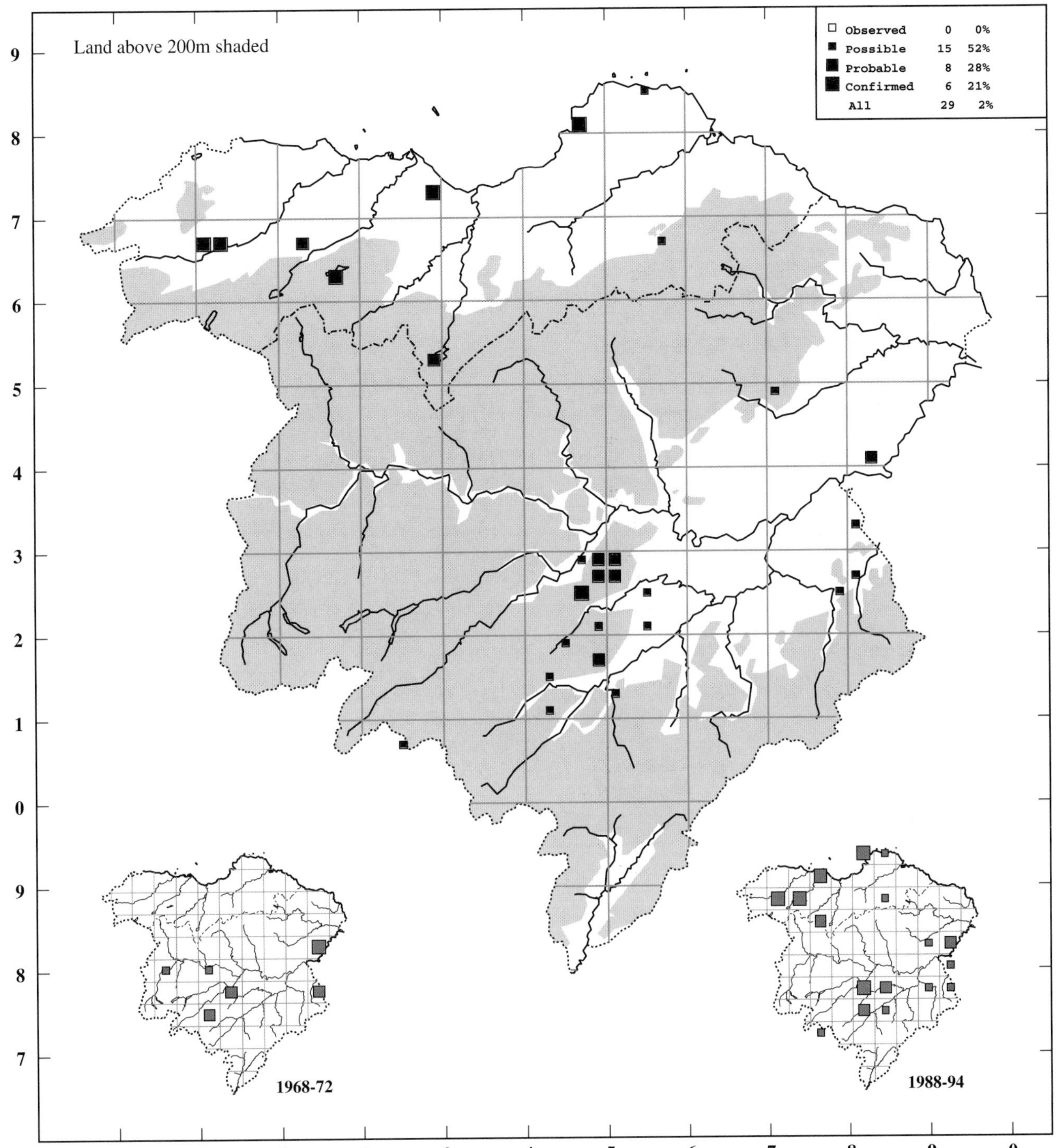

Land above 200m shaded

□	Observed	0	0%
■	Possible	15	52%
■	Probable	8	28%
■	Confirmed	6	21%
	All	29	2%

1968-72

1988-94

113

Dotterel
Charadrius morinellus

Associated with the high tops of the Cairngorms, possessing an extremely confiding nature and having an unusual sex life, the Dotterel is a bird that is irresistibly attractive to birders, a Blue Riband bird. Breeding mostly occurs on mountain summits in the Highlands where female Dotterels actively court a number of males, leaving them with clutches of eggs while they move on to the next male. Indeed some females have actually moved to Norway in the same summer in search of males after laying clutches in Scotland! Prostrate alpine heaths dominated by sedges and mosses on mountain plateaux above 700m are the preferred nesting habitat although areas with a cover of short grasses and dwarf shrubs can be used. Dotterels arrive in Scotland in early May and depart in August and September to winter on the North African steppes.

Living on remote summit plateaux, Dotterel are not found in localities often visited by birders and consequently there is only a handful of breeding records from SE Scotland. It is possible that they are under-recorded. A scatter of *Atlas* records occurred between the coast and the fringes of the Pentlands, Moorfoots and Lammermuirs which were where parties of Dotterels (maximum 18 at Eweford (NT67T) in May 1993) stopped off to feed and even display, before resuming their journey north. The records include two reports of birds just passing over, astute observers noting their calls.

The high tops of the Southern Uplands, and even the summits of the Lammermuirs, are also used as staging posts. The hill shepherds say they are virtually annual, small trips of up to eight birds arriving during the first ten days of May, although up to 20 were reported in the 1970s. Although most birds act in an identical manner to those lower down, hill top records are much more regular and they are, of course, on potential breeding habitat which resembles that in the Highlands. Accordingly these records have been assigned as possible

and probable records, the latter for birds in pairs and displaying. In a good year, such as 1989, at least six pairs were located on four different summits in May.

Some birds have remained to breed and Dotterels have nested on at least two occasions in recent years, always on classic ground above 750m. A nest was found by hill-walkers in 1975. Unfortunately it was found to have been deserted after a spell of bad weather two weeks later. In 1989, during the *Atlas* period, another nest was located. While it was noted that one egg had gone missing, the later fate of the nest is not known and it may have failed.

The Southern Uplands are clearly just on the margin of the Dotterel's range and in periods when the British population is high, as it appears to have been in the late 1980s, breeding is more likely to take place. However, the high summits are not often visited by birders and it is possible that there are more occasions when Dotterels attempt to nest than have come to light.   ***R.D.Murray***

Corncrake
Crex crex

The rasping call of the Corncrake, sounding exactly like its scientific name, repeated endlessly throughout the night, was once a familar sound of the British countryside. Rarely seen, but more often heard, Corncrakes have become extinct across much of the British mainland, the outer isles and western Ireland holding the now tiny remnant of what may once have been a large population.

The catastrophic decline in range and numbers of the Corncrake is well known. On summer evenings a century ago Corncrakes would be heard from every hayfield. Mechanisation speeded up haycutting so that adults and chicks were unable to evade the cutting blades. The later move to the use of silage, rather than hay, for feeding stock made matters worse as silage is cut well before Corncrakes are able to hatch their young, let alone rear them. The demise of working horses also meant that there was less need for hay crops. Increased specialisation of agriculture has resulted in more arable cropping in the lowlands and less mixed cropping in uplands, and firmly closed the door on potential Corncrake habitat.

The species was all but extinct as a breeder in Lothian by the mid-1950s and in the Borders just ten years later. This pattern has been repeated throughout its European range and despite large numbers in Russia, the ongoing westernisation of agriculture means that the Corncrake is still a species of global conservation concern. Intensive research by the RSPB seems to have suggested the measures necessary to prevent the extinction of the species in Britain.

Corncrakes are rarely seen but males give their presence away by the far-carrying territorial calls. Not surprisingly there were no instances of proved breeding in the *Atlas*. Half of the small number of records were treated as probable, typically single males calling in one site for more than a week. Whether these isolated individuals were able to attract a mate from Britain's tiny population is debatable. Elsewhere in Scotland, however, there have been cases of isolated proved breeding, so this potentiality should not be written off. As the territorial calls are most persistent at night it is quite possible that some further birds were missed. A special RSPB survey in 1993 received considerable publicity and a few records, two of which were confirmed as Corncrakes, were elicited from the public.

Corncrake

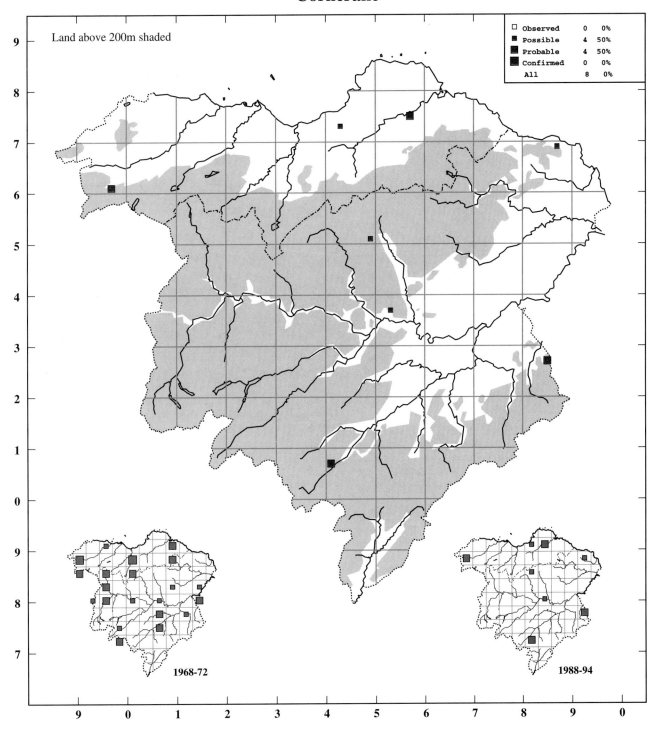

Land above 200m shaded

□ Observed	0	0%
■ Possible	4	50%
▣ Probable	4	50%
▤ Confirmed	0	0%
All	8	0%

1968-72

1988-94

Records in the *Atlas* period came from just eight 10-km squares, compared to 21 in the *Old Atlas*. With no proved breeding and probable breeding in just four squares in 1988-94, compared to two squares with confirmed breeding and eleven with probable breeding in 1968-72, the decline is clear, particularly given the longer period of the current survey compared to the *Old Atlas*. Two individual squares were occupied during both periods but this may have just been a chance event as males appear to turn up at random wherever there may be suitable habitat. However, a territorial male reported by a farmer at Teviothead (NT40) in 1993, and later confirmed, had been recorded by the farmer the previous year. While chance may have thrown up 10-km squares occupied in both *Atlas* periods, the possibility of different males appearing in the same tetrad in consecutive years is very slim. As birds often only return to a site where they have been successful in previous years, it hints that

successful breeding could have taken place at Teviothead in 1992.

Even when the chance of birds being overlooked is taken into account it is hard to believe that any Corncrakes have bred in SE Scotland in recent decades. There is certainly no convincing evidence to indicate that this may have occurred. At best, in a good summer, less than a handful of birds might be present, while in poor summers there will be none. While this view may be pessimistic there is little doubt that more birds have turned up in SE Scotland in the 1990s than were seen in the whole of the 1970s and 1980s combined. This may be related to the partial recovery of the Scottish population on the Hebrides. If the recovery continues there is every chance that summering birds may become more frequent and that the call of the Corncrake may once more become a sound heard regularly in the countryside of the area.   *P.R.Gordon*

115

Moorhen
Gallinula chloropus

Moorhens are amongst the most adaptable of waterfowl, at home on waters from the largest lakes to tiny ditches and drains. They inhabit eutrophic still waters but can take freely to the slower flowing canals, rivers and streams. Fast-flowing water in hilly country is avoided, as are deep upland lochs and reservoirs. Some cover is needed for a nest-site and for roosting but in some sites a clump of rushes can suffice. A study on the Water of Leith (Gardner *et al.* 1984) showed areas of river with a minimal gradient, a gentle current and emergent or overhanging vegetation were preferred. Moorhens are omnivorous, eating a wide range of plants and invertebrates. They maintain a territory all year although some may move downhill from higher areas in winter.

Moorhens are easy to record. Even at sites with dense cover or with shy individuals, presence could be registered by alarm calls. Young Moorhens can be conspicuous and retain the brown juvenile plumage for some months, so young birds comprised 70% of all confirmed reports.

The Moorhen prefers lower altitudes and despite the 'moor' element in its name (the name is derived from 'Mere-hen'), all moorland is avoided and birds are mostly found above 300m only on the higher Ettrick Forest lochs. While the range is controlled by the distribution of water features, birds are missing on parts of certain rivers. They occur fairly continuously along the lower Water of Leith (NT27), lower Esk (NT36&37), Tyne (NT57) and Whiteadder (NT85). However, along the middle Water of Leith (NT16), the middle Tweed above the Ettrick (NT23,33&43), the Teviot between Hawick and Ancrum (NT51), the Liddle (NY48,59) and the Blackadder (NT74) there are many gaps. Some of these rivers have dense cover where finding birds might have been difficult but birds are reported from other streams where cover is equally dense.

Predation may be important. The Water of Leith survey (Gardner *et al.* 1984) showed a drop from 6-8 territories in 1978 to none in 1983 after the arrival of Mink. Declines noted along the Almond and Tyne (*LBR* 1987), Gladhouse Reservoir (*LBR* 1989 & 1992) and at Lindean (A.Buckham *pers.comm.*) are also associated with Mink. While there is no evidence of Mink having a pronounced effect on national distribution and numbers (*New Atlas*), local effects may present themselves by these vacant areas of rivers. Intensive farming with heavy grazing of river banks and unsympathetic bank management may also be important. The lack of nest-sites and cover in 'over-tidy' farmland may preclude Moorhens. In contrast, urban habitats next to rivers do not inhibit Moorhens, as in the lower Esk and Water of Leith.

There is a hint of a range contraction in the 10km-square maps since 1968-72, with birds now missing from seven 10-km squares and very scarce in others. The *New Atlas* noted such contractions at the margins of the range on a national basis and it is noticeable that most of these are on the edges of high ground, particularly in the Highlands, Southern Uplands and Northumberland. Land drainage is mentioned as a possible explanation in some areas but this would be unlikely in areas like Liddesdale and the Upper Tweed where there is an abundance of undrained marshy ground near rivers.

Moorhens were reported from 574 tetrads compared to 290 sites in the *Bird Reports* between 1979-1995. The disparity shows that Moorhen are under-recorded in the *Bird Reports* although some sites, like the Union Canal and Tweed, are linear and would fall into more than one tetrad. Moorhens were also reported from 52 sites in Lothian in the 1986 waterfowl breeding census (Brown 1987), a large contrast to the 15-25 sites reported annually in the species accounts. While both presence and numbers are regularly reported from particular waters in SE Scotland, the many small ponds, rivers and ditches where Moorhens breed pass unreported or will only be encountered during the type of systematic search engendered by the *Atlas*.

50% of sites in Lothian and 80% of sites in Borders have only ever had a single pair reported. Few sites hold large numbers and Bavelaw (*c.*13 pairs 1988-95), Gladhouse (ten pairs), Linlithgow (ten pairs) and Bemersyde (ten pairs) stand out as does the Union Canal where 24 territories were counted along 5km of the canal. The 290 *Bird Reports* sites suggest a breeding population of *c.*200 pairs in Lothian and *c.*350 pairs in Borders with min-max figures of 468-701 pairs in total. As the sites with good populations tend to be more regularly included in the *Bird Reports*, and as most sites only held single pairs, the disparity between the 290 reported sites and the 573 tetrad registrations probably refers mainly to single pairs. This produces an additional *c.*370 pairs across the whole area and brings the total to about 900 pairs.

The *New Atlas* abundance map shows only low to moderate numbers in SE Scotland. However, there is a huge disparity between the local density of 14 pairs per occupied 10-km square, mostly based on counts, and the estimated national density of 118 pairs per occupied 10-km square probably based on CBC densities of 3.8 pairs/km^2. While local densities are almost certainly low compared to further south, it is hardly credible that *average* British Moorhen densities are 10 times greater than that seen in SE Scotland.

Estimates of breeding success taken from 448 broods between 1984 and 1995 in the Borders averaged 2.55 young per brood within a range of 1.86-3.53. Unfortunately there are no published British figures for Moorhen broods to compare this with (*BWP*).

R.D.Murray

Moorhen

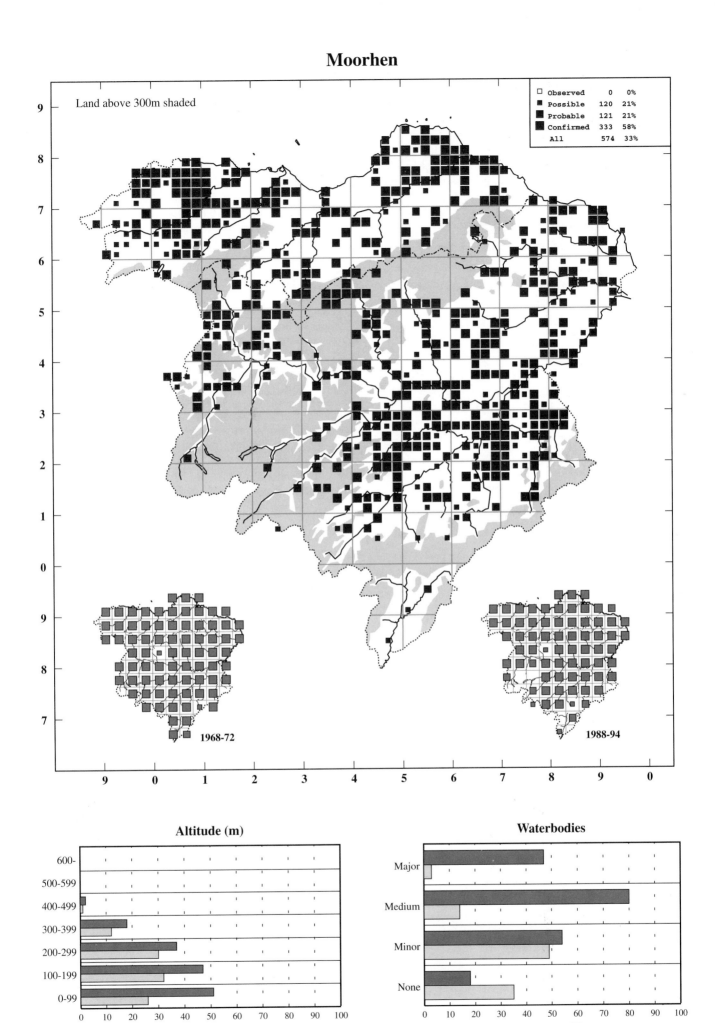

Land above 300m shaded

	Observed	0	0%
	Possible	120	21%
	Probable	121	21%
	Confirmed	333	58%
	All	574	33%

1968-72

1988-94

Altitude (m)

600-
500-599
400-499
300-399
200-299
100-199
0-99

█ % of tetrads occupied   ▢ % of records of species

Waterbodies

Major
Medium
Minor
None

█ % of tetrads occupied   ▢ % of records of species

Coot
Fulica atra

As the tamest and most approachable of the rail family, the Coot is a widespread and familiar inhabitant of still waters in Britain. Submerged vegetation provides both plant and invertebrate food for Coots and such vegetation flourishes best in shallow, eutrophic waters at low altitudes. Upland sites are occupied, provided they have submerged plants, but the deeper, steep-sided upland reservoirs are shunned.

Being fairly conspicuous birds, Coots were both easy to survey and to prove breeding. Three-quarters of all records were of confirmed breeding which when broken down were mostly sightings of young (60%) and occupied nests (20%).

The size of the water is important to Coots with medium to large sized waterbodies much preferred . Almost all of the smallest ponds are unoccupied. Altitude is less important (see graph), a broad range of altitudes being occupied, presumably wherever there are suitable waters. Coots occupy most waters in the area, except for the unvegetated, stony, steep-sided reservoirs with constant changes in water level like Bonaly (NT26D) and West Water (NT15B) in the Pentlands, and Talla and Fruid in the Tweedsmuir Hills. In contrast the small reservoirs on the northern Lammermuirs such as Stobshiel (NT56B) and Whiteadder have all held Coots, although numbers are small and subject to fluctuations.

The differences in the Coot and Moorhen maps and between the numbers of sites from which the two species are recorded in the *Bird Reports* (250 for Moorhen and 200 for Coot) may be due to Coots avoiding small waters. Moorhens can use small waters, such as ditches, marshes and overgrown farm ponds that may be too small for Coots.

The map shows some patchiness in the distribution across SE Scotland, with clusters in West Lothian, Edinburgh and the Ettrick Forest. In West Lothian the sites are linked by the Union Canal which holds good numbers of birds, the Winchburgh to Linlithgow stretch holding 21 pairs in 1990. Coots occur on all the Edinburgh lochs and along the eastern end of the Union Canal, demonstrating their tolerance of human activity. Even at higher altitudes Coots are virtually ubiquitous, occupying all the Ettrick

Forest lochs with the exception of Windylaw Loch (NT31S) and the tiny Goose and Back Lochs (NT31M) which may be too thickly vegetated.

Rivers are used along the Tweed in NT83&84 and along the Teviot in NT62,72&73. Occupancy can be erratic. The Teviot held ten territories between Nisbet and Kelso in summer 1992. A part of this stretch, between Nisbet and Sunlaws, which held five pairs in 1992 only had one pair in 1994. Similarly the Tweed around Fireburnmill (NT83E) held ten pairs in 1992, but only four in 1994. These variations are related to changes in river levels. 1992 was very dry, presenting Coots with slow moving water overgrown with mats of Water Crowfoot which provided abundant feeding. The exceptionally large flood in May 1993 largely destroyed the nests of all breeding waterfowl and consequently few birds were found in 1994, an average-to-dry summer.

The 10-km maps show some contraction on the uphill margins of the range in Tweeddale since the *Old Atlas*. Coots stopped breeding in NT11&12 (Fruid), NT22 (St. Mary's/Lowes) and NT33 (Glen House) by the late-1970s, with the last reports of breeding from NT13 (Rachan) in 1987, NT23 (Hallmanor) in 1988 and NT14 (Mount Bog and Garvald) in 1989. The last successful breeding in NT24 (Portmore) was in 1986. This site suffers from serious disturbance from the commercial fishery. This withdrawal, which may also have affected the Moorhen's distribution, may also be seen in Northumberland and around the eastern edge of both the Highlands and Welsh hills (*New Atlas*). The contraction may involve the loss of just 1-2 pairs in each square. The additional squares occupied in the 1988-94 period often hold just single sites in squares adjacent to those already occupied. These may possibly have been overlooked in the *Old Atlas*.

Coots were recorded from 200 sites in the *Bird Reports* between 1979 and 1995, *c.*150 in Borders and *c.*50 in Lothian. The difference between the number of these sites and the 240 tetrads is mostly due to the difference between multi-tetrad sites and multi-site tetrads, the former slightly outweighing the latter.

Some lochs may hold more non-breeding birds than nesting birds. The status of these birds is obscure but *BWP* hints that young birds may have to wait some years before managing to hold a breeding, as opposed to a feeding, territory. Counts must be treated as dealing with a potential breeding population rather than the number of birds that actually breed. The waters that hold the largest numbers of Coots, between 15-27 pairs, such as the Hirsel, Hoselaw, Williestruther (NT41V), Wooden (NT72C) and Yetholm Loch in Borders and Bavelaw, Duddingston, Gladhouse and Linlithgow in Lothian, are the most subject to these high ratios of non-breeders. Broods counted indicate a rather variable rate of success with every pair breeding some years (even producing double-broods) while in other years the majority of birds fail. The data from casual sightings of some 933 broods in Borders between 1984-95 show a mean of 2.95 young/brood within a range of between 2.65 and 4.06.

The *Bird Reports* provide min-max figures of between 361 and 867 pairs, if every water was occupied in every year between 1979-1995. The mean is about 600 pairs, *c.*200 pairs in Lothian and *c.*400 in Borders. Details of about 300 pairs appear annually in the *Bird Reports*, 200-250 pairs at *c.*50 sites in Borders with 40-90 pairs at *c.*25 sites in Lothian. **R.D.Murray**

Coot

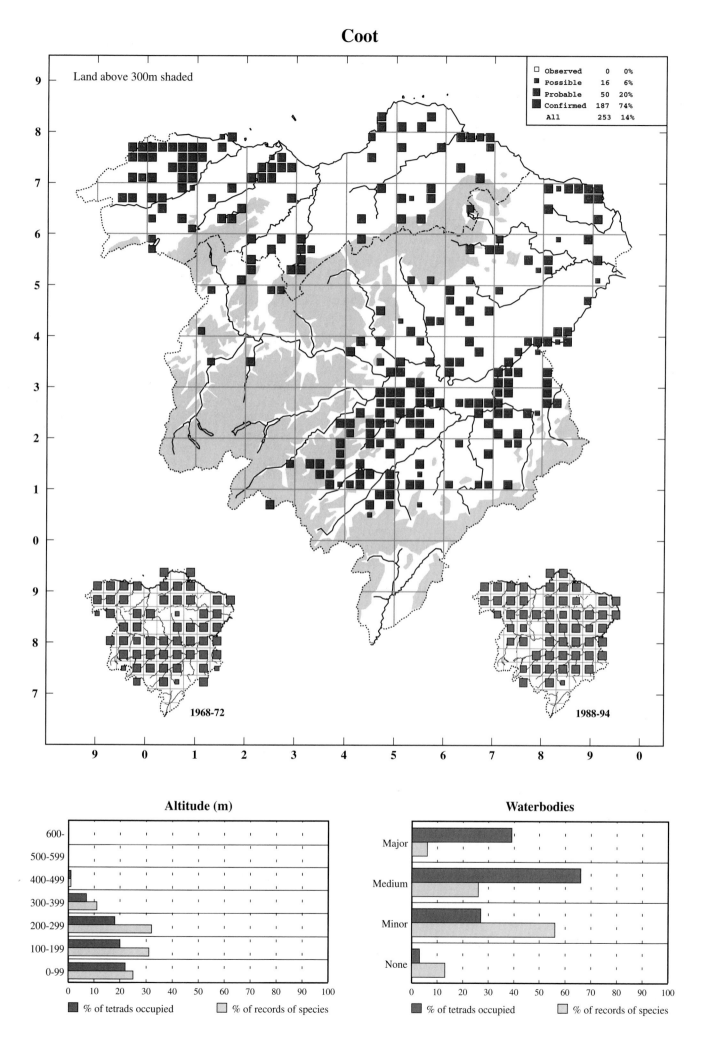

□ Observed	0	0%
Possible	16	6%
Probable	50	20%
Confirmed	187	74%
All	253	14%

Land above 300m shaded

1968-72

1988-94

Altitude (m)

■ % of tetrads occupied   □ % of records of species

Waterbodies

■ % of tetrads occupied   □ % of records of species

Oystercatcher
Haematopus ostralegus

The noisy piping calls and conspicuous display flights of the Oystercatcher proclaim spring along the coasts, valleys and fields of northern Britain. Originally limited in the breeding season to coastal shingle, dunes and rocky shores, with some nesting in stony sections of broad rivers, this pied wader began to spread inland in Scotland in the 19th century so that it now also nests in open agricultural land, especially arable crops. It has thus become a familiar species throughout Scotland. On the coast Oystercatchers feed mainly on marine molluscs and worms, but inland the food is mainly earthworms and fly larvae.

As it is so conspicuous the Oystercatcher was easy to find in SE Scotland and pairs were obvious in the early part of the breeding season as they stood together in fields or by rivers, or flew over in noisy piping parties. Half of the records were of probable breeding, based on pairs, agitated birds, or display. About a third were confirmed breeding, mainly records of chicks or indications of occupied nests. The actual nests are not always easy to find. During incubation, the incubating bird slips off the nest quietly and runs some distance as an observer approaches, and eggs can be very hard to locate in stonebeds by rivers or amongst crops. Soon after the chicks hatch they leave the shallow nest scrape and hide next to small plants or stones when the parents call the alarm. The behaviour of the adults then is quite different from earlier as they fly around the intruder calling loudly, distracting attention away from the crouching chicks.

The map is likely to accurately reflect the distribution of the Oystercatcher in SE Scotland. It is widely distributed, occurring in all but a few marginal 10-km squares. Many of the concentrations can be traced to the river valleys, notably the lower Tweed and the haughs south from here to the Teviot and in the Kale valley (centred on NT72 which has Oystercatchers in every tetrad), the watershed between the North Esk and the Lyne (NT15&25), the Tweed above Broughton and the area near Biggar (mainly NT02&03), and the upper Almond in West Lothian (NS96&NT06). With the exception of the upper Tweed, all of these areas are dominated by arable agriculture on broad flat haughlands close to rivers. The populations in NT03 near Biggar are part of the large Clyde Haughs area which has one of the highest densities of inland nesting waders (A.D. Wood *pers. comm.*) and shows on the *New Atlas* abundance map as one of the areas of highest Oystercatcher abundance in Britain.

The species is absent from only a few areas, the built up areas of Edinburgh and Midlothian precluding nesting, as do the large plantations of Craik (NT30&31) and Wauchope (NT50&60). The slopes and tops of the higher hills do not hold Oystercatchers, 90% of all records coming from below 400m, although they do occur deep into the hills if there are well grazed fields on flatter land. There are some agricultural areas where the species is scarce, such as east of Hawick (NT51), and parts of the Merse (NT84&95) and East Lothian (NT57&67). While birds may have been overlooked in NT51, these parts of the Merse and East Lothian may be too intensively devoted to cereals and other crops, with too few interspersed grass fields to provide feeding areas for Oystercatchers.

There are few nesting Oystercatchers on the coast, most occurring in East Lothian east of Aberlady, with a concentration around Tyninghame where protection is offered. They nest on several of the islands, but not the steeper sloping ones such as Craigleith and the Bass Rock. The records classified as observed refer mostly to pre- or post-breeding flocks, or non-breeding birds. Most of these are near the coast and in habitats unsuitable for breeding in Edinburgh and the Musselburgh area due to disturbance.

The graphs show a strong relationship with rivers, with 80% of large rivers holding Oystercatchers. Most birds are found where the more numerous medium-sized and small rivers occur, nesting mainly in arable fields close to the water. With such catholic tastes in nesting habitats, they occur equally in all altitudes up to 400m, with fewer above that level. There are signs of range expansion and consolidation since the *Old Atlas*, with new 10-km squares occupied close to Edinburgh, but the number of nesting pairs in these areas is small. However, the other new 10-km squares now have an average of 15 occupied tetrads. If such an increase has occurred here then a large increase across the whole area since the early 1970s is suggested. *Andrews* stated that the increase in Lothian started in the 1950s and accelerated in the 1960-70s. In Borders, where nesting in the Merse was first noted in the 1930s, large scale increases have occurred since 1970 (R.D. Murray *pers. comm.*).

Being a conspicuous species associated with rivers, there have been some numerical studies in SE Scotland. Oystercatchers are well represented on the Borders WBS plots, with average densities of 2.25 prs/km on the Gala Water (1991-94), and 0.66 prs/km on the Tweed at Melrose, over six of the *Atlas* years. The Borders river census in 1987 counted 1,054 birds in March and 118 territories in June/July, which equates to just 0.35 prs/km (*Bird Reports*). Because Oystercatchers occur in fields away from the river, these densities do not represent the actual numbers. There are no statistics for the areas with the highest densities locally, but densities of 1.7prs/ km^2 were recorded in the Eddleston valley in 1996 (R.D. Murray *pers. comm.*). O'Brien (1996), reporting on the survey of waders breeding in lowland Scotland, based on sample sites, put the average density of Oystercatchers in areas where they occur at 1.9 prs/km^2, with a maximum of 13 prs/km^2. Personal observations on the Gala Water suggest a density of 3prs/km^2 close to the river, including all habitats. With SE Scotland showing medium to high abundance of Oystercatchers (*New Atlas*), a density of 2.0 prs/km^2 for all tetrads with at least probable breeding is assumed. Adding one pair per tetrad with possible breeding gives a local population estimate of around 7,000 pairs. This total fits well alongside the recent population estimate for Scotland of 82,493 (O'Brien 1996). The British total in the *New Atlas* (33,000-43,000) now seems woefully inadequate.

M.Holling

Oystercatcher

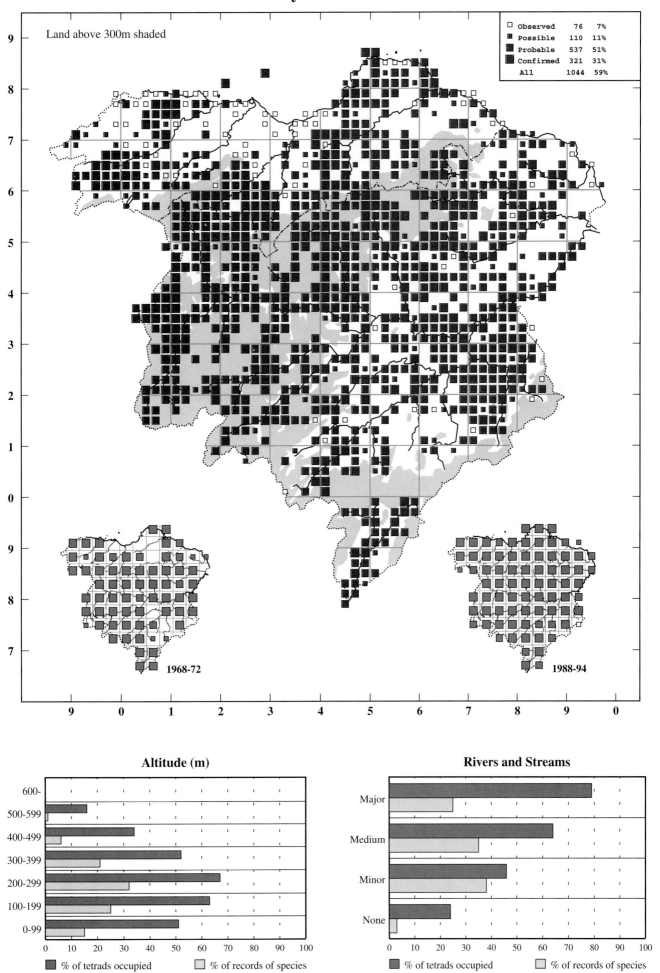

Ringed Plover
Charadrius hiaticula

Familiar to most people as a bird of sandy beaches, the Ringed Plover nests sparingly on the shorelines of much of Britain, both on coasts and along rivers, lakes and reservoirs. The broad bands of black-and-white and the countershaded body gives the Ringed Plover the ability to disappear into the confusing background of sand and shingle to brood its equally-well camouflaged eggs.

While being well camouflaged, their innate nervousness can give them away as the adults call when nesting territories are approached. The adult often moves quickly off the nest, long before an observer gets near, calling quietly. The call is quite diagnostic and a quick search often quickly reveals the presence of birds. Probable records were mainly of pairs seen in suitable habitat. Half of the confirmed records were of hatched young with the remainder equally divided between nests with eggs and adults engaged in distraction display.

Coastal birds occur along the East Lothian coast from Cockenzie (NT47I) into Berwickshire at Redheugh (NT87A) and the sandy bays interspersed by low rocky headlands offer many nesting opportunities. However, the beaches at North Berwick and Dunbar are rendered useless by human disturbance. Further west the coast is either mostly muddy or too heavily urbanised although even in these areas Ringed Plovers have been successful at Leith Docks (NT27T) and Musselburgh Lagoons (NT37L) in sites sufficiently undisturbed to encourage birds to breed. To the east the cliff coast of Berwickshire eventually runs out of beaches other than at the Linkim shore (NT96H). A few pairs were found on Inchkeith (NT28W) in 1994 and breeding occurred on Fidra (NT58D) earlier in the 1980s.

The inland sites were mostly on river shingles, the banks of large lochs and reservoirs and in industrial settings. River shingles were used on the Tweed between Kelso and Norham (NT73,83,84) and at Hopecarton (NT13F). Lochs and reservoirs were used at Cobbinshaw and Crosswood (NT05); West Water, Baddinsgill and North Esk (NT15); and Talla, Fruid, Megget, Loch of the Lowes and St. Mary's Loch. Industrial sites include: active and disused sandpits at Leadburn, Shiphorns and Cowieslinn (NT24&25) and Roslin and Bilston (NT26); a shale bing at Polkemmet (NS96G); an open-cast mine pool at Whitburn (NS96M); and a demolished factory at Bathgate (NS96). Breeding has also occurred on a golf course at Bathgate (NS96) and on farmland at Gladhouse (NT25).

Comparison with the *Old Atlas* shows losses and gains in local 10-km squares, hardly surprising in a species that often nests on ephemeral habitats. Eight squares show losses, two of which may have been in a neighbouring recording area. Five of the losses are from inland river sites on the upper Tweed (NT01&02), Ettrick (NT31) and Kale (NT71&72) where there have been no records of birds during the period of the *Bird Reports*. These losses have been more than balanced by gains in a number of inland 10-km squares where breeding may, at best, be transitory (NT36,42,56&66), possibly like some of the lost sites. More important and perhaps more permanent gains have been made in the industrial sites in West Lothian (NS96&NT06) and north Peeblesshire (NT25), on river sites on the lower Tweed (NT83), on Inchkeith (NT28) and on the Pentland reservoirs (NT16).

The *New Atlas* abundance map is understandably patchy but the sites at Aberlady, Tyninghame and Musselburgh stand out as having high numbers, with the Pentland Reservoirs having moderate numbers. Ringed Plovers were surveyed nationally by the BTO in 1973/74 and again in 1984. Coverage was fairly complete in both periods for Lothian (Brown & Brown 1985) but poor for Borders. The 90 pairs found in Lothian in 1973/74 had risen to 113 pairs by 1984, 90% of them coastal. 22 pairs were recorded in Borders in 1984. 78% of the Lothian coastal birds bred on beaches, mostly where there was a mix of sand and shingle. Brown and Brown thought that disturbance was a major restriction to breeding along the coast and that a much larger population might be maintained but for disturbance. Aberlady and Tyninghame, which offered protection, held 60 pairs, just over half of the Lothian population. Inland sites could suffer from disturbance from bank fishermen at reservoirs while industrial sites suffered a lack of environmental stability.

The Aberlady population has dropped since the early 1980s from 27-36 pairs to just 6-10 pairs between 1988-94. The fate of the Tyninghame population is not known but numbers reported from there may have fallen in a similar manner *(Bird Reports)*. The numbers at Musselburgh have dropped due to changes in the land-use of the lagoons.

The map suggests that the coastal population has maintained its range, if not its numbers, since 1984. Inland breeding, particularly in West Lothian, on the Pentland and Tweedsmuir reservoirs and along the lower Tweed have definitely increased. A mean of all counts on the map suggests *c.*98 pairs during the 1988-94 period, 66 in Lothian and 32 in Borders. A full-scale survey, which is urgently needed, may increase this number to between 115-150 pairs, probably a slight decline from the less than complete total of 135 pairs counted in 1984. At a likely 125 pairs, SE Scotland holds just 1.5% of the British population.   ***R.D.Murray***

Ringed Plover

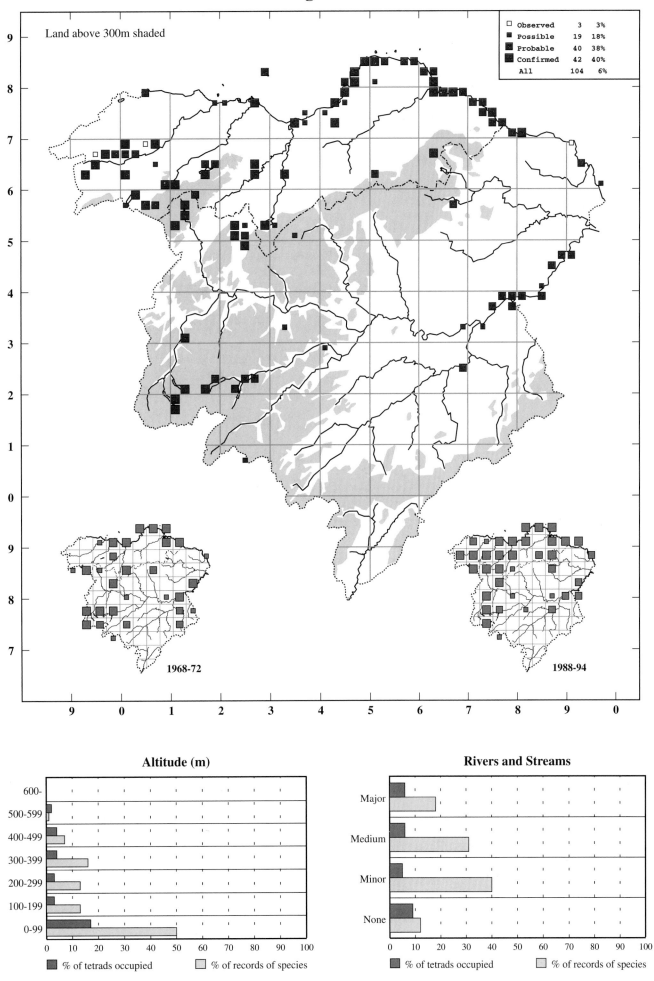

Land above 300m shaded

☐ Observed	3	3%
■ Possible	19	18%
■ Probable	40	38%
■ Confirmed	42	40%
All	104	6%

1968-72

1988-94

Altitude (m)

■ % of tetrads occupied   ☐ % of records of species

Rivers and Streams

■ % of tetrads occupied   ☐ % of records of species

Golden Plover
Pluvialis apricaria

The sound of the plaintive and musical calls of the Golden Plover tell the observer he has arrived on high, wild, open country, clad with heather, cotton grass, moss or sedges. For nesting, Golden Plovers prefer vegetation of about 15cm height or less, so that moors managed for Red Grouse with heather re-growing in patches after burning are favoured, and small ground invertebrates for food are more easily seen. In SE Scotland the local breeding population starts to appear on the hills from February or March, often with big snow patches still present. Later, in April, flocks of the blacker-fronted "*altifrons*" form can be seen halting here during their migration further north.

In the *Atlas* fieldwork "Goldies" were usually detected by birds first calling and then seen on some low rise in their territory. Hatching commences in May and June, after which birds are much more likely to be sight-recorded (Yalden & Yalden 1991). This is when most of the *Atlas* work on higher ground was done and so Golden Plovers in SE Scotland are probably well recorded by the survey. Nearly half of all registrations were of probable breeding; anxious birds, pairs seen, or territory. A third of tetrads had confirmed breeding, almost half of this due to injury-feigning or distraction behaviour, with young seen being the next most frequent evidence. Records of possible breeding were few and mainly around the periphery and slightly below the main breeding moors. These may involve birds which had not gained suitable territories, or were waiting to breed later when failed or early breeders may vacate territories (Parr 1979, Ratcliffe 1990). The few observed records were mostly on the coast or low ground and were probably birds still on passage.

The map and graphs show the Golden Plover distribution to be clearly associated with two factors; high ground and heather. About half of all tetrads above 400m have Golden Plovers. At 300-400m a quarter of tetrads have Golden Plovers, but more Golden Plovers occur at this level than at any other, as higher land is scarcer. The map of heather distribution shows a great similarity to the Golden Plover map, though the bird is actually using only two thirds of tetrads with extensive heather. The second graph shows that 55% of Golden Plovers occur in tetrads with abundant heather, but they may also be using other vegetation in these tetrads, and the graph shows that significant numbers live where heather is scarce or absent.

In the south-western and northern Lammermuir Hills (NT55&66) the Golden Plover is surprisingly not present in all of the open, good quality moors, perhaps due to deep heather, or perhaps because these moors are drier due to lower rainfall (see rainfall map). In the Broughton Heights (NT13,14), the western, southern and eastern fringes of the Moorfoots (NT24,33,44), and the mid and northern Pentlands, there is extensive heather without Golden Plovers. Steep gradients could be a reason for this, and also human disturbance in the Pentlands. In the high hills round the Manor Water catchment (NT12,13,22,23) Golden Plovers are on the more level exposed tops, but not on the steeper sides even where more heather survives the heavy grazing. Unusually for SE Scotland, in an area south of the Lammermuirs (NT65,74.75) good heather extends, below 300m altitude, and Golden Plovers inhabit this. In the southern hills around Roan Fell (NY48,49) Golden Plovers are better spread than the heather map would predict, where a cushion-like mix of cotton-grass, cloudberry and some heather clothes the hills. Likewise on the high hills near Hart Fell (NT01,11) there are Golden Plovers with little heather, on short montane sedge-grass-moss vegetation. The Roan Fell and Hart Fell hills are in the highest rainfall areas of SE Scotland.

Comparison of the two 10-km maps reveals a worrying trend of range contraction. The appearance of three newly occupied squares in the north is more apparent than real, involving just four tetrads altogether, with no confirmed breeding. This is outweighed by the loss of seven squares elsewhere. There is no doubt at all that afforestation of formerly suitable habitat can account for most or all of these losses; in the Cheviots, Wauchope, Craik, Coulter Fell, Broughton Heights, and Monynut Edge. The *New Atlas* change map shows a great preponderance of losses in SE Scotland closely agreeing with the present map. Further in the past, overgrazing, resulting in loss of heather to grass, must have caused losses of Golden Plover habitat on the border hills and those around the sources of the Tweed, Yarrow and Ettrick.

The diminished Golden Plover range in SE Scotland sadly fits a similar picture elsewhere. Golden Plovers have declined in Britain and Europe due to afforestation, conversion of moors to grass, and reduction of rotational burning for Red Grouse (Ratcliffe 1976, *Trends*). Breeding success on grassy moors is lower than on heather or bog (Crick 1993). Frequent hill walkers can affect Golden Plover distribution (Yalden & Yalden 1989) and this is probably significant in the Pentlands, and perhaps in the hills around Peebles and the Lammermuirs. Predation of nests by crows and foxes is greater on moors in a zone extending out from plantation edges (Ratcliffe 1990), and winter mortality could be another factor in the national decline (*New Atlas*, Yalden & Pearce-Higgins 1997).

Densities of breeding Golden Plovers in Britain are typically 5-8prs/km^2 on good moors, but range down to below 1.0prs/km^2 in N, W and S Scotland (Ratcliffe 1990, *New Atlas*). One of the highest British densities of 10prs/km^2 was recorded on part of the Moorfoots with rotational heather burning (Campbell 1978), and the *New Atlas* abundance map shows high Golden Plover numbers in SE Scotland only in a small part of the Moorfoots and a tiny spot on Roan Fell. High densities are probably unusual for SE Scotland. Density estimates were made in the *Atlas* fieldwork in three areas based on linear transects in June by this author giving 2.0prs/km^2 on Broad Law-Dollar Law (NT12), 2.5prs/km^2 on Wedder Lairs (NT55) – both on short montane sedge-grass-heather, and 1.2prs/km^2 on Cooms Fell-Watch Hill (NY48,49) on cotton grass-heather moor. These accord well with results of NCC surveys of ten moorland plots in and near SE Scotland giving a mean of 2.2 (range 0.8-5.2) prs/km^2 (Easterbee & Pitkin 1984). JNCC (*in litt.*) found similar results in 1990 around Coulter Fell.

Using a value of 2prs/km^2 for all tetrads with confirmed and probable breeding, and none for those with possible, produces a population estimate for SE Scotland of 1,600 pairs, four fifths in Borders and one fifth in Lothian. This forms a notable 7% of the British total, which dropped from 29,400 pairs in 1968-72 to 22,600 pairs in 1988-91(*New Atlas*). **H.E.M.Dott**

Golden Plover

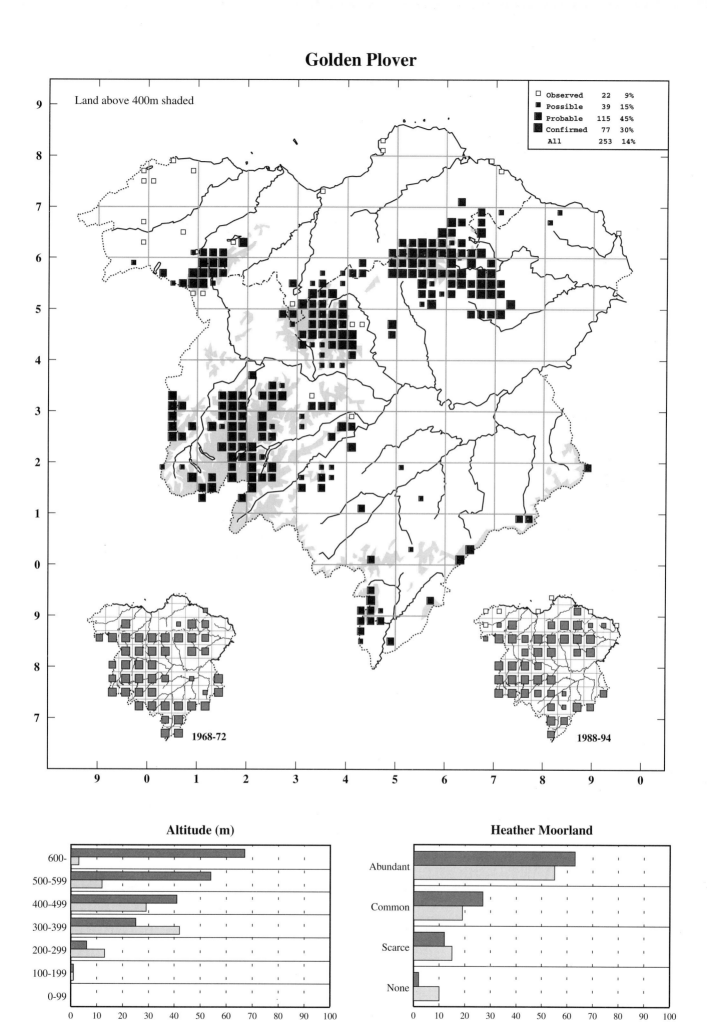

Lapwing
Vanellus vanellus

Towering and tumbling during its spectacular skydance while constantly uttering its 'pees-weep' call has endeared the Lapwing to farmers and the public alike. It is a common and familiar sight on arable and pasture land through much of Britain but has been suffering in recent years from declines associated with the intensification of farming in most of its range.

The conspicuous display flight and familiar calls of Lapwings mean that the species was very easy to record in the *Atlas*. Almost all records (90%) are of probable and confirmed breeding. Probable breeding records were an equal mixture of pairs, displaying birds and anxious adults while half of the confirmed reports were of hatched young with the remainder being split between sitting birds and adults carrying out distraction display.

Lapwings are known to show a marked preference for mixed farming and this is confirmed by the habitat graph which examines the distribution of arable/improved grassland and unimproved grassland in tetrads where Lapwings occur. They are most frequent in tetrads where there is extensive areas of both types of farmland, occurring in over 80% of such squares. Lapwings do not occur when both types of farmland are absent and are more likely to be absent when there is no arable/improved grassland. They can manage, however, when unimproved grassland is absent.

Arable fields that have been ploughed early in the spring but are surrounded by invertebrate-rich permanent pasture or rough grazing provide suitable nest sites in the ploughed areas and the good feeding and shelter in the surrounding fields. This need for permanent pasture means that many of the intensively farmed lowlands that now specialise in a combination of autumn-sown cereal and silage grasses are becoming unsuitable for Lapwings. Intensification is probably responsible for the gaps in the lower grounds in parts of the Tyne valley (NT46&57), around Dunbar (NT67&77), Eyemouth (NT96) and the Merse (NT84&85). The main gaps between 100-300m are mostly in areas dominated by forestry along the middle Tweed (NT24,33,34&43), Craik Forest (NT21,30&31) and Newcastleton and Wauchope Forests (NT40,50&60 and NY58&59).

While Lapwings can occupy about three-quarters of tetrads on the lower and middle ground, the percentage of occupied tetrads falls away above 400m and very few birds are found above 500m. While most of the tetrads in the Pentlands and Lammermuirs are almost fully occupied, the higher tops of the Moorfoots (NT34), but more particularly the Tweedsmuir Hills (NT02,11,12&22), that rise above 400m display gaps. Which factors prevent Lapwings moving further into the hills are not documented but some combination of poorer feeding and poorer climatic conditions seems likely as well

as the presence of unsuitable habitats like heather moor which Lapwings avoid. A study of breeding birds on hill summits around Culter Fell in 1989 certainly found no Lapwings present at 500m (JNCC *in litt.*). The slightly lower percentage of tetrads occupied at the lowest levels is probably entirely due to the presence of urban areas, as Lapwings clearly shun Edinburgh and the surrounding conurbation (NT26,27&37).

Lapwings occupy almost 100% of the 10-km squares in SE Scotland, just as they did in the *Old Atlas*, and so this reveals little information other than a lack of overall change on the grossest scale. The *New Atlas* abundance map is much more informative and reveals that Lapwings occur in our area at some of the highest abundance levels in Britain. A large swathe of the area from the edge of the Lothian coastal strip south to the Tweed, including much of the Pentlands, Moorfoots and Lammermuirs is shown to have the highest level of abundance. Apart from the area around Edinburgh, the highest ground in the Tweedsmuir Hills and the forestry dominated areas in southern Roxburgh, the remainder of SE Scotland holds moderate to good numbers of Lapwings.

Local studies indicated a density of 1.2prs/km^2 on arable farmland near Tranent in 1984 (da Prato 1985) while Murray (*pers.obs.*) found 106 pairs on 40km^2 of mixed pasture and rough grazing between Peebles and Leadburn in 1996, a density of 2.6prs/km^2. Local BBS results average about about 3.0prs/km^2. As might be expected upland sites hold lesser densities of Lapwings, a study of 10 upland plots in 1983 finding densities averaging just 1.0prs/km^2 in the Moorfoots (Easterbee & Pitkin 1984). These values are all higher than the 0.7-1.0prs/km^2 used in the *New Atlas* calculation of the British population but as much of the area has the highest abundance levels, just such a difference might be expected. O'Brien (1996) found a value of 2.2prs/km^2 for lowland habitats in mainland Scotland which included plots in SE Scotland. On the basis of a value of 2.5-3.0prs/km^2, the local population would be in the region of 11,600 -13,900 pairs.

Figures by O'Brien (1994) based on local results calculated 17,475 pairs in SE Scotland using an estimate of the area of 'lowland' over an area that almost certainly included the 30% of lowland SE Scotland below 300m that is devoid of Lapwings (vacant arable tetrads, tetrads covered by forestry and urban habitats). When such areas are disregarded, a figure of 12,200 pairs remains of O'Brien's total. A compromise figure of 12,500 pairs would represent about 5.5% of the British population, a figure well ahead of the 2% of mainland Britain that SE Scotland occupies.

R.D.Murray

Lapwing

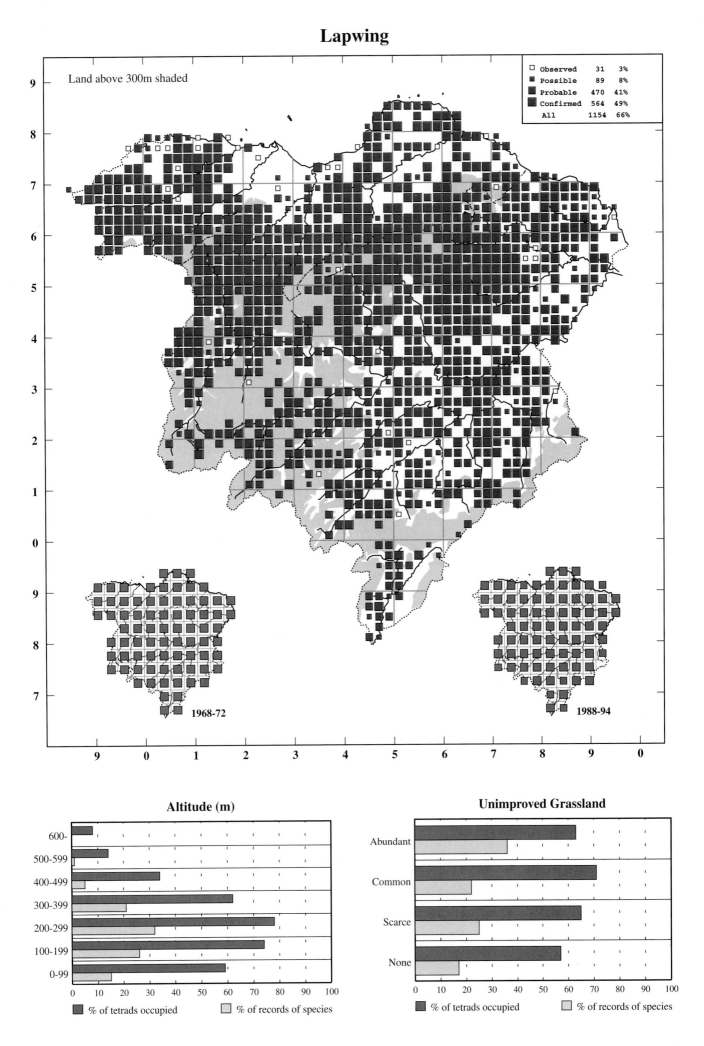

□	Observed	31	3%
■	Possible	89	8%
■	Probable	470	41%
■	Confirmed	564	49%
	All	1154	66%

Land above 300m shaded

1968-72

1988-94

Altitude (m)

■ % of tetrads occupied   □ % of records of species

Unimproved Grassland

Abundant

Common

Scarce

None

■ % of tetrads occupied   □ % of records of species

127

Dunlin
Calidris alpina

In Britain Dunlins breed typically in hummocky, uneven moorland usually with wet pools. The main strongholds are in the Outer Hebrides, the Flow Country, and the Northern Isles. Elsewhere Dunlins are scarce, local or sporadic breeders over the uplands of Britain, often at high altitude, though occasionally at sea level. This enigmatic distribution, suggestive of particular requirements, is reflected in SE Scotland by sparse occurrence in a variety of localities. Small invertebrate food is extracted by Dunlins from wet or damp ground, hence the need for wet ground in or near the territory.

Many of the upland tetrads were criss-crossed in such a way that most Dunlin territories were probably near enough to cause at least one of the pair to call, fly near, perch ahead of, or lead away the observer. However, much Dunlin breeding habitat is remote, and some Dunlin territories are likely to have been missed. Probable and confirmed records accounted for 55% of all tetrads with Dunlins. Probable records were mainly two or more birds seen, while of confirmed a third were young seen and two thirds were due to injury-feigning or other pronounced leading-away behaviour, this normally indicating presence of eggs or young (Nethersole-Thompson & Nethersole-Thompson 1986, Ratcliffe 1990).

The map shows an interesting variety of sites, from sea level to the highest land in SE Scotland. The observed registrations at the coast are probably due to late migrating birds, and those at reservoirs are perhaps birds making feeding trips from nearby breeding moors, or displaying and courting while territories are still being established. Confirmed and probable breeding occurs in three main categories of site: firstly on damp heathery moorland with a loch or reservoir within 3-4km distance; secondly on mountain or moor often high up near summits on smooth montane heather-, sedge- or moss-sward, and interrupted by uneven ground containing damp hollows with pools or peat hags; and thirdly on coastal sites with saltings or rough grass.

In the first category are the Pentland Hills tetrads in and near NT15, which are damp moors and slopes bordering West Water, Crosswood, Cobbinshaw and Harperrig Reservoirs, and the top of East Cairn Hill in close flying distance to Harperrig Reservoir. Further south is Culter Fell (NT02) above Culter Water Reservoir, and five tetrads in NT11which are high hills close to Loch Skeen, Gameshope Loch and Fruid Reservoir. Hutlerburn Hill (NT42) is beside Akermoor Loch, and NT31Y is moorland by Hellmoor Loch. At many of these water bodies one or more Dunlins are seen feeding or resting, presumably off-duty birds from the hill or moor nest sites.

In the second group are Hundleshope Heights (NT23), eastern Moorfoot hills (NT34), Roan Fell Flow (NY49), and Lammermuir tetrads around NT65, all high peaty hill tops without water bodies close. The Lammermuir birds may use Watch Water Reservoir or nearer minor wet sites, as Dunlins have been noted feeding at small Lammermuir streams (*Bird Reports*). The Broad Law and Dollar Law tetrads in NT12 are very much high mountain sites, though Broad Law birds might descend down to Megget or Talla Reservoirs.

In the third category, coastal sites, Dunlins probably attempted to breed at Aberlady and Tyninghame in grassy saltings where they have bred previously. At Musselburgh where landscaping has changed habitats frequently, a pair laid eggs in 1987 and 1988 but failed in both years. At Thorntonloch (NT77) a displaying pair was seen in early and late May in 1989. All the coastal sites tend to suffer some human disturbance.

The altitude graph shows that Dunlin occurence peaks at two levels, at 200-400m and at over 600m. These relate to moorland and high mountain sites respectively. Notably, almost 60% of all tetrads over 600m have Dunlins, and some were found at 800m. No breeding Dunlins were found at 100-200m, between the coastal and upland nesters. The habitat graph shows a high proportion of Dunlins where heather is extensive, not unexpectedly as most extensive heather is at the higher levels prefered by Dunlins. However, the birds are not necessarily breeding on the heather as the graph also suggests, montane sward and damp mossy moor being alternative habitats.

Evidence for any change in the Dunlin's local range is scant. The numbers of occupied 10-km squares in the two small maps are similar, although their distributions are slightly different. Less coastal breeding was recorded in the 1968-72 survey, but more was recorded in the hills along the Scottish-English border. This is probably a real loss due to afforestation. Stroud *et al.* (1990) showed that plantations on moors reduce breeding by Dunlins in a zone more than 400m outwards from forest edges, and so loss of Dunlin habitat is considerably greater than the area planted. At some better watched localities, Dunlin range appears to have changed little; at reservoirs and damp moors in the Pentland and Lammermuir Hills and at Aberlady Bay and Tyninghame on the coast, Dunlins have bred off and on since the 1920s (*R&B*, *Thom*, Munro 1988), though at the coast sites there were long spells without breeding probably due to disturbance (*Andrews*, *Bird Reports*). Dunlins have declined in low areas south and east of the Great Glen (*Thom*) and in afforested moors in SW Scotland and NW England (*New Atlas*).

Dunlins can breed almost colonially, and high densities are recorded in specialised habitats in the Flow Country and Western Isles (Ratcliffe 1990, *New Atlas*). In SE Scotland, however, all tetrads with confirmed or probable breeding are likely to contain only 1-2 pairs, with 5-6 pairs in the two tetrads at West Water Reservoir. This low suggested density is supported by NCC surveys in the 1980s. Ten plots on moorlands spread in and near SE Scotland gave densities from no Dunlins (the majority) to 0.41 prs/km^2, mean 0.3prs/km^2 for plots with Dunlins (Easterbee & Pitkin 1984). Also JNCC (*in litt.*) found no Dunlins on moors and hill-tops near Culter Fell (NT02&03) in 1990. The map therefore suggests that SE Scotland has 45-50 pairs of Dunlins in any one year, with 50-60 pairs being more realistic, allowing for some pairs that were probably missed. Although this is only 0.5% of the 1990 British population estimate (*New Atlas*), there are now serious declines in some of the main Dunlin areas (SNH, RSPB unpubl.), so that our local Dunlins and the wild places they inhabit should be valued.

H.E.M.Dott

Dunlin

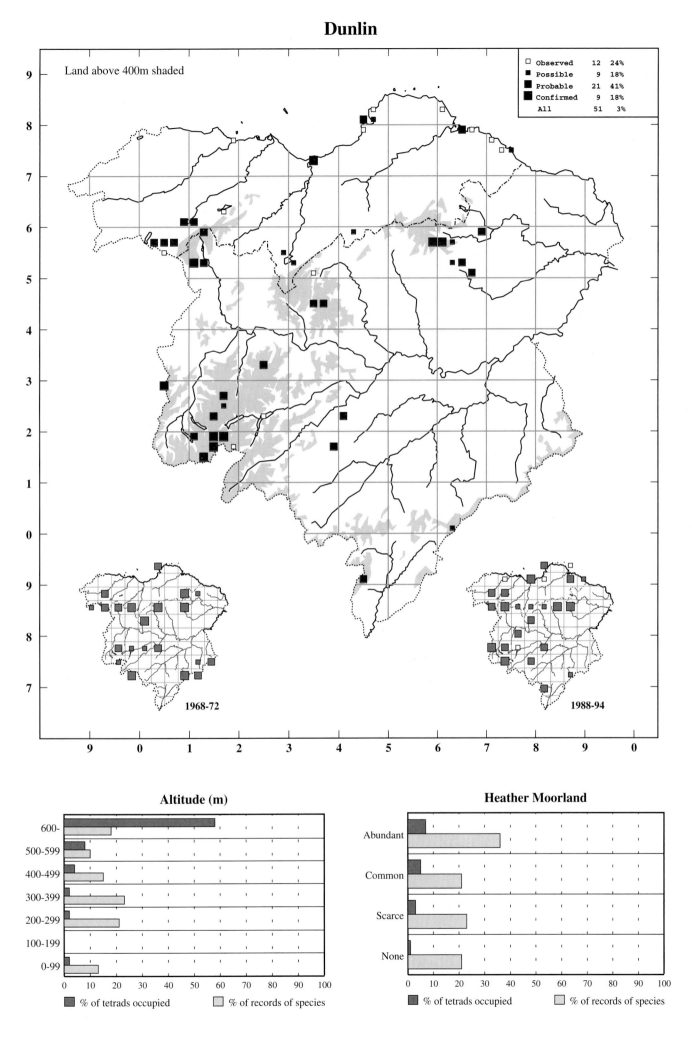

□ Observed	12	24%	
■ Possible	9	18%	
■ Probable	21	41%	
■ Confirmed	9	18%	
All	51	3%	

Land above 400m shaded

1968-72

1988-94

Altitude (m)

600-
500-599
400-499
300-399
200-299
100-199
0-99

■ % of tetrads occupied   □ % of records of species

Heather Moorland

Abundant
Common
Scarce
None

■ % of tetrads occupied   □ % of records of species

Snipe
Gallinago gallinago

The vibrating' thrum' from a tiny speck high in the sky or the 'ticka-ticka' chipping call from the depths of an area of marsh or wet moorland are usually the first signs of the presence of Snipe. A secretive bird that stays hidden, even on the closest approach, they are more often heard than seen.

Snipe nest in wet places and are most active under the cover of darkness and so are relatively difficult birds to record. The resulting map probably underestimates the range and the population of our area. Snipe are best surveyed within three hours of dusk or dawn (O'Brien 1996) making it more likely that birds may have been missed in remote tetrads. Most of the possible breeding records were of flushed birds or birds giving the chipping song. Drumming birds dominated probable records while the relatively few confirmed records were shared by adults doing distraction display or records of young.

Snipe occurred in about half the tetrads where unimproved pastures were widespread, mostly between 250-450m. At these altitudes rough grazing offers damp, invertebrate-rich pastures for feeding with nearby rushy areas for nesting. Low intensity management reduces disturbance by farm operations while the low stocking rates mean that trampling of the nest or young is reduced and the sward is not grazed so hard as to remove cover. While Snipe were still present on the highest areas, they were less widespread, possibly through a lack of good damp feeding areas on steeper slopes.

The map shows similarities to the map of unimproved grassland in the hills to the north of the Tweed. There is less correspondence further south where Snipe are absent on the rough grazing above 450m on the steep Tweedsmuir Hills, in the large blocks of forestry in south Roxburghshire and in the Cheviots where severe grazing and better drainage may make areas unsuitable for Snipe. These areas are also remote and observers may not have been able to reach these areas during the periods of maximum Snipe activity and thus missed many birds. A broad band of tetrads runs across the northern hills from the Pentlands to the Lammermuirs. The very highest

ground is vacant, as are the Leader and Gala valleys where improved grassland and arable farming penetrate along the lower ground. The broadest swathe occurs in the southern Lammermuirs where the flatter, more undulating topography allows large areas of damp grassland to exist between Lauder (NT54), Gordon (NT64) and Duns (NT75). Further south Snipe are widespread on the lower hills between the valleys of the Yarrow, Ettrick and Teviot, often on the flatter summits not occupied by forestry.

The fields of arable and improved farmland on low ground are mostly vacant with only the damp rushy meadows at Aberlady Bay (NT48) known to hold any numbers of Snipe. 'Improvements' to the drainage characteristics of most fields reduce their suitability for Snipe through a loss of soil invertebrates and because intensive grazing removes cover and increases risk of trampling. A total conversion to arable cultivation would result in the wholesale loss of Snipe, as has happened in many parts of England (*New Atlas*).

Comparisons with the *Old Atlas* unexpectedly show the range of Snipe to have marginally improved since 1968-72, with three 10-km squares gained to two losses. The number of occupied tetrads in Tweedsmuir (NT02), Hawick (NT41) and possibly Chirnside (NT85), (eight, ten and three respectively) suggests that Snipe were overlooked there in the *Old Atlas* survey. With agricultural 'improvements' and the spread of forestry there is little likelihood that anything other than a reduction of range could have occurred since 1968-72. The 10-km square grid is too coarse, as yet, to record such losses.

The *New Atlas* abundance map shows areas of highest numbers matching the areas with high densities of occupied tetrads in the Lammermuirs, the northern Moorfoots between Middleton and West Linton, the Ettrick Forest and the hills around Fauldhouse in West Lothian. The hills in southern Roxburgh, which may have been less thoroughly surveyed, show up poorly and yet are surrounded by areas of high abundance in the Lowther Hills, Eskdalemuir and Langholm and around Kielder. As the grassland habitats are rather similar in all of these areas, the concern about the coverage for Snipe in these areas is perhaps justified.

Snipe population estimates are rightly couched in vague terms with broad margins for error. The BTO used figures of 0.4-0.5prs/km² in the *Old Atlas* and 0.16prs/km² in the *New Atlas* for their calculation of the declining national population (*Trends*). Locally, da Prato (1985) found a low 0.2prs/km² in his arable Tranent study. In moorland areas, sample plots in SE Scotland (SNH 1984) had mean densities of 0.7prs/km² while work near Culter Fell (JNCC *in litt.*) found 0.75prs/km². Local BBS returns in 1994-95 suggest a higher 1.0prs/km², from just 15% of the plots. Rossiter (1988) found a density of 0.5prs/km² in all occupied areas of Northumberland. The BTO estimates include large areas of southern Britain that are very poorly populated by Snipe, perhaps resembling the Tranent area, and as our area does have locally high abundances of birds, a value of 0.75-1.0prs/km² might seem more appropriate. This would produce a local population of 1,740-2,320 pairs.

O'Brien (1996) calculated an average of 0.8prs/km² for lowland Scotland as a whole, which seems high when most Snipe occur in uplands, to give an estimate for Scotland of 41,000 pairs. His local estimate for SE Scotland was 3,725 pairs, rather higher than our estimate based on 0.75-1.0prs/km². The *New Atlas* estimate of 30,000 pairs for Britain has recently been superseded by a figure of 55,000 pairs (Stone *et al.* 1997). **R.D.Murray**

Snipe

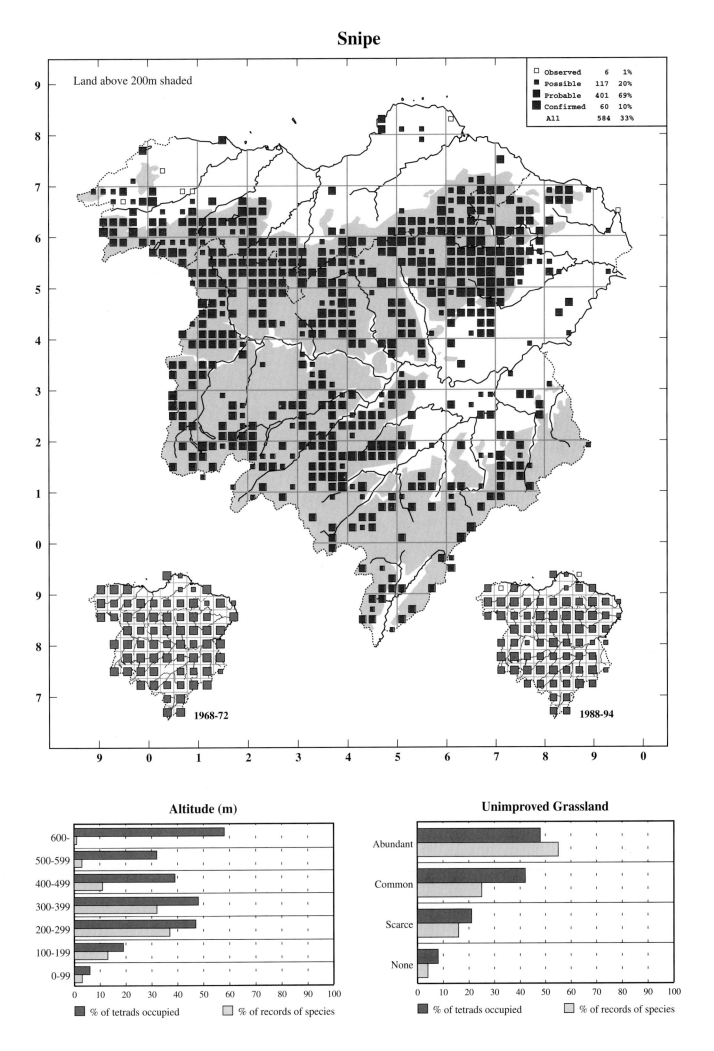

	Observed	6	1%
	Possible	117	20%
	Probable	401	69%
	Confirmed	60	10%
	All	584	33%

Land above 200m shaded

1968-72

1988-94

Altitude (m)

■ % of tetrads occupied   ☐ % of records of species

Unimproved Grassland

Abundant

Common

Scarce

None

■ % of tetrads occupied   ☐ % of records of species

131

Woodcock
Scolopax rusticola

A dark silhouette in the gloaming, flitting at tree-top height along a forest track and giving a quiet croaking call followed by a high pitched 'twisk', sums up the usual encounter with a Woodcock. They are well camouflaged, spend most of their time in thick forest, are mostly active under cover of darkness, and are hardly ever seen in daylight except when accidentally flushed or during their 'roding' display flight at dawn or dusk.

Possible records were mostly of birds accidentally flushed. Most probable records came from questioning local residents or by searching for roding birds at dusk. The few confirmed records were of fledged young or reports of breeding from gamekeepers and forest rangers. There can be little doubt that large numbers were missed as many tetrads had no coverage whatsoever at the appropriate time of the day. Remote tetrads must have suffered the most in that respect.

Woodcocks breed in woodlands near patches of invertebrate-rich damp soils that allow good feeding. While any kind of woodland can be used, deciduous woods on richer soils offer better feeding and probably result in higher populations. Some ground cover is also needed to help conceal the nest, so closed-canopy conifer plantations and over-grazed woodlands are less suited to the Woodcock's requirements. Some records from wet flushes in some of the upland valleys, some distance from the nearest wood, hint that birds can travel some distance to find good feeding.

The difficulties in detecting Woodcocks have produced a map that may only sketch the local distribution in broad strokes. Some knowledge of the coverage is essential as certain observers made extra efforts to find birds in their areas (NS97&NT07; NT35&36, NT50, NT72) while others made little or no effort. Other areas were also better covered during organised overnight 'blitzes' in specific areas (NT30,62,70&71) by groups of tetrad surveyors. Coverage was better in Lothian and there the map may well be a reasonable reflection of the real distribution. The wooded valleys of the the Esk (NT26,35&36), upper Tyne (NT46), upper Water of Leith (NT16) and Almond (NT06) and the plantations of the Bathgate Hills (NS97&NT07) are the main concentrations of occupied tetrads. Pockets also exist at Gosford-Aberlady (NT47&48) and Tyninghame (NT67). In Borders the picture is more sketchy with concentrations at Craik (NT30) and Leithope (NT60&70), found during weekend atlasing field trips, while records from the Kelso area were reported during evening surveys for Quail. Otherwise the Borders show a scatter of records in areas where observers lived (NT14 &75) or where birders regularly visit (Dawyck in NT13, Hirsel in NT84). The main conifer forest areas were not surveyed to any great extent but good numbers were found to be present when searched for.

Comparisons with the *Old Atlas* show large changes with four 10-km squares gained to 14 losses. As the four gains held just five occupied tetrads, these may be of little importance. Other than near Musselburgh (NT37), losses were in the areas that are known to have been badly covered by the current effort as far as crepuscular species like Woodcocks are concerned and yet have much likely habitat. It seems likely therefore that some of these losses may be because of poor surveying rather than real losses.

The *New Atlas* abundance map shows high numbers around Linlithgow, the Esk valley and Dunbar, where the map opposite shows concentrations of occupied tetrads. A 'hot-spot' in Wauchope Forest is puzzling as there are so few records from that forest in our survey. Where the BTO obtained this information from is unclear. In British terms, SE Scotland is shown to have a greater concentration of high abundance areas than anywhere in Britain. *Thom* also considered the area to hold good numbers.

Doubts have been cast on the value of using roding males as indicators of the size of the population because Woodcocks are polygynous and only a proportion of the males rode, usually the higher-ranking males (Hoodless 1995). However, as the majority of Woodcock records refer to roding males, that is the only information available to us. Records from 10-25 sites are reported each year in the *Bird Reports*. Most sites have records of 1-2 roding birds but a number, especially those in the Borders, hold higher numbers. The record count was at the largely coniferous Bowmont Forest (NT72J) in 1995 when 19 roding birds were seen. Nine were seen along 5km of the Logan Burn between Flotterstone and Loganlea in 1981 (NT26B&G), while large estates like Duns & Floors Castles (NT75S&73C), the Hirsel, Monteviot (NT62M) and Abbey St.Bathans (NT76Q) hold 5-8 roding birds.

The BTO used density figures of 0.1-0.25prs/km^2 and 0.07-0.18prs/km^2 in their atlases for calculating the British population. da Prato's Tranent study area (1985) only revealed 0.15prs/km^2. In a much smaller area, however, *Andrews* mentions Roslin Glen (NT26R) as having a density of 11prs/km^2. The larger sites in the *Bird Reports* suggest that occupied 1-km squares (e.g. not just the forest habitat) held the equivalent of 1-2prs/km^2, with the Bowmont Forest (3km^2) recording 5-6prs/km^2. Using 1.0pr/km^2 for each occupied tetrad would give a population of 1,200 pairs in SE Scotland, despite poor coverage. The area also has at least 600km^2 of commercial forest of which only a fraction was properly surveyed. Even at 0.5prs/km^2 such a density might add another 300 to this total. With all the uncertainties a figure of 1,400-1,500 pairs seems as reasonable a guess as any.   ***R.D.Murray***

Woodcock

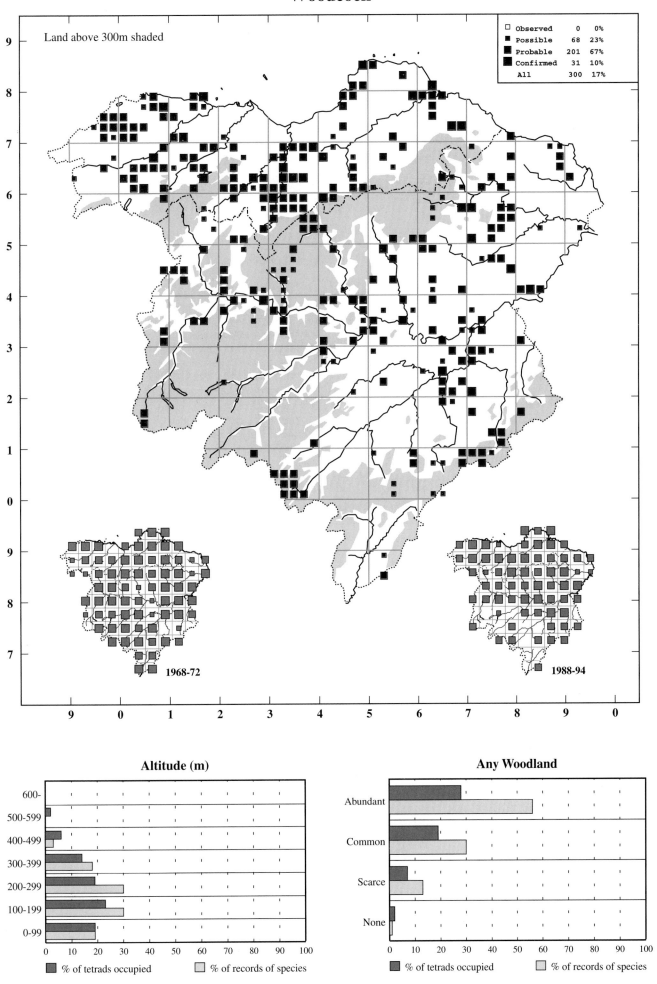

Land above 300m shaded

□ Observed	0	0%
■ Possible	68	23%
■ Probable	201	67%
■ Confirmed	31	10%
All	300	17%

1968-72

1988-94

Altitude (m)

600-
500-599
400-499
300-399
200-299
100-199
0-99

0 10 20 30 40 50 60 70 80 90 100

■ % of tetrads occupied   ☐ % of records of species

Any Woodland

Abundant
Common
Scarce
None

0 10 20 30 40 50 60 70 80 90 100

■ % of tetrads occupied   ☐ % of records of species

Curlew
Numenius arquata

Open expanses of grass and heather moor are the Curlew's favourite haunts, over which its bubbling song resounds in spring. This habitat is generally found above cultivated land, but Curlews can also nest low down where rushy ground remains and even in cultivated land, though usually with poor success. By late July the breeding grounds are deserted for shores and coastal fields until the following spring. Though familiar locally, the Curlew is not abundant worldwide, with Britain holding 40% of European birds (Tucker *et al. 1994*) and a substantial part of the world population.

Fieldwork results produced probable breeding in 60% of all occupied tetrads. This high figure is mainly due to the song given in display flight and loud alarm calls, usually uttered at a distance from the intruder while birds slip off nests or young hide, so that confirmed breeding is a low 20%, due mostly to young seen or distraction display. Confirmed breeding therefore under-represents the distribution, but taken with probable records, both give a truer picture of breeding distribution.

The map shows the great majority of breeding tetrads to be above the 200m contour, with some lower tetrads occupied mainly in the Tweed-Teviot basin and in Liddesdale. The Curlew map also shows a close similarity with that of unimproved grassland. The graphs confirm these associations. Notably, 80% of all tetrads from 200-600m have Curlews, and 50% of those at 100-200m have them, emphasising the universal nature of Curlews in SE Scotland except on lowlands. Above 600m Curlew occupancy drops, with evident gaps around Hart Fell and Broad Law (NT11&12). The other large gaps on high ground without Curlews are all where extensive forestry occurs (NT21,30,31,50,60, & NY58,59). The second graph shows a clear association of Curlews with abundant unimproved grassland, birds decreasing as grassland area becomes smaller. Curlews also show a positive relationship with extent of heather (not shown), though more Curlews are found where heather is scarce or absent than where common or abundant, emphasising that grassland is where most Curlews occur in SE Scotland.

Below 200m the Curlew is more localised, with some south of the Lammermuirs (NT63&64) where extensive unimproved grazing still occurs, south of the Tweed (NT52,62,72&73) where there is mixed rough and improved grazing with damp mossy haughs along the river courses, and in southern and western West Lothian (NS96,NT06) where patches of rough moorland are still dispersed amongst improved pasture and bordering forestry. The few breeding tetrads on lowlands in Lothian and the Merse may indicate pioneer birds attempting to nest in arable land or remnants of marshy grassland. Tetrads with observed records are evident along and near the coast. A study in East Lothian using individually marked

Curlews (Evans 1988) showed that those remaining at the coast through the summer were immature birds without breeding territory. The *Bird Reports* reveal that small groups appear in May at favoured coastal spots, increasing in June to flocks of up to 100-200 birds, presumably passage birds and local failed breeders. The observed records are likely to represent such immature, passage and failed birds.

The two 10-km maps show little change since 1968-72, the main differences being an East Lothian square (NT47) gained, and several squares in the East Lothian and Berwickshire lowlands improved from possible breeding to probable or confirmed. This suggests an extension of Curlew breeding into lower ground here since 20 years ago. The *New Atlas* change map supports this. What the 10-km maps do not show is that *within* upland squares Curlews have been lost in the last 20-30 years where moors have been afforested, and where improved pasture has advanced into upper glens and slopes. The tetrad map shows gaps in these places. In Britain the Curlew's range expanded slightly in the first half of the 20th century, but trends are now less clear (*Trends*), and in Europe there has been some decline (*BWP*).

Curlew densities decrease from uplands to lowlands (Ratcliffe 1990). A Scotland-wide study (Galbraith *et al.* 1984) found averages of 2.9prs/km^2 on rough grazing above 300m, 2.4prs/km^2 on rough grazing below 300m, 0.6prs/km^2 on dry pasture, and 0.3prs/km^2 on arable land. In lowland Scotland generally O'Brien (1996) found 1.4 prs/km^2. Ten sample moorland plots in and near SE Scotland gave a mean density of 3.3prs/km^2, with over 5prs/km^2 in the south Pentlands and east Moorfoots (Easterbee & Pitkin 1984). With these known densities, and bearing in mind that the uplands of SE Scotland are part of a major area of nationally high Curlew abundance (*New Atlas*), a population estimate can be made based on the numbers of tetrads occupied at different altitudes. Using 3.5prs/km^2 for tetrads above 300m, 2.5prs/km^2 for tetrads 200-300m, and 0.5prs/km^2 for those (excluding observed) below 200m, an estimate of 11,450 territorial pairs for SE Scotland is obtained, with perhaps 200-300 non-territorial immature birds at and near the coast.

The figure of 11,450 pairs for SE Scotland is 32% of the latest British population estimate (Stone *et al.*1997), a quite unrealistic proportion. O'Brien (1994) estimated Lothian and Borders to have 12,075 pairs in "lowland" alone (including land capable for improved pasture), though his "new method" (O'Brien 1996) would reduce this figure. The British population is evidently greatly underestimated and in need of revision, as O'Brien (1996) has hinted.   ***H.E.M.Dott***

Curlew

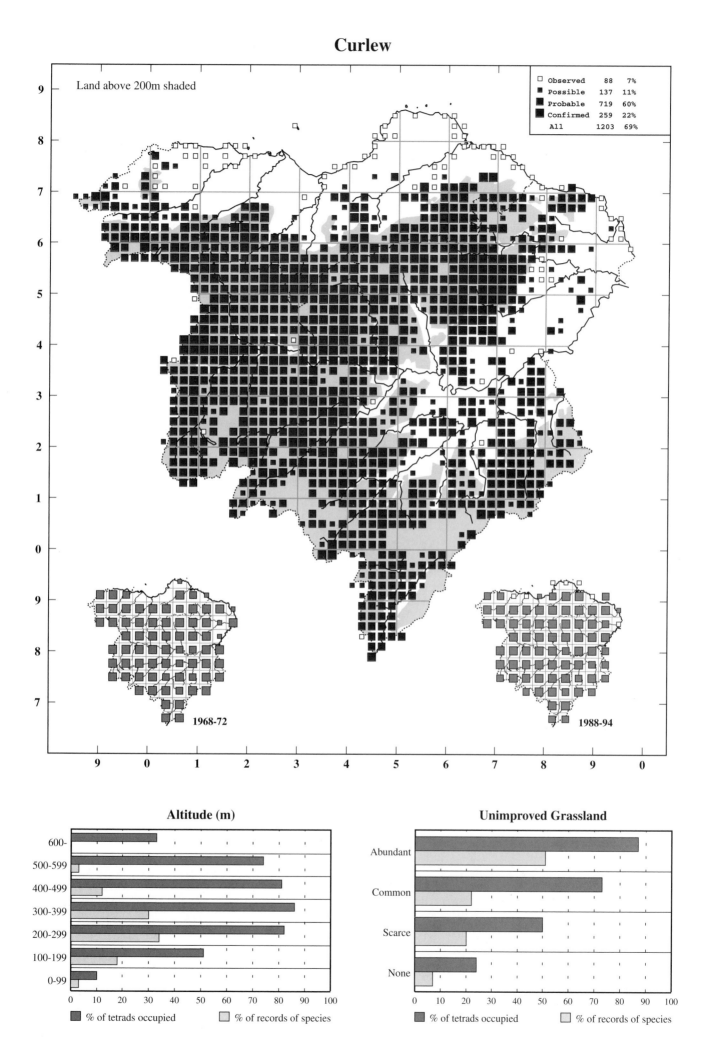

Land above 200m shaded

	Observed	88	7%
	Possible	137	11%
	Probable	719	60%
	Confirmed	259	22%
	All	1203	69%

1968-72

1988-94

Altitude (m)

600-	
500-599	
400-499	
300-399	
200-299	
100-199	
0-99	

■ % of tetrads occupied ☐ % of records of species

Unimproved Grassland

Abundant	
Common	
Scarce	
None	

■ % of tetrads occupied ☐ % of records of species

Redshank
Tringa totanus

The sentinel of many a coastal salting, wet moorland or marsh, the scolding *tuu-tuu* alarm of the Redshank in response to any human intruder or predator, is well-known across many parts of Britain. It is commonest along the shore outside of the breeding season, the British Isles hosting the breeding population of Iceland and other Arctic areas, but considerable numbers do breed in Britain, with Scotland holding the majority of the population.

The loud and familiar alarm calls of the Redshank mean that birds are usually fairly easy to detect if they are present. In the survey some caution was needed in coastal areas where passage birds may have been present and most records from such areas were considered to be of observed status, unless there was some suitable habitat available and more definite evidence of breeding found. Possible breeding records were typically birds seen in potential habitat. Probable records were mostly of pairs or anxious birds although territorial behaviour and display were also prominent. Confirmed records were shared by adults performing distraction displays and sightings of hatched juveniles.

Redshanks were found in three main habitat types, along the coast, near water features and in damp grasslands. A very few birds breed in the saltmarshes at Aberlady and Tyninghame and in the more secluded bays east of Dunbar. Larger numbers nest near inland water features, mostly streams, rivers or reservoirs, usually in the adjacent damp fields. The association with reservoirs can be seen at the Pentland reservoirs in NT05,06&16. While river breeding is most obvious along the lower Tweed (NT63,73,83,84&94) and the Yarrow (NT22&23), Redshanks are most widespread in valley haughlands well into the hills, as along the Whiteadder Water in NT66 or the Kale Water in NT71. These haughs and areas of undulating terrain, moulded into humps and hollows by the ice sheets, form much of the habitat for the main block of occupied tetrads that stretches along the northern hills. Such areas of mostly rough grazing, with the hollows dominated by mosses and the fields by rush-lined drains, cover large parts of the Pentlands, Moorfoots and Lammermuirs and together provide the more continuous distribution seen across the northern hills. Limited clumping in the Ettrick Forest marks the remnants of what may once have been a similar area prior to the afforestation of Craik. This preference is seen in the habitat graph which shows a strong association with rough grazing, about two-thirds of all Redshank records coming from areas where rough grazing is common or abundant. While wetlands might be considered important for Redshanks, and birds do occupy half of all tetrads that hold large wetlands, more than three-quarters of all tetrads with Redshanks in SE Scotland actually contain no wetland feature recognisable on the 1:25,000 map series.

These damp grassland habitats are very prone to piecemeal drainage by farmers, as well as afforestation, and it would seem likely that some habitat loss has occurred and is still occurring in our area. Comparisons with the *Old Atlas* map do show a net loss of occupied 10-km squares since 1968-72. The coastal areas show both gains and losses that are probably meaningless because the *Old Atlas* map may have included passage birds. These are shown on the current map as observed records. The inland squares show losses high up in the watershed of the Tweed (NT01&02), the Bowmont (NT81&82) and in Liddesdale (NY58), all areas where afforestation has probably removed suitable habitat, as it may have done at Craik and is suspected also to have happened in Northumberland (*Day*). While no losses are indicated in the lowlands since the *Old Atlas*, losses did occur in lowland areas in Northumberland through drainage. While there is currently little evidence for change in such areas in SE Scotland, the future will almost certainly show losses as more of the damp fields are 'improved' and losses accumulate until no breeding occurs in a 10-km square. The altitude graph shows two-thirds of Redshank tetrads are at the 200-400m level, the altitude where arable and improved grassland gives way to rough pasture.

The *New Atlas* abundance map indicates that SE Scotland holds reasonable numbers of Redshanks with much of the main range in the area shown as having moderate to good numbers. A few areas have the highest abundances: in the southern Pentlands around Cobbinshaw (NT05), around Portmore and Gladhouse (NT25), Carfraemill (NT55), the Westruther-Longformacus area (NT65) and Teviothead (NT40). This abundance is confirmed on the map opposite by the density of occupied tetrads in these squares.

The *Bird Reports* contain published details of at least 30 sites that have held more than two pairs since 1979. While numbers are variable, some sites such as Bavelaw-Threipmuir and Aberlady have had as many as 15 pairs, while areas like Whitrig (NT63H), Teindside (NT40I) and the Whiteadder WBS site (NT66H,I&M) have had 8-12 pairs. In Goosander surveys in 1986, 38 pairs of Redshanks were found along the Tweed between Peebles and Coldstream with 13 pairs along the Whiteadder between Preston and the reservoir. Density figures quoted by the BTO in both the *Old Atlas* and *New Atlas* refer to values around 0.20-0.25prs/km^2 when calculating a British population of about 30,000 pairs, more than half of which must breed in Scotland. O'Brien (1996) found evidence for 12,000 pairs in 'lowland' Scotland, in habitat that included improved grassland and arable farmland below 300m. However, the map and altitude graph show Redshanks have a preference for unimproved, rough grazing at higher altitudes and accordingly most were outwith the area analysed by O'Brien. He calculated the mainland Scottish lowland population on the basis of 0.1prs/km^2, although some areas achieved 5prs/km^2.

O'Brien (1994) assessed that 'lowland' SE Scotland held about 450 pairs. This figure seems inappropriate for all of SE Scotland, as most Redshanks do not breed in such habitats. Our minimum figure must be 400 pairs as birds occurred in just over 400 tetrads if observed records are excluded. Galbraith (1984) found Redshank density in rough grazing varied from 0.7prs/km^2 below 300m to 0.1prs/km^2 above that height, rising to 2.0prs/km^2 in damp grassland at all levels. As 70% of Redshank tetrads occurred around 300m, a median figure of 0.4prs/km^2 might be appropriate for the area. This would give a local population of 660 pairs, higher than O'Brien's figure but more realistic on habitat grounds and 2.1% of the British figure.

R.D.Murray

Redshank

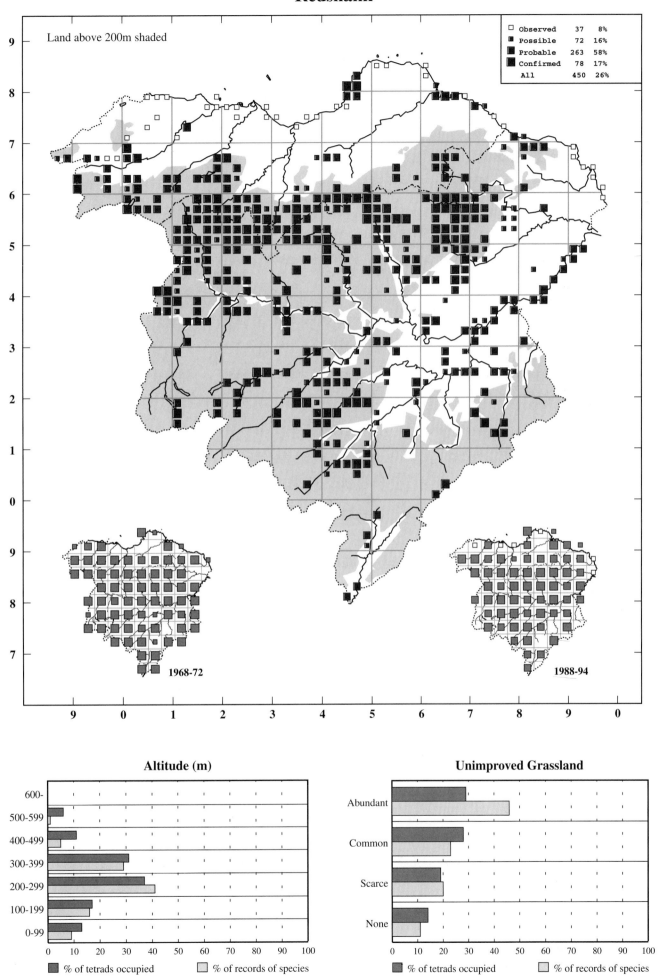

Land above 200m shaded

☐ Observed	37	8%
▣ Possible	72	16%
▨ Probable	263	58%
■ Confirmed	78	17%
All	450	26%

1968-72

1988-94

Altitude (m)

■ % of tetrads occupied   ☐ % of records of species

Unimproved Grassland

■ % of tetrads occupied   ☐ % of records of species

137

Common Sandpiper
Actitis hypoleucos

The bobbing body, characteristic piping call and fluttering flight of the Common Sandpiper are well known to those frequenting rivers, streams, lochs and reservoirs in the north and west of Britain. Habitat preferences are for more open-edged upland waters with stretches of shingle and rocky banks, adequate feeding and cover to provide hiding places for the nest and young. The short breeding season is of no more than three months, mid-April to mid-June. Failed breeders and passage birds are commonly seen on coastal estuaries and along the shoreline where no breeding occurs.

The Common Sandpiper is a fairly easy bird to find. It is restricted to watercourses and waterbodies and when disturbed tends to fly noisily along its territory. It is most obvious during courtship and when protecting its young through distraction displays. A high proportion of records were of probable and confirmed breeding. Records of pairs and anxious adults dominated the probable records, sightings of young and the distraction display the confirmed records. The small number of observed records were mostly in coastal or near-coastal sites and were considered to refer to passage birds.

Common Sandpipers were found from sea-level up to 600m but two-thirds of all records were between 200-400m. This is the area where the major break of slope between the hills and the lower ground occurs in SE Scotland. In such areas shingle and gravel often forms the major substrate along the rivers, boulders predominating upstream where stream flow is faster and sand and mud downstream where flow is slower in the lower gradients. In the analysis of rivers the smallest representation is in small streams; both the percentage of tetrads and percentage of bird records. While a much greater proportion of tetrads with larger rivers held Common Sandpipers, it was medium-sized streams that showed the largest representation of the actual bird records.

On the map it is easy to trace the pattern of breeding pairs along the river and stream courses, especially along the upper tributaries of the main rivers. In this respect the valleys of lower and middle Tweed and Teviot, Leader (NT53&54), Bowmont Water (NT82), Whiteadder (NT75&85) and Eye (NT86) stand out in the lowlands below 300m. Above 300m where the hill valleys are closer together the density of occupied tetrads increases in the valleys of the upper Tweed (NT01,02,11,12&13), South Esk (NT25&35), Yarrow and Ettrick (NT21,22,32&42), upper Teviot (NT30,40&41) and Liddel (NY48,49&59). The greatest density of tetrads are in Lammermuirs along the upper reaches of the Leader (NT55) and Whiteadder systems (NT66&67). The cluster in the northern Pentlands (NT15,16&26) are in a mixture of streams and reservoirs. There is a general absence of birds from the Blackadder, Tyne, Water of Leith, Almond and lower Esk which tend to lack shingle and be either intensively farmed, enclosed by woodland or pass through urban areas. Only the Tweed has many Common Sandpipers on its lower reaches, probably because it is so wide that even when wooded the river is not enclosed, and it also has considerable areas of shingle and is only built-up along short stretches.

In the *New Atlas* and *Trends,* population monitoring suggests that the British population has been steady over the course of the last few decades. However, personal population estimates in the Lammermuirs over the past several years have indicated a significant decline which has no apparent cause nor which has been noticed elsewhere in SE Scotland. Local declines have, however, been noted in the West Midlands, around Manchester and in Devon (*Trends*) but no regional trends are visible across Britain as a whole, and in Scotland there was little change in the range between the BTO breeding atlases.

The *New Atlas* abundance map shows the upper and middle Tweed to hold the highest concentrations in SE Scotland, the rivers of the remainder of the main area holding above average numbers. The good numbers known to occur on the upper Teviot (Murray 1988) are also indicated although shown as not being of the highest category.

Studies in the Peak District have recorded Common Sandpiper densities of up to 4.7prs/km along streams (Holland *et al.* 1982), while the WBS national figures that include large areas unsuited to Common Sandpipers suggests a mean of 0.6prs/km (*New Atlas*). Cowper (1973) found densities of around 1.0pr/km along the upper courses of the Esk drainage while local WBS returns on the Gala Water have produced similar figures (Holling *pers.comm.*). The sawbill counts along 340km of the Tweed drainage in 1987 (Murray 1988) encountered 339 Common Sandpiper territories, an overall density of 1.0prs/km and including many areas where there were no Common Sandpipers reported. The best figures in this count were along 46kms of the Teviot which held 1.9prs/km, the maximum being 2.8prs/km upstream of Hawick. Most still water sites hold 1-2 pairs each but long linear waters like St. Mary's Loch and Fruid Reservoir have had over 12 pairs reported on just one side of the water. Sandpits such as those at Shiphorns and Leadburn (NT24&25) also hold a few pairs (*Bird Reports*).

Most occupied tetrads have a river or stream traversing the square and probably average well in excess of two kilometres of river bed. With overall counts of 1.0pr/km from several areas of SE Scotland, a likely figure per tetrad of 2.0prs/tetrad may be appropriate for all probable and confirmed breeding reports. If a lower figure of 1.0pr/tetrad is assigned to those squares with possible records, a local population of 900 pairs is indicated. This compares with the 339 pairs found in the big Tweed drainage survey of 1987, which, in searching for sawbills, did not focus much attention on the hill areas where the map opposite shows the greatest density of tetrads to occur. The additional numbers known to be present on lochs, reservoirs and sandpits points to a total population of 1,000 pairs for SE Scotland, or 6% of the British population.

An interesting project for future research might be a comparison with the densities found in the Esk drainage study by Cowper in the 1960s and 1970s. **I.R.Poxton**

Common Sandpiper

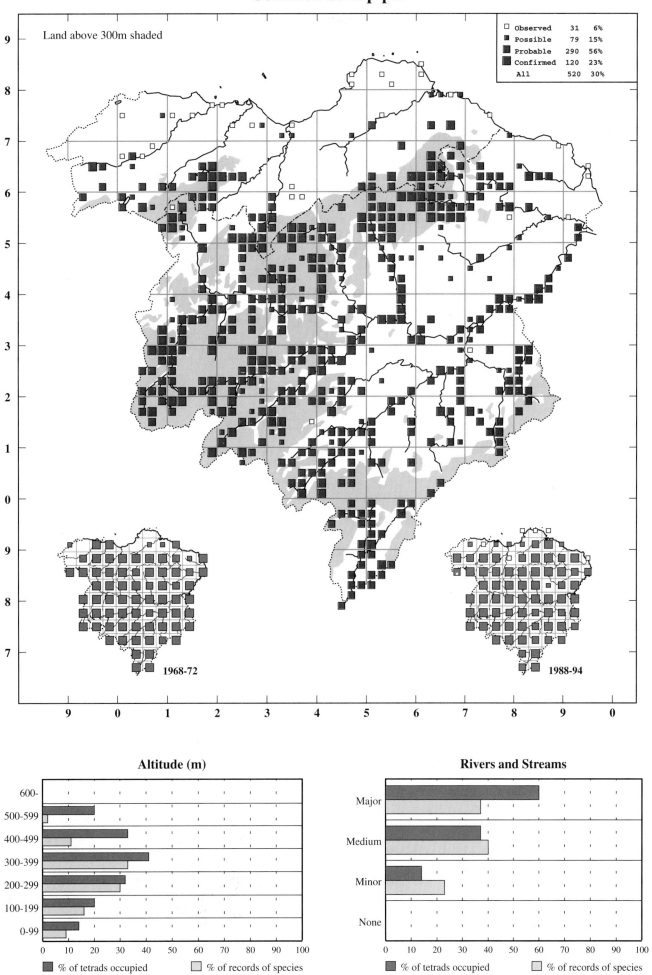

Land above 300m shaded

☐ Observed	31	6%
◪ Possible	79	15%
◩ Probable	290	56%
■ Confirmed	120	23%
All	520	30%

1968-72

1988-94

Altitude (m)

Categories: 600-, 500-599, 400-499, 300-399, 200-299, 100-199, 0-99

■ % of tetrads occupied   ▢ % of records of species

Rivers and Streams

Categories: Major, Medium, Minor, None

■ % of tetrads occupied   ▢ % of records of species

139

Black-headed Gull
Larus ridibundus

The least marine of our seabirds, Black-headed Gulls nest in a variety of habitats in Britain ranging from rocky islands and saltmarsh on the coast to lakes, reservoirs, marshy ponds and hill pools far from the sea. Coastal nesting is more common in southern Britain but in Scotland colonies are mostly inland. Colony sizes range from a few pairs up to tens of thousands. Colonies can be prone to desertion, usually in response to predation.

Foraging birds were recorded as observed and being easy to locate accounted for 92% of tetrads. The few probable records were only used when nesting was suspected, but impossible to prove, or where pairs persistently alarm-called, but there was no further proof of breeding. Breeding was confirmed in just 6% of tetrads.

Foraging birds were very widespread and were present everywhere except in the highest hills (NT12), areas of blanket forestry (NY59,NT30&60) and in intensively farmed areas of East Lothian and Berwickshire (NT57&85). Birds were almost ubiquitous in tetrads within 40km of the giant Bemersyde colony (NT63B&C). As observed records are controlled to some extent by the presence of a nearby colony, the lack of colonies near the Cheviots and in coastal East Lothian may be a reason for the gaps seen there.

Although breeding sites are scattered over the area, SE Scotland is dominated by the huge colony at Bemersyde of 14,320 pairs (in 1991), holding 72% of all the nests in the area (see pie-chart). The next three largest colonies, accounting for 14% of the total are in the Pentlands: Bavelaw, a mean of 1,090 pairs in 1988-95; North Esk Reservoir (NT15N&P), a mean of 959 nests; and West Water Reservoir (NT15B), a mean of 767 nests. The next largest is Hule Moss, mean 524 (2.6%). The remaining 11% of the total (*c*.2,200 nests) is shared amongst 47 other sites, ranging from a mean of 300 nests at Cobbinshaw to three sites where only one pair has ever been found, typically only in a single year (see Appendix).

Confirmed breeding mostly occurs between 200-400m but the impact of Bemersyde on the altitudinal distribution of observed records is so profound as to render meaningless discussion of the altitudinal distribution of birds in the area. It merely reflects the landscape around Bemersyde where gulls from that colony forage.

Large colonies are persistent and have records extending back to at least the start of the *Bird Reports* in 1979 (see Appendix). Colonies of less than 100 pairs are more transient and the smallest colonies even more so. Some 75 sites are known to have held breeding Black-headed Gulls between 1979 and 1996 of which only 37 were extant after 1990 (the fate of another 11 is uncertain). Several colonies were abandoned due to human factors, such as drainage at Outerston (NT35I) or gravel pit operations at Shiphorns (NT25K), but Mink are suspected to be responsible for the abandonment at Mount Bog (NT14A&B) and Medwyn Mains (NT14J) and are known to be the cause of the temporary abandonment at North Esk Reservoir (NT15N&P) in 1978 and 1979, the birds returning after trapping controlled the predators (M.Jones *pers.comm.*).

Colonies located in large marshes, such as those at Bemersyde and Bavelaw, appear to be the most secure. Smaller marshes, which are more prone to drying out, can lead to colonies being more easily predated. The position of a colony can shift at reservoir sites such as West Water or Cobbinshaw due to the vagaries of water levels, but the constant shifting of the St. Mary's Loch colony, with five sites in nine years, is probably due to a combination of human disturbance and mammalian predation. River shingle nests, mostly in the upper reaches of the river systems, are almost always temporary. Black-headed Gulls seem to readily and opportunistically prospect new sites. Some may be successful, such as that at Hule Moss when the water level was raised in 1992, but most fail, as happened at Acreknowe, Fruid, Kirkhouse, Shielswood, Whitton and Wooden (see Appendix for locations).

Surveys in Lothian in 1919, 1938, 1958 & 1981, summarised in *Andrews*, suggest approximately 1,000 pairs have been present during each of these periods, mostly at Cobbinshaw, Threipmuir (Bavelaw) and Harperrig. North Esk Reservoir only appeared in the last of these counts and Bavelaw increased dramatically after 1984, probably after the water level there was stabilised. The current Lothian population of just over 3,000 pairs is a considerable increase on that of much of the 20th century. The increase at Bemersyde also dates from the early 1980s when there was an apparent jump from 1,100 pairs in 1981 to 9,000 pairs in 1983. This change may largely be the result of poor estimates prior to the first systematic count in 1983. The colony definitely expanded through the 1980s but has changed little in extent through the 1990s.

Comparison of the 10-km square maps reveals little in a species so prone to establishing and abandoning colonies, except that more 10-km squares have been abandoned than colonised. The population of SE Scotland has certainly increased considerably since the early 1980s, increasing from about 3,900 pairs in 1979-81 to a mean of 19,713 in the 1988-95 period.

With such a concentration of birds at just one site, Bemersyde is clearly of local and national importance. Indeed Bemersyde is currently the largest colony in Scotland, and could also be the largest in Britain. Protection is ensured not just because it is an SWT reserve but paradoxically through egg-collecting for the "plover-egg" market, which ensures a sound economic reason for the owners, the Haig estate, to maintain the well-being of the colony. While a full census of all colonies in the area is needed, the conservation status of Bemersyde demands that thorough, accurate and regular counts be made, preferably from the air as ground-based observers are unable to see all nests and so cannot render a really accurate total.

With the latest British population estimate of 167,000 pairs (Stone *et al.* 1997), SE Scotland currently holds 13.5% of the British population. Remarkably, Bemersyde may hold just over 1% of the European population (*BWP*). **R.D.Murray**

Black-headed Gull

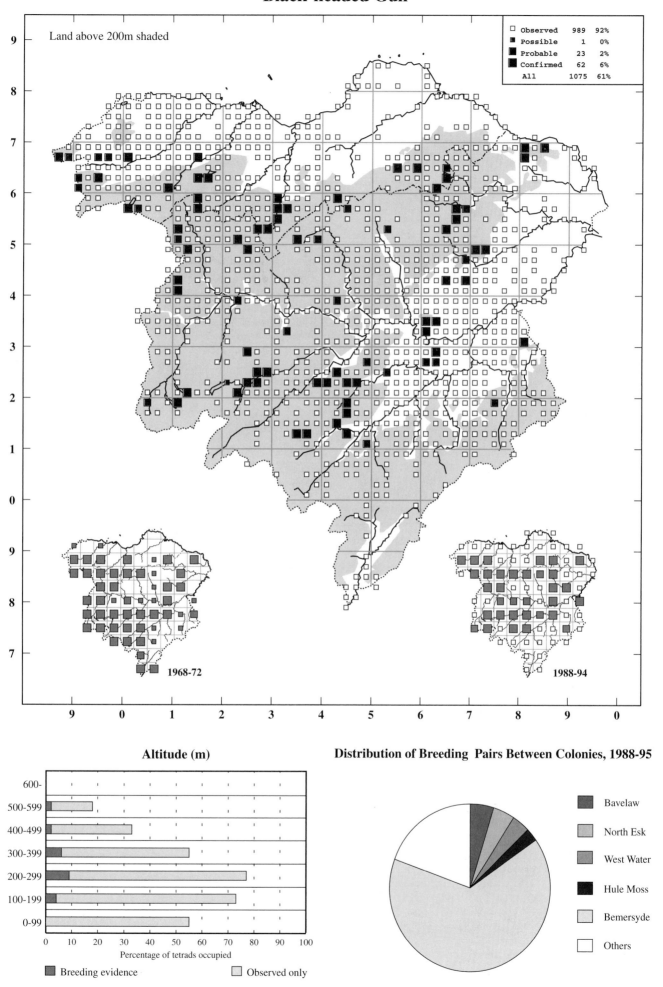

Land above 200m shaded

	Observed	989	92%
	Possible	1	0%
	Probable	23	2%
	Confirmed	62	6%
	All	1075	61%

1968-72

1988-94

Altitude (m)

Percentage of tetrads occupied

■ Breeding evidence   □ Observed only

Distribution of Breeding Pairs Between Colonies, 1988-95

- Bavelaw
- North Esk
- West Water
- Hule Moss
- Bemersyde
- Others

Frederick J Watson 98

Common Gull

Larus canus

Despite its name, the Common Gull is far from being a common breeding species in Britain. Indeed amongst the gulls it ranks a very poor fifth in SE Scotland, well behind the Kittiwake and Black-headed Gull. It is a bird of moorlands, typically nesting at or near an upland loch or reservoir. As a bird of northern and western Britain, the Common Gull is right on the edge of its range in the Southern Uplands, the only large colonies further to the south and east being in Northumberland. Foraging birds often visit nearby lochs, rivers and cultivated ground near the breeding colony.

The Common Gull was one of the species that *Atlas* fieldworkers were asked to record as either observed or as confirmed breeding. As with other gull species, it was known that Common Gulls forage widely in summer and that it was necessary to distinguish between birds associated with breeding and others either feeding in the area or simply passing through, features that the *New Atlas* methodology was unable to distinguish between. Despite requesting records in these categories a number of possible and probable records were submitted in justifiable circumstances where proving breeding on the banks of an upland reservoir might have necessitated a time-consuming search along the shores, or where Common Gulls were located in large Black-headed Gull colonies and proved to be as anxious as the mobbing Black-headed Gulls. As with all other gulls, over 90% of the records were of foraging birds, a proportion that clearly justified the decision to use the observed category.

The map shows that breeding Common Gulls are closely associated with upland reservoirs. In the Pentlands breeding was proved at Harperrig, Bavelaw, North Esk (NT15N&P) and West Water (NT15B) Reservoirs, often amongst Black-headed Gull colonies, and was probable at Cobbinshaw (NT05D). In the Tweedsmuir Hills breeding was also proved at St. Mary's Loch and was probable at Megget Reservoir (NT12Q,V&W) and Talla. In the Lammermuirs breeding occurred around Watch Water Reservoir (NT65N,S&T).

Away from breeding sites observed birds were fairly widespread in the northern hills and more loosely along the coast. The spread of this distribution is reflected in the altitude diagram which shows

birds occurring most frequently between sea-level and 400m with the largest proportion between 200-300m, mostly on the fringes of the northern hills. Birds are much more scattered in the southern hills. Other than in the Lammermuirs, there is no great concentration of foraging birds close to any colonies, the birds being concentrated along the water courses of the Tweed and Lyne (NT13&14), Eddleston Water and South Esk (NT24,25&35), Gala Water (NT43&44) and Whiteadder/Blackadder drainage (NT64,65&66). To what extent these birds are from the few breeding colonies or simply late migrants roosting at the big spring roosts sites at West Water, Portmore and Gladhouse and foraging in the immediate vicinity of the roosts, is unclear but with the low numbers of breeding birds in the area, the latter option is probably more correct.

The Common Gull is a relatively recent colonist of SE Scotland. Although suspected of breeding in Borders in the last century (Evans 1911), the first confirmed breeding records came in Borders near Houndslow (NT64I) in 1960 (Meiklejohn *et al*. 1960) and at Cobbinshaw and Whiteadder Reservoirs in Lothian during the *Old Atlas*. *Andrews* also mentions Auchencorth Moss (NT15) and Fala (NT45J) as breeding sites in the 1970s. The *Old Atlas* suggests the bird was actually a more widespread breeding species than at present and shows proved breeding records in at least seven Borders 10-km squares. As is often the case with such records in the *Old Atlas*, no substantiation is available which raises doubts as to the nature of the evidence obtained.

Breeding has occurred in most years since 1980 and the numbers of sites and of birds have been steadily increasing into the 1990s. Since the early 1980s breeding has been almost annual at West Water and Harperrig, with occasional breeding at St. Mary's Loch, Cobbinshaw and North Esk Reservoir. Isolated cases of breeding occurred at Harehope (NT24C) in 1983, on the Tweed near Tweedsmuir (NT02R) in 1984, around the Dirrington Laws (NT65W) in 1985 and at Talla in 1987. In most cases just one to three pairs were involved although between five and eight pairs have bred at the most regular sites at West Water and Harperigg. Through most of the *Atlas* period the breeding population of SE Scotland was probably around 10-15 pairs at about five sites in any single year. However, a real change occurred at Megget Reservoir in 1994 when a new colony of about 20 pairs appeared at a site that had only previously held six pairs in 1991. By 1997 this colony had grown to about 60 pairs, easily eclipsing all other sites in the area.

The colonisation of SE Scotland may be part of a trend of spread towards the south and east that was evident to *B&R* from earlier in the century. While the *Old Atlas* shows that Common Gulls may have been more widespread in southern Scotland in 1968-72 than at present, there is no real sign that the losses of 10-km squares, particularly in SW Scotland, have any great significance in a species that readily switches colony sites. It seems apparent that SE Scotland has been colonised in the last 20-30 years. This matches the experience in Northumberland where breeding first occurred in 1967. A total of 17 pairs, at several sites, bred in the early 1990s (*Day*). With a SE Scotland breeding population of about 75 pairs, the breeding population is small but actively growing.

R.D.Murray

Common Gull

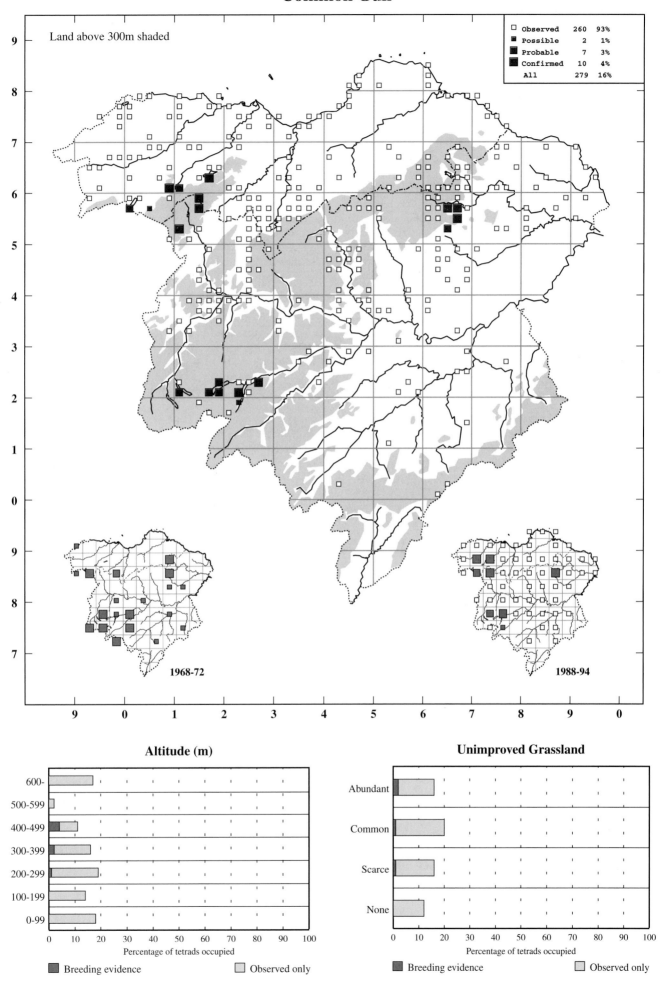

Land above 300m shaded

	Observed	260	93%
	Possible	2	1%
	Probable	7	3%
	Confirmed	10	4%
	All	279	16%

1968-72

1988-94

Altitude (m)

Percentage of tetrads occupied

■ Breeding evidence   ■ Observed only

Unimproved Grassland

Abundant

Common

Scarce

None

Percentage of tetrads occupied

■ Breeding evidence   ■ Observed only

143

Lesser Black-backed Gull
Larus fuscus

The Lesser Black-backed Gull and the closely related Herring Gull are part of one northern, circumpolar superspecies with many component populations, some of which interbreed. The two forms present in Britain normally behave as separate species. They have some different habits, an obvious one being that the great majority of British Lesser Black-backed Gulls migrate south from this country in winter, although a small and increasing proportion of them remain here. They have a slightly greater tendency to forage inland than Herring Gulls. They are colonial nesters, often in company with Herring Gulls, usually on rocky or grassy coasts or islands, occasionally inland at lochs or moors, and have a recent growing liking for nesting on roofs of buildings. Nationally they are less numerous, but currently are increasing faster than Herring Gulls.

The map and first graph show that possible, probable and confirmed breeding is confined to a limited number of tetrads, while observed records account for 97% of all occupied tetrads. These observed records have an immense spread far from breeding areas, from the coast to the inland extremities of the area, with some interesting features. On the low ground they are most concentrated over most of West Lothian, the city of Edinburgh and near Musselburgh, all being areas where some inland urban nesting occurs. They are scarce in lowland Berwickshire where Herring Gulls are numerous. Some records are grouped along rivers such as the Whiteadder, Tweed, Ettrick, Teviot and Liddel, extending up to the headwaters, particularly where reservoirs are also present (Fruid, Megget and St. Mary's Loch, NT01,11,12&22). The most mountainous, steep-sided hills as in NT12,13,22&23 and the high watersheds on the southern boundaries are not frequented, whereas the smoother more moor-like northern hills are, as are lower moors in NT64&74. Almost all these far-inland birds are of adult-type plumage, and may be scavenging for fish at rivers and sheep or rabbit carrion in the hills, with some roosting at reservoirs. Most sightings are single birds, but sometimes pairs were re-sighted in the same locations in hill areas as if holding territories (R.D.Murray *pers.comm.*).

The breeding tetrads are in three types of location: on islands, the mainland coast, and on buildings. By far the largest colonies are on the Forth islands. Only six of these islands are shown on the map. In the Appendix full details of counts for all islands are given since the 1950s, and the second graph shows the increasing numbers in different parts of the Forth area for certain years Counts are presented as "pairs", which are difficult to assess in the field, as explained for the Herring Gull article. Inchkeith has the largest colony of nearly 3,000 pairs. Inchcolm has now probably surpassed the Isle of May as the second largest colony.

The figures show that at mid-century the Lesser Black-backed Gull was a scarce species, confined to four outer-Forth islands. Since then it has spread inexorably to virtually every island and islet. In the 1960s it was suspected that the big colonies of mixed Lesser Black-backed and Herring Gulls were inhibiting breeding by terns, and a programme to humanely reduce numbers of these two gulls on the Isle of May, Fidra and Inchmickery was begun by the conservation organisations in 1972 and continued for many years. This caused a drop in the counts for the Isle of May in the 1970s.

Since then, however, increases have continued on virtually all the islands, including those where culling occurred. Only on the Bass Rock has the spread been limited perhaps due to pressure from the spreading Gannets there. All the islands hold mixed colonies of this species with Herring Gulls, and the latter have always outnumbered the Lesser Black-backs, usually by several times. On Inchmickery, Inchcolm and perhaps now on the Lamb, Lesser Black-backed Gulls have become as numerous as Herring Gulls in recent years.

In contrast with the islands, only a few pairs nest on the Berwickshire coast, near Fast Castle (NT87), St. Abb's Head and Eyemouth (NT96). These only account for some 3-7 nests in total, with none in some years. No nesting on the Lothian coast (buildings excepted) has ever been known; two pairs were seen among Herring Gulls on the tidal islet of Eyebroughy in 1981, without evidence of breeding.

Nesting on buildings accounts for all other tetrads with breeding on the map: three well inland in West Lothian, some in central Edinburgh (NT27) and two next to the coast at Granton (NT27I) and Musselburgh (NT37L). Roof-nesting by Lesser Black-backed Gulls was unreported in SE Scotland until 1989 (Holling 1991) although it may have passed undetected a year or so prior. By 1994 no less then ten different locations were known with from two to 36 pairs at each site. Lesser Black-backs outnumber Herring Gulls at virtually all roof colonies and seem to be the first colonists, with Herring Gulls joining later. The West Lothian colonies at Bathgate, Livingston and Ratho Station are all on industrial buildings, while in Edinburgh they are on warehouses, bus depots, town centre blocks and domestic housing, and in Musselburgh they nest on housing only (Dott 1994a,1996).

In the 19th century only the Bass Rock and St. Abb's Head were known to have Lesser Black-backed Gulls, each site having a few pairs. In the 1930s Craigleith and the Isle of May were colonised (*R&B*, Eggeling 1960). By the 1950s the spread on the islands was commencing (Appendix), but on the coast numbers always remained small, at between none and seven pairs (da Prato 1986, *Bird Reports*). This is many fewer than the roof-nesting birds which numbered some 130 pairs in 1994 (Dott 1996), and speaks volumes about the relative security of these two types of nesting site. The 10-km map from the *Old Atlas* shows a scatter of possible and one confirmed (NT21) breeding records in the south and west of the region which must surely have been non-breeding birds taken by observers as pairs perhaps breeding, as there are no details known of any inland breeding there.

In 1996 the Lesser Black-backed Gull population of the Firth of Forth stood at about 7,850 breeding pairs (4,500 in SE Scotland only) plus an unknown number of non-breeding birds. This consists of 7,700 pairs on the islands, *c.*4-5 pairs or the coast, and 130 pairs on buildings. The Forth and SE Scotland total is a substantial 9.5% of the British population of 83,500 pairs (*New Atlas*), 5.5% in SE Scotland alone. While the population in Britain is increasing overall with regional differences (*New Atlas*, Raven & Coulson 1997), in SE Scotland the rate of increase is high.   ***H.E.M.Dott***

Lesser Black-backed Gull

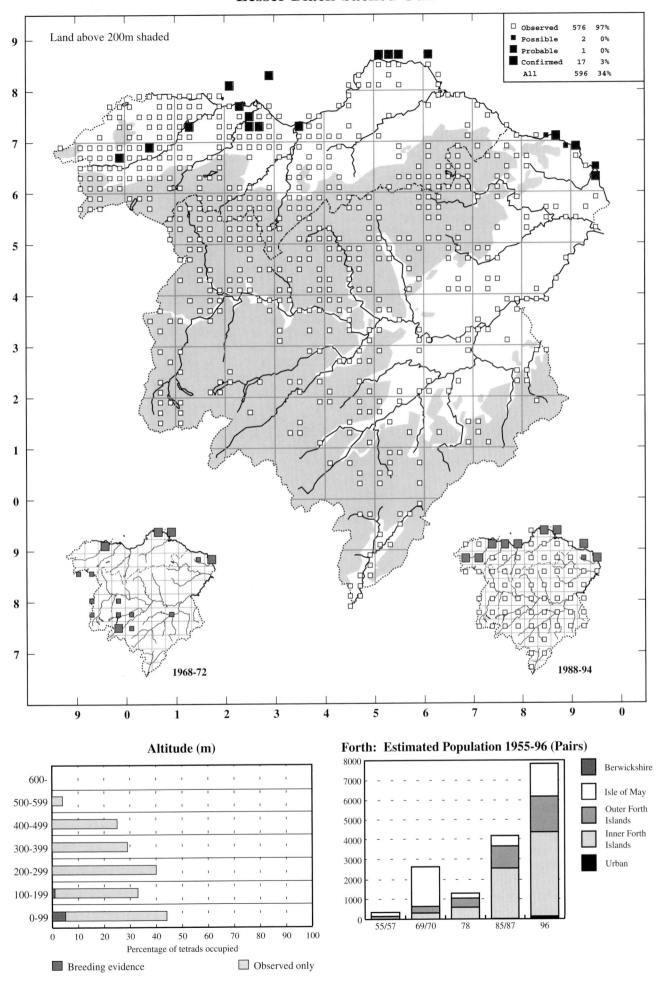

Land above 200m shaded

□ Observed	576	97%
■ Possible	2	0%
◼ Probable	1	0%
◼ Confirmed	17	3%
All	596	34%

1968-72

1988-94

Altitude (m)

Percentage of tetrads occupied

■ Breeding evidence □ Observed only

Forth: Estimated Population 1955-96 (Pairs)

Berwickshire
Isle of May
Outer Forth Islands
Inner Forth Islands
Urban

55/57 69/70 78 85/87 96

Freverickjthiatsons

Herring Gull
Larus argentatus

The Herring Gull is a highly adaptable creature, making use of a wide range of habitats and habits. It breeds on steep coasts and rocky or grassy islands, and can use dunes, sandspits and inland moors and lochs, if disturbance is low. Nesting on building roofs has become a regular habit, in seaside towns especially. It typically nests colonially, often in company with Lesser Black-backed Gulls. This century it has increased enormously in Britain, taking advantage of many human-derived food sources, although more recently it has declined in many parts.

In the *Atlas* survey proof of breeding was normally easy to obtain, except on some high complex roofs which were difficult to view. Thus confirmed breeding occurred in 90% of all tetrads where Herring Gulls were suspected of breeding, although observed records accounted for 93% of all records, as the map and graph show. The observed records were birds seen from the coast to far inland, often singly, widely over the countryside south to the Tweed and tributaries, with greater density over West Lothian, Edinburgh, Berwickshire, the northern hills, and near some rivers and reservoirs. These were mostly birds in adult-type plumage, but whether breeders or non-breeders is unknown. Fewer of this species than of Lesser Black-backed Gulls were found in the extreme west and south.

Records of breeding on the map can be considered in three categories: on islands, on the mainland coast, and on roofs of buildings. The islands hold by far the largest numbers, with about 5,000 pairs on Inchkeith alone. The coast holds much fewer, while roof-nesting is a recent habit with only small colonies. The numbers of Herring Gulls breeding in the Forth area from the 1950s onwards are displayed in the Appendix, and the second graph shows the numbers breeding in different parts of the area for certain years.

In practice counting is very problematic, especially in mixed species colonies. The majority of the counts of "pairs" were of apparently occupied nest-sites, or sometimes of total birds halved to represent pairs. In 1985-87 and 1994 painstaking counts of nests were made, mainly by NCC and SNH workers. The figures show clearly that Herring Gulls were far less numerous 40 years ago than now, and

that they nested predominantly on islands in the outer Firth of Forth, spreading into the Firth by degrees through the 1950s-70s. From 1972 to the early 1990s culling of both adult gulls and their eggs occurred on the Isle of May, Fidra and Inchmickery in order to protect the Forth tern populations. This caused a reduction in numbers, especially on the Isle of May, where 38,000 Herring Gulls (15,000 pairs plus 8000 non-breeding birds) were present in 1972 before culling (Eggeling 1974). Some of the spread to other islands in the 1970s may have been boosted by birds leaving the three islands where culling occurred (Lloyd *et al.* 1991). Overall on the Forth islands, numbers have never regained their high pre-cull levels of the early 1970s, though they are rising recently but at a much lower rate than formerly (see Appendix). Going back further, no Herring Gulls nested on the Isle of May until the first pair in 1907 (Eggeling 1960), while some bred on the islands near North Berwick in the early 20th century (*Andrews*) and on the Bass Rock in the 19th century (*R&B*). For unknown reasons, numbers have decreased considerably in the last two decades on Craigleith and the Bass Rock, though on the latter spread by Gannets must be a causal factor.

On the mainland coast, Herring Gulls only breed on the steep shores and cliffs of Berwickshire; all breeding symbols on the Lothian mainland, westwards from NT67, are in fact birds breeding on roofs. There has never been confirmed breeding on the Lothian coast except a nest (later destroyed) on the ground in Leith Docks in 1993, and a pair showing territoriality at Bilsdean in 1984 and Tantallon in 1986. The annual counts at St. Abb's Head are of consistent accuracy made by the reserve staff, and, with minor fluctuations, they show a continual decline over the past 40 years, probably due to disturbance by visitors to the reserve. Counts for the rest of the coast are fewer, with none more recent than 1987, and give a sketchier picture of fluctuating numbers mainly at a level below those of the 1950s. There are no established reasons for this mainly downward trend on the coast in contrast to most of the islands. Some gull-egg collecting by humans has been practised on the coast (but decreasingly), while Fox and Mink populations have risen through the 1980s-90s and predation may have increased. Herring Gulls have been breeding on the Berwickshire coast since the 1870s or earlier (*R&B*).

The Herring Gulls on roofs of buildings are of relatively recent origin and mostly nest in small groups or even as single pairs. Those on the North Sea coast in Eyemouth, St. Abbs and Dunbar are the longest established, since the 1970s, and nest mainly on domestic houses, though in Eyemouth *c.*40 pairs were on factory roofs in 1997. The remainder, in East Lothian coastal towns, Edinburgh city, and three West Lothian towns well inland (Ratho Station, Livingston, Bathgate) nest on domestic and industrial buildings in company with more numerous Lesser Black-backed Gulls (Dott 1994a,1996). Single pairs have occasionally nested in unexpected places; one at Rosslynlea Reservoir in 1973 (*Andrews*), one in Shiplaw sand quarries (NT25K) in 1983, 26km from the sea (*Bird Reports*), and one on a roof in Duns (NT75W) in 1994. The two inland symbols on the *Old Atlas* map opposite must indicate where birds seen together have been assumed to be possibly breeding pairs, but no substantiated breeding records for those areas are known.

The Herring Gull population in 1996 is about 15,650 breeding pairs in all Forth islands and SE Scotland (10,800 in SE Scotland only), plus a substantial number of non-breeding birds. This is comprised of 14,450 pairs on the Forth islands, 1,000 pairs on the mainland coast (estimated), and 200 on roofs of buildings. The Forth and SE Scotland total forms a substantial 9.7% of the British total of 161,000 pairs (*New Atlas*), or 6.7% in SE Scotland only. Herring Gulls have declined nationally by nearly 50% since 1969, though with differing trends in different regions (*New Atlas*), while in SE Scotland they are rising slightly on most islands and in towns, and decreasing overall on the coast and some islands. **H.E.M.Dott**

Herring Gull

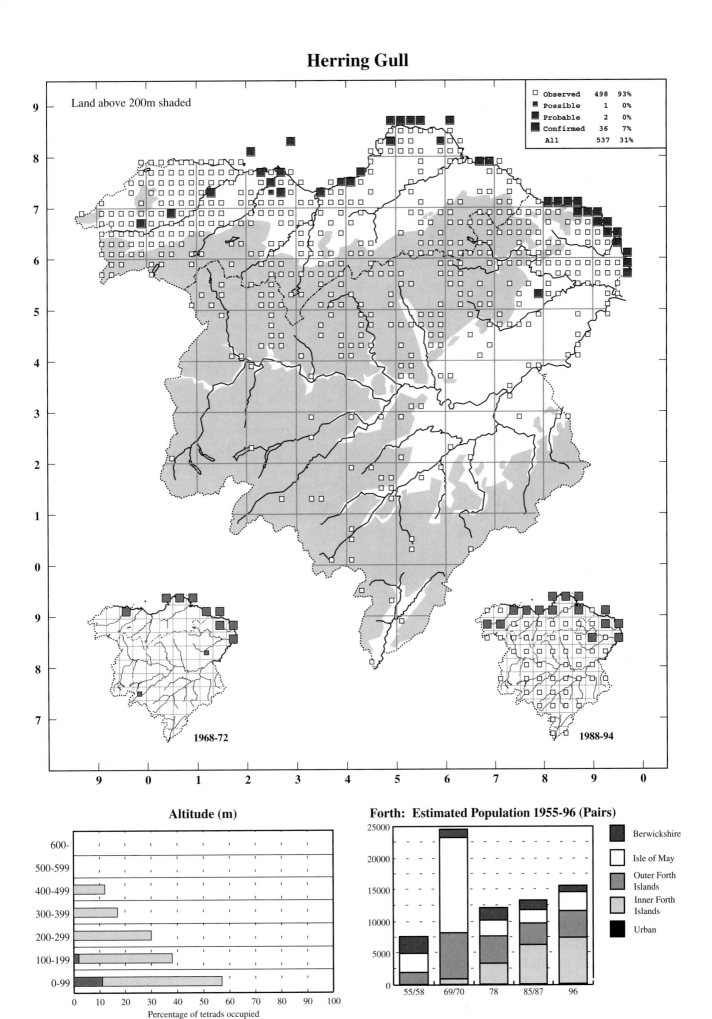

Land above 200m shaded

☐ Observed	498	93%
■ Possible	1	0%
▨ Probable	2	0%
◼ Confirmed	36	7%
All	537	31%

1968-72

1988-94

Altitude (m)

Percentage of tetrads occupied

■ Breeding evidence   ☐ Observed only

Forth: Estimated Population 1955-96 (Pairs)

55/58 69/70 78 85/87 96

■ Berwickshire
☐ Isle of May
▨ Outer Forth Islands
▨ Inner Forth Islands
◼ Urban

147

Great Black-backed Gull

Larus marinus

This huge bird seeks nesting places that have a combination of rock and grass and a degree of protection from human disturbance, particularly islands, stacks or headlands. A few nest inland by lochs or moors in northern Scotland. Nesting on buildings is known but rare. With the exception of the Kittiwake it is the most maritime of our gulls. The stronghold of the British population is in the north and west of Scotland where the bird snatches food from the sea or from fishing boats, predates seabirds and their eggs, and generally scavenges in coastal areas.

In the Firth of Forth the Great Black-backed Gull is one of the scarcest breeding seabirds, and at its southern limit of breeding on the British east coast. In winter there is a spread from NW Scotland to other coasts including the Forth, and immature birds can be seen here all year round. The size and voice of this gull mean that it is not easily overlooked even among other gulls. Lothian and Borders seabird sites are surveyed annually, and there is no doubt that all breeding sites of this species were located during the *Atlas* fieldwork.

The map shows confirmed breeding limited to four island tetrads off the East Lothian coast, with a single probable breeding tetrad on the Berwickshire coast. In addition there are a considerable number of observed records which display a pattern rather different from that seen in other gulls. Most of these are along the North Sea coast from Berwick to Aberlady with a few further into the Forth, but a surprising number are along the lower Tweed with a scatter all the way up to the headwaters of many rivers. This may be an extension of winter behaviour by non-breeding birds that routinely feed along the river system well inland, some following the Salmon migration and roosting on the reservoirs. Some of these scattered tetrads are also well into the Lammermuir, Moorfoot and Pentland Hills where sheep carrion and afterbirths may be the attraction, with reservoirs nearby for roosting. The single probable breeding record on the coast near Fast Castle (NT87K) was due to one pair showing signs of territorial behaviour during 1994 but with no other evidence of breeding. To date there has never been any proved breeding on mainland SE Scotland.

Breeding was confirmed on four islands during the survey: Craigleith, Lamb, Fidra and Bass Rock but was not annual on each of them. Breeding also occurred on the Isle of May in Fife. Numbers on the islands have fluctuated considerably, with only Craigleith and the Isle of May having pairs every year, as the graph opposite shows. A trend of increase and spread is becoming more evident in the last few years. Since the end of the *Atlas* fieldwork, Great Black-backed Gulls have nested successfully on four additional islands where breeding has never previously been confirmed: on Inchcolm in 1995, Inchmickery in 1996, and Inchkeith and Inchgarvie in 1997; one nesting pair on each new occasion. This constitutes a spread in distribution onto islands further west into the Firth of Forth, and could be related to the cessation of Great Black-backs breeding in a dockyard at Rosyth near the Forth Bridges before 1994 (Raven & Coulson 1997).

In the 19th century the species was believed to have been near extinction in Britain, but from late that century it expanded markedly in Britain and elsewhere (*New Atlas*). A few pairs are reputed to have nested on the Bass Rock in the early 19th century (*B&R*) but since then no Great Black-backed Gulls are known to have nested anywhere on the east coast of Scotland south of Moray until the 1960s, when an increase and expansion southwards took place (Lloyd *et al.* 1991), with first nesting in Aberdeenshire in 1962, Isle of May 1962, Lothian 1965, Banff 1968, Angus 1969 and in Kincardineshire by 1980 (*Thom*).

In the Forth colonisation was gradual. On the Isle of May only one to three pairs nested from 1962 through to 1990, before increasing as the graph here shows. In Lothian the first known successful breeding was by a pair on Craigleith in 1965, although breeding may have occurred there in the few years prior (Smith 1966). Craigleith held 1-2 pairs annually through the 1960s-70s and 3-4 pairs in the 1980s. The first breeding on Fidra was in 1978, on Lamb in 1983 and on the Bass Rock in 1986. A symbol for possible breeding on the *Old Atlas* map far inland at St. Mary's Loch must have been a bird mistakenly assumed in possible breeding habitat. A pair reported as nesting on a roof in Edinburgh in 1995 (Raven & Coulson 1997) has not been substantiated and in fact no Great Black-backed Gulls are known to nest on roofs in SE Scotland to date.

The Great Black-backed Gull population stood at 18 breeding pairs in the Firth of Forth, 12 of these in SE Scotland, at the end of the *Atlas* survey in 1994. By 1997 these figures had increased to 25 and 13 breeding pairs respectively. The highest figure comprises a mere 0.13% of the British population of 19,000 pairs (*New Atlas*).

H.E.M.Dott

Great Black-backed Gull

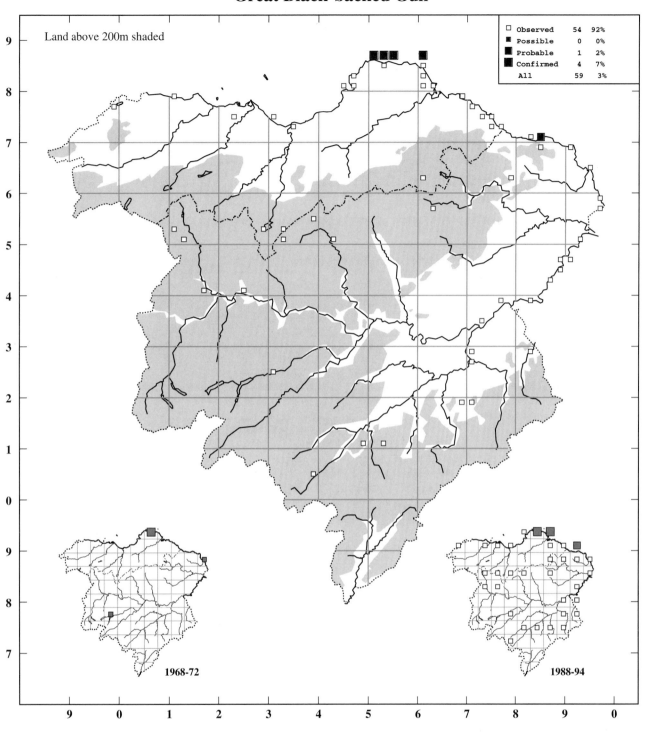

Land above 200m shaded

	Observed	54	92%
	Possible	0	0%
	Probable	1	2%
	Confirmed	4	7%
	All	59	3%

1968-72

1988-94

Forth Breeding Population 1985-96 (Pairs)

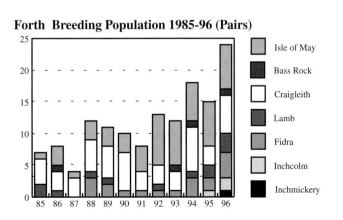

- Isle of May
- Bass Rock
- Craigleith
- Lamb
- Fidra
- Inchcolm
- Inchmickery

Kittiwake
Rissa tridactyla

Spending most of the year at sea and coming to land just for nesting, the Kittiwake is the only species amongst Britain's breeding gulls that truly deserves the name "seagull". Its gentle appearance and the manner in which pairs share the tiny nest stuck on a vertical cliff-face mean that the Kittiwake is held in great affection by the public. The name is onomatopoeic, recalling the greeting ceremony when one of a pair returns to the nest.

Living in conspicuous colonies, Kittiwakes were easy to record for the *Atlas*. Records were shared between confirmed breeding, identifying the colonies, and observed, indicating the coastal feeding range of the species. Within the confirmed breeding category, registrations were evenly divided between occupied nest, nest with eggs and nests with young.

Like many seabirds the local distribution of the Kittiwake is controlled by the availability of suitable nesting sites. This largely restricts Kittiwakes to the Forth islands to the west of Dunbar and the Berwickshire cliffs to the east. On the islands breeding takes place on Fidra (NT58D), The Lamb (NT58I), Craigleith (NT58N) and the Bass Rock (NT68D) in Lothian, and Inchcolm, Inchkeith (NT28W) and the Isle of May in Fife. Coastal breeding is almost wholly confined to the Berwickshire cliffs and then only on the highest, steepest or least accessible cliffs between Redheugh (N87F) and St. Abb's Head and at Fancove Head (NT96L). The presence of ground predators on the mainland prevents colonisation of anything but the steepest cliffs. The only non-cliff mainland nesting Kittiwakes are at Dunbar harbour (NT67U) where the walls of Dunbar Castle have been colonised, despite there being higher and steeper cliffs at Tantallon (NT58X), Cove (NT77V) and Lamberton (NT95U). Clearly other more subtle factors affect the decision of what constitutes a suitable cliff to a Kittiwake.

The observed records indicate that Kittiwakes are seldom seen on the coast away from the vicinity of a colony. This particularly applies to the coasts west of North Berwick where there are few observed records, even from coasts adjacent to breeding islands. The few records are of singles in the vicinity of gull roosts at Aberlady and Musselburgh, and of feeding flocks moving up the Forth between Dalmeny and Queensferry (NT17). The two inland tetrads with registrations refer to single records of wayward individuals in April 1988 at Gladhouse and April 1994 at Hule Moss.

Comparison with the 10-km map of the *Old Atlas* indicates losses from two squares, NT17 and NT77. Unfortunately there is no record of breeding ever having taken place in that earlier period in either 10-km square, and so it seems likely that both records are erroneous and should be ignored. A pair was, however, seen on Inchgarvie (NT17J) in 1993 although there was no evidence of breeding.

There are records of Kittiwakes breeding on the Bass Rock as far back as 1661, on the Isle of May at about the same period and at St. Abbs since the 1830s (*R&B*). It is clear, however, that there has been an enormous population increase and expansion throughout the 20th century, mainly due to protection, the Kittiwake having been shot by "sportsmen" and collected for the millinery trade. This persecution was so great that only 200 pairs bred at St. Abbs in 1909 (Evans 1911). Craigleith and the Fast Castle cliffs (NT87K) were colonised in the 1930s when birds also moved onto the harbour ruins and buildings at Dunbar, and briefly onto a pier at Granton (*B&R*). The great population increase really started in the 1950s. St. Abb's Head and the surrounding cliffs, which appear to have held two-thirds of all Forth Kittiwakes since at least the 1940s, had 4,602 pairs in 1957. This figure doubled to 8,293 pairs by 1976 and then doubled again to 16,208 pairs by 1988. The Lamb (1959), Inchkeith (1960), Fidra (1964) and large areas of the Berwickshire coast were no doubt colonised in response to population pressures at St. Abbs and to a lesser extent the Isle of May.

Colony counts (see Appendix) show that the population changes at most sites run roughly in concert with one another (see graph) with numbers rising and reaching temporary plateaux (or even dropping) before rising further, in a series of steps between 1970 and 1985, peaking between 1985 and 1992, and then falling by about a quarter of peak values into the mid-1990s. The peak is not synchronous at different sites and may indicate that some birds move between colonies in the face of overcrowding.

What is undisputed is that overall numbers have declined since the peak around 1989. As not all sites are counted every year, particularly the Berwickshire coast away from St. Abbs, estimates of population levels have been made (see graph and Appendix) over five year intervals which suggest the Forth population reached over 40,000 pairs in 1990 before falling to *c*.35,000 in 1995, about 27,000 in Lothian and Borders. In 1995 the Forth held 7% of Britain's birds.

The cause of the changes, both the long-term increase and recent decline, are probably associated with changes in availability of herring, sprats and sand-eels. Studies in Northumberland and Shetland (Coulson & Thomas 1985, Harris & Wanless 1990) show a strong correspondence between food supply, colony attendance and breeding success. Productivity in SE Scotland during the 1990s, at 0.48 chicks per pair, has only been moderate (Thompson *et al.* 1997) and suggests that the days of the huge increases of Kittiwakes are over for the time being.

A glance at the Appendix shows a major need for a full census of the Berwickshire colonies, last counted in 1982. Considering that these cliffs hold about a quarter of the Forth population, an up-to-date count is urgently needed.

R.D.Murray

Kittiwake

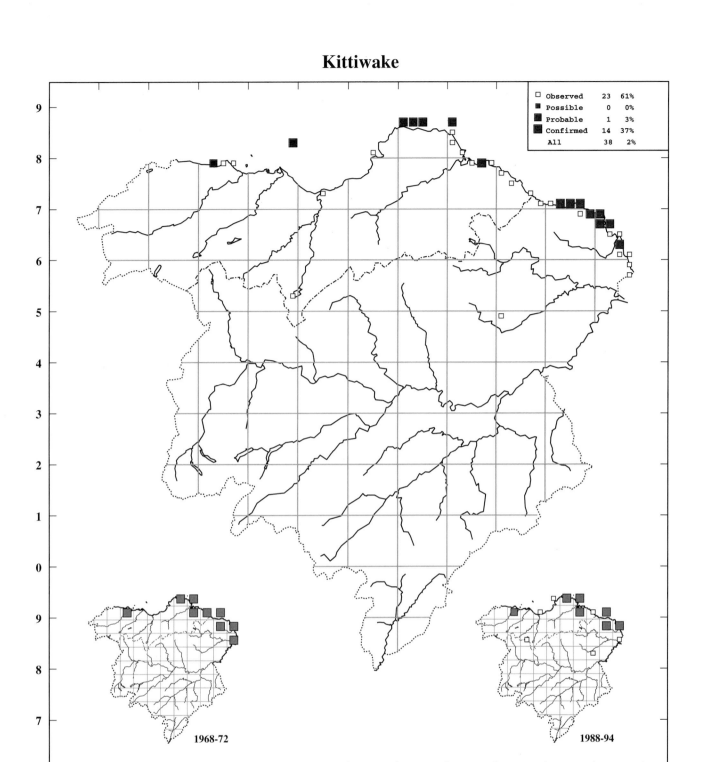

□ Observed	23	61%	
■ Possible	0	0%	
▨ Probable	1	3%	
▦ Confirmed	14	37%	
All	38	2%	

1968-72

1988-94

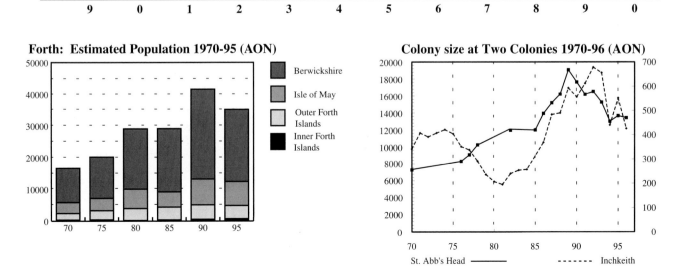

Forth: Estimated Population 1970-95 (AON)

- Berwickshire
- Isle of May
- Outer Forth Islands
- Inner Forth Islands

Colony size at Two Colonies 1970-96 (AON)

St. Abb's Head ———   - - - - Inchkeith

Common Tern
Sterna hirundo

The Common Tern has a wide distribution across the northern hemisphere and is a lower latitude counterpart of the Arctic Tern, although their ranges overlap. With a diet of fish and some invertebrates, it is strongly associated with water and although this can be both salt and fresh water, in Britain the species is mostly maritime. A colonial breeder, often in mixed colonies with other terns, Black-headed Gulls or even Ringed Plovers, Common Terns nest on the ground on rocky, gravelly or sandy substrates, with or without vegetation. Artificial habitats are also increasingly used and in some areas have been deliberately provided to improve breeding performance.

Most coastal colonies are monitored annually but minor sites may have been missed in some years, particularly the sporadic inland breeding attempts. In the *Atlas* period breeding was only confirmed at a small number of sites. Probable records mostly involved pairs seen in suitable habitat where short-lived breeding attempts could have occurred. Single birds seen at potential inland breeding sites, usually reservoirs, were classified as possible breeders. The high number of observed records reflects the coastal movements of the Common Tern. These movements extend well inland to the river systems during passage periods, the birds using river valleys as corridors across southern Scotland and possibly to prospect breeding sites.

In 1988-94 the vast majority of the Forth breeding birds were at only two sites in Lothian and one in Fife. On Inchmickery (NT28A), where numbers varied between 91 and 182 pairs, there has been a gradual downwards trend from a maximum of 780 pairs in 1973. At Leith Docks (NT27T) nesting was first recorded in 1967 and in the *Atlas* period from 106-694 nests were found annually, the numbers increasing, albeit erratically. In a good year this may be the largest Common Tern colony in Scotland and one of the top five in Britain. Birds here nest on a flat-topped, concrete mooring island, safe from ground predators. It is, however, very exposed and many eggs are probably blown away when incubating adults are disturbed. Two other artifical sites were used between 1988-94 with up to 20 pairs breeding on floating pontoons at the Port Edgar marina (NT17E) while five pairs nested on the stone islands that support the Forth Railway Bridge just outside the *Atlas* area in Fife. East Lothian coastal sites saw fairly regular breeding between 1988-94. Elsewhere, on another small Forth island (un-named for security reasons), 110 pairs nested in 1994, the same year that 13 pairs made a late season attempt to breed on Eyebroughy (NT48Y).

There have been a few changes in the main coastal distribution since the *Old Atlas*. Breeding has ceased on Fidra (NT58), at one time the species' local stronghold, and also at Aberlady where 500 pairs bred during the *Old Atlas* period. These losses are compensated by new colonies at Port Edgar, the Forth Bridge, Leith Docks and the un-named islet.

Inland breeding has never been widespread and only a few pairs are ever involved, mostly at upland reservoirs or river sites. In the *Atlas* period breeding only occurred in 1988 at West Water Reservoir (NT15B) where nesting was annual between 1976-88 and reached a maximum of six pairs in 1978 before declining to 2-3 pairs for much of the 1980s (Brown & Brown 1978, *Bird Reports*). While birds apparently prospected at other inland sites at Portmore Loch and the Megget (NT12W), Watch Water (NT65T) and Whiteadder (NT66M) Reservoirs, there was no definite proof of breeding.

Historically the Forth Common Tern colonies have been short-lived and mobile, flourishing for a few years at one site then, gradually or more suddenly, moving to another location. On Fidra 400-500 pairs bred between 1969-73 and again in 1981-84 but the island has been vacant since. Numbers at Aberlady peaked at 500 pairs in 1972 and, while present in recent years, the species has not definitely bred since. Inchmickery held 700-800 pairs between 1960-1980, and formerly some bred along the coast and offshore islets between Aberlady and Tyninghame. Various other Forth islands and islets have been occupied sporadically in the 19th and 20th centuries. Inland nesting occurred at Harperrig and Gladhouse Reservoirs between the 1930s and 1950s.

Loss of eggs and chicks to gulls, crows, foxes and other mammal predators is a frequent problem for this species. At some mainland sites this has been particularly acute and trapping of mink and electric fences to exclude foxes have been tried, but to little avail. Culls of adult gulls and the pricking of gull eggs have also been carried out at some island colonies in order to reduce pressure for space and predation on terns. Human disturbance at some mainland sites has been greatly reduced by fencing and wardening but natural events such as sandblow, tidal flooding and vegetational succession have all had a part to play in reducing success at some sites. Food shortages have been cited as occasionally causing problems and may, indeed, have a local effect, although nearby colonies have been successful in the same season.

In the *Atlas* period the total population in the Forth varied from 341 pairs to 1,029 pairs in 1993, the best year, when 806 pairs bred in Lothian and 223 pairs on two Fife islands. In that year the Forth total represented a high 8% of the British population.

P.R.Gordon

Common Tern

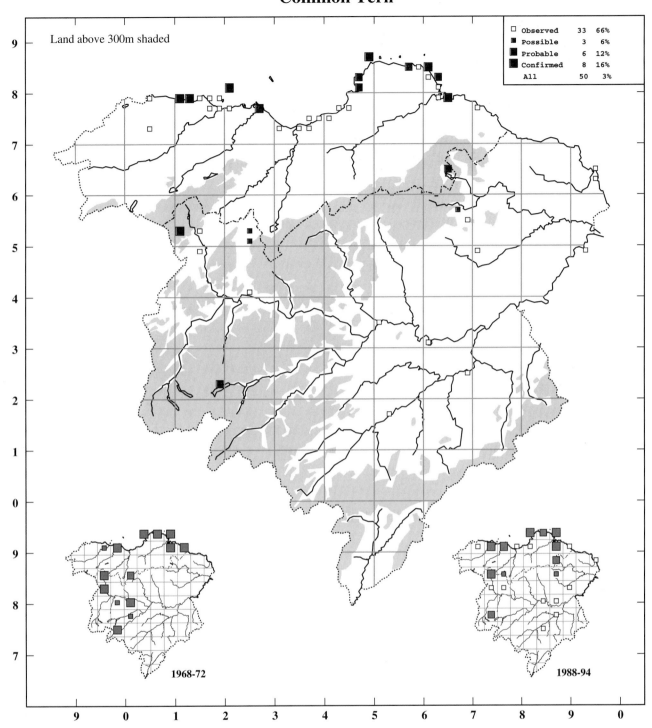

Land above 300m shaded

□	Observed	33	66%
◼	Possible	3	6%
◼	Probable	6	12%
◼	Confirmed	8	16%
	All	50	3%

1968-72

1988-94

Sandwich Tern

Sterna sandvicensis

Our largest tern, the Sandwich Tern arrives in Britain earlier in spring than the others and stays later into autumn, with very occasional birds seen in winter. It is entirely marine in Britain, though elsewhere it breeds at inland seas. It nests on shingle, dunes and on islands. Like all terns and more so than most, Sandwich Terns can desert a breeding colony of a number of years and shift to a new one, unpredictably and for no apparent reason. The Firth of Forth receives large additional numbers of this species in July to September from as far as Sands of Forvie to the north and the Farne Islands to the south.

Sandwich Terns were observed foraging in 50% of all the coastline tetrads of Lothian and Borders. Probable breeding (pairs seen) was recorded at Aberlady, but no breeding in fact occurred there. Confirmed breeding occurred at just three sites. A pair nested at Leith Docks for the first time ever in 1994 and 1996 among Common Terns, but were unsuccessful both times. Breeding was successful on Inchmickery and a smaller island (not named for security reasons), but numbers have collapsed on both. On Inchmickery *c.*300-500 pairs nested in 1988-91, *c.*120 in 1992, and none in 1996-97, as the Appendix details. On the smaller island, where breeding only commenced recently, over 200 pairs in 1993 crashed to 2 in 1996 when tides and bad weather flooded nests, and none nested in 1997. Thus in 1997 no Sandwich Terns nested in SE Scotland.

In the 19th century when their eggs were collected for food, Sandwich Terns apparently bred at times on the Bass Rock, Lamb, Inchmickery and Car Craig, and on Lamb again in 1921-1928 (*R&B*). On the Isle of May they nested with other terns in the early 19th century but deserted it by 1850. They recolonised there in 1926, rose to a peak of *c.*1,500 pairs in 1946 in a four-tern-species colony (Eggeling 1960), and then declined as the gull population rose before disappearing in 1957. Sandwich Terns bred on Car Craig from the 1930s to 1950, on Inchgarvie and Inchcolm in the 1950s where rats were a problem, attempted breeding on Eyebroughy, and bred in erratic numbers on Fidra from 1952 to

1971 (Sandeman 1963, ENHS). On Inchmickery numbers peaked at over 600 pairs several times in 1959-1987 (ENHS,LBR) with birds sometimes switching between there and Fidra. On the mainland, pairs nested unsuccessfully at Aberlady Bay in the 1970s and at St Baldred's Boat (NT68C) in 1968 (*Andrews*). Reasons for changes in numbers may be complex, as discussed in the Arctic Tern article.

The peak Forth population in the *Atlas* period was almost 500 pairs in 1991, 3.5% of the British population, before declining to none in 1997. In Britain Sandwich Terns increased greatly during 1969-87 (Lloyd *et al*.1991) but have dropped by 25% since then (Thompson *et al*. 1997). The local changes have occurred despite increasing efforts to conserve terns. Measures include provision of shingle, supression of rank growth before birds arrive in spring, and culling of adjacent Herring and Lesser Black-backed Gulls.

H.E.M.Dott

Sandwich Tern

Roseate Tern
Sterna dougallii

A beautifully tinted tern, the Roseate is internationally rare and endangered. Much of its scattered range is tropical. The Firth of Forth is presently its most northerly breeding station on the globe. Like other terns, it shifts breeding sites unpredictably. Roseates may have been extinct as breeding birds in Scotland in the early 20th century (*B&R*) though there have been colonies of a few hundred pairs before and since.

In the Forth area Roseate Terns nested at three locations during 1988-94, and were recorded as probable at an East Lothian site where they did not nest. On the RSPB reserve island of Inchmickery, nesting pairs dwindled from 5-20 in the 1980s to none during 1990-93, 1-2 pairs 1994-6, and then none in 1997. On another island (not named for security) nesting began in the 1980s, rose to about 15 pairs in the 1990s as Inchmickery was almost deserted, with some nesting continuing since. At a mainland site one pair hatched young in 1989 only. The Isle of May was recolonised in 1995 by a single pair, both birds of which had been ringed as chicks in Ireland, after a forty-year absence. There were only three coastal observed records in the *Atlas* survey.

Roseate Terns bred on the Isle of May in the early 19th century, but did not return there until the 1930s. They reached 15-20 pairs in

1946, before deserting again from 1956 to 1995. Early in the 20th century Car Craig and Inchmickery had Roseate Tern colonies, the former having up to 250 pairs in the late 1940s but was deserted suddenly in 1951 as Herring Gulls became established. Inchgarvie briefly became the main colony in 1952 with *c.*500 pairs but was abandoned two years later due to rats. This left Inchmickery as the main colony with over 400 pairs from 1957 to the 1960s, with small numbers also on Fidra. Herring Gulls were becoming numerous on both these islands and in 1972 a programme of gull culling was begun to aid the terns. In spite of this, Roseate Terns ceased to breed on Fidra from 1971, while on Inchmickery numbers dwindled from 100 pairs in 1976 to none by 1990. There has been sporadic breeding on Lamb in 1936, Eyebroughy 1950-51, Inchcolm 1954, St. Baldred's Boat 1969, and Aberlady Bay 1970-73 and 1979 (Sandeman 1963, *Andrews*, unpublished reports).

In total, up to about 20 pairs have attempted breeding in any year since 1988 in the Forth. There are recently no other Scottish colonies, so this forms 100% of the Scottish and *c.*23% of present British totals. Conservation measures are being tried for these most northerly breeding birds, including different kinds of shelters for nests and for chicks.

H.E.M.Dott

Arctic Tern
Sterna paradisaea

The smaller sized terns are amongst the loveliest of all seabirds, none meriting this more than the Arctic Tern. Its main breeding range lies on the most northerly coasts and tundras of the world. Light and acrobatic in wheeling, hovering and diving for fish, it also covers gigantic distances. Its amazing migrations from Arctic to Antarctic have been described again and again. In Britain it favours sandy shingle bars and exposed rocky islets for nesting, but it is also attracted into mixed-species tern colonies on more vegetated sites.

In the Forth area the most important Arctic Tern colony is currently on the Isle of May, which rose to over 500 pairs in the *Atlas* period, outnumbering the Common Terns there (see Appendix). All other confirmed breeding is on the mainland, in keeping with the species' liking for sand and shingle flats. The two mainland colonies, struggling presently to continue, are in protected areas at Aberlady and Tyninghame, the former being in two sub-colonies most years. A single pair bred with unknown results in the large Leith Docks Common Tern colony in 1988 and 1993. There were no other confirmed breeding sites during the *Atlas* work or since, although two adults on Inchmickery in late June 1992, one with a fish, suggests either courtship or the presence of young. Observed records were scattered along the East Lothian coast near colonies. Four tetrads with "probable" records were situated near other Arctic and Common Tern colonies.

Recent numbers at the two mainland colonies combined are shown in the Appendix and reveal a steep decline in the 1990s, when only one chick is believed to have fledged in 1990-97. In the 1970s and 1980s numbers were better, with Arctic Terns reaching over 100 and *c.*60 pairs at the two sites, outnumbering Common Terns by 9:1 (*Andrews, Bird Reports*). Human disturbance at these sites has been well reduced by fencing and signs, but flooding by high tides and sand-blow over nests remain serious problems. Predation of eggs and chicks by Carrion Crows and Foxes has worsened and food shortages have been suspected in several years, and so the outlook for all shore-nesting terns looks tenuous in spite of efforts to alleviate the problems. At these same two sites, terns have nested through much of the 19th and 20th centuries although Common Terns were then the main species (*R&B, Andrews*). In the 1960-70s Arctic Terns nested occasionally at St. Baldred's Boat and Peffer Sands with little success, and at Leith Docks single pairs bred intermittently on five occasions between 1974-95.

Arctic Terns have featured on fewer of the islands than most terns, although it is difficult to discover a few isolated pairs in large terneries. Fidra had some breeding Arctic Terns in most years from 1955 to 1986 among abundant Common Terns, with at least 50 nests in some years. On Inchmickery it is not known whether Arctic Terns have ever bred, though one or two adults have been seen occasionally. On the Isle of May Arctic Terns nested before 1850 (*R&B*). They reappeared in the 1930s, grew to 800 pairs in 1936, but declined and disappeared after 1957 (Eggeling 1960), to reappear again in 1980 and then increase as described. The decline and desertion by four species of terns in the 1950s on the Isle of May coincided with a huge increase of breeding Herring and Lesser Black-backed Gulls. Culling began in 1972 which greatly reduced the gulls, and terns reappeared in the 1980s. However, the reasons for changes in tern numbers may be complex, as changes in the availability of young Herring, and in island vegetation due to big changes in Rabbit numbers, may also have been significant, as discussed by Wanless (1988).

In 1996 the Forth held 636 pairs of Arctic Terns, with just six of these in SE Scotland and the rest on the Isle of May. This total represents 1.4% of the British population.   ***H.E.M.Dott***

Little Tern
Sterna albifrons

This tiny seabird is the second rarest tern in Britain. It is entirely coastal in this country although it nests far up rivers in other continents. Of all our terns the Little Tern has the strongest tendency to nest on shelly sand and shingle spits, so close to high water level that flooding by high spring tides is a sadly frequent occurrence.

In the 1990s the Little Tern has become the rarest tern in SE Scotland. In the *Atlas* period breeding occurred only at two locations, with display observed at a third site in one year only, all on the mainland coast. In 1991 to 1994 only 7-13 pairs attempted to breed and failed to fledge any chicks. In 1995 and 1996 one pair attempted and failed, and in 1997 no Little Terns attempted to breed anywhere in SE Scotland.

This is a sad decline after an increase in preceeding decades. The *Old Atlas* shows breeding in five 10-km squares in 1968-72. In the early 1970s numbers were low in the two main colonies but there was erratic nesting at two other sites in eastern East Lothian. From 1979 to 1986, 24-78 pairs nested at the two main sites together and managed to fledge young in about half those years. In the best year, 1982, there were 29 and 49 pairs at the two colonies (*Andrews, Harris et al.*1987). In 1987 to 1990, when a pair was seen displaying at a third site in one year, 11-47 pairs at the two sites fledged some young in each year, after which numbers fell away as the Appendix shows. Little Terns bred at similar coastal locations early in the 20th century and reputedly nested on Inchmickery in 1881 (*R&B*). They have been seen at the Isle of May but never nested there.

The reason for the increase at the main colonies in the 1970s-1980s was due to measures taken to prevent human disturbance by wardening, fencing and explanatory notices. Human disturbance is now a reduced problem at these protected sites, though elsewhere it is probably preventing establishment of colonies. The complete breeding failure through the 1990s has been due to a combination of traditional problems of high tides flooding nests, sand-blow overwhelming nests, hard weather, perhaps a shortage of small fish, and recently eggs and young being predated by Carrion Crows, Foxes and possibly Stoats, Weasels and Hedgehogs. Staff and helpers are trying to address these problems. As though these are not enough problems for Little Terns, larger terns will attempt to take their food or even destroy their chicks (Clunas 1982).

SE Scotland's 1988-94 breeding population averaged less than 1% of Britain's total, and is now nil, hopefully only temporarily. Britain's population has declined lately after a rise in 1969-1987 (Carter 1995).   ***H.E.M.Dott***

Guillemot
Uria aalge

Presently rivalling the Fulmar to be Britain's most numerous seabird, the Guillemot breeds in relatively few, but often very large colonies. Its preferred breeding stations are high cliffs with long ledges onto which Guillemots pack so tightly that scores or hundreds may be touching shoulder to shoulder. This makes pairs or incubating birds, slightly crouched on their single egg or small chick, hard to pick out except by long hours of watching. Rock stacks and slopes of broken rocks are also used, but all breeding sites chosen are normally inaccessible to ground predators or humans. The busy clamour of birds calling, waves breaking, and the constant arriving and departing of birds, make enthralling watching. Colonies are deserted in July, much earlier than with most seabirds. The young birds are less than half grown at this stage and are closely attended by the male for a while, usually out of sight of land.

As all the island and most mainland seabird breeding places in SE Scotland are monitored annually, no Guillemot breeding locations should have been missed in the *Atlas* survey. The few observed symbols on the map probably all represent foraging birds, as most are at sites quite unsuitable for breeding. The only possible record, in NT87F, might indicate a prospecting bird. In the Forth area there are six tetrads with breeding colonies on the mainland, all in Berwickshire, and six island colonies; five shown on the map and the Isle of May lying off Fife Ness.

Guillemot counts for the Forth area are displayed in the Appendix. In the past, counts have sometimes been recorded as totals of birds on cliffs and sometimes as "pairs" or "sites", assessed variously by sightings of eggs, young, incubating adults, or birds taken to represent pairs. Count accuracy can be somewhat variable due to the problems of arranged brief boat visits in weather that cannot be organised! Counts at St. Abb's Head and the Isle of May since the early 1980s are more consistent due to resident workers being able to choose suitable dates, time and weather. However, over the long term the validity of all the counts is certainly sufficient to show real trends.

The history of local Guillemots, like that of some other seabirds, is one of relentless rise to higher and higher levels. New protection law in the early 20th century must have been a cause of increase then for this species whose eggs were much harvested. Changes in food availability may also be a factor as Guillemots at breeding time do not go far from the breeding cliffs to find food (*New Atlas*). Removal of larger fish by fishermen may have allowed smaller fish to prosper, aiding birds that take these.

As the Appendix shows, the cliffs of St. Abb's Head and the Isle of May are the two locations holding by far the largest numbers of Guillemots. These two sites, with the Bass Rock, are also the oldest Guillemot colonies in SE Scotland and are the furthest out from the Forth Estuary towards the North Sea. Guillemots have been breeding on the Isle of May and Bass Rock since the 17th century or before, and at St. Abb's Head since at least the early 19th century. The colonies then held hundreds rather than thousands at all three sites (*R&B*).

Westward colonisation towards the inner Firth of Forth began with first recorded breeding on Craigleith in 1934 (*R&B*). Some decades later this westward progress was continued with first confirmed breeding on the Lamb in 1963, on Fidra in 1972 and on Inchkeith in 1976. Thus the continual increase in population was accompanied by a colonisation of new islands progressively further into the Forth. The graphs opposite show the rise in the Guillemot population and the proportions of this which occur in different parts of the Forth area; where counts are not available for certain islands or sites in the required years (see Appendix) estimates are made using the nearest years' counts.

The total numbers of Guillemots in Britain have been increasing all through the 20th century to the 1980s, though with very different rates in various regions (Lloyd *et al.* 1991). In the 1990s the increase has slowed and decreases have occurred in some areas with a complexity of possible reasons (*New Atlas*). In the Firth of Forth there have been impressive rises. At St. Abb's Head, Bass Rock and Isle of May the steepest rises must have been in the early 20th century when few counts were available, whereas recently their rates have slowed but are still increasing, as annual sample plots at St. Abb's Head and the Isle of May confirm. At Craigleith and the Lamb (see graph) the rise in numbers was very steep during early colonisation, but has slowed at both, and may be near stabilisation on Craigleith presumably as suitable new breeding sites become exhausted. On Fidra and Inchkeith numbers are still rising, but on these and all the inner Forth islands the amount of cliff habitat is limited and further large increases here do not seem probable. However, we can expect the Guillemot to be flexible in where it increases its numbers in future, as Harris *et al.* (1996) have shown that a considerable proportion of local Guillemots can move from one colony to another. The high cliffs on mainland East Lothian around Tantallon have so far never been known to hold Guillemots.

For the whole Firth of Forth, counts indicate the Guillemot population in 1996 to be 69,600 birds. This can be considered as 36,000 on the Berwickshire coast and 33,600 on all the Forth islands, or, 36,000 in Borders, 9,050 in Lothian and 24,550 in Fife. The most recent British population estimate is 1,047,000 birds in 1985-87, when the Firth of Forth held a significant 5.2% of this. Some studies indicate that to convert totals of birds to numbers of breeding pairs, a factor of about 0.67 should be used (Lloyd *et al.* 1991). This method suggests that the Forth's 69,600 birds in 1996 represent 46,600 pairs. ***H.E.M.Dott***

Guillemot

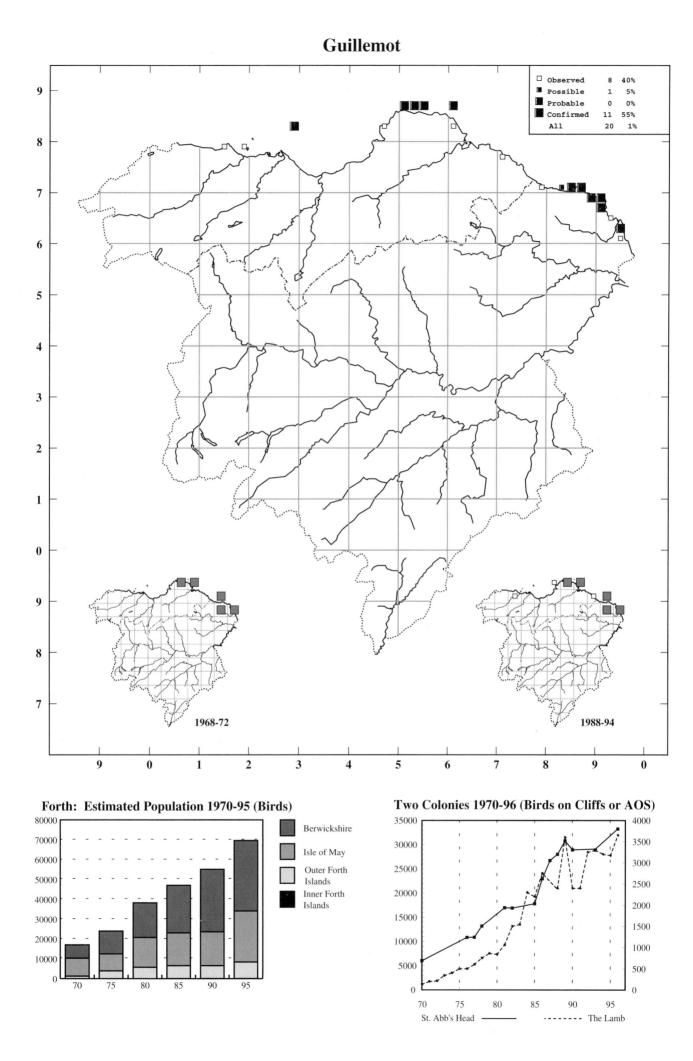

□ Observed	8	40%	
▪ Possible	1	5%	
▨ Probable	0	0%	
■ Confirmed	11	55%	
All	20	1%	

1968-72

1988-94

Forth: Estimated Population 1970-95 (Birds)

Berwickshire
Isle of May
Outer Forth Islands
Inner Forth Islands

Two Colonies 1970-96 (Birds on Cliffs or AOS)

St. Abb's Head ——— The Lamb ------

157

Razorbill
Alca torda

Like other auks, this is a totally marine seabird, only coming to land in order to nest. In the breeding season Razorbills are found at nearly all the same locations in Britain as the Guillemot, but almost invariably in much smaller numbers. They lay their single egg in recesses among jumbled rocks below or around cliffs and rock stacks, and also on visible nicks and ledges on open cliffs and rock towers. They do not breed in jostling close-packed groups, but may be scattered and less conspicuous amongst the more numerous Guillemots. A few breed away from Guillemot colonies, as they are less limited to true cliffs than the latter. As with Guillemots, Razorbills desert land early, in July, when the young are less than half grown, after which the young are fed at sea, usually out of sight of land.

Razorbills are not easy to count. As they do not pack tightly together, those on cliffs can usually be distinguished as pairs, or single members of pairs, occupying a site, and if with an egg or small chick they may be distinctive by their crouched posture. Thus in SE Scotland Razorbills have most often been censused as numbers of apparently occupied sites (AOS) or "pairs", rather than as individual birds. However, Razorbills breeding in out-of-sight crevices or among jumbled boulders present problems, and may only be detectable as birds entering or leaving such places. As with other auks some of the birds at a colony may be non-breeders.

Razorbills, as with other seabirds in SE Scotland, have been well monitored in recent years, and no breeding sites should have been missed during the *Atlas* survey. The map shows two symbol categories only, confirmed and observed. The five tetrads showing observed must refer to birds foraging near shores, possibly including pre-breeding immature birds.

The breeding locations fall clearly into two groups, mainland and island. The mainland sites are all in Berwickshire, clustered around St. Abb's Head, including west from there beyond Fast Castle to Hirst Rocks (NT87F), and a group south of Eyemouth around Fancove Head (NT96L). The island sites comprise four clustered near North Berwick: the Bass Rock, Craigleith, Lamb and Fidra, the Isle of May lying off Fife, and newer colonies on inner Forth islands at Inchkeith, Inchmickery, and Inchcolm.

The Appendix shows all Firth of Forth counts gathered together, which hitherto have been only recorded in scattered sources. Many of the counts were made in the sometimes unkind weather and limited time of pre-arranged boat trips, while more recent ones from the Isle of May and St. Abb's Head made by resident staff are more consistent. Over the long term, however, all the counts are valid to show changes and trends. The graph opposite displays counts at five-year intervals for different parts of the Forth area, including some estimates for individual colonies if counts for required years were not available. The tremendous population increase is revealed, with the Isle of May and St. Abb's Head holding the great majority of birds.

There is confusion in history over the names used for Razorbill and Guillemot, but Razorbills were certainly breeding on the Bass Rock in the 18th century and on the Isle of May and St. Abb's Head in the 19th century, and perhaps since long before. Numbers were probably between 50 pairs and the lower hundreds at all three locations in the 19th century (*R&B*). Razorbills and their eggs were taken as food until banned by new laws in the early 20th century. This harvesting may have suppressed any potential rise in numbers then.

As the Appendix shows, a spectacular rise in population began at St. Abbs and Isle of May about the late 1970s. This has continued right through the 1980s and into the l990s and is still ongoing, though there may be a recent slowing of the increase at St. Abbs. On the Bass Rock, where good counts have been fewer, trends are unclear. Pressure on good nest sites may be greater there due to other seabirds.

Away from the traditional colonies there is no hint of anything but increase and spread. Starting about the 1950s, Razorbills have been colonising westwards further and further into the Firth of Forth. Craigleith was colonised about l951, followed by the first confirmation on the Lamb in 1962 (*Andrews*). Breeding then began on Inchkeith in 1970 just before Fidra in 1974, although Inchkeith is well west of the latter. Increases on these four islands have continued, though with fluctuations in counts as the second graph shows for two of the islands. Very recently the Razorbill has appeared on Inchmickery and Inchcolm, still further west into the Forth. Here they have colonised without the Guillemot, whereas on other Forth islands this century Guillemots preceeded Razorbills, except on Inchkeith. On Inchmickery although one pair of Razorbills laid an egg in 1992 they have not apparently bred since. On Inchcolm laying by two pairs was confirmed in 1995.

In Britain as a whole, Razorbills increased overall between 1969 and 1987, but unevenly in different regions, and with a number of possible influences. Since the 1980s numbers have stabilised or declined in some studied colonies but wider trends are not known (Lloyd *et al.* 1991, *New Atlas*). Increases in SE Scotland have been pronounced from the 1970s into the 1990s, but appear to have slowed recently at the two largest colonies while still increasing in the newer, smaller colonies. Recent counts are lacking for the Berwickshire coast outwith St. Abb's Head NNR.

Overall, the Firth of Forth population stands at about 4,250 "pairs" in 1996. This consists of *c.*2,750 pairs on all the Forth islands (mostly on the Isle of May) and *c.*1,500 on the Berwickshire coast, or, 400 pairs in Lothian, *c.*1,500 in Borders, and *c.*2,350 in Fife. The latest British population estimate for 1985-87 is of 148,000 birds (*New Atlas*), and using the conversion factor for relating "pairs" to birds recommended by Lloyd *et al.* (1991), the Firth of Forth then held 2.6% of Britain's birds. This would be 4.3% with the Forth's 1996 population, such has been the local rise.

H.E.M.Dott

Razorbill

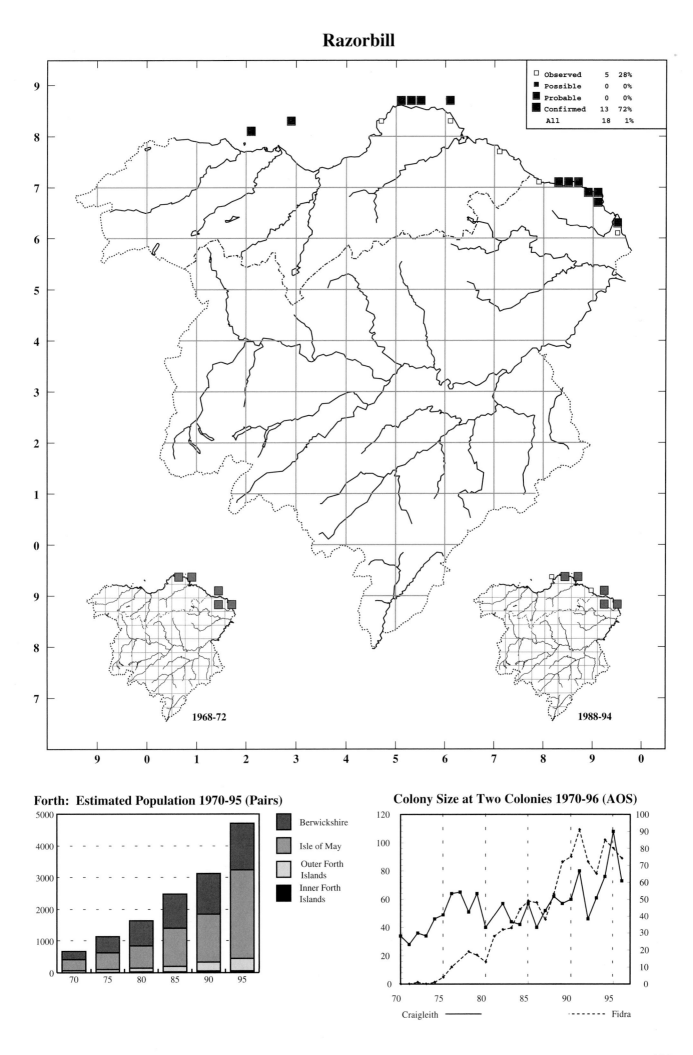

	Observed	5	28%
	Possible	0	0%
	Probable	0	0%
	Confirmed	13	72%
	All	18	1%

1968-72

1988-94

Forth: Estimated Population 1970-95 (Pairs)

Berwickshire
Isle of May
Outer Forth Islands
Inner Forth Islands

Colony Size at Two Colonies 1970-96 (AOS)

Craigleith ——— Fidra - - - - - -

Puffin
Fratercula arctica

Much loved by the public, the Puffin is known to many only from pictures. Yet it is more numerous than our familiar gulls, and currently vies with the Kittiwake to be Britain's third most abundant seabird. In summer Puffins are concentrated into relatively few and sometimes enormous breeding colonies. They nest underground in burrows or under loose rocks, giving safety from predatory gulls, and to avoid ground predators such as rats, foxes, cats or mustelids, the colonies are usually on islands or sometimes on inaccessible cliffs or headlands. In winter Puffins become one of our most oceanic of seabirds, spreading across the North Sea and the Atlantic Ocean with few remaining near our coasts.

Puffins are notorious amongst seabird enthusiasts for being difficult to census meaningfully. In the breeding season, especially during incubation and chick rearing, few Puffins are usually visible at a colony on land or water, and the numbers that do occur vary erratically with time of day, weather or other factors. Large numbers can appear at the beginning or near the end of the breeding season and sometimes on calm evenings. Counts of birds cannot reliably be converted to represent pairs, but if an approximation is needed, one bird from such counts is thought to represent a minimum of one breeding pair (Lloyd *et al*. 1991). Counting total numbers of burrows is also a poor option for censusing, as only a proportion of burrows are used by birds in any one year, and this proportion varies greatly from one colony or year to another. At any colony Puffins can be subject to unexpected breeding failures for unknown reasons, causing up to 30% decreases in a year with recovery the next (Harris & Murray 1981).

The Forth area has a fair number of Puffin colonies, some small and recently established. Most are on the islands and only a few on the Berwickshire coast. Breeding has been confirmed on nine Forth islands in the *Atlas* period (three in Fife not shown on the map). On the Berwickshire coast, there is one tetrad at St. Abb's Head with confirmed breeding, and three others with probable breeding. Proof of breeding is not easily recorded except by intensive fieldwork and it is possible that breeding may have occurred but not yet been detected in the tetrads near Fast Castle (NT87K), Heathery Carr (NT87Z) and Fancove Head (NT96L), where some Puffins have been seen coming ashore for some years (*Bird Reports*). The four observed records may be stray birds foraging or prospecting.

In spite of the defiance by the Puffin to be censused properly, all available Forth Puffin counts are collected together in the Appendix. Although the counts have variously been of birds, "pairs" or occupied burrows, they are valid to show long-term changes and trends. The greatest numbers breed on the Isle of May, perhaps four times as many as all the other colonies put together. Craigleith and recently Inchkeith are also important. The islands in the outer Forth are the longest established and the innermost ones the most recent, with the only evidence of breeding on Inchgarvie so far being a bird taking fish onto it in 1993. The mainland has been

less intensively studied and although Puffins have been stated as "breeding" at St. Abb's Head since the early 19th century, no proof was recorded until an adult with a chick was seen in 1988 and a dead chick found in 1990. In spite of the numbers of birds seen at St. Abb's Head (see Appendix), less than 20 pairs were thought to be breeding in the 1980s (SAHSR). Elsewhere in Berwickshire breeding has yet to be proved. The first graph opposite shows the increase in the Forth population since 1970 in five-year intervals, including estimates for some colonies based on the nearest years' counts available, and examples of two colonies are in the second graph.

Changes in the Puffin numbers have been remarkable. At St. Abb's Head, Bass Rock, Craigleith and Isle of May Puffins have been breeding in small numbers since the early 19th century or before. St. Abb's Head had from a few to *c*.50 pairs and the Bass Rock tens of pairs in the 19th century, Craigleith 20-30 pairs in 1889 and the Isle of May 20-40 pairs in the 1880s (*R&B, B&R,* Eggeling 1960). The Appendix shows that there was little change between the 19th century and the first half of the 20th, before a spectacular increase on the Isle of May and Craigleith starting in the 1960s, closely followed by the establishment of new colonies on Inchkeith and Fidra with steep rises continuing and more new colonies establishing thereafter. Between 1959 and 1985 the Forth population increased almost 200-fold (Harris *et al*. 1987). Only St. Abb's Head and the Bass Rock have shown little or no increase respectively, perhaps due to lack of sites safe from ground predators at the former and intense competition from other seabirds at the latter. Increase at the Isle of May has been the most dramatic, at around 20% per annum through the 1970s and involving immigration from elsewhere, including the Farne Islands (Harris 1984). This increase slowed abruptly after 1981 and there has been no increase there since 1985 (Harris in *New Atlas*). The rates of increase may be slowing now on other islands, but more good counts are needed.

In Britain overall, Puffin numbers are thought to have been lower in the early 20th century than before and after. From 1969 to 1987 there may have been a marginal increase with many different trends at different colonies, but at present data are insufficient to determine any overall trend. Reasons for changes are complex and influences may operate locally or generally and in summer or in winter quarters (Lloyd *et al*.1991, *New Atlas*).

The Puffin population of the Firth of Forth in 1995 comprises about 26,100 birds at colonies (probably involving at least this number of pairs - Lloyd *et al*. 1991). This total consists of *c*.150 on the Berwickshire coast and *c*.25,950 on all the islands including *c*.20,100 on the Isle of May, or, *c*.4,600 in Lothian, *c*.150 in Borders and *c*.21,350 in Fife. The Forth area's total of 26,100 birds forms 2.9% of the most recent (1985-87) estimate of the British population of 900,000 birds (*New Atlas*).   **H.E.M.Dott**

Puffin

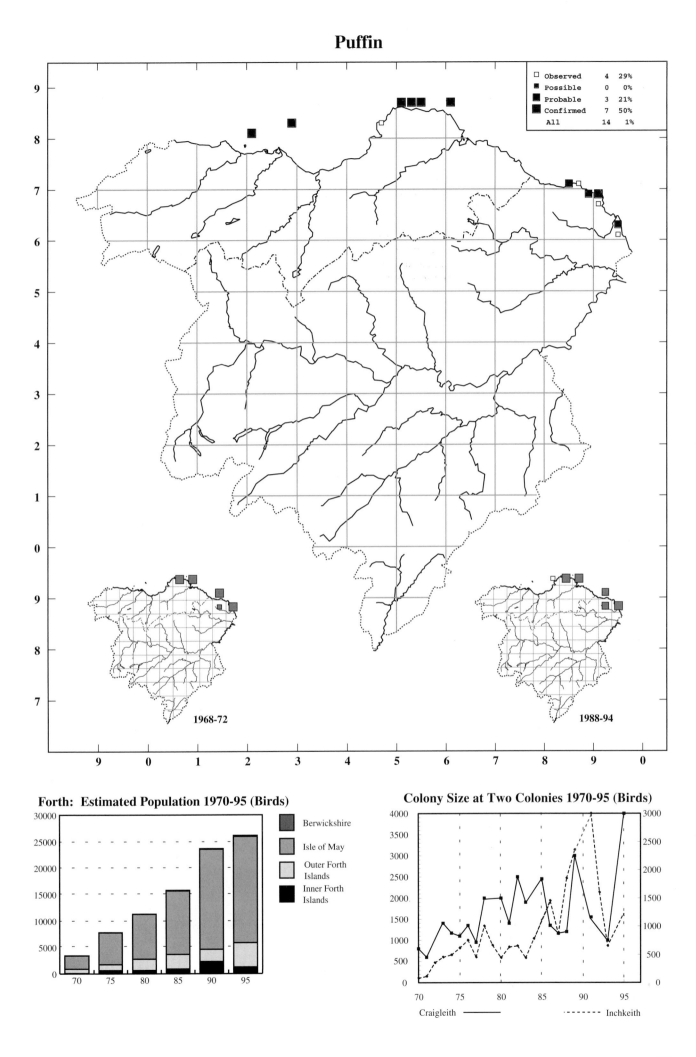

☐ Observed	4	29%
■ Possible	0	0%
■ Probable	3	21%
■ Confirmed	7	50%
All	14	1%

1968-72

1988-94

Forth: Estimated Population 1970-95 (Birds)

- Berwickshire
- Isle of May
- Outer Forth Islands
- Inner Forth Islands

Colony Size at Two Colonies 1970-95 (Birds)

Craigleith ———   Inchkeith - - - -

161

Feral Pigeon

Columba livia

The Rock Dove, the ancestor of the Feral Pigeon, once nested across much of the British Isles. Centuries of domestication, initially as a source of fresh winter meat but latterly in the hobby of pigeon-racing, have led to wholesale hybridisation between the wild population and feral birds that have escaped from doocots and pigeon lofts. Although a few apparently purely wild birds persist in the more remote parts of northern and western Britain, the remainder of the country is populated by a hybrid swarm of all manner of colours, sizes and patterns.

Feral Pigeons are relatively easy to record when they are associated with buildings. Observers routinely looked inside farm outhouses, in derelict buildings and under bridges for signs of pigeon nests. Consequently most confirmed records were of occupied nests, with both fledged young and nests with young distant runners-up. Probable records were mostly of pairs in suitable habitat while possible records were mostly of single birds in suitable habitat. The fairly large number of observed records mostly involved birds which may have been homing pigeons or birds passing through a tetrad. Cliff nesting birds were more difficult to get to grips with as their nests were often hidden in caves or cracks in the cliff-face.

While Feral Pigeons were reported in almost half of the tetrads, it is likely, judging from some of the gaps in the coverage where they must almost certainly be present, that some observers failed to record birds, the 'doo' being a sort of second-class bird not worth recording. Such an effect was so marked in the Northumberland Atlas (*Day*) that it was not worth producing a map for the species. Such a factor may be responsible for the gaps in the distribution in West Lothian (NS97) and East Lothian (NT46,47,57&67) rather than a real lack of birds. Despite this effect it is believed that the map fairly accurately reflects the principle features, if not the finest detail, of the Feral Pigeon's range in SE Scotland.

The map, not unnaturally, bears some resemblance to the map of human settlement. Most birds nest in buildings and the main urban areas can be seen in the Feral Pigeon map although the density of occupied tetrads is low in the Edinburgh suburbs, presumably because there are fewer nest-sites in modern housing and some observers may have thought that birds there were from local pigeon lofts. Most of the occupied tetrads, however, reflect a more rural aspect to the Feral Pigeon in that they frequently inhabit farms and farm buildings. Indeed pigeons are often considered a nuisance on many farms and active measures are often taken to kill them. Feral Pigeons clearly favour lowland arable farms across much of SE Scotland where suitable nest-sites coincide with abundant grain. However, the population clearly extends well into the hills where animal fodder helps to supplement the more natural diets. This is supported by the altitude graph that shows a steady drop in representation with altitude, with 75% of all records from below 250m where arable land is concentrated and Feral Pigeons present in about 65% of all tetrads below 200m.

Although difficult to distinguish because of adjacent occupied tetrads, all of the coastal tetrads that are dominated by cliffs between Torness (NT77) and Lamberton (NT95) hold breeding Feral Pigeons in habitats resembling that of their 'wild' ancestor. The lack of birds on the cliffs around Tantallon (NT58X) is odd and suggests that birds may have been overlooked there. Feral Pigeons are also present on most of the Forth islands, breeding in the ruins of the Second World War defences, as well as cliff sites.

There would appear to have been huge changes in the local distribution of Feral Pigeons in SE Scotland if the differences from the *Old Atlas* 10-km square map are taken at face value. This shows that despite the loss of breeding birds from just a single 10-km square, no fewer than 28 other squares appear to have been colonised since 1968-72. This is not a marginal colonisation with Feral Pigeons breeding in one or two tetrads adjacent to occupied 10-km squares, as on average the 'new' 10-km squares, hold a minimum of eight occupied tetrads. It is likely that observers simply did not record Feral Pigeons in these 10-km squares during the *Old Atlas*, on the basis that Feral Pigeons are not 'real' birds! This certainly happened in the Northumberland Atlas (*Day*) and may have happened in some tetrads in this publication. There is no knowledge of any great spread of Feral Pigeons into the areas shown as vacant in the *Old Atlas* and local farmers will tell you that the 'doos' have been on their farms for many years back to their childhood. While the *New Atlas* says that birds have recently spread into these rural environments, there is no evidence to suggest that such is the case in SE Scotland. Certainly the numbers of centuries-old doocots hints that doos have bred in rural areas for hundreds of years and site names such as Dowlaw (NT87K) indicate a long history of occupation.

The *New Atlas* abundance map shows considerable numbers in the main inhabited part of the local range. Much of West Lothian, the Edinburgh-Penicuik area, East Lothian north of the A1, the Eye valley and a large area between Kelso, Jedburgh and Lauder have the highest densities of Feral Pigeons.

The *New Atlas* made only a cursory attempt to calculate the national population, suggesting about 100,000 pairs. Counts along the Berwickshire coastline in winter suggest a likely 500-1,000 pairs breed just on the coastal cliffs while offshore islands like Inchmickery (250 birds), and Inchgarvie (100 pairs) hold considerable numbers. Many individual farm steadings across much of the area appeared to hold between 10-50 birds during the survey, even well away from arable areas. Central Edinburgh alone may hold in excess of a thousand pairs, with perhaps a similar number around Leith Docks (H.E.M. Dott *pers. comm.*), while most towns and villages may hold between 10-100 pairs. The local BBS surveys in 1994-95 found an average of 16 contacts on 40% of the 1-km plots. With 'fly-bys' included in these numbers a suitable reduction would still leave 2-3prs/km². Such figures would suggest 6,500-10,000 pairs in our area. If that number is realistic, the BTO national estimate is far too low. The lack of precision in this estimate suggests that even the humble Pigeon should not be ignored and that counts may be worthwhile to provide a more accurate and reliable estimate of local numbers.

R.D.Murray

Feral Pigeon

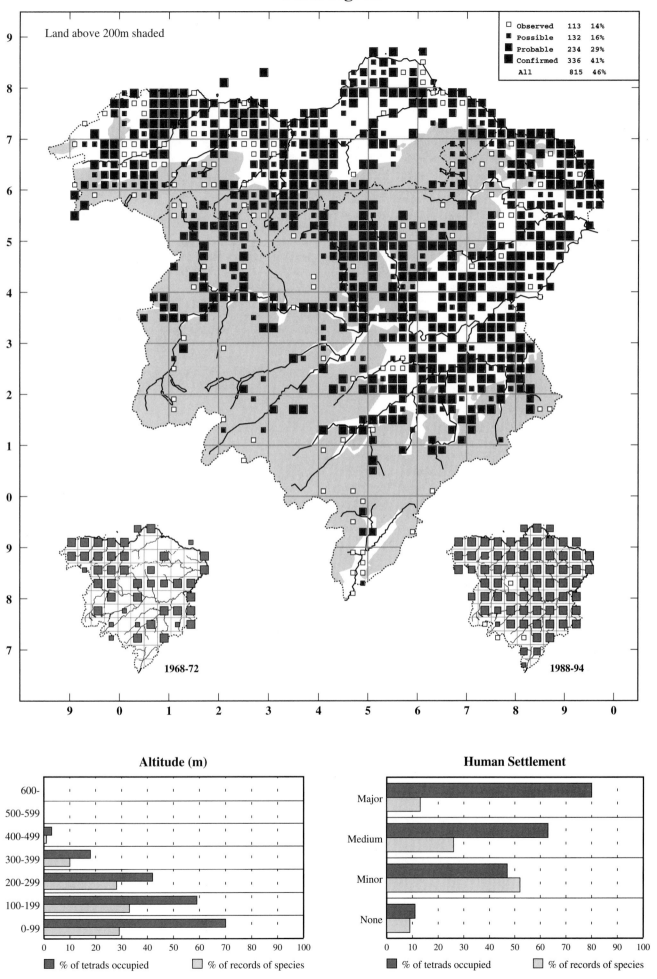

Land above 200m shaded

☐ Observed	113	14%
◱ Possible	132	16%
◩ Probable	234	29%
■ Confirmed	336	41%
All	815	46%

1968-72

1988-94

Altitude (m)

Human Settlement

■ % of tetrads occupied   ▨ % of records of species

Stock Dove

Columba oenas

The Stock Dove was probably a bird of open warm temperate woodlands and forest steppes prior to the opening up of the European forest by man for farming. The additional edge habitats have clearly benefited the species and allowed it to spread from its original limited range to colonise much of western Europe. In Britain it is now a bird of open parkland, breeding in the woodland but feeding in grassy clearings, woodland edges and in neighbouring fields. It is versatile in its nesting habits and readily uses rock faces, buildings and old burrows, as well as the more usual tree holes and old nests.

While Stock Doves are not shy, they do tend to be unobtrusive, their presence usually being given away by the characteristic cooing and a frequent habit of flying in pairs. This feature may have been responsible for the fact that three-quarters of all probable records were of pairs. With nests hidden out of sight in cavities, breeding was relatively difficult to detect, only a fifth of all records being of confirmed breeding. With juveniles being difficult to distinguish from adults in the field, most proof of breeding came from birds entering or leaving likely nest-holes. These factors almost certainly mean that Stock Doves were under-recorded in the *Atlas*, particularly at confirmed level.

The map shows a species strongly associated with lowland farming areas. This is confirmed by the altitude graph where it occurs in about half of all tetrads below 200m, despite only being represented in just a quarter of all tetrads. Above 200m it is wholly confined to the river valleys, showing a deep penetration along the valleys as far as the upper Tweed (NT12&13) and Teviot (NT40), mostly in the wooded policies of large country houses. The density of occupied tetrads in parts of West Lothian (NT07,16&17), Midlothian (NT25&36) and East Lothian (NT46,47&67) suggests that the mosaic-like mixture of wooded estates and arable farming characteristic of these areas suits Stock Doves well. Similar conditions certainly exist in the middle Tweed (e.g. NT63) but the density of occupied tetrads is generally lower in the Tweed basin. While this difference may indeed be real it is also likely that birds may have been overlooked in the relatively less intensively surveyed Merse. The absence of birds from several large estates along the lower Tweed that seem perfect for Stock Doves is hardly credible and supports the speculation that birds were under-recorded. The Stock Dove shows considerable penetration into urban areas in Edinburgh and the Esk Valley, presumably in the remnant valley woods, parks and large suburban gardens. The preference for more open areas of mixed and deciduous woodland is supported by the habitat graph that shows a greater percentage of Stock Dove records coming from woods where such habitats are just scarce or common, despite the apparent popularity of tetrads where such woods are abundant.

The presence of some large winter flocks of up to 250 birds around Musselburgh and Dalmeny (NT17) (*Bird Reports*), in a species that according to ringing returns is particularly sedentary and rarely controlled more than 8km from the place of ringing (*Bird Reports*), supports the impression of where the largest numbers of birds are, as given by the density of occupied tetrads. This is confirmed by the *New Atlas* abundance map that shows small areas of the highest numbers in Dalmeny and the Aberlady area with good abundance along much of the Lothian lowlands. The Tweed valley shows up poorly in comparison.

Stock Doves first bred in Scotland in East Lothian in 1866, having spread northwards from their strongholds in the south and east of England. Indeed, the colonisation of Scotland may have been part of a much larger spread into much of western Europe that has occurred in the last 150 years or so. O'Connor & Shrubb (1986) found the expansion of Stock Doves to be correlated with the expansion of arable farming and this reached its fullest extent in the 1950s before the introduction of modern agrochemicals that control weeds and regulate plant growth. The weedy fields, more open crops, summer fallows and winter stubbles were ideal for Stock Doves. The organochlorine poisons used as seed dressings in the 1950s and 1960s wreaked havoc with the population and led to a decline in numbers and a shrinkage of the range. Numbers recovered by the 1980s but are not thought to have attained their previous levels due to the general intensification of farming (*Trends & New Atlas*).

Comparison of the 10-km maps gives a mixed message. While there is only an overall reduction of just one 10-km square since 1972, there has been a redistribution with seven squares showing gains to eight with losses. Stock Doves are present in an average of seven tetrads in NT52,57&75, suggesting that they were overlooked there in 1968-72. Elsewhere the gains and losses have been mostly confined to the upland edge of the range, the new squares averaging just three tetrads. Most losses were in 10-km squares that held possible and probable records in 1968-72 or are boundary squares where breeding may have occurred outwith SE Scotland in the past. A similar loss from the upland edge and northern limits of cultivation is also evident in the *New Atlas* change map.

This shrinkage of range in a species associated with arable farmland from the upland edge of cultivation, particularly in the south and west of the area, is seen in a number of other 'farmland' birds such as Grey Partridge and Yellowhammer. Changes in farm practice are probably responsible, the reduction of cereal growing for feeding stock in winter on the upland edge resulting in a loss of feeding for birds with a liking for cereals fields.

While unobtrusive in summer, the widespread reports of winter flocks in the range of 20-120 individuals (*Bird Reports*) suggests reasonable numbers of birds are scattered through the area. While most breeding season reports are of just 1-2 pairs at any site, there are a number of places that have held up to 13 pairs: the Hermitage of Braid (NT27K), 13 pairs, the Balerno area (NT16), 12 pairs and Floors Castle (NT73C), 9 pairs, being the best sites.

The *New Atlas* British population estimate suggests an average of 1.3prs/km^2 across the country. Locally, da Prato (1985) found a density of 2.0prs/km^2 south of Tranent, located in areas with good numbers of occupied tetrads, while local BBS results in 1994-95 suggest 2-3prs/km^2 in occupied squares. A value of 2.0prs/km^2 would produce a local population of 3,900 pairs for SE Scotland. Given the likely level of under-recording, a figure of 3,900 pairs seems appropriate.   ***J.G.Mattocks & R.D.Murray***

Stock Dove

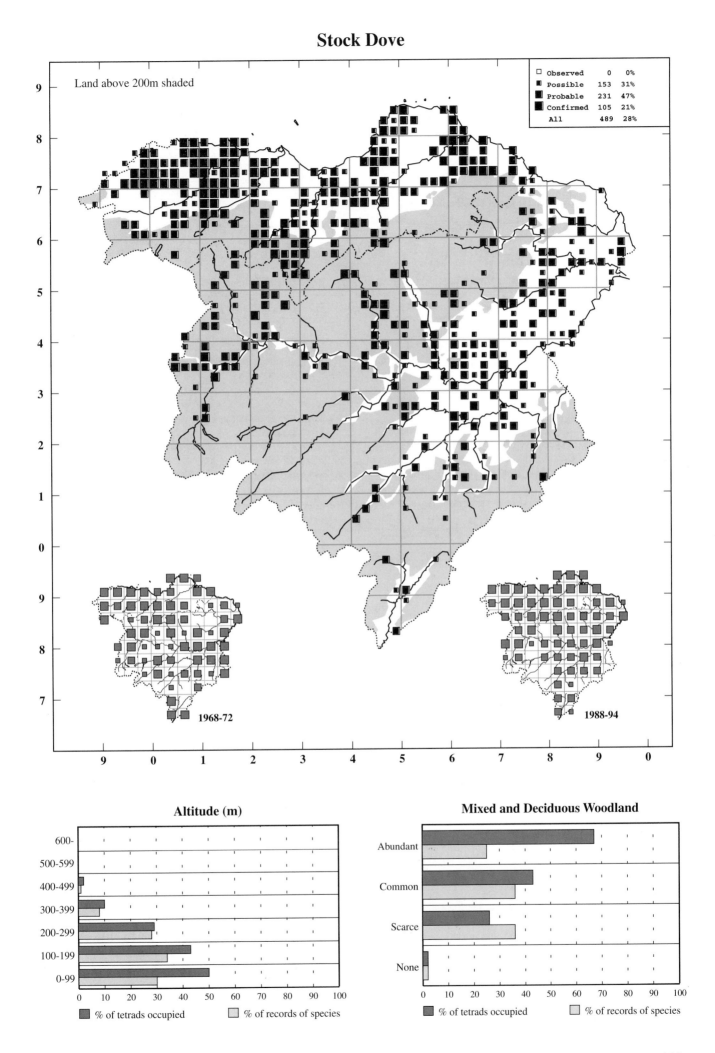

Land above 200m shaded

	Observed	0	0%
	Possible	153	31%
	Probable	231	47%
	Confirmed	105	21%
	All	489	28%

1968-72

1988-94

Altitude (m)

600-
500-599
400-499
300-399
200-299
100-199
0-99

0 10 20 30 40 50 60 70 80 90 100

■ % of tetrads occupied   □ % of records of species

Mixed and Deciduous Woodland

Abundant
Common
Scarce
None

0 10 20 30 40 50 60 70 80 90 100

■ % of tetrads occupied   □ % of records of species

Woodpigeon
Columba palumbus

The cooing of a Woodpigeon in full song is one of the familiar sounds of a summer day. Originally purely woodland birds, Woodpigeons have adapted well to farmland environments that keep them well fed throughout the year. This has allowed them to spread and they now breed across most of the British Isles in very considerable numbers.

Woodpigeon nests were usually very easy to find. When surveying most tetrads a quick visit to the first small conifer plantation would be rewarded by the sight of a current nest or the remains of a nest from a previous year. The large number of confirmed reports were made up mostly by occupied and used nests, with discarded eggshells also being important. Probable records were mostly of pairs followed by territorial singing and males engaged in display flighting.

There are two requirements needed to fulfil the habitat needs of Woodpigeons: trees to nest in and fields to feed in, if food is not available within the woodland. The habitat data show that Woodpigeons occupy almost all tetrads where woodland is available. Indeed only 1.5% of Woodpigeon records came from tetrads where there was no evidence of woodland present in the habitat survey (from maps and aerial photographs). There is only a small difference in the levels of occupation between tetrads with coniferous woodland on the one hand, and mixed and deciduous woodland on the other. While over 90% of tetrads with either type of woodland hold Woodpigeons, the lowest level of occupation (91%) is in tetrads where coniferous woodland is extensive. 100% of tetrads with extensive mixed and deciduous woodlands hold birds. Fieldwork during the *Atlas* indicated that extensive commercial forests in SE Scotland generally lack or hold low numbers of Woodpigeons. The absence of feeding within the forest, or within a reasonable distance of the nest-site, are the most likely reasons for Woodpigeons not using such forests. Conifer woodlands are used as suitable nesting sites as long as feeding can be found nearby.

The range of the Woodpigeon closely resembles the map of 'all woodlands'. The Pentlands (NT05), Moorfoots (NT34), Lammermuirs (NT55&66), Tweedsmuir Hills (NT02,11,12&22) and Tinnis Hill-Din Fell area (NY48&49) are essentially treeless and match the gaps in the Woodpigeon distribution. The small vacant areas in the hills below 400m on the map are in treeless moors. This is supported by the altitude graph which shows a drop-off in occupation of tetrads above 400m but while half of all tetrads above 400m have records of Woodpigeons, these represent just 7% of all records, the vast majority being found at lower levels. The slightly lower occupation rate (93%) in the 0-99m altitude band

than at 100-299m is mostly in a few coastal habitats and Edinburgh. The gap in the North Berwick area (NT58) can only be explained by birds being overlooked.

There are, however, distinct areas where the density of occupied tetrads is lower than that seen elsewhere in the 'all woodland' map and there are generally more possible and probable records. These mark the large areas of commercial forestry in southern West Lothian (NS95), Craik (NT30&31) and Wauchope (NT40,50&60). Woodpigeons are definitely uncommon in these forests, with few singing or flying birds, and nests almost impossible to find, the potential sites being endless. As discussed above, the lack of feeding in such areas and their distance from arable fields may be the main limiting factor in these areas. Urban areas are almost fully occupied. Birds were recorded breeding over most of Edinburgh, other than the depths of industrialised Leith and Seafield (NT27T&Y).

Woodpigeons occupied 100% of the local 10-km squares in the *Old Atlas*, as they do today and so no useful data can be gathered from any comparison. The *New Atlas* abundance map is more helpful in that it confirms the relative lack of numbers along the southern watershed of the Tweed basin where the hills and commercial conifer forests dominate the landscape. There are several areas of the highest abundance in much of West Lothian, East Lothian north of the A1, the lower and middle Tweed and Teviot valleys and in the Biggar-Broughton area. In British terms however SE Scotland may only hold moderate numbers of Woodpigeons as the abundance map shows about a third of the area with just low to poor abundance. The BTO surveys suggest that Woodpigeon numbers have been increasing in recent years (*Trends*), with indices doubling. There are also signs that the spread of plantations have allowed birds to colonise new areas (*Thom*).

National densities, according to the *Old Atlas*, were between 9-15prs/km², but this figure was refined in the *New Atlas* to 10prs/km². In 1984 da Prato (1985) found *c.*13prs/km² in the Tranent area, while local BBS returns in 1994-95 suggest a slightly lower value of 7-9prs/km². The *Bird Reports* list a number of sites that regularly hold 10-20 pairs with a few, such as Muiravonside (NS97S), Beecraigs (NT07C) and Lochcote (NS97R), holding between 40-50 pairs. There can be little doubt that the tetrads on the southern margin of the local range will have lower densities, but overall a figure of 10prs/km² might be appropriate, giving SE Scotland 61,500 pairs, 2.3% of the British population. **R.D.Murray**

Woodpigeon

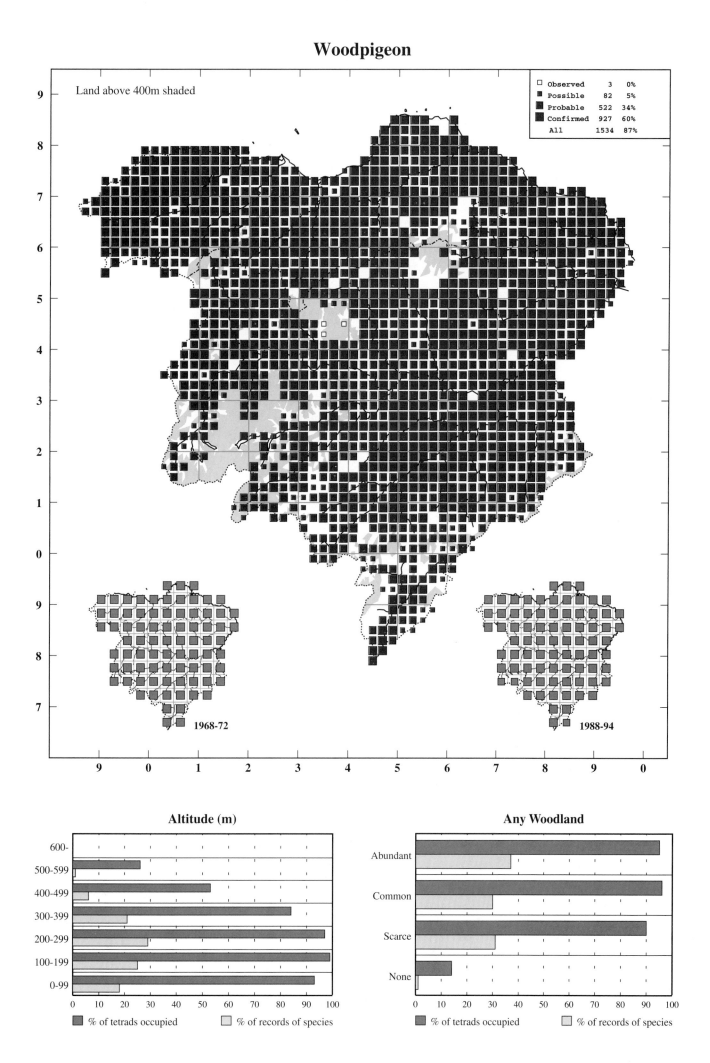

Land above 400m shaded

□ Observed	3	0%
■ Possible	82	5%
■ Probable	522	34%
■ Confirmed	927	60%
All	1534	87%

1968-72

1988-94

Altitude (m)

Any Woodland

■ % of tetrads occupied   □ % of records of species

■ % of tetrads occupied   □ % of records of species

167

Collared Dove

Streptopelia decaocto

In 1955 the first Collared Dove nested in Britain. Today the Collared Dove breeds in every part of the British Isles with an estimated population of 230,000 pairs. It has since become such a familiar part of our environment that it becomes difficult to appreciate that the Collared Dove was once a twitchers delight! The Collared Dove is one of a number of species that have shown remarkable range changes within recorded ornithological history although few have done so with such rapidity. Several waterfowl such as Pochard, Tufted Duck and Goosander and even common species such as Stock Dove were once either absent or rare breeders in much of Scotland.

The cooing of Collared Doves, allied to their display flighting, makes them fairly easy to record even when birds are hidden in distant gardens. Most possible records were of single birds seen or heard singing in suitable habitat while probable records were mostly of pairs or territorial display and singing. Fledged young formed about half of all confirmed records with birds on occupied nests also being important.

The unfilled ecological niche that the Collared Dove exploited in its dramatic colonisation of Europe was that of a small dove within gardens and cities. Habitat data show a close relationship to human settlement, much stronger than that of the more notorious town dweller, the Feral Pigeon. Collared Doves are present in 74-82% of tetrads that had village, town or city landscapes. Indeed they favour settlement to such an extent that only 4% of records were in tetrads where buildings were absent. As might be expected, human settlement is a feature of the low ground and Collared Doves accordingly occur mostly below 300m, with three-quarters of all records actually below 200m altitude.

The map confirms these comments in that there is a close correlation between the Collared Dove map and that of human settlement in SE Scotland. Collared Doves seem to be present in most of the top two categories of human settlement which are villages, and urban and suburban landscape. As the habitat graph indicates, however, their mastery of urban living is not complete and does not allow them full rein within Edinburgh. The map shows a number of vacant tetrads in Granton-Pilton, Leith, Corstorphine and the Princes Street-Meadows area, as well as in Livingston new town (NT06).

The lack of birds away from tetrads with human settlement is striking and may be responsible for the marked difference in the densities of occupied tetrads between Lothian and Borders. The CBC data indicate that urban areas form the core of Collared Dove numbers in Britain, with rural areas being populated with the overspill from built-up areas (*New Atlas*). The differences in the density of occupied tetrads may well be the result of this with the more heavily urbanised Lothians having Collared Doves in many more rural tetrads compared to the more sparsely populated Borders where birds are more or less confined to towns and villages. It is not surprising that the least favoured rural areas in Lothian are away from human settlements while the most favoured rural parts of the Borders are in the vicinity of larger settlements and in the Merse where cereal-growing is widespread and where Collared Doves are known to be common in the vicinity of grain-storage facilities.

Despite limited human settlement at higher altitudes Collared Doves have been able to move well into the hills wherever a suitably large house or small village allows, as witnessed by the birds at Redfordgreen at 380m (NT31T), Cloich at 330m (NT24E), Tweedsmuir at 260m (NT02&12), Heriot at 260m (NT45C) and Hindhope at 250m (NT71Q). The *Bird Reports* indicate that some of these higher altitude sites have only been colonised during the period since the publications started in 1979.

Not surprisingly, a comparison with the *Old Atlas* shows a large net gain of occupied 10-km squares across the area since 1968-72. There have been three apparent losses but two were in boundary 10-km squares where the possibility exists that the 1968-72 records may have originated from outwith SE Scotland. The 20 squares colonised since 1968-72 are mostly in rural areas and add weight to the idea that Collared Doves colonised towns first and only moved into rural areas due to population pressure in the favoured urban habitats. The squares at Whitburn-Bathgate (NS96), Livingston (NT06), Greenlaw (NT74) and Grantshouse-Reston (NT86), which were unoccupied in 1968-72, now have over half their tetrads holding breeding birds. Most of the other squares where Collared Doves were absent in the *Old Atlas* have relatively few occupied tetrads and are in much more rural areas.

In national terms SE Scotland does not hold large numbers of Collared Doves, with the *New Atlas* abundance map indicating that the 31% of our area that actually holds birds is mostly in the moderate to low abundance range. Indeed only two points of high numbers are shown, around Musselburgh-Tranent (NT37&47) and around East Linton-Whitekirk area (NT67&68). The lower Merse area shows up as holding as many birds as much of the area around Edinburgh and in West Lothian. However, judging from the density of occupied tetrads in the 10-km squares in Lothian, there can be little doubt that the squares in the Merse will not hold comparable numbers, despite the *New Atlas's* hint. The high Merse counts may be simply due to the field surveyors encountering a flock of Collared Doves in the vicinity of a grain store during the timed visits.

The *New Atlas* calculated the British population using densities of 0.9prs/km^2, precisely the same as da Prato's (1985) finding for his Tranent study in 1984. Local BBS plots produce figures that equate to 1-2prs/km^2. The *Bird Reports* show there is little interest in reporting Collared Dove numbers. Linlithgow has held 18 pairs and Reston 12 pairs, but most rural sites hold, at most, 1-3 pairs. At 1.0-1.25prs/km^2 the local population would reach 2,200-3,300 pairs, about 1.25% of the British population.   ***R.D.Murray***

Collared Dove

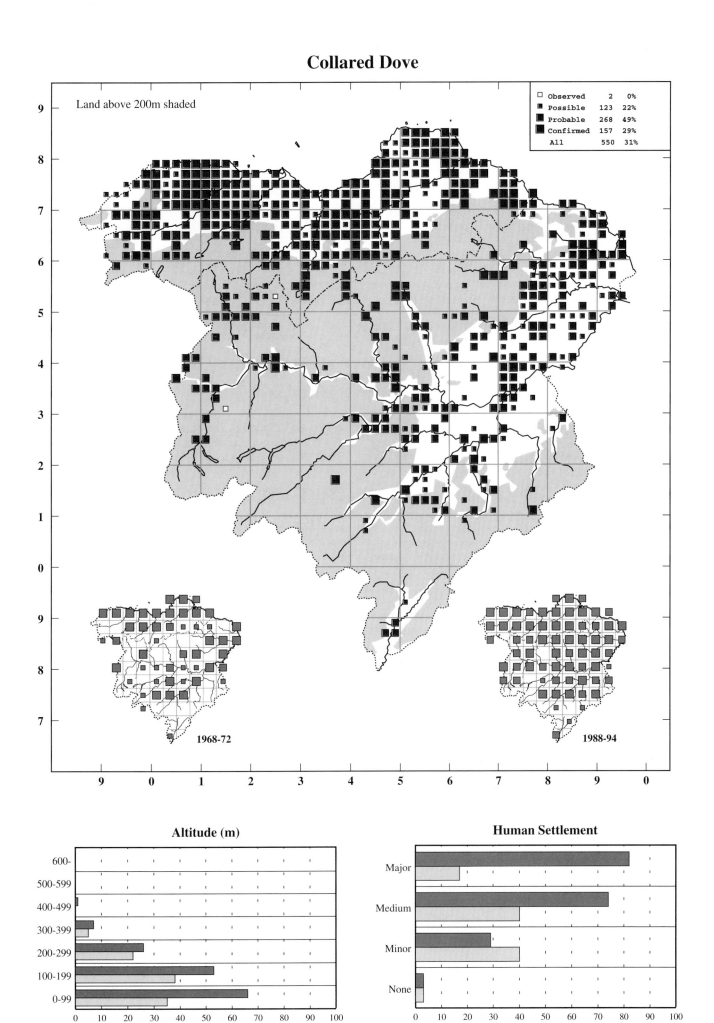

□ Observed	2	0%
▪ Possible	123	22%
▪ Probable	268	49%
■ Confirmed	157	29%
All	550	31%

Land above 200m shaded

1968-72

1988-94

Altitude (m)

600-
500-599
400-499
300-399
200-299
100-199
0-99

■ % of tetrads occupied   ▫ % of records of species

Human Settlement

Major
Medium
Minor
None

■ % of tetrads occupied   ▫ % of records of species

Cuckoo
Cuculus canorus

Although not a commonly seen bird, everyone is well acquainted with the call of the Cuckoo. In much of northern and western Britain it is mainly a bird of the open countryside, especially uplands where it parasitises the Meadow Pipit. The name Penicuik, the "hill of the Cuckoo" in ancient Cumbric, suggests that Cuckoos may have been present in SE Scotland since that tongue was last spoken locally, at least 800 years ago. Dunnocks are parasitised elsewhere in Britain, but in SE Scotland there has only been a single instance of Dunnock parasitism reported in recent years. The other main host in Britain, the Reed Warbler, has only bred in the area since 1997.

While the song is unmistakable, the long tail, low flight and attendant mobbing passerines mean that the Cuckoo can be misidentified by inexperienced observers as a Sparrowhawk. The main arrival from Africa, in late April and early May, is when Cuckoos are most vocal. The decline in singing later in June could mean that silent Cuckoos may be overlooked and that some could have been missed in the more remote tetrads that were only surveyed late in the season. Also juveniles are often not on the wing until late July when *Atlas* survey work was much less intensive.

Amongst the more widespread species in SE Scotland, the Cuckoo at 57% coverage, has the highest percentage of possible records, as opposed to probable and confirmed records, of any species in this *Atlas*. Only the Grasshopper Warbler and Barn Owl approach this level of possible registrations. Evidence for confirmed breeding is extremely difficult in a species that does not have a nest or carry food for its young, and with sightings of juveniles running at just a handful per year (*Bird Reports*), there are few chances to obtain proof of breeding. Two-thirds of all probable records were of territorial behaviour, mostly males singing against each other and males singing later in the year or in a following season. Pairs formed a fifth of probable registrations.

The map and altitude graph show that most Cuckoos occur in the uplands above 200m, occupying about 40% of all tetrads between 250-550m. Occupied tetrads are most numerous in the Lammermuirs, Moorfoots, Pentlands and on the fringes of the Tweedsmuirs, reaching 20 occupied tetrads per 10-km square in the middle Tweed hill area between Broughton and Walkerburn (NT13,23&33). The lesser density of tetrads in the Cheviots may reflect the late coverage of much of the Cheviots, well after the main period when Cuckoo song had passed its peak. Note that most registrations there were only of possible records, indicating a lack of follow-up visits to raise their status. There is every likelihood that the Cheviots have a comparable density of occupied tetrads to those in the northern hills.

Despite these observations on the map distribution, the real factor that controls much of the Cuckoo distribution is the range of its main host in SE Scotland, the Meadow Pipit. Over 90% of Cuckoo registrations occur in tetrads where Meadow Pipits are also present, and an additional 6% in tetrads where Meadow Pipits occur in adjacent squares. The residual 4% of records may be of passage birds or Cuckoos with alternate hosts, a rarity in SE Scotland. The absence of Meadow Pipits from the lowlands and the rarity of "Dunnock-Cuckoos" in the area are the main reasons why Cuckoos are mostly confined to the hills, rather than some other limiting factor in the landscape.

Despite CBC results that show British Cuckoo numbers as being stable, there is an overall impression that Cuckoos have been in decline through much of the 20th century (*Trends*). The *New Atlas* reiterates this difficulty of hard evidence, showing declines on the western and northern margins of the range in areas where *New Atlas*

coverage was weakest. While comparison between the 10-km maps in SE Scotland show no overall change in the range of the Cuckoo, the quality of records certainly gives an impression that Cuckoos are much more difficult to locate now than they were in 1968-72. Despite lasting seven years and visiting every tetrad, the current project could only prove breeding in 21% of the 10-km squares. Yet in just five years and with no need to visit all parts of the 10-km squares, breeding was confirmed in 44% of the same squares in the *Old Atlas*. Possible registrations tell a similar story with only 4% of squares with possible breeding in the *Old Atlas* but 23% in the current project. For virtually all other species where the 10-km maps show differences, the present survey shows up as indicating more thorough surveying. The suspected decline is thought to be the result of a loss of invertebrate prey due to the intensification of farming, specifically in our area through the 'improvement' of pastures on the hill margins. Adverse changes to habitats in their wintering range may also have had an impact on populations.

The *New Atlas* abundance map shows really low densities across much of the area. Only the Tweedsmuir Hills are shown to hold reasonable numbers, precisely in the 10-km squares in the upper Tweed with a high number of occupied tetrads on the map opposite.

The *New Atlas* British population estimate suggests an overall density of 5-10 pairs per occupied 10-km square, but in view of the low numbers of tetrad registrations in much of SE Scotland and the very low numbers hinted at by the *New Atlas* abundance map, such a figure is highly unlikely across most of our area. It is probably exceeded in the best squares such as NT13, 23&33, but taking into account the large territories, the great mobility of Cuckoos and the fact that Cuckoos are rarely seen in consecutive years in many peripheral areas, an overall figure of 5 pairs per occupied 10-km square might be more realistic. This equates to 335 pairs. Working on a tetrad basis, it is likely that many peripheral 'possible' records were of passage migrants and that most actual breeding takes place in the hill areas. If just 1-2 pairs were present in each tetrad in these peripheral areas, adding the probable and confirmed records would produce 200-400 pairs. If the 280 possible tetrads represent perhaps another 200 pairs, a total of 400-600 pairs is produced. Both estimates suggest between 350-500 pairs are present annually, about 2-3% of the national estimate. **I.R.Poxton**

Cuckoo

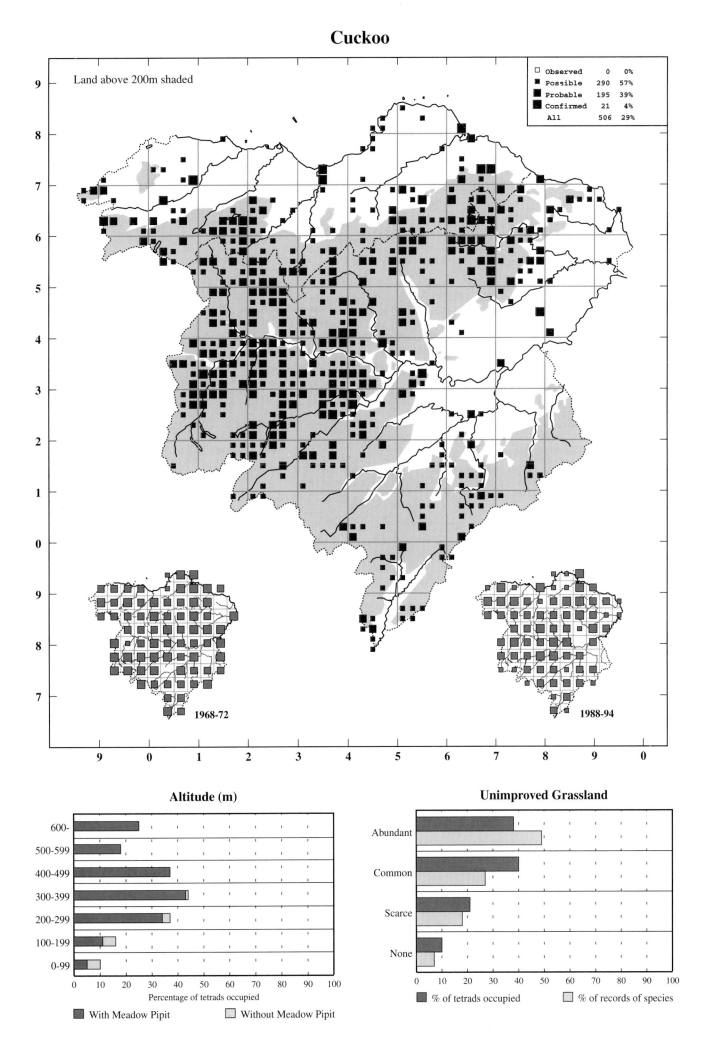

Land above 200m shaded

		Observed	0	0%
■	Possible	290	57%
■	Probable	195	39%
■	Confirmed	21	4%
	All	506	29%

1968-72

1988-94

Altitude (m)

Percentage of tetrads occupied

600-
500-599
400-499
300-399
200-299
100-199
0-99

■ With Meadow Pipit   ■ Without Meadow Pipit

Unimproved Grassland

Abundant
Common
Scarce
None

■ % of tetrads occupied   ■ % of records of species

Barn Owl

Tyto alba

Barn Owls are inhabitants of open agricultural ground in SE Scotland. The essential habitat requirement is a foraging area of long grass where small mammal prey is available. In arable areas such grassland is usually limited to woodland edges, hedgerows, ditches and track verges. Pheasant or fox coverts, old railway lines and river banks are also used. On higher ground large areas of rough grazing are available but prey densities are usually too low due to competition for grass from sheep and cattle. Grazing pressure is reduced when land is fenced for forestry and then the numbers of small mammals become sufficient to support Barn Owls, even at higher altitudes above 200m. Land given over entirely to intensive cereal production, intensive grazing and closed canopy forestry is shunned. Nest sites may also limit distribution. Three types are preferred: buildings, large tree holes and rock cavities. In Scotland Shawyer (1987) found that more than 80% of Barn Owls used buildings, the remainder being shared between tree-holes and caves.

Voles and shrews form the greatest part of Barn Owl diet. Owl numbers and success are influenced by the 3-4 year changes that occur in vole populations. Success is usually good in high vole years but breeding may not take place at all in a poor year.

Barn Owl records for the *Atlas* came from three main sources: from landowners when seeking permission to enter private land (subject to a degree of scepticism but often proving reliable); casual supplementary records of birds seen in car headlights; and hunting birds at dawn or dusk in late spring when large young are being fed and the adults are especially active. Probable records were dominated by territorial birds while confirmed records were shared between occupied nests, nests with young, sightings of fledged young and adults carrying food for young.

The map shows that Barn Owls are widely, but thinly, distributed in the Merse, from the coast upstream to Hawick on the Teviot and to Selkirk on the Tweed. This matches the maps by both Shawyer (1987) and Taylor (1993). The greatest density of records is in the area between Coldstream, Morebattle, Jedburgh, Melrose and Gordon. The lower Merse between Coldstream and the sea seems to hold fewer birds, something not indicated by either Taylor or Shawyer. There are outliers beyond this area at Wauchope, Craik and Leithope Forests. Another group occurs to the north and west of the Moorfoots in a band along the edges of the higher ground from the Esk valley near Dalkeith through Penicuik and Eddleston to Broughton. The birds around Newcastleton in Liddesdale are part of the large Dumfries & Galloway population.

The altitude data show that Barn Owls are spread fairly evenly across lowland habitats, occupying about a fifth of all land up to 300m with a fairly even number of birds at each 100m interval between these altitudes. Less than 10% occur above 300m. This altitude cut-off is almost certainly related to habitat, Barn Owls

showing a very strong affinity with areas where arable and improved grassland is abundant. Indeed almost 90% of records came from tetrads where such farmland was abundant. As abundant arable farmland is rare above 300m, so are Barn Owls. This agrees with Taylor's (1993) study in SW Scotland which found good densities of owls on enclosed pastoral farmland at 50-150m altitude, mostly under hay, silage and pasture. Arable fields were restricted to a few barley fields. Small woodlands, often coniferous, were frequent.

Comparisons with the *Old Atlas, Winter Atlas* and *New Atlas* maps suggest that shrinkage has occurred from parts of the local range. Barn Owls were reported from 53 squares in 1968-72 but only 40 in the winters of 1981-83 and 43 in 1988-91. Losses have been greater in the west and south with 29 of 46 squares occupied in 1968-72 compared to only 21 in 1988-91. Many squares in West Lothian, Tweeddale and SW Roxburghshire are now heavily forested. They may have held owls when the woodlands were at the plantation stage but are now closed-canopy forests with few nest sites. In this *Atlas* Barn Owls were found in 55 squares in 1988-94 (47 in 1988-91). However, 29 have reports from only one or two tetrads, leaving 26 squares with reports from three or more tetrads. Densities outwith the central Borders area are therefore probably very low.

Taylor identifies three core areas for Barn Owls in Scotland that fall within our area: the "Esk & Liddle valleys" where there is a high density of birds, Newcastleton being on the margins of this area; the "Tweed Valley" which appears to have a good density of birds; and the "South Lothians". He comments that the latter areas have many sites with suitable habitat but that it is generally patchily distributed. These core areas are where conservation efforts should be focused.

Both this *Atlas* and the *Bird Reports* suggest that the "South Lothians" population has declined greatly since Taylor's study. Indeed ten sites that Taylor knew of around West Linton in the 1980s are now known to be vacant. Only a handful of birds are thought to persist in the Lothians and Peeblesshire. Little is known of the Liddesdale population and so it is readily apparent that the central Borders now holds the bulk of the local Barn Owl population.

The *New Atlas* population figure, based on Hawk Trust surveys, suggests that occupied 10-km squares hold between 4-8 pairs. Using just those squares with probable and confirmed breeding, this translates to 144-288 pairs in Lothian & Borders. This compares to Shawyer's population estimate of 96 pairs in the 1980s. However, as he received little co-operation from local birders, his conclusions may be more suspect than the present data. Birds probably or definitely bred in nearly 90 tetrads in the *Atlas* but this number is cumulative over the seven-year period of the survey and may exaggerate the true numbers. The population may fluctuate between 125-200 pairs, depending on the vicissitudes of any particular year.

R.D.Murray

Barn Owl

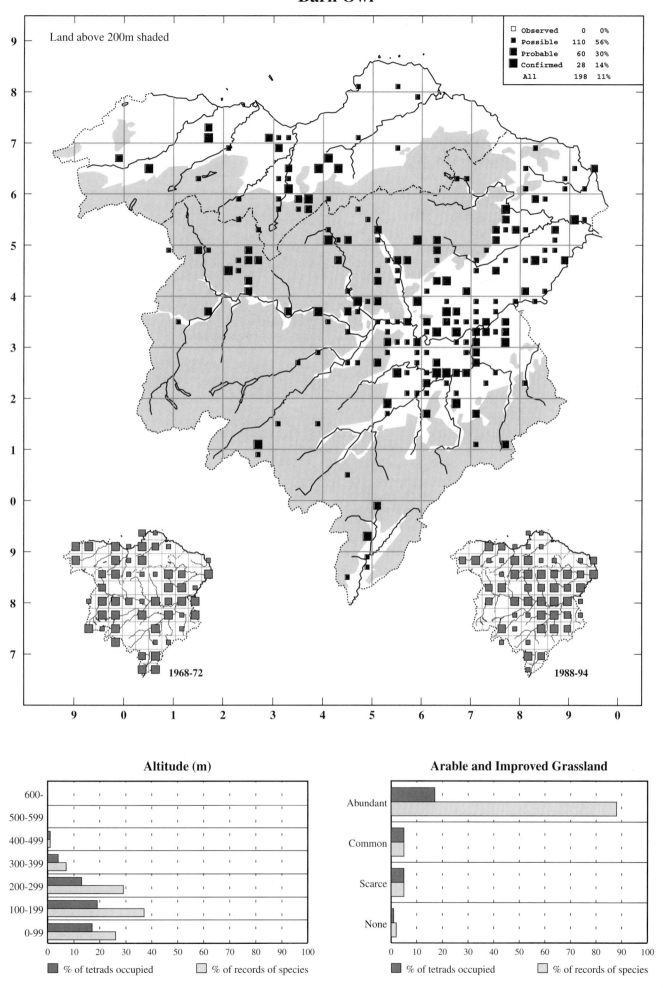

Land above 200m shaded

☐ Observed	0	0%
▪ Possible	110	56%
◾ Probable	60	30%
■ Confirmed	28	14%
All	198	11%

1968-72

1988-94

Altitude (m)

600-
500-599
400-499
300-399
200-299
100-199
0-99

0 10 20 30 40 50 60 70 80 90 100

■ % of tetrads occupied   ☐ % of records of species

Arable and Improved Grassland

Abundant

Common

Scarce

None

0 10 20 30 40 50 60 70 80 90 100

■ % of tetrads occupied   ☐ % of records of species

173

Little Owl
Athene noctua

The Little Owl has a distribution centred on the warm temperate parts of the western and central Palearctic, living mostly in open woodland and grassland habitats. While its range extends north to the shores of the Baltic and North Seas, wholesale mortality in severe winters apparently prevents it penetrating further into the cooler temperate areas of Europe (Voous 1960). It seems likely that the creation of open grasslands for farming in prehistoric times may have allowed the Little Owl to spread into north-west Europe, but not before the flooding of the English Channel which prevented it from reaching Britain. Being sedentary and lacking any great ability to disperse far, the Channel formed an insuperable barrier until there were a series of introductions during the 19th century. The most successful of these was in Northamptonshire in the 1870s and it is from that nucleus of birds, as well as later introductions, that the British population has developed. Currently British Little Owls are the most northerly in the world, and those that reach Scotland the most northerly of all.

Despite almost all textbooks on British birds claiming that Little Owls are "characteristic" of agricultural land, they are exceedingly rare in SE Scotland, averaging about three reports annually, including winter records, between 1979-95 (*Bird Reports,* see graph). Typically birds are seen or heard at a site on a single occasion and despite some sites being searched later, they are rarely re-located. A number of records were obtained during deliberate searches for nocturnal birds for the *Atlas,* usually when listening for Quails and Grasshopper Warblers (NT74U,85Z&86I). Others have been seen briefly in car headlights on posts at the side of the road. The probable records consist of a bird relocated a week or so later (NT73Y), a pair that summered (NT86Q) and single birds that were seen in the same general areas in different years (NT96D & NT67M*). The only confirmed breeding record during the *Atlas* period was of a dead juvenile found in July 1989 at Morham near Haddington (NT57K). The precise origin of the dead individual is not known, but with a July date it is a safe assumption that it was local.

As Little Owls are so rare and rather sedentary, the few winter records can be mentioned to help flesh out the picture. These were in Bowhill (NT42I), Gattonside (NT53M), Lauder (NT54I), Carfraemill (NT55B), Dykegatehead (NT85Q) and Causewaybank

(NT85U). Even including these records, Little Owls have been found in just 20 tetrads over an eight-year period.

The resultant map indicates a very thin scatter of records along the coast near Dunbar and in the St. Abbs-Reston area, and inland in the Gordon-Greenlaw area and south of the Tweed between Kelso and Yetholm. Unexpectedly there are outlying records well into hills near St. Mary's Loch and Hawick that are supported by winter records from similar habitats at Bowhill and Carfraemill. While being unexpected it should be noted that Little Owls were regular in the Moffat valley, just over the watershed from St. Mary's Loch, for several years in the 1970s.

One feature of several sites where Little Owls were recorded is that while the general habitat feature was arable farmland, birds have often been found in or near islands of old pasture and rough grazing. The old pasture sites are all heavily grazed, especially by Rabbits, a mammal whose burrows Little Owls have been known to use as nest-sites in Borders in the past. Old pasture may also provide good feeding for earthworms and beetles.

Little Owls first bred in Scotland near Edrom (NT85H) in 1958. There are, however, a number of records from Berwickshire that suggest that birds may have been breeding in 1949 at Charterhall (NT74T) (Home 1950). It is believed that breeding became more widespread in Berwickshire in the 1960s with birds nesting near Pease Bay, Duns and at other sites. Unfortunately the sites, dates and numbers were kept secret for security reasons and as a result there is no evidence in the literature after 1960 that any breeding occurred at all. As most of the observers have since died or moved elsewhere it is possible that none of this information will ever come to light. In Lothian breeding was first recorded near Borthwick (NT35U) between 1968-75 but may have occurred earlier near Barns Ness where a juvenile with some down on the head was seen in 1959 (*Andrews*).

In recent years outwith the *Atlas* period, breeding has been confirmed at just two other sites, with single pairs near North Berwick between 1979-82, and at a site near Dunbar between 1984-87 (*Bird Reports*).

The *New Atlas* shows that limited expansion has occurred on the northern margins of the Little Owl's range in Britain, mostly in Cumbria. The Northumberland Atlas (*Day*) also shows some expansion, mostly along the Tyne valley. Scottish records, however, continue to show only a very limited presence in SE Scotland and around Dumfries (*Scottish Bird Reports*), continuing the level of occurrence that has become standard since Little Owls colonised Scotland 30 years ago.

Little Owls are on the extreme limit of their range in Scotland and being mostly nocturnal give a very enigmatic picture of their presence. While it seems that they do occur regularly in the area it is very doubtful that the population is any more than a handful of pairs, of which birders rarely catch a glimpse. *R.D.Murray*

* Note that this tetrad has been moved to a central position (tetrad M) in the 10-km square to protect the confidentiality of the site.

Little Owl

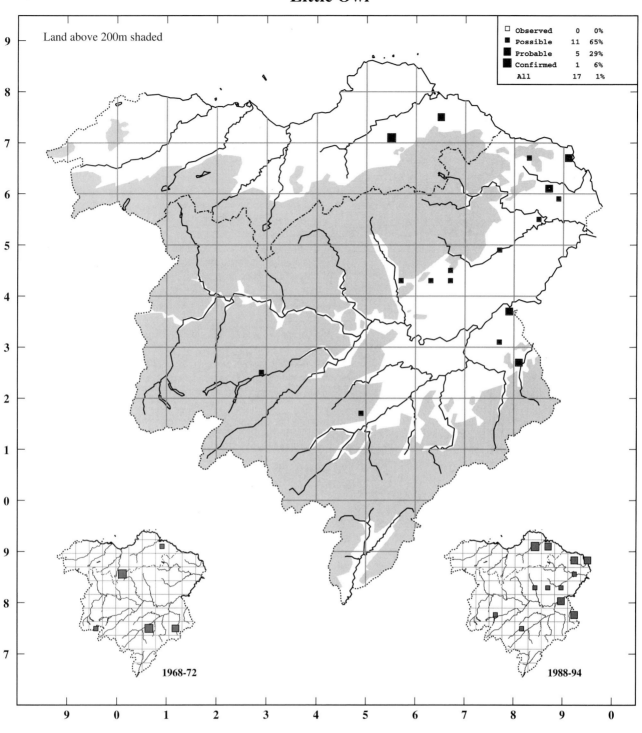

Land above 200m shaded

	Observed	0	0%
	Possible	11	65%
	Probable	5	29%
	Confirmed	1	6%
	All	17	1%

1968-72

1988-94

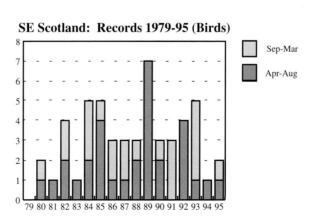

SE Scotland: Records 1979-95 (Birds)

Sep-Mar
Apr-Aug

79 80 81 82 83 84 85 86 87 88 89 90 91 92 93 94 95

175

Tawny Owl
Strix aluco

The Tawny Owl is by far the most numerous owl and the most familiar to members of the public, owing to its tolerance of human presence in towns and villages. Its loud hooting and contact calls ring out on the long still nights of winter, but it is rarely seen as it is almost totally nocturnal. It requires trees for roosting and nesting, and good populations of small rodents for food, although small birds can be important prey. Unlike most other owls, it is very sedentary and once a territory is established, individuals remain there. Young birds of the year are driven out of the territory at the end of the summer and there is consequently another period of intense territorial activity and calling in August and September.

Fieldwork for the *Atlas* missed these months of high territorial activity, and, with such a nocturnal species, many Tawny Owls must have been overlooked. Almost a third of records relate to single birds, usually heard on just one occasion, mostly near dawn or dusk, although Tawny Owls are occasionally heard during the day in the breeding season. A few roosting birds will have been found or flushed. Most records relate to probable breeding, with three-quarters of these being recorded as territory: owls heard on more than one occasion or calling against each other. Despite the nocturnal habits, a high percentage of confirmed breeding was obtained, due to the habit of juveniles calling persistently for food from mid-evening onwards. Only a few nests were found. Newly fledged birds were sometimes found sitting out in the open in the early morning.

The map shows the species to be widespread throughout the region. The patchy distribution below the 300m level may relate partly to variations in fieldwork effort at dawn and dusk. The valleys of the North and South Esk in Midlothian (NT36 and parts of NT25,26&35) stand out as being especially good for this species. Other good areas are from Duns (NT75) to Grantshouse (NT86) especially along the valleys of the Eye and lower Whiteadder, the upper Gala and Leader catchments, parts of West Lothian and along the valley of the middle and upper Tweed. There are Tawny Owls in Edinburgh, especially around the Water of Leith, the Meadows, Duddingston and Craigmillar. Many of these areas, however, coincide with places which received additional coverage at dusk, due to being close to observers' homes or near centres used as bases for fieldwork weekends. Well covered tetrads usually produced Tawny Owls if there was suitable habitat; finding the resident Tawny Owls in less visited areas was more a matter of luck. The gaps in the distribution coincide with open habitats: the hills and the

intensively cultivated arable lands of central East Lothian (NT57) and the Merse (part of NT74). The *New Atlas* shows areas of high abundance of this species to the south of Edinburgh and along the upper and lower Tweed, which does not entirely match the tetrad map.

The altitude graph shows Tawny Owls occupy about half of all tetrads between sea level and 300m. However, these altitude bands actually held over 80% of all Tawny Owl records and here the species is probably ubiquitous where there are sufficient trees to make up a territory. The slightly lower occupation levels below 100m may be related to the scarcity of woodlands in the urban and arable habitats which predominate there. There are no Tawny Owls above 500m, and the records show a cut-off at 450m. This rapid drop-off is related to habitat factors, woodland being less common above 300m. The habitat graph shows that between a third and half of all tetrads with woodland cover support Tawny Owls. This may well be an underestimate, due to the factors discussed above. Detailed habitat analysis (not shown here) shows birds prefer tetrads where woodland is common or abundant. Thus tetrads where mixed and deciduous woodland is scarce only have 40% occupancy compared to 70% where such woodlands are widespread and abundant. It is quite possible that the species was overlooked in the remaining 30% of these tetrads. The 15% occupancy of tetrads with no deciduous or mixed woodland will relate to areas with coniferous trees only. Tawny Owls do occur in older coniferous plantations, moving in when the canopy closes (*Trends*). The map shows them to be present in some large plantations, such as Craik (NT30) and Newcastleton (NY58) but not in Wauchope (NT50&60). This difference may be an artifact of coverage. *Atlas* fieldworkers stayed after dusk in the first two forests but not the latter, although the presence of some nest boxes at Craik may have had an effect, and much of Wauchope is at slightly higher altitude.

At 10-km level there has been minimal change in the distribution of Tawny Owls, with a few new squares occupied in this survey compared to the *Old Atlas*. This is probably due to afforestation (NY59) and poorer coverage in the earlier survey (NT47&86).

There is little information on the density of Tawny Owls in different habitats, but habitat data support the view that better numbers occur in more extensive mature woodland than in the more open habitats characteristic of much of SE Scotland. The *New Atlas* refers to an average of just ten pairs per 10-km square. However, with an average of 10-11 occupied tetrads per 10-km square in SE Scotland, and with some 10-km squares, such as those with larger areas of woodland (as at Dalkeith in NT36) having up to 22 occupied tetrads, the *New Atlas* value is probably low for our area. The number of territories reported in the *Bird Reports* can be up to around 150 in a year, and as this is only a sample of the total population of an inconspicuous species, it indicates a healthy total number of pairs. The best site counts of calling birds are at Duns Castle (NT75S&X; 6-9), the Hirsel (5-9), Craigurd (NT12G&H; 4-7) and the Hermitage of Braid (NT27K; 3). These indicate densities of 3-6prs/km^2 in mostly parkland habitats. *Thom* quotes densities of 0.17prs/km^2 in farmland and 2.2prs/km^2 in upland spruce forest.

There are about 300 tetrads with abundant woodland where Tawny Owls are recorded, and if we assume a density of only 1.0prs/km^2 in these squares, with one pair in each of the other tetrads, a total of 1,600 pairs for SE Scotland is calculated. This does not take into account pairs unrecorded because not all tetrads were visited at suitable times, so is likely to be a low figure. The discovery of Tawny Owls in most well-searched areas supports this assertion. The British population is put at just 20,000 pairs (*New Atlas*), and although there are pockets of high abundance of Tawny Owls in our area according to that survey, it is unlikely that SE Scotland contains 8% of the British population. It seems that the national total is far too low. **M.Holling**

Tawny Owl

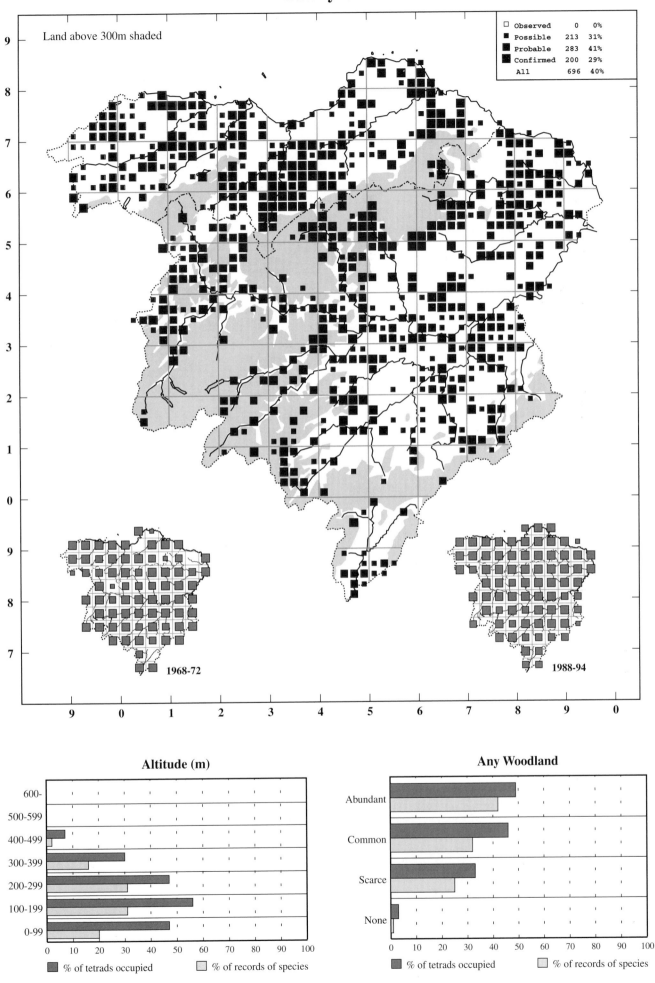

Land above 300m shaded

☐ Observed	0	0%
■ Possible	213	31%
■ Probable	283	41%
■ Confirmed	200	29%
All	696	40%

1968-72

1988-94

Altitude (m)

■ % of tetrads occupied　　☐ % of records of species

Any Woodland

■ % of tetrads occupied　　☐ % of records of species

Long-eared Owl
Asio otus

The Long-eared Owl is perhaps one of the most overlooked species breeding in Britain, owing to its strictly nocturnal behaviour and habit of roosting in dense vegetation. It usually nests in old crow nests, or other stick platforms in trees, and is generally associated with coniferous woodland although it seems to be most commonly found where small coniferous woods adjoin open rough grassland. Long-eared Owls feed mainly on small mammals, especially voles, which they catch over open ground. Although these owls can be detected by the long cooing hoot of the male in early spring, it is more usual that the first evidence of presence is when the high-pitched hunger call of the young, likened to the noise of a gate with squeaky hinges, is heard.

Records of Long-eared Owls in the *Atlas* were usually obtained by chance, with almost half of all records being of single birds in habitat and occasional reports of hooting. Most of the probable records were of territorial birds. There were no records of the wing-clapping display flight. There is a high percentage of confirmed records for such an elusive species, the loud and far-carrying calls of fledged young or of large owlets in the nest alerting fieldworkers to their presence. In SE Scotland, young birds can be heard from about 9pm onwards, but most start to call after sunset. Birds are more likely to be heard on still nights, when the calls can be heard over 1km away. In fact, the majority of confirmed records came from just a handful of dedicated *Atlas* workers who visited suitable habitats in the late evening in late May through to early July specifically to listen for young, and from Raptor Study Group workers who found nests either by accident or by careful searching. This explains the clusters of confirmed records in West Lothian (NT05&06), the Pentlands, south of Dalkeith (NT36) and around the headwaters of the Gala and Leader in NT35,44,45&55. Other records come from well monitored reserves such as at Aberlady, Tyninghame and Tailend Moss (NT06D).

The map shows a concentration of records around the hill edges in southern West Lothian and Midlothian and in the Moorfoots and western Lammermuirs, with a scattering around Duns (NT75). Records in East Lothian are mainly coastal. It is along the hill edges that most conifer plantations and shelter belts occur. South of the Tweed there are just a handful of records at isolated sites. However, the difficulties of finding this species and the reasonably high success of finding young when specifically searched for, suggests that the map seriously underestimates the distribution in the southern part of SE Scotland. There are rather few records to relate the distribution with habitat criteria, but the data (see second graph) indicate birds prefer tetrads where unimproved grassland is common or abundant, with two-thirds of birds found in such tetrads. Personal experience suggests that the best chance of finding broods is to visit open rough grazing areas where there are small coniferous plantations, or edges of larger conifer forests bordering rough grassland. Altitude is not important, but in SE Scotland the habitat typically occurs between 200m and 400m and this is where over 60% of Long-eared Owl registrations were reported. It is thought that the distribution of Long-eared Owls may be limited by the occurrence of the larger Tawny Owl which competes for food (*New Atlas*) and this may prevent Long-eared Owls occupying more woodland sites, especially in lowland areas.

Comparison with the distribution in the *Old Atlas* offers little as the maps are so dependent on chance findings. The earlier map shows a very scattered distribution compared to this *Atlas*. There has also been a 50% increase in the number of occupied 10-km squares since the *Old Atlas*. This may be partly related to the long survey period, but is more likely to be the result of more

fieldwork aimed at locating Long-eared Owls. There has been a great redistribution of occupied squares, only just over a quarter of the present 10-km squares being used in both periods, with a shift towards the northern hill areas where fieldwork was more intense. The differences between the two surveys can probably be explained by a relative lack of fieldwork at the right time of day in the most suitable months in the earlier survey.

The map shows a composite picture for a seven-year period, but it is unlikely that it exaggerates the picture as most Long-eared Owls are believed to be sedentary (Mikkola 1993). During the *Atlas* period, between five and 22 sites for this species were reported to the local Bird Recorders in any one year, with peaks in 1990 and 1991, probably related to increased coverage at this time (*Bird Reports*). In poor vole years, there will be fewer young raised, and unsuccessful pairs are not monitored, or even found, if broods are the most usual means of establishing the presence of birds. In such years few owls would be recorded other than casually.

Where studied, densities of between ten and 50 pairs per 100km^2 have been recorded (Mikkola 1993), but in this survey the highest number of tetrads with Long-eared Owls in any one 10km-square is just five (in five 10-km squares). Assuming just one pair per tetrad, this *Atlas* map suggests a population in SE Scotland of under 100 pairs, but given the above densities and the lack of coverage in the south of the area, it could be as high as 300. Clearly, any additional systematic censusing of an area could reveal better information as to numbers in SE Scotland. All Long-eared Owls should be reported to local Bird Recorders.   ***M.Holling***

Long-eared Owl

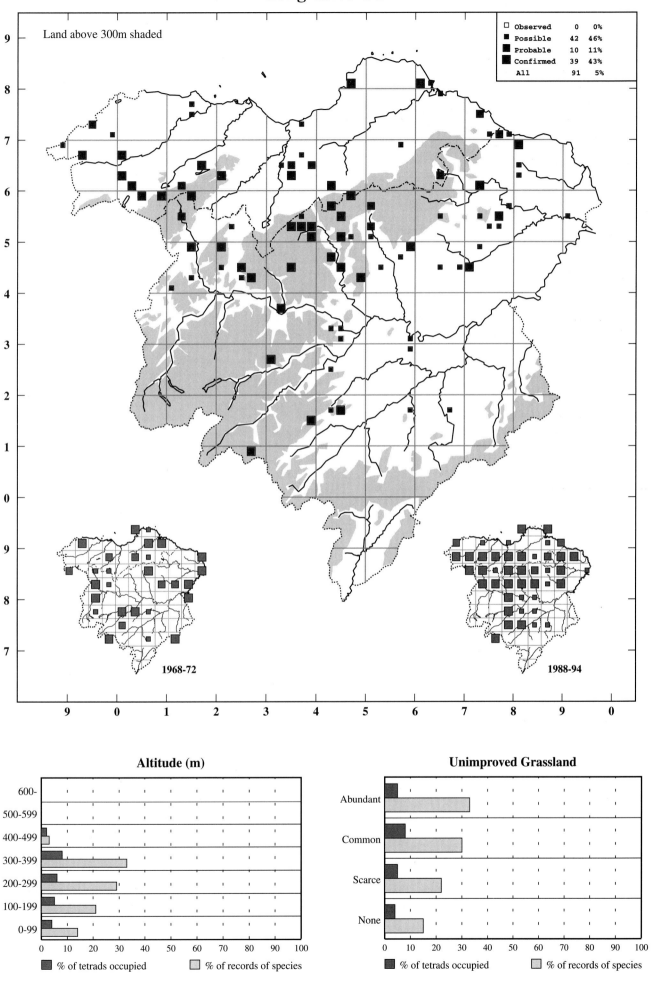

Land above 300m shaded

□	Observed	0	0%
■	Possible	42	46%
■	Probable	10	11%
■	Confirmed	39	43%
	All	91	5%

1968-72

1988-94

Altitude (m)

- 600-
- 500-599
- 400-499
- 300-399
- 200-299
- 100-199
- 0-99

0 10 20 30 40 50 60 70 80 90 100

■ % of tetrads occupied   ☐ % of records of species

Unimproved Grassland

- Abundant
- Common
- Scarce
- None

0 10 20 30 40 50 60 70 80 90 100

■ % of tetrads occupied   ☐ % of records of species

Short-eared Owl
Asio flammeus

The Short-eared Owl is essentially a nomadic species. Outwith the breeding season it will travel far and wide in search of food, often hunting over rough grassland in coastal areas. During the breeding season, it is found in areas supporting a substantial population of small mammal prey (usually Short-tailed Field Voles) and is found in open habitats such as heather and grass moorland and young forestry. Although it can take a wide variety of prey, both small mammals and birds, the size of the breeding population is largely determined by the numbers of voles, which usually peak every three to four years. During the breeding season, most hunting is done in the early morning and evening, but when prey is in short supply Short-eared Owls are often forced to be more diurnal. As ground nesters, they are susceptible to ground predators, agricultural or forestry damage, fire and human disturbance.

Since Short-eared Owls are frequently encountered by day in very open habitats, they were not difficult to locate during fieldwork. However, in years when prey is plentiful, some birds remaining more crepuscular in habit may have been overlooked. Nearly half of all records were of possible breeding and refer to single birds in suitable habitat. The few observed records were near the coast and probably involve migrants. Pairs in suitable habitat and territorial behaviour accounted for the majority of the probable records. It was more difficult to prove breeding, since the incubating hen usually sits tight, so birds may have been overlooked at the egg stage. Intensive fieldwork by raptor workers in some areas helped to uncover many of the confirmed breeding records. Nearly half of these referred to adults carrying food for young.

Records of Short-eared Owls came from nearly a fifth of all tetrads. They were well represented in the Lammermuirs, Moorfoots and the Ettrick Forest hills, more scattered in the Pentlands, Tweedsmuirs and western Cheviots, and almost absent from the bare, heavily grazed eastern Cheviots and the West Lothian moors which are now largely covered with closed canopy conifers. NT34 in the Moorfoots is a stronghold, with records in 19 out of the 25 tetrads over the seven-year period. Breeding was confirmed on the lower-lying edges of the hills in places such as near Gladhouse Reservoir and Crosswood Reservoir (NT05), and was probable in some lower-lying parts of West Lothian, for example north of the River Almond (NT06), where rough grassland or young coniferous plantations provide enough prey. However, the altitude data show that Short-eared Owls occurred in about a third of all tetrads between 300-500m, confirming the widespread but scattered hill distribution outlined above. Almost half of all tetrads with owls occurred between 300-400m, with three-quarters between 250-450m. These are the altitudes where the most favoured habitats occur. The map

confirms it is the lower hill plateaux, not the tops, which are favoured. Thus there are few records from the highest Tweedsmuir Hills in NT11&12.

The strongest relationship with a habitat type is with rough grazing, despite the relatively low percentage of this widespread habitat actually occupied. However, over 60% of birds were recorded in tetrads where rough grazing was abundant (see graph). In heather moors between a third and a half of all tetrads held Short-eared Owls (not shown). The best occupation rates were in tetrads where each of the three most favoured habitat types, coniferous woodland, unimproved grassland and heather moorland, was present, offering ideal cover, food and nest sites.

Comparison with the *Old Atlas* shows Short-eared Owls having been lost from a number of 10-km squares, but this loss has been matched by gains elsewhere. The losses are scattered but may reflect intensification of farming in lower lying areas, and maturation of conifer plantations. The gains are mostly at the edges of the Lammermuirs and Ettrick Forest, perhaps where newer plantations were established during the fieldwork period. However, the map exaggerates the position because it shows records accumulated across seven years. The number of records submitted to *Bird Reports* varies annually, partially dependent on observer effort but also due to varying numbers of Short-eared Owls breeding in SE Scotland. The table below shows this variation over a ten-year period for Borders. Thus 1990-92 appear to have been good years, with widespread records, while in years such as 1987 and 1995 fewer pairs were reported and no nests or broods were found at all. The table shows how the number of records swings from just a handful to nearly 60 in 1990 when confirmation of breeding was received for a record 14 pairs. It is notable that after this successful year even more pairs were reported in 1991, although the number of nests declined to only three. Most records refer to singles or pairs, but two counts of at least 20 in an area have been received, at Tweedsmuir (NT02) in June 1981 and in the Watch Water-Dirrington area of the Lammermuirs (NT65) in March 1993.

Records reported to *Borders Bird Report* 1986-1995.

Year	Territorial Pairs	Nests/broods
1986	15	2
1987	20	0
1988	21	5
1989	22	1
1990	57	14
1991	61	3
1992	29	9
1993	22	5
1994	25	3
1995	10	0

The *New Atlas* gives a British population estimate of 1,000-3,500 pairs, based on at least five pairs per 10-km square in suitable habitat, when food is plentiful. Locally, some squares may, at times, hold considerably more than this, for example the Watch Water area of the Lammermuirs (NT65) where 12 tetrads recorded at least probable breeding. Lockie (1955) recorded territories as small as 17.8ha when food was plentiful, which would produce 5.6prs/km^2. However, since nearly half of the records refer only to possible breeding, even in good years a maximum of 200 pairs is indicated, especially as the map shows a cumulative picture over seven years. In poor vole years, the population may be as low as 20 pairs, a figure supported by the low numbers noted in the *Bird Reports* in some years. ***O.C.McGarry***

Short-eared Owl

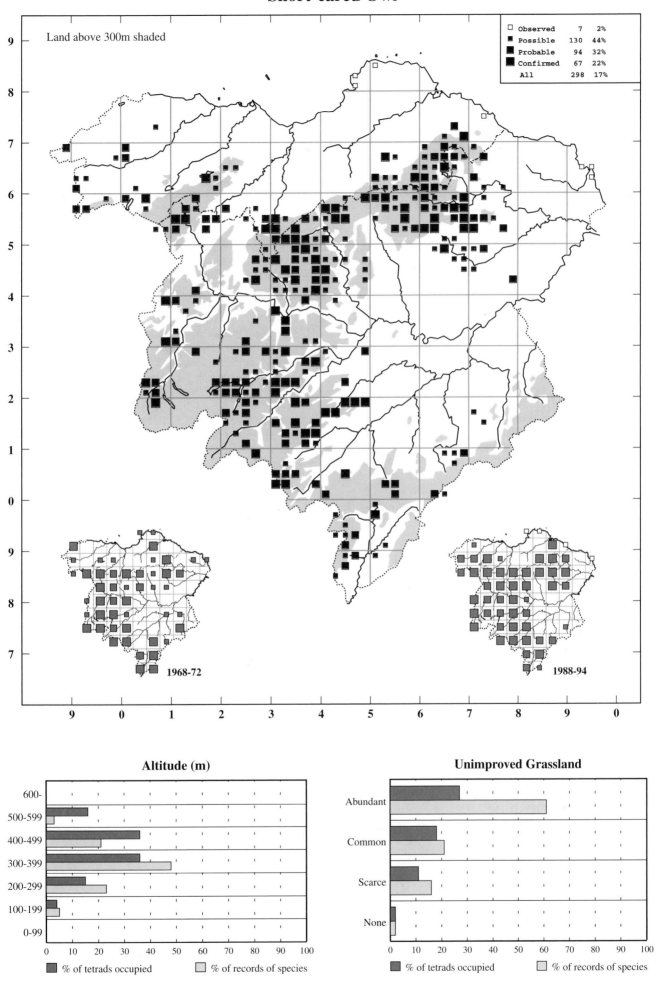

Land above 300m shaded

☐ Observed	7	2%
◼ Possible	130	44%
◼ Probable	94	32%
◼ Confirmed	67	22%
All	298	17%

1968-72

1988-94

Altitude (m)

600-
500-599
400-499
300-399
200-299
100-199
0-99

0 10 20 30 40 50 60 70 80 90 100

◼ % of tetrads occupied   ☐ % of records of species

Unimproved Grassland

Abundant

Common

Scarce

None

0 10 20 30 40 50 60 70 80 90 100

◼ % of tetrads occupied   ☐ % of records of species

Swift

Apus apus

High speed parties of screaming Swifts are an essential part of our fine summer days. In Britain Swifts are late arrivers and early departers, getting their young on the wing when aerial insects are most available, and then off again to obtain year-round summer weather elsewhere. After this they may never alight again, day or night, until they return to a nest chamber the following year. Nesting in buildings has all but replaced the original sites in crags and cliffs in Britain, but in Russia crags, caves and tree holes are used.

Swifts were readily located in the fieldwork. There were twice as many tetrads with confirmed as with probable breeding, suggesting that observers took time to watch for Swifts entering cavities. Three quarters of confirmed records were of birds entering presumed nest chambers. All cavities seen used were in buildings except for two in stone bridges.

The preponderance of observed records is due to Swifts flying considerable distances from nesting areas to where flying insects may be found in the prevailing weather of the day. Swifts were encountered over farmland, open country, lee sides of slopes and woods, and over water bodies. The map shows a denser occurrence of observed records within 10-20km of Edinburgh and of Midlothian and West Lothian towns, suggesting a limit on usual flying distance from these places, and similarly around Hawick (NT40,51). The graph shows a fall-off in observed records above 300m. Many of the higher records were on the nearest parts of the hills to the towns. The map shows an unmistakable clustering near river courses, notably the Tweed and its tributaries. This cannot be all due to settlements or observers' travel routes being mainly along rivers, as these are widely spread in the middle and lower Tweed and Teviot valleys while Swift occurrences are clustered closer to the rivers. Presumably Swifts find more insect prey in a zone near these rivers. The second graph shows no clear association of foraging Swifts with settlements, though there are marginally more at medium and minor sized settlements.

The distribution of breeding tetrads, as expected, shows similarity with the map of human settlement. The settlement graph confirms this, showing the numbers of Swift breeding tetrads increasing markedly with increasing size of human settlements. Edinburgh city holds the largest concentration of breeding tetrads, but the settlement map reveals that Swifts do not occupy the suburbs, mainly being newer buildings. They do breed in the central city, Leith, part of Corstorphine, and along the Water of Leith to Colinton and Currie, all places which contain older buildings. Similarly, in the 10-km square NT06, the new buildings of Livingston occupy much of the northern half of this square, but Swifts breed in only a small part of it. Otherwise, most Swift breeding tetrads clearly fit individual towns, for example Fauldhouse (NS96F), Bathgate (NS96U), Musselburgh (NT37G,L,R), Pencaitland (NT46J,P), Dunbar and West Barns (NT67P,U,Z), Reston (NT86R,W), Bonchester Bridge (NT51V,W) and Newcastleton (NY48Y).

Some clumps of contiguous breeding tetrads on the map, mostly in Borders, are deceptive, and are not the major Swift locations they appear to be. This is because Swifts were found to make use of some quite isolated large country houses and old substantial farm houses for nesting. For example the apparent large stronghold at NT75, with 11 connecting breeding tetrads, has the town of Duns occupying a quarter-tetrad area (2.3% of the tetrads), the two villages Preston and Gavinton occupying 0.6% of the tetrads, with over 97% of the tetrads being only farmland and woods. The six tetrads together in NT45-55 have the little village of Oxton in one, while the other five are countryside with a few isolated buildings, such as the roadside hotel at Carfraemill where Swifts nest. Town Yetholm

in NT82 shows as four breeding tetrads on the map, but only occupies 1.7% of their combined area. As a whole, in Edinburgh, Midlothian and West Lothian, Swifts are mainly urban birds breeding within the towns. In Borders and East Lothian, Swifts breed in the towns, small villages, and on isolated buildings in countryside, perhaps reflecting the smaller amount of urban habitat available.

Comparison of the two 10-km square maps shows loss of breeding range in the west and south since 1968-72, but numbers of Swifts concerned must have been small. Large scale forestry in those squares has matured in the period and may have discouraged Swifts from isolated buildings formerly in the open. A few 10-km squares in the north-east appear to have gained breeding Swifts but again the numbers involved are small. There are no records of Swifts ever having bred on the Forth islands.

In Britain as a whole, nothing is known with certainty about changes in numbers or distribution (*Trends*) and estimation of population is presently impossible in a reliable quantitative way, immature Swifts being present yearly in unpredictably changing numbers (*New Atlas*). It is supposed that the spread of building in the 19th century led to expansion of range then. In recent times the replacement of tall old buildings by modern ones, lacking holes and crevices, is known to be reducing available nesting sites (*BWP*). One study at the Hirsel shows a slow rise and then a fall in Swift breeding success over the past 40 years (Thomson *et al.* 1996).

Local information on Swifts is more about migration and passage than breeding (*Bird Reports*). Late May-June counts for a few Borders towns are: Kelso, 50 birds in 1990; Hawick, 22 in 1990; Newcastleton, 30-35 in 1991; Earlston, 40 in 1992; Grantshouse, 30 in 1994; and Lauder, 30 in 1997. All are surprisingly low as some of these are sizeable municipal towns. A count of all Swifts in big screaming groups over Haddington (NT57) on 30 July 1995 was 90 birds (this author), possibly mainly local adults, as young are known to leave the area quickly on fledging (*New Atlas*). The largest counts of big feeding collections of Swifts when insects attract them to water bodies are: 1,000 Gladhouse in June 1980, 1,000 Cobbinshaw 29 May 1983, 500 Gladhouse 29 May 1983, and 400 Linlithgow Loch 23 May 1985. In general SE Scotland has very few Swifts compared to most of England, only Edinburgh showing good numbers on the *New Atlas* abundance map.

The *New Atlas* estimates the British population to be *c.*80,000 pairs based largely on guesswork. From local counts, and knowledge of human settlement in the tetrads, there are probably *c.*1,500-1,800 'pairs' of Swifts in SE Scotland including immature prospecting birds, *c.*2% of the British population. Up to a quarter of these are in Edinburgh. Some monitoring of Swifts at selected local sites would be worthwhile, especially as there are now new insights into the behaviour of male, female and immature Swifts (Kaiser 1997).

H.E.M.Dott

Swift

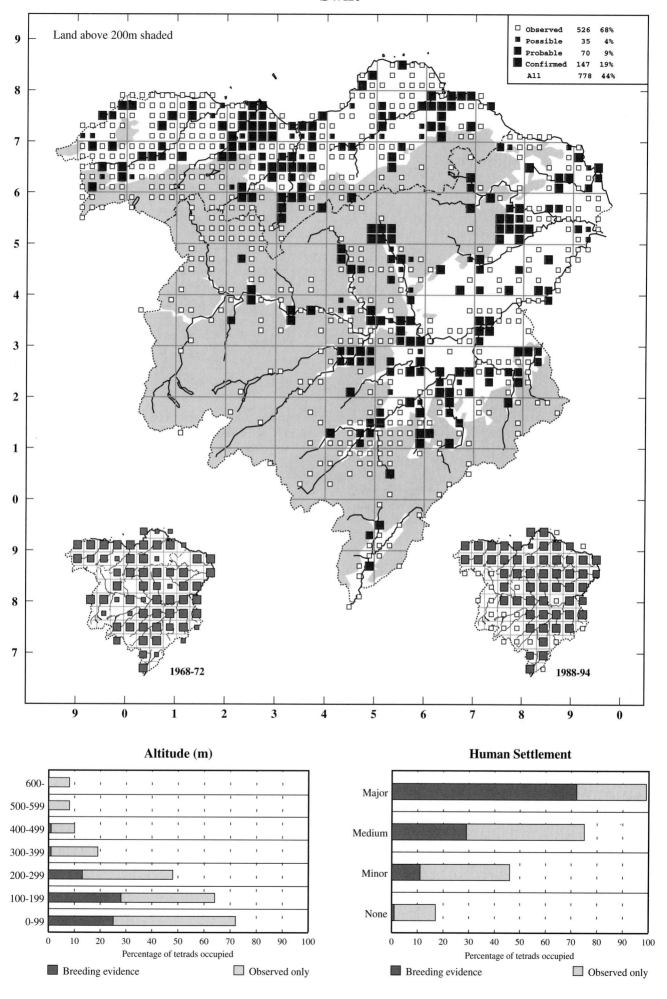

Altitude (m)

Percentage of tetrads occupied

Breeding evidence   Observed only

Human Settlement

Percentage of tetrads occupied

Breeding evidence   Observed only

183

Kingfisher
Alcedo atthis

While Kingfishers are instantly recognisable to vast numbers of the public, it must be one of the birds least often seen by that same public. Birdwatchers do not often fare much better as Kingfisher sightings usually involve hurried glimpses as a bright blue spark shoots past at great speed over a river. Indeed, the best placed to observe Kingfishers are the more stoic anglers who remain rooted to one spot on the river or canoeists who force everything to flee on their travels downriver. Slower-moving rivers with vertical sandy banks for nest sites and a ready supply of small fish are the primary needs of the Kingfisher. Overhanging branches for shady perches above a sunlit pool on the river margin offer the ideal feeding opportunity.

While Kingfishers may be amongst the most brightly coloured of birds, they are remarkably inconspicuous and amongst the most difficult of species for birders to find. The main cue to the presence of a Kingfisher is the repeated "chee" call that birds give as they fly up or downstream. While seeing a perched bird is rare, finding a nest is rarer still. With these difficulties, it is hardly surprising that half of all records involved possible breeding, mostly observations of single birds in suitable habitat. Probable records were dominated by sightings of pairs or birds on the same water on different occasions. About half of all confirmed records were of occupied nests, the remainder shared between sightings of juveniles or adults carrying fish to feed their young.

In a species tied absolutely to rivers or ponds for their food, it is hardly surprising that the analysis of Kingfisher records shows that 95% of all reports were from tetrads with large and medium-sized rivers. A finer analysis of the gradients of the rivers indicates that birds prefer rivers located in tetrads with flatter gradients. The map shows that Kingfishers occur across most of the drainage system, being present on all four major rivers in Lothian and along a significant part of the Tweed. Birds are generally absent from the upper reaches of rivers, the steeper gradient presumably being unsuited to a species that prefers to feed from the stiller pools of rivers. The absence of birds from some of the Teviot tributaries, as well as those from Liddesdale, could be more related to their relative remoteness during the survey as much as any actual lack of birds. Indeed, there is more than a hint from the map that the sites where birds were recorded may be related as much to the accessibility of the river bank, rather than any other single factor. It is noticeable that records cluster near towns as in Livingston (NT06), Edinburgh (NT27), Peebles (NT23&24), Selkirk to Melrose (NT42,43&53) and Kelso (NT73) or where birders are frequent visitors as at Tyninghame (NT67) and the Hirsel (NT84). In other words, Kingfishers are reported where many people frequent the river banks. The corollary of this is that they could occur just as frequently in the less accessible parts of the river system that are less frequently visited by either birders or the more general public and that the gaps seen along the rivers could be more apparent than real.

Comparison with the 1968-72 *Old Atlas* map shows that a large increase has occurred in the numbers of occupied 10km squares, the total having more than doubled from 16 to 38 squares. Kingfishers are known to be sensitive to hard winters, with large-scale mortality occurring when the small streams and the margins of larger rivers where the birds feed freeze over, preventing feeding. Although birds can move to the coast, it is well known that Kingfisher numbers drop drastically after hard winters (*Trends*). While there is little information on the history of the Borders population, it is clear that the numbers in Lothian were high (*c.*20 pairs) in the 1930s. This gradually declined until breeding ceased in the late 1940s, perhaps in response to the hard winter of 1947. *Andrews* makes it clear that

Kingfishers had become a rare autumn and winter visitor between the 1950s and 1980s with scarcely 10 records per year. Breeding recommenced in Penicuik in 1975 and numbers seem to have crept gradually upwards since. It is likely that this trend was mirrored in the Borders as records there have also increased during the period of the *Bird Reports* since 1979. The picture from the *Old Atlas* therefore probably shows Kingfishers at or near their lowest ebb in the area, with possibly only three records of breeding in the five years of the survey. With hard winters becoming relatively infrequent, Kingfisher numbers continue to increase with little sign that the severe weather of winter 1995-96 has had any lasting impact on the local population.

The *New Atlas* abundance map shows that Kingfishers are definitely scarce or even rare in SE Scotland, as few were clearly encountered during the limited two hour per tetrad survey visit and probably none at all on the key squares timed visits. Indeed the map shows just a single bird may have been encountered during the timed visits, in NT52. With such a low density in the area, the *New Atlas* calculation of the British population, based on 3-5 pairs per occupied 10-km square, would clearly be unsuitable. With records from the 80 tetrads spread across 36 occupied 10-km squares, the use of such a figure would grossly inflate our local population to more than 100-180 pairs. Any calculation of local numbers must consider the manner in which the map exaggerates the distribution by showing seven years accumulated records. As recent copies of the *Bird Reports* annually record about 10-12 cases of breeding, summer records from upwards of 35 sites and winter records from another 10-15 sites, a figure of 45-60 pairs of Kingfishers in SE Scotland may be a more realistic estimate. **R.D.Murray**

Kingfisher

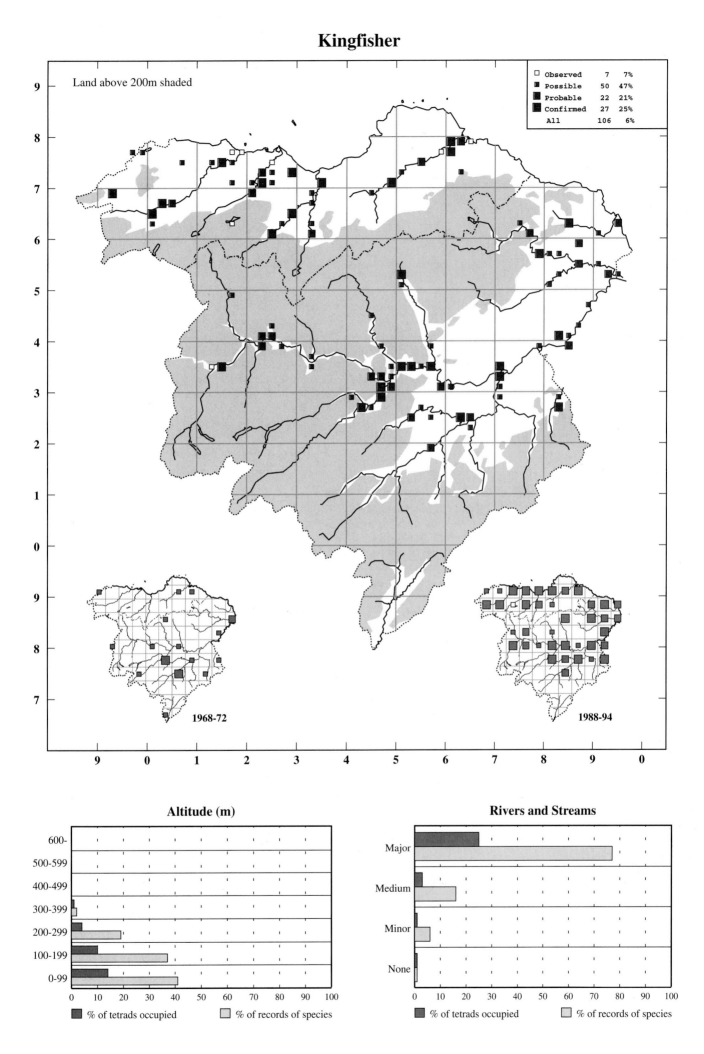

Land above 200m shaded

☐ Observed	7	7%
◼ Possible	50	47%
◼ Probable	22	21%
◼ Confirmed	27	25%
All	106	6%

1968-72

1988-94

Altitude (m)

600-
500-599
400-499
300-399
200-299
100-199
0-99

◼ % of tetrads occupied   ☐ % of records of species

Rivers and Streams

Major
Medium
Minor
None

◼ % of tetrads occupied   ☐ % of records of species

185

Green Woodpecker
Picus viridis

Despite its bright green and yellow plumage the Green Woodpecker can be surprisingly inconspicuous and difficult to locate in areas where densities are low. Its far-carrying "yaffle" call is better known and gives the bird its country name of "rain-bird" as the call was thought to herald rain. In Britain, the species is commoner in the south and east in well-wooded parkland landscapes and open deciduous woodlands. It nests in holes excavated high in deciduous trees but feeds mainly on the ground. Ants are the preferred diet, if available.

In SE Scotland Green Woodpeckers are local and half of the records received were of single birds only, many of these being calling birds. In fact, very few records were received from outwith the yaffling period, which normally ends in May. Little more than 10% of records related to confirmed breeding, mostly of fledged young or occupied nest holes. The remaining 40% of records in the probable category were largely due to evidence of territory, often two or more sightings or yaffling heard in the same area. In areas which received poorer coverage, it is probable that some Green Woodpeckers were missed. The species is mainly sedentary yet there are some winter records from areas where there is no evidence in this *Atlas*, perhaps indicating small unrecorded populations or movements in response to hard weather.

Despite these factors, the map shows distinct clusters, many of these relating to areas of mature deciduous woodland or parkland. West of Edinburgh, Green Woodpeckers are found in the hills around Beecraigs (NS97) and in estates such as Hopetoun (NT07Z) and Dalmeny (NT17N). Wooded parts of Edinburgh (NT27) are occupied at Corstorphine Hill, Hermitage of Braid and Holyrood Park. The wooded estates and deans between Whittingehame and Spott (NT67) and Tyninghame are the main centres of the East Lothian population. Elsewhere in Lothian, Green Woodpeckers are found mainly along the flanks of the hills, especially around the northern Pentlands near the headwaters of the Water of Leith and North Esk. There are two concentrations in Borders, in the Whiteadder woods from Ellemford (NT76F) to Foulden (NT95H), and in the middle Tweed from Leaderfoot (NT53S) up to Dawyck (NT13S). Elsewhere Green Woodpeckers are restricted to scattered single sites, mainly estate policy woodlands and mature deciduous woodlands, such as the Haining (NT42Z), Ancrum (NT62H), Gordon (NT64L), Charterhall (NT74T) and the Hirsel (NT84F). There are a few isolated records from sites deeper into the hills, like Portmore (NT24P), Fountainhall and Stow (NT44), Oxton (NT45W), Shielswood Loch (NT41P), Calaburn Farm (NT41T) and Hownam (NT71U). The *New Atlas* abundance map shows the Tyninghame and Whiteadder populations as the main centres for this species in SE Scotland.

The altitude graph expands on this distribution, with all but 10% of records below 300m and the majority of tetrads with Green Woodpeckers lying around the 200m contour. The slopes at the hill edges at this altitude hold much of the remaining semi-natural deciduous woodland of SE Scotland, and tend to be grazed rather than planted with arable crops, providing feeding opportunities in the short grass and bracken under trees. This pattern is similar to that in Northumberland (*Day*). Only in the open woods of NT76 around Abbey St. Bathans is this species more widespread than the Great Spotted Woodpecker.

Although quite well distributed in SE Scotland, the Green Woodpecker is a relative newcomer to the area, the first breeding being as recent as 1951 in Selkirkshire (*Thom*). There has been a 43% increase in the number of occupied 10-km squares since the *Old Atlas*, confirming the increase in numbers reported over the last three decades. Birds appear to have been lost from Liddesdale, which matches a loss from throughout the upper Solway area shown in the *New Atlas*. Detailed reference to *Andrews* and *Murray* shows that there appear to have been some losses from the South Esk valley and some of the Berwickshire Deans where the species may have once been commoner. During the *Atlas*, Green Woodpeckers became extinct in the Fountainhall and Stow area, with no records since summer 1992, despite a mainly mild 1992-3 winter. It is likely that at low density the species is prone to small scale extinctions and re-colonisations.

Considering that the Green Woodpecker colonised the area less than 50 years ago, and despite setbacks during hard winters when snow cover on the ground leads to increased mortality, the species has made remarkable inroads and seems well established. The extension of deciduous woodland cover through hardwood plantings may help to increase the low density of birds currently in the area.

Thom, referring to an SOC Enquiry in the early 1980s, reported between 55-90 pairs in SE Scotland. From the *Bird Reports* most sites hold one pair, and although a few hold two or three, some of these sites span more than one tetrad. Given the volatility of the population, it is reasonable to assume that each tetrad on the map represents one pair. This puts the SE Scotland population at about 150-200 pairs. A full survey of all known and likely Green Woodpecker sites would be useful to establish a more accurate figure and a list of occupied sites.   ***M.Holling***

Green Woodpecker

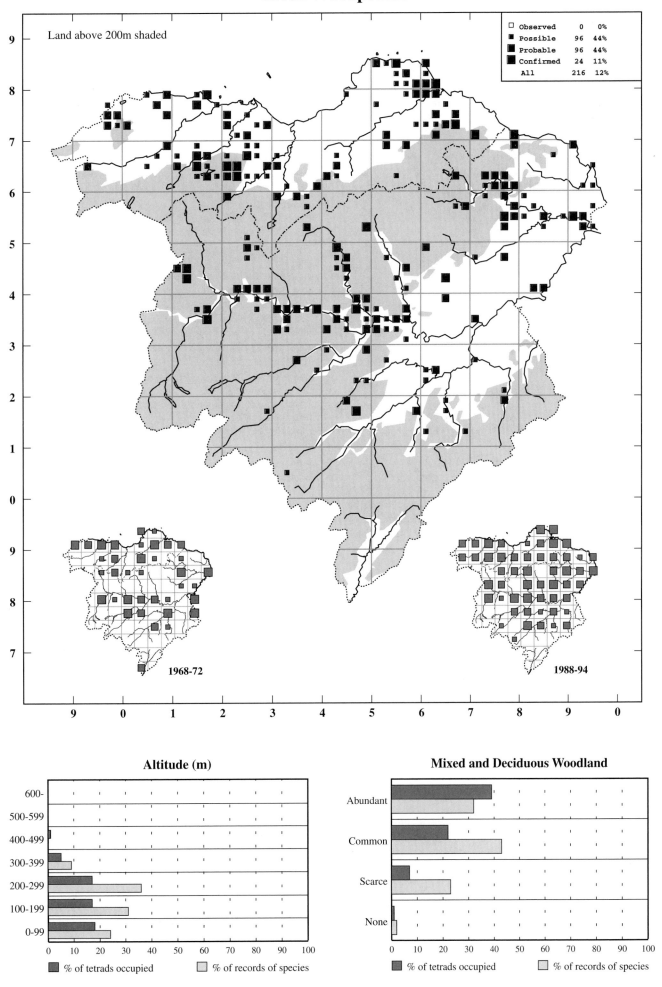

	Observed	0	0%
	Possible	96	44%
	Probable	96	44%
	Confirmed	24	11%
	All	216	12%

Land above 200m shaded

1968-72

1988-94

Altitude (m)

Mixed and Deciduous Woodland

■ % of tetrads occupied   □ % of records of species

■ % of tetrads occupied   □ % of records of species

187

Great Spotted Woodpecker
Dendrocopos major

The Great Spotted Woodpecker often betrays its presence as it flies away with characteristic undulating flight and loud, sharp "tchick" calls; it is less frequently seen climbing tree trunks or hammering away at dead wood to extract its insect food from beneath the bark. In spring, territories are proclaimed by drumming on dead trunks and branches. Most mature woodlands, large or small, hold this species, which excavates its own nest hole in dead and dying wood.

Almost a third of all tetrads have Great Spotted Woodpeckers, indicating the availability of sufficiently mature trees. Records received were evenly split between possible, probable and confirmed. Most probable records referred to territorial behaviour or anxiety calls, usually the repeated "tchick" call from close to a nest hole. As this species tends to be solitary, only a small proportion of records were of pairs. Proof of breeding came from three main sources. Fledged broods accounted for almost a third of confirmed breeding records, with the remainder being records of occupied nests, often detected due to the calls of the young within, or of used nest holes. Checking old trees, especially birches, for previously excavated holes, was an efficient way of confirming the presence of this species.

The map shows clusters of records, often based around the policy woodlands of large houses, such as at Tyninghame, around Floors Castle (NT73C) and the Hirsel (NT84F). Other records in these mainly cereal growing areas relate to the use of mature trees in hedgerows and small game coverts. Well wooded river valleys such as the North and South Esk (NT26&36), the middle Tweed, the Rule (NT51) and the Jed (NT61) show up well. Many of these valleys contain large amounts of Elm, much of which was dead during the survey period. This dead wood provides both food and nesting opportunities, and it may be that the Great Spotted Woodpecker has been able to spread into new habitats over the last 20 years because of the effects of Dutch Elm disease.

Both the map and the altitude graph show that most Great Spotted Woodpeckers occur below 200m, and detailed analysis of the data shows that 80% of records occur below 250m. They are consequently found mainly in lowland Lothian, Berwickshire and northern Roxburghshire. Elsewhere they penetrate the hills only up the river valleys, occurring where there are stands of mature broad-leaved trees. Although Great Spotted Woodpeckers are recorded in coniferous woodland, the map shows that they are virtually absent from the main plantations in the Tweed valley, Craik, Newcastleton and Wauchope. These forests have little mature timber and many were planted on the open hill where there were few old trees still standing. It may be that, as these forests mature and diversify, Great Spotted Woodpeckers will move into them. The graph of occurrence against woodland shows that no Great Spotted Woodpeckers occur if there is no woodland in a tetrad, emphasising the complete dependence of this species on trees, unlike the Green Woodpecker. The fact that four-fifths of all Great Spotted Woodpeckers were found in tetrads where woodlands are common or abundant also supports this association.

Comparing the distribution with that in the *Old Atlas*, there has been considerable infilling of the range. This may be partially an artifact of better coverage in this survey, or may be real due to the spread of Dutch Elm disease since the *Old Atlas*. There does, however, appear to have been a loss from the upper Tweed and Yarrow in NT12 and NT22 respectively, but this may relate only to odd pairs in the earlier survey. The *New Atlas* shows a loss of both this and the Green Woodpecker from parts of southern Scotland to the south and west of our area. Despite this, proof of breeding for the Great Spotted Woodpecker in this *Atlas* was quite easy to obtain compared with the *Old Atlas* (a 33% increase in cases of confirmed breeding). Squares occupied now which were vacant or only had possible breeding in the *Old Atlas* now have an average of six occupied tetrads per 10-km square, with NT61 (south of Jedburgh) now having no fewer than 15 occupied tetrads. This suggests that the Great Spotted Woodpecker was much easier to find in this *Atlas*, and that it may be more common than hitherto, supported by anecdotal reports from many local birdwatchers (H.E.M. Dott & R.D. Murray *pers. comm.*). BTO data also show a huge increase in numbers since the *Old Atlas* (*Trends*).

The history of the Great Spotted Woodpecker in Scotland is an interesting one, related to changes in tree cover. It changed from being widespread in the 18th century to being possibly extinct by the middle of the 19th, due to deforestation (*Thom*). It then recolonised most of lowland Scotland, including SE Scotland, in the late 1800s. For instance, nesting was recorded again in Lothian, at Penicuik, in 1901 (*Andrews*). This return to the area was probably related to planting of amenity and policy woodlands. Numbers have fluctuated since then, and may have peaked during the 1980s in Scotland with the increase in rotting wood because of Dutch Elm disease. The *New Atlas* abundance map shows a similar pattern to this *Atlas*, but numbers are only low to moderate in SE Scotland.

About 90-100 sites for Great Spotted Woodpecker were reported annually to the *Bird Reports* during the *Atlas*, which is effectively only a sample of the total population. Some sites carry good numbers, with 11 territories at Floors Castle (NT73C) and five territories at both the Hirsel and Marchmont (NT74J&P) in 1995. The total number of pairs can be estimated from this *Atlas* by dividing the population by habitat groupings, as the more woodland in a tetrad, the greater the chances of there being more than one pair present. Thus, assuming a conservative density of 1.0 prs/km² for the top category woodland (228 tetrads), and just one pair for each of the other tetrads, gives an estimate of almost 1,200 pairs. The *Old Atlas* used a mean of 15-20 pairs per occupied 10-km square which would give a similar figure of 810-1,100 pairs, taking into account boundary squares. Only a more detailed sample survey on a 10-km square level could confirm these figures.   *M.Holling*

Great Spotted Woodpecker

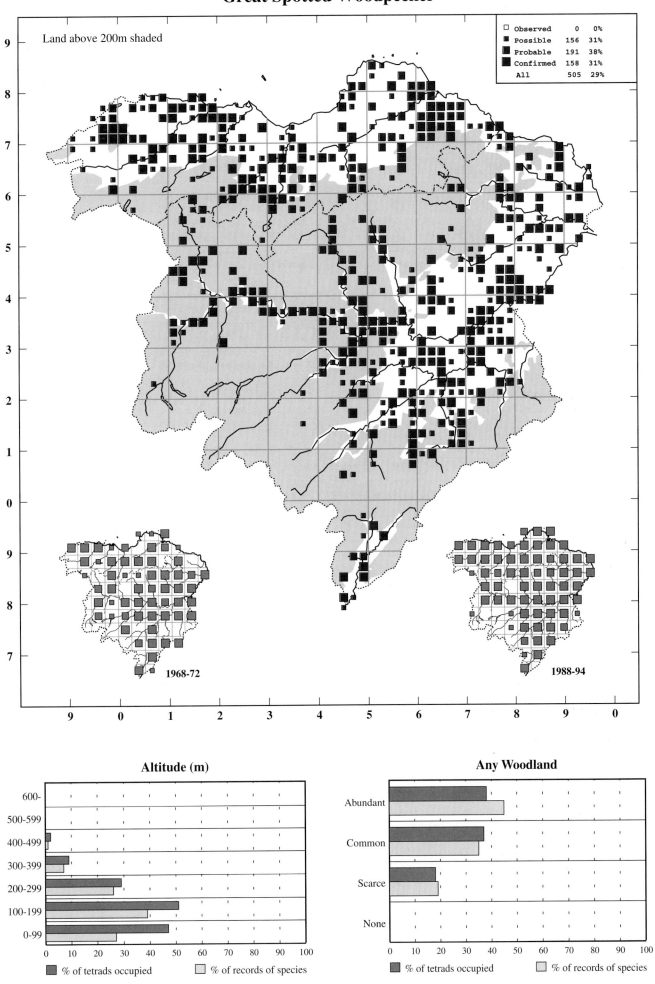

Land above 200m shaded

☐ Observed	0	0%
■ Possible	156	31%
■ Probable	191	38%
■ Confirmed	158	31%
All	505	29%

1968-72

1988-94

Altitude (m)

% of tetrads occupied
% of records of species

Any Woodland

% of tetrads occupied
% of records of species

189

Skylark
Alauda arvensis

All types of open country are attractive to Skylarks. They will occupy open terrain from the coastal cliffs, dunes and saltmarshes, through all types of farmland including intensively cultivated arable land and open scrub up to the summits of the highest hills. This lack of specific habitat requirements, other than open terrain, has allowed the Skylark to become amongst the most widespread species in both Britain and SE Scotland; Skylarks featuring in the top ten most widespread species both nationally and locally. The only essential habitat demand is that it must provide areas of short herbage to feed and nest in. Even intensively cultivated ground is occupied and some birds nest in the hedge remnants between the fields, avoiding the risk of nests being destroyed by farm operations. The principal foods include seeds, green vegetation and insects.

Skylarks are one of the easier species to record. Their loud distinctive song, delivered in flight from a considerable height, makes them very obvious and this led to three quarters of all registrations for possible and probable breeding involving singing and displaying birds. Evidence of confirmed breeding was more problematical with nests being difficult to find, young tending to appear later in the season when *Atlas* activity was less intense and the fact that adults do not always carry food visibly when feeding young. Thus the relatively low 25% of the evidence referred to proved breeding.

The map shows Skylarks are absent from only three habitat types: islands, urban areas and commercial forestry. Penicuik (NT26), Edinburgh (NT27), Dalkeith (NT36), Haddington (NT57), Prestonpans (NT47) and Galashiels-Melrose (NT53) stand out on the map where the open areas between the settlements have presumably vanished under the tide of increasing urbanisation. Conversely other areas that are apparently well built up on large-scale maps, such as in the Livingston, Bathgate, Broxburn area (NS96&NT06) must have sufficient open spaces and temporary 'wasteland' left to allow the presence of Skylarks to be registered in the *Atlas*.

Commercial forests planted in the 1950s and 1960s when the policy was for blanket coverage of conifers, with little or no open space, have produced substantial blank areas on the map. The large forests in the middle Tweed (NT23&33), Upper Ettrick (NT21),

Craik (NT30), Newcastleton (NY58), Wauchope (NT50&60), Beecraigs (NT07) and Leithope (NT70) stand out as largely lacking Skylarks. It is possible that Skylarks will re-occupy these areas as the forests are felled and replaced with woodlands with more progressive forestry practices that allow a mosaic of open habitats and forest of different ages which should have sufficient open ground to suit Skylarks, provided the spaces are sufficiently large. Thus urban areas account for about 50 blank tetrads, while forestry may occupy another 120, approximately 10% of the area. The remaining gaps are less easy to account for, particularly the area round Hawick (NT41&51), Stow (NT44) and Ettrickfoot (NT43).

The *New Atlas* abundance map shows areas of moderate to high numbers in the East Lothian cereal belt but the highest abundance category in the Pentlands, Lammermuirs, the head of the Tweed and the flanks of Cheviot. This presents a problem as the *New Atlas* categorically states that highest densities are achieved on mixed and arable farmed lowlands while their map demonstrates that in SE Scotland at least, equally high or even higher abundance occurs on moorlands and on hill margins where open improved and rough grassland is the norm. This is compounded by the area of lowish abundance that is shown in the area between Coldstream and Jedburgh that might well fit with the *New Atlas* concept of optimum habitat. Clearly some difficulty exists here. Great concern has surfaced in recent BTO publications (*BTO News*) about the effect of the intensification of farming on the birds of arable farmland like the Skylark, mainly due to the large scale drop in the CBC index for Skylark which started in the early 1980s after a period of stability (*Trends*). Perhaps the lower than expected abundance in some of these areas of intensive arable farming makes the good values achieved in the less intensively farmed grasslands stand out more.

A little work has been done on Skylark densities in SE Scotland at Aberlady Bay where P.R.Gordon found densities of 60prs/km^2 on open natural grassland (*Andrews*) while cultivated land in the Tranent area (da Prato 1985) yielded an average of 11prs/km^2. During the 1993 Lowland Wader Survey, H.E.M.Dott (*pers.comm.*) found densities of 17prs/km^2 near Harperrig on tall rough grazing but only 1-2 prs/km^2 on short intensively grazed grass. Densities of over 20prs/km^2 were found on high level wet moorland at Cooms Fell-Watch Hill (NY48J&49F) by H.E.M.Dott (*pers.comm.*) during *Atlas* work. BBS returns suggest about 10-15prs/km^2.

While Aberlady compares well with some of the highest densities reported in Britain of up to 90prs/km^2, and a CBC average of 18prs/km^2 was quoted in the *Old Atlas*, their working figure for an occupied 10-km square used a much lower value of 5-10prs/km^2. The *New Atlas* used a similar value of 7prs/km^2 in its calculation of the British population. The density figure produced by da Prato in the Tranent study seems appropriate for the better arable land in SE Scotland and agrees well with the general value derived from the recent BBS surveys. Densities on the upland moors and grasslands do seem to have higher values although this may be balanced by the lower values to be expected from tetrads dominated by forestry. If a value slightly less than da Prato's figure is used to represent the whole area, an overall density of about 9prs/km^2 for our area would give a local population of 54,400 pairs or 800 pairs per occupied 10-km square. This is not too different from the *New Atlas* estimate of about 730 pairs per occupied 10-km square.

In view of the concerns about population levels in Britain, the BTO launched a Skylark Survey in 1995. This survey should provide a better picture of the nature of the crisis as well as a better understanding of the precise habitat preferences of the species. *R.D.Murray*

Skylark

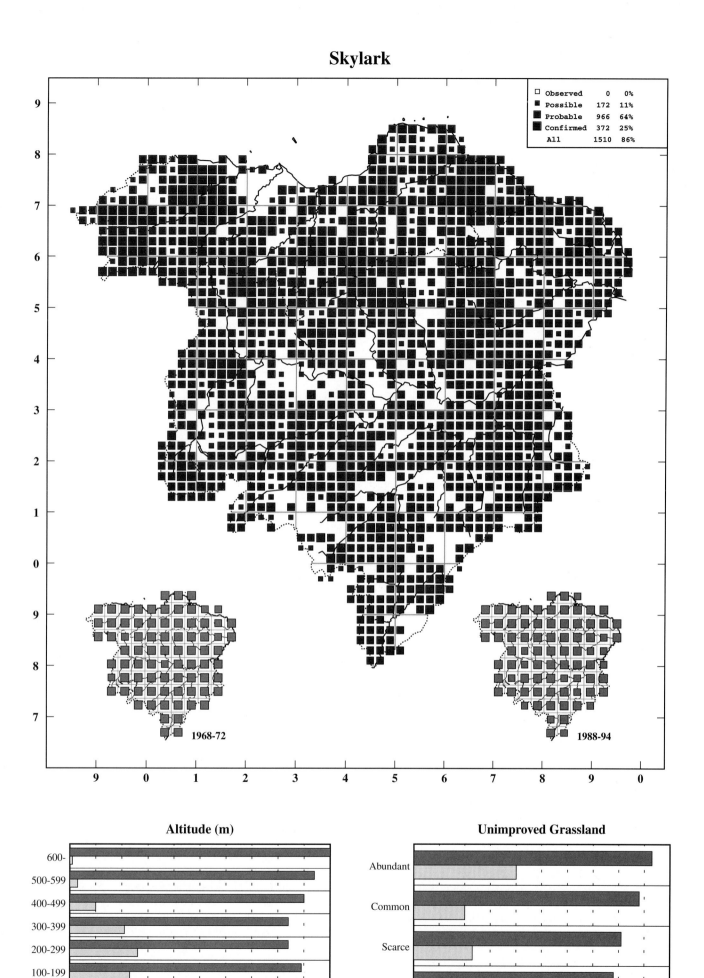

Observed	0	0%
Possible	172	11%
Probable	966	64%
Confirmed	372	25%
All	1510	86%

1968-72

1988-94

Altitude (m)

- 600-
- 500-599
- 400-499
- 300-399
- 200-299
- 100-199
- 0-99

■ % of tetrads occupied   □ % of records of species

Unimproved Grassland

- Abundant
- Common
- Scarce
- None

■ % of tetrads occupied   □ % of records of species

Sand Martin
Riparia riparia

The Sand Martin is a long-distance migrant that winters in sub-Saharan Africa and is one of the earliest summer visitors to return to Britain in spring. It is mainly a bird of the riverbank, nesting colonially in sandy banks but is also common in sand-pits where sand and gravel is extracted for the construction industry. It catches flying insects on the wing over rivers and streams. It is susceptible to the droughts that afflict the sub-Saharan savannas where European populations overwinter, and numbers vary over the years as droughts reduce the numbers of flying insects. The reduction of food resources depresses Sand Martin survival during winter and increases mortality on the spring passage.

They are relatively easy to see, especially along waterways, although colonies are not always easy to locate. Colonies are prone to destruction by floods and locations change as banks become overgrown, flooded or are subject to high levels of nest parasites. Abandonment can occur in the middle of a breeding season but new sites spring up nearby. This is particularly true of sand-pits where operations can force birds to move, although operators are usually very considerate of their breeding birds and avoid undue disturbance. These shifts make it difficult to keep track of the location of colonies from year to year. While Sand Martins were reported from 40% of the tetrads, over half of the registrations involved observed records, birds foraging for food. The remaining records were mainly of proved breeding, mostly birds flying in an out of occupied burrows.

The map clearly shows a strong relationship with the river system, especially along the Tweed and its main tributaries, as well as in Liddesdale in the extreme south and along the Tyne in the north. Colonies occur in clusters along the rivers that mark areas of haughland, the flatter open sections of the valleys where sands and gravels have been deposited since the end of the last glacial phase. These haughs are usually separated by sections where the river valleys are characterised by erosion and do not have deposits of sand for birds to nest in. This pattern can be seen along the Tweed where the haughs at Drumelzier (NT13) are separated from those between Peebles and Walkerburn (NT23&33) and again between Selkirk and Melrose (NT43&53). The pattern is repeated further down the Tweed. The open haughs are mostly farmed while the vacant sections are often narrow, steep-sided and wooded and less suitable for Sand Martins. Similar haughs are evident along the Ettrick in NT32, the Tyne in NT47, Teviot in NT51&62, the Whiteadder in NT85 and the Eye in NT86. In Liddesdale colonies are almost continuous along the Liddel and Hermitage Waters (NY48,58&59).

There are several groups of tetrads away from rivers that indicate the position of sand-pit colonies in West Lothian (e.g. North Couston NS97K, 260 burrows in 1993), Midlothian (Loquhariot NT36Q, 378 in 1993), East Lothian (Blinkbonny NT56G, 140 in 1993), Tweeddale (Shiphorns NT25K, 137 in 1994), Roxburghshire (Eckford NT73I, 300 in 1988) and Berwickshire (Causewaybank (NT85U&Z, 350 in 1990). The fluvio-glacial sands are mostly found along the fringes of the hills where the melting remnants of the most recent ice sheet poured out sediment-laden meltwater onto the surrounding lowlands. Mining activity to expose the sands, however, is mostly in an arc round Edinburgh where the greatest demand for the product lies. Sand-pits often have large faces and this usually results in larger colonies than in natural river banks where exposures of sand cliffs are short and often only a few metres in height. One coastal colony was found, in a sandy sea-cliff at Winterfield near Dunbar (NT67P, four burrows in 1993).

While birds are tied to sites with exposed sand banks, the observed records indicate that birds do not stray far from rivers to feed. There are few observed records more than two tetrads away from a recorded breeding site and hints that birds rarely travel more than 4km to feed. In Lothian there are more observed records that are neither on, or near, a river or near a breeding site.

Sand Martins are lowland birds with 90% of breeding sites and 84% of all records below 300m, foraging birds flying into slightly higher tetrads accounting for the difference. Sand Martins clearly prefer larger river courses with half of all tetrads where large rivers were present having registrations and 88% of all breeding records coming from tetrads with large or medium-sized rivers.

Sand Martins were almost ubiquitous in the *Old Atlas* when the British population may have been at an all-time high. Numbers crashed in 1969 and later crashes occurred in the mid-1970s and again in 1985 when the population fell to 16% of the 1968 level (*Trends, New Atlas*). Numbers have improved since and the *Atlas* survey was conducted when numbers were recovering. The 10-km square maps show that birds bred in all but three squares in 1968-72. By 1988-94 birds were absent from nine squares and no breeding took place in a further 13 squares. The *New Atlas* abundance map shows a large area of the highest numbers in the Tweed drainage between Berwick and Selkirk with a spur of moderate numbers extending towards Broughton on the upper Tweed. Numbers elsewhere are rather low, including all of the Lothian lowlands.

The 1983 Lothian count (Brown & Brown 1984a) found 516 burrows in 12 colonies. By 1993 (Speak 1994) this had increased to 1,193 burrows in 15 colonies. Both counts took place when the CBC data suggest that numbers were at moderate levels (*Trends*), in contrast to the 1987 counts in Borders of 2,605 burrows in 64 colonies which occurred just after population levels had troughed in 1985-86 (Murray 1988). Counts of comparable stretches of river on the middle Teviot and Tweed in 1994-95 suggest that numbers were at 190% of the 1987 levels, in line with known increases in the British population. If this is extrapolated to the whole Borders count, the total would rise to c.4,700 burrows for 1994-95. These counts of burrows, either censused or estimated, total c.6,000 pairs. There can be little doubt that colonies have been missed, especially on the Liddel Water that was never counted and so the population present in 1994 is more likely to have been in the order of 7,000 pairs, or 2.8% of the British population. With birds colonising small hill streams in 1997, perhaps due to pressure on the core areas along the river haughs, an even higher population is hinted at. A census of colonies would be desirable to establish the distribution and scale of the population at a period when numbers are high.   *P.W.Speak*

Sand Martin

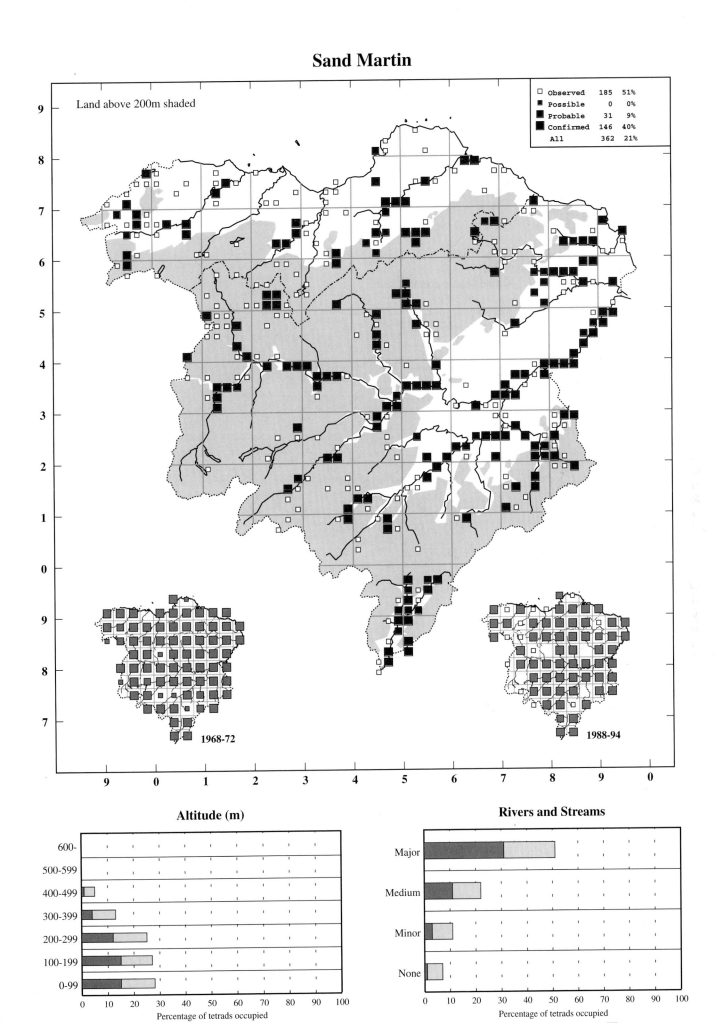

Land above 200m shaded

	Observed	185	51%
	Possible	0	0%
	Probable	31	9%
	Confirmed	146	40%
	All	362	21%

1968-72

1988-94

Altitude (m)

Percentage of tetrads occupied

■ Breeding evidence   ☐ Observed only

Rivers and Streams

Percentage of tetrads occupied

■ Breeding evidence   ☐ Observed only

FJWatson

Swallow
Hirundo rustica

The Swallow, the herald of summer, is a familiar part of rural landscapes through much of Britain with its swooping flight in pursuit of flying insects, constant twittering and habit of nesting in buildings. While flying insects can be found almost anywhere, concentrations of favoured prey mostly occur over farmland, lakes and rivers and woodland edges. Swallows are more thinly distributed in extensive areas of moorland and forestry, probably due more to a lack of suitable nest sites than a lack of prey. The central parts of cities are shunned, presumably due to a lack of feeding opportunities.

Swallows are conspicuous and rather easy to record. The high proportion of confirmed breeding is due to the ease with which Swallow nests can be found, occupied nests forming two-thirds of all confirmed reports. Sightings of young, in the nest or recently fledged, accounted for a further quarter of confirmed records. The durability of the nest means that old nests were worth looking for, forming 10% of breeding reports. Observers were advised to automatically check buildings for Swallow nests when surveying a new tetrad. This was especially important in upland squares where it was usual for the only building in a tetrad to hold a nest, even if only a tiny shed for fodder,.

Swallows can feed and breed in most areas where flying insects are common. The habitat graph shows a strong relationship with tetrads where arable land and improved pasture with stock were widespread. As arable land becomes scarce only a slight fall (15%) in Swallow representation is seen, possibly because Swallows are able to feed in the presence of stock on all pastures, the stock being a major attraction to flies. It is only in tetrads with no arable land, mostly in areas of extensive moorland and forest in the hills that the numbers of Swallows fall dramatically. The altitude graph shows that Swallow representation drops above 300m in areas where arable farmland becomes scarce.

The map nevertheless confirms the catholic habitat requirements of the Swallow and its ability to find prey and nest-sites over much of SE Scotland. Only hill areas are sparsely settled with the Pentlands

(NT05), the Tweedsmuirs (NT11,12,13,22&23), the Moorfoots (NT34), the Lammermuirs (NT56&76) and Liddesdale (NY49&58 &NT30,50&60) having 10-km squares with only a third of the tetrads occupied, although no 10-km square is truly unoccupied. These gaps represent moorlands and forested areas with no human habitation whatsoever that might offer a nest-site for Swallows. Indeed these gaps in the Swallow map correlate well with the gaps in the settlement map that show tetrads where there are no buildings. The only other major gap on the map is in Edinburgh (NT27) where the density of housing may preclude the prey that Swallows depend on. A minor gap can be seen at Prestonpans (NT47B&C). It is likely that elsewhere settlements either have patches of suitable habitat or are near enough to feeding areas for Swallows to penetrate.

Just over half of all observed records are adjacent to vacant tetrads, producing an edge-of-range effect, birds from nesting areas clearly being able to forage into those parts of SE Scotland where breeding was not possible. This limitation may well be the lack of nest-sites which may be the main constraint on the breeding distribution. These foraging birds were mostly seen on the fringes of urban areas and the edges of the hills and commercial forests.

Although not shown on a graph, there is a strong relationship between Swallows and the presence of buildings. While city areas, where the density of housing may preclude suitable feeding areas, had a somewhat lower percentage of occupied tetrads compared with the suburbs and villages, tetrads with no buildings whatsoever have a very much lower representation. Many of these sites without human habitation comprise the 15% of observed reports where Swallows were seen foraging but were unable to nest.

Comparison with the *Old Atlas* maps is not informative as Swallows bred in all of the 10-km squares in both periods. If the use of buildings for nesting does restrict the range, however, there may well have been some minor contraction of range in the remoter valleys or in areas of forestry where farm buildings have been abandoned and fallen into ruin.

Local data are poor but where sites have been reported on over several years, the story is usually one of decline. For instance, Scoughall (NT68C) held ten pairs in 1982 but only four or five from 1983-1987 while Longformacus (NT65Y) had up to 30 pairs in 1986 but by 1991 only four pairs were present. West Craigie (NT17N) was more variable, rising from six to ten pairs before falling to four pairs over a five-year period (*Bird Reports*).

The *New Atlas* abundance map shows a curious pattern of small isolated areas of high abundance around Linlithgow, Musselburgh, East Linton, the lower Tweed and the middle Teviot. The common factor may well be water bodies that provide plenty of food for Swallows. Otherwise much of the area achieves only moderate abundance across the lower ground and poor abundance on or near higher ground. This lower than average abundance pattern is supported by da Prato's (1985) data from farmland near Tranent where Swallows occurred at less than 1.0prs/km², well below the value of 2-2.6prs/km² quoted from CBC studies in both the *Old Atlas* and the *New Atlas* for the British population. Data on Swallow numbers in Northumberland (*Day*) yielded a slightly higher value of 1.5prs/km² from an area with a similar density of occupied tetrads to SE Scotland. This suggests our population may be between 6,000-8,500 pairs.

The poor data collected locally suggest a strong need to start logging the numbers of Swallows nesting in some parts of SE Scotland. McGinn's (1977) study of farm nests in NT51 near Hawick should be repeated. There is a need for a base-line at several sites that might be used for future comparisons to determine whether there have been declines in our area or not. ***R.D.Murray***

Swallow

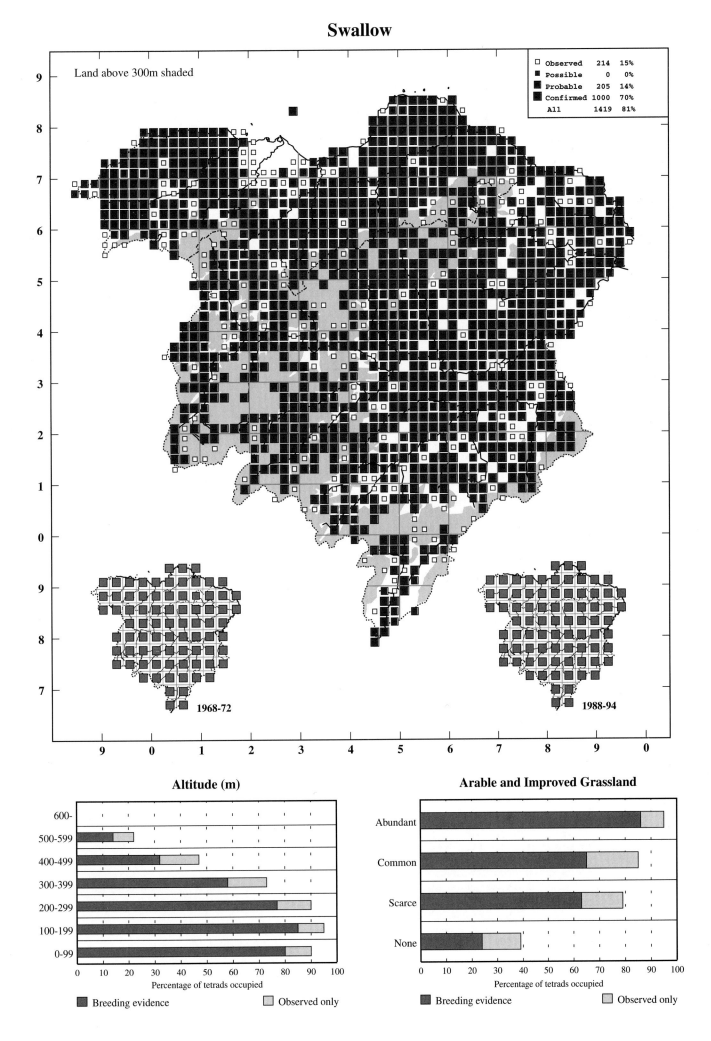

□ Observed	214	15%
■ Possible	0	0%
■ Probable	205	14%
■ Confirmed	1000	70%
All	1419	81%

Land above 300m shaded

1968-72

1988-94

Altitude (m)

600-
500-599
400-499
300-399
200-299
100-199
0-99

Percentage of tetrads occupied

■ Breeding evidence   □ Observed only

Arable and Improved Grassland

Abundant
Common
Scarce
None

Percentage of tetrads occupied

■ Breeding evidence   □ Observed only

195

House Martin
Delichon urbica

Cheerfully twittering round the eaves of houses in summer, the House Martin is a familiar presence around settlements throughout much of Britain. The mud nests stuck to the walls of houses, just below the eaves, can be a blessing or a curse to householders, depending on their outlook and the precise location of the nest. Few willingly accept a nest just above the doorstep! While familiar in modern Britain, they were undoubtedly rarer in the past before stone buildings were common, and the species was limited to natural nest-sites on cliffs and in caves. Small numbers still breed in natural sites along the British coast. House Martins are the last of the hirundines to return to Britain, the majority not arriving until May. Two or three broods may be attempted and young in the nest have been reported well into October.

With such close ties to human habitation and obvious nests, House Martins were easy to record in the *Atlas* fieldwork. Buildings were routinely inspected for nests in new tetrads and such is their durability that even old nests could be used as proof of breeding. The ease in finding House Martin nests produced one of the highest levels of confirmed breeding in the *Atlas* which, if the observed records are ignored, amounted to 86% of all records. The significant number of observed records shows the areas where House Martins were seen foraging but not recorded as breeding. Almost all tetrads with observed records are adjacent to those with breeding, presumably birds foraging away from the nest sites. The altitude and habitat distribution of observed records is similar to that for breeding records and is therefore not shown in the graphs.

While House Martins might have been expected to show a strong correlation with the distribution of human settlement in SE Scotland, the map indicates otherwise. This is less surprising when the finer details of their habitat requirements are examined. Bryant in the *New Atlas* lists three primary factors: suitable nest sites, a ready supply of flying insect food and clement climate to aid feeding. While urban areas may supply an abundance of good nest sites, most fail in supplying the other needs. This is most obvious in Edinburgh where birds nest in only *c.*40% of the tetrads, mostly in the suburbs. Smaller towns and villages do hold breeding birds, however. The habitat graph confirms this with just 12% of records from heavily built-up tetrads, compared to 53% in tetrads with few buildings. The need for good conditions to catch food rules out the uplands and this is confirmed by the large voids in the Pentland, Moorfoot, Lammermuir, Tweedsmuir and Cheviot Hills. While they may be generally absent from the hills, Bryant points out that conditions can be locally favourable in upland glens. The presence of House Martins at high altitudes along the Dewar valley in the Moorfoots (NT34M), at Manorhead (NT12Y) and Fruid (NT11E) in the Tweedsmuirs and more widely in the upper Whiteadder in the Lammermuirs (NT66), shows that altitude *per se* does not exclude the species. Again the altitude graph confirms this with breeding in about half of all tetrads up to 300m, sharply dropping above that.

Interestingly, the percentage of bird records peaks between 100-300m, suggesting the lowest lying ground, as well as hills,

present problems for House Martins. This is most marked in the lower Tweed and parts of East Lothian where up to half the tetrads in a 10-km square can fail to hold House Martins. The patchiness in these cereal-growing districts may be the result of a combination of low rural housing density, restricting the availablility of nest sites, and the intensive nature of the farming, reducing the amount of insect food available. Birds are even absent in the vicinity of rivers in parts of the cereal belt (NT52,63,72,74&95) where insects are probably plentiful. Densities are better along the hill fringes of the Borders and best in the Esk valley in Midlothian, the Almond valley in West Lothian and in coastal West Lothian, all areas where stock-rearing may be more widespread.

The *New Atlas* abundance map confirms the low numbers of birds in both hill areas and the mid-lower Tweed, although not the areas of lower tetrad density in East Lothian and Berwickshire. While no part of SE Scotland holds really high numbers, the Lothian lowlands and the middle Tweed valley between Galashiels (NT43) and Broughton (NT13) are shown as holding moderate numbers. That the upper Tweed should hold greater numbers than further down seems paradoxical but emphasises the paucity of birds in the Merse.

Small numbers of cliff-breeding birds can be found along the cliff coast of SE Scotland. Counts in the *Bird Reports* (see Gordon 1991) suggest 200-250 nests along the well-surveyed cliffs at Tantallon (NT58&68; 60-100 nests), Dunbar (NT67; 30-70 nests) and Bilsdean (NT77; 80-100 nests). In Borders up to 250 nests have been counted along the lower cliffs between Dunglass and Redheugh (NT77&87) while the Lamberton cliffs (NT95) have held over 100 nests. It is likely that many more may be found along the higher, less accessible cliffs and caves between Fast Castle and St. Abb's Head. In total, as many as 600 pairs are known to breed along the coast.

Being present in 100% of squares, comparison with the *Old Atlas* yields no data on the House Martin's local history. While anecdotal evidence may point to local and regional decreases, there is little evidence that such has occurred and it seems the British population is stable (*Trends*). The *New Atlas* shows some range shrinkage in the least hospitable areas of Britain, the north and west, but locally there is almost no useful information in the *Bird Reports*. Counts of individual colonies are known to be unreliable indicators of local population trends (*Trends*). Sample counts across specific areas such as 1-km squares, tetrads or 10-km squares would be of more use than site counts and if repeated might provide useful data on local densities and changes in abundance. However, Tatner (1978) has pointed out that an area of at least 30km^2 is needed to produce reliable density values.

Tatner found an average density of 2prs/km^2 in reliably surveyed parts of Britain while the *New Atlas* used a value of 1-2prs/km^2 for their calculation of the British population. Local BBS returns indicate densities of 1-2prs/km^2. Using 1.0-1.5prs/km^2 such values would produce a local population, in occupied tetrads, of 2,800-4,200 pairs.   ***R.D.Murray***

House Martin

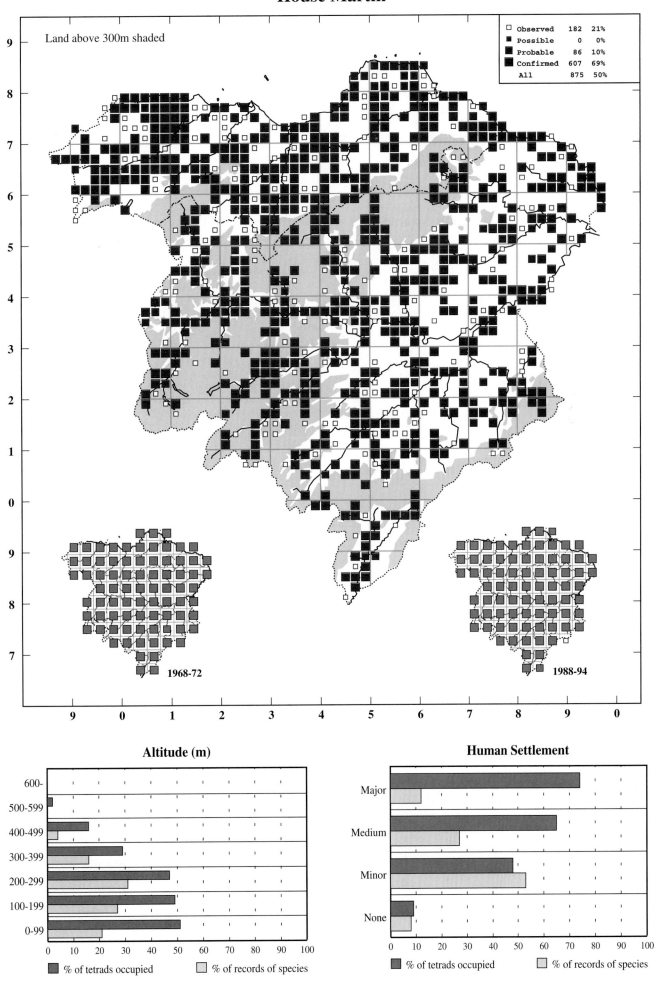

Land above 300m shaded

☐ Observed	182	21%
■ Possible	0	0%
■ Probable	86	10%
■ Confirmed	607	69%
All	875	50%

1968-72

1988-94

Altitude (m)

- 600-
- 500-599
- 400-499
- 300-399
- 200-299
- 100-199
- 0-99

■ % of tetrads occupied   ■ % of records of species

Human Settlement

- Major
- Medium
- Minor
- None

■ % of tetrads occupied   ■ % of records of species

197

Tree Pipit
Anthus trivialis

The Tree Pipit requires open ground for nesting and tall trees from which the song flight can begin. It is often associated with hillside birch woodland in many areas of Scotland but this is not the case in SE Scotland where this habitat is relatively uncommon. Tree Pipits are summer visitors, arriving between mid-April and early May. They are ground nesters, rearing only one brood in Scotland.

The song flight from a tree-top or tall bush is distinctive and conspicuous, and Tree Pipits are easily seen during fine weather in May and June. Adults often perch conspicuously, calling anxiously if an observer is near and adults carrying food provided the bulk of a rather low percentage of confirmed breeding records. This figure may be due to the relative remoteness of the breeding areas and fewer visits in July towards the end of the fieldwork season.

Tree Pipits show a strongly localised distribution. In Lothian the only concentrations are in the birch woods, mosses and conifer plantations of West Lothian. Sites such as Cairnpapple Hill and Beecraigs Wood (NS97), the plantations at Fauldhouse (NS96) and Woodmuir (NS95) and the patchy woodland south of West and Mid Calder (NT06) can be identified on the map. Elsewhere Lothian sites are quite isolated and there are only five areas where occupied tetrads occur adjacent to one another. The number of sites identified in this survey is considerably more than the five listed in *Andrews* who suspected the bird was very much under-recorded in the *Bird Reports*. The other possibility, of an increase in numbers, is less likely.

In contrast the Borders has several major concentrations in the extensive areas of commercial forestry in the middle Tweed valley between Peebles and Selkirk (NT23,24,33&43), in Craik (NT20,21&30), along the northern Cheviots in Newcastleton (NY58&59), Wauchope-Kielder (N50&51) and Leithope Forests (NT60&70). Smaller concentrations can be seen in Tweedsmuir (NT01&02), Cloich (NT 24) and Bowmont Forest (NT72).

There is a striking resemblance between the map of Tree Pipit and that of coniferous woodland in SE Scotland with all of the major forestry areas represented on the species map. This can be seen on the habitat graph where 37% of all areas with extensive conifer plantations hold Tree Pipits. Indeed three-quarters of all records are in areas where coniferous woodland is common or abundant. The fact that most conifer plantations occur on the fringes of high ground probably forms the major factor controlling the altitudinal range with four-fifths of all records occurring between 200-500m.

Tree Pipits would be more widely distributed but for the fact that they use commercial forestry only during two periods in the woodland succession. They breed in plantations of up to ten years of age, the habitat preferred in the forests at the headwaters of the Teviot and Slitrig Waters (NT40&50) where good densities (up to

eight per tetrad) were achieved in young spruce plantation. As the canopy develops, the open grassy areas are shaded out and so Tree Pipits are virtually excluded from 10-30 year-old plantations unless there are substantial rides, as in parts of Craik Forest (NT20,21,30,31). They are only able to move back into the forest when clear-fell becomes available at the end of the rotation. Clear-fell seems ideal habitat for Tree Pipits with open ground for feeding and nesting and elevated perches provided by the occasional standing tree or upturned root.

Clear-fell is almost invariably occupied by birds, something not true of young plantations where occupation can be very patchy. It was noticeable during fieldwork in 1991-92 that almost every block of clear-fell in the Elibank and Newcastleton Forests was occupied. The rotation of our large areas of forestry should ensure plenty of habitat for this species in the future.

Comparison with the *Old Atlas* map shows a substantial number of gains and a few losses. These are probably mostly related to the succession of forest growth, with losses in areas where development of closed-canopy precludes Tree Pipits, and gains where clear-fell and new plantations have allowed birds to colonise. The gains are mostly in the areas of newer forestry development in the Tweedsmuir Hills and around the Lammermuirs. Losses are more scattered. There is no reason to believe that any great change has occurred in Scottish populations (*Trends*), although declines have been seen in England. In the longer term, however, the population of SE Scotland must have increased substantially throughout the 20th century as woodland cover of any type was distinctly scarce in 1900, before modern forestry practices were developed.

The *New Atlas* abundance map shows that Tree Pipits are not particularly numerous in SE Scotland, the only 'hot-spot' being in Craik. Elsewhere only moderate to low numbers are present.

Counts of Tree Pipits over large areas of ground are rare in the *Bird Reports*. However, there is a number of counts of between 5-10 pairs from fairly discrete areas of forestry that suggest that even the highest figures mentioned in the *Old Atlas* of 30-40prs/km² may be achieved locally in parts of Craik, Elibank and Bowmont Forests. These may amount to an overall figure of 2-3prs/km² in actual occupied 1km squares. Very much lower figures, 0.1-0.3prs/km², were used to estimate the national population. While many of the outlying, more isolated, tetrads only held single pairs there are considerable numbers in the core areas (*c.*150 tetrads) that may reach 2-3pr/km²·, or 10 pairs per tetrad. This suggests a likely population of around 1,600 pairs. This represents just over 1.5% of the British population, a low figure in line with the abundance data.   ***R.D.Murray***

Tree Pipit

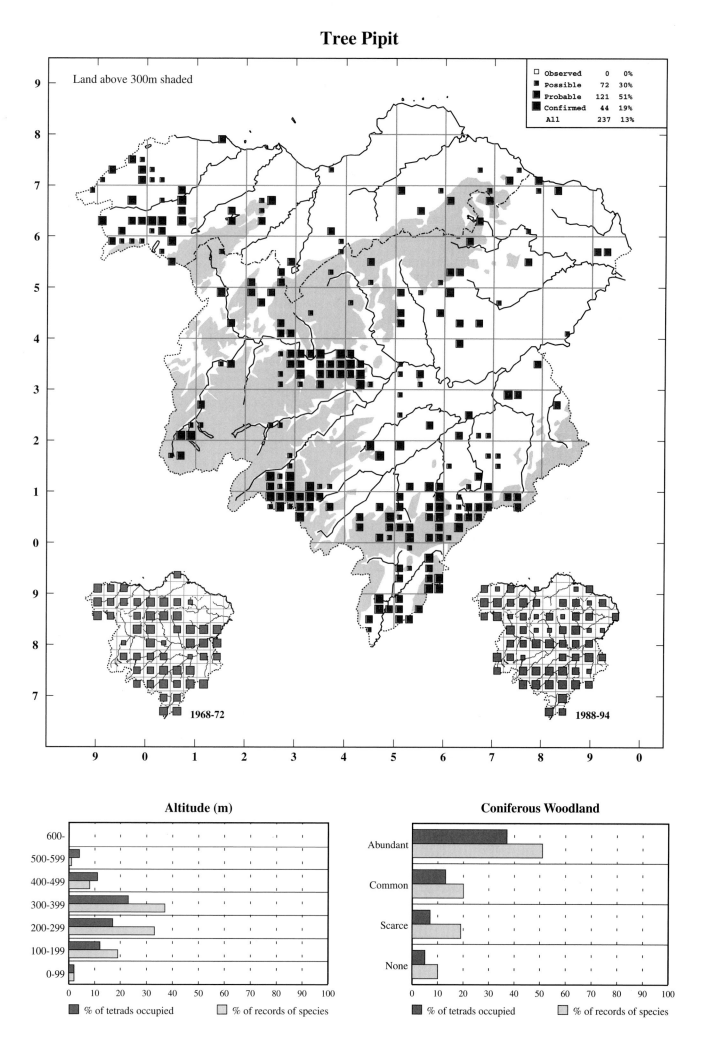

Land above 300m shaded

☐ Observed	0	0%
◪ Possible	72	30%
◼ Probable	121	51%
◼ Confirmed	44	19%
All	237	13%

1968-72

1988-94

Altitude (m)

600-
500-599
400-499
300-399
200-299
100-199
0-99

0 10 20 30 40 50 60 70 80 90 100

◼ % of tetrads occupied   ☐ % of records of species

Coniferous Woodland

Abundant
Common
Scarce
None

0 10 20 30 40 50 60 70 80 90 100

◼ % of tetrads occupied   ☐ % of records of species

Meadow Pipit
Anthus pratensis

The Meadow Pipit is perhaps the species that typifies the high hills and moors of SE Scotland. It is able to inhabit a range of open habitats right down to sea level but is certainly at its most abundant in the uplands. This liking for open habitats extends from coastal saltmarsh and cliffs, through old pasture in the lowlands into young forestry, cultivated grasslands, heather moor and rough grazing in the uplands. Above 500m it is the commonest nesting bird, passerine or non-passerine. The habitat requirements are simple, comprising patches of open grassland in which to nest and to find the invertebrate food. Scrub is suitable, as is young forestry and even wide rides in older forestry plantations, as long as there are open grassy areas.

Meadow Pipits are easy to record by virtue of their towering display flight, distinctive alarm calls and their habit of anxiously hanging around their nest areas with beakfuls of insects when feeding young. These factors have produced probable and confirmed breeding in all but 7% of cases. Two-thirds of all confirmed breeding records were of birds feeding young. Sightings of fledged young were also important. Probable records were shared equally between pairs, territorial behaviour and display.

Meadow Pipits are found in over three-quarters of the area of SE Scotland. The lower limit of the main range corresponds well with the 200m contour. They avoid the lower ground along much of the middle and lower Tweed and the valleys of the Leader, Gala, Ettrick, Teviot, Rule and Bowmont, as also the Almond, Water of Leith and Esk in Lothian. There is generally more penetration into lower ground in arable areas in West Lothian than elsewhere, possibly due to the more rolling landscape and a mosaic of arable and stock-rearing farms that provide rough grassland on stream margins and steep slopes. These habitats are more limited along the lower Esk and Tyne and absent on much of the lower Tweed.

At low levels the Meadow Pipit avoids arable farmland, even where grass for silage is important. Its main presence in these low-lying areas is the result of patches of old pasture and rough grassland associated with coastal habitats such as saltmarsh at Aberlady (NT48K&Q) and Tyninghame (NT68A&F), dunes between Aberlady and Torness (NT77M), coastal slopes on the Berwickshire cliffs (NT87A,F&K), reclaimed land at Musselburgh (NT37L,R&S), old grasslands on volcanic crags at Blackford (NT27K), Arthur's Seat (NT27S&W), the Braids (NT26P&U) and Traprain Law (NT57X), golf courses at Silverknowes (NT27I) and Coldstream (NT84K), and flood-plain grasslands at Nisbet (NT62S&X) and Kelso (NT73G&M). Each low-lying tetrad will have some remnant of open habitat, mostly ancient grassland.

Meadow Pipits are almost ubiquitous above 200m, occurring in 87% of all tetrads. They avoid some of the river valleys where the valley-bottom grasslands are presumably too intensively worked to produce the longer grass needed by Meadow Pipits. They are even present in most extensive older forestry, showing that rides between the woodland coupes are sufficient habitat for a few pairs. Only at Kershope (NY58), Craik (NT30) and Leithope (NT60) are there gaps due to commercial forestry. The other gaps within the distribution may simply be due to birds being missed.

The habitat data show a strong correlation with unimproved grassland and with heather moor. Indeed Meadow Pipits are present in almost all tetrads where either or both habitats are common and abundant and even in half the tetrads where these habitats are scarce.

As might be expected from such a widespread species, comparison with the *Old Atlas* shows little difference over the 20-year period.

The only gap apparent in the *Old Atlas* contained Meadow Pipits in the current survey. The *New Atlas* abundance map shows that the highest numbers of birds are in the hills, especially in the higher parts of the Pentlands, Lammermuirs and Tweedsmuir Hills. The Moorfoots and Cheviots have high, but not the highest abundance, categories, possibly due to the greater cover of commercial forestry there. Interestingly it is not the highest parts of the Pentlands that stand out but rather the lower, more open, moors around Harperrig and Cobbinshaw. The areas of very low abundance are in the lowlands where birds are mostly absent or have very low tetrad densities.

The *Old Atlas* quotes overall densities of 1,000pairs/10-km square while the *New Atlas* national estimate produces figures of about 750/10-km square (7.5prs/km^2). Using such numbers, a population of between 49,000 and 65,000 pairs might be appropriate for SE Scotland. However, these are overall density figures for the British Isles, rather than for areas like SE Scotland where Meadow Pipits may be more abundant, having so much more suitable habitat.

Scottish figures suggest much higher densities of between 20-40prs/km^2 for both heather moor and rough grassland, not dissimilar to Northumberland which had up to 21prs/km^2 in habitats comparable to SE Scotland (*Day*). In neighbouring Lanarkshire, sheepwalk held 13prs/km^2 while young plantation held more birds at 34-41prs/km^2 (H.E.M.Dott *unpub. report* 1996). Local figures show considerable variation. Not surprisingly da Prato (1985) recorded extremely low densities of <1.0prs/km^2 in East Lothian arable land. This is in great contrast to 102prs/km^2 on the heather moor at Red Moss (NT16R) (Keymer 1980) and over 100prs/km^2 during *Atlas* work on heather-cotton grass moor on Cooms Fell (NY48E, H.E.M. Dott *pers.comm.*). Sheep walk and rough grassland hold lower numbers with just 14prs/km^2 at Harperrig (NT06, H.E.M. Dott *pers. comm.*). Coastal grassland at Aberlady has held 25-40prs/km^2 (*Andrews*). Local BBS data suggest an average figure of 32prs/km^2 in occupied plots on all types of habitats within the area.

Analysis of the habitat data on rough grassland and heather moor provides a means for breakdown of occupied tetrads by habitat. The calculations used a figure of 100prs/km^2 where heather is abundant, 50prs/km^2 where heather moor and rough grazing are common, decreasing to 25prs/km^2 where these habitats are scarce and just 5prs/km^2 where they are absent. These values suggest a local population of 127,000 pairs, an overall density of 24prs/km^2, and *c.*6.7% of the British population. ***R.D.Murray***

Meadow Pipit

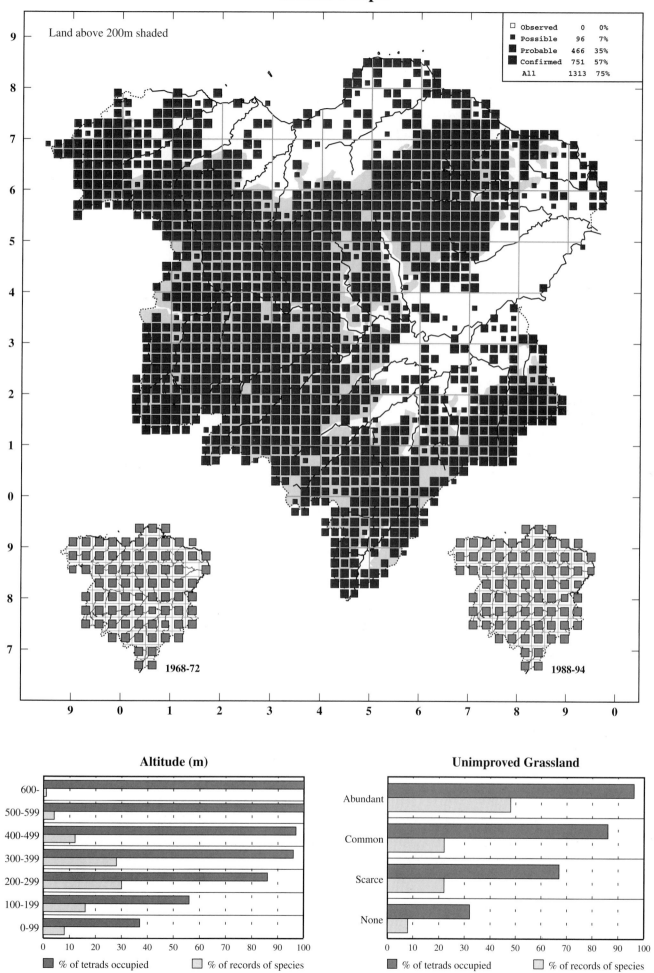

Land above 200m shaded

☐ Observed	0	0%
■ Possible	96	7%
■ Probable	466	35%
■ Confirmed	751	57%
All	1313	75%

1968-72

1988-94

Altitude (m)

Unimproved Grassland

% of tetrads occupied   % of records of species

% of tetrads occupied   % of records of species

201

Rock Pipit
Anthus petrosus

The Rock Pipit takes over the pipit niche from the Meadow Pipit along our rocky shorelines. It is easy to imagine, in a Britain unaltered by man, the Rock Pipit occupying the open land along the shore, separated by the forests from the open uplands where the Meadow Pipit held sway, with the Tree Pipit taking over in the woodland glades. While Meadow Pipits have taken well to some farmland, Rock Pipits are still mostly confined to their ancestral habitat, almost always staying in sight of the sea. While they can occupy most types of shoreline in autumn and winter, Rock Pipits are mostly confined to coasts where rocks and cliffs dominate during the breeding season. They feed on the rock platform exposed at low tide, along the high water mark, and on the grassland immediately behind the shore and on the open cliff. Like most pipits, the food is almost entirely invertebrates, Rock Pipits benefiting additionally from access to marine crustaceans along the shore. The nest-site, like most pipits, is often in dense grass although Rock Pipits can also nest in crevices in the cliff.

With its parachuting flight-display and its more metallic pipit song allied to the *tsip* alarm call given whenever the bird takes flight, the Rock Pipit is fairly easy to detect on a coastal walk. Again, as with most pipits, confirmation of breeding can be easy to obtain as birds with young typically perch anxiously in the vicinity of the nest with large beakfuls of insects. The conspicuous display plus the easy confirmation of breeding have resulted in all but 18% of reports being of probable or confirmed breeding. Rock Pipits were registered in 2% of the area, along approximately half of the actual coastline, as the map clearly shows. The remaining 40 coastal tetrads are presumably unsuited to breeding on account of the fact that the substrate is mostly mud and sand, although Rock Pipits do occupy these 'soft' shore habitats in winter as at sites like Cramond Island.

The map confirms this dichotomy between the 'soft', unsuitable shorelines of the inner Forth from the 'hard', rockier shorelines mostly found along the outer Forth. The shore around Eyebroughy (NT58D) appears to be the area where the shoreline switches between 'soft' and 'hard'. In the west the exceptions to this pattern are on Cramond Island (NT17Z) and Inchkeith (NT28W) and along the shore between Musselburgh and Port Seton where the shoreline is more varied with rock and sand alternating. Along the outer Forth, Rock Pipits are absent from the tetrads with predominantly sandy shores at Scoughall (NT68G) and Belhaven (NT67P). Birds may

have been missed at Tantallon (NT58X) where suitable habitat exists and birds held territory in 1983.

Historically Rock Pipits bred as far west in the Forth as Grangemouth (*R&B*). The current distribution, however, is similar to that found in the *Old Atlas*, differing mostly in the lack of a record from NT48 in the current survey. The earlier presence was probably at Gullane Point, where Rock Pipits last bred in 1981. The records from NT37 (Musselburgh Lagoons-Prestonpans) seem to be new. While Musselburgh may have been recently colonised *Andrews* noted a decline on some of the Forth islands, notably the Bass Rock where numbers fell from 10 pairs in the 1960s to just 2-4 pairs in the 1990s. However, this could be related to the huge increase in Gannet numbers and the resultant loss of both feeding and nesting habitat for Rock Pipits. *Thom* and the *New Atlas* state that there has been a decline along the North Sea coasts. The absence of birds from some 10-km squares along North Sea coasts seen in the *New Atlas*, bearing in mind the time constraints of the methodology, may be more apparent than real. Certainly detailed surveys such as those in SE Scotland do not support that there has been a reduction in range or numbers. This point was also raised in Northumberland (*Day*) where there has been little change in Rock Pipit status in the last 60 years.

Despite the species accounts for Rock Pipit in the *Bird Reports* being rather cursory, particularly during the breeding season, there have been sufficient counts to provide a fairly accurate picture of the Rock Pipit population. The Forth islands are routinely counted during seabird counts while St. Abb's Head has been regularly surveyed since 1985 and found to regularly hold 11 pairs. Elsewhere there are occasional casual counts from specific areas of shore such as the Belhaven-Dunbar Harbour area (NT67U&Z) with 8-11 pairs, Fancove Head area (NT96L&M) with 10 pairs and Fast Castle to Midden Craig (NT87K) with 9 pairs. These counts indicate that for much of the outer Forth there are around 5-8 prs/km of rocky coastline, with up to 10 prs/km on coasts with high cliffs.

The map clearly shows an east-west decline in representation, the shore to the east of Belhaven being solidly occupied while that further west is more patchy, suggesting a real decline in the quality of the shoreline as far as Rock Pipits are concerned. This is supported by the rather small counts from the shores to the west of Dunbar. In total there are about 40km of good rocky shoreline to the east of Dunbar, including 12km of high cliff. Using an overall population density of 7 prs/km would give a local population of 280 pairs. Further west numbers are low and may only total 10-20 pairs. The Forth Islands are well counted and add another 5-15 pairs, using minimum-maximum figures from the *Bird Reports*. Thus the SE Scotland population lies in the area of 295-325 pairs.

The *Old Atlas* analysis used values of 50 pairs per occupied 10-km square. The use of this method seems limited as in our area five of the 12 squares have records from only 1-2 tetrads. However, dismissing those squares produces a figure of 350 pairs, not too dissimilar from the estimate given above. *BWP* suggests a figure equivalent to 5-10 pairs per tetrad which gives a likely 200-400 pairs. The *New Atlas* quotes a variety of densities that seem to be rather low compared to the estimates for our area (0.9-6.0 pairs per kilometre of shore) but confirms the 10-km square estimate used in the *Old Atlas*, using it as a basis for calculating the British population.

The outer Forth coastline, with a wide rock platform, extensive grassy slopes and vertical cliffs, clearly provides excellent habitat for the Rock Pipit. As Rock Pipit habitat appears to be very poorly understood in Britain and with a reasonably-sized, but not too large population, this species might well be one to provide a good subject for local study. **R.D.Murray**

Rock Pipit

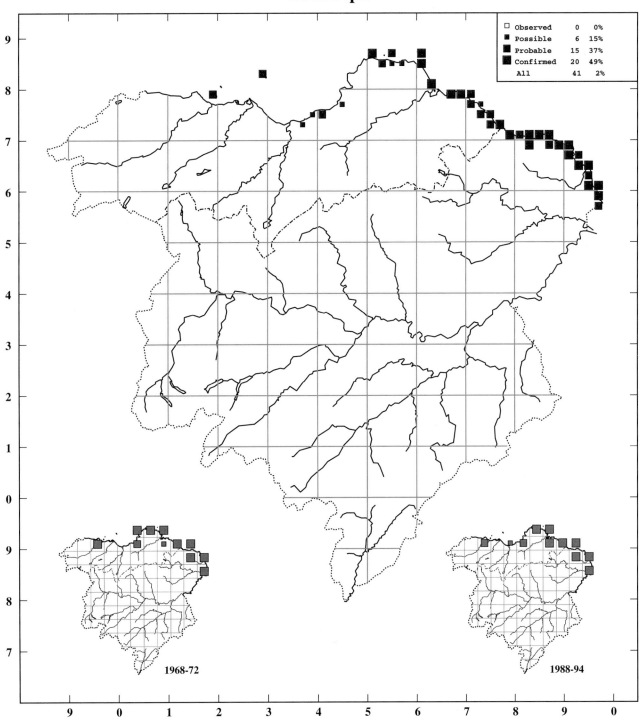

□ Observed	0	0%
■ Possible	6	15%
■ Probable	15	37%
■ Confirmed	20	49%
All	41	2%

1968-72

1988-94

Cliffs, Crags and Quarries

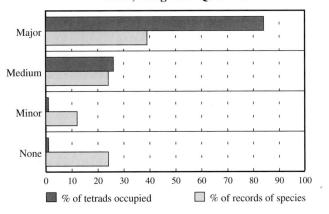

■ % of tetrads occupied   □ % of records of species

Yellow Wagtail
Motacilla flava

The brightest-coloured, most migratory and the rarest of the wagtails to breed in Britain, the Yellow Wagtail is at the northern limits of its British breeding range in Scotland. Yellow Wagtails display a great deal of racial differentiation in Eurasia with distinctive populations replacing each other in different habitat zones. The yellow-headed British population, *M.f.flavissima*, is well differentiated from the more widespread dark-headed races, although there are other yellow-headed races in central Asia and eastern Siberia.

Where present, Yellow Wagtails are not difficult to find with their bright colouration and, if known, a distinctive flight call. Proof of breeding later in the season is usually easy to acquire as calling adults often fly between feeding areas and nests with beakfuls of insect food. Accordingly two-thirds of all records were of probable and confirmed breeding, mostly territorial adults, adults carrying food or fledged juveniles. Observed records indicate sightings of probable passage birds in areas where birds are not known to breed. Not unexpectedly a number are on the coast where some caution is required due to the presence of breeding birds.

The map shows breeding mostly on the coast and the lower Tweed and Teviot valleys. Coastal breeding occurs in the eastern parts of East Lothian and Berwickshire although the number of instances in any year rarely exceeds four or five pairs, usually in the the Dunbar to Thorntonloch area (NT67&77). Elsewhere nesting is more sporadic and in the *Atlas* period only occurred at Musselburgh (NT37), Drem (NT57), Tantallon (NT58) and Eyemouth (NT96) on single occasions. The nesting habitat along much of this area seems to be the interface between the rough grassland along the shore and the arable farmland further inland.

Inland breeding is mostly limited to the haughs of the Teviot below Denholm (NT51) and the Tweed below Kelso (NT73). The habitat resembles that on the coast, feeding along the river and old riverside pastures and nesting in adjacent barley fields. The lack of haughland on the Tweed below Coldstream, where the river has steep, heavily wooded banks, forms a downstream limit although Yellow Wagtails re-appear further downstream at Paxton and Berwick (NT95) on the tidal haughs of the Tweed that are mostly in England. The range is fairly continuous along the Teviot and Tweed, only interrupted by Kelso (NT73) and between Ancrum and Denholm (NT62). Similar habitats on the Rule (NT51V), Jed (NT61F), Oxnam (NT61Z&71E), Bowmont (NT82J) and Blackadder (NT64I) sometimes hold birds and this hints that breeding could be more widespread but overlooked. The breeding in damp moorland at Deadwater near Kielder (NY69D) was just in England and echoes the nest that was found in similar habitat at Fruid Reservoir (NT11E) in 1987. The strongest habitat correlation for Yellow Wagtails is with arable land, most occupied tetrads occurring where arable farmland is abundant.

Historically, breeding in SE Scotland has been sporadic with just a few instances on the fringes of Edinburgh between 1888-1926 and in 1951 (*Andrews*). More widespread nesting did not occur until 1969 with the first Borders record in Liddesdale and the first nesting near Dunbar in 1981. The *Old Atlas*'shows confirmed breeding in several 10-km squares in Borders. Unfortunately, like many *Old Atlas* records from Borders, there is no documentary support for many of these records. As the first known breeding only occurred in 1969, some must be regarded as doubtful, and perhaps refer to the Grey Wagtail. While breeding has been proved in odd places like Fruid and Deadwater in recent years, it is difficult to accept that Yellow Wagtails nested in the Lammermuirs in NT65 or in Craik Forest in NT30. There is no doubt, however, that there has been an expansion since the mid-1980s. Breeding also occurred at Lumsdaine (NT96U) and Saughtree (NY59U) in the pre-*Atlas* period.

The *New Atlas* abundance map shows that Yellow Wagtails are very scarce with only a few areas of the lowest values indicated. The species is certainly rare enough for all records to be published in the *Bird Reports*. The coastal population is very small with four to eight pairs in any year between Tyninghame and Thorntonloch. Numbers are larger inland with territories spaced along the river haughs about every 300m where there is continuous occupation. The *Bird Reports* show that *c.*20 territories are regular in most years between Kelso and Coldstream, with *c.*10 territories along the Teviot haughs. Other birds are present on the lower part of the Tweed and Whiteadder in NT84,94&95 of which about 4-5 pairs breed within SE Scotland. While the odd pair may have been present in the early 1980s, widespread breeding was first apparent in 1986-87 when the first survey of breeding riparian birds took place (Murray 1988). The larger numbers now present are not thought to have occurred much before the mid-1980s. With the occasional breeding pair elsewhere, SE Scotland may hold between 40-50 pairs annually.

Thom documents that Yellow Wagtails were formerly common in western Scotland with perhaps several hundred pairs in Ayrshire and the Clyde valley. Although these declined in the early 20th century, up to 50 pairs were still present in the early 1980s before declining further during the late 1980s. No birds were reported in 1995, despite searches in the former breeding habitats (*Scottish Bird Reports*). While it may be coincidence that the decline in the west matches the increase in the east, the two events could be related. There has been a recent general range contraction in western Britain with only limited spread in eastern Britain (*New Atlas*).

A few dark-headed birds, resembling males of the Blue-headed race *M.f.flava,* nest along the Tweed. As females are indistinguishable from the dominant *flavissima* birds, it is not known whether the pairs formed are with *flava* or *flavissima* females. There are no indications of hybrid males. In most years one or two paired males are seen, mostly east of Kelso. Such breeding is rare in Britain with only three cases reported in the *New Atlas*, all in northern England. Dark-headed birds resembling the *flava* and *beema* races, and yellow-headed birds that resemble the *lutea* populations, were present in the Clyde area in the 1980s. While the precise genetic background of these birds was not resolved, the differences were ascribed to broad individual variation rather than to an influx of exotic genes from elsewhere (I.Gibson *pers.comm.*). These birds should be studied as they are anomalous and may illuminate features of the complex genetic variation within the Yellow Wagtail populations.

R.D.Murray

Yellow Wagtail

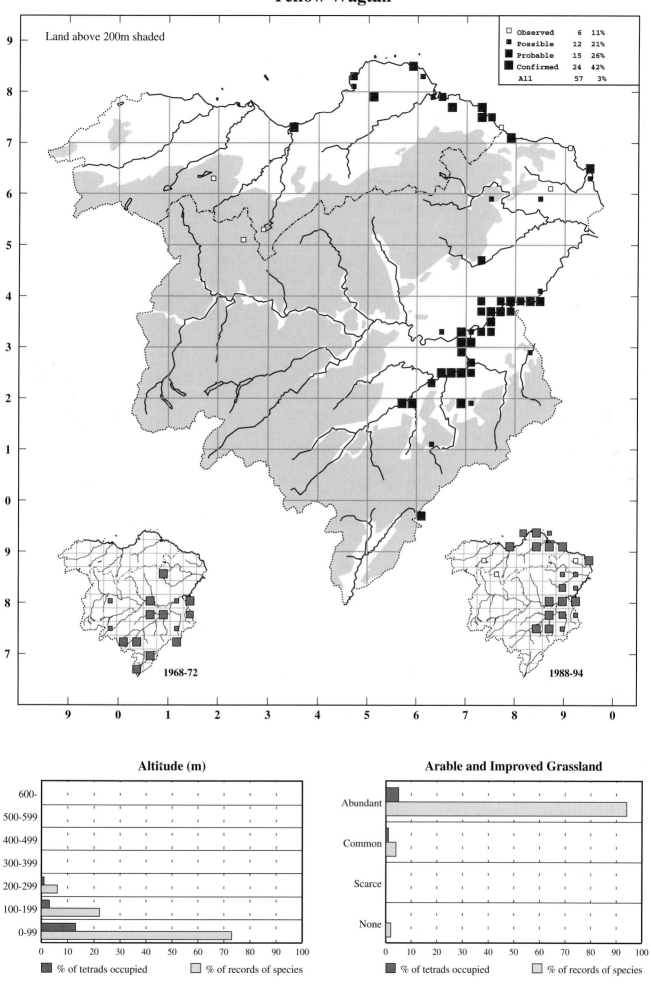

Land above 200m shaded

□ Observed	6	11%
■ Possible	12	21%
■ Probable	15	26%
■ Confirmed	24	42%
All	57	3%

1968-72

1988-94

Altitude (m)

600-
500-599
400-499
300-399
200-299
100-199
0-99

0 10 20 30 40 50 60 70 80 90 100

■ % of tetrads occupied   □ % of records of species

Arable and Improved Grassland

Abundant

Common

Scarce

None

0 10 20 30 40 50 60 70 80 90 100

■ % of tetrads occupied   □ % of records of species

Grey Wagtail
Motacilla cinerea

Arguably our most beautiful and graceful wagtail, the Grey Wagtail with its contrasting grey, black and lemon colouration, strikingly long tail and dipping flight, is tied in the breeding season to the presence of flowing water. Hunting for aquatic insects in, along and above streams and rivers, it is mostly a bird of fast-flowing water where its main prey, mayflies, stoneflies and caddis-flies, are most numerous. Grey Wagtails are short-distance migrants, moving to lower altitudes or further south in the British Isles in winter.

The association with rivers means that they are not difficult to find if the riverbank is walked for even a short distance, although in rivers that flow through woodland birds are somewhat less obvious than in more open countryside. Probable records were dominated by reports of pairs while the high level of confirmed records were shared between adults with food for young and fledged juveniles.

Grey Wagtails are widespread in SE Scotland and found wherever there are rivers. The map shows a definite association with the river systems and the main elements of the drainage are discernible in the pattern of tetrads. It is easier to detect the pattern of the river system across the low ground (e.g. the lower Tweed in NT73,84&95) but in the higher areas where birds also inhabit the many tributaries, the pattern is less clear. 75% of all records occur between 100-400m while only 13% of records occur below 100m. This preference for middle altitudes, at first impression, appears to be contradicted by an equally strong association with larger rivers. The river graph shows that Grey Wagtails prefer medium to large rivers rather than the smaller waters, often associated with higher altitudes. However, as the numbers of the various river invertebrates preyed upon by Grey Wagtails are undoubtedly related to the area of stony substrate, it is clear that wider streams will hold more food.

The liking for higher altitudes is probably related to their need for fairly fast-flowing waters and as this feature is associated with gradient, it comes as little surprise that birds are more often found along rivers with fairly steep gradients. Our range in altitude variable is only a rough proxy for this, but over 50% of tetrads with a range in altitude of 100-400m are occupied, while 34% with a range less than 100m are occupied and 46% with a range over 400m. It appears that ideally Grey Wagtails favour fairly steep but wide rivers and in this respect the shingle-bedded courses of the rivers that drain the hills of SE Scotland are extremely suitable. Grey Wagtails also favour streams with some presence of trees (Buckton &Ormerod 1997), their diet being supplemented by invertebrates that fall from the branches or fly in the air above the water surface. However, there is no corroboration of this feature evident on the map. Their liking for fairly fast-flowing streams means that they are absent in areas where there are no streams and rivers or where the streams are so small or so slow-flowing that they lack suitable food.

Such gaps are evident in much of coastal East Lothian (NT47&58) and considerable areas of the Merse (NT73,74,84 and 85). The flatter-topped summits of the hill areas also stand out, the drainage there presumably being too narrow and peaty to offer many feeding opportunities.

With birds present in most 10-km squares, comparison with the *Old Atlas* shows limited change, mostly in coastal East Lothian and Berwickshire where five coastal squares show gains. While the gains in four squares are founded on just one tetrad in each, the gain in NT86, where birds were present in eight tetrads along the Eye Water, suggests that birds were overlooked there in 1968-72.

The *New Atlas* abundance map shows that SE Scotland holds pretty large numbers of Grey Wagtails with much of the middle and upper Tweed and all tributaries shown as having the highest abundance levels. Smaller areas along the Almond, Water of Leith, Eye Water and in Liddesdale also hold these high numbers. In contrast, the vacant areas of East Lothian and the Merse hold poor numbers. Grey Wagtails are prone to changes in population levels in response to hard winters (*Trends*) although numbers rapidly recover. Such changes are apparent in WBS sites in SE Scotland (*Bird Reports*) although spring flooding may also have an impact locally.

Counts along parts of the river system published in the *Bird Reports* show some variation between different parts of the drainage, varying between 0.4prs/km in many areas to higher levels such as 1.2prs/km on the Tweed at Melrose and 1.1prs/km on the Teviot upstream of Kelso. The river survey in 1987 (Murray 1988) found 153 territories along 342km of the main system, an average of 0.45prs/km with a peak of 1.5prs/km on the Teviot upstream of Hawick. Cowper (1973) found 37 pairs along the *c.*80km of the Esk drainage, an average of 0.46prs/km, remarkably close to the Tweed figure. Miller & Porteous (1989) found *c.*15 pairs along 20km of the Water of Leith between Balerno and Leith in 1988, an average of 0.75prs/km of river or *c.*2prs/occupied tetrad. The *New Atlas* quotes averages of 2-4 pairs per occupied tetrad from studies in Wales and Devon, areas that hold similar numbers of birds according to the *New Atlas* abundance map. The calculation of the British population is based on a figure of 2 pairs per occupied tetrad, a figure based on Welsh work that does not appear to be typical nationally. A figure of 1.25 pairs per occupied tetrad would give a local population of just over 1,000 pairs. This would represent just 3% of the British population, which given that our area apparently holds large numbers is too low, and strongly suggests that the *New Atlas* figure used for the calculation of the British population is considerably too large. It is noticeable that the Devon Atlas (Sitters 1988) used a value of 1-2 pairs per tetrad, more akin to the 1.25 pairs per tetrad used here.

R.D.Murray

Grey Wagtail

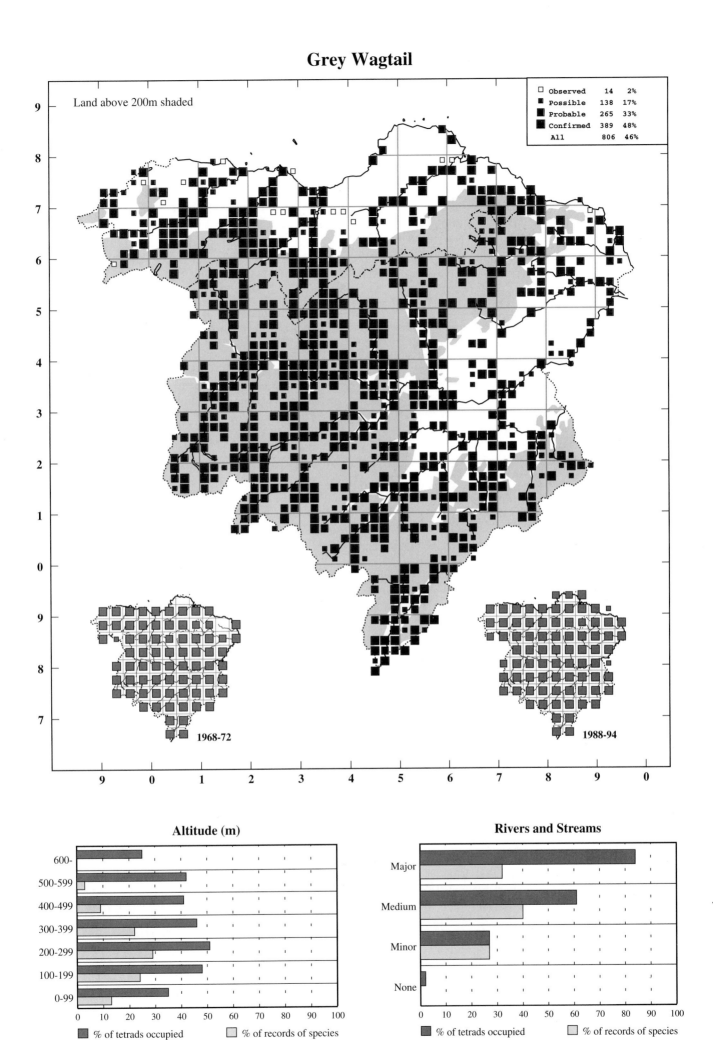

	Observed	14	2%
	Possible	138	17%
	Probable	265	33%
	Confirmed	389	48%
	All	806	46%

Land above 200m shaded

1968-72

1988-94

Altitude (m)

600-
500-599
400-499
300-399
200-299
100-199
0-99

■ % of tetrads occupied   ☐ % of records of species

Rivers and Streams

Major
Medium
Minor
None

■ % of tetrads occupied   ☐ % of records of species

Pied Wagtail
Motacilla alba

Strutting across a lawn, then scurrying after some insect before flitting up to catch a passing fly, the Pied Wagtail is a widespread and familiar inhabitant around human settlements and along roads. By no means confined to the presence of humans, Pied Wagtails occur in open conditions wherever there is insect food available for feeding and some niche in which to raise their young. Pied Wagtails even roost in and around human settlements outwith the breeding season, possibly enjoying the slightly warmer microclimate associated with towns, as well as the obvious shelter of trees and buildings.

There were no difficulties in collecting evidence of breeding for Pied Wagtails, the birds being distinctivly plumaged and having familiar calls. In general a high level of proof of Pied Wagtail breeding was obtained, confirmed records being split between adults carrying food for young and sightings of fledged juveniles. Half of all probable records were of pairs, another third showing evidence of territoriality.

With the Pied Wagtail ranked just outside the ten most widespread species in SE Scotland, it is no surprise that the species is almost universal across the area. In such cases it is more revealing to discuss where birds are absent rather than where they are present. Birds seem to be absent from the high hills and this is confirmed by the altitude graph that shows that the percentage of occupied tetrads drops from 80-90% of tetrads below 300m, to 30-50% between 400-600m. There is only a single record above 600m. The absence of Pied Wagtails is most marked on the maps in the cores of the Pentlands, Moorfoots, Lammermuirs and Tweedsmuir Hills. The southern fringe along the Cheviots also shows vacant squares, particularly in the hills west of Newcastleton (NY48&49). The absence of birds from the heart of these hill areas may be related to food and a lack of nest-sites. Voids are also visible in the forested areas of Craik (NT30&31), Elibank (NT33), Wauchope (NT40,50&60) and Newcastleton (NY58&59) where the lack of open terrain may be a limiting factor to Pied Wagtails.

While a lack of Pied Wagtails in high hill areas and forests might be expected, the gaps in the lowlands are more difficult to explain, especially as birds are so widespread in farmland with arable and improved grass, the dominant form of land use at these levels. Indeed Pied Wagtails show a strong correlation with arable farming, being found in 90% of all tetrads where such farms are common or abundant, but in less than half of tetrads where they are absent. There are large vacant areas west of Haddington (NT47), around Swinton-Whitsome (NT84) and between Kelso and Earlston (NT63), as well as many smaller gaps made by single tetrads such as west of East Linton (NT58V). This may fit with the *New Atlas* statement that Pied Wagtails show a preference for mixed farms and are thinly distributed in areas of intensive cereal production. While wall-to-wall cereals are not common in SE Scotland, there are a few tetrads

in the areas listed above where such habitat exists and it may be that the insecticide sprays associated with this form of farming could be enough to remove the insect prey that is essential for Pied Wagtail success. The removal of hedges and dykes, and hence nest sites, may also play a part. Curiously, birds are also absent from suburban Edinburgh, but not from the city centre. Small numbers breed on the Forth islands and were recorded in the *Atlas* on Fidra, Craigleith and the Bass Rock.

As Pied Wagtails occur in all 10-km squares in SE Scotland and also had a similar distribution in 1968-72, comparisons between the maps yield no information. Indeed there is no hint that there has been any significant change in the range of the species in the 20th century. The *New Atlas* abundance map shows that SE Scotland holds excellent numbers of Pied Wagtails and is one of the best areas of Britain for the species, Pied Wagtails being more abundant in northern and western Britain. There is some variation in numbers within the area, with low abundance in coastal West Lothian and Edinburgh (NT07,17&27), East Lothian (NT47,48&68) and in the forest areas of southern Roxburgh. Only moderate numbers are shown in the Merse (NT84,94&95). The highest numbers occur along the hill fringes of the Pentlands and Moorfoots in western Peeblesshire, the Lammermuirs, and along the middle Tweed and Teviot.

Little is known about Pied Wagtail numbers in SE Scotland except in relation to their spacing along water courses. The river survey in 1987 (Murray 1988) found 173 territories along 342km of the major river courses, approximately 0.5prs/km overall, with 1.3prs/km along the Tweed and Teviot haughs. Other counts in the *Bird Reports* detail 1.0prs/km along the Teviot between Ancrum and Kelso (30km) and on the Tweed between Makerstoun and Floors (6km). WBS plots at Melrose, Fountainhall, Paxton and the Whiteadder above the reservoir, yield values of 1-3prs/km. More birds must occur in these sites away from the riparian habitats and certainly hint that densities are higher per square kilometre. Away from rivers, St. Abb's Head has held densities of between 1-4prs/km^2 while Musselburgh Lagoons hold 2-3prs/km^2 (Andrews 1989). On the other extreme da Prato (1985) found that the Tranent cereal area, close to the vacant area near Haddington on the species map, held only 0.5prs/km^2, in an area where the *New Atlas* shows that low numbers occur. Unfortunately no density figure is available from a site where the *New Atlas* shows Pied Wagtails to be numerous. Local BBS results, from plots across the area, suggest 2-3prs/km^2, considerably higher than the overall British densities of 1.1prs/km^2 used to calculate the British population in the *New Atlas*. However, this should be expected in an area the *New Atlas* shows to hold amongst the best numbers of Pied Wagtails in Britain. Using a value of 2.5prs/km^2, SE Scotland would hold *c.*14,000 pairs, about 5% of the British population.   ***R.D.Murray***

Pied Wagtail

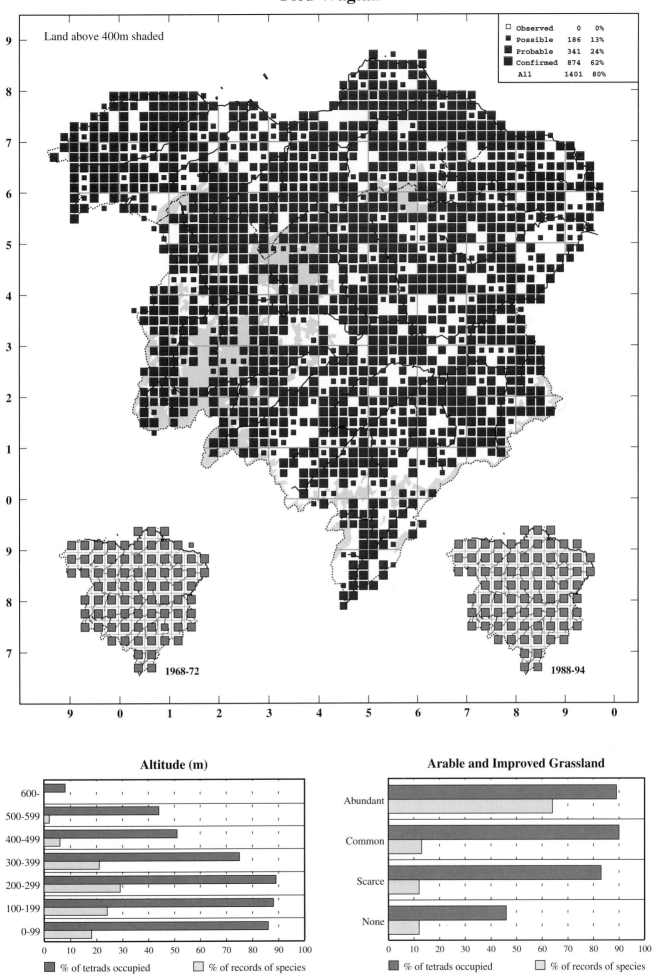

Land above 400m shaded

☐ Observed	0	0%
■ Possible	186	13%
■ Probable	341	24%
■ Confirmed	874	62%
All	1401	80%

1968-72

1988-94

Altitude (m)

- 600-
- 500-599
- 400-499
- 300-399
- 200-299
- 100-199
- 0-99

■ % of tetrads occupied   ☐ % of records of species

Arable and Improved Grassland

- Abundant
- Common
- Scarce
- None

■ % of tetrads occupied   ☐ % of records of species

Dipper
Cinclus cinclus

The Dipper's bobbing black and white appearance and chuckling, gurgling song strongly evoke the image of the fast flowing burns and rivers where it is found. If the flow is fast enough, Dippers can be found in streams bounded by both open and wooded habitats. Large invertebrates form the main diet and these are caught underwater. The prey is associated with fast-flowing productive streams. Dippers are thus found in upland Britain, occurring in low ground only where weirs and bridges provide the faster flow the prey requires. The large bulky nests are built in banks, behind waterfalls, and often under bridges and in waterside walls.

Territorial behaviour is most conspicuous in the spring and a check of suitable rivers usually provided sightings. Bridges were routinely checked to locate nests. Dippers are sometimes double brooded, but once young birds have fledged both adults and juveniles become much more difficult to see. Some may have been overlooked on more remote waters visited later in the season. Confirmed breeding records provided over half the records, with most of these being of fledged young. Probable records were mainly of pairs or territorial behaviour.

Dippers breed along most rivers and streams in hilly areas above 200m, and were recorded in 40% of all tetrads above that height. Closer to headwaters at around 500m, Dippers occur in over half of all tetrads. At lower levels only the faster flowing streams such as the Dunglass and Pease Burns in NT77 and the Eye at Eyemouth (NT96) are occupied. They are missing from the lower stretches of the Almond (NT17) and the Tweed which are deeper, muddier, slower flowing, less oxygenated and therefore less suitable for the Dipper's prey. While the majority of rivers, large and small, hold Dippers, just 20% of tetrads with only small burns hold Dippers. Presumably these are the drains and small streams at lower altitudes that lack the fast flow and stony substrate required by Dippers and their prey. In the lower ground the occupied tetrads clearly follow the rivers but in the hills the number of suitable streams increases so that most tetrads hold Dippers.

Dippers are missing along long stretches of the Almond (NS96,NT06&17), the Ale (NT52) and, surprisingly, parts of the Ettrick (NT21,31&32). On the Tweed down from Leaderfoot (NT53X) they are almost absent except at Mertoun (NT63A), Makerstoun rapids (NT63W), Kelso (NT73B&G), and Coldstream (NT83J&P,NT84F&K). Most of these sites are associated with weirs, and one tetrad represents the Leet Water at the Hirsel. Occupied tetrads apparently away from rivers are actually associated with narrow rivers such as the Eden in NT63&73, or are in the hill ranges.

Much has been published about the loss of Dippers from waterways flowing through large conifer plantations due to water acidification (e.g. Ormerod *et al.* 1986). Such an effect is not obvious in SE Scotland except for NT50 where the headwaters of the Slitrig

and Rule lack Dippers. However, close comparison of the Dipper map and where forestry surrounds burns in Craik Forest (NT30) shows that although hill burns are abundant, Dippers are absent from many tetrads. They are, however, present in some urban areas such as on the south side of Edinburgh (NT27) where burns flow down from the Pentlands.

The *New Atlas* abundance map shows that Dippers are more numerous in the Southern Uplands than anywhere else in Britain, illustrating the familiar horseshoe shape of the deeply dissected hills of SE Scotland. There has been little change in distribution since the *Old Atlas*, despite the anomalous absence from NT52 (Ale Water near Lilliesleaf), surely a case of birds being overlooked. However, they are now found in NS96 (south and west of Bathgate) and NT86 (Eye Water). The number of tetrads now occupied on the Eye makes it seem unlikely that it was absent in 1968-72, so perhaps then too it was overlooked.

The Dipper has been the subject of a number of local surveys and is well represented in the two WBS plots active during the *Atlas* period. Average densities of 0.33 and 1.75prs/km were obtained on the Tweed at Melrose (1989-94) and on the Gala Water (1991-94) respectively (*Bird Reports*). Murray (1988) in the 1987 sawbill census reported a total of 160 territories and an overall density 0.51prs/km but this included large stretches of the lower Tweed where Dippers are absent. The highest density of 2.0prs/km was recorded near Stobo on the upper Tweed and Abbey St. Bathans on the Whiteadder. Extensive work has been done on the Dipper population on the Esk, which included nest counts and productivity measurements (Cowper 1973, Ballantyne & Vick 1980, Wilson 1996). In 1966, Cowper (1973) recorded 0.14prs/km in the whole Esk system (400km). In 1979-90, the South Esk (52.6km) held an average of 0.85prs/km with a maximum of 1.66prs/km between Carrington and Lothianbridge (Wilson 1996). On the Water of Leith, densities of 0.60prs/km have been recorded (Miller & Porteous 1989). There can be significant reductions in numbers following flooding, such as happened after a spate on the South Esk in October 1990 (Wilson 1996). No local studies on the effect of different substrates on Dipper densities have been made, but substrate type may affect the availability of prey and in turn the number of Dippers.

To estimate the population, different densities for different stretches of river are required. If it is assumed that Dippers above 200m (70% of records) occur at 1.5prs/km, with 0.5prs/km below that, and that each occupied tetrad contains 2km of river habitat, then a population of 1,555 pairs is indicated. The *New Atlas* estimate of the British population is a rather wide 7,000-21,000 pairs. This equates to 5-15prs/10-km square and 350-1,050 pairs for SE Scotland. This seems low based on observed local densities related to altitude and gradient. A figure of around 1,500 pairs seems more appropriate, about 7% of the British population using the higher BTO figure.

M.Holling

Dipper

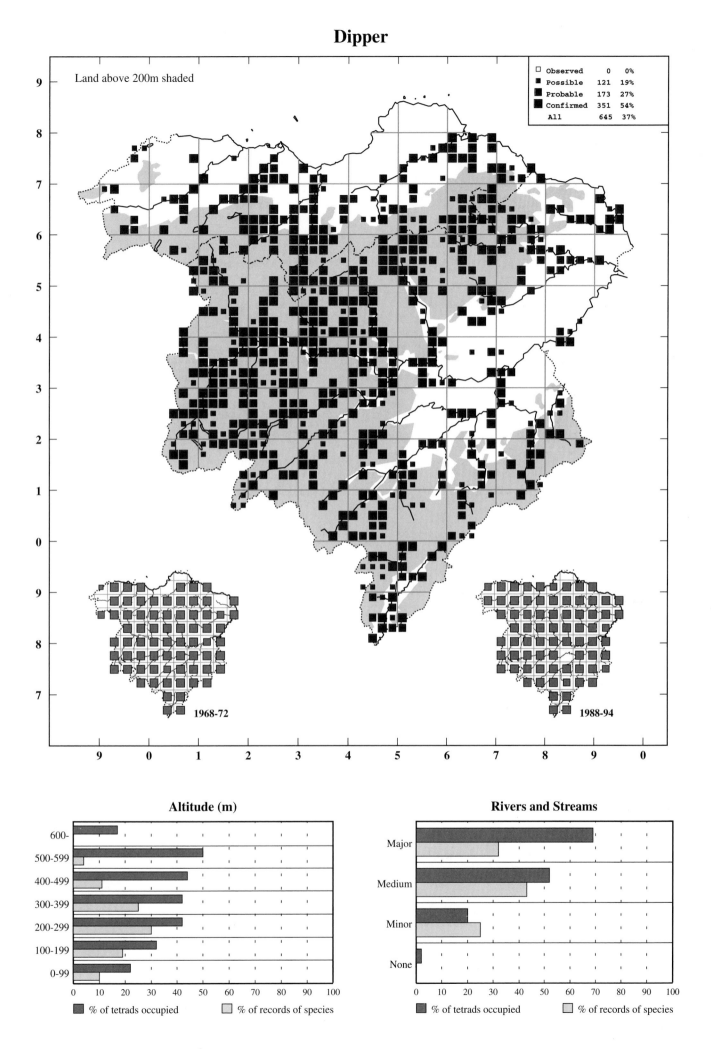

Land above 200m shaded

□	Observed	0	0%
■	Possible	121	19%
■	Probable	173	27%
■	Confirmed	351	54%
	All	645	37%

1968-72

1988-94

Altitude (m)

Rivers and Streams

■ % of tetrads occupied   ☐ % of records of species

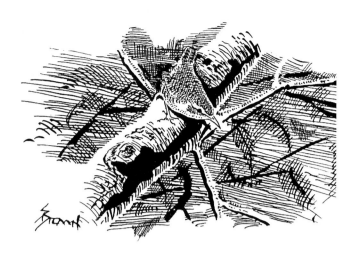

Wren

Troglodytes troglodytes

The Wren was the commonest bird in Britain during the 1988-91 *New Atlas* survey. It is common because it is perhaps our most adaptable species, able to find a living space in a variety of different habitats ranging from woodland, where it is most abundant, to farmland, moorland edges, cliffs, and islands. Perhaps by virtue of its tiny size it is able to live in the skimpiest of cover and eke out a living feeding on small invertebrates. The Wren was not only the commonest species but also the most widespread, occurring in 97% of the 10-km squares in Britain, including some of the smallest and most remote islands and on many hostile mountain areas.

Despite their small size, Wrens are amongst the most vocally conspicuous of all species. They are highly territorial and their explosive song carries well across many habitats as does their compulsive ticking whenever they feel threatened. This resulted in probable and confirmed breeding formimg all but 7% of records. Probable records are dominated by territorial behaviour although anxious birds ticking on the approach of fieldworkers were also important. Around half the cases of confirmed breeding were of fledged young. Adults carrying food for young also formed an important fraction of confirmed records.

Wrens were found in 95% of the tetrads in SE Scotland, making them the most widespread species in the area. The Wren was recorded in about 50 more tetrads than the next most ubiquitous species, the Chaffinch and Carrion Crow. With a species as common as this, it is perhaps more revealing to discover where Wrens do not occur. The 83 tetrads where Wrens were not recorded were dominated by featureless grassy or heather moorland. The most extensive area was on the hill summits near Tweedsmuir (15 tetrads around NT01,11&12), Dinley Fell in Liddesdale (10 tetrads around NY48&49, the central Lammermuirs (9 tetrads in NT55,56&66) and the flanks of the Cheviot (7 tetrads around NT81). These areas are mainly featureless, and this lack of physical variety may not create microhabitats that give Wrens a toehold. Deep heather, 'rough areas' on grassy hills and small banks along burns present opportunities that Wrens can exploit. In 1995 Wrens were searched for, and found, in seven of the nine vacant tetrads in the Lammermuirs and in eight vacant tetrads in Liddesdale (P.Vandome *pers. comm.*). There is no reason to believe that they were not there in 1994 or earlier when the sites were surveyed for the *Atlas* and it seems possible that Wrens were overlooked in several other tetrads. It is a possiblity that Wrens may be less vocal at extremely low densities and the pair or so that may occupy these tetrads could sing less and be easily missed.

The lack of birds from high moorland is supported by the altitude graph that shows Wrens occur almost everywhere up to 400m, and even at 500-600m are still to be found in over 70% of all tetrads. It is only above 600m that representation really drops. Wrens are also universal in woodland areas, large or small. Their ability to live in less than optimal habitats is indicated by the fact that they can be found in over half of all tetrads that lack woodland cover.

Other than these open moorlands, the only group of tetrads that had Wrens missing were a few of the Forth islands: Fidra, The Lamb and the Bass Rock. It should be noted, however, that *Andrews* mentioned up to 5 pairs of Wrens nesting on the Bass in 1986. Perhaps their habitats have been lost, possibly like the Rock Pipit, in the face of the continuing expansion of the Gannet colony.

Comparisons with the *Old Atlas* shed little light on the Wren. The single 10-km square that lacked Wrens in 1968-72, the Berwickshire cliffs NT87, produced birds in all four tetrads in the 1988-94 survey. Birds were almost certainly overlooked in the *Old Atlas*.

The *New Atlas* does, however, shed light on Wren abundance in SE Scotland for the first time. As might be expected the hills stand out as areas of low abundance, although as the tetrad map suggests there are only small areas of the very lowest abundance. Areas of highest abundance are surprisingly small, and mainly limited to north of the A1 road in East Lothian, the Eye Water, lower Tweed and along the Tweed/Teviot valleys between Galashiels, Jedburgh and Kelso. Areas of moderate abundance mostly surround those of highest abundance.

The *Old Atlas* quotes average CBC densities of 22prs/km^2 in farmland and 60prs/km^2 in woodland areas, the precise figure for woodland being dependent on variables such as tree species, age and ground cover. Over 100prs/km^2 have been recorded in small woodland CBC sites in both East Lothian and Midlothian (*Andrews*) while 50-100prs/km^2 were found in Grampian woodlands (Buckland *et al.* 1990). Extrapolating small woodland results up to a square kilometre can produce rather unlikely densities that are rarely, if ever, reached in reality. Farmland can be very poor with only 4 prs/km^2 in the da Prato (1985) study near Tranent, where the heavily-trimmed hedges provided extremely poor cover. It is noticeable, however, that da Prato's study was in an area of moderate to poor abundance. The 1994-95 local BBS results suggest a figure of about 15-20 prs/km^2 for all habitats in SE Scotland. A value of 3,000 pairs per occupied 10km-square, 30prs/km^2, was used by the BTO for their assessment of the British population in both of their *Atlas* projects. This would produce a figure of about 195,000 pairs in SE Scotland.

As SE Scotland clearly shows a less than average abundance in the *New Atlas* abundance map there would be some expectation that numbers might be below the national average and a figure of about 20-25prs/km^2 may seem appropriate for our area. Using such figures, the local population can be estimated as between 134,000-167,000 pairs, based on the number of occupied tetrads. As Scotland comes lowest on the rankings for CBC for both woodland and farmland (*Trends*), a median figure of 150,000 pairs might be appropriate. While this seems a huge figure, the lack of a severe winter throughout the *Atlas* period will have allowed Wren numbers to be at a high level.

Clearly there is no ready way to assess the validity of these numbers and they will vary to a high degree according to the mortality rates of the Wren which can vary greatly between winters. Whatever the precise value, however, there can be little doubt that the Wren will remain as one of the commonest birds in the area.   ***R.D.Murray***

Wren

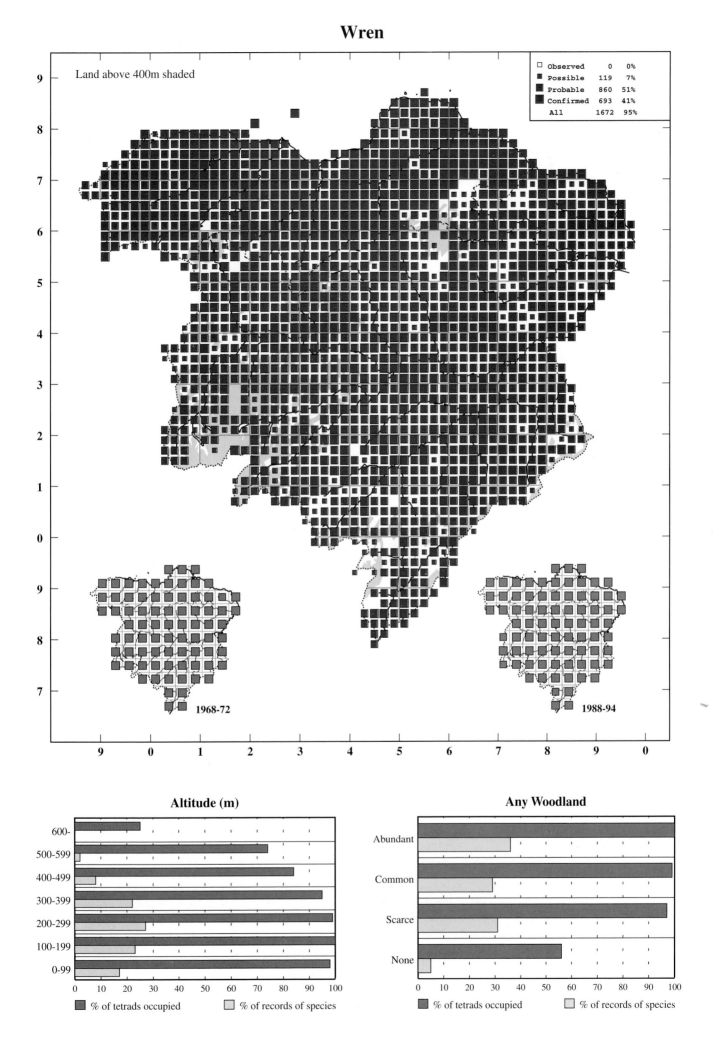

☐ Observed	0	0%
Possible	119	7%
Probable	860	51%
Confirmed	693	41%
All	1672	95%

Land above 400m shaded

1968-72

1988-94

Altitude (m)

600-
500-599
400-499
300-399
200-299
100-199
0-99

■ % of tetrads occupied   ☐ % of records of species

Any Woodland

Abundant
Common
Scarce
None

■ % of tetrads occupied   ☐ % of records of species

213

Dunnock
Prunella modularis

The Dunnock is a bird of edge habitats, being associated with woodland scrub, forest edge, parkland, hedges and gardens. It nests in cover but feeds unobtrusively on the margins of adjacent, more open, habitats. While it does breed in areas of coniferous forestry, where it prefers the margins of rides, clear-fell and young plantation, it is less frequently encountered than on the margins of mixed and deciduous woodland. Dunnocks are often secretive and usually nest low down, hidden in thick cover.

Dunnocks have a unique breeding behaviour with some pairs monogamous, some polyandrous (one female and two males), some polygynous (one male and two or more females) and some polygynandrous (two or more males with two or more females) (Snow & Snow 1981). Male territories can overlap or be inclusive and as a result, surveys that employ the normal CBC methodology to estimate numbers, can easily underestimate the actual total present. There is also some difficulty about just what is being recorded with numbers of pairs, territories or birds all as potential counting units.

Dunnocks are widespread, being found in about three-quarters of all tetrads in SE Scotland. Probable records were mostly of territorial behaviour, while confirmed records were split evenly between adults with food for young and fledged juveniles. The high percentage of confirmed records is remarkable, given the unobtrusive nature of the species. *Atlas* workers became aware of a hiatus in Dunnock song and activity during May that was not apparent in the literature, which made birds difficult to detect for a short period. This presumably coincided with the incubation period of the second brood.

The map is characteristic of a species that is abundant at lower altitudes, almost all of the low ground below 300m being occupied.

This is confirmed by the altitude data which show over 80% occupancy of tetrads up to 300m, falling to half of all tetrads between 300-400m. Above that level the numbers fall rapidly but birds were still found in a small number of tetrads above 500m, although *Thom* states that 500m is the highest altitude on record for breeding in Scotland. Nevertheless the higher ground of the main hill groups is clearly devoid of breeding Dunnocks almost certainly as a result of their treelessness, as even a small clump of scrub can suffice for a Dunnock territory. The Lammermuir and Tweedsmuir Hills are most prominent in that respect, with the large treeless expanse of the Lammermuirs forming a definite void. A few birds do inhabit the more wooded valleys that penetrate to the heart of the Tweedsmuirs. The wooded fringes of the Pentland, Moorfoot and Cheviot Hills, and to some extent the Ettrick Forest, allow Dunnocks a wider distribution at these fairly high levels. Large areas of plantation forestry, particularly in Craik (NT20,21,30&31) and Newcastleton (NY58), stand out at these higher altitudes, although some of the southern plantations may suffer from under-recording as a result of survey work being done during May when Dunnocks scarcely sing.

The association of Dunnocks with wooded habitats can be clearly seen in the habitat graph for all woodlands where 70-80% of tetrads with any type of woodland are occupied. Tetrads with larger areas of woodland are preferred, but the fact that Dunnocks like edge habitats means that this preference is not marked, tetrads where woods are scarce holding over a quarter of all records. Only a tiny fraction of the records come from tetrads with no woodland.

At low altitudes, in the intensively farmed areas of the Merse, and possibly East Lothian, there are tetrads with Dunnocks missing or not confirmed as breeding. Birds were recorded as nesting on Cramond Island and the Bass Rock, and possibly breeding on Craigleith.

Trends shows a real decline in Dunnock numbers in Britain since about the early 1980s. However, comparison with the *Old Atlas* shows no change since 1968-72 in overall range, though confirmation of breeding was not obtained in the present survey in some high squares in the south, perhaps relating to maturation of much coniferous forest there since the earlier survey. The *New Atlas* abundance map shows SE Scotland to hold rather poor numbers of Dunnocks, despite their ubiquity. Good numbers are only shown in small areas around Hopetoun House (NT07), northern East Lothian (NT48,58&68) and the St. Abbs-Eyemouth area (NT96). Elsewhere the lowlands and valleys have moderate to good abundance with the hill fringes being mostly areas of low abundance.

A few areas in SE Scotland have regular counts of Dunnocks, mostly reserves such as Aberlady which holds 23-34 territories, Bawsinch 13-18 pairs, Roslin Glen 6-10 pairs and St. Abb's Head 9 pairs. The highest count was at the Hermitage of Braid and Blackford Glen which had a count of 38 singing males. These figures equate to between 12-20prs/km^2, similar to da Prato's (1985) 17prs/km^2 in the Tranent area, not dissimilar to Petty *et al.* (1995) who found *c.*20 birds/km^2 in coniferous forest at Kielder in Northumberland. Local BBS data suggest 8-11prs/km^2 in all habitats. The *New Atlas* uses a figure for its national population estimate of 8prs/km^2 across all of Britain, a huge reduction from the 15prs/km^2 used by Sharrock in the *Old Atlas*. As there is some indication of a drop-off in the occupation of tetrads with altitude in SE Scotland, which may imply a drop-off in density, a population estimate can be made treating tetrads up to 200m as holding 15prs/km^2, those between 200-400m with 10prs/km^2 and those above 400m with 5prs/km^2, producing a total of 63,000 pairs. The average of 8prs/km^2 used by Snow in the *New Atlas* to calculate the British population does seem low, especially when compared to the *Old Atlas* figure.

J.G.Mattocks

Dunnock

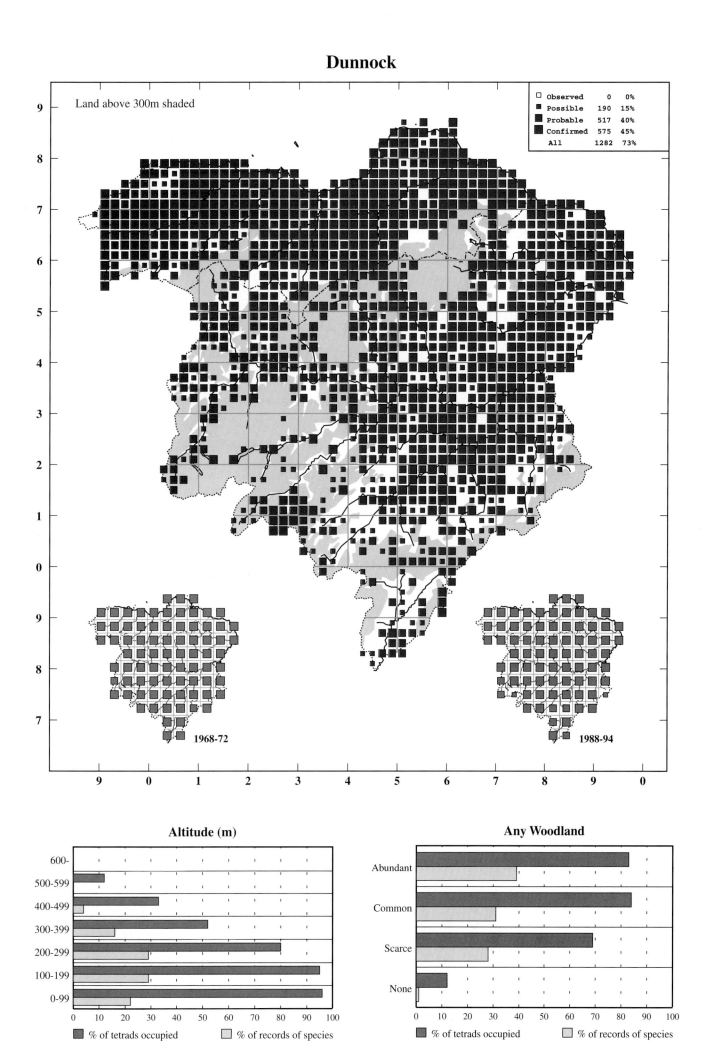

Land above 300m shaded

□ Observed	0	0%
■ Possible	190	15%
■ Probable	517	40%
■ Confirmed	575	45%
All	1282	73%

1968-72

1988-94

Altitude (m)

600-	
500-599	
400-499	
300-399	
200-299	
100-199	
0-99	

■ % of tetrads occupied   ☐ % of records of species

Any Woodland

Abundant	
Common	
Scarce	
None	

■ % of tetrads occupied   ☐ % of records of species

Robin

Erithacus rubecula

An inhabitant of all types of woodland, the Robin is perhaps *the* most familiar of British birds. It has been able to adapt successfully from natural woodlands to landscapes managed by man, most particularly the garden. This, combined with its boldness, has brought it into contact with many people who would otherwise hardly notice the bird. The Robin is sufficiently versatile to live in most woodland environments from dense conifer plantations, to the sparce woodland created by a few birches or rowans in a cleugh in hilly areas, to highly urban gardens and parks. Part of this versatility can be ascribed to its catholic diet, enabling it to switch between insects, fruit and seeds, as season, abundance and scarcity allow.

The very familiarity of the Robin made it one of the easier species to record for the *Atlas*. The song and ticking alarm call are well known and easily registered, and while the spotted young are less familiar, the boldness of the adults when feeding and defending their young meant that proving breeding was not difficult. Over 95% of registrations were of probable and confirmed breeding. Probable records were mostly of territorial singing, birds singing against one another being easy to record in most tetrads. Anxious 'ticking' adults were also important. Around 60% of confirmed records were of fledglings with another 30% concerning adults carrying food for young.

Robins are one of the most widespread species in SE Scotland, ranking fifth alongside the Woodpigeon, behind Wren, Carrion Crow, Chaffinch and Willow Warbler. As might be expected from their habitat requirements, Robins were mostly absent from those tetrads that were totally devoid of woodland of any description, mainly the hill summits. The map clearly shows vacant tetrads in the open areas of higher ground in the Pentlands, Moorfoots, Lammermuirs, Tweedsmuir and Liddesdale. Isolated tetrads on the edges of some of these hills, such as Meggethead (NT12Q), Mount Main (NT34Z) and Mayshiel (NT66C), show that Robins can maintain a presence, provided there is some modicum of woodland cover, mostly in these cases in the form of tiny shelterbelts or trees around shepherds' cottages.

The altitude graph supports this relationship, with birds present in 93% of all tetrads below 400m with just 5% of the records coming from tetrads above that altitude. With a species so universal on the lower ground, Robins show strong relationships with most lowland habitat types. Amongst the strongest correlation, however, is with woodlands, Robins being present in 94% of tetrads that have woods, of whatever size, with just 1% of birds being reported in what must be essentially treeless tetrads. Human settlement also relates highly, with birds being present in 97% of tetrads that held buildings.

The few vacant tetrads on lower ground, probably due to birds being overlooked, seem to have a random distribution. There are no significant areas that lack Robins on the lower ground, even within the intensively worked arable areas of East Lothian and the Merse, indicating that there are no tetrads without some habitat that can hold this versatile species. Robins even extend onto some of the Forth islands. Breeding has only been proved on Inchkeith and Inchcolm (both in Fife) but birds have also been recorded on Inchmickery, Cramond Island and Inchgarvie (Fife) during the breeding season.

As with all widespread species, comparison of the 10-km square maps shows very few differences. As for the Wren, only one 10-km square, the Berwickshire cliffs in NT87, shows Robins present in the recent period but not in 1968-72, presumably because they were overlooked in the 1968-72 survey.

The *New Atlas* abundance map for SE Scotland clearly shows that Robins are much less abundant in our area than they can be further south and west in the British Isles. There are only a few areas of high abundance; around Linlithgow-Bathgate, Dalkeith, much of East Lothian north of the A1 road, St.Abbs-Eyemouth and in the Jed and middle Teviot valleys. Areas of moderate abundance extend around these centres to much of the lowlands but miss out Edinburgh, the Dunbar coast and the Merse between Kelso and Berwick. These last three areas are shown as being as poor for Robins as are the hills on the *New Atlas*.

In Scotland, Robin densities vary considerably according to details of the woodland habitat, from the poorest in overgrazed conifer plantations with little ground cover at 10prs/km², to the best in policy woodland in lowland areas at 300prs/km² (*Old Atlas*, Thom). The *New Atlas* quotes maximum mean densities of 33prs/km² in farmland and 66prs/km² in woodland, but adopts an overall figure of about 16prs/km² in calculating the British population.

Work in East Lothian farmland (da Prato 1985) showed densities of 60-160prs/km² in small woods and shelterbelts, with an overall figure in an area which is mostly arable farmland of 7prs/km². The BBS survey suggests *c.*10prs/km². Although just outwith SE Scotland, the study of Sparrowhawk and Merlin prey species in Kielder (Petty *et al.* 1995) found Robin densities of 39prs/km² in an area that the *New Atlas* abundance map shows to hold very high numbers.

As the *New Atlas* abundance map clearly shows few areas of high or even moderate abundance in SE Scotland it might be better to adopt a lower overall value of perhaps about 10prs/km² for our area, a little above da Prato's mean for the Tranent area. Such a figure would yield around 61,000 pairs of Robins in our area, just over 1% of the British population, on 2.6% of the country. However, if commercial forestry areas such as Kielder hold substantial numbers of Robins, the growth of forests like Craik, Wauchope and those of the upper Tweed will mean that very large numbers may be present in parts of SE Scotland in the near future. With SE Scotland's 600km² of commercial forestry holding Kielder densities of Robins, there might develop a population of almost 90,000 pairs just in these forests alone. Making an allowance for the higher densities possibly present in the conifer forests and raising the overal local density to 15prs/km², the SE Scotland Robin population is estimated to be around 92,000 pairs.
R.D.Murray

Robin

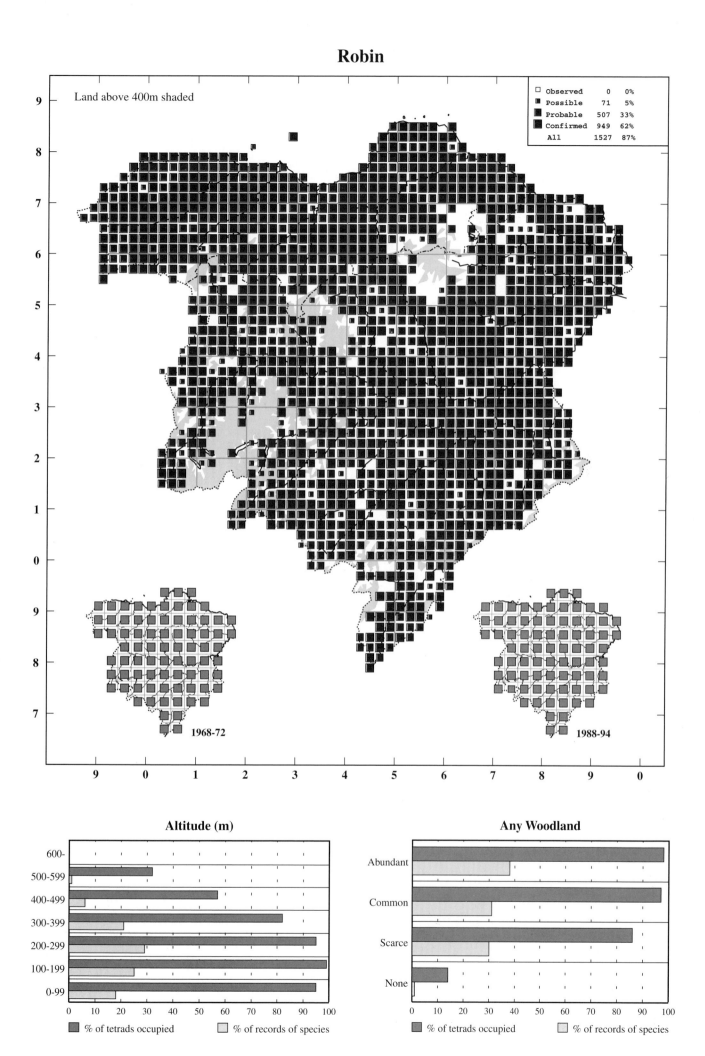

Observed	0	0%
Possible	71	5%
Probable	507	33%
Confirmed	949	62%
All	1527	87%

Land above 400m shaded

1968-72

1988-94

Altitude (m)

600-	
500-599	
400-499	
300-399	
200-299	
100-199	
0-99	

■ % of tetrads occupied   □ % of records of species

Any Woodland

Abundant	
Common	
Scarce	
None	

■ % of tetrads occupied   □ % of records of species

Redstart
Phoenicurus phoenicurus

The Redstart is a bird of open woodland in Britain, mostly in woodlands at the break of slope between the hills and the lower ground. An insectivorous summer visitor, it occurs mainly in the north and west of Britain where suitable topography offers abundant habitat in the northern and western oakwoods. Redstarts are hole nesters and so old woodlands with plenty of tree cavities offer the best opportunities for breeding, although nest-boxes and holes in buildings are also used.

Birds were fairly easy to detect, when *Atlas* workers were familiar with the song. The song is distinctive and far-reaching and although song peaks in mid-May, some birds still sing well into late June. The high percentage of possible records, mostly singing birds, could have been improved to territory but many remote areas never received follow-up visits. Probable records were dominated by territorial behaviour or anxious adults, while confirmed records were mostly of adults feeding young and fledged juveniles.

The Redstart is surprisingly widely distributed across one-fifth of SE Scotland. Mature deciduous woodland is the preferred habitat, particularly those remnant woods situated along the steeper banks of the main rivers that are unsuited to both farming and commercial forestry. These woodlands tend to be narrow and thus afford an extensive edge from which the birds can forage for their insect prey. Many woods are heavily grazed which allows birds room to forage beneath the canopy. Redstarts also occupy wooded cleughs well into the hill areas. Some birds can be found in very open areas, apparently using just a few mature trees that have grown up from old hedgerows planted in the last century. The liking for small to medium sized woods is confirmed by the habitat graph that show 73% of all records come from tetrads that hold these sizes of woods.

The map shows a strong relationship with the river valleys at the edge of the hill areas and this is supported by the altitude data that show that two-thirds of records are between 100-300m. This is particularly evident along the middle and upper parts of the Tweed, the Leader (NT54,55), the Liddel Water (NY48,49&59), the Esk (NT35) and along the Jed and Rule valleys (NT51&61). The linear patterns along the northern edge of the Lammermuirs and Moorfoots, particularly NT46 &67, are where woods growing in gullies on the steep ground of the Southern Upland Fault are used by Redstarts. Away from these steeper-sided sites Redstart registrations are scarcer and mostly confined to the wooded policies of large houses such as Carberry Tower (NT36U), Mellerstain (NT63P), Floors Castle NT73C&D), the Hirsel (NT84A&F) and Mordington (NT95N).

Not all valleys are occupied, despite having areas of apparently suitable habitat incorporating both steep slopes and deciduous woodland, as is confirmed by the habitat graph that shows just 20-40% of tetrads with woods are occupied.This is true of the main Lothian drainage away from the hills and of the lower Eye and Tweed. Agriculture may play some role in this, birds being mostly absent from areas where the growing of cereals predominates. Redstarts could be found in lines of single Beech trees bounding grazing land, so the nature of the landscape against which the woodland edge abuts may be vital, pastoral areas providing a greater abundance of insects. This would certainly be true of the areas where Redstart numbers are more common.

Though Redstarts are generally perceived to be a scarce species in the area and consequently observers submit all breeding season records to the *Bird Reports*, the *Atlas* uncovered many more birds than had hitherto been expected. This perception of scarcity may be related to the fluctuations in Redstart numbers over the last 30 years as it is one of the species that is thought to have suffered as a result of desert formation in the Sahel area in Africa where birds winter. Comparison with the *Old Atlas* shows birds were a little less widespread then, but the CBC index in 1973 had fallen to just 25% of 1960s. The recovery since has been slow but reached good levels by the mid-1980s, and during the period of the *Atlas* stood at an all-time high (*Trends*), unlike some other Sahelian species that underwent further declines in the mid-1980s. It seems likely that the population in SE Scotland has not been higher in living memory.

The *New Atlas* abundance map shows that highest numbers occur along the middle Tweed between Melrose and Broughton with moderate numbers across much of the Tweedsmuir Hills and the valleys of the Teviot and lower Whiteadder and Eye Waters. Much of Lothian, the Merse and Liddesdale are shown to hold few birds.

Redstart numbers are typically low at most sites in SE Scotland, and while well over 250 sites have been mentioned in the *Bird Reports*, few held more than 1-2 pairs, the average being 1.8 singing males per site. The most dense concentration of birds is undoubtedly around Dawyck where 21 singing males were located in 1987 in about 2km^2 of deciduous woodland situated in two tetrads (NT13M&S). Other areas that have held notable concentrations of Redstarts include nine males at Lewenshope (NT32Z&33V) and Abbey St. Bathans (NT76L&R) and seven at Neidpath (NT23J&24F), with many more sites with 5-6 males. With a mean of 1.8 males per site and some tetrads holding more than one site, a value of 2.5 pairs per tetrad or 0.62prs/km^2, therefore seems a conservative figure on which to calculate the likely population of SE Scotland. This produces a figure of about 1,000 pairs.

The calculations used by the BTO in their original estimates of the British population for the *Old Atlas* used figures of 0.45prs/km^2. These estimates were raised, in line with increases in the CBC index, to give figures of 0.68prs/km^2 in the *New Atlas*, close to the value seen in SE Scotland based on actual site counts and the numbers of tetrads where birds were present. However, on this basis the area has only 1.3% of the British population, far too low for both the apparent numbers indicated in the *New Atlas* abundance map and by proportion of the British mainland occupied by SE Scotland. The discussion on population levels in the *New Atlas* clearly flags problems with national population estimates which have been grossly inflated in the past. Local figures hint that the current national estimate of 90,000 pairs is still too large. **R.D.Murray**

Redstart

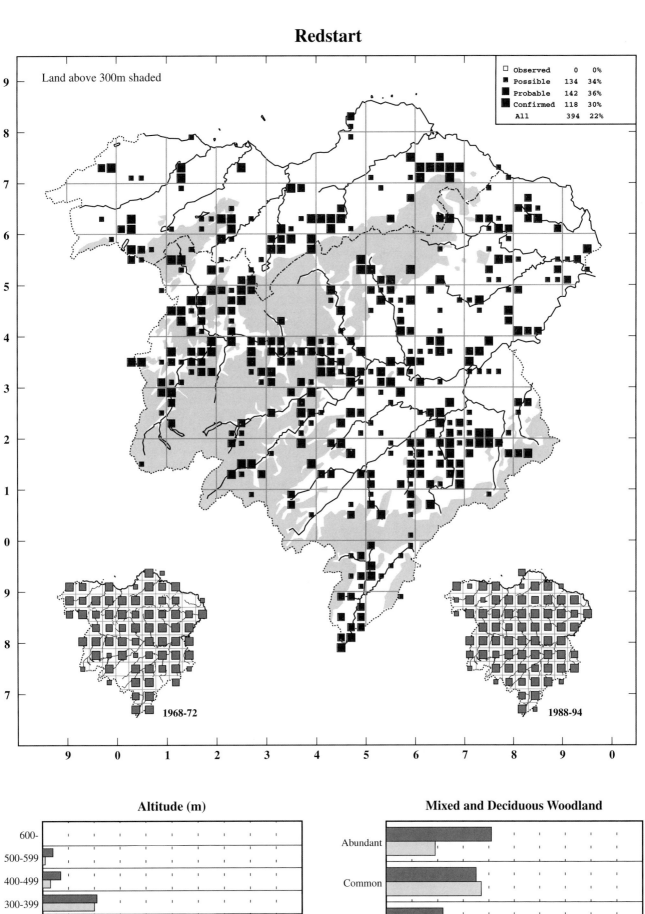

Land above 300m shaded

□ Observed	0	0%
▪ Possible	134	34%
◼ Probable	142	36%
◼ Confirmed	118	30%
All	394	22%

1968-72

1988-94

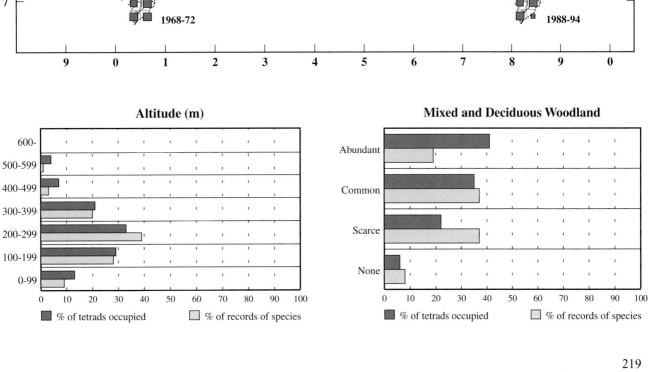

Altitude (m)

600-	
500-599	
400-499	
300-399	
200-299	
100-199	
0-99	

0 10 20 30 40 50 60 70 80 90 100

■ % of tetrads occupied   □ % of records of species

Mixed and Deciduous Woodland

Abundant	
Common	
Scarce	
None	

0 10 20 30 40 50 60 70 80 90 100

■ % of tetrads occupied   □ % of records of species

Whinchat
Saxicola rubetra

A small brown bird scolding from a perch on top of a bracken frond or a fence-post, that is revealed through binoculars to be surprisingly colourful, must be the way that many people first encounter a Whinchat. It is a migrant that arrives in grassland and scrub habitats just as the first flush of insects emerge. Any habitat with a combination of open grassland, high perches and patches of denser vegetation for nests can be occupied, be it moorland edge, rough pasture, roadside verges, young plantation or clear-fell. High vantage points such as shrubs, bracken, heather or fence-posts are used to spot insects on the ground. It is mostly a bird of northern and western Britain, typically on higher ground where such habitats are more likely to occur than in the more intensively cultivated lowlands.

Whinchats are easy to find through their use of high perches for singing and hunting. Pairs also readily alarm. About 75% of all observations involve probable and confirmed breeding. Probable records are mostly of pairs although territorial behaviour and anxiety are also important, confirming what has been said of the species' behaviour. Confirmed records are mostly split between fledged young and adults with food for their young.

Both the map and the altitude diagram show that Whinchats are mostly absent from the lowest ground with only 14% of records below 200m, mostly the clusters in East Lothian (NT36,37,46&47) and West Lothian (NS96). Some of these are associated with abandoned railway lines and the scrub habitats at the summits of hills associated with Carboniferous volcanic intrusions such as Corstorphine Hill (NT17W), the Eildon Hills (NT53L) and Garleton Hills (NT57C). Most occupied tetrads are above 200m and show a strong relationship with large areas of heather moorland and rough grazing, with nearly 60% of tetrads dominated by such habitats holding Whinchats. Birds are absent from the highest tetrads above 450m, leaving gaps in the heart of the Lammermuirs and around the summits of the Tweedsmuir Hills, indicating a definite preference for the valleys rather than summits of the hills. The less exposed, grass and bracken-covered slopes of the Cheviots (NT71,81&82) are extensively inhabited as are the grass-heather-bracken moors and glens of the northern and eastern Lammermuirs (NT65&66). Young plantation can hold large numbers of Whinchats for a few years until the canopy closes. Few areas of forestry on the map show particularly large densities of occupied tetrads, indicating that the young plantation stage in the succession has mostly passed.

Several 10-km squares have an extremely high density of occupied tetrads, particularly the Upper Ettrick (NT21), Leithen valley (NT34), Spartleton Edge (NT66) and the Kale valley (NT71). Each has a good mix of heather moor and rough pasture with extensive areas of bracken, the ideal habitat for Whinchats. The *New Atlas* abundance map highlights these areas as having excellent numbers of Whinchats, possibly some of the most extensive areas of the highest Whinchat abundance in Britain, particularly in the Tweedsmuir Hills between the Ettrick and Tweed, in the southern Pentlands and the western flank of the Cheviot. The map confirms the virtual absence of birds from the main areas of arable farmland in East Lothian and the Merse. Modern arable farming practices and Whinchats clearly do not mix!

Comparison with the *Old Atlas* shows a retreat from the more intensively farmed areas, particularly along the Tweed where there has been a definite contraction of range with four previously occupied 10-km squares (NT63,74,84&95) now vacant, and two squares (NT73&96) with confirmed breeding in 1968-72 now reduced to possible breeding. Other changes suggest expansion although, in fact, very few birds are probably involved. The confirmed breeding in NT17 was a one-off record. Few birds are present in NT37 and NT85&86 where high quality hedges are the preferred habitat. The number of 10-km squares remains almost identical over the 20-year period, marginal losses almost balanced by marginal colonisation. *Andrews* noted several sites where numbers have fallen, as in the Moorfoot valley (NT25) which showed a fall from 37 to 20 pairs between 1980-1983, or disappeared altogether as at Aberlady. At Holyrood Park numbers fell from 10 pairs to 1-2 pairs, and then none after grazing ceased in 1978. Such losses fit the national picture where Whinchats have been lost from large areas of farmland in southern and central England through intensification of farming (*New Atlas*).

The *New Atlas* uses a density of 10-20 pairs per occupied 10-km square in calculating the national figures for Whinchat, equivalent to 0.1-0.2prs/km^2. As our local densities are certainly high judging from the abundance map, this overall figure is likely to be low for our area, particularly as half of the 10-km squares in SE Scotland have ten or more occupied tetrads. There are not many figures on local densities but in recent years Swanston (NT26I&N) has held 11 pairs on 0.8km^2, while the Moorfoot valley (NT24Z&25V) has 5-9 pairs/km^2 (*Bird Reports*). Other population figures published in the *Bird Reports* over the *Atlas* period indicate several sites with considerable numbers: Heatherhope (NT81D): 22 pairs; Leithen Valley (NT34F): 20 pairs; Monynut Water (NT76): 18 pairs in 3.5km; 'north Pentlands' and Caddon Valley (NT44A): 15 pairs each; Whiteadder Water (NT66): 13 pairs; Outer Huntly (NT42L) and Fruid: 12 pairs each; and Whitrope (NY59E): 11 pairs. Such numbers suggest that the *New Atlas* population estimate based on 0.1-0.2prs/km^2 is very low indeed and unlikely to pertain to our area. *Day* found densities of *c*.0.75prs/km^2 in Northumberland and calculated their local population on the basis of 0.75-1.25prs/km^2. This still seems slightly on the low side for SE Scotland, when the numbers at the above sites are considered. At 1.25prs/km^2, the local population would be around 3,100 pairs, or 10-20% of the British population.

R.D.Murray

Whinchat

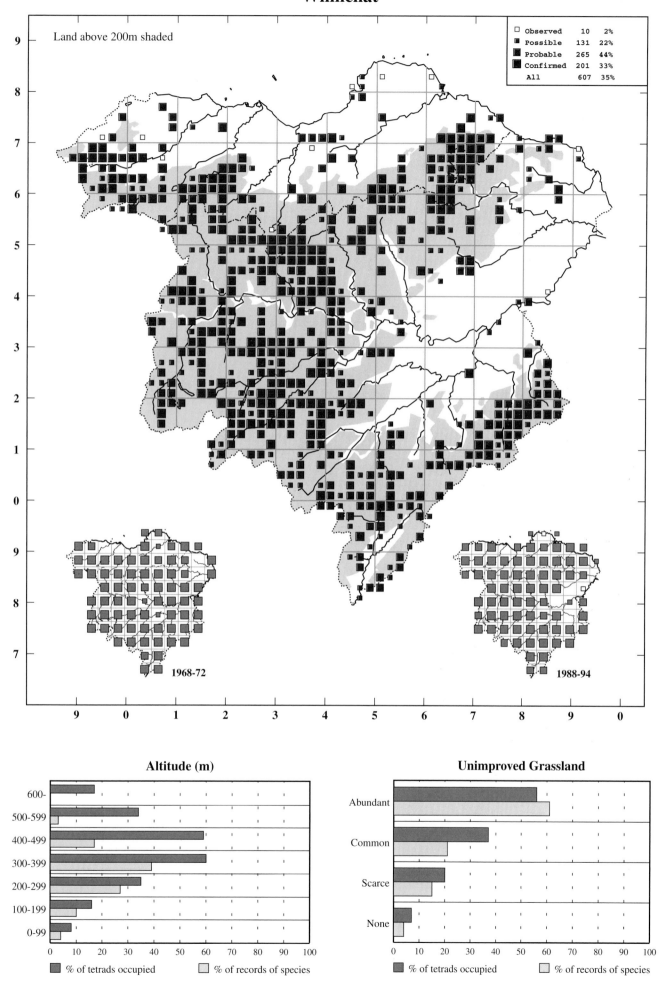

	Observed	10	2%
	Possible	131	22%
	Probable	265	44%
	Confirmed	201	33%
	All	607	35%

Land above 200m shaded

1968-72

1988-94

Altitude (m)

% of tetrads occupied   % of records of species

Unimproved Grassland

% of tetrads occupied   % of records of species

Stonechat

Saxicola torquata

The Stonechat is usually portrayed in illustrations perched on top of a gorse bush. This stereotyped image certainly has more than a grain of truth in it although birds can be found in habitats where gorse is absent. Gorse is perhaps symbolic of a liking for rough, uncultivated ground, often well-grazed by sheep or rabbits to create a short sward. Low shrubs can provide high perches from which the Stonechat can sally forth to snatch its insect prey from the short grass. It is a bird of western coastal grasslands and heaths in Britain but scarce or absent along the North Sea coasts. In parts of Scotland numbers nest well away from the coast in areas of rough grazing and heather moor.

Once located, Stonechats announce their presence by loudly alarming from high perches such as bushes, fence posts and bracken stems. As they can be double or even treble-brooded it is not just the breeding pair present that give alarm but also their sometimes large number of young. The difficulty is in locating the breeding site. Local birds typically inhabit the deeper valleys in the hills that possess a combination of well-grazed rough grass, heather and bracken. Some valleys will hold Stonechats while similar neighbouring valleys are vacant. This appears to be a national trait as it is commented upon in the *New Atlas*. Over half of all the records were of confirmed breeding, most of which involved sightings of fledged young. Most probable breeding records were of pairs.

Stonechats are very scarce breeders in SE Scotland. The map shows registrations in only 40 tetrads, mostly in the Pentlands, Moorfoots Lammermuirs and the northern part of the Tweedsmuir Hills. Altitude data show a distinct preference for areas between 300-500m where three-quarters of all records originate. With such small numbers of occupied tetrads, habitat correlations are poor but most birds seem to be found in tetrads where both rough grazing and heather moor are common or abundant.

To fully understand the map it is necessary to understand the history of the Stonechat in SE Scotland. The *Old Atlas* 10-km map was surveyed when the Stonechat was in the process of recovering from the severe winter of 1962-63 and shows a bird of coastal scrub (NT27,48,58&77), grazed hills (NT02,03,05,16,26), heather moor (NT65) and young forestry (NT30,31,41&51). *Bird Report* records indicate further colonisation through the 1970s on the coast at NT47,68,87&96 and inland at NY59,NT50,60,80&81. The Stonechat reached its widest distribution around 1978, before

declining after the hard winter of 1978/79 when temperatures fell to -27°C. A fair population survived that winter but almost the entire population was wiped out in the prolonged hard weather of winter 1981/82. Two or three pairs managed to hang on into 1984 but there were no reported cases of breeding from 1985 to 1987 and only a handful of birds reported at other times of the year. The table below shows the extremely low levels of the mid-1980s with the numbers of birds seen outwith the breeding season usually marching in step with the breeding population, despite the occasional large movement of passage birds.

Breeding season records 1980-95

	80	81	82	83	84	85	86	87	88	89	90	91	92	93	94	95
Territorial	18	10	2	3	2	0	0	0	3	4	9	2	13	11	10	21
Other	7	7	11	9	8	3	5	5	15	39	10	10	11	31	12	32

The map shows the recolonisation of the area by Stonechats since 1988 when the first returning birds bred at Carnethy Hill (NT26A). These were followed in 1989 by records from the Medwin valley (NT05W), Loganlea (NT16W), Tailend Moss (NT06D) and Eildon Hills (NT53L). The first records from the Moorfoots and Lammermuirs were in 1990 and the Tweedsmuir Hills in 1992. The Cheviots have yet to be re-colonised.

The map has clustering of records in the Pentlands in NT16&26 where the birds are concentrated in the Glencorse-Loganlea valley and just over the watershed at Black Springs at Threipmuir. The tetrads in the Moorfoot and Tweedsmuir Hills seem more spread out but birds are actually inhabiting adjacent valleys that are more widely spaced due to the greater height of the hills in between. Thus Hopecarton and Drumelzier in NT13, and Hundleshope, Black Burn and Glenrath in NT23 are just over a watershed from one another. A similar situation appears to exist in the Moorfoots with records in the Moorfoot valley (NT25V), Longcote Burn and Soonhope Burn in NT24, and Leithen Water and Leithen Doors Burn in NT34, separated by the main Moorfoot massif. The young may simply disperse over the watershed into the nearest valley to find vacant habitat. There are outlying probable and confirmed records at Tailend Moss (NT06), Medwyn Water (NT05), White Hill (NT03) and Monynut (NT76). Birds were discovered between the Yarrow and the Teviot during Merlin research work in 1994 but not followed up to confirm breeding. These may represent the first stages of the recolonisation of the Ettrick Forest area.

The differences of the fates of coastal and inland Stonechats in SE Scotland, and indeed on the whole east coast of Scotland, is interesting. Prior to the crash, inland birds were mostly partial migrants, moving out of the area in the depths of winter and during periods of hard weather. Coastal birds were more sedentary. The severe winters between 1978 and 1982 totally wiped out the coastal birds while a few inland birds have survived to recolonise the hills in the current period. The breeding record at Dowlaw (NT86J) in 1995 was the first definite sign of a return to the coast and was followed up by broods seen at Dowlaw and St. Abbs in 1997. It will be interesting to see whether any future coastal population retains its sedentary habits.

The *Bird Report* records indicate that only one or two pairs breed in each tetrad. Breeding, or even the presence, of Stonechats is not indicated every year in the *Bird Reports*, almost certainly because most sites were not often re-visited in subsequent years. The local population is probably around 30-50 pairs of which only a fraction are reported on annually. Old records suggest substantial scope for expansion of these numbers. Lothian alone was thought to hold 45 pairs in 1976 (*Andrews*), while single valleys in the Cheviots were documented to hold 5-10 pairs (*BBR 1980*). These figures and the amount of apparently suitable habitat suggest that SE Scotland might be capable of supporting several hundred pairs, providing the population is not checked by severe winters.   ***R.D.Murray***

Stonechat

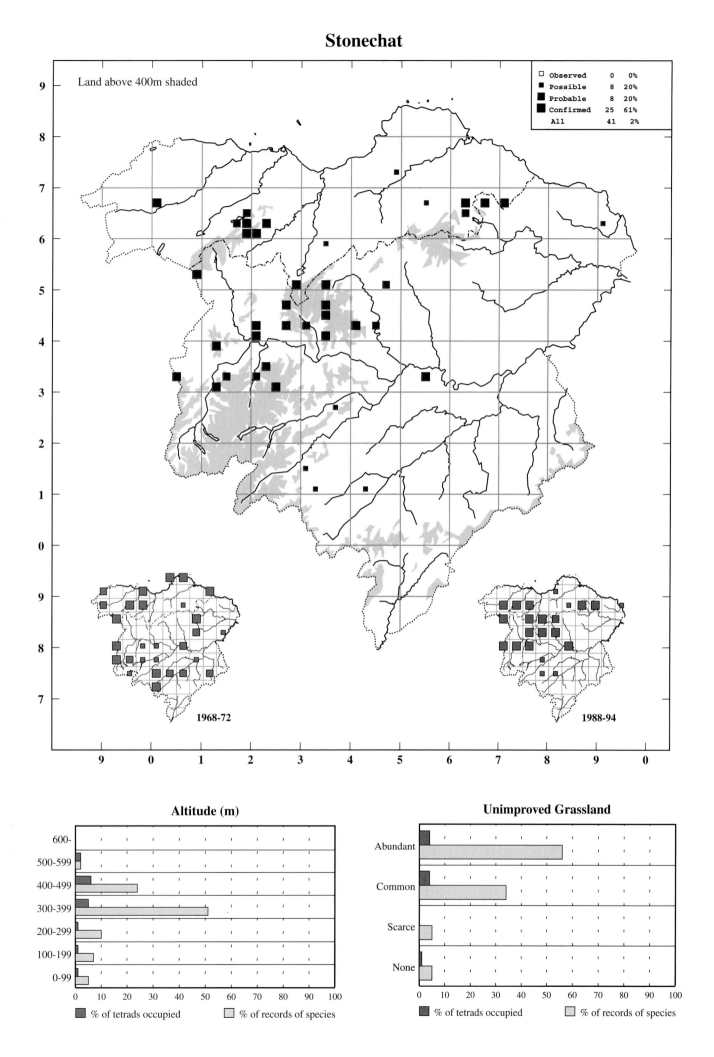

□ Observed	0	0%
■ Possible	8	20%
■ Probable	8	20%
■ Confirmed	25	61%
All	41	2%

Land above 400m shaded

1968-72

1988-94

Altitude (m)

- 600-
- 500-599
- 400-499
- 300-399
- 200-299
- 100-199
- 0-99

■ % of tetrads occupied   % of records of species

Unimproved Grassland

- Abundant
- Common
- Scarce
- None

■ % of tetrads occupied   % of records of species

223

Wheatear
Oenanthe oenanthe

The Wheatear is a characteristic bird of the upland areas of northern and western Britain, where it nests up to 1,200m in the Highlands. It needs open habitat comprising areas of short grass, where it forages for insects, and high perches which allow it to spot potential prey. It is particularly associated with sheepwalk where the grazing keeps the sward short , and with cliff tops and sand dunes where the wind and spray stunt growth. It can be associated with Rabbits whose grazing keeps the herbage short and whose burrows serve as nest-holes. Dry-stane dykes, ruins, rocky outcrops and screes also provide nest sites.

Amongst the earliest of migrants, the first Wheatears arrive in SE Scotland in late March, the bulk of the population appearing by the third week of April. The return passage starts in late July and most local birds have left by mid-September. There is no reason to believe that the odd winter records involve local birds.

Birds were not difficult to locate during fieldwork because of their loud and distinctive alarm calls and habit of perching conspicuously. The preferred open habitats also allowed fledged broods to be easily located. Probable records were mostly of territorial pairs and alarming birds. Half of all confirmed records were of broods, with another quarter being adults carrying food. Passage birds in spring caused difficulties as it was impossible to know whether a bird was setting up a territory or merely moving through. The sprinkling of observed records mostly involves such birds.

The map shows that Wheatears in SE Scotland breed in most areas above 300m in the Pentland, Moorfoot, Lammermuir, Tweedsmuir and Cheviot Hills. The altitude diagram confirms this with two-thirds of all records occurring above 300m. Above this altitude between 60-75% of all tetrads recorded breeding Wheatears, the strength of the association increasing with altitude. There is a strong relationship with unimproved grassland, most specifically rough grazing. Above 300m there are gaps in the Lammermuirs (NT55&56) where heather is dominant, and in Craik Forest (NT20,30&31) and Tweedsmuir (NT01) where forestry dominates. Below 300m the preferred habitats are primarily on the moors in the higher parts of West Lothian (NS95&96), Arthur's Seat (NT27R), the golf links around Gullane (NT48&58), the coastal heaths and grasslands of Coldingham Moor and St.Abbs (NT86&96) and the sheepwalk of the Greenlaw Moor-Westruther area (NT64&65).

A comparison with the *Old Atlas* reveals no change in the main upland breeding areas, but definite losses from the marginal breeding areas at lower levels in the Merse and middle Tweed and in the northern foothills of the Moorfoots. The loss of unimproved grasslands has probably been marked in these areas as farming has become increasingly intensive since the 1970s. The reduction of grazing on Arthur's Seat saw a collapse of the population there from 10 pairs to five pairs and then just 1-2 pairs since grazing ceased altogether in 1978 (*Thom*). The conversion of unimproved pastures to silage or cereals would be more dramatic and exclude Wheatears altogether, as may have happened in NT36&46. Wheatears certainly have no association with wheat, the name meaning "white-arse" in Old English.

The population of southern Britain has been in decline since the 19th century due to factors such as afforestation, less intensive grazing and the reduction in Rabbit numbers as a result of myxomatosis (*Trends*). The Scottish population has been more stable, despite local reductions in forestry areas (*Thom*). While the main breeding areas in SE Scotland seem unlikely to suffer any significant losses while sheep stocks remain high, parts of the range may be vulnerable to further spread of commercial forestry.

Wheatears can be locally common and a number of sites are known to hold good numbers of birds. In Lothian studies by L.L.J. Vick in the Moorfoot Valley (NT24Y&Z, NT25V&W) showed a population of up to 45 pairs and densities of 9-15prs/km^2 (*Thom*), while up to 17 nests (15prs/km^2) are known from the Swanston area (NT26I&N) and 14 pairs in the Whiteadder valley (NT66H,I&M). In Borders 34 territories were estimated along the road between Talla and Megget Reservoirs (NT12), while the glens at Kingledores (NT02Y) and Glenrath (NT23B&F) have held 12 and 14 pairs respectively. These latter figures indicate that densities of 3-5prs/km^2 may be common.

The *New Atlas* abundance map shows that Wheatears are moderately common in SE Scotland, with areas of highest numbers in much of the Tweedsmuir Hills and in parts of the Moorfoots. The BTO used a figure of 40 pairs per occupied 10-km square to calculate the British population in both breeding atlases. This translates as 0.4prs/km^2, extremely low when compared to the numbers and densities apparent in the sites quoted above. While such sites may be exceptional, many glens are known to hold a few pairs and so a conservative figure of 2prs/km^2 can be used to estimate the local population. Such a figure is not dissimilar to the local BBS returns that showed *c*.2prs/km^2. This suggests that about 5,000 pairs may be present in SE Scotland, equating to 8-9% of the *New Atlas* estimate of the British population. As the national figure is based on the very low 0.4 prs/km^2, our figures suggest that there may be many more Wheatears in Britain than the BTO estimate states.   *J.Palfery*

Wheatear

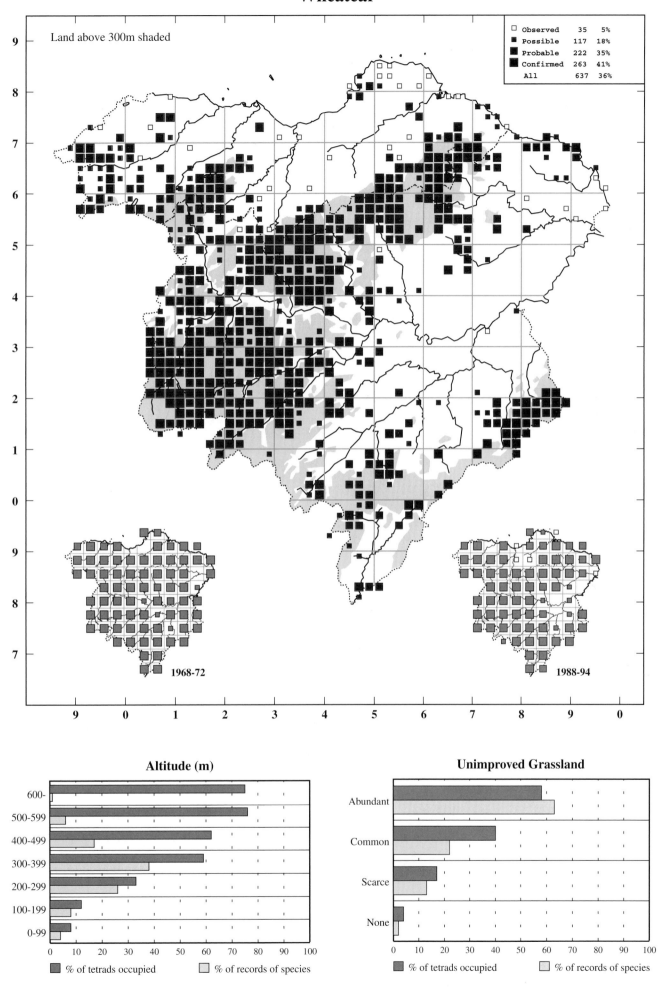

Land above 300m shaded

☐ Observed	35	5%
■ Possible	117	18%
■ Probable	222	35%
■ Confirmed	263	41%
All	637	36%

1968-72

1988-94

Altitude (m)

■ % of tetrads occupied   ☐ % of records of species

Unimproved Grassland

■ % of tetrads occupied   ☐ % of records of species

Ring Ouzel
Turdus torquatus

Ring Ouzels are restricted to the uplands of Scotland, Wales and the north and northwest of England where they breed on heather moorland with sheep pasture and scattered stunted trees, typically with some steep-sided gullies or crags. They are most often found at around 250m above sea-level, nesting on the ground in heather. Depending on latitude Ring Ouzels are found anywhere between sea-level and 1200m where suitable habitat exists.

Although a shy and relatively localised bird, the recording of breeding Ring Ouzels is not too difficult if likely territories are visited in suitable weather during that time of the breeding cycle when males are singing. Mornings and evenings on still days when it is not too cold are ideal. While song and the alarm calls can be heard at any time of day, it seems possible that birds may have been overlooked in some areas that may have been surveyed at both the wrong time of day and time of year when singing was subdued or absent. Probable records were dominated by alarming adults, pairs and territorial behaviour, while confirmed records were shared between adults carrying food for young and fledged juveniles.

In SE Scotland the basic distribution in the Pentlands, Moorfoots and Lammermuirs was established by an SOC survey in 1985-86 (Poxton 1987). The more extended survey for this *Atlas* confirmed this distribution, showing the Moorfoots and Lammermuirs to hold many territories with rather fewer than previously in the Pentlands. A third major concentration is evident in the Tweedsmuir Hills with lesser pockets in the Liddesdale hills and around Cheviot. The map and graph show a strong relationship with areas around the 400m contour with some records occurring down to 300m, mostly in the eastern Lammermuirs where a combination of the drier climate and land management allows heather to be dominant in certain areas at lower altitudes. Within the Pentlands and Tweedsmuir Hills there is some correlation between areas of steep ground and Ring Ouzel tetrads, perhaps indicative of the birds liking for steep cleughs. The flatter parts of the southern Pentlands and the flat whaleback summits of the Tweedsmuirs appear to lack Ring Ouzels, as do the partially-forested Minch Moor (NT33) and parts of the Ettrick Forest. Note, however, that Ring Ouzels were still present in parts of the southwestern Moorfoots that are dominated by forestry.

In the 1985-86 survey, considerable variations in breeding densities were observed. In apparently identical habitats, especially in the Pentland Hills, some valleys had high densities with less than 500m between nests while other valleys had none (Poxton 1986, 1987). This produced an almost colonial pattern of territories. The habitats recorded were steep-sided valleys with ample heather and bracken for nesting and sheep-cropped pasture for feeding.

The habitat data show a strong relationship between Ring Ouzels and heather moorland, over half of all tetrads with extensive heather holding birds. Indeed almost 60% of all birds were found on such moors. As heather becomes rarer in a tetrad, so does the likelihood of it holding Ring Ouzels. Not surprisingly, rough grazing also rates highly in Ring Ouzel tetrads with over 80% of records coming from tetrads where such habitat is common or abundant.

It is widely acknowledged that there has been a marked decline of Ring Ouzels across Britain over the last few decades. Comparisons with the *Old Atlas* confirm a decline in range with a loss of 13 squares, compared with a gain of just two. All squares, whether gains or losses, are at the periphery of the range and may only involve a handful of tetrads and certainly there does not seem to have been any impact on the core of the range. The reasons for this decline are uncertain. Suggestions have included increased visitor pressure in the hills, afforestation, competition with the Mistle Thrush and the Blackbird, the sibling species of the Ring Ouzel, as well as climatic warming. None of these reasons can properly explain the more recent decline seen in SE Scotland where birds have all but disappeared from several valleys since the 1985-86 survey, despite a lack of any discernible alteration in the habitat or its management. In the author's opinion the decline has little to do with what occurs in the breeding range in summer, and the causes may more likely be found in the wintering range in North Africa, where a nine-year drought together with some environmental change such as over-grazing of Juniper, has perhaps increased winter mortality. A survey organised by the RSPB started in 1997 to investigate this decline further.

The *New Atlas* abundance map indicates that SE Scotland holds a considerable proportion of the British Ring Ouzel population, comparable with the best areas of the eastern and northern Highlands and the Pennines. Five local centres of abundance can be seen corresponding to the Lammermuir, Moorfoot, Tweedsmuir, Cheviot and Liddesdale Hills. The Pentlands show up poorly, a fact confirmed by the low number of occupied tetrads on our map. The Cheviot population is larger on the English side of the boundary (*Day*).

In prime habitat it is difficult to give accurate estimates of population densities in terms of pairs per square kilometre, as breeding territories tend to be arranged linearly along water courses with nests about 500m apart. In moorland areas dissected by many streams, as in the Moorfoots, densities of up to 34prs/km^2 have been found (Poxton 1987). Taking this figure for the best areas, and with a knowledge of the extent of suitable habitat in the remaining tetrads with Ring Ouzel registrations, an estimate of the SE Scotland population is in the order of 300 pairs. Supporting this estimate, the count for the northern hills in 1986-87 revealed 143 territories, while a partial survey for part of the Borders in 1994 (*BBR* 15:44-45) revealed 122 territories.

The *New Atlas* population estimate used figures of 10-20prs/km^2 per occupied 10-km square which suggests a local population of 350-700 pairs. However, just less than half of all occupied squares on the map have Ring Ouzels in just one or two tetrads. Omitting these squares would bring this total down to 210-420 pairs, more in line with the 300 pairs estimated from local surveys. With the 300 pairs in SE Scotland representing just 2.5-5% of the *New Atlas* British population estimate, but clearly seen to be a large element of the British population in the abundance map, the BTO's calculation of the British population seems to be very much overestimated.

I.R.Poxton

Ring Ouzel

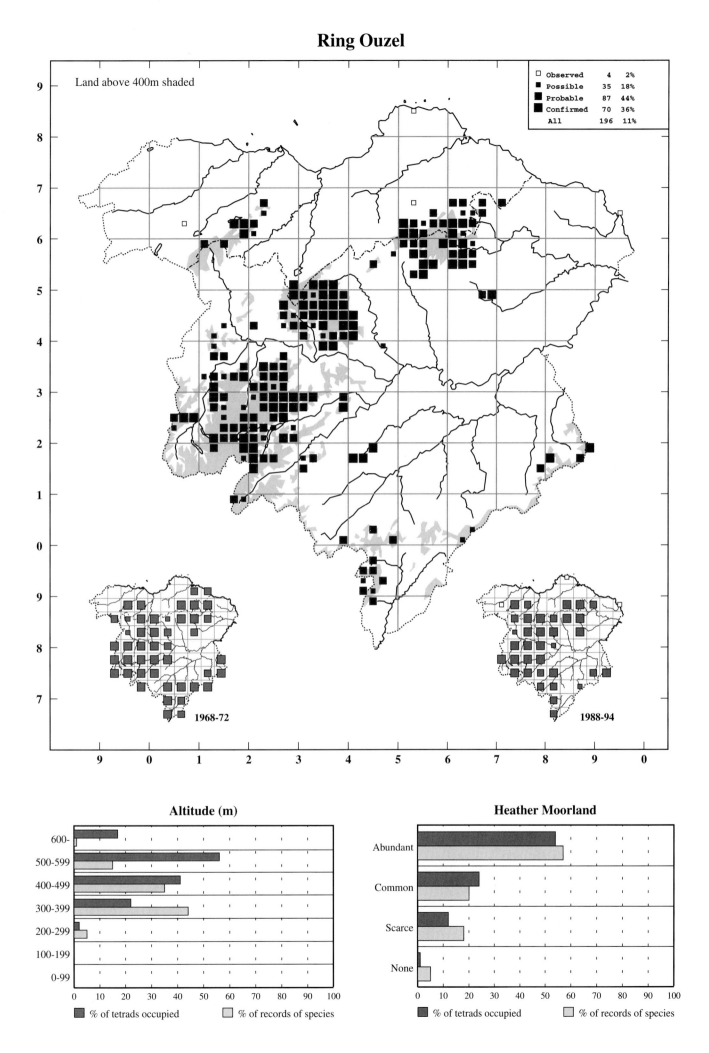

Land above 400m shaded

□ Observed	4	2%
■ Possible	35	18%
■ Probable	87	44%
■ Confirmed	70	36%
All	196	11%

1968-72

1988-94

Altitude (m)

■ % of tetrads occupied   ☐ % of records of species

Heather Moorland

■ % of tetrads occupied   ☐ % of records of species

Blackbird
Turdus merula

The Blackbird belongs to that select group of birds that are instantly recognisable to most of the population of Britain. It is in the top three most common breeding species in Britain, only the Wren and Chaffinch being more numerous, and being larger and more conspicuous, makes it familiar to most people. The Blackbird is also common throughout Britain, being found in almost every habitat with the exception of high mountains where it is partly replaced by the Ring Ouzel. It is naturally a bird of woodland edge and scrub that has adapted successfully to man-made habitats, ranging from farmland hedgerows to the most urbanised settlements. It has a very catholic diet, switching between invertebrates, seeds and fruit.

Blackbirds were fairly easy to record and consequently only 6% of records fell outwith the probable and confirmed categories, mostly involving tetrads near the upper limit of the range in the hill country and in dense plantations where Blackbirds were fairly uncommon. Only a handful of species had a higher rate of confirmed breeding due to the ease with which adults carrying food and fledged young could be observed. Probable breeding records were mostly of paired birds and alarming adults.

The map shows that Blackbirds are extremely widespread in SE Scotland, ranking eighth equal with the Song Thrush on that score. The principal gaps in the distribution occur in the Pentland, Moorfoot, Lammermuir, Tweedsmuir and Cheviots Hills, in areas mostly devoid of woodland vegetation. Some of the more isolated moorlands such as Coldingham Moor (NT86P&U) and Shiningpool Moss (NT65W&NT75B) stand out from the otherwise fully-occupied areas of lower ground. In some areas of the hills the Ring Ouzel takes over the thrush niche, possibly excluding the Blackbird, but there are many tetrads where neither lives and other tetrads where both occur, although rarely in the same location within the tetrad.

Blackbirds are so successful that they breed on several of the Forth islands, namely Inchmickery (NT28A), Inchkeith (NT28W), Craigleith (NT58N) and Inchcolm (Fife).

The altitude graph supports the near-universal nature of the Blackbird's distribution in lowland SE Scotland, with birds present in 90% of all tetrads below 400m. The lack of suitable habitat above 400m is demonstrated by the fact that only 5% of occupied tetrads occur above that altitude. The Blackbird's ability to prosper in man-made environments can be seen in the habitat graph which shows that all but 10% of Blackbirds were registered in tetrads where arable farming is a dominant activity. Although Blackbirds do breed in areas dominated by commercial forestry there are a number

of tetrads in such habitats where Blackbirds appear to be either absent or only registered as possibly breeding. These are mostly even-aged, closed canopy forests at fairly high altitudes such as Craik (NT30&31), Newcastleton-Wauchope-Leithope (NY59,NT60 &70) and Tweedsmuir (NT01&02). Isolated tetrads elsewhere in similar habitat, such as along the Leithen Water (NT34C,D&I), also lack Blackbirds.

Not surprisingly, with such a widespread species there is no difference in the 10-km square distributions between the *Old Atlas* and the current survey, the Blackbird breeding in all 10-km squares in both periods.

The *New Atlas* abundance map mirrors the local tetrad map in showing centres of low abundance in all of the hill areas, surrounded by fairly wide areas of moderate to low abundance. Blackbirds are only really abundant in lowland areas, the Lothian coastal plain and the Tweed valley being easily differentiated from the emptier hill areas. Although Blackbirds are widespread on the middle ground, the abundance map clearly suggests that only moderate numbers extend into the passes between the hills along the Esk, Lyne, Eddleston, Gala and Leader Waters. The scarcity of birds in the areas of extensive commercial forestry in southern Roxburghshire is also evident. In national terms therefore, there are only about average numbers of Blackbirds in SE Scotland.

While Blackbirds are ubiquitous they do not occur uniformly in all woodland habitats. Local studies show a wide variation in density of up to 200prs/km^2 in regenerating scrub (*Andrews*), and *c.*100prs/km^2 in urban gardens at three sites (200ha) in and around Edinburgh (da Prato 1989). Farmland densities are much lower with just 8prs/km^2 in open farmland near Tranent (da Prato 1985). Numbers are also low in commercial forestry, and Blackbirds were not among the 13 most frequently found species in conifer forests at either Kielder or Cowal (Patterson *et al.* 1995). Local BBS returns suggest an average of *c.*10-12prs/km^2.

Nationally, the CBC figures show 26prs/km^2 in farmland and 60prs/km^2 in woodland, with Scotland firmly at the low end of the density rankings in Britain (*Trends*). In estimating the British population the *New Atlas* figure was based on 16.5prs/km^2. Given that some occupied 10-km squares in SE Scotland contain fair numbers of vacant tetrads, and that numbers are probably very low in commercial conifer forests, a lower value of around 11prs/km^2 is used to assess the local population at 64,000 pairs or 1.5% of the national population.   *R.D.Murray*

Blackbird

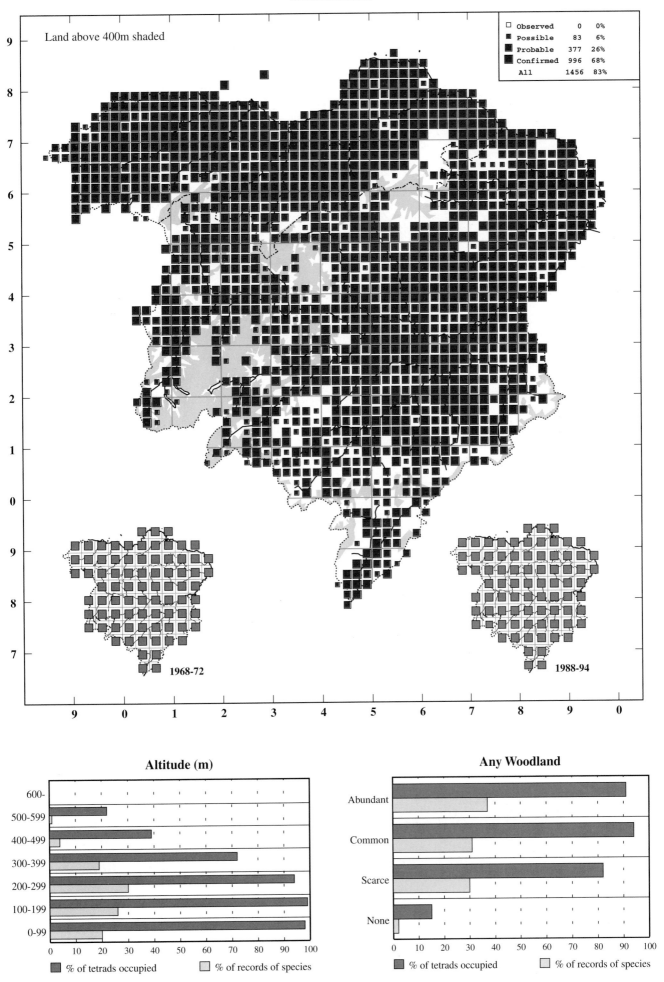

Land above 400m shaded

☐ Observed	0	0%
■ Possible	83	6%
■ Probable	377	26%
■ Confirmed	996	68%
All	1456	83%

1968-72

1988-94

Altitude (m)

■ % of tetrads occupied
■ % of records of species

Any Woodland

■ % of tetrads occupied
■ % of records of species

229

Fieldfare
Turdus pilaris

The Fieldfare is a widespread and numerous winter visitor to Britain. This large thrush, conspicuous in winter with its loud and far-carrying 'chacking' calls, largely vacates Britain in April when migrating flocks move north and eastwards through the country. However, since the first breeding in the 1960s, a very small number have remained to breed in Scotland and northern England.

Just a little over 40 records were submitted during the *Atlas* period over the seven years, but this number is higher than usually reported because *Atlas* fieldworkers were exploring areas not normally visited. All reports were chance discoveries as there is no history of regular occupation in the area. Large flocks, some well over 1,000 birds, move through SE Scotland in April and smaller groups are often reported in early May. There appears to be a large scale undocumented passage route across SE Scotland in spring, possibly birds moving from Ireland and returning to Scandinavia (SBR). These records were not collected for the *Atlas*. Most records submitted referred to single birds in potential breeding habitat, with a few records of singing males. The probable records were all of alarming birds in suitable habitat, but no further evidence was obtained. In some cases, birds found on one date were searched for again, but usually could not be relocated. Additional records submitted to the *Bird Reports* were used to supplement the data gathered during *Atlas* fieldwork.

Two records of confirmed breeding were received, both in 1994 and both of birds carrying food for young. In neither case was a nest or fledged birds found. At Baddinsgill Burn in the Pentlands (NT15C) an adult was watched collecting food from the banks of the burn and then seen flying behind a small pine plantation, but it could not be relocated. In May, at Deadwater near Kielder on the English border (NY69D), an adult was also seen carrying food, but it flew into England and also was not seen again. These are the second and third confirmed breeding records for Borders, following one recently fledged juvenile on the Corsehope Burn near Heriot (NT45B) in June 1985. There have been no breeding records for Lothian.

Despite the scarcity of this species in summer, there is a clear pattern to the distribution of records. Most records are in the hill ranges with concentrations in the Pentlands, Moorfoots and Lammermuirs, with a few in coastal and lowland Berwickshire. The altitude graph supports this observation with the bulk of sightings between 200m and 400m. Birds seem to occur in isolated hill glens with a few trees but some are in more open sites along the edges of shelter belts. There is no shortage of this kind of habitat in SE Scotland and breeding pairs could easily be going unrecorded. On the continent, Fieldfares tend to nest in small colonies. In SE Scotland, there are only isolated pairs or individuals, and Fieldfares can hardly be considered established yet.

Very few sites record Fieldfares in more than one year, although those that do tend to be near birders' houses or at well watched sites. Thus, near Blyth Bridge (NT14H), pairs or territorial birds were recorded in three out of the five years between 1984-1988 and three sites were found near Stow (NT44) in 1993-94. There are also a number of records in the Gladhouse area, including observations in two consecutive years. There are only four instances of birds being seen more than once in the same season during the *Atlas* period. A bird held territory near Blyth Bridge in 1988, and one heard singing in late May 1990 at nearby Wester Happrew (NT14Q) preceded a record of three Fieldfares roosting with local Mistle and Song Thrushes in early September – this is highly suggestive of local breeding. In 1989 a record of a bird seen at the Dye Water in the Lammermuirs (NT65E) in May was followed by an alarming bird at the same site in June. Finally a singing male was present near Auchencrow (NT86K) for ten days in late May 1994.

The Fieldfare is a recent colonist to the area, and only one record of possible breeding was mapped in the *Old Atlas*. The second graph plots the number of all known sites where potentially breeding Fieldfares were reported in Lothian and Borders from the *Bird Reports* and this *Atlas*, and shows that the number has varied from zero to a maximum of nine in 1989. Although there appears to have been an increase in records since 1987, most of this may be due to *Atlas* fieldwork rather than a true increase in the numbers of breeding Fieldfares. Only two summer records of Fieldfares were reported in 1995: a single bird in the Moorfoots in early August and another in central Edinburgh at the end of that month. This drop may be because of the cessation of *Atlas* fieldwork in 1994. The annual breeding population in SE Scotland probably normally falls between zero and five pairs, perhaps up to ten in some years, with most pairs going unrecorded in any one year. The British total is thought to be fewer than 25 pairs (*New Atlas*) but this will also probably be an underestimate of the true population.

To document the future of this species locally, all records of singles and pairs seen between May and August should be reported to the local Bird Recorders. Where possible, attempts should be made to relocate the birds. The species is monitored annually by the Rare Breeding Birds Panel.

M.Holling

Fieldfare

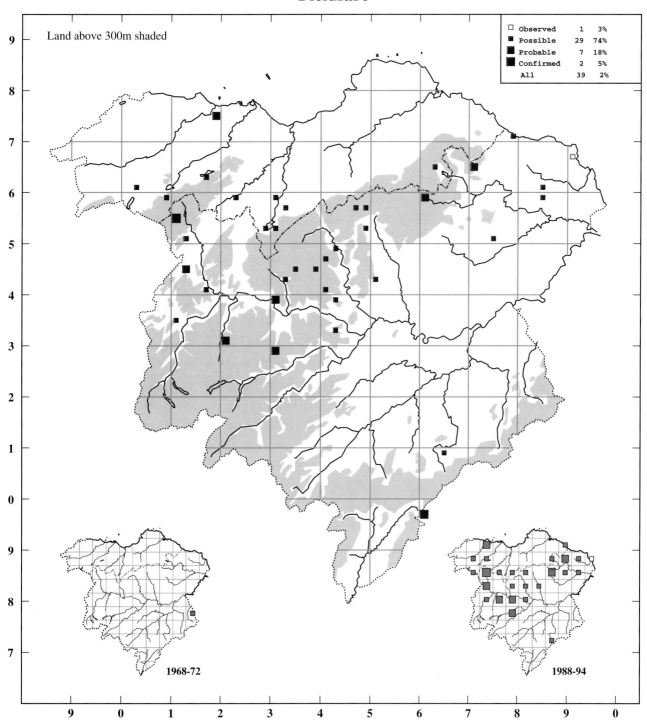

Land above 300m shaded

	Observed	1	3%
■	Possible	29	74%
■	Probable	7	18%
■	Confirmed	2	5%
	All	39	2%

1968-72

1988-94

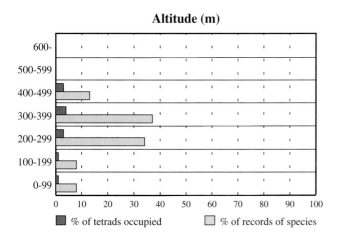

Altitude (m)

■ % of tetrads occupied ☐ % of records of species

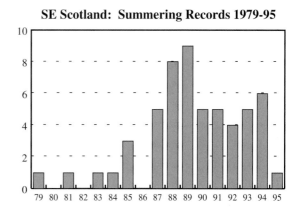

SE Scotland: Summering Records 1979-95

Song Thrush
Turdus philomelos

Like all thrushes, the Song Thrush is primarily a bird of woodland-edge habitats, occupying a range of environments that includes wooded policies, conifer plantations, gardens and hedgerows. Song Thrushes avoid treeless habitats such as open moorland and rough grazing and so are scarce or absent in hill country. The diet is more dependent on invertebrates compared to that of the Blackbird, Song Thrushes being renowned for their liking for snails. In reality snails are only a 'fallback' prey when other soil invertebrates are difficult to obtain. The problem of finding sufficient food is probably the reason why almost all Song Thrushes quit SE Scotland in winter, leaving a few birds along the coast and in Edinburgh where food is presumably easier to obtain. They are amongst the first birds to return after winter, sometimes appearing in the first week of February.

Evidence of Song Thrush breeding was fairly easily obtained. Only 9% of records were in the possible category, mostly in upland areas where Song Thrushes become scarce. Given their habit of singing loudly from conspicuous perches it is not surprising that three-quarters of all probable records were of birds holding territory. Confirmed breeding was mostly through sightings of fledglings and of adults carrying food for their young. The main problem with the use of song for recording was that song tended to be confined to limited periods near dawn and dusk and rather rarely during the day. This may have had an effect on recording in the more remote locations, especially as most survey work in these areas was conducted in May and June when song intensity is also reduced.

The Song Thrush is one of the top ten most widespread species in SE Scotland, being found in almost the same number of tetrads as the Blackbird. The principal blank areas on the map are open, treeless hill habitats in the Pentlands (NT05&15), Moorfoots (NT34), Lammermuirs (NT55,56&66), Tweedsmuir Hills (NT01,02,11,12, 13,22&23), and the southern hills (NY48,49&NT81). Small outlying moors such as that along the Monynut Edge (NT76) also stand out as being vacant. The altitude graph shows that it is present in at least 80% of tetrads up to 400m, dropping to just 30-50% of tetrads above that level, presumably using hill cleughs and the upper edges of commercial forestry as suitable habitat. However, numbers above 400m are small, representing just 7% of all Song Thrush records.

Low-lying tetrads in East Lothian (NT57&58) and the Merse (NT73,74,84,85&95), dominated by intensive arable farmland, show vacant tetrads, but as many of these areas have extensive systems of hedgerows, it is not clear what is operating to exclude Song Thrushes from these areas. Birds were also present on Inchkeith (NT28W) but not on any other island. The 'all woodlands' habitat graph confirms that birds are present in 80-95% of tetrads that hold any amount of woodland in the area.

In the *New Atlas* maps the Song Thrush shows only moderate to low abundance through much of SE Scotland with only a few areas of higher abundance centred on the lower Esk and Tyne, middle Tweed and Teviot and near Biggar. It is interesting however that the largest area of moderately high abundance is at 200-300m elevation across the middle-to-upper Tweed and Teviot where forestry is widespread.

With both Blackbird and Song Thrush occupying a similar number of tetrads in the area, a comparison of their distributions is useful in teasing out the subtle distinctions between their requirements. Blackbirds occupy nearly all of the lowland tetrads with intensive arable farming where Song Thrushes are fewer or even absent. Near Tranent in arable farmland da Prato (1985) found Blackbird densities of 8prs/km^2 compared with only 5prs/km^2 for Song Thrush. An even larger difference was found in urban areas, da Prato (1989) recording 25 Song Thrush territories in 3 sites covering 200ha in Edinburgh and Tranent, which held 203 pairs of Blackbirds. Song Thrushes, on the other hand, are present in the huge conifer plantations that are less suitable for Blackbirds. Work on spruce forest populations in Kielder (Patterson *et al.* 1995) showed Blackbirds scarce where Song Thrushes were present in 10-12% of the plots in early spring. Fieldworkers were also very impressed by the good numbers of Song Thrushes that were present in areas like Craik Forest, both early in the season, when birds were actively singing, and later when broods were flying. CBC regional rankings show that Scotland lies sixth out of seven for numbers of Song Thrushes in farmland compared to other parts of Britain but is ranked third for woodland habitats (*Trends*).

Occupying 100% of the 10-km squares means that comparisons with the map from the *Old Atlas* are not helpful. However, the expansion of commercial forestry into areas previously dominated by moorland must have allowed Song Thrushes to expand into new areas of southern Roxburghshire.

Song Thrush numbers in Britain have been giving cause for concern (*Trends*) for some years with estimates that the population has dropped from over three million in the *Old Atlas* to less than one million in the *New Atlas*. While such a drastic decline may well have occurred in southern England, there is little evidence in SE Scotland that any such drop has occurred locally. Indeed the large numbers found in conifer plantations, in areas where there could only have been few birds in earlier years, makes a mockery of the epitaphs for the Song Thrush that periodically appear in the ornithological literature.

With only moderate abundance, the SE Scotland population is likely to be a minor element of the British total. The *New Atlas* uses a figure of 4prs/km^2 across the whole of Britain compared with da Prato's figure of 8prs/km^2 for farmland around Tranent, and *c.*12.5prs/km^2 in urban habitats around Edinburgh, areas of high abundance in the *New Atlas*. Counts published in the *Bird Reports* from wooded sites in lowland Lothian (Blackford, Roslin, Prestongrange and Bawsinch) show a range of figures around 10-14prs/km^2, while mainly open habitats at Aberlady manage just 0.5prs/km^2. Local BBS data suggest 4-5prs/km^2. A value of 5prs/km^2, close to the national figure, would give a local population of 29,000 pairs.

R.D.Murray

Song Thrush

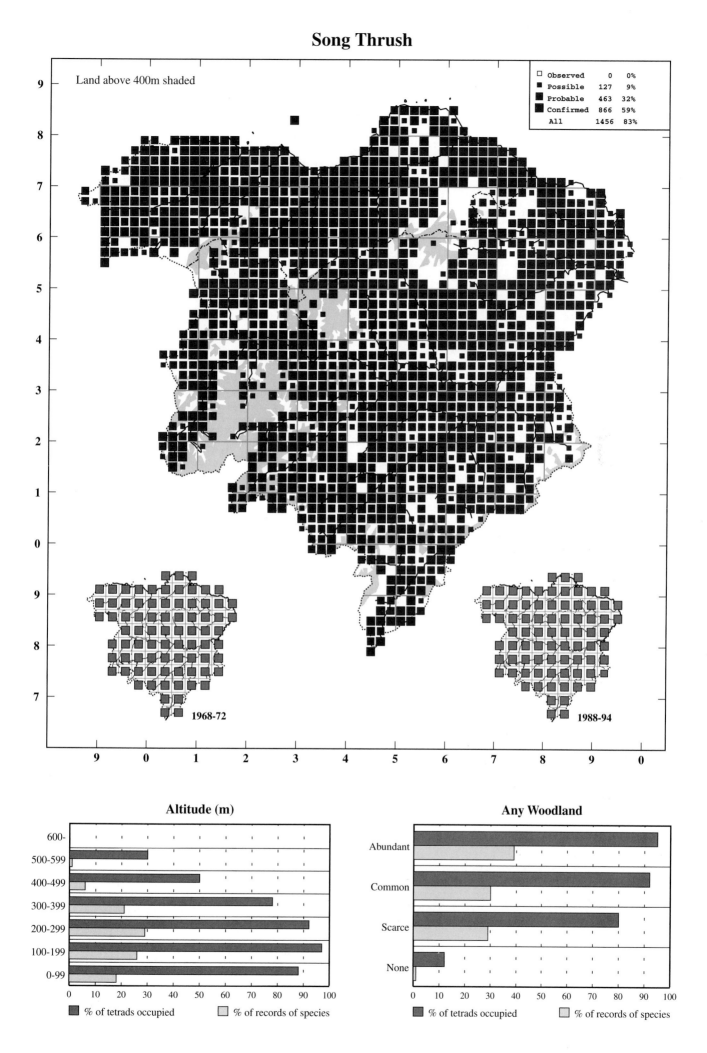

Land above 400m shaded

□ Observed	0	0%
■ Possible	127	9%
■ Probable	463	32%
■ Confirmed	866	59%
All	1456	83%

1968-72

1988-94

Altitude (m)

■ % of tetrads occupied   ■ % of records of species

Any Woodland

■ % of tetrads occupied   ■ % of records of species

Mistle Thrush
Turdus viscivorus

This large conspicuous thrush is found throughout Britain where it is usually considered a rather shy bird of parks, gardens and open deciduous woodland, nesting high in trees. However, it is also commonly found on the edges of coniferous plantations and in open country where it can nest on small crags, in walls and in isolated trees. When disturbed it gives a characteristic rattling alarm call and flies to a high perch, or if in open country flies out of sight. In spring and summer it is usually found in pairs but from late summer through to early spring it is regularly seen in small flocks, although parties of over 50 birds occur annually. In southern Britain many Mistle Thrushes are sedentary, but in Scotland they undergo local movements and move to lower ground or fly further south in Britain for winter.

The clear and diagnostic song of the Mistle Thrush, its noisy alarm calls and its size and shape make this a relatively easy species to survey. However, later in the breeding season, once singing stops, it can be elusive and could have passed unrecorded in some areas. Probable records were shared by territorial and alarming birds while confirmed records were mostly adults carrying food for their young and the fledged young themselves.

Mistle Thrushes were fairly common in SE Scotland but were more frequently recorded in the western half of the area where birds are widespread along the foothills and valleys of hill areas. Indeed the altitude data show that three-quarters of birds were in tetrads between 100-400m and that birds were present across two-thirds of tetrads at these levels. The Pentlands, Moorfoots, southern Lammermuirs and the valleys penetrating the Tweedsmuir hills show a considerable density of occupied tetrads with the numbers in the northern Moorfoots (NT25&35) being conspicuous on the map, as is the finger of tetrads in the upper Tweed valley (NT01,02,12&13). Birds are absent from the highest, most treeless parts of the hills as witnessed by the gaps in the Tweedsmuirs (NT11,12,22&23), the Pentlands (NT05&15), the Lammermuirs (NT55,56,65&66) and Cooms Fell in Liddesdale (NY48&49). This again is confirmed by the tiny numbers of tetrads above 400m, just 8% of all registrations. Lowland areas are thinly occupied, comprising just 15% of occupied tetrads, except for parts of West Lothian immediately west of Edinburgh (NT07&17) which show densities of tetrads comparable to those seen in the Moorfoots. Elsewhere, however, the cereal areas of East Lothian and the Merse show a relatively low density of occupied tetrads although birds can exist in such areas in the excellent woodland policies around large country houses such as Floors castle (NT73C,D,H&I), the Hirsel (NT84F&G) or on the steeper banks of the Tweed (NT84X&Y). While birds are present in central Edinburgh, gaps are also evident

in the ring of suburbs to the west, south and east of the city where the lack of large parks and woodlands may exclude Mistle Thrushes. The close-ranked extensive conifer plantations of Craik (NT30) and Wauchope (NT50&51) also seem to be lightly occupied and this is supported by the habitat data that indicate that there were similar rates of occupancy for mixed and deciduous woods and for coniferous woods where they are scarce or common, but in the abundant category a lower rate of occupancy for coniferous woods (70%) than for mixed and deciduous woods (78%). Because of the general similarity the graph shown is for any woodland.

Like all widespread species, comparisons between the *Old Atlas* and *New Atlas* yield little information, but there was a minor spread on the Berwickshire coast (NT87) where birds may have been missed in 1968-72. The *New Atlas* abundance map shows areas of highest abundance between the Pentlands and the northern Moorfoots, western Tweeddale and the middle Tweed, where the density of occupied tetrads was also high. In contrast it shows an area of good numbers in the eastern Lammermuirs that appears as only moderately filled in NT76, while the area to the west of Edinburgh that has many occupied tetrads is shown to have few birds. Other discrepancies exist in western West Lothian and in the upper Teviot and Ettrick. These are areas of low numbers on the BTO map but of moderate tetrad density on the map opposite. Whatever the difference in the details of the maps, there is broad agreement that Mistle Thrushes are reasonably numerous across SE Scotland.

Mistle Thrushes are the least abundant of the common thrushes, Simms (1978) quoting ratios of 1:6 with Song Thrush and 1:18 between Mistle Thrush and Blackbird in parkland where all three species breed together. These ratios will be very different in upland woods where Mistle Thrushes occur in greater numbers. Average breeding densities of 2-5prs/km^2 are quoted by Simms in farmland and woodland, reaching a maximum of 10prs/km^2. *Andrews* noted 4-7prs/km^2 in small areas of woodland (<1km^2) in Lothian where the best totals are at Gladhouse which regularly holds 5-6 pairs (4.3prs/km^2). da Prato (1985) only found 0.5prs/km^2 on arable land near Tranent, but Holling (*pers.comm.*) noted 3prs/km^2 in the Gala Water WBS plot and local BBS returns indicate 2-3prs/km^2. At 2.5prs/km^2 a local population of 10,500 pairs is indicated, 4.5% of the British population, a little high for SE Scotland's proportion of the British mainland but in line with the abundance figures seen in the *New Atlas*.

Singing Mistle Thrushes are easy to count in the early spring and sample densities in a range of habitats could provide a more accurate population estimate in the future.   ***I.R.Poxton***

Mistle Thrush

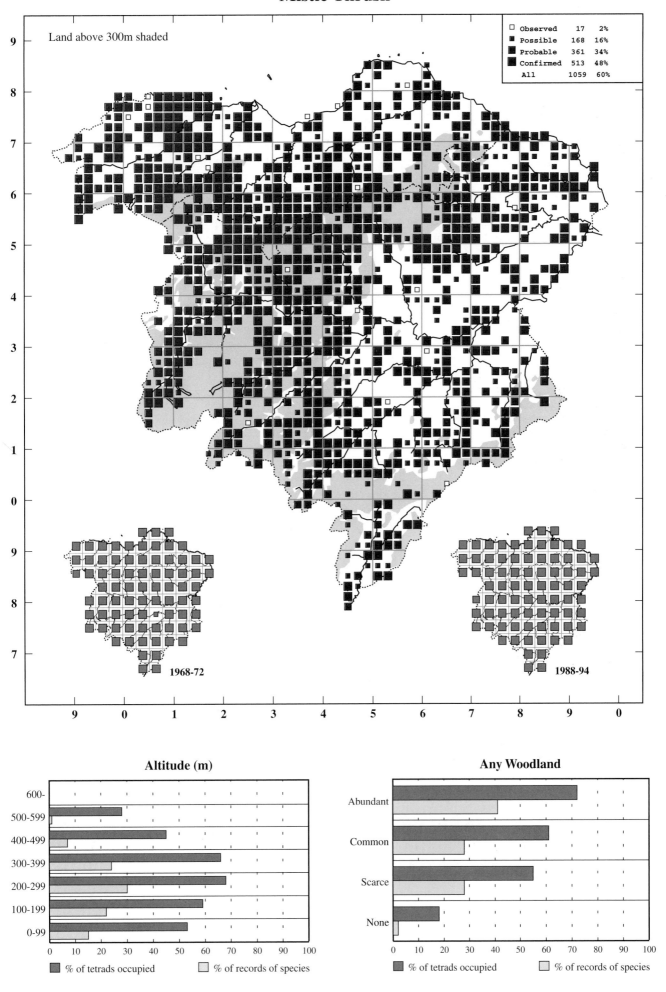

Land above 300m shaded

☐ Observed	17	2%
■ Possible	168	16%
■ Probable	361	34%
■ Confirmed	513	48%
All	1059	60%

1968-72

1988-94

Altitude (m)

■ % of tetrads occupied   ☐ % of records of species

Any Woodland

■ % of tetrads occupied   ☐ % of records of species

235

Grasshopper Warbler
Locustella naevia

A constant churring from an area of tall ground cover, too loud to be a grasshopper and often continuing throughout the night, is typically the only indication that a Grasshopper Warbler is present. Even seeing the bird scuttling mouse-like through deep grass is difficult, as it can be extremely elusive and anxious not to be detected. Any habitat with a tall rank herb layer can be attractive to Grasshopper Warblers, ranging from any ungrazed open ground such as young plantation or low scrub to wet marshy margins of water bodies. Thick ground cover, low song perches and plenty of invertebrate food are essentials.

Grasshopper Warblers are difficult to find. Only the song gives away their position but unfortunately much of the singing occurs at night. In the remoter parts of SE Scotland and in the large areas of commercial forestry, this must have led to the species being under-recorded. Many supplementary records were extracted from the *Bird Reports* to present a fuller picture. Half of all records were of birds singing on just a single occasion, particularly in the remoter parts of the Borders, where re-visiting a tetrad, possibly at night, was not feasible to upgrade a record to probable by registering it as a territory. The probable records are almost wholly of territorial birds, many being instances of birds singing against each other. Confirmed records, at a lowly 8%, were mostly of adults carrying food for young and fledged young.

The map shows a species thinly spread through mostly low-lying areas of SE Scotland. The distribution is patchy, occurring in pockets of suitable habitat along the Almond drainage (NT06,07&17) in rank canal and riverside vegetation, the upper Tyne (NT36&46) in hedges and scrub along the abandoned railway line, the middle Tweed (NT53) in young plantation and basin mires, the Kale Water (NT72,73,82) in hedges and the fringes of wet habitats, the low-lying parts of East Lothian (NT57&58) in tall meadow and scrub and on the Berwickshire coast (NT85,86&96) in hedges and young plantation. In general the more isolated records in the southern part of the map are associated with young conifer plantation. With a small number of records and such diverse habitats used by Grasshopper Warblers, all habitat relationships proved to be rather weak. In terms of altitude, 70% of of all records were from areas below 200m, although birds were present in just 20% of the tetrads located between sea level and 200m. The range in Lothian must be a truer reflection of the actual distribution than will be the case in the

Borders, especially in the remoter areas. With their habit of nocturnal singing, survey visits during daylight hours must have missed many birds. Indeed, many of the few records in the south were recorded on overnight visits to remote areas by survey teams, such as at Craik (NT31), Scotch Kershope (NY58) and the Kale Valley (NT71). Others were heard when touring likely areas for Quail on summer nights.

Grasshopper Warblers can be erratic, both in their appearance at a site and in site fidelity in later years (Parslow 1973, *Day*). Numbers may be dependent on the strength of the spring passage. In years when there are good numbers at coastal migration points, there are usually good numbers and the converse is true of poor springs. Although more birds are being reported now compared to the 1980s, there is constant variation between years (see graph). Poor site fidelity means that of 160 sites in SE Scotland where Grasshopper Warblers were reported between 1979 and 1993, only 43 had birds reported there in more than a single year (*Bird Reports*). The *Old Atlas* ascribes this lack of fidelity to habitat change between years (ploughing, change of crop, etc.) but the strength of the spring passage may be a better explanation, although the vagaries of the recording effort by birders may play a part.

There has been a massive reduction of Grasshopper Warblers in Britain since the *Old Atlas* period (*Trends*). Numbers increased in the 1960s but crashed between 1971-74 and again in 1984. The reasons for these population changes are not known. Despite the *New Atlas* showing considerable losses in our area since 1968-72 (23 losses, seven gains), the current *Atlas* survey shows that Grasshopper Warblers actually occurred in three more 10-km squares in the 1988-94 period compared to 1968-72. The *New Atlas* methodology, with its emphasis on the two-hour visits to tetrads, was not structured to best gather records of this species. Whether there has been any long-term variation in the *range* of this species in our area is therefore questionable. Bearing in mind the erratic nature of site occupancy and the variation of numbers from year to year, it is unlikely that the historic literature is helpful in answering this question.

The numbers of Grasshopper Warblers reported in SE Scotland in any year between 1988-94 varied between 30-48 birds at 18-31 sites, comprising a total of *c*.150 sites over the whole period (*Bird Reports*). Most only held single birds and many, particularly those along the coast, may only have been passage migrants that sang for a brief period before moving on. In total, 43 sites held birds in more than a single year but many other sites were never re-visited in later years and so it is not possible to say with certainty which sites had passage birds, and which may have held birds in other years and which stayed to hold territories. A few sites have regularly attracted numbers of Grasshopper Warblers over a number of years: Aberlady (2-4), Alemill (2-6 at NT96B), Bawsinch (1-3 at NT27W), Ormiston (2-11 at NT46E), St. Abbs (1-5) and Turnhouse (1-4 at NT17S); while some others discovered on one-off visits have held more than 1-2 birds (e.g. 3 at Swinside NT71H).

In his study of farmland around Tranent da Prato (1985) found densities of 0.34prs/km^2. Grasshopper Warblers rarely register on the BBS survey. The erratic, fluctuating nature of Grasshopper Warbler numbers means that only an approximate number can be estimated. From the *Bird Reports* a likely figure might be between 50-150 singing males in any year, depending on the strength of the passage in late April and early May, although with under-recording in many areas the actual total may be two or three times higher. The *New Atlas* optimistically suggests 10 pairs per occupied 10-km square but with birds present in 58 squares this would raise the total to nearly 600 pairs, probably too great. A total population of perhaps 250 pairs may be on the high side but realistic when the problems of such a furtive species are considered.   ***R.D.Murray***

Grasshopper Warbler

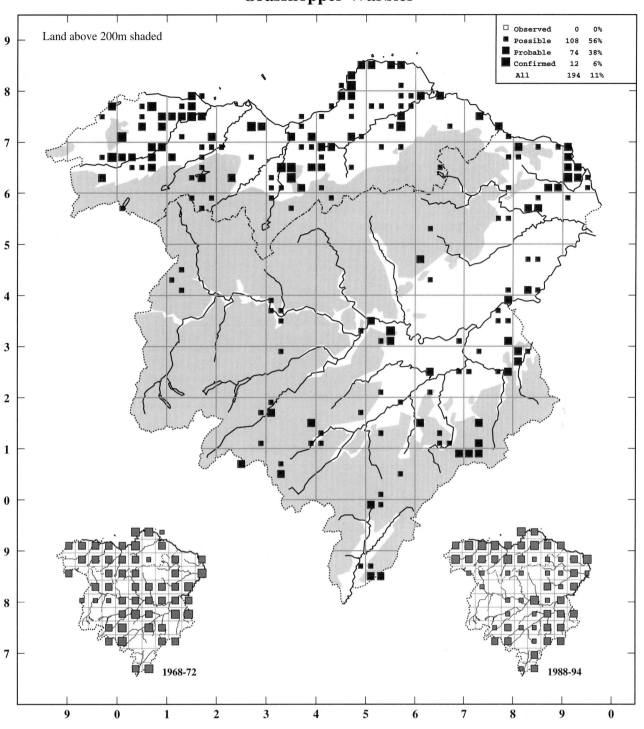

Land above 200m shaded

□	Observed	0	0%
■	Possible	108	56%
■	Probable	74	38%
■	Confirmed	12	6%
	All	194	11%

1968-72

1988-94

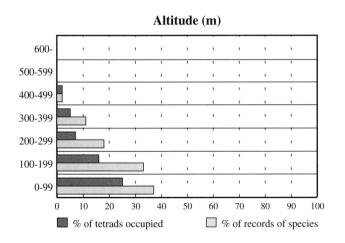

Altitude (m)

■ % of tetrads occupied   ▫ % of records of species

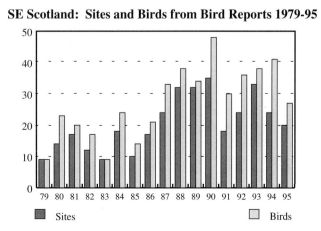

SE Scotland: Sites and Birds from Bird Reports 1979-95

■ Sites   ▫ Birds

Sedge Warbler
Acrocephalus schoenobaenus

A loud chatter or a scolding 'chuck' from a patch of dense cover usually announces the presence of a Sedge Warbler. Cover is the common denominator of Sedge Warbler habitat, be it a reed-bed, willow carr, thick hedgerow, dense scrub or even an oil-seed rape field, a habitat recently colonised by the species. Although song can be given in a display flight, the rapid chattering is more typically delivered from within cover between late April and June.

Due to their song and the often linear habitats they inhabit, Sedge Warblers were not difficult to find. Evidence was mostly associated with song, with most of the possible records referring to singing birds and two-thirds of the probable records to territorial birds. With nests typically well hidden in scrub it is not surprising that 90% of the confirmed records were of adults with food for their young.

The map of Sedge Warbler distribution shows features that resemble the map of arable and improved grassland for SE Scotland. While dense populations of Sedge Warblers are associated with wetlands such as Aberlady, Bavelaw, Gladhouse, Yetholm and others, their ability to live in drier habitats has allowed them a much wider distribution. The resemblance of the local range to that of the distribution of arable farmland supports the view that Sedge Warblers live widely in hedges, the overgrown corners of farmland, 'waste' ground such as disused railways and bings, and along the ungrazed margins of the river system where scrub can develop. Oil seed rape fields, a habitat preference recently acquired, are now widely used in areas of intensive arable farming. These microhabitats within the overall classification of arable land are by no means continuous and so the Sedge Warbler distribution is generally discontinuous and patchy. There is a noticeable cluster of tetrads around the valley of the Almond in West Lothian (NS96,NT07&17) with less marked concentrations between the South Esk and Tyne (NT36,46&57), Dunbar (NT67) and in the middle Tweed (NT63&73). Away from the low ground, Sedge Warblers are able to penetrate right up into the hills along the river valleys, birds being registered near the sources of many rivers, but markedly so up the Lyne, Yarrow, Ettrick, Teviot, Gala, Leader and Kale, mostly in riverside scrub.

The association with rivers and lowlands is supported by the altitude data that show that birds were present in just over half of all tetrads below 200m and that almost 90% of birds were found below 300m. As Sedge Warblers occur in a number of habitat types, relationships can be demonstrated with a number of variables. Birds are present in about half of all tetrads with small to medium sized waterbodies, with 40% of birds in tetrads with small ponds and lochs (see graph). A weaker relationship occurs with wetland habitats but even then about half of tetrads with such habitat are still occupied.

With Sedge Warblers being widespread and present in most 10-km squares, only a little information can be gained from comparison with the *Old Atlas*. Only one marginal 10-km square (NT01) shows a loss, while seven others have evidence of breeding now where none occurred in 1968-72. Most are marginal, involving only nine tetrads in all, except for NT44 which has better representation with six tetrads. Some gains and losses at the margins of the local distribution are to be expected but a slight range expansion is shown. Great changes have taken place in the British Sedge Warbler population since the *Old Atlas* with a widespread decrease through the 1970s and a recovery in numbers since 1985 related to climate in the sub-Saharan wintering grounds (*Trends*). The marginal gains may suggest that the recovery may have surpassed the levels seen at the time of the *Old Atlas* in SE Scotland.

The *New Atlas* abundance map indicates that SE Scotland holds good numbers of Sedge Warblers with three large areas of high abundance along the Berwickshire coast, up the Tweed to the Selkirk-Melrose area and along the Tyne drainage. While there is general agreement, the *New Atlas* map shows much of the southern Roxburghshire as being devoid of Sedge Warblers. *Atlas* fieldwork in these areas discovered pockets of high Sedge Warbler numbers both within the forestry areas, often on clear-fell and restocked areas, (three tetrads in NT30 at Craik held 34 singing males) and in wetlands (two tetrads in NT21 at Ettrick have held up to 24 singing males). As much *Atlas* fieldwork occurred there in the summers of 1992-94, after work for the *New Atlas* was completed, these records do not appear in the national publication. Similarly the concentration in West Lothian fails to show up on the abundance map. Whether birds are widespread there at low densities or whether there are weaknesses with the *New Atlas* count methodology is not known.

Local data from da Prato (1985) recorded Sedge Warblers at a mean density of 4prs/km² in arable farmland with scrub near Tranent in an area of moderate to high abundance on the BTO map. The *Bird Reports* show much higher numbers are present at sites such as Bavelaw (1988-94 mean 20prs/km²), Aberlady (18prs/km²), Gladhouse Reservoir (14.0prs/km²) and St.Abb's Head (14prs/km²). Away from these hot-spots, local BBS results suggest densities of 3-4prs/km². This is much higher than the overall 1-1.5prs/km² the BTO used for its assessment of the British population but as SE Scotland is shown as an area of good abundance in the *New Atlas*, a higher value than the average might be expected. Using the BTO densities would indicate about 3,200-3,600 pairs in our area while these locally-derived densities, even using a conservative figure of 3prs/km² for each occupied tetrad, would give a local population of 6,750 pairs, or about 2.7% of the British population. ***R.D.Murray***

Sedge Warbler

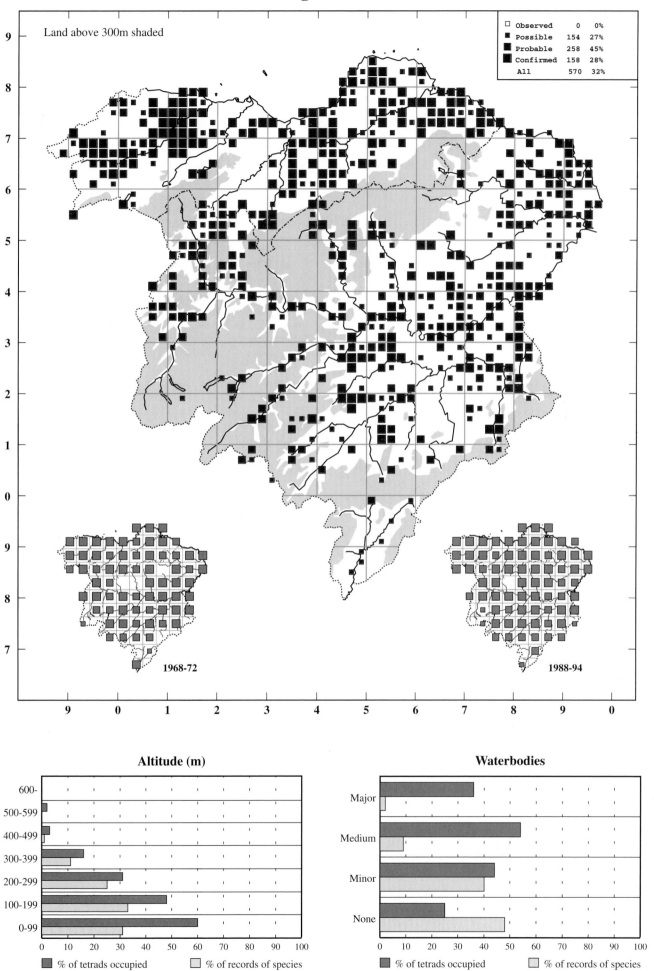

Land above 300m shaded

☐ Observed	0	0%
■ Possible	154	27%
■ Probable	258	45%
■ Confirmed	158	28%
All	570	32%

1968-72

1988-94

Altitude (m)

% of tetrads occupied   % of records of species

Waterbodies

% of tetrads occupied   % of records of species

Lesser Whitethroat

Sylvia curruca

While most British *Sylvia* warblers are skulkers, preferring to sing from hidden perches rather than in the open, the Lesser Whitethroat is more skulking than most. It is so inconspicuous that to many local birders it is hardly known and more familiar as a passage migrant in spring or autumn than as a breeding species. While it is a bird of parkland and farmland with tall, mature and dense hedges elsewhere in Britain, the population that lives on the northern limits of its range in Scotland seem to prefer thorn and gorse scrub, which compounds the difficulty of actually detecting the birds. The scrub-covered areas were often on warm south-facing banks, typically associated with regenerating scrub on or near old railway embankments, old quarries and the like.

This difficulty in finding Lesser Whitethroats was so acute that da Prato (1980) was prompted to describe the evidence that had been gathered to that date on the population in Lothian. Apart from the problems of finding birds in the densely-vegetated habitat, the song period of local Lesser Whitethroats was decidedly short or apparently non-existent in some cases. Indeed the only singing that occurred in one census plot was when an unmated cock appeared later in the season when the resident birds already had young. Byars *et al.* (1991) found that while Lesser Whitethroats in Strathclyde could be extremely vociferous, being audible up to 200m, the song period was only intense over a two-week period in early May, diminishing in both volume and intensity thereafter. The low density of birds in Scotland, and the resultant reduction in the need to sing to defend a territory, may be the the prime reason for the lack of song. In Lothian da Prato found that the best evidence for breeding was the numbers of dispersing juveniles caught in mist-nets in July and August.

The *Atlas* records reflect the problem of the short period of intense singing with about half of all records being only of possible status, almost entirely of birds heard singing on just one occasion. Raising the status of the evidence in a tetrad was more difficult but just over half of all probable records were of territorial birds, either birds found singing more than once or where birds were singing against one another in adjoining territories. A quarter of probable records were of anxious birds giving the distinctive alarm call from deep cover. Confirmed records, mostly fledged young and adults feeding young, were scarce but in percentage terms little different from that seen in other *Sylvia* warblers.

Lesser Whitethroats are mostly birds of low altitudes, 91% of all records occurring below 200m. Although inhabiting scrub, this is mostly in the setting of arable farmland, 87% of all records coming from tetrads where arable and improved grassland is abundant.

The map shows an essentially coastal distribution, 85% of occupied tetrads being in 10-km squares on or adjacent to the coast. This pattern is repeated in the altitudinal distribution where 91% of all records are between sea-level and 200m. The coastal records are fairly evenly distributed along the coastal lowland from Dalmeny to Eyemouth. The only obvious gaps are at Coldingham Moor (NT87) where grass and heather moorland reaches the coast, Prestonpans (NT37&47) and the built up areas of coastal Edinburgh. While heavily urbanised areas may preclude Lesser Whitethroats, the large city parks with dense unmanaged growth in Edinburgh at Duddingston, The Hermitage of Braid and Corstorphine Hill clearly provide the scrub cover needed, even within the city. The section of coast between Aberlady and Dirleton (NT48&58) stands out as a cluster and indeed it is in that area that the most continuous stretch of suitable habitat apparently exists in the dune scrub, spinneys and hedgerows lying just inland of the coastal dunes and golf links. Inland records are correspondingly rare. In da Prato's discussion of the detectability of Lesser Whitethroats in areas of low density, he hints that the small scatter of records in West Lothian and in the Tweed drainage, between Hawick, Galashiels, Lauder and Yetholm, may be the tip of a larger iceberg.

Comparison of the current Lesser Whitethroat range with that of the *Old Atlas* shows a huge expansion from just five 10-km squares in 1968-72 to 28 in the current project. The first confirmed breeding in Lothian was at Cousland (NT36Z) in 1972 and birds are thought to have bred ever since. The precise date of the first Borders record is not known but it is certain that breeding was taking place in the 1970s. Expansion seems to have been rapid and by 1986 *Andrews* and *Murray* could each list about 20 sites where breeding was known to have occurred. Breeding seems longest established in the Cousland-Tranent, Aberlady-Gullane and St. Abbs-Eyemouth areas and birds may have expanded outwards from these sites of initial colonisation. A similar range expansion has been seen nearby in Cumbria since 1970 and in neighbouring Northumberland since 1972 and birds have more recently been found breeding in NE Scotland, Speyside and even Caithness (*Trends, Day*).

In his review of the Lothian Ringing Group's records to 1980, da Prato estimated that the numbers of dispersing juveniles captured by the Group suggested that there could be as many as 50-100 pairs breeding in Lothian alone by that year, a number that was not even suspected by what was then known of the species locally. Since then da Prato (1985) found 20 territories in his Tranent study area alone, a density of 1.12prs/km^2. 20-25 pairs were estimated to be present in the Gullane-Yellowcraig area in 1989, while Aberlady regularly holds 5-7 territories (*Bird Reports*). Indeed wherever birds or sites have been closely studied, a much larger concentration of birds has been revealed than hitherto suspected. Away from these hot-spots much lower numbers are recorded, typically just 1-2 singing males. Whether these mask other birds is uncertain and as some tetrads undoubtedly refer to wandering unmated males singing in June and July, there is no simple formula to multiply the numbers of tetrads by the numbers known to exist in the hot-spots. However, even using a figure of 2 territories per occupied tetrad or 0.5prs/km^2, this would suggest 180-200 pairs regularly breeding in SE Scotland.

R.D.Murray

Lesser Whitethroat

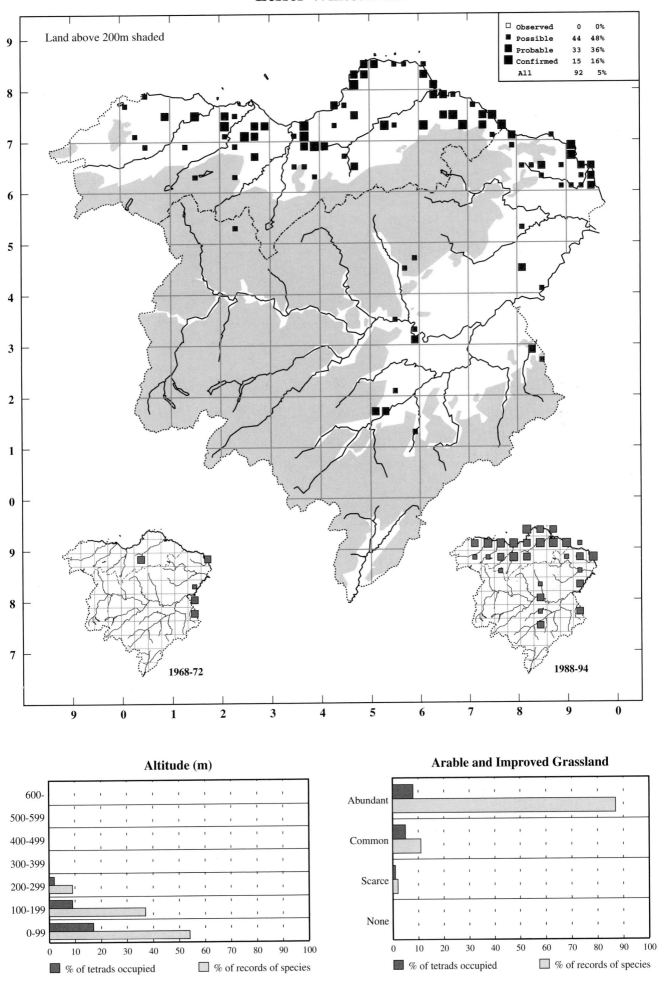

	Observed	0	0%
	Possible	44	48%
	Probable	33	36%
	Confirmed	15	16%
	All	92	5%

Land above 200m shaded

1968-72

1988-94

Altitude (m)

■ % of tetrads occupied   ■ % of records of species

Arable and Improved Grassland

■ % of tetrads occupied   ■ % of records of species

241

Whitethroat
Sylvia communis

Whitethroats are one of our more schizophrenic birds, alternating between bouts of skulking deep within dense cover and the need to suddenly show themselves from the top of a hedge or even to song flight. Their scratchy song starts in early May and can be heard mostly in arable areas from hedges and all manner of scrub. Thick ground cover is always needed so Whitethroats normally avoid woods where shading prevents a good growth of brambles and other plants suitable for feeding and nesting.

The linear nature of much of the habitat in SE Scotland, in hedges and the scrub along used and abandoned railway lines, helped in searching for this species. The song is readily identifiable, as are the scolding alarm calls, and this territorial behaviour accounted for 75% of all possible and probable records. Advertising flight displays also helped in the detection of birds. One third of all records were of confirmed breeding, mostly of adults feeding young.

Whitethroats are birds of arable land and this is reflected in the habitat and altitude data, which show most are found below 200m where arable farming is dominant. Indeed three-quarters of all birds were below 200m, a larger proportion than in some other birds of arable farmland such as the Yellowhammer. Although *Thom* dismisses hedges as being an important habitat for Whitethroat in Scotland, there is little doubt that in SE Scotland many birds do in fact live in such habitats, despite the poverty of over-trimmed hedges in certain parts of the area (da Prato 1985). Habitat data show that while Whitethroats occupy only half of the areas where arable is abundant, some 88% of all records came from such areas.

The low ground is fairly solidly occupied along most of the coastal lowlands from West Lothian to the Tweed except for the obvious gap on the heather and grass moor at Coldingham Moor (NT86&87) and in the urbanised parts of Edinburgh. Even in the city Whitethroats have managed to penetrate fairly well in all the suburbs and even along the Water of Leith towards Leith. Further inland the density

of tetrads drops, particularly in the Merse. This difference in density is seen in a number of other farmland species and could be partly due to the Merse being less thoroughly surveyed than the Lothians during the survey. However, the *New Atlas* abundance map also suggests that birds are much more numerous along the coast with few inland and so the difference may be real, possibly related to the intensity of farming, including the use of pesticides in the Merse.

The range only extends into inland areas via the rivers where fingers of occupied tetrads go short distances up the valleys of the Cheviot, Lammermuir and Tweedsmuir Hills. The only large area of higher ground occupied is in the Leader valley (NT54&55) where the range is almost continuous across the Moorfoots, failing only at the highest parts of Soutra. The Leader valley is slightly unusual in having a considerable extension of arable land between the Moorfoot and Lammermuir Hills almost linking with that of Midlothian just to the south of Pathhead. Further inland still, records are few and far between and may include occasional migrants. While altitudinal factors may be involved in these parts, the lack of extensive areas of arable ground may be more critical because although there are hedges in many stock-rearing areas, the grazing below these hedges may remove many critical features of the habitat needed by Whitethroats. This may account for the lack of birds in Liddesdale and the middle Tweed where stock-rearing dominates.

The *New Atlas* abundance map shows that Whitethroats are relatively scarce in SE Scotland when compared to further south and east in Britain. Even within the third of our area that actually holds Whitethroats, abundances are low to moderate with only two small pockets of high abundance around Musselburgh-Tranent and Aberlady-Drem.

Comparison with the *Old Atlas* shows some withdrawal from marginal 10-km squares in the hill areas, mostly to the south and west but also in NT65 in the Lammermuirs, all stock-rearing areas where hedges may be more overgrazed than they were in the past. Judging from the current occupancy in the upland 10-km squares it is reasonable to assume that only small numbers of birds in just a few tetrads were involved in these losses. With the large-scale reductions in the British Whitethroat population from the peak in the 1960s, it is hardly surprising that there should have been some withdrawal from marginal parts of the range, especially at higher altitudes (*Trends*). The pattern seen in the Borders hills matches that seen elsewhere in the hills of northern and western Britain in the *New Atlas*.

Whitethroat numbers in SE Scotland must have changed in recent years as the national population recovered from its lowest levels in the mid-1980s. This was when da Prato (1985) surveyed the birds of the Tranent area and found overall densities of 5.0prs/km^2 in an area that the *New Atlas* shows to hold high numbers of Whitethroats. Recent BBS survey results indicate about 3.0prs/km^2, although admittedly on a small sample. Nationally the *Old Atlas* calculated the British population on a basis of 2.0prs/km^2, the *New Atlas*, in a period of population recovery, using a slightly higher 3.0prs/km^2. If an overall figure of 3.0prs/km^2 is used for lowland tetrads below 200m, with 1.0prs/km^2 for higher elevations, a local population of 6,200 pairs is obtained, about 2% of the British population.

R.D.Murray

Whitethroat

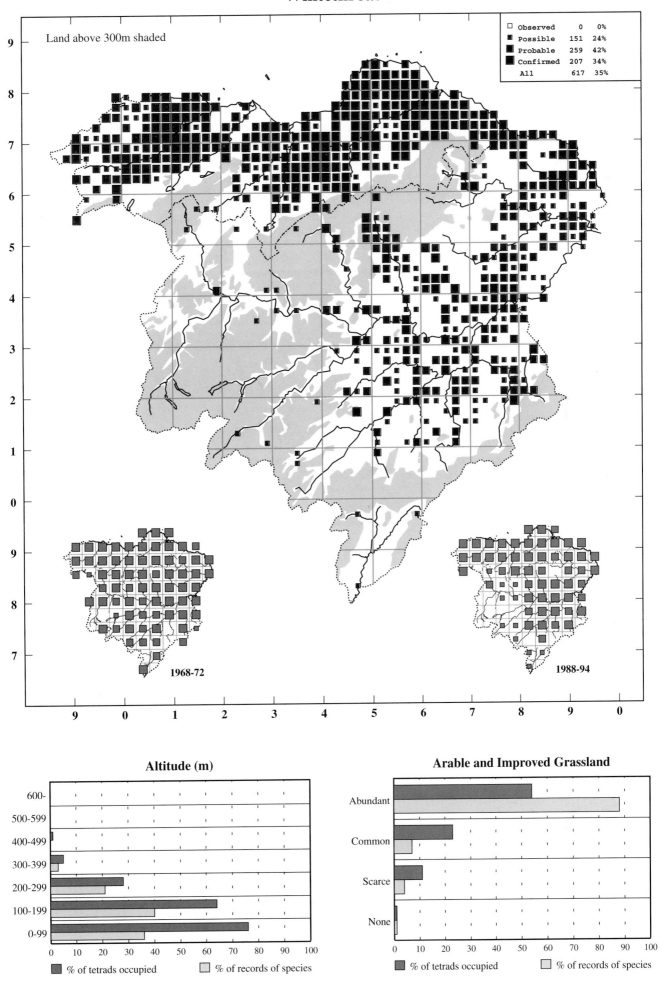

Land above 300m shaded

☐	Observed	0	0%
■	Possible	151	24%
■	Probable	259	42%
■	Confirmed	207	34%
	All	617	35%

1968-72

1988-94

Altitude (m)

- 600-
- 500-599
- 400-499
- 300-399
- 200-299
- 100-199
- 0-99

■ % of tetrads occupied   ■ % of records of species

Arable and Improved Grassland

- Abundant
- Common
- Scarce
- None

■ % of tetrads occupied   ■ % of records of species

243

Garden Warbler
Sylvia borin

The Garden Warbler is not so often seen as it is heard. Unlike many warblers this species lives up to its name, its babble of sweet, melodic and vigorous tones flowing effortlessly from the depths of tall bushes in open deciduous woodland and in large shrubby gardens. These woods typically have dense ground cover for nesting, through which this subdued-coloured, rather nondescript bird can forage for the insects and fruit it needs to feed its young.

As with any *Sylvia* warbler, many of the records came from singing birds. Unfortunately Garden Warbler song closely resembles that of the Blackcap, a species with which it is incompletely ecologically isolated resulting in competition between them for living space. Blackcaps arrive earlier in the spring and usually manage to exclude Garden Warblers by prior occupation of the habitat. Exclusion is done through song, the song of one species being so similar to the other that it can exclude males of both species. Garden Warbler song is usually more continuous, having shorter gaps between the individual phrases and is generally higher pitched, Blackcap being deeper and more mellow. In some cases, however, it is necessary to actually see the bird to convince yourself which species is present. Song was the main criterion for most possible and probable records through the singing of individual birds, birds singing against one another, or singing over the period of a week or more to register a territory. As in many skulking species, confirmed records were less frequent and mostly of adults carrying food for their young.

Garden Warblers live in mixed and deciduous woodland and preferentially inhabit areas where such habitats are relatively common or abundant as the graph illustrates. Despite this a third of records came from tetrads where these habitats were scarce, reflecting its ability to live in smaller and more open areas of deciduous woodland. While the map resembles that of the distribution of mixed and deciduous woods, both the map and the altitude data show a strong modification towards the edges of the hills between 100-300m where 65% of the records occur. These are mostly in the valleys along the fringes of the Pentlands, Moorfoots and Lammermuirs, and in the middle and upper parts of the Tweed and Teviot drainage. The valley woodlands of the Almond (NT06,16&17), lower Eye and Whiteadder (NT75, 85&86), middle Tweed (NT53,63&73) and Teviot-Jed (NT61&62) have good densities of occupied tetrads, as does the northern slope of the Lammermuirs near Dunbar (NT67). A quarter of all records were over 250m where the range penetrates the hills along valleys of the Tweed, Eddleston (NT24), Gala (NT44), Teviot (NT40), Rule (NT50), Jed (NT60) and Liddel (NY59), with outliers right at the head of some of the streams where the policy woodlands around large country houses provide suitable habitat. With only 9% of the birds found below 50m, approximately within 5km of the coast on the map, the relative lack of birds along the coast is striking. It is possible that this is an effect of the competition with the Blackcap which is more common at lower levels. Blackcaps may occupy the prime habitats at lower levels, leaving the less desirable territories to the later-arriving Garden Warbler.

Garden Warblers are not very numerous in SE Scotland according to the *New Atlas* abundance map, with only isolated patches of high numbers on the lower Eye and Whiteadder (NT95&96), around Melrose (NT53) and Gosford-Aberlady (NT47&48). The last area is surprising as there are few occupied tetrads there. It is also surprising that the numbers of birds that extend up the Tweed and Eddleston Water and along the north face of the Moorfoots are sufficient to register as moderately abundant on a national basis.

Comparisons with the *Old Atlas* show that change has taken place since 1968-72. While two 10-km squares well up on the extreme western fringe of our area have lost their Garden Warblers, some 14 squares show gains. The two squares showing losses since 1968-72 may only represent individual isolated tetrads. In contrast, over 50 tetrads, 10% of all occupied tetrads, are found in the 'new' 10-km squares. These are mostly between the middle Tweed and the hills and some show a good density of occupied tetrads, particularly NT52 where half the tetrads had birds present. This is a significant gain which is commented on in the *New Atlas* as 'little change' and 'some expansion in Scotland'. A 10% increase in our area over a 20-year period hardly seems to be adequately described, especially as it has been matched by similar increases in Kintyre, Lochaber, the Great Glen and Tayside, as the BTO maps suggest. This expansion is more significant when it is considered that Garden Warblers were relatively numerous over the period of the *Old Atlas* survey, according to the CBC. Numbers then crashed during the period of sub-Saharan droughts and have only recovered slowly since the late 1970s (*Trends*). Woodland numbers are now at 1968-72 levels although farmland numbers are still recovering (*New Atlas*).

The numbers of Garden Warblers reported annually vary a great deal (*Bird Reports*) with most sites holding one or two singing males, but at least 20 sites known to have held more than four or five males. Outstanding are the Hirsel with 18-20 singing males in 1983 and 1987, Floors Castle (nine in 1989) and the disused railway at Penicuik (nine in 1991). Nationally, Garden Warblers were calculated to occur in densities of about 1.0prs/km². This accords well with da Prato's (1985) figure of 0.8prs/km² from the Tranent area during a period only part way through the current recovery. Birds are scarce on local BBS plots but suggest a density of 1-2prs/km². As the abundance map shows the Tranent area to have only moderate numbers, a figure of 1.25prs/km² is used to produce a figure of 2,400 pairs in our area, about 1% of the British population.   ***R.D.Murray***

Garden Warbler

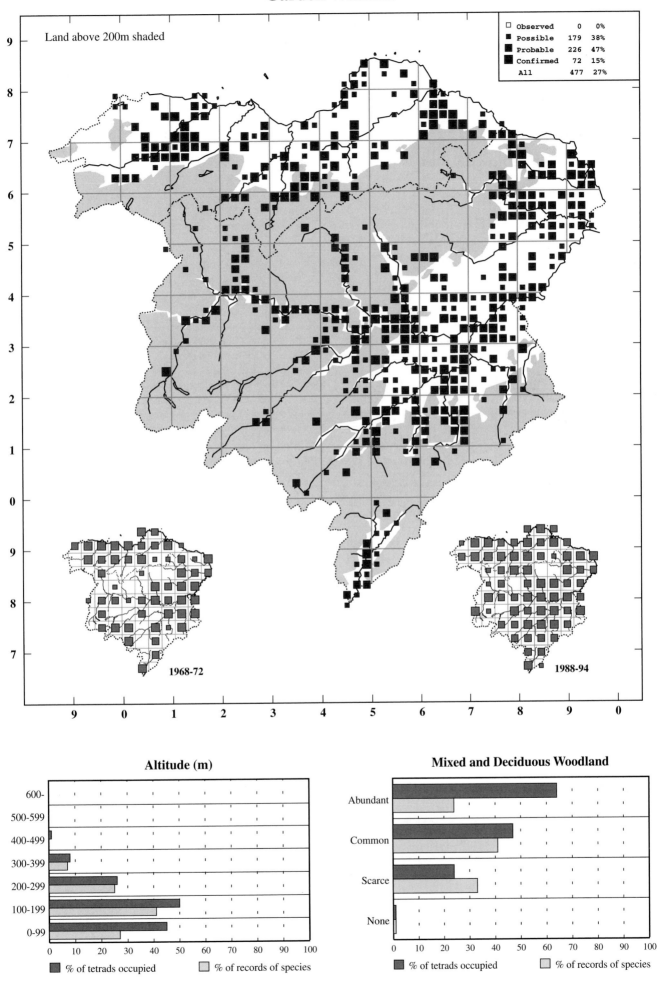

□ Observed	0	0%
■ Possible	179	38%
■ Probable	226	47%
■ Confirmed	72	15%
All	477	27%

Land above 200m shaded

1968-72

1988-94

Altitude (m)

■ % of tetrads occupied   □ % of records of species

Mixed and Deciduous Woodland

■ % of tetrads occupied   □ % of records of species

Blackcap
Sylvia atricapilla

A mellow warble with the deeper tones of a Blackbird is usually the first sign that Blackcaps have returned in mid-April. While it is visually the most recognisable of all our local warblers, the song can easily be confused with its close relative the Garden Warbler. The song, however, is less frenetic, more relaxed and flute-like with longer gaps between the phrases. The similarity between the songs is not accidental as Blackcaps and Garden Warblers indulge in interspecific competition, the song being used to maintain mutually separate territories. Blackcaps prefer taller, more continuous woodlands and are less likely to be found in scrub. Arriving earlier in spring gives Blackcaps an advantage in that they can be well established before Garden Warblers arrive in early May. Their ability to winter or return earlier in the spring appears to be based on their more frugivorous diet and ability to find food if insects are scarce, and a much shorter journey from their winter grounds in the Mediterranean, Garden Warblers travelling from sub-Saharan Africa.

Blackcap records in the *Atlas* were invariably associated with their far-reaching song. While most songs can be recognised as Blackcaps, a few birds were so similar to Garden Warblers that a sighting was necessary to confirm the identity. A third of all records were only of singing birds. It is likely that many of these referred to territorial birds but being in more remote tetrads there was little opportunity to upgrade the record through a subsequent visit. Half of all records were of probable breeding, mostly territorial birds. The smaller number of confirmed records was equally divided between sightings of adults with food or fledged young.

Blackcaps live in mixed and deciduous woodland and preferentially inhabit areas where these habitats are common or abundant. Indeed 86% of tetrads where such woodlands are available held Blackcaps. In contrast only a quarter of tetrads where deciduous woods were scarce were occupied. Nevertheless a third of Blackcap records came from these tetrads, reflecting its ability to live in smaller, more open areas of mixed and deciduous woodland.

The map and altitude data show Blackcaps mostly confined to mixed and deciduous woods below 200m, along the river valleys and in wooded policies. Three-quarters of all records occurred below 200m with few extending any distance into the hillier parts of SE Scotland and then only in the valleys where they are almost invariably found in the gardens of large houses. The concentration of occupied tetrads is dense in Lothian, in an arc north of the hills from about Bathgate to Dunbar. Blackcaps are absent on the higher ground to the west of Bathgate, in parts of central Edinburgh and in the most intensively cultivated parts of East Lothian. While urban habitats and a lack of woodland might explain the vacant tetrads in the east, the absence of birds in the west is less easy to explain, although the higher more exposed terrain may play a part. The lack of woodland, other than hedges, in areas of intensive cultivation of the Merse is doubtless responsible for the patchy distribution in the eastern Borders.

The 10-km square maps show eleven gains since the *Old Atlas* with only three marginal 10-km squares lost. While most of the new squares are at the hillier margins of the range and may involve just one or two tetrads per 10-km square, there have been large gains to the west of Hawick (NT41), at Lilliesleaf (NT52) and at Gordon (NT64) where between 30-60% of tetrads are occupied. If these changes took place in other 10-km squares occupied in both surveys, a major change in Blackcap numbers must have taken place since 1968-72. This may be supported by the upward climb of the CBC index for Blackcap (*Trends*) and the spread of the range seen in the *New Atlas* change map where large areas of western Scotland and Ireland have been colonised since 1968-72. The factors that have influenced this change remain obscure although there are suggestions that it may have a basis in the ability of the Blackcap to alter its winter range and to enhance both winter and migratory survival rates (*New Atlas*).

Blackcaps only occur in moderate numbers throughout their range in SE Scotland, according to the *New Atlas* abundance map. The best numbers are shown to be in Mid and East Lothian and in the middle Tweed and Teviot between Galashiels, Kelso and Jedburgh. Despite the density of occupied tetrads apparent in West Lothian and the lower Tweed, the *New Atlas* suggests these areas have fewer birds.

While the numbers reported annually fluctuate to some extent, perhaps depending on the strength of the spring passage and breeding season success, good numbers of Blackcaps are now being reported from sites across Scotland, with a mean of 90 birds at 55 sites being reported in Borders alone. At least 30 sites in the area have held over five singing males, with 18 males between Cramond and Queensferry (NT17) in 1992 and 16 males at both the Hermitage of Braid (NT27K) in 1989 and The Hirsel in 1987 (*Bird Reports*). This is a remarkable change since earlier in the 20th century where it was definitely rare in Lothian. For instance, there are only three known records at the much-watched Duddingston reserve prior to the 1960s (Anderson & Waterston 1961), while the diaries of G. Sandeman show birds appearing at the Hermitage of Braid and Blackford only since the 1960s and Dalmeny since the 1970s. The above figures show the species is now commonplace at all these sites.

Measurement of the local population using the figure of 0.8prs/km² derived from da Prato's (1985) study in Tranent encounters problems in that his site was predominantly a farmland landscape with scrub in limited places and that Blackcap numbers have increased considerably, perhaps doubled, since 1984. The *New Atlas* uses a figure equivalent to 2.8prs/km² to calculate the British population. Recent BBS studies indicate Blackcaps densities of 3-4prs/km². As the *New Atlas* abundance map shows mostly average numbers in the parts of SE Scotland inhabited by Blackcaps, a figure of 2.8prs/km² would give a population of 6,750 pairs, just over 1% of the British population.

R.D.Murray

Blackcap

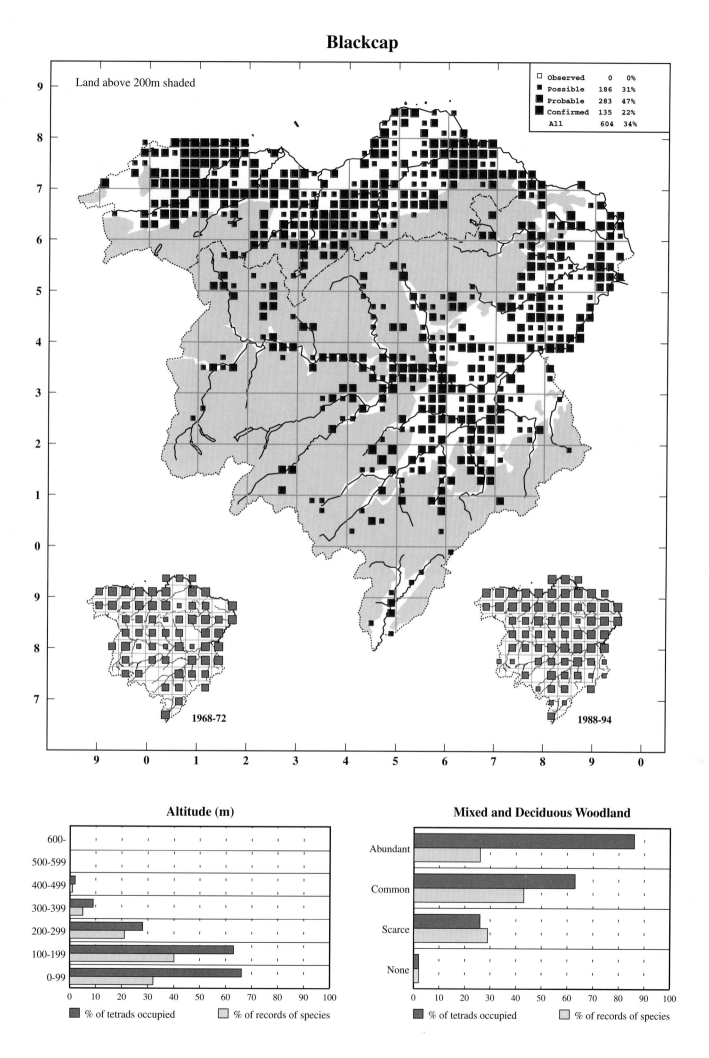

Land above 200m shaded

	Observed	0	0%
	Possible	186	31%
	Probable	283	47%
	Confirmed	135	22%
	All	604	34%

1968-72

1988-94

Altitude (m)

% of tetrads occupied   % of records of species

Mixed and Deciduous Woodland

% of tetrads occupied   % of records of species

Wood Warbler

Phylloscopus sibilatrix

The trill of the Wood Warbler from the high canopy of a sun-spattered woodland represents a real landmark in the year to many birders, the true arrival of summer. With a relatively late arrival at the end of April, Wood Warblers always seem to catch the first of the real summer, rather than the false starts to summer that can characterise the arrival of the other *Phylloscopus* species. This is a bird of the upland oakwoods of western Britain that maintains a toehold in eastern Britain in ancient woodland remnants and the better policy woodlands. It has a preference for close-canopy woodland, often in even-aged stands of oak and beech, but occasionally birch and ash. The closed canopy reduces the extent of the shrub layer, offering the Wood Warbler open air-space between the sparse ground layer where it nests and the canopy where it feeds.

Wood Warblers were invariably located by their diagnostic, far-reaching trill. As the preferred high canopy woodland tends to occur as discontinuous habitat islands, there was rarely more than one singing male in a wood and most possible registrations are of single birds singing. As many woodlands were not revisited during the brief song period, the chance to upgrade song to territory was missed. Accordingly, possible breeding runs well ahead of probable breeding. Some possible records may refer to passage migrants, especially in coastal areas. There were few confirmed breeding, as Wood Warblers become harder to detect once singing stops.

As Wood Warblers prefer a particular type of woodland, it is hardly suprising that less than a fifth of tetrads with mixed and deciduous woodland was occupied. The exact habitat needs of the species may be the main factor in restricting numbers in SE Scotland with four-fifths of all Wood Warblers found in just 18% of tetrads where such woods were relatively common or abundant. That two-thirds of all Wood Warbler records were between 100-300m is less surprising as mixed and deciduous woodlands are most common in the valley woods along on hills fringes, rather than in lowlands.

The map shows a species tied very strongly to the ancient woodland remnants that survive along the steeper banks of river valleys. The Esk in NT26,35&36 is prominent, as is the middle Tweed in NT24,33&43, the Jed in NT61&62, the Rule in NT50&51 and the Liddel in NY48. Elsewhere, large estates and houses stand out as habitat oases in otherwise barren land for Wood Warblers, as at Gosford and Luffness House (NT47N,P&U), Pressmennan (NT67G), Woodhall Dean (NT67R&W), Ayton Castle (NT96F), Floors Castle (NT73C), Stobs Castle (NT50D) and Craigurd (NT14G&H). Other large estates such as Hopetoun (NT07P), Dalmeny (NT17N,P,T&U), Tyninghame (NT68A,B,F&G), Monteviot (NT62H&M) and the Hirsel, that are excellent for other warbler species, appear to have either no records or just the occasional birds singing in spring. The need for a lack of a shrub layer covering the ground perhaps rules out these estates, as they all share extensive plantings of ornamental Rhododendrons.

The *New Atlas* abundance map shows SE Scotland to hold rather low numbers of birds. Only four areas appear to have moderate numbers: NT13 at Dawyck, NT33&43 in the middle Tweed, NT36 at Eskbank and NT67 at Pressmennan and Woodhall Dean. The remainder of the area is shown to have the lowest abundance figures.

Comparison with the *Old Atlas* shows that occupied squares have almost doubled since 1972. There has been some status change in at least half of all 10-km squares with 28 gains and eleven losses. This increase is understated as there are a number of records from the 1979-87 period where birds were recorded from sites not registered in the present survey (*Bird Reports*). Losses are mainly on the fringes of the Merse and around Craik Forest. Gains are frequent in the middle and upper Tweed, around Denholm and Jedburgh and in Liddesdale. The losses in the east, where Wood Warblers are scarce, may represent single singers not present in the recent period and migrants in the coastal squares during the 1968-72 survey. The gain in the middle Tweed is extraordinary, especially in NT43 which currently has the greatest density of tetrads in the area. It is inconceivable that birds were not present there in 1968-72, especially as all sites are mostly unmodified since then. This also applies to Liddesdale and the Rule-Jed valley woods. There is no hint of any such range expansion or increase in numbers in the middle Tweed so the assumption must be that Wood Warbler were somehow overlooked in these areas in the *Old Atlas* or that numbers can be very erratic, even in major strongholds.

The *Bird Reports* show that 160 sites have held birds since 1979, 20% of which were vacant or not checked independently during the *Atlas* period. This matches the 150 tetrads with birds in the survey. About half of all sites have never held more than single males. The 1984-85 BTO Wood Warbler survey counted birds in a sample fourteen 10-km squares across the area (Murray 1985, Brown 1986). Four had no birds, but the remainder held 41 singing males. A repeat of this survey during the *Atlas* period might have found 44 singing males although there is a great deal of re-distribution. Numbers of singing males can fluctuate between years but the best counts in 1988-94 were at Roslin Glen NT26R (7), Plora Wood NT33N (6), Venlaw NT24K (5), Dawyck NT13S (5) and Elibank NT33Y (5). Prior to 1988, 12 singing males at Saltoun-Humbie (NT46S&T) in 1980 and Bowhill (NT42D&I) in 1986, were the best totals. Mean counts for all 160 sites between 1979-94 indicate a population of 225 males. As some sites are only occupied in single years, the minimum figure is between 170-190 singing males.

The BTO Wood Warbler Survey in 1984 (Bibby 1989) produced figures of 9 pairs per occupied 10-km square for Scotland. The extremely patchy local range shows that the use of such figures requires caution, as half of the 10-km squares in the area only have registrations in one or two tetrads. NT43 on the other hand may hold as many as 25 singing males. Local data show a mean figure of 5 singing males per occupied 10-km square. Bibby's figure of 9 pairs per 10-km square for Scotland clearly includes the much denser populations in the west and north, which according to the *New Atlas* are as abundant as the best in the British Isles. The *New Atlas* abundance map emphasises this regional difference with all areas of SE Scotland, other than NT43, shown in the low to moderate categories. At half the Scottish figure that Bibby found, just 4 pairs per 10-km square, the area would hold 196 pairs, a figure extremely close to the 170-190 pairs derived from site counts during the period. ***R.D.Murray***

Wood Warbler

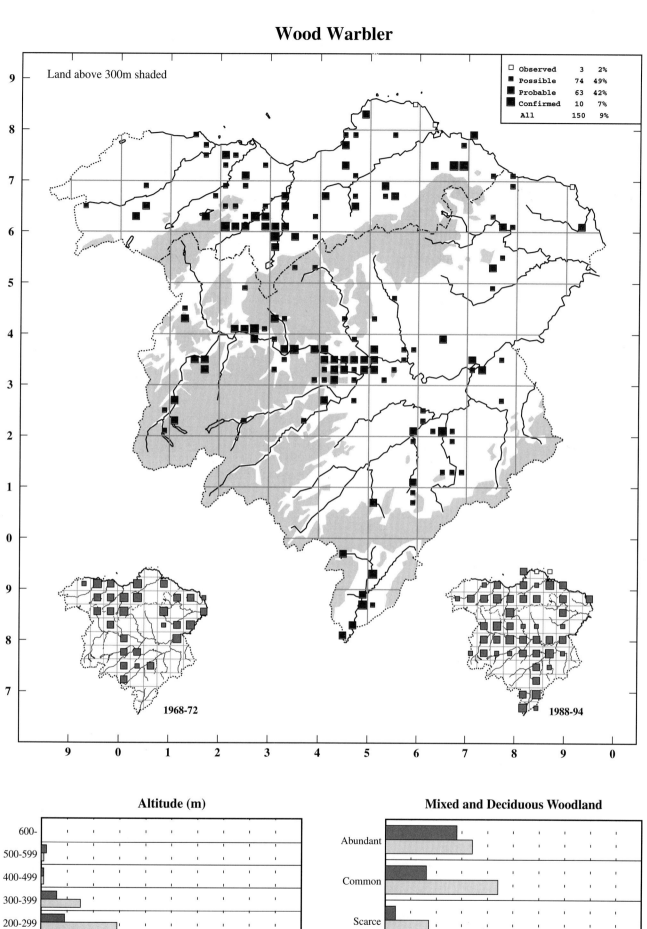

Land above 300m shaded

	Observed	3	2%
	Possible	74	49%
	Probable	63	42%
	Confirmed	10	7%
	All	150	9%

1968-72

1988-94

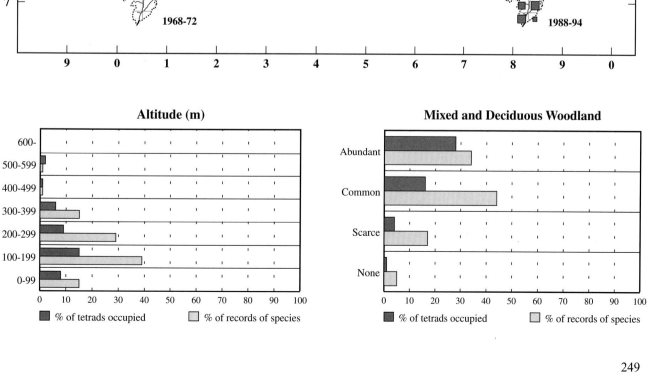

Altitude (m)

600-
500-599
400-499
300-399
200-299
100-199
0-99

0 10 20 30 40 50 60 70 80 90 100

■ % of tetrads occupied   □ % of records of species

Mixed and Deciduous Woodland

Abundant
Common
Scarce
None

0 10 20 30 40 50 60 70 80 90 100

■ % of tetrads occupied   □ % of records of species

Chiffchaff
Phylloscopus collybita

Like all warblers it is the song that draws attention to the Chiffchaff, the bright two-syllable phrase reiterating the bird's name through the canopy of tall woodland in summer from late March onwards. Some form of dense shrubbery is important to Chiffchaffs, and while deciduous woodlands are preferred they can inhabit even extensive stands of conifers, provided a few large deciduous trees are present.

The song of the Chiffchaff is both easy to identify and far-reaching. Almost all records in the *Atlas* related to song, with most of the possible registrations being of singing birds and most probable records relating to territorial singers. Silent Chiffchaffs are hard to find, picking them out from the multitudes of Willow Warblers being a thankless task. The few confirmed records of fledged young or adults feeding young were probably birds stumbled upon rather than searched for.

Chiffchaffs are birds of mixed and deciduous woodland, the graph showing 74% of all records coming from tetrads where such woods are common or abundant. While tetrads with large areas of woodland are clearly preferred, the lack of birds from the remaining habitat that exists is puzzling. While some essential requirement for Chiffchaffs may be lacking, the vacant habitat may reflect Scotland's position on the edge of the range of the Chiffchaff in Britain.

The map shows a relationship between Chiffchaffs and the more extensive areas of deciduous woodland around the wooded policies of the larger estates such as Dalmeny (NT17), Gosford (NT47), The Hirsel (NT84) and Floors (NT73). There is some continuity of tetrads along parts of the Esk, upper Tyne, Whiteadder, lower to middle Tweed and Jed, mostly in the remnant semi-natural oakwoods that line the steeper banks of these rivers. The best density of occupied tetrads is near Dalkeith (NT36) and Dunbar-Stenton (NT67) in similar habitats, with areas of Berwickshire holding

slightly lower numbers of occupied tetrads. Three-quarters of all records were in tetrads below 200m with a few fairly far up the valleys of the North Esk, Tweed, Yarrow, Ettrick, Gala, Whiteadder and Jed. Some coastal tetrads between Dunbar and Eyemouth show Chiffchaff records that may be attributed to passage migrants rather than to breeding birds.

The *New Atlas* sounds slightly sceptical about the increase in Chiffchaff numbers in Scotland reported by Scottish local recorders in *Thom*. However, there is no doubt that Chiffchaffs have made significant gains in SE Scotland, with 22 additional squares occupied since the *Old Atlas*. There were losses in four squares giving a net increase of 38% in the number of occupied squares in *c*.20 years. Many of the gains are marginal, in hilly areas where only one or two tetrads held Chiffchaffs and it is likely that the losses were of a similar magnitude, involving just a few tetrads in each square. Several of the new 10-km squares, however, have 15-30% of their tetrads occupied, while in the Jed valley (NT61) no less than 45% of the tetrads had reports of Chiffchaff. While the additional fieldwork involved in the *Atlas* may be an explanation for the better numbers of birds, it is difficult to believe that Chiffchaffs could have been missed in the better occupied 10-km squares such as NT61, or those near Edinburgh such as NT37 (Musselburgh) and NT58(Gullane-North Berwick). A similar increase in the number of 10-km squares is also seen in neighbouring Northumberland (*Day*) where there were gains in 17 squares as against 4 losses.

This increase is certainly seen in the literature where Chiffchaffs were noted as extremely uncommon prior to the 1960s. This is true of the well-watched Duddingston reserve (Anderson & Waterston 1961) where Chiffchaffs have only become annual since the 1970s, and also in the diaries of G.L. Sandeman and H.E.M. Dott that cover the 1930s-1990s period and show a great expansion into areas previously unoccupied during the 1960s and 1970s. These observations are also supported in the Edinburgh Bird Club Bulletins of the 1950s which treat Chiffchaff as an unusual species well worth mentioning.

The *New Atlas* abundance map suggests that Chiffchaff numbers in SE Scotland are rather poor with much of the occupied area showing only low to moderate abundance compared to south-west Britain and Ireland. Certainly the great majority of local reports in the breeding season refer to single singing birds and only about 20 sites have ever had more than three singers since 1979 (*Bird Reports*). While numbers do fluctuate between years, the large estates generally have the biggest counts with 11 males at Floors (NT73) and ten pairs each at Bowhill (NT42), Duns Castle (NT75), the Hirsel (NT84) and Pressmennan (NT67).

These large estates hold good densities of 6-13prs/km^2, in contrast to da Prato's (1985) Tranent study where Chiffchaff were hardly present at 0.2prs/km^2, although his survey was done in a period when Chiffchaff numbers had reached an all-time low in the CBC (*Trends*). The *New Atlas* uses a mean of 3.0prs/km^2 in its estimate of the British population while local BBS returns suggest 2-3prs/km^2. As the *New Atlas* abundance map shows numbers to be moderate to low in our area, values of 1.75prs/km^2 for tetrads below 200m and 0.5prs/km^2 for higher altitude tetrads, would suggest about 2,000 pairs for our area, just 0.25% of the British population. While only small numbers might be expected in SE Scotland, this percentage seems very small and could hint that the national estimate is rather high.

R.D.Murray

Chiffchaff

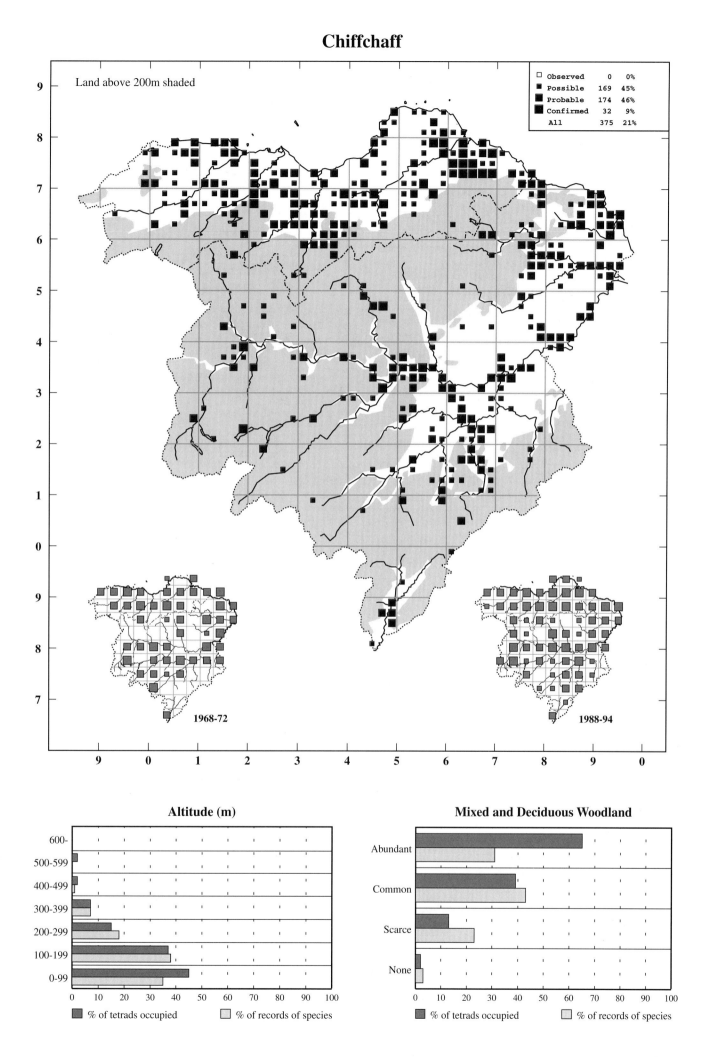

Land above 200m shaded

☐ Observed	0	0%
■ Possible	169	45%
■ Probable	174	46%
■ Confirmed	32	9%
All	375	21%

1968-72

1988-94

Altitude (m)

■ % of tetrads occupied　　☐ % of records of species

Mixed and Deciduous Woodland

■ % of tetrads occupied　　☐ % of records of species

Willow Warbler
Phylloscopus trochilus

Early summer in Scottish woodlands often belongs to Willow Warblers, the successive songs from different birds interlocking and weaving a seemingly endless melody from dawn to dusk. As one of the commonest birds in Britain, it inhabits most types of woodland and any tall scrub that provides both insect food and a nest site near the ground.

Willow Warblers were easy to record by virtue of their abundance and their distinctive song. As birds are frequently heard singing against one another it was very easy to obtain territorial registrations. This is reflected in the low number of possible records (7%) and the fact that three-quarters of all probable records were of territorial behaviour. The high numbers of confirmed records were mostly of adults feeding young or fledged young, the young being readily identifiable by their yellowish underparts and feet.

Willow Warblers inhabit most types of woodland, including coniferous forests and scrub. Indeed, the habitat data show that over 90% of all tetrads in SE Scotland that had any type of woodland, be it scarce or extensive, held Willow Warblers. The altitudinal distribution indicates that they can extend right up into the hills where over half the tetrads above 500m held Willow Warblers, a feat matched by only the Wren and Chaffinch amongst woodland birds. Despite this, 91% of the birds occurred below 400m where 90% of all tetrads were occupied.

This range of habitat preference has allowed the Willow Warbler to become the fourth most widespread species in SE Scotland. The main gaps in the distribution mark the essentially treeless habitats above 500m of the inner core of the hills. Even a handful of birches or rowans high up a rocky cleugh is enough to provide a Willow Warbler with a territory so only the truly treeless areas of the south-west Pentlands (NT15), Moorfoots (NT34), Lammermuirs (NT55,66&76), Cheviots (NT81&82), Liddesdale (NY49) and the Tweedsmuir Hills (NT02,11,12 &22) show areas of vacant tetrads. The only significant areas below 400m unoccupied by Willow Warblers are on the fringe of the Lammermuirs in NT55,65&66, and on the fringe of Cheviot (NT81&82). These are, respectively, treeless heather moor and treeless sheepwalk. Even Edinburgh has been colonised, the only vacant squares being in deepest Leith, Wester Hailes-Sighthill and Musselburgh. The odd vacant lowland tetrads elsewhere appear to be in treeless areas of very intensive arable farmland where the few hedges present have been trimmed so hard as to offer no opportunities for Willow Warblers. Edge habitats along roads, rides and planting coupes in blanket conifer plantations, regardless of age, form useful habitat with birds widespread in the high-level forests at Craik (NT30) and Wauchope (NT50&51).

Like many widespread species, comparison between the two 10-km square maps reveals little as the bird occurs in 100% of the squares. The *New Atlas* abundance map is more helpful. While showing the gaps in the hill areas, the Lammermuir 'hole' extends further southwards to the Merse in parts of NT63,64,74&75 suggesting that the arable land here holds few birds. Another similarly poorly-off area for Willow Warblers is in the south Roxburghshire conifer forests around NT40&50, although these forests do in fact hold good numbers of birds. Areas of high abundance are present in much of West Lothian away from the Pentlands, East Lothian north of the A1, the Berwickshire coast, between Galashiels and Jedburgh, and the southern Pentlands between Biggar and West Linton. There is no obvious reason for these centres of high abundance.

The *Bird Reports* note over 20 males singing in many areas of woodland and as many as 65 counted in sites such as Bavelaw-Red Moss. Most of these areas equate to less than a single kilometre square and indicate that densities of 20-30prs/km^2 are fairly widespread with sites like Bavelaw, Whim Wood (NT25B), the Hermitage of Braid (NT27Q) and Ladyurd (NT14H) holding much higher densities of 30-60prs/km^2. Open areas yield much smaller numbers with a WBS plot along the Gala Water managing 5.5prs/km^2 (M.Holling *pers. comm.*). Variations in abundance are seen in da Prato's Tranent study (1985) where Willow Warblers only achieved a density of 3prs/km^2 in intensively managed farmland compared to 163prs/km^2 in small areas of scrub, giving an overall value of 11prs/km^2. This is near the figure used by the BTO for its calculations for both the *Old Atlas* and *New Atlas*. Local values from the BBS survey indicate a similar 13prs/km^2 from 84% of the plots. Census work near Hexham (Galloway & Meek 1983) found 46prs/km^2, while studies in the forested areas of Kielder (Petty *et al.* 1995) showed densities approaching 90prs/km^2 in some years.

The Kielder density alone would yield over 50,000 pairs on the 600km^2 of conifer woodland in SE Scotland. However, Kielder does contain more young plantation, which can hold really large numbers of Willow Warblers, than does Borders and so lesser densities seem more appropriate. A moderate figure of 12-15prs/km^2, close to the national average, would produce a figure of between 74,000-93,000 pairs in SE Scotland, but as the *New Atlas* abundance map clearly shows the area to have above-average numbers, a value of 18prs/km^2 might be more appropriate to take account of the large areas of forestry where birds are abundant, producing a figure of 112,000 pairs or 4.9% of the British population.   ***R.D.Murray***

Willow Warbler

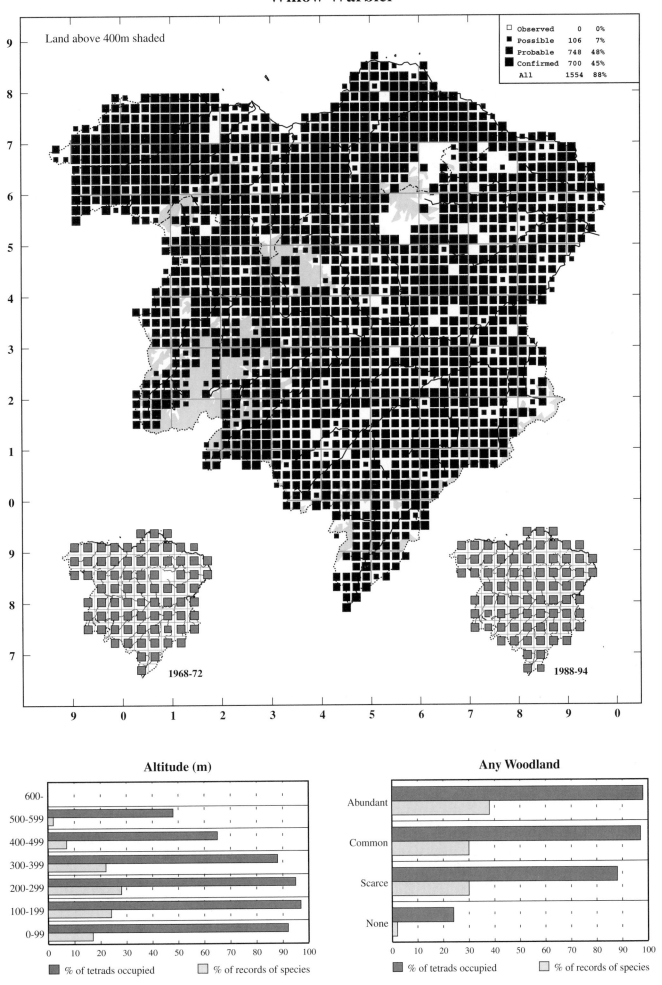

Land above 400m shaded

☐	Observed	0	0%
◼	Possible	106	7%
◼	Probable	748	48%
◼	Confirmed	700	45%
	All	1554	88%

1968-72

1988-94

Altitude (m)

% of tetrads occupied   % of records of species

Any Woodland

% of tetrads occupied   % of records of species

Goldcrest
Regulus regulus

A flicker of movement high in a conifer accompanied by a highly-pitched sibilant call is usually the first sign that a tiny Goldcrest is present. While not confined to coniferous forest, there is little doubt that such woodlands are their preferred habitat. Goldcrests are seemingly never still in their search for food, always flicking from branch to branch, sometimes hovering, at other times flycatching. The tiniest bird in Britain has a surprisingly loud but high-pitched call adapted to penetrate the layers of branches and leaves that normally surround them.

The distinctive contact calls of Goldcrests mean that they are often easy to find. They are usually numerous in their preferred habitats and territoriality is easy to establish when birds sing against one another, providing two-thirds of all probable records. Goldcrests are also easy to 'pish' or 'squeak' out of cover. Probable records also included numbers of pairs and alarming birds. About a third of confirmed reports were of the large and fairly noisy broods that are frenetically fed by the adults, with most of the remainder of adults carrying food.

Goldcrest populations occasionally crash because of severe winter weather and this happened during the winter of 1990-91, possibly due to prolonged icing of conifer branches when short thaws were followed by sharp frosts. In the following spring Goldcrests were extremely hard to find, one observer seeing only three birds between March and June, despite intensive *Atlas* work. It was only after broods appeared in June that the reporting improved. Recovery can be very rapid and numbers are often restored within two to three years.

Goldcrests are primarily birds of coniferous forest with just 13% of records coming from tetrads where coniferous woodland was absent. This was mostly mixed woodland, including those around Dalmeny (NT17), in Edinburgh (NT27) and parts of coastal East Lothian (NT47&58). While almost any size of woodland may be used, 76% of all records came from tetrads where such woods were common or abundant.

Being mostly tied to coniferous woodland means that although it is widespread in SE Scotland, occurring in two-thirds of all tetrads, the distribution more closely resembles the map of coniferous forests

rather than that of either mixed and deciduous woodland or indeed all woodland. Similarly, the Goldcrest's altitudinal distribution resembles that of conifer woodland occupying 78% of all tetrads between 100-400m. The main gaps in the range correspond to the treeless hill areas above 400m (8% of records) and wherever arable farming is very intensive, mostly below 100m (14% of records). Surprisingly, there are small gaps within the larger areas of commercial conifer forest (NT30,50&NY58). Perhaps these areas are dominated by trees too young to hold Goldcrests at present but a more likely explanation is that they were surveyed during the 1991 Goldcrest crash and never revisited.

The areas of highest numbers in the *New Atlas* abundance map in SE Scotland are in the the middle and upper Tweed and the Ettrick drainages where conifer forests dominate. Pockets of good numbers are also present along the southern flank of Coldingham Moor (NT86) and around Livingston (NT06). Areas of low numbers were in the arable parts of the lower Tweed around Kelso (NT73,74&84) where woodlands are scarce. Surprisingly, low abundance is also seen around Teviothead and the Hermitage Water (NT40&NY49) where there are some large plantations, especially in NT40. This is almost certainly due to fieldwork being done in that area during the 1991 population crash.

Comparisons with the *Old Atlas* 10-km square map provide little information in such a widespread species. Two additional squares are now occupied, NT87 at Dowlaw where Goldcrests inhabit the wooded Dowlaw Dean, and NT71 on the Cheviot slopes, where new plantations have allowed birds to colonise since the 1968-72 period.

The *Old Atlas* used a figure of 5.7prs/km^2 to calculate the British population while the *New Atlas* used 2.4prs/km^2. Local BBS plots suggest densities of 9-14prs/km^2 while the da Prato's (1985) study near Tranent found only 0.9prs/km^2 over what is poor ground for Goldcrests. Prime Goldcrest habitat, commercial conifer forestry, covers at least 600km^2 of our area and in such habitats they can occur at very high densities indeed. The *New Atlas* quotes studies with as many as 400-600 prs/km^2. The *Old Atlas* states that densities in excess of 100prs/km^2 are common in plantations. Work at Kielder in 1991-92 (Petty *et al.* 1995) found densities of 150-900birds/km^2 (mean 200prs/km^2) in Sitka Spruce plantations. Deciduous woodland, on the other hand, holds relatively low numbers of Goldcrests, some western oakwoods in Scotland holding up to 26prs/km^2 (Williamson 1974).

These widely varying figures, tied in with the presence of large areas of forestry, make a calculation of the local population very difficult. Just the *c.*600km^2 of commercial forest, occupying *c.*540 tetrads, even at densities of 150prs/km^2, would produce around 90,000 pairs, 16% of the *New Atlas* British population estimate. This is higher than the 100prs/km^2 used as the basis for the calculation of the population in Northumberland (*Day*) but lower than the mean found by Petty *et al.* (1995). The remaining 634 tetrads are calculated at 6prs/km^2, an additional 15,000 pairs, although with large areas of coniferous woodland outwith the big plantations a higher value might have been used. This 105,000 pairs estimate is made on lowish density figures, some of which were found during a period of low Goldcrest numbers after the 1990-91 crash. As Goldcrests did very well in the following years and had increased by 500% on farmland CBCs by 1995 (*BTO News* 204:12), it seems possible that the local population may be much higher, at least 150,000 pairs. The *New Atlas* calculation of the British population certainly seems out of date and it is likely that Goldcrests may have returned closer to the 1.5 million pairs calculated in the *Old Atlas*, although its estimate was not updated by Stone *et al.* in 1997 despite significant changes to the national indices. On such a figure SE Scotland would have about 7% of the British population, in line with the numbers indicated in the *New Atlas* abundance map.   ***R.D.Murray***

Goldcrest

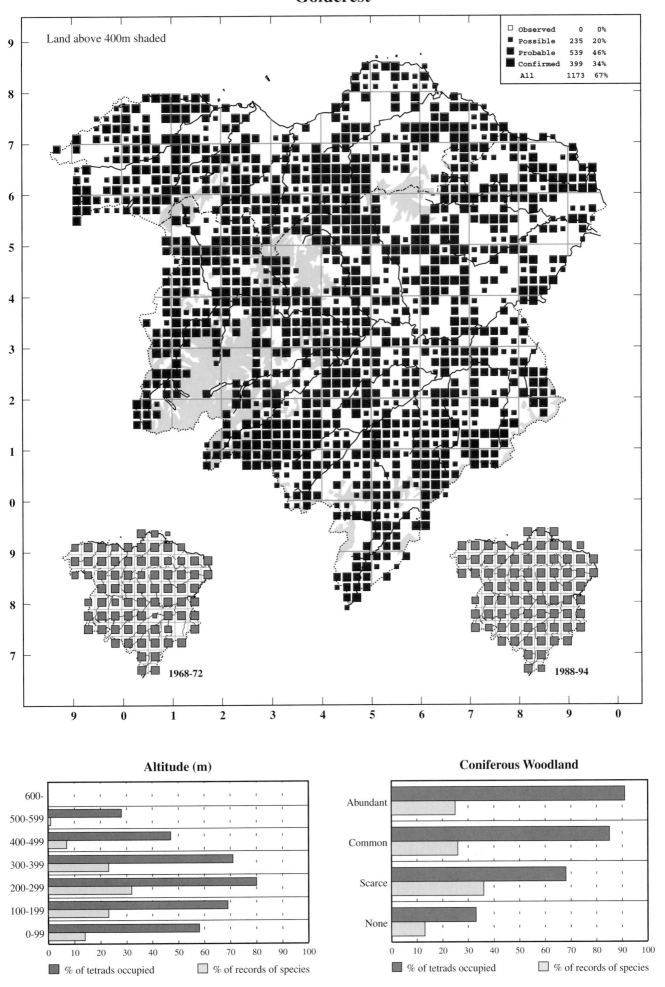

Land above 400m shaded

□ Observed	0	0%
■ Possible	235	20%
■ Probable	539	46%
■ Confirmed	399	34%
All	1173	67%

1968-72

1988-94

Altitude (m)

■ % of tetrads occupied   ■ % of records of species

Coniferous Woodland

■ % of tetrads occupied   ■ % of records of species

Spotted Flycatcher
Muscicapa striata

A rather nondescript brown and grey bird in deciduous woodland with a thin scratchy call and a song that has been described as 'insignificant' is surprisingly conspicuous only due to its habit of sallying forth from an exposed perch, often into a beam of sunlight, to chase and snatch a flying insect from the air before returning to its perch. Spotted Flycatchers are confiding and, allied to their habit of nesting amongst climbing plants that sprawl along the walls of gardens, show that brightness of song or appearance is not the only way of attracting attention.

The lack of an attention-catching song meant that being seen in appropriate habitat was relatively more important in recording this species than for most passerines. This was true of both possible and probable records where sightings of singles or pairs formed approximately half of all records. As in many insectivores, confirmed records came mostly from adults carrying food and from fledged young.

Habitat data show Spotted Flycatchers are widespread in mixed and deciduous woods. While four-fifths of all large woodlands held Spotted Flycatchers, these woods are rare and account for less than a fifth of all bird records. Tetrads where such woodlands are common held about half of the birds with the smaller, possibly more open woodlands holding two-fifths of the birds recorded in the area. A small number of records came from areas where no woodlands were present, the birds inhabiting tall scrub or gardens.

The map shows a distribution characteristic of a mixed and deciduous woodland species that is widespread but not particularly common. The fragmented nature of the habitat produces a patchy map with only occasional areas where there are better densities of occupied tetrads. Woodlands in SE Scotland are squeezed between the arable farming that dominates the lowlands and the grass and heather of the uplands. This is supported by both the map and the altitude data which indicate that about half of the low ground is vacant, mostly in coastal East and West Lothian and into the Merse. With 80% of all records below 300m, the hill areas show up as clear gaps in the Lammermuirs, Moorfoots and Tweedsmuir Hills, despite the ability of Spotted Flycatchers to penetrate well into the hill glens such as the head of the Tweed (NT11), the Yarrow and Ettrick (NT21) and the Teviot (NT30). These upland sites are typically in the groups of sycamores that often surround remote farms, cottages and old hunting lodges. While the range is not continuous across the higher southern and western hills, there is some continuity across the passes between the northern hills at Leadburn (NT25), Middleton (NT35) and Soutra (NT45). There is some avoidance of areas dominated by blanket coniferous forest although many of those

areas do tend to be above the range of altitude that Spotted Flycatchers seem to prefer.

By British standards Spotted Flycatchers are relatively numerous in SE Scotland, according to the *New Atlas* abundance map. Areas of the highest abundance occur all round the Moorfoot-Lammermuir Hills, extending north-eastwards from Biggar along the northern flanks of the hills to Haddington and Dunbar, in the Eye and Whiteadder valleys, and in a broad swathe up the Tweed and Teviot drainage from Kelso-Jedburgh westwards to Peebles and Biggar. This mostly matches those parts of SE Scotland between 100-300m and corresponds to the altitudinal levels that hold two-thirds of all records.

As with most widespread species, comparison with the *Old Atlas* 10-km square map offers few hints, with two squares gained in NT45 and NT87 the only changes (apart from the loss of NT20 where breeding in 1968-72 could well have been outside SE Scotland). In fact Spotted Flycatchers were recorded in no fewer than 15 tetrads in NT45. In the adjacent NT44, where birds have always been present in recent years (M. Holling *pers.comm.*), the *Old Atlas* only managed a possible record, so they were surely overlooked between 1968-72. With national populations exhibiting a downward trend, although less so in Scotland (*Trends*), range expansion would seem unlikely.

Although Scotland leads the British CBC regional rankings (*Trends*) and the *New Atlas* abundance map shows SE Scotland as having good numbers of Spotted Flycatchers, the actual density values used in the *New Atlas* indicate a species that is not numerous. This fits with published figures where the *Old Atlas* cites CBC data densities of 1.0prs/km^2 on farmland and 10prs/km^2 in woodland in a period when birds were more numerous. The *Old Atlas* and *New Atlas* calculated the British population on a basis of 0.3-0.6prs/km^2. In line with the better numbers found in our area da Prato (1985) found 0.9prs/km^2 in arable farmland around Tranent while the local BBS plots yield higher levels of 2-3prs/km^2 from a small sample. Using a density of 1-2prs/km^2, an estimate of the local population of 3,500-7,000 pairs is derived, about 4% of the British total.

There is some anecdotal evidence that Spotted Flycatchers may have undergone a more recent, and significant, decline since 1994, with many local birders commenting on the paucity of birds. Some regular surveys of woodlands with good numbers may be desirable to monitor numbers in future.   ***R.D.Murray***

Spotted Flycatcher

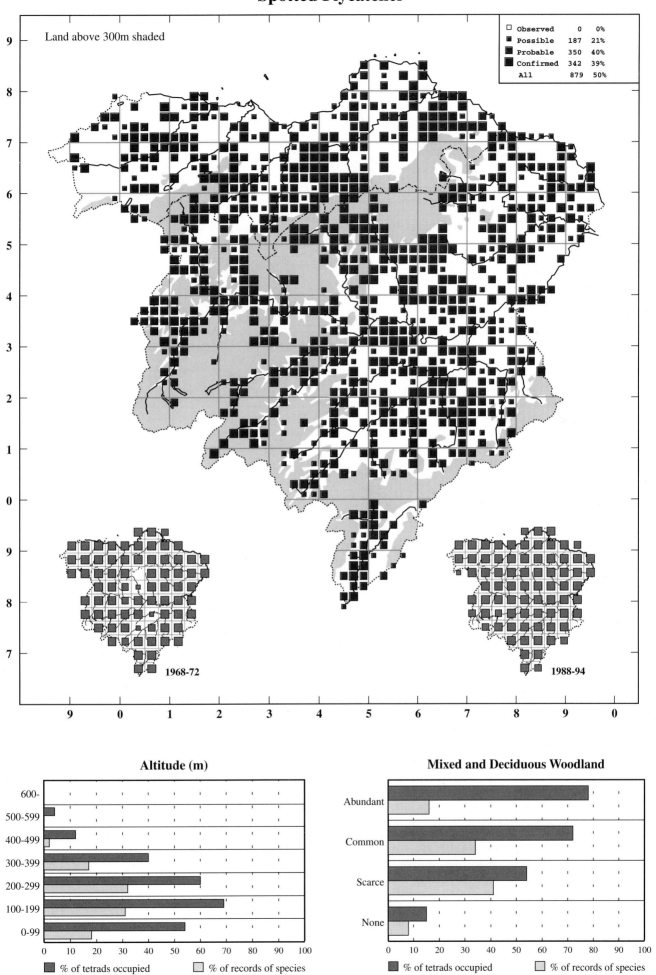

Land above 300m shaded

	Observed	0	0%
	Possible	187	21%
	Probable	350	40%
	Confirmed	342	39%
	All	879	50%

1968-72

1988-94

Altitude (m)

600-
500-599
400-499
300-399
200-299
100-199
0-99

0 10 20 30 40 50 60 70 80 90 100

% of tetrads occupied   % of records of species

Mixed and Deciduous Woodland

Abundant
Common
Scarce
None

0 10 20 30 40 50 60 70 80 90 100

% of tetrads occupied   % of records of species

257

Pied Flycatcher
Ficedula hypoleuca

Pied Flycatchers are birds of the wooded valleys fringing the upland areas of western and northern Britain where ancient woodland has survived centuries of deforestation, clinging to the steep sides of the valleys. Pied Flycatchers show a preference for sessile oakwoods that hold plentiful numbers of caterpillars and flying insects, have numerous perches, plenty of nest-holes and a low ground cover that allows extensive flight areas under the canopy. Nest-sites can be a limiting factor on the numbers occupying any wood and the provision of nest-boxes can increase densities dramatically.

Pied Flycatchers are not easy to record. They arrive in late April and early May and leave by August and have a very limited song period, mostly confined to two or three weeks in May. The song is quiet and easily lost in the background of the woodland chorus and may be relatively unfamiliar to many local observers as Pied Flycatchers are rather scarce. This low density also reduces the need for a long song period, as singing is stimulated by competition to some extent. It is therefore likely that some birds may have been missed in areas that were not surveyed at the crucial period when singing was at its peak. Another factor that militates against recording Pied Flycatchers is that the occupation of some territories tends to be sporadic, perhaps an effect of being on the edge of the range where males are less able to attract females and hence move on after a period of futile singing. Other sites, especially those that have been successful in the past, continue to attract birds, presumably including offspring returning to their natal areas in later years. The relatively low level of proved breeding, only 26%, is a reflection of all of these factors.

The map represents an inventory in SE Scotland of two types of woodland, large wooded estates and semi-natural valley oakwoods. It is possible to pick out the wooded policies of Portmore (NT24P&25K), Penicuik House (NT26G&H), Traquair House (NT33H&I), Faldonside (NT42V), Torwoodlee (NT43X), Butterdean (NT47L), Monteviot (NT62L&M), Tyninghame (NT68F) and Duns Castle (NT75S&X). Loose colonies of Pied Flycatchers are not untypical, especially when centred on a nest-box scheme. The three adjacent tetrads in NT62 is just such a colony centred on boxes along the Ale Water at Ancrum and in Monteviot estate. Elsewhere birds have been recorded along the oakwoods that line the steep sides of glens just before their emergence onto the flood plains of middle Tweed at Horseburgh, Plora Wood and Thornilee (NT33&43); the lower Ale Water at Ancrum (NT62); the Rule (NT51) and Jed Waters (NT61); and the middle Whiteadder at Abbey St. Bathans and Elba (NT76). In Lothian birds were recorded along both the North and South Esk at Roslin, Arniston, Auchendinny and Carrington. The records from Liddesdale (NY48,58,59), mostly recorded during the few June visits to the area specifically for the *Atlas*, suggest that this area may hold a very healthy population of Pied Flycatchers. Isolated records are also present along the Tyne, Almond, Leader, Yarrow and Liddel Waters.

Numbers are known to be higher in western Britain than in areas further east like SE Scotland. The *Bird Reports* and the reviews by *Andrews* and *Murray* indicate a few other areas where breeding may have occurred immediately before the *Atlas* period. In Lothian breeding may have taken place at Redside Burn, Cousland and Crichton along the Esk and at Humbie in East Lothian, while in Borders, Ladykirk, Paxton, Stobo, Netherurd, the Hirsel, Peel and Wells are mentioned. Most are near areas where breeding was reported between 1988-94.

The altitude graph shows Pied Flycatchers to be concentrated between 200-300m, in the areas where the relict oakwoods are most frequently encountered. Their strongest association is with mixed and deciduous woodland where over half the birds were in medium-sized rather than small or large woodlands, reflecting the open nature of the woodland required for feeding.

Comparison with the *Old Atlas* shows that the numbers of 10-km squares where Pied Flycatchers are recorded has nearly doubled since 1968-72. Some of this will be an effect of the longer survey period accumulating records but it is very likely that there has been a substantial increase in the numbers present each summer in recent years. The main spread seems to have been in the middle Tweed between Peebles and Galashiels and in Liddesdale. Elsewhere the gains mostly involve single or perhaps just a few tetrads. Numbers are generally low and in most tetrads only a single male or pair was found. Loose colonies of up to six pairs have been reported from Roslin and in nest-boxes at Ancrum.

This local increase in records appears to be in line with small increases seen nationally (*Trends*) although both *Trends* and the *New Atlas* state that much of the increase is the result of more birds breeding in nest-boxes than previously. As few birds use boxes in SE Scotland, these publications suggest that areas like SE Scotland may be being colonised by the surplus populations from areas such as the Wood of Cree in Dumfries & Galloway or in the Trossachs where hundreds of pairs of Pied Flycatchers use nest-boxes each year (*Scottish Bird Report*).

SE Scotland: Males and Nests from Bird Reports 1979-95

	79	80	81	82	83	84	85	86	87	88	89	90	91	92	93	94	95
Males	1	9	4	6	5	4	6	4	5	7	4	9	15	14	18	13	9
Nests	-	1	1	-	-	4	-	4	5	9	8	3	6	2	-	1	2

The data above from the *Bird Reports* suggest that the number of reports in SE Scotland in any year is in the region of 10-20 singing males of which about a third may breed. The reports probably underestimate the real numbers, whereas the map, compiled from seven years data, overestimates the number in any year. It is likely that the actual number falls between the two figures and the area probably holds 30-50 singing males in most years. Two factors seem to limit the population: the scarcity of the habitat and the lack of nest-sites within that habitat. To ensure a good population, or perhaps to increase the population, effort should be made to both preserve the habitat and encourage nest-box schemes. With such a small population this species might well be worthy of further study as it would be fairly easy to visit all sites in a breeding season.

R.D.Murray

Pied Flycatcher

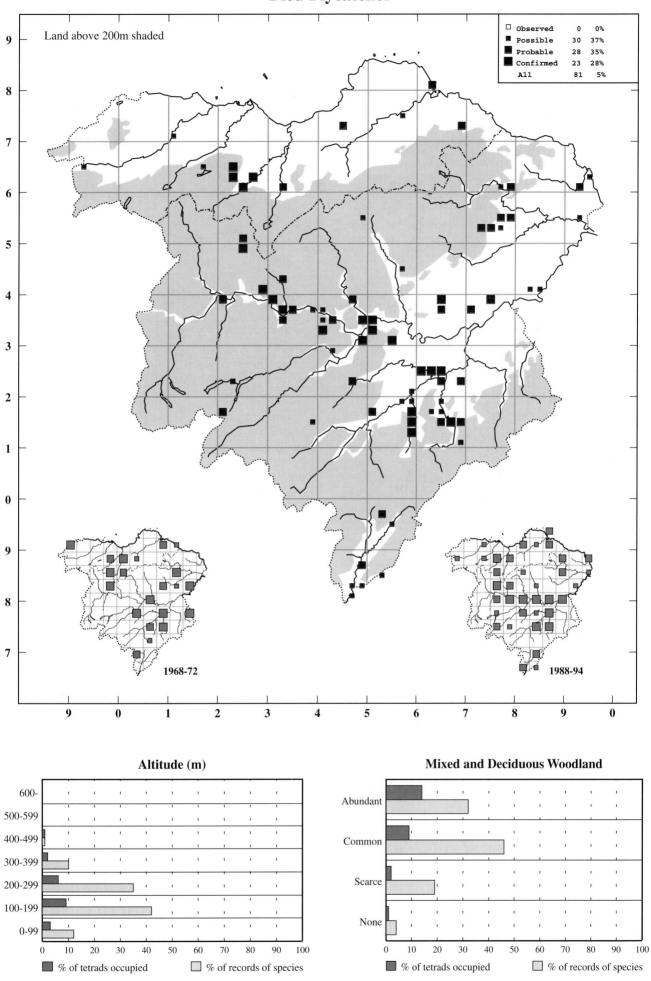

Land above 200m shaded

	Observed	0	0%
	Possible	30	37%
	Probable	28	35%
	Confirmed	23	28%
	All	81	5%

1968-72

1988-94

Altitude (m)

600-
500-599
400-499
300-399
200-299
100-199
0-99

0 10 20 30 40 50 60 70 80 90 100

■ % of tetrads occupied   ☐ % of records of species

Mixed and Deciduous Woodland

Abundant
Common
Scarce
None

0 10 20 30 40 50 60 70 80 90 100

■ % of tetrads occupied   ☐ % of records of species

Long-tailed Tit
Aegithalos caudatus

Tiny bundles of black, white and pink feathers with a tail perhaps two or three times the length of their bodies flitting through the trees, is the usual encounter with Long-tailed Tits. For most of year they move in flocks, occasionally with as many as 50 birds, but more typically 1-15. Birds pair off in the breeding season to build their feather and lichen nests bound together with spider-silk.

The usual cue that Long-tailed Tits are present is the 'tsee-tsee-tsee' contact calls they constantly make on their feeding forays through deciduous woodland. When one bird is found, its partner is often visible, and as failed breeders often act as 'helpers' at neighbouring successful nests (that usually belong to siblings), the registration of pairs formed the most important element of probable breeding records. The higher than usual rate of confirmed breeding is almost wholly the result of the flocking behaviour of young Long-tailed Tits after leaving the nest, when flocks of adults and young move noisily through woodland.

Long-tailed Tits are birds of mixed and deciduous woodland, all but a handful of records occurring in tetrads where such habitats are present. Tetrads where such woodlands were common or abundant held 70% of all records. Three-quarters of all records were also in tetrads below 200m, probably because that is where these woodland habitats are most frequent. However, considerable areas of woodland fulfilling these criteria are vacant, so other factors must be restricting their range in our area. They are known to like woodlands where a broken canopy allows a growth of bushy shrubs and small trees which provide hidden nest sites and good numbers of invertebrates.

The map shows a distribution characteristic of a species that inhabits mixed and deciduous woodland but is scarce, although widespread. The fragmented nature of the habitat produces a patchy map with only occasional areas where there are better densities of occupied tetrads. With few records above 200m, the hills make up the major areas where Long-tailed Tits are absent. There are considerable numbers of tetrads with mixed and deciduous woodland above that altitude so there may be an additional factor preventing birds moving into these higher level woods. On the lower ground the arable areas of the Merse (NT74,84&85) and East Lothian (NT47,57&58) also hold few records. On the other hand Lothian shows an area of fairly continuous distribution along the flanks of the northern hills with the Balerno area (NT16), the middle Esk (NT36) and the Garvald-Dunbar area (NT67) standing out as having particularly good densities of tetrads. The range in the Borders is more fragmented although it is fairly continuous along the valleys of the Tweed and neighbouring rivers around Galashiels-Melrose (NT43&53) and Kelso-Jedburgh (NT62&63).

The *Old Atlas* 10-km square map shows some interesting changes, many of which are minor changes at the margins of the local range where the addition or withdrawal of a record from a single tetrad would show up as a loss or gain. Five of the seven 10-km squares that show a loss are shared with neighbouring areas where the 1968-72 record may have been outwith SE Scotland. The nine gains are more interesting as most appear to be towards the heads of valleys that were only occupied further downstream in 1968-72. Thus tetrads near the source of the Lyne and North Esk (NT14&15), Tweed (NT12), Teviot (NT30&41), Gala (NT44) and the Dye (NT65) appear to have been 'colonised' since the *Old Atlas*. It is of interest to point out that the remaining two 'lost' 10-km squares are in similar situations at the head of the Yarrow (NT22) and Whiteadder (NT66). As *Trends* indicates a buoyant population during the *Old Atlas*, some prior withdrawal from the range margins resulting from a severe winter and subsequent recolonisation cannot be responsible for this expansion. With no significant increase in the cover of mixed and deciduous woodlands at the valley heads since 1968-72, a real colonisation must have occurred.

The *New Atlas* abundance map reveals that Long-tailed Tits are numerically scarce in the area compared to the southern half of England. Despite the better density of occupied tetrads in Lothian compared to the central Borders, the *New Atlas* shows the Borders to have the higher abundance, particularly in the middle Tweed between Selkirk, Galashiels and Kelso. Moderate numbers are shown to occur around Broughton (NT13), the middle Esk and between Aberlady and Dunbar (NT47,57&67).

The low population level is also revealed by the *Bird Reports* where the largest numbers of birds at any site were six pairs at the Hirsel in 1994 and five pairs each at Muiravonside (NS97S) in 1985, Floors (NT73B&C) and Roslin (NT26R) in 1989 and Aberlady in 1992. Three pairs have been seen at Pease Dean (NT77V), Elba (NT76V), Abbey St. Bathans (NT76L), Bawsinch (NT27W), Hermitage (NT27K), Dalkieth (NT36I&P), Penicuik (NT25E&J) and Crichton (NT36W).

Local breeding season data are almost totally lacking for this species in the *Bird Reports*, birds being absent from most local study plots. *Thom* mentions densities between 4-26prs/km^2 in western oakwoods in Scotland but nationally Long-tailed Tits were calculated to average 0.6-1.0prs/km^2 in both the *Old Atlas* and *New Atlas* in occupied 10-km squares. Using a density of 0.5-1.0prs/km^2, this would produce a local population of 800-1,600 pairs across SE Scotland. **R.D.Murray**

Long-tailed Tit

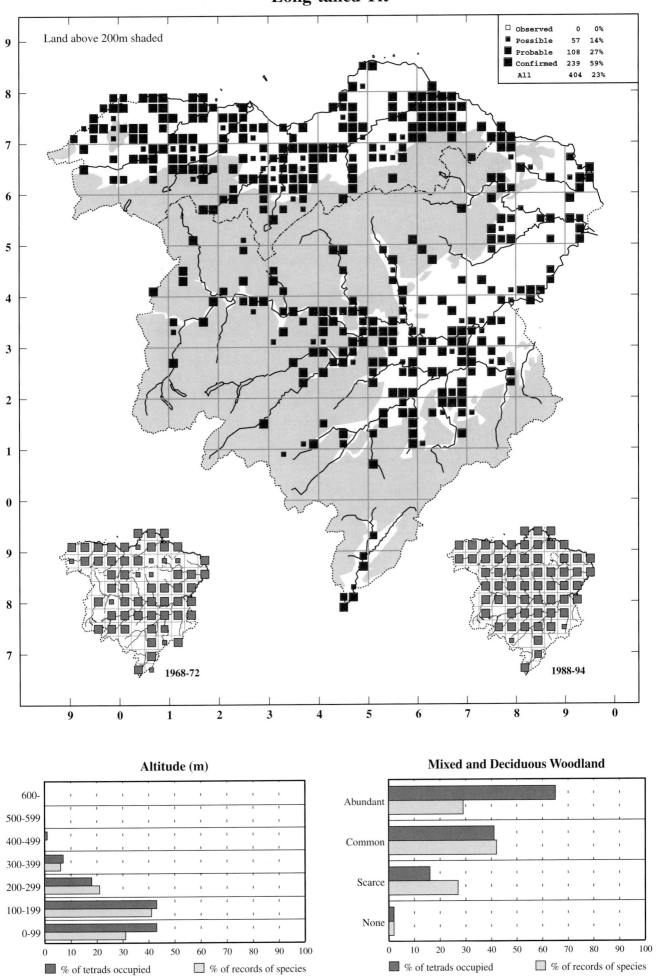

Land above 200m shaded

☐ Observed	0	0%
■ Possible	57	14%
■ Probable	108	27%
■ Confirmed	239	59%
All	404	23%

1968-72

1988-94

Altitude (m)

600-
500-599
400-499
300-399
200-299
100-199
0-99

■ % of tetrads occupied   ☐ % of records of species

Mixed and Deciduous Woodland

Abundant
Common
Scarce
None

■ % of tetrads occupied   ☐ % of records of species

Marsh Tit
Parus palustris

The Marsh Tit is a species with a rather misleading name, open deciduous woodland, parks and gardens being the principal habitat in Britain. Although it can be seen in marshy woodland, it is the trees that are the attraction, not the wet conditions. Marsh Tits present an identification problem due to their close resemblance to their relative, the Willow Tit. Attention should be paid to the slight plumage features that distinguish in areas where both occur, but particular attention should be paid to any vocalisations, the voices being diagnostic. The principal contact call is *pitchou* for Marsh Tit, compared to the more nasal *chay-chay* call of the Willow Tit.

Marsh Tits are by no means easy to record. They tend to be unobtrusive, often moving quietly through woodlands in the shrub layer close to the ground. While the call is often cited as one of the principal methods of locating this species (*Winter Atlas*), local experience suggests that birds are often silent, perhaps as a result of the low densities of Marsh Tits towards the edges of their range and a reduced need to call to proclaim territory. About half of the reports were of probable breeding, mostly of pairs earlier in the season and anxiety calls later on. Confirmed reports make up about a third of all records, consisting almost entirely of adults carrying food for young or adults with fledglings. Several resulted from observers 'squeaking and pishing' in suitable habitat to elicit a response from hidden birds. Sites where birds had been reported in winter, when birds move around in flocks with other tits and hence are generally easier to locate, were systematically searched.

The map indicates a species tied very closely to the ancient woodland remnants on the steeper banks of the middle and lower Tweed, lower Teviot, Whiteadder, Blackadder and Eye. The gaps in distribution along these rivers mostly correspond to parts of the river that are flatter and have lost their woodland cover to cultivation. This is particularly true of the larger gaps along the Tweed (NT63&73) and Teviot (NT62&72) which are largely devoid of woodland or where woods are mostly coniferous plantations not favoured by Marsh Tits. Birds are also present in the rich wooded policies surrounding the large estate houses of the Merse such as the Hirsel, Duns Castle (NT75S), Floors Castle (NT73C), Monteviot (NT62M),

Ladykirk (NT84X) and Ancrum House (NT62H), some of which are coincidentally also along the main rivers. There is a small outlying group of birds in the Pease Dean-Dunglass gorge woodlands (NT76Z,77Q&V) that form the boundary with East Lothian. It is uncertain whether breeding still occurs in East Lothian as none have been found in recent years despite searches where birds were reported during the *Atlas* at Woodhall Dean (NT67W), Pencaitland (NT46P), Innerwick (NT77G) and River Tyne (NT57H&S) (Holling 1997). However, the habitats in which birds have been seen in Lothian match those in Borders in all essential features.

Marsh Tits are extremely sedentary. Adults are very site faithful and it is apparently mostly first-winter birds that join wandering winter tit flocks. With over 85% of all Marsh Tit ringing recoveries being within less than 4km (*Winter Atlas*), winter records are also of interest. Most are near tetrads where birds were recorded in the main survey or in close proximity to the main range, often extending further upstream in river valleys already occupied. This is true of the Ale and Rule but most particularly the Tweed where winter records are frequent upstream from Melrose, regularly reaching Bridgeheugh near Selkirk (NT43Q). Exceptional records at Yair (NT43H) and Peebles (NT23P) also occurred during the *Atlas* period.

Older records from the *Bird Reports* covering the period 1979-1987 indicate a possible contraction of range. There are a number of sites in the westernmost part of the range, mostly between Gala and Lilliesleaf (NT42,43,52&53) and also in the Yetholm area (NT82) where birds were reported in 1979-87 but not recently. While it is possible that birds might have been missed in the more remote Yetholm area, it is less plausible that birds have been overlooked in recent years around Galashiels where there is a reasonable density of observers. Although birds still come to winter feeders at Bridgeheugh and Lilliesleaf (E.Middleton, P.Tabor *pers.comm.*) some decline is indicated.

In Britain there has been a long-term shallow decline in Marsh Tit numbers during the 1980s which may have stabilised in recent years (*Trends*). The *New Atlas* suggests interspecific competition for both food and nest-sites with other tit species, whose populations have been increasing steadily, as the potential cause of the decline. This decline has been accompanied by a contraction of range in Britain as a whole, with 17% of the 10-km squares occupied by Marsh Tits in 1968-72 being vacant in 1988-91 (*New Atlas*).

The Borders was apparently only colonised in the 20th century with birds being identified in Berwickshire in the 1920s. However, the second Scottish breeding record only occurred in Berwickshire in 1945, with the first Roxburghshire record in the 1960s (*Thom*). Breeding followed in Selkirkshire at Faldonside, Boleside and Langlee during the 1970s and early 1980s, but has not been reported there since (*Murray*). Marsh Tits first bred in East Lothian in 1966 but there has been no confirmation of breeding since (*Andrews*) although it has been suspected. Comparison of the 10-km square maps suggests a substantial (30%) spread since 1968-72. This hardly fits with local knowledge, and suggests that Marsh Tits were missed in the *Old Atlas*, hardly surprising for an unobtrusive bird which occurs in few tetrads of several 10-km squares. If the Marsh Tit truly has colonised SE Scotland in the 20th century it is entirely a possibility that it might disappear again in the face of decline and contraction within the core of the range further south.

There is evidence of birds in about 60 tetrads. Only single pairs have been noted at the majority of sites but some of the large estates such as the Hirsel and Floors can hold 5-6 pairs each. 80-100 pairs are almost certainly present in the area. As Marsh Tits are so rare here and these birds represent the entire Scottish population, a more detailed study of the numbers and distribution might be warranted.

R.D.Murray

Marsh Tit

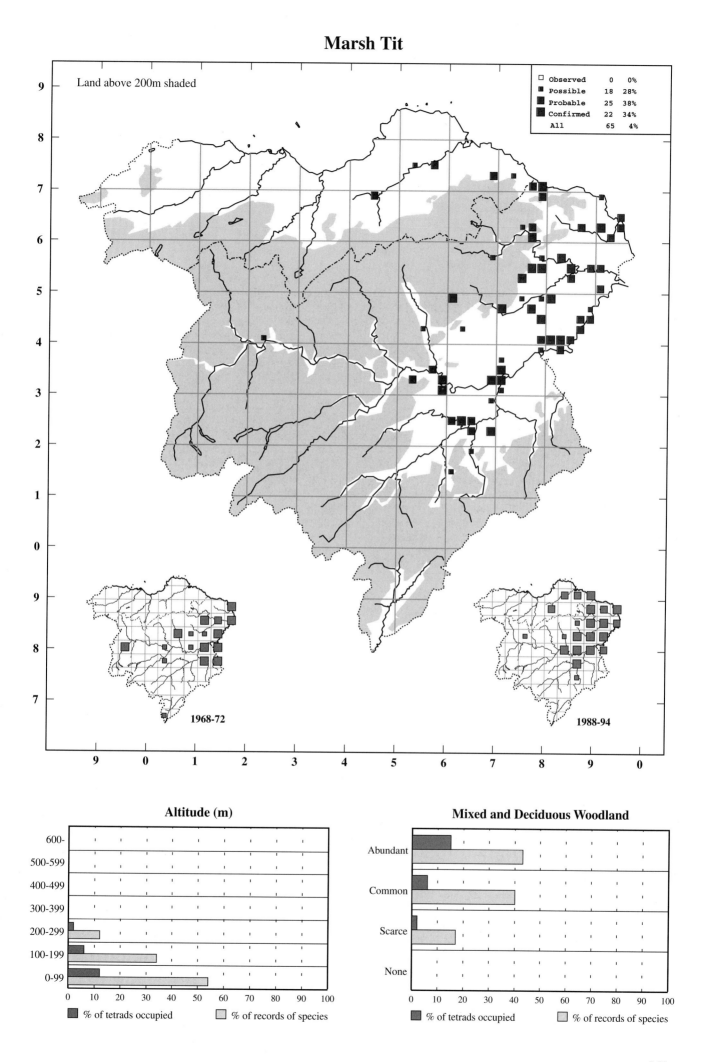

Land above 200m shaded

	Observed	0	0%
	Possible	18	28%
	Probable	25	38%
	Confirmed	22	34%
	All	65	4%

1968-72

1988-94

Altitude (m)

Mixed and Deciduous Woodland

■ % of tetrads occupied   ☐ % of records of species

■ % of tetrads occupied   ☐ % of records of species

Willow Tit

Parus montanus

As the name suggests, the Willow Tit is a bird of marshes and carrs where willows often predominate. Unfortunately the Willow Tit belongs to a pair of cryptic species that has caused and still causes problems with identification. It was not until the start of the 20th century that ornithologists were able to distinguish between the Willow and Marsh Tit in Britain. Consequently the early history of the two species is hopelessly confused and often based on unreliable identifications. The dull cap, more rounded tail, slightly larger black bib and the pale panel on the closed wing are all features that help to separate the Willow Tit. Most of these features are, however, difficult to see in the field. The wing-panel (which is not always present) and the *chay-chay* call are really the only diagnostic features that readily distinguish the two species.

Willow Tits are extremely rare in SE Scotland and records are bedevilled by the identification problem. Nevertheless a very small population lives in eastern Berwickshire on the lower part of the Whiteadder, the lower Eye Water and at two estates, the Hirsel and Duns Castle (NT75S). This population appears to be contiguous with that of Northumberland to the south where the bird is known to be rather scarce. There have been reports from eastern Berwickshire since the *Borders Bird Report* started in 1979, and although there have often been misgivings about some of the identifications, the presence of Willow Tits has been confirmed by ringers who trapped birds at Alemill (NT96B) and the Hirsel.

The map shows just a few records in Berwickshire, reflecting the difficulties of both finding and identifying this species. In Berwickshire breeding was confirmed in 1990 with a brood in a nest-box at the Hirsel and a pair were seen excavating a nest-hole at Duns Castle in 1993. Other records were of pairs and singles. Knowledge of the wider range outlined above comes from records from the pre-*Atlas* period and from reports outwith the breeding season. The sites indicated fulfil the habitat requirements described for Willow Tit in the literature of extensive patches of damp woodland along the banks of rivers, with stands of willows on the inside bends of the incised meanders, a feature of the wooded coastal deans along the Eye and Whiteadder. The Hirsel and Duns Castle also have damp woodlands round the Hirsel Lake and the Hen Poo.

The breeding record in the west, of fledged young, came from an area of willow carr at Ettrick, and was a great surprise considering the distance from the coastal population in Berwickshire. It is, however, in a 10-km square where breeding was reported during the

Old Atlas in 1968-72. Accordingly it is conceivable that breeding has occurred continuously there since that period but been totally overlooked until the area was searched during the current survey in 1992. It would appear that this site might be an outlier of the Dumfriesshire population, whereas the eastern population could be regarded as an outlier of that in Northumberland.

The *Old Atlas* shows breeding in a number of 10-km squares where no birds were found in the 1988-94 period. As with many *Old Atlas* records there is no documentary evidence of these reports but they suggest nesting occurred immediately west of Coldstream in the Gordon (NT64) and Greenlaw (NT74) areas with possible breeding in the Hawick area (NT50&51). While there is no confirmation of these records, Willow Tits did breed at Stobs Castle (NT50E) in 1976 immediately adjacent to the Hawick area. The *Old Atlas* also shows possible breeding to the south of Newcastleton (NY48) in an area where a pair was seen just over the area boundary in Cumbria in winter 1993-94.

In Lothian there are old records of breeding prior to 1935 (*R&B*) with West Lothian as a stronghold for the species. However, *Andrews* states that Willow Tits have only been recorded from two sites since 1951, at Beecraigs in 1972-73 and at Ormiston in 1984. Both of these records were in winter and there has been no hint of breeding. These winter records are reminiscent of the occasional reports away from the coast at Peebles, Hopes, Longformacus and Hule Moss in the 1979-87 period and at Pease Dean, St. Abbs and Gordon Moss in winter during the *Atlas* period. These suggest some dispersal in what is essentially an extremely sedentary bird, possibly from the population in SW Scotland.

The Willow Tit is a declining species in Scotland and has withdrawn from a large area south of the Highlands over the last 100 years (*Thom*). While birds may be easily overlooked, there is little doubt that it no longer breeds as it once did in Angus, Perthshire, Stirling and Lothian. Reports from the Clyde area (*Clyde Bird Reports*) indicate that numbers there are at a very low ebb, Willow Tits being limited to a handful of sites. The numbers in Ayrshire and Dumfries and Galloway seem more stable.

The SE Scottish population is clearly tiny and can hardly number more than ten pairs. A full survey of this species, and its cogener the Marsh Tit, would be useful to detail the precise distributions and numbers of the two species that are right on the northern limits of their British ranges.　　　　　　　　　　　　　　　**R.D.Murray**

Willow Tit

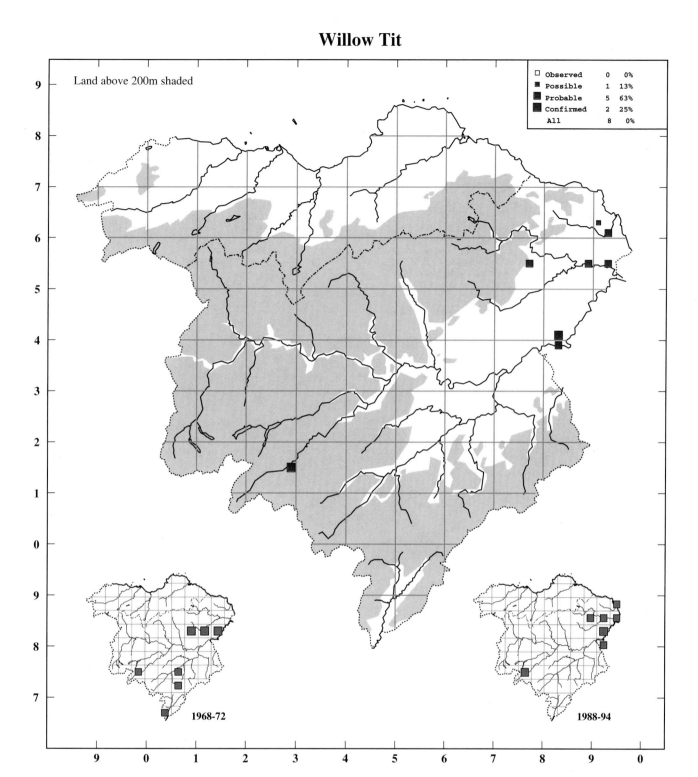

Land above 200m shaded

	Observed	0	0%
	Possible	1	13%
	Probable	5	63%
	Confirmed	2	25%
	All	8	0%

1968-72

1988-94

Coal Tit
Parus ater

Conifer forests are reputed to be 'lifeless' places, but are only lifeless for those who cannot listen. Perhaps the most familiar sound of such forests is the Coal Tit's disyllabic 'see-too-see-too' coming continuously from the tops of spruces, firs and pines. Coal Tits are adapted to a life in conifers, with their fine bills suited to finding food between needles or in the bark, their acrobatic skills allowing them to search for food where others cannot reach, and their habit of caching food when it is abundant for periods when foraging is poor. They eat whatever is plentiful, invertebrates in summer and seeds in winter.

Coal Tits were not particularly difficult to find. Although often in dense cover, their curiosity makes them readily drawn into the open by 'squeaking and pishing' by observers, aiding the recording of pairs, territorial birds and anxious parents. The song is also diagnostic and easy to imitate, further enhancing recording. About half of the probable records were of territorial birds singing against one another, most of the remainder being pairs. Confirmed records ran at a high level of over 50% of all records and were mostly of the numerous and noisy young being seen, or adults carrying food to them.

Conifers are so favoured by Coal Tits that it was often worthwhile listening for them in mixed woodlands wherever there were patches of a few pines, yews or other conifer species. While most wooded tetrads, regardless of size or type, held Coal Tits, the birds were somewhat more strongly associated with coniferous woodlands, the habitat data showing that 15% of Coal Tit records were in tetrads where there was no significant area of conifers while 19% of birds were reported in tetrads where there was no mixed and deciduous woodland. However much Coal Tits might favour mixed and deciduous woodlands, they have to share such woods with the other species and so tend to be more strongly associated with coniferous woodlands where they are the dominant, if not the sole, species of tit.

Coal Tits are the most widespread tit species and are able to flourish in woods up to 600m at significantly higher altitudes than the other tit species. The ability to live in coniferous woodland allows them to penetrate the higher altitude woodlands above 300m, occurring in about half of all forests above that level. The optimum zone, however, is between 100-400m from where three-quarters of all records came, above the competition of the Great and Blue Tit. The fall-off in representation above 400m, with just 8% of the Coal Tit

records coming from only two-fifths of wooded tetrads at that altitude, suggests there are difficulties living at these high altitudes.

The Coal Tit, one of the twenty most ubiquitous species in the area, is widespread at higher levels, being absent only in the islands of high ground that rise above 400m dominated by treeless grassland and moor, in the Pentlands (NT05&15), Moorfoots (NT34), Lammermuirs (NT55,56&66), Tweedsmuirs (NT02,11,12&22), Liddesdale (NY48&49) and the Cheviots (NT81&82). At lower altitudes, where Coal Tits are absent from 30% of tetrads below 100m, the range is less continuous and more patchy. The gaps are mostly in areas of intensively cultivated arable farmland such as around Tranent (NT47), Drem (NT57), Innerwick (NT77) and Stichill (NT73&74) where there are few trees and which lack even the minimum of habitat for Coal Tit, a shelterbelt. Where shelterbelts are present they are often deciduous in these areas and the tit niche may be occupied by other tit species, to the exclusion of Coal Tits. They are also absent from much of central and eastern Edinburgh, in marked contrast to western and southern Edinburgh where the wooded islands of Corstorphine Hill, the Braids, Colinton Dell and Dean Village and generally more wooded gardens allow birds to penetrate deeply into the city.

The *New Atlas* abundance map confirms the main gaps in the map opposite, showing the hill areas, the city and the arable areas of the lower Tweed as vacant. Areas of high abundance occur in a wide arc between the middle Esk, upper and middle Tweed, lower Ettrick and Yarrow and middle Teviot, between the Teviot and Cheviot Hills, the lower Tyne and around Livingston and Whitburn. As large areas of forestry occur in most of these areas this is to be expected. More surprising, however, are the areas of low abundance shown in the areas of prime habitat that extend across southern Roxburghshire between the Craik and Wauchope Forests. Experience indicates that these forests hold vast numbers of Coal Tits, as do many of the neighbouring and more-or-less contiguous forests in Eskdalemuir, Kielder and the Ettrick Forest. A similar 'gap' was noted for the Goldcrest and it is likely that these areas might have been surveyed for the *New Atlas* in 1991, after the hard winter of 1990-91 which had a drastic effect on Goldcrest populations. Although Coal Tits are less affected by such weather, the CBC does show fluctuations (*Trends*) and they may also have crashed there after severe hoarfrosts coated branches with thick ice for several weeks in winter.

In large coniferous stands of trees the Coal Tit can be very numerous indeed and the *Old Atlas* quoted densities of up to 100prs/km^2. These are close to the numbers found in predator-prey studies in neighbouring Kielder (Petty *et al*. 1995) where 65-470birds/km^2 were noted in different years, the mean being 95prs/km^2. As there are about 600km^2 of these forests in SE Scotland these areas alone would hold large numbers of Coal Tits. A modest 30prs/km^2 would yield 70,000 pairs in the 580 tetrads where conifers are common and abundant. Away from forested areas da Prato (1985) found only 0.8prs/km^2 in mainly arable farmland. Nationally the *Old Atlas* used 3.5prs/km^2 and the *New Atlas* 2.6prs/km^2 for their calculations of the British population. The *Old Atlas* CBC mean was 12.5prs/km^2, similar to the 13prs/km^2 found on local BBS plots where Coal Tits were found to be the most abundant of the tit species in SE Scotland. A figure of half these values, 7prs/km^2 would indicate 17,500 pairs for the tetrads other than large plantation, suggesting a local population of 98,000 pairs. Jardine in *Day* makes it clear Coal Tit populations fluctuate greatly according to food supply, so the figure may well vary from year to year. This figure would give the area a massive 16% of the British population. The BTO British population estimate is probably far too low, perhaps calculated on figures from a year when Coal Tit numbers were low, or based on CBC statistics biased to areas where they are least common.   ***R.D.Murray***

Coal Tit

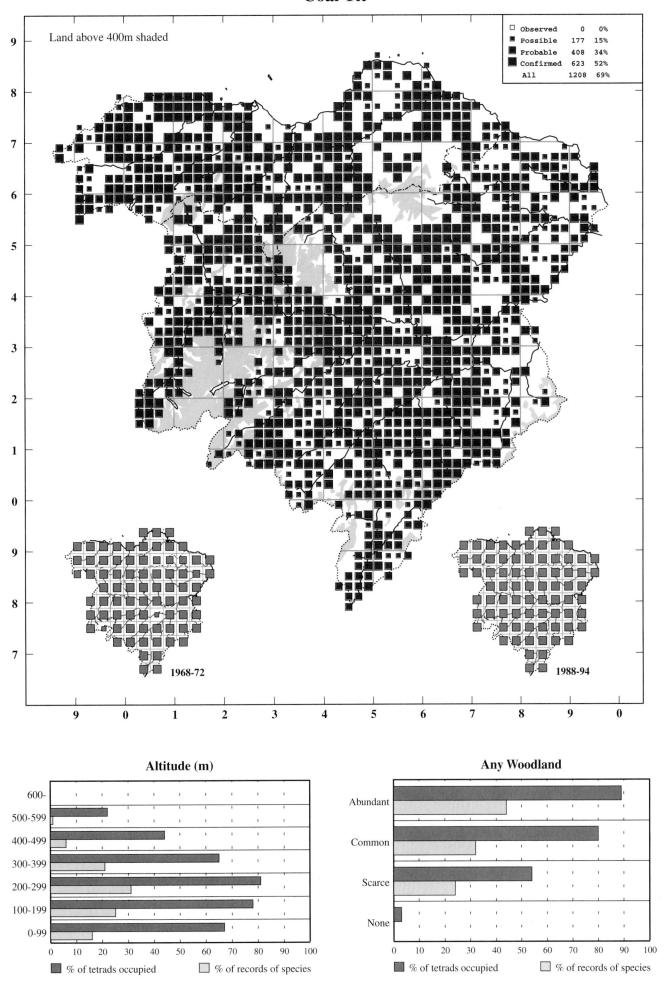

Land above 400m shaded

□ Observed	0	0%
■ Possible	177	15%
■ Probable	408	34%
■ Confirmed	623	52%
All	1208	69%

1968-72

1988-94

Altitude (m)

600-	
500-599	
400-499	
300-399	
200-299	
100-199	
0-99	

■ % of tetrads occupied   □ % of records of species

Any Woodland

Abundant	
Common	
Scarce	
None	

■ % of tetrads occupied   □ % of records of species

267

Blue Tit
Parus caeruleus

One of the most loved and familiar of our small birds, the Blue Tit is found on almost the entire British mainland, only missing from the remoter parts of the Scottish Highlands and the Flow Country. The Blue Tit usually reaches its greatest abundance in deciduous woodlands, and is generally absent or scarce in conifer woods. It is more abundant in southern than in northern Britain. Caterpillars are the all-important food for nestling and young Blue Tits. Summers with few caterpillars and winters with severe weather can both cause temporary reductions in Blue Tit numbers. Holes in trees are the prime nest sites, but holes in walls and buildings are also used as well as nest-boxes.

This was an easy species for which to find proof of breeding, and the map shows a huge preponderance of confirmed records. Confirmed and probable records together account for an impressive 93% of all occupied tetrads, and most of the 20% probable records almost certainly represent breeding pairs as well. Of all the confirmed records, over half were due to sightings of the noisy food-demanding young, and over a quarter to adults carrying food.

The solidness of the Blue Tit's distribution is conspicuous, indicating that wherever suitable habitat occurs the Blue Tit is there in easily detectable numbers. The comparison of the Blue Tit map with that of deciduous and mixed woodland is striking, showing a close match. The small differences that are evident relate to altitude. Most of those tetrads with deciduous or mixed woodland that lack Blue Tits are above the 300m contour, for instance in the Lammermuir Hills, the Culter Fell-Tweed source area (NT02&03), and the slopes of the Cheviot Hills (NT70&82).

Blue Tits are absent from the high open ground, and from large pure coniferous stands at both high and low altitudes, as in Craik Forest (NT30), the Tweed source area (NT01), both sides of Talla Reservoir (NT12), Elibank & Traquair Forest (NT33), and Wauchope Forest (NT50&60). There are open treeless areas as low as 200m at Coldingham Moor (NT86), the eastern Lammermuirs, and upper glens of the Teviot tributaries without Blue Tits. Only a very few low places seem to have a genuine scarcity of Blue Tits, as at the flat arable fields near Drem (NT57J), the exposed grazing land around Falside Hill (NT37Q&V), in the intensely arable Merse, and in a few coastal pockets.

Blue Tits are present right through the city of Edinburgh and all other towns. The Forth islands have no breeding Blue Tits, and even sight records on the islands for this most sedentary species have always been extremely rare. The *New Atlas* abundance map shows gaps in the high and forested areas similar to those detailed here. It also shows spots of high abundance in some rural lowland places. The 'alternative' map (*New Atlas* p459) differs, showing highest abundance in and around Edinburgh.

The altitude graph confirms that Blue Tit tetrad occupancy is high up to 300m altitude, falling away quickly above this height. Indeed, 85% of all Blue Tit tetrads were below 300m, and 95% of all tetrads below 200m have Blue Tits. The second graph strongly confirms the association with deciduous and mixed woods, with 98% occupancy of tetrads with large and medium-sized woods, dropping only to 77% occupancy of small woods. Thus Blue Tits use almost all available deciduous and mixed woodland in SE Scotland, unlike Great Tits. When a similar graph is made for all woods, including coniferous, (not shown) the Blue Tit occupancy rate falls considerably for all wood size categories.

Being a widely spread species, comparison of the two 10-km square maps shows no significant change in Blue Tit distribution over the past twenty years in SE Scotland. The lack of confirmation in squares NT40 and NT86 in the earlier map must indicate poor coverage then, as the suitable habitat in those squares is of long standing, especially in NT86 where Blue Tits are in 23 of the 25 tetrads. In Britain as a whole, the Blue Tit's range has not changed either, except in the far north early this century (*New Atlas*), and on certain islands (*Thom*). Blue Tit numbers nationally increased slightly up to the 1970s, after which trends are less clear (*Trends, New Atlas*).

Blue Tit densities vary enormously from few pairs in poor habitat to over 200prs/km^2 in good woodland with nest boxes (*Thom*), and over 100prs/km^2 in natural woods as far north as NE Scotland (Buckland *et al*. 1990). In SE Scotland 155prs/km^2 and 104prs/km^2 have been recorded in Roslin Glen and small woods near Tranent respectively, and 67prs/km^2 in mature gardens near Ormiston (*Andrews*, da Prato 1985, Scott 1992). However, such data are not applicable to general countryside. A large part of East Lothian dominated by arable land held 5prs/km^2 overall (da Prato 1985), while SE Scotland BBS plots give results averaging about 16prs/km^2. In general, Blue Tit density in SE Scotland must be below the national average, as the *New Atlas* abundance map shows that high abundance is clearly concentrated in the southern half of Britain.

For Britain as a whole, the *Old Atlas* uses a national average of 42.7prs/km^2 for woodland and 14.6prs/km^2 for farmland, and suggests an overall figure for Britain of 2,000 breeding pairs per occupied 10-km square (20prs/km^2). For SE Scotland a lower average density of 15prs/km^2 for occupied tetrads would indicate a population of 70,440 pairs. Alternatively, dividing the British population estimate of 3,300,000 territories (*New Atlas*) in proportion to SE Scotland's part of Britain's area suggests there would be 83,000 pairs, but this figure should probably be reduced as this area has below average abundance. The two estimation methods give fairly close results. This suggests that 75,000 pairs of Blue Tits would be a reasonable estimate for SE Scotland, 2.3% of Britain's population.

H.E.M.Dott

Blue Tit

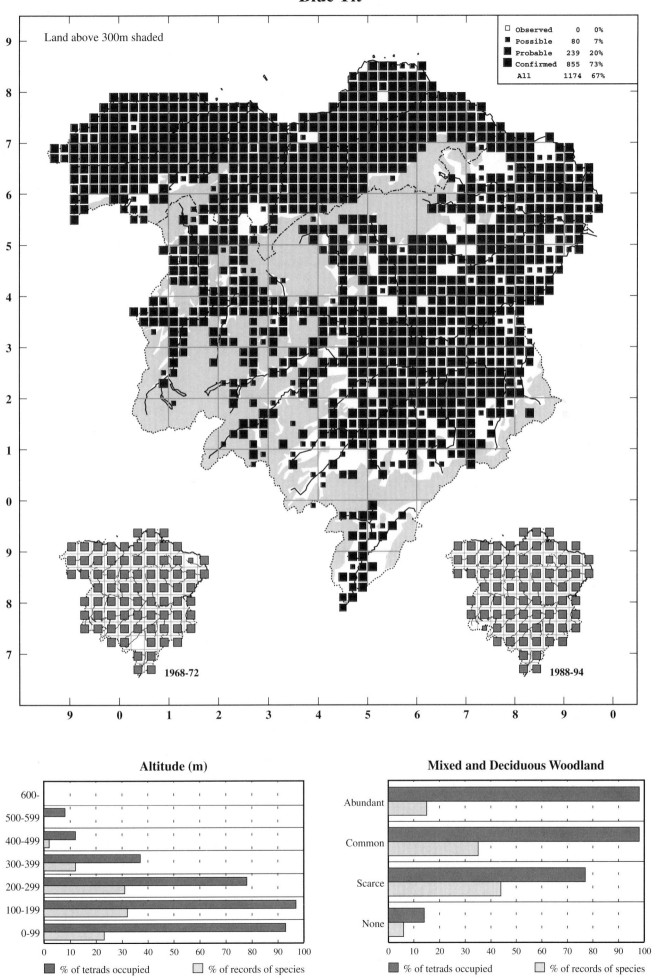

Land above 300m shaded

☐ Observed	0	0%
Possible	80	7%
Probable	239	20%
Confirmed	855	73%
All	1174	67%

1968-72

1988-94

Altitude (m)

600-	
500-599	
400-499	
300-399	
200-299	
100-199	
0-99	

■ % of tetrads occupied   ☐ % of records of species

Mixed and Deciduous Woodland

Abundant
Common
Scarce
None

■ % of tetrads occupied   ☐ % of records of species

269

BJH

Great Tit

Parus major

This, the largest of our tit species, is half as numerous as the Blue Tit in Britain although it has almost the same distribution, being absent on the mainland only in the remoter NW Highlands and Flow Country. The Great Tit is most abundant in deciduous woods, rather than in gardens, and its abundance increases towards the south in Britain. It is very scarce or absent in pure coniferous plantations. It nests primarily in tree holes, but will use holes in walls and buildings, including such places as hollow metal gate posts and inside broken roadsign poles.

Great Tits were easy to detect in the fieldwork and breeding was readily proved, with noisy fledged young providing 50%, and parents carrying food 32%, of all confirmed records. Confirmed and probable records combined accounted for a high 88% of all occupied tetrads.

The map shows Great Tits to be clearly concentrated in the low ground, thinning out with altitude well below the 300m contour. The distribution maps of the Great Tit and that of deciduous and mixed woodland show a strong similarity, except that the higher reaches of woodland in the hills are unoccupied by Great Tits, as are a fair proportion of the smaller sized woods in the Merse and in other low ground. Thus although Great Tit distribution clearly relates to that of deciduous and mixed woods, a proportion of these are unoccupied. Great Tits are absent from all high open land, and from extensive coniferous plantations at high or lower altitudes (in the forests detailed on the Blue Tit page). The Great Tit occurs all through the city of Edinburgh except for parts of Leith and Seafield. It is completely absent from the Forth Islands, where even sight records in any season are extremely rare.

The altitude graph shows Great Tits present in 84% of all tetrads up to 200m, decreasing from this height upwards to a very few at 400-500m. 89% of tetrads with Great Tits are below 300m. The second graph shows that from 96% occupancy of all tetrads with large deciduous and mixed woods, there is a fall-off with decreasing wood size and only half of the tetrads with small woods are occupied. Despite this, more Great Tits live in small and middle sized woods as there are fewer large deciduous and mixed woods

in SE Scotland. A similar graph with data from all woods including coniferous (not shown), shows a weaker relationship between Great Tits and woods, confirming the picture that the species is absent from most large conifer plantations.

The Great Tit distribution is extremely similar to that of the Blue Tit, but with the Great Tit clearly more sparsely spread within the range. This is an interesting state of affairs, as when the two are in competition for nest sites the Great Tit usually gains the upper hand (Minot & Perrins 1986). The food requirements of both species in all seasons are quite similar (e.g. Gibb 1954, Betts 1955) and yet the Blue Tit is twice as numerous in Britain. The map suggests that the Great Tit may be a little less able to exploit certain sub-optimal habitats where there may be less cover. Thus, it is absent from some higher glens where tree growth becomes sparse towards river sources and where Blue Tit distribution extends slightly further, as in the upper Esk around Gladhouse (NT25&35), the upper valleys of the Hermitage (NY49), Liddle (NY59) and Ettrick (NT21) Waters, and drainage from the Cheviots (NT61&71). Even more striking, however, is the relative sparseness of the tetrad density of the Great Tit evident in parts of Lothian and the Tweed-Teviot basin and particularly in the low-lying Merse, indicating that the Great Tit does not utilise such a wide range of small shelter belts, tree strips or other cover in SE Scotland as does the Blue Tit. A similar sparse distribution of Great compared to Blue Tit is revealed in Northumberland (*Day*).

The two 10-km square maps show no certain evidence for change in SE Scotland since 1968-72. The squares NT30 and NT65 hold Great Tits now but only in two and three tetrads respectively, indicating either a small range expansion or that birds were simply overlooked in 1968-72. In Britain generally there has similarly been no change in distribution except for a marked spread in north Scotland in the early 20th century (*Trends*) and on certain islands (*Thom*). A slight increase in numbers since the 1970s may no longer be continuing (*Trends, New Atlas*).

In optimum woodland habitat Great Tit density in Britain can reach as high as 100-150prs/km^2 (*New Atlas*). In SE Scotland, however, the highest measured densities are only 70prs/km^2 in Roslin Glen (*Andrews*) and 56prs/km^2 in very small woods near Tranent (da Prato 1985). Over a large mainly arable part of East Lothian, however, overall density was just 3.0prs/km^2 (da Prato 1985), and local BBS plots suggest about 6-9prs/km^2 on average. The Great Tit abundance maps in the *New Atlas* show almost no high abundance in SE Scotland, even in the best lowland parts, and high densities are only widespread in the southern half of England.

The *Old Atlas* gives average British densities of 27.7prs/km^2 and 8.5prs/km^2 for woodland and farmland respectively, and considers that the overall British average may be "more than" 1,000 pairs per occupied 10-km square (10prs/km^2). For SE Scotland it is evident that density must be less than the British average. Using a figure of 7prs/km^2 for occupied tetrads would indicate a SE Scotland population of 26,500 pairs of Great Tits. Another method of estimation would be to divide the British population estimate of 1,600,000 territories (*New Atlas*) by SE Scotland's proportion of Britain's area, indicating 40,000 pairs, with a reduction as the area has below national average density; say 35,000 pairs. A compromise of these two methods suggests *c.*30,000 pairs of Great Tits in SE Scotland, 1.9% of Britain's total.   *H.E.M.Dott*

Great Tit

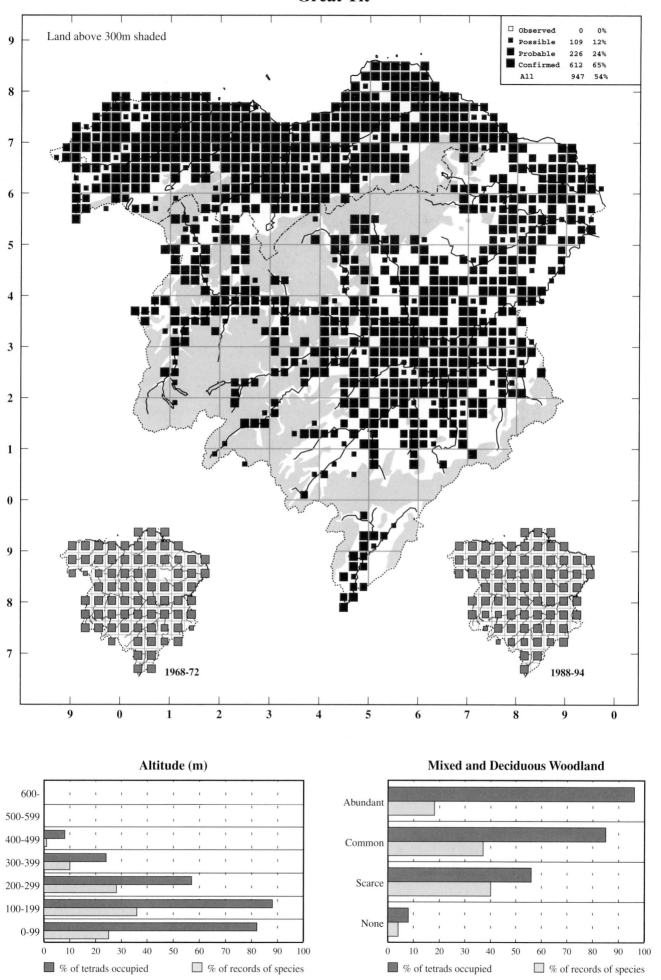

Land above 300m shaded

		Observed	0	0%
☐	Observed	0	0%
	Possible	109	12%
	Probable	226	24%
	Confirmed	612	65%
	All	947	54%

1968-72

1988-94

Altitude (m)

600-	
500-599	
400-499	
300-399	
200-299	
100-199	
0-99	

☐ % of tetrads occupied ☐ % of records of species

Mixed and Deciduous Woodland

Abundant	
Common	
Scarce	
None	

☐ % of tetrads occupied ☐ % of records of species

Nuthatch
Sitta europaea

The Nuthatch is a bird of mature deciduous woodland, parks and gardens. Large mature nut-bearing trees are essential with oak, beech and hazel providing the main winter food for the bird which gets its name from the habit of lodging nuts into the bark of trees prior to hammering them open with its stout bill. Nuthatches nest in tree holes, using both natural holes and those created by woodpeckers and man. They have a habit unique amongst Palearctic birds of reducing the hole size by applying mud to the margins in order to prevent larger species entering the hole either to usurp the resident birds or to predate the eggs or young.

Nuthatches are newcomers to SE Scotland and are still very rare. Discovery of sites in the area was either through hearing calls, reports of birds at feeders, or by pure accident, such as when birds were found breeding in a nest-box at the Hirsel. There is some reason to believe that the frequency of calling is depressed when they occur at low densities and so detection in a large area of woodland can be difficult. Reports from non-birders, especially those of birds at nut-feeders, have so far often proved to be correct. In some unconfirmed cases birds have been found at nearby locations in subsequent years.

The first Scottish breeding records came from the middle Tweed at the Hirsel (NT84F) and Floors Castle (NT73C) in 1989 (Murray 1991c). Birds have bred annually at both sites since. Spread away from those sites did not occur until 1992 when a bird was heard at Benrig (NT63A) in April and one started visiting a bird-table at Gattonside (NT53M) in the autumn. Numbers at the Hirsel and Floors increased while Hirsel birds appeared in Coldstream during the winter. Numbers increased significantly in 1994 when there were five territories at the Hirsel and at least three pairs at Floors. Singles were seen at Ashkirk (NT42R) in April, Minto (NT52Q) in May and at Mellerstain (NT63P), Wells Estate (NT51Y) and Langlee (NT53C) during the autumn and winter period. Hirsel birds were also reported at Coldstream Hospital (NT83J), Coldstream (NT83P) and the Lennel (NT84K) between August and December.

Away from the middle Tweed area there has been a series of intriguing reports from the coastal area where birds were reported from St. Abbs in May and July 1994. Taken alongside four confirmed reports from the same area in April 1987 and unconfirmed reports from Lumsdaine (NT86U) in 1985, Ayton (NT96F) in 1986 and Dunglass (NT77Q) in 1992 there is a strong hint that a small breeding population is in the area, perhaps in the steep-sided wooded deans of the Eye, Dunglass or Pease Burns near Cockburnspath and the Buskin and Mill Burns at Coldingham.

Single birds from a bird-table in Longformacus (NT65Y) in April 1986 &1993, at Peebles (NT23P) in April 1991 and at Dawyck (NT13S) in September 1995 suggest some dispersal away from the core areas and that there is every possibility that birds are present in the Dye and Whiteadder valleys and perhaps extending into the upper Tweed area. In Liddesdale, after being seen at bird tables at Redheugh (NY49V) in winter 1993-94, a pair had a territory straddling the border, although nesting just in Cumbria, near Kershopefoot (NY48W) in 1994.

Subsequent to the *Atlas* period, the Floors and Hirsel populations have built up to seven and six pairs respectively and breeding has been confirmed at Langlee (two pairs), Mellerstain (two pairs), Monteviot (two pairs at NT62M), Coldstream and Lees (NT83P) while pairs have been seen at Gala Policies (NT43X), the Lennel (NT84K) and Paxton House (three pairs at NT95G). Singles have also been reported from Abbotsford (NT53B), Pirn (NT44N), Lauder (NT54I), Denholm (NT51U), Hawick (NT51C) and Duns Castle (NT75S) and in winter at Birgham Wood (NT74V).

Although there are earlier non-breeding records in Scotland (*Thom*), the spread into the Borders is a part of a larger-scale expansion of the population into northern England (Murray 1991c). Large areas of Northumberland and Cumbria have been colonised in recent decades and the range limit gradually crept towards to the Scottish border during the 1980s. The expansion has been most marked in Northumberland from where the Borders birds are presumably derived, and while expansion in Cumbria has been slower, perhaps due to the topography, the Liddesdale breeding record in 1994 shows that the colonisation is also approaching Dumfries & Galloway (Dean 1987 & *Day*).

The rate of expansion in Borders from the two pairs in 1989 is now marked. By the end of the *Atlas* period in 1994 at least ten pairs were present but this rose to a minimum of 18 pairs by 1996 and may have been in excess of 20 pairs by 1997 (see graph and Appendix). The number of sites has increased from the original two to at least eight where breeding has been proved, with birds singing at another six. As broods of up to six young can be produced, a potential annual production of about 100 young is indicated. Large areas of suitable, but vacant, habitat appear to exist in the large estates, gallery woodland along the main rivers and in gardens, so there is every possibility that Nuthatches will rapidly colonise the whole area. The first Lothian record should occur in the next few years, the woodlands of the Esk and possibly Woodhall Dean being the best bets.

R.D.Murray

Nuthatch

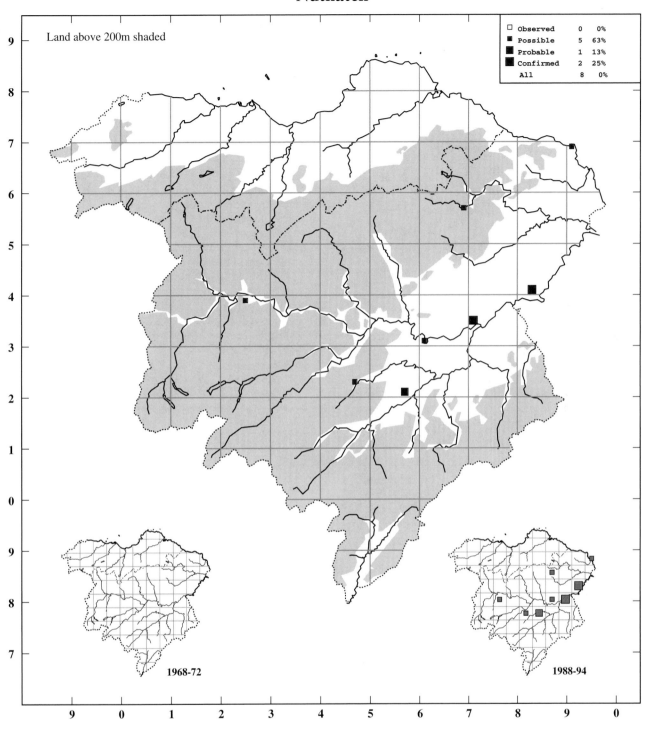

Land above 200m shaded

□	Observed	0	0%
■	Possible	5	63%
■	Probable	1	13%
■	Confirmed	2	25%
	All	8	0%

1968-72

1988-94

SE Scotland: Estimated Breeding Pairs 1989-97

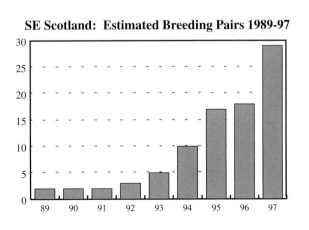

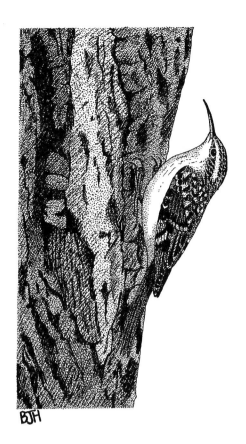

BJH

Treecreeper
Certhia familiaris

Foraging upwards across the vertical surfaces of tree trunks, the Treecreeper moves around like a small avian mouse exploiting a niche all of its own. Superbly camouflaged amongst the irregularities of colour and texture of the bark, it carefully searches upwards in the wrinkles and cavities of the trunk and branches for hidden invertebrates.

Such camouflage presents problems when searching for Treecreepers. They are quiet and furtive birds that do little to attract attention to themselves other than sing. While their song is diagnostic it is not always easy to distinguish amongst other background calls and song. The large percentage of possible records, a third of all reports, is tribute to the difficulty of locating Treecreepers and then being able to promote that record to probable or confirmed. Most were of birds in suitable habitat or singing males. As territories are rarely contiguous and birds are difficult to relocate, territoriality only accounted for half of the probable records with sightings of pairs making up much of the remainder. As usual, adults carrying food or feeding young were important in confirming breeding records, although one in six reports were of occupied nests, mainly birds disappearing into cavities in the bark.

Treecreepers mainly live in mixed and deciduous woodland and like most woodland passerines showed a marked preference for tetrads where mixed and deciduous woodlands are extensive or common. Nevertheless, about a third of all records came from tetrads where such habitats are scarce, suggesting Treecreepers are able to cope with even small woodlands. The relatively low percentage of occupied tetrads where mixed and deciduous woodlands are scarce suggests that Treecreepers are rather selective in their habitat preferences. As most mixed and deciduous woodland occurs below 300m it is no surprise that just 9% of birds were reported in tetrads above that altitude. While Treecreepers do live in coniferous woods, providing there are some deciduous species present, there are few records from areas where conifers are dominant.

The map is typical of a scarce species that lives in mixed and deciduous woodlands in SE Scotland. Such woodlands are fragmented across the low-lying areas of the Lothian coasts and the Merse with fingers reaching into the wooded valleys of the Tweed and Lothian drainage systems. This fragmented distribution is further broken up as Treecreepers apparently fail to occupy all available woodland habitats. There is some penetration into the uplands between 200-250m, almost wholly in wooded policies or large gardens towards the head of the river valleys such as at Carlops on the North Esk (NT15T), Rosebery on the South Esk (NT35D), Longformacus on the Dye (NT65Y), Carfrae on the Leader (NT55C) and to Mossfennan on the Tweed (NT13A). The highest and most remote penetration into the hills is at Ettrick (NT21S) where the Treecreeper shares a tiny enclave of ancient woodland with the Willow Tit. While there is a degree of range continuity along the upland and inland river valleys, it is in the lowlands that the inability of Treecreepers to live in tetrads where mixed and deciduous woodland is scarce and localised produces the greatest fragmentation of its range. Other than in western areas between Linlithgow, Livingston and Edinburgh (NT06,07,16,17&27) and around Stenton-Dunbar (NT67), Treecreepers seem to be rather patchily distributed in lowland areas. Clearly, Treecreepers are unable to live in many of the smaller blocks of woodland in areas of predominantly open arable farmland as can their allies the tits. In such areas most Treecreepers occur in the wooded policies of large estates.

Comparisons with the *Old Atlas* show losses along the southern and western edges of the range. While the presence in some of these marginal 10-km squares may have been from records of birds in neighbouring areas, the group of 10-km squares in the upper Tweed and Ettrick do hint at some range contraction, especially as there is no suggestion that woods have been felled in these areas. Adjacent squares, where Treecreepers are only represented in single tetrads, support the case that the bird is very scarce in the upper valleys. Missing a few scarce residents or any withdrawal of range would in any event appear as a loss. In the British population there is no suggestion of anything other than a gradual increase (*Trends*) in recent years and although both the *New Atlas* and the Northumberland Atlas (*Day*) show losses in 10-km squares at the upper ends of main valleys, neither make particular comment upon it. *Trends* does note that birds move into the more marginal farmland habitats in periods when numbers are high, only for them to retreat again into the optimal woodland habitats when population pressure drops. Perhaps these squares were occupied during such a period and that numbers in the valleys were low during the course of the *Atlas* survey, possibly after the hard winter of 1990-91 when the populations of other small resident woodland species crashed.

The *New Atlas* abundance map shows the Tweed valley holds good numbers of Treecreepers, with pockets of the highest abundance around Coldstream, Kelso, Monteviot, St. Boswells-Galashiels and Innerleithen-Peebles. Lothian generally shows moderate to lower abundances. SE Scotland appears to hold around average abundances.

There seems to have been little work on densities of Treecreepers in Britain. No studies are quoted in either the *Old Atlas* or its successor although they use values of 0.6-1.2prs/km^2 in their estimate of 200,000 pairs for the British population. Local data are also unhelpful in that da Prato (1985) only found 2 territories in his Tranent study while only one bird was seen on the local BBS plots in 1994-95. The *Bird Reports* record few sites that hold more than one or two territories. Roslin Glen (NT26R), the Hirsel (NT84A&F), Floors Castle (NT73C) and the Hermitage of Braid (NT27K) have held 4-7 territories between 1979-1995. While the Roslin site has been calculated to hold the equivalent of 21prs/km^2 (*Andrews*) that figure is of little help in determining the regional population. The BTO average density of 0.6-1.2prs/km^2 would give a population of 1,100-2,200 pairs across the area. ***R.D.Murray***

Treecreeper

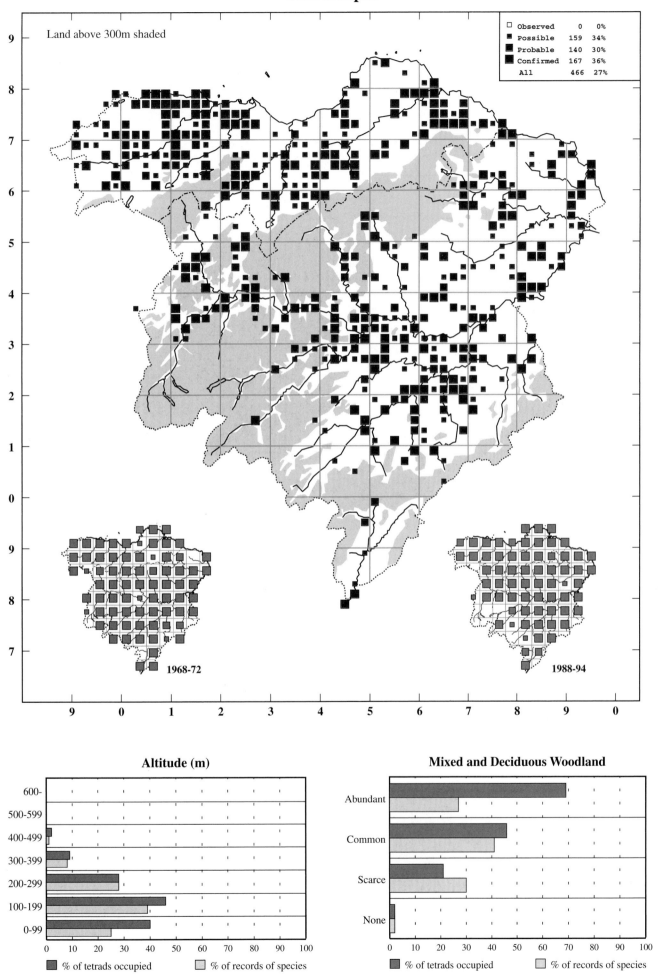

Land above 300m shaded

1968-72

1988-94

Altitude (m)

600-
500-599
400-499
300-399
200-299
100-199
0-99

0 10 20 30 40 50 60 70 80 90 100

◼ % of tetrads occupied   ☐ % of records of species

Mixed and Deciduous Woodland

Abundant
Common
Scarce
None

0 10 20 30 40 50 60 70 80 90 100

◼ % of tetrads occupied   ☐ % of records of species

275

Jay
Garrulus glandarius

A scolding screech from the depth of woodland cover or a flash of a white rump as a bird flap-glides across a woodland path are the usual encounters with Jays. While these colourful members of the crow family might be thought of as flashy and conspicuous birds from their field guide pictures, in reality it is usually difficult to even glimpse a Jay and rare to get a really good view. Their onomatopoetic name, however, makes them easy to identify when heard.

The Jay is one of the few species in the *Atlas* where possible records outnumber probable and confirmed records combined. Jays are secretive by nature but when persecuted the desire not to be seen seems to be raised by a magnitude or so and makes the bird exceedingly difficult to detect. It is not a familiar bird in our area and most observations were made by experienced observers who recognised the distant calls or the glimpses of furtive birds. Possible records were made up equally of birds in suitable habitat or calling birds. Probable records were shared between pairs and territorial birds recorded on more than one visit. Confirmed breeding was rare. It seems likely that the picture obtained between 1988-94 may underestimate the actual population, such are the difficulties of making contact with Jays.

Jays are birds of mixed and deciduous woodland, preferably woodlands that hold good numbers of nut-bearing trees, such as oak, hazel and beech, to provide feeding over the winter period. Such good-quality woodlands are uncommon in SE Scotland but the Jay distribution resembles an attenuated version of the mixed and deciduous woodland map of the area, Jays apparently living only in the highest quality woodlands. These are in the wooded policies of the large estates or remnant ancient woodland clinging to the steeper banks of the river systems. This can be seen in the Jay distribution with policy woodlands at Dalmeny (NT17), Bowhill (NT42), Monteviot (NT62), Floors Castle (NT73), Charterhall (NT74), Duns Castle (NT75), the Hirsel (NT84) and Ayton Castle (NT96). In ancient woodland remnants Jays occur along the Tweed between Innerleithen and Yair (NT33&43), Leaderfoot (NT53) and at Pressmennan (NT67).

While high-quality woodlands may be scarce in SE Scotland it is equally likely that Jays are uncommon because of persecution. Predation of Pheasant nests makes them unpopular with sporting interests and keepers routinely remove Jays when present. There is no doubt from historical accounts (Evans 1911, Nash 1935, *R&B*) that Jays largely vanished from much of SE Scotland by the end of the last century as a direct result of persecution. Records were exceedingly rare for much of the first half of the 20th century and it is almost certain that Jays became locally extinct, at least in Lothian, during this period. As the numbers of gamekeepers has steadily decreased since the Second World War, so has the Jay expanded its numbers and range and recolonised parts of the SE Scotland.

Jays can also live at very low densities in coniferous woodland and along some of the Tweed valley records come from sites where the narrow linear oakwoods border large blocks of commercial forestry. In sites such as Elibank (NT33) and Yair (NT43) along the Tweed and at Beecraigs (NT07) in West Lothian, Jays mostly inhabit the conifer forests and visit the neighbouring oak and beech woods to collect food. These sites may provide more secure living space, free from the persecution that might occur if they had to live permanently in the vicinity of keepering. Small plantations are a feature of many of the estates mentioned above and it is possible that the combination of reduced keepering and the development of afforestation together have aided the return of the Jay.

Whether the Jay actually ever totally disappeared from SE Scotland is uncertain. It almost certainly vanished from Lothian (*Andrews*) and possibly from the Borders (*Murray*) but there is a slight possibility that small numbers may have persisted in the lower Tweed and Teviot where immigration from the more stable Northumbrian population was possible (*Day*). A small number of 10-km squares produced records in the *Old Atlas*, mostly bordering on the more numerous populations of Northumberland and Dumfriesshire. Since then there has been a dramatic spread with gains in 26 squares as opposed to losses in just five. The spread into the Tweed valley has occurred since the mid-1970s while the West Lothian records date from the early 1980s. East Lothian only seems to have been colonised in the 1990s. Jays are similar to Magpies in their dispersal habits, judging from their records in the *Bird Reports*, and show an increase in sight records in winter as the young are pushed out of their natal areas by the renewed territorial behaviour of their parents in winter and spring. Such dispersal can only encourage the discovery of new habitats and there can be little doubt that Jays will thrive in years to come.

The *New Atlas* abundance map confirms that Jays are rare here, most of SE Scotland being blank. This probably means that few were encountered on formal *New Atlas* survey work and that the majority of 10-km square records may have come via supplementary records submitted from the tetrad atlas survey.

The *Bird Reports* have shown a steady increase in Jay numbers. There are usually records from many more sites in winter, when birds are easier to find, than in the breeding season. It is likely that many are overlooked in summer. While most sites only hold one or two birds, some sites hold more. In the mid-1980s, when a birder worked at Bowhill estate, that area was known to hold up to 12 pairs. The Hirsel, Elibank and Yair Forests regularly have three to four pairs. With records from only 87 tetrads, the population of SE Scotland is probably only between 80-100 pairs at present. This may well double in the next decade.   ***R.D.Murray***

Jay

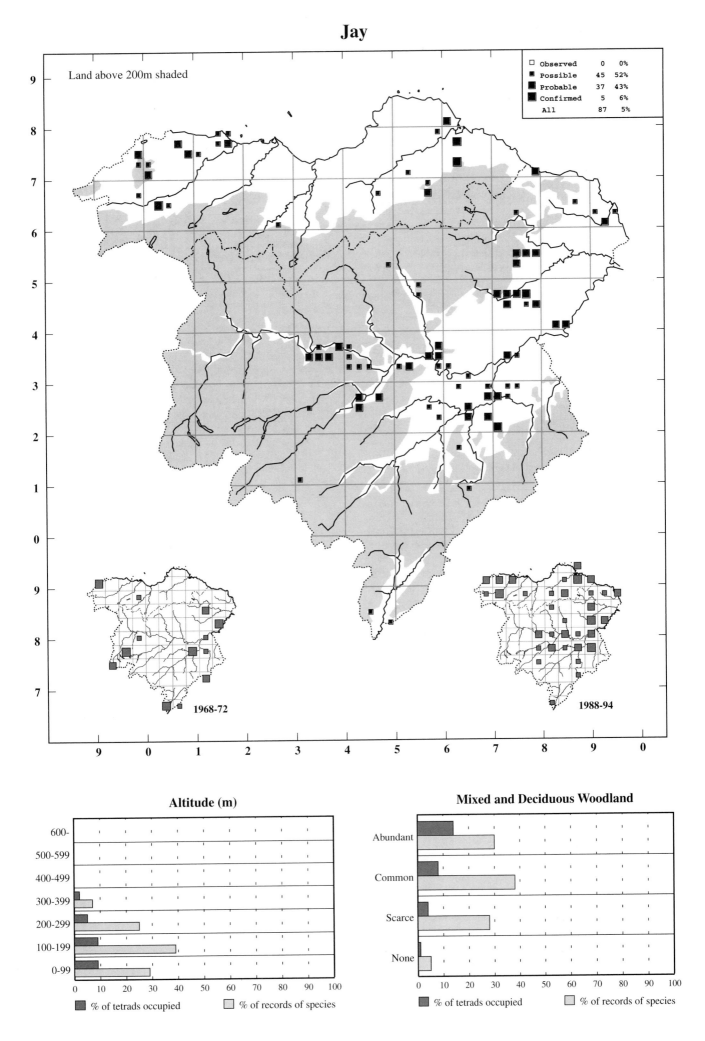

Land above 200m shaded

□ Observed	0	0%
Possible	45	52%
Probable	37	43%
Confirmed	5	6%
All	87	5%

1968-72

1988-94

Altitude (m)

600-	
500-599	
400-499	
300-399	
200-299	
100-199	
0-99	

■ % of tetrads occupied   ☐ % of records of species

Mixed and Deciduous Woodland

Abundant	
Common	
Scarce	
None	

■ % of tetrads occupied   ☐ % of records of species

Magpie
Pica pica

The Magpie's loud chatter and black and white cut are more and more frequently noticed nowadays, though suburban areas have long been favoured habitat. Magpies require open grass along with cover of gardens, trees or scrub. They have different strategies for siting nests: they may use dense twiggy or thorny growth such as hawthorn, thick evergreens for concealment such as fir, holly and exotics like monkey puzzle, or may nest in conspicuous single trees close to a farm-house or busy city road perhaps giving some safety from their enemies, Carrion Crows. Food is mainly invertebrates in summer and seeds or fruits in winter taken from grass pasture or lawns. Though eggs and young birds are taken from nests Magpies have no overall effect on numbers of songbirds lasting from one season to the next, except perhaps in small parks or gardens isolated from other good habitat (Gooch *et al*.1991, Groom 1993). Magpies have increased in Britain greatly through the 20th century. Though they avoid treeless country and extensive woods, their spread has taken them into some more open countryside, into conifer plantations, and further into city centres.

In the *Atlas* fieldwork, finding confirmation of breeding was not equally easy in all parts of the range. In West Lothian and Midlothian most Magpie nests are in hawthorn and other deciduous trees and are easily seen especially before leaf growth. In Borders and nearby parts of East Lothian they favour small dense stands of conifers, making nests difficult to locate (Dott 1994b). In the city both deciduous trees and evergreens are used, and recent Magpie colonists along the East Lothian coast use coastal growth including large Sea Buckthorns for nesting. Magpies are less obvious during incubation, and in Borders appeared to be more secretive and easy to miss in their favoured conifers, so they may be slightly under recorded in Borders, particularly in the probable and confirmed categories. Of all confirmed tetrads, 43% were due to fledged young seen and 46% to nests seen. The possible category formed a quarter of all tetrads and were mostly in the range fringes, sometimes in high locations, and may include young pioneering birds and some breeders whose partners or nests were not seen.

The map shows an extraordinary distribution, different from any other in this book, being continuous in West Lothian and Edinburgh and sparce or absent everywhere else. The solid West Lothian cover stops abruptly at the southern Pentlands, though reaching into the northern end of those hills (NT16). From Edinburgh there is a spread into and around the towns of the lower North and South Esk Rivers. Three extensions of the Magpie distribution are evident: along the Pentlands towards the source of the North Esk (NT15), up the flank of the Moorfoot Edge through to the headwaters of the Heriot, Gala and Leader Waters (NT35&45), and along the coast of East Lothian. Borders and East Lothian are largely empty of Magpies with some strangely far flung records and loose groupings in the Lammermuirs and the coast, and a separated population in the descents from the Cheviot Hills (NT60-82) which have only a few equally isolated neighbours over the watershed in Northumberland (map in *Day*). The altitude graph shows that nearly 90% of Magpies live below 300m, while a few live considerably higher and all of these are where there are conifer shelter strips or plantations as at Monynut (NT76J), Byrecleugh (NT65J), Soutra (NT45U), and Manorhead (NT12Y) and all with some improved or short-cropped grass nearby. The second graph shows that *c*.90% of Magpies are found where arable or improved grass are abundant or common, and almost none occur where no such land is present.

With suitable farmland and trees widespread through East Lothian and Borders, the distribution cannot be explained by natural factors. East coast climatic influence does not explain the scarcity as the *Old* and *New Atlases* show continuous Magpie range along most of the British east coast. The explanation is in the previous history of Magpie control by gamekeepers. Magpies disappeared from SE Scotland by about the 1840s due to keepering (*Thom*). This control decreased greatly since as far back as both world wars but Magpies have only recently begun to spread here. They were rare in East Lothian and scarce in Edinburgh in the 1950s (*Edinb. Bird Bull*), and occasional visitors at Duddingston and not common in the east of the city in 1960 (Anderson & Waterston 1961). Spread is now pronounced with records for new Magpie locations south and east of Edinburgh and in Borders and East Lothian steadily appearing in the *Bird Reports*. A huge spread since 1972 is evident by comparing the 10-km square maps opposite. There are a few disappearances, however, in south and west Borders, towards where the *New Atlas* shows considerable losses further south and west outwith SE Scotland. These are unexplained. In Britain generally there has been an ongoing 20th century increase and spread (Parslow 1973, *Trends*).

On a national scale of Magpie abundance the *New Atlas* shows SE Scotland to have extremely low levels with slightly higher levels in West Lothian and Edinburgh, agreeing well with the tetrad map. In contrast central and southern England and Wales are shown with continuous large areas of high abundance. British mean Magpie densities have increased greatly, reaching over 5prs/km^2 in farmland, over 10prs/km^2 in woodland and suburbs, and 32prs/km^2 in one English city (Birkhead 1991, Gooch *et al*. 1991) and have since increased further (Gregory & Marchant 1996). SE Scotland is far below these averages. West Lothian mixed farmland held Magpies at 1.75prs/km^2, Edinburgh suburbs at 2.25prs/km^2, and more urban Edinburgh at 1.50prs/km^2 (Dott 1994b). Using the mapped occupied tetrads and allowing 2.0prs/km^2 for those in Edinburgh and West and Midlothian, 0.5prs/km^2 for those in East Lothian and Borders, and 0.25prs/km^2 for tetrads showing possible breeding, the SE Scotland Magpie population is estimated to be *c*.1,870 pairs, a small 0.3% of Britain's population. Increase and spread is still occurring here, though the long British increase seems now to have slowed or ceased (Gregory & Marchant 1996). **H.E.M.Dott**

Magpie

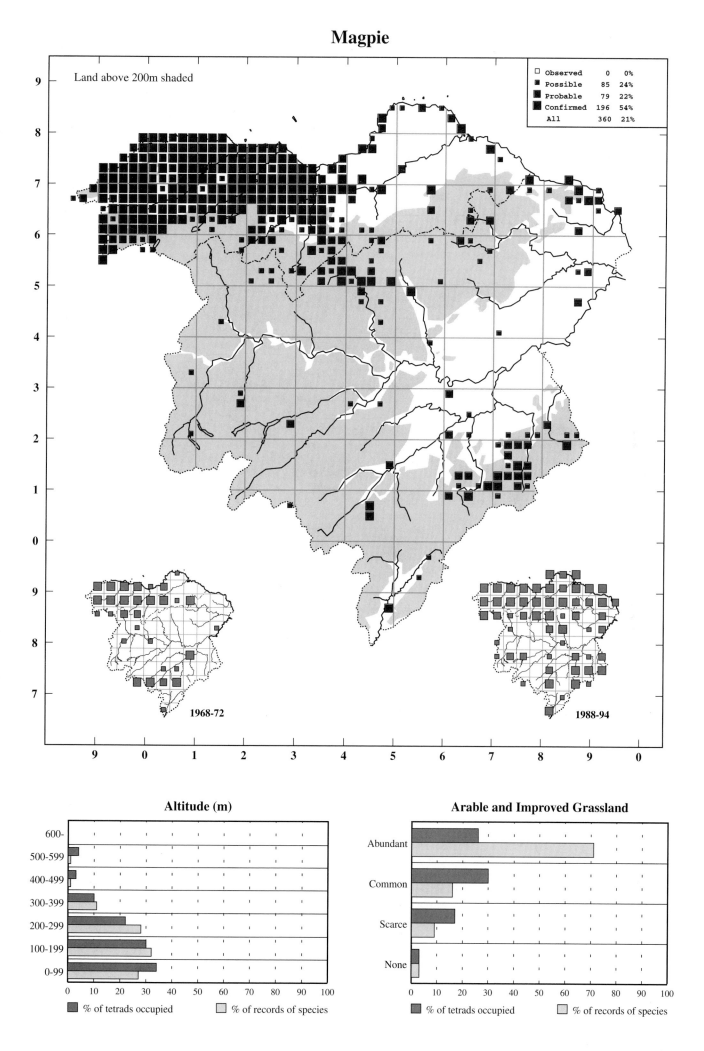

□	Observed	0	0%
■	Possible	85	24%
■	Probable	79	22%
■	Confirmed	196	54%
	All	360	21%

Land above 200m shaded

1968-72

1988-94

Altitude (m)

- 600-
- 500-599
- 400-499
- 300-399
- 200-299
- 100-199
- 0-99

■ % of tetrads occupied   ■ % of records of species

Arable and Improved Grassland

- Abundant
- Common
- Scarce
- None

■ % of tetrads occupied   ■ % of records of species

279

Jackdaw
Corvus monedula

Our smallest crow is a familiar bird in urban as well as rural settings in SE Scotland because of its liking for nesting in buildings where any sizable cavity can be used. The spread of central heating systems makes chimneys redundant, thus providing ideal nest-boxes for Jackdaws. Natural nest-sites, in tree holes and in cliffs, are not neglected either, but humans have doubtless allowed Jackdaws enormous scope for population increase and spread.

With their relative approachability and familiarity, Jackdaws were easy to record for the *Atlas*. The few observed and possible records were mostly noted from the fringes of the range in the barer hills or in the more open arable areas where nest-sites might be rare or absent from a tetrad. Jackdaws often feed or move around in small parties and one fifth of records, mostly of the pair category, came from such flocks. Jackdaw nests are very easy to locate and family parties are usually noisy and obvious and hence about two-thirds of all records were of confirmed breeding.

Jackdaws are adaptable birds that can find a living in most types of environment provided there are suitable nests sites. One colony near Birgham (NT83E) uses Rabbit burrows dug in a sand cliff above the Tweed to furnish the necessary nest-holes. Mixed and deciduous woodlands, most types of arable farmland and areas of improved grass provide abundant feeding areas and nest-holes in trees and buildings. The *New Atlas* mentions Scottish studies where Jackdaws used a mosaic of microhabitats within an area at different times of the year to provide the continuity of feeding necessary. Much of SE Scotland appears to provide this mosaic. The habitat data indicate that Jackdaws have a liking for tetrads where arable and improved grass are abundant, the bird being found in 90% of such tetrads in the area. There is also a liking for mixed and deciduous woodlands, birds being found in at least three-quarters of all tetrads where such habitat is present (graph not shown). However, while almost all tetrads where such woodlands are abundant are occupied, the largest number of Jackdaws (43% of all records) prefer tetrads where woodlands are small or scarce. This indicates a need for only a mimimum of woodland for nests along with plenty of open environment for feeding.

Where the open habitats offer no possibility of a nest-site, Jackdaws will be absent. This is most obvious in the treeless uplands above 350m where grass and heather dominate and cliffs, which might provide a nest-site, are rare. Accordingly there are few Jackdaws found at such levels unless human habitation offers an opportunity such as at the head of the Tweed where birds nest in buildings at Tweedshaws (NT01N) and Fruid (NT11E). The uplands form all of the major gaps in the map. Jackdaws are also absent in areas of commercial forestry (NT01,20,21,30,31,33,40,50&60), These woodlands generally lack both nest-holes and convenient areas of arable and improved pasture for feeding. On the lowlands the occasional vacant tetrad occurs in areas where tree-holes or suitable buildings must be absent. The absence of birds from coastal Edinburgh in Granton, Leith, Portobello and Joppa (NT27&37), as well as all of the Forth islands, may mark a lack of suitable feeding opportunities, as there is certainly no lack of nest-sites on buildings and cliffs.

With Jackdaws currently present in every 10-km square except NT20, comparison with the *Old Atlas* provides only limited information. In 1968-72 Jackdaws were absent in the central Moorfoots in NT34 and were present as just possible breeders in the central Lammermuirs in NT66. The current tetrad map shows that they really only have a toehold in both of these 10-km squares although the probable breeding sites in The Bell wood (NT66R) and at Cranshaws (NT66V) may have existed in 1968-72.

Jackdaws are more numerous in SE Scotland than in many places in Britain, other than the extreme west coasts, according to the *New Atlas* abundance map. Apart from the hills and conifer forests, much of the area has moderate to good numbers of Jackdaws with East Lothian north of the A1 and the Eye and Whiteadder valleys in Berwickshire producing the highest abundance values. The Almond valley in West Lothian and the middle Teviot drainage in Roxburgh also hold good numbers. Presumably all of these areas hold the habitat mosaic that Jackdaws prefer.

Both the *Old Atlas* and *New Atlas* used figures based around 1.6prs/km^2 in their calculations of the British population. This is rather close to the 1.26prs/km^2 obtained by da Prato (1985) for the mostly arable Tranent area. Local BBS returns equate to 3-5prs/km^2, a much higher value than the other statistics suggest. A coastal population at St. Abb's Head has a density of 5-6prs/km^2, and there are many sites and small towns that regularly hold colonies of 20-30 pairs according to the *Bird Reports*. The *New Atlas* abundance map suggests Jackdaws are much more numerous in SE Scotland than the average 1-2prs/km^2 national average and may be around 4prs/km^2. The occupied tetrads in SE Scotland would therefore hold about 19,000 pairs, *c.*5% of the British population.   ***R.D.Murray***

Jackdaw

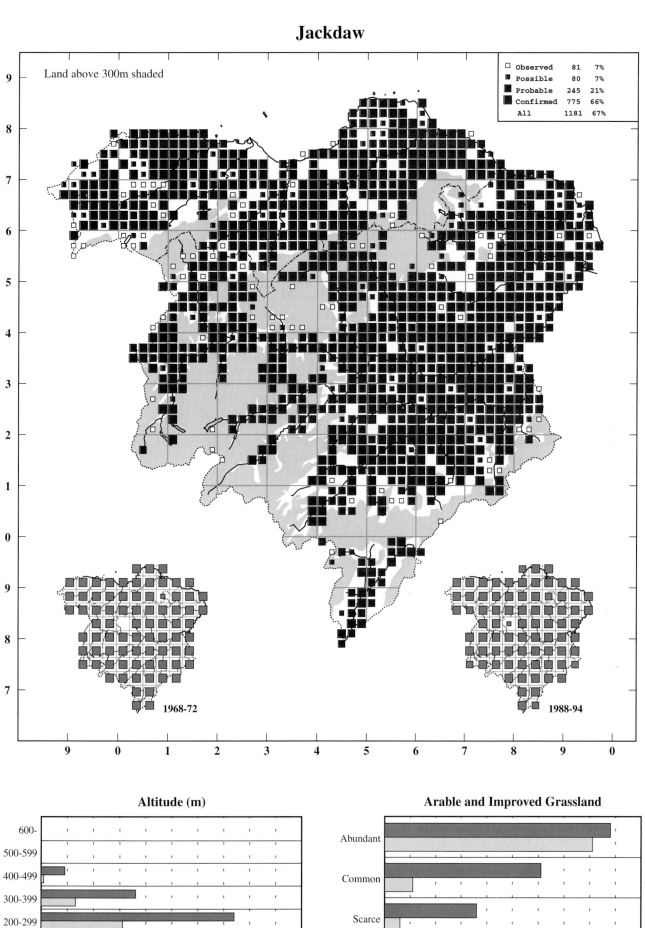

□	Observed	81	7%
▪	Possible	80	7%
◼	Probable	245	21%
■	Confirmed	775	66%
	All	1181	67%

Land above 300m shaded

1968-72

1988-94

Altitude (m)

■ % of tetrads occupied □ % of records of species

Arable and Improved Grassland

■ % of tetrads occupied □ % of records of species

Rook
Corvus frugilegus

The Rook is widespread across the Old World in temperate latitudes from Europe to China. Rooks are large and noticeable at all times of year, whether at nesting colonies, in winter feeding flocks or at roost. They are present in all areas of agricultural land in the lowlands of Britain, being uncommon only in the Highlands and islands. While Northern Ireland has the highest densities in Britain, Scotland has the biggest rookeries. They feed mostly on invertebrates, particularly in the nesting season, and so prefer non-arable farmland with pasture although they do utilise grain seasonally. They require mature trees for their nest colonies so a mixed landscape of lowland arable fields and pastures with amenity woodlands and shelterbelts represents the ideal habitat for Rooks.

Rooks are essentially sedentary, the breeding range almost exactly matching the winter distribution (*Winter Atlas*). Winter flocks can number tens of thousands, whereas few colonies exceed 500 nests. In the 1975 national survey (Sage & Vernon 1978) over half of the nest-sites were in Scots Pine followed by Beech, Sycamore, Oak and Elm in order of popularity. In a West Lothian study, Bennie (1984) found Sycamore (46%), Pine (20%), Beech (16%) and Elm (8%) were the preferred species. Nests in pines can be difficult to count accurately as old nests often amalgamate as they are enlarged each year.

In the *Atlas* survey fieldworkers were asked to only record Rooks as observed, to map their feeding range, or as confirmed breeding, to locate their colonies. Colonies were generally easy to find, being conspicuous to the eye and ear. However, once the foliage appears and the rookeries go silent after the young fledge in mid-May, they can be easily missed in a site not surveyed until later in the season. Experience with randomly chosen 1km-squares in the 1996 BTO census showed that colonies can be missed, even in well worked places, a view previously expressed by Murray (1991a).

The map shows Rooks do not breed in the uplands of the Lammermuirs, Moorfoots, Pentlands, Tweedsmuir or Cheviot Hills. This is supported by the altitude diagram which shows that almost 90% of breeding tetrads were situated below 300m. According to Castle (1977), the highest rookeries in Britain were at 340m in Berwickshire and Midlothian, but during the *Atlas* period there were three rookeries at sites between 360-380m: at Tollishill (NT55J) and Blackhope (NT35F) with the highest at White Barony (NT24T). This drop-off in occupation rate at altitude is almost certainly related with the Rook's liking for farming areas with arable and improved grasslands. The habitat graph shows very clearly that Rooks both nest and feed in areas where such habitats are common and abundant and so positive is this association for breeding birds that 87% of colonies were found in tetrads where these habitats were abundant. Very few colonies, just 3%, were in tetrads where this habitat was scarce or absent. Within arable areas blank tetrads might be expected where there is a lack of suitable nesting trees. This may be responsible for the voids in NT56&63, although it is more likely that some rookeries were overlooked in these squares. Nest colonies are also absent from the areas of blanket forestry in southern West Lothian (NS95&NT05), Craik (NT30&31), Newcastleton (NY58), Wauchope (NT50&60) and the middle Tweed (NT33). Habitat analysis shows that only 9% of rookeries were in tetrads where

conifers were extensive (not shown). Northern Edinburgh, lacking suitable feeding areas, also has no rookeries, although the more open southern half of the city does.

The main period of mortality for Rooks occurs in summer. Their reliance on worms causes problems in summer as their prey is driven underground by heat and dryness. Rooks can use the moister soils of upland areas that are less subject to drying out, and in summer forage in pastures well into the hills. The presence of crane-flies and other insect larvae in these habitats boosts food supplies at a critical time of year. Of all occupied tetrads above 300m, 77% had observed-only records, rising to 96% above 400m. Below 300m breeding tetrads outnumber observed tetrads by 6:5. The feeding range is limited by the need to return to a roost but birds fly as much as 20-25km from their colony to feed at the head of the Tweed and Ettrick. Similar records exist in the upper valleys of other hill areas.

Comparison with the *Old Atlas* shows a decline of breeding range since 1968-72. Three squares, involving just seven tetrads, have been colonised compared to 16 squares lost. Some of those lost are in marginal areas where breeding might have occurred outwith SE Scotland but all are in the hill fringes where other species that rely on arable farmland have shown similar declines. Rooks can feed in these areas, as the observed records show, but it is possible that changes in farming practice in these glens now prevent Rooks from being full-time residents. The loss of the few cereal fields and land to forestry may be critical. The *New Atlas* abundance map shows that Rooks occur in good numbers across the lower-lying parts of our area, with a few pockets of the best abundance at Tyninghame and along the Tweed between St. Boswells and Kelso.

Surveys show numbers peaked in the early 1950s, with a dramatic fall in numbers by the 1975 national count (Sage & Vernon 1978). The decline in SE Scotland from the 1944-46 count was 52% but numbers have gradually recovered, the 1980 sample census showing a local rise of 10% (Sage & Whittington, 1985). The 1996 sample count indicates further recovery, although still short of the 1944-46 figures (Marchant 1997). The Clyde survey of 1987-88 (Wood 1990) reported a doubling of numbers since 1975, but Northumberland showed a continuing decline in nest numbers since 1980 of about 50% (*Day*). Locally, there have been several surveys which confirm a decrease followed by recovery. Munro (1970) found a 66% reduction in numbers of colonies in Edinburgh from 1957 to 1970. Bennie (1984 & 1985) showed a density increase in West Lothian from 9.3 nests/km^2 to 13.3 nests/km^2 from 1975-83. There was a steep rise of 51% in Tweeddale since 1975 (Murray 1991a). This dramatic increase, and the Clyde results, were thought to be partly products of serious under-recording in the 1975 census.

The population in SE Scotland can be calculated from 1975 census figures of 34,204 nests. Using Marchant's (1997) figure of a 43% rise for the UK by 1996, a population of 48,911 pairs with a density of 7.1 nests/km^2 is indicated, although the under-recording in the 1975 survey, where whole 10-km squares were omitted (Murray 1991a), suggests a higher figure of 55,000 pairs, or 4.3% of the latest British population estimate (Marchant 1997).

N.Crowther

Rook

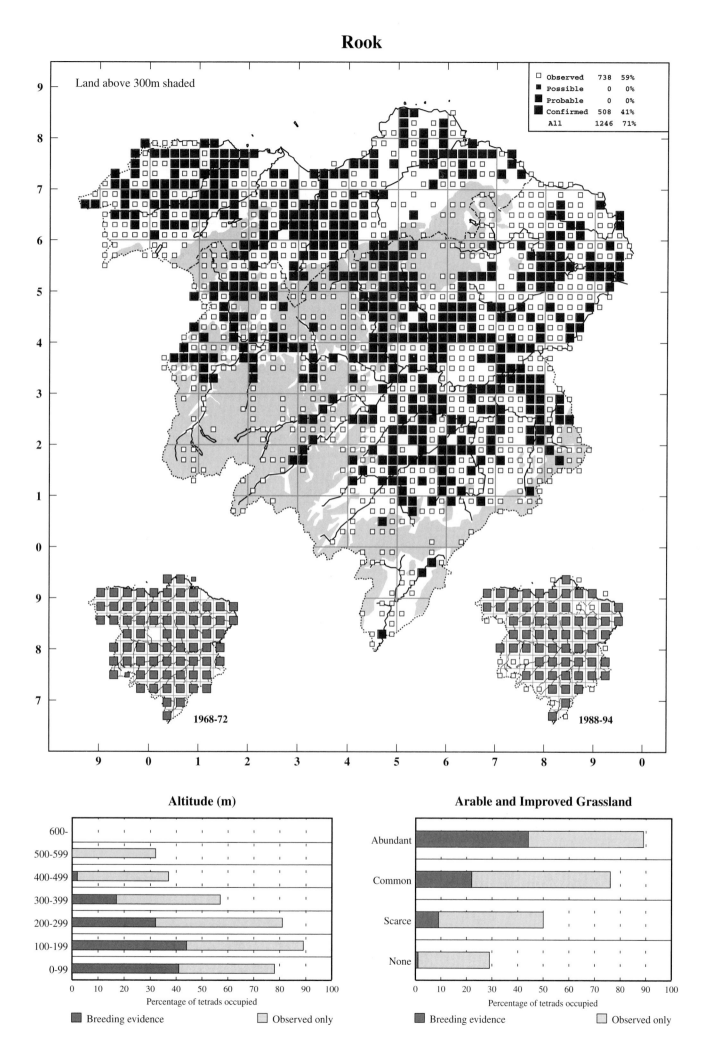

Land above 300m shaded

	Observed	738	59%
	Possible	0	0%
	Probable	0	0%
	Confirmed	508	41%
	All	1246	71%

1968-72

1988-94

Altitude (m)

Percentage of tetrads occupied

◼ Breeding evidence   ▢ Observed only

Arable and Improved Grassland

Percentage of tetrads occupied

◼ Breeding evidence   ▢ Observed only

283

Carrion Crow and Carrion x Hooded Hybrid Crow

Corvus corone corone and *C. c. corone* x *C. c. cornix*

The Carrion Crow is a highly adaptable bird, being able to seek out a living in a great variety of habitats. All types of farmland and countryside are used and Crows now nest right through suburbs and city centres, only moors and mountains offering few nesting places. Edges of woods and strips of trees are used but not normally extensive dense woods, although they have begun to do so in some coniferous plantations. In rural areas Crows choose tall trees but avoid those close to human dwellings, while in towns they may nest high over busy streets, perhaps thus avoiding attention. Crows eat ground invertebrates, worms, grains, seeds, carrion, birds' eggs and young, periwinkles and worms on shores where larger shellfish will be dropped on rocks to break them, and in towns all manner of scraps and garbage. Crows may not breed till their third or fourth year, and these younger birds form loose roaming groups or flocks, forming a significant part of the population.

Crows and their nests are often conspicuous and confirmed and probable records together formed 87% of the total. Half of confirmed records were of nests seen while a third were of young. Observers were asked to record Hybrid Crows, resulting in 38 tetrad reports, shown on the smaller map. The main map incorporates all Carrion and Hybrid records, but as perhaps every breeding Hybrid Crow had a Carrion Crow mate, the findings from the main map can be discussed as though for the Carrion Crow.

No pure Hooded Crows were recorded for the *Atlas*, despite very small numbers being noted in the *Bird Reports* each winter, mostly near the coast, their origin remaining obscure. The *Atlas* Hybrid records are widely scattered, with slight concentrations in Edinburgh and the hill edges south of Edinburgh near Leadburn, where winter records also come from. The continued presence of Hybrids strongly suggests a pool of Hooded-type genes, and interestingly, for many local hill-country farmers "Hoodie" is still the regular name for all Crows as distinct from Rooks or Jackdaws, possibly an indication of a time when grey-and-black forms were more widespread. *R&B* describe the Hooded Crow as a winter visitor and "breeding sparingly and occasionally in the Lothians". The *New Atlas* marks a few pure Hooded Crows in SE Scotland, but it is fairly subjective whether an observer judges a pale shade of grey to indicate a Hooded or a Hybrid Crow.

The main map shows a very widespread and solid distribution with 92% of all tetrads having Crows. However, two habitats have fewer Crows: high open land and large coniferous forest. The Lammermuir Hills have the most wide open expanses and form the largest gap without Crows. Other hill masses such as the Moorfoots (NT34), Pentlands (NT15) and Tweedsmuir Hills (NT11,12) with much bare grazing or heather, also have steep gullies which can harbour odd trees, and Crows will utilise even a single stunted bush-sized tree far into hills or moors if available. Most of the northern Pentlands have Crows where fairly frequent shelter strips or remnants of these provide nest sites. The areas with major coniferous forests such as in NY58, NT30,31,50,60, and NS95 all show absence or scarcity of Crows. Some tetrads within large coniferous expanses such as Craik Forest (NT30) hold a few breeding Crows, using the few mature deciduous trees that still stand beside abandoned farm buildings, now surrounded by plantation. In SE Scotland Carrion Crows have hardly begun to

nest in large coniferous plantations as happens elsewhere, though the habit may be just beginning (Dott 1994b).

The whole of the city of Edinburgh and Leith and other towns are occupied by Crows, and most of the islands in the Forth have a pair of breeding Carrion Crows at least in some years. Most of the 5% of tetrads with only observed records are on the flanks of hills, and will be due to Crows seen foraging a little higher than the breeding tetrads reach. The small but wide scatter of tetrads with Crows only possible, observed or absent are harder to explain and some may simply be where birds were overlooked. However, Crows are legally trapped in lambing and game bird areas, or casually shot in farming regions in general. This will not usually have any effect on Crow distribution as other birds quickly move in, but may temporarily have a local effect. This may be true of NT06L, a game rearing area, where breeding Crows were absent despite being searched for. Similarly, the lack of Crows around Hawick (NT41) is puzzling and could be due to control or under-recording or both.

The graph confirms that tetrads up to 300m are almost totally inhabited by Crows, with 60% occupancy even as high as 500-600m. Habitat data indicate that 60% of tetrads with Crows in SE Scotland are where arable or improved grassland is abundant, with another 12% where such land is common.

In Britain as a whole the Carrion Crow has increased greatly as persecution has declined, especially since the 1940s, and has spread into towns and some upland conifer plantations (*Old Atlas, Trends*). Some increase is still continuing though more on mixed and grazing farmland than in other habitats (Gregory & Marchant 1996). Increase has probably occurred in SE Scotland also although evidence is lacking. The species is too widespread for the 10-km square maps to reveal any significant local change, and the *Bird Reports* receive few contributions on breeding numbers.

At the time of the *Old Atlas* British Crow densities were 3.2prs/km^2 in farmland and 4.7prs/km^2 in woodland, and an average of 2.5prs/km^2 was used for estimation of national numbers. Though densities have now risen higher (Gregory & Marchant 1996), in SE Scotland Crows appear to be well below the national average. In mainly arable land in East Lothian, da Prato (1985) found 2.0prs/km^2 over a 17km^2 study area. In Tranent town there were *c*.3.3prs/km^2, and in high-rise housing in Edinburgh *c*.0.8prs/km^2 (da Prato 1989). Dott (1994b) found 2.5prs/km^2 in Edinburgh and in mixed farmland in West Lothian, *c*.1.5prs/km^2 in Edinburgh fringes, 0.2prs/km^2 in East Lothian arable land, and 0.25-0.5prs/km^2 in hill grazing land in Borders. Taking all occupied tetrads below 300m (the approximate upper limit of arable and improved grassland) at 2.25prs/km^2 and all above at 0.35prs/km^2, the Carrion Crow population of SE Scotland is estimated to be 10,500 breeding pairs, plus a large unknown number of non-breeding younger birds, a surprisingly low 1.1% of Britain's estimated Carrion and Hooded Crow territories.

H.E.M.Dott

Carrion Crow or Carrion x Hooded Hybrid Crow

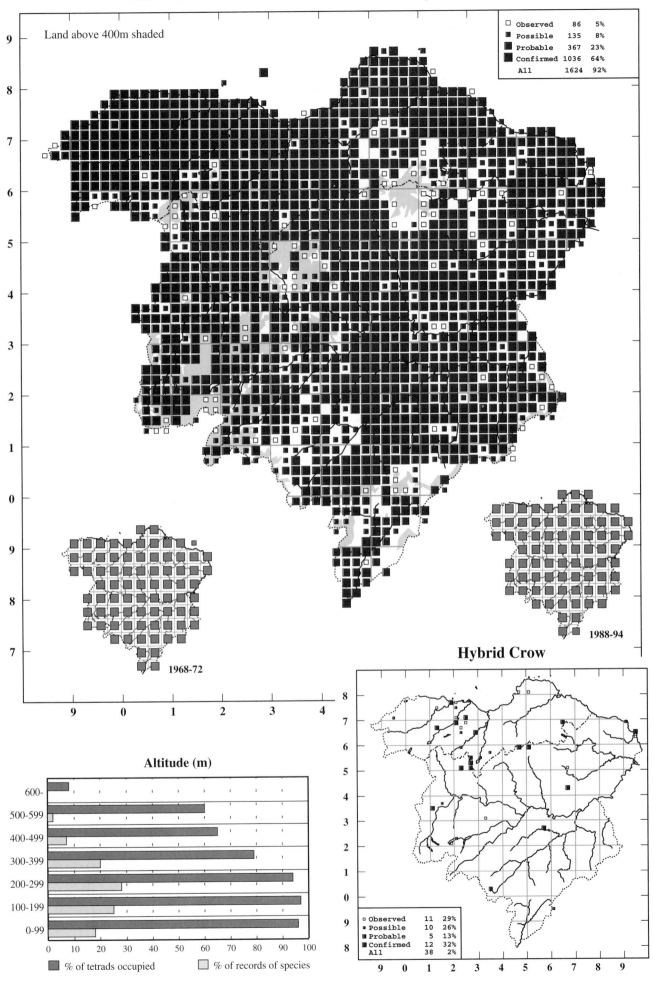

	Observed	86	5%
	Possible	135	8%
	Probable	367	23%
	Confirmed	1036	64%
	All	1624	92%

Land above 400m shaded

1968-72

1988-94

Altitude (m)

■ % of tetrads occupied   □ % of records of species

Hybrid Crow

	Observed	11	29%
	Possible	10	26%
	Probable	5	13%
	Confirmed	12	32%
	All	38	2%

285

Raven
Corvus corax

A large black bird appearing over a ridge, uttering deep croaking calls and perhaps tumbling in an acrobatic aerial display marks the sight of a Raven in its windswept hill homeland. Ravens are found mainly in western Britain in upland and coastal habitats, nesting on cliffs and in trees. They feed largely on carrion, and sheep carrion is an important food source throughout the range in Britain. Timing their breeding season to take advantage of the peak of winter mortality amongst sheep, goats and deer, Ravens are one of the earliest nesting species. Some clutches can be laid in the late autumn, although young birds usually fledge in April.

Ravens are rather scarce birds in SE Scotland, and rarely recorded in *Atlas* fieldwork. Over half of all records were assigned to the observed category because the birds were seen flying over a tetrad, often for some distance. These records referred to individuals, pairs and even small parties of families or non-breeders. Due to the early breeding season and the wandering nature of Ravens during the rest of the year, these records could not be upgraded to represent more definite breeding evidence. Most other records were of individuals or pairs using the habitat, but with no further evidence of breeding. There were only four tetrads where breeding was confirmed, based on nests found or recently fledged juveniles. Some nesting attempts will have failed before the start of the *Atlas* fieldwork season and will not have been recorded. The map therefore almost certainly underestimates the likely breeding population.

To protect these few nesting pairs, the map shows distribution only at the 10-km square level. There is a clear centre of population in the south-west from above the headwaters of the Tweed and Yarrow in the Tweedsmuir Hills (NT11) across to the Moorfoots (NT44). Fewer birds were recorded in the Pentlands, the Lammermuirs and around the Cheviot. There is a further group of tetrads on the Berwickshire coast west of St. Abb's Head. All of the hill areas are heavily grazed by sheep with sheep carrion providing food. There is, however, a natural shortage of nesting sites owing to the almost complete lack of suitable cliffs and crags. There is a wider range of prey available at the coast and no shortage of cliff nest sites. The altitude analysis (not shown) has 90% of records at 300m and over with 69% between 300m and 500m. This is the height of most of the exclusively sheep grazing country. The occupancy rate increases with altitude (see graph).

Comparison with the *Old Atlas* reveals a mixed picture of some range expansion and some contraction. The total number of 10-km squares has increased by three if squares with observed records only in 1988-94 are included, but the range has changed notably. In the two surveys there were similar concentrations in the Tweedsmuirs and some increase eastwards in the Moorfoots. However, some contraction is indicated in the recent period further

south and east in the Cheviot Hills, where there were just two occupied squares in 1988-94. Two factors may be responsible for this loss. Most of the 10-km squares are on the margins of the recording area and in 1968-72 the records may have been in Northumberland or Dumfries and Galloway rather than Borders. Secondly, much of this area is now under forestry. The *New Atlas* shows a large area of losses around the English border, coinciding with the Border and Kielder forests. However, there have been gains in the east, in parts of the Lammermuirs and on the coast. These differences are probably related to habitat changes during the intervening 20-year period. Large scale afforestation will have removed previously suitable habitat, especially in the southern part of Borders, and improved animal husbandry during this period also reduced the supply of available carrion. Mearns (1983) documented a 70% decrease in Ravens in southern Scotland due to these two reasons. Since then though, there has been a balancing increase in the numbers of sheep in other areas, which have seen such high levels of grazing that heather has been lost from large areas of hill. This increase will have provided more food for Ravens. It is likely that, as the commercial forests mature and the canopy is opened up by felling, Ravens will move back into these areas, making use of trees for nesting and eating deer carrion (C. Rollie *pers. comm.*).

The Raven was formerly common and widespread in SE Scotland, breeding in Edinburgh on the Castle Rock and Arthur's Seat, and on the islands off North Berwick (*Andrews*). *Thom,* summarising the status of Ravens in the 20th century, states that breeding did not occur in West or East Lothian, and ceased in Midlothian in 1976. By 1981, breeding was confined to Peeblesshire, and throughout the 1980s there were only two or three pairs in Borders, in the Tweedsmuir Hills. In this survey, the four confirmed breeding records came from the Tweedsmuirs (two sites), the Berwickshire coast and the Pentlands. The coast was recolonised in 1990, where a recently fledged juvenile was seen in December. The Berwickshire coast now supports three pairs, as it did previously prior to 1972 (Mearns 1983). Breeding in Lothian recommenced in 1993 (*Bird Reports*). The increase in the number of records from a wider range of sites seems to have occurred in 1989-90.

Despite the increase in sightings, the species is still very scarce as a breeder. The *New Atlas* gives a population for Britain of 7,000 pairs, but since then Ratcliffe (1997) has reduced the estimate to just 4,300 pairs in Britain and Ireland. In SE Scotland in 1988-94, there was a minimum of only four breeding pairs, with no more than 16 pairs present, (based on tetrads with probable breeding records). More detailed monitoring by the Lothian & Borders Raptor Study Group in 1997 revealed 11 breeding pairs with two of these in Lothian. Such detailed, regular checking of sites is essential to keep a handle on the changing fortunes of the species. *M.Holling*

Raven

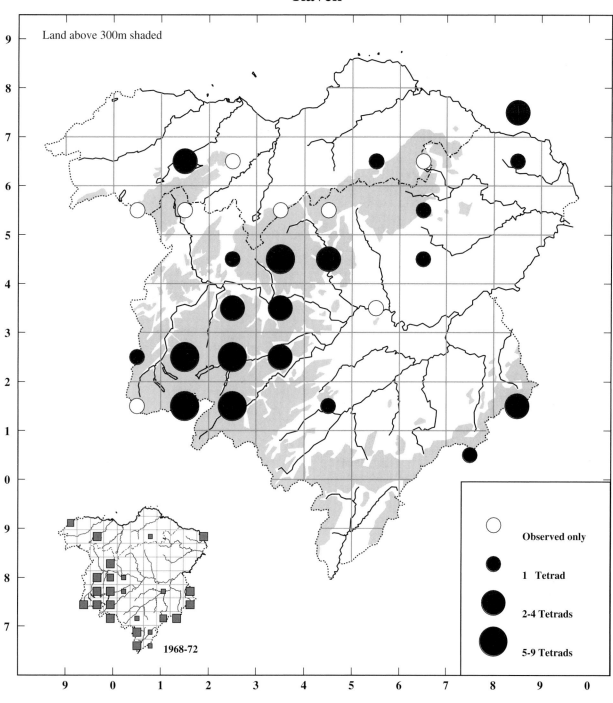

Land above 300m shaded

1968-72

Observed only

● 1 Tetrad

● 2-4 Tetrads

● 5-9 Tetrads

Altitude (m)

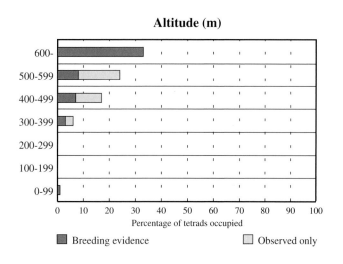

Percentage of tetrads occupied

■ Breeding evidence ☐ Observed only

287

Starling

Sturnus vulgaris

Love them because of their jaunty, almost arrogant song, behaviour and appearance, or hate them because of their aggressiveness in driving off smaller birds from food in the garden and messily nesting inside your house, Starlings are a familiar part of the avifauna of SE Scotland. Their ability to adapt to human settlements and farmland has allowed them to become widespread and abundant and one of the most successful birds on the planet, travelling through introductions to all of the continents bar Antarctica and South America.

Starlings, through their ease of identification, their tameness and their liking for nesting in human habitations were easy to record. Their noisy young and the ceaseless efforts needed to keep them fed, with parents travelling like arrows straight between the feeding grounds and their nests, resulted in confirmed breeding records forming the majority of records. Indeed an 82% rate of confirmed breeding records was not surpassed by any other species.

Open ground, from which the invertebrate food demanded by their young can be obtained, and some kind of nest-hole, seem to be the basic habitat requirements of Starlings. The open ground can be in arable farmland, improved or rough grassland, open woodland, cliff tops or urban parks and gardens, although permanent pasture is preferred. The nest site is typically either in a building or a natural tree-hole but could equally be in a cave or cranny in a cliff, a nest-box, old Sand Martin burrow or an old, or even usurped, woodpecker hole.

Starlings rank as the 14th most widespread species in the area and their local range bears a striking resemblance to that of the distribution of arable and improved grassland, being common and widespread up to 300m but distinctly rare above 400m. The gaps on the map are generally above 300m where grassy or heather moorland dominates and to a lesser extent in the areas of extensive commercial forestry (NT30,31,33,40,50&60). The preference for arable farmland is quite distinct with the percentage of occupied tetrads steadily increasing with the increase in the amount of arable land within the tetrad, rising from just 13% in tetrads where there is no arable land to 92% of all tetrads where arable is abundant. This is also confirmed by the fact that 75% of all bird records come from tetrads where arable is abundant. The Starling map also bears comparison with that of settlement in the area. The presence or absence of buildings may control their ability to penetrate upland areas where there is undoubtedly good feeding in summer but a general lack of suitable nest-holes. A farm steading in the hills can allow Starlings to forage over large areas of hill pasture. Such habitats are productive as is witnessed by the large parties of juvenile Starlings that move into the uplands in June and July to take advantage of the emergence of crane-flies and caterpillars (*Bird Reports*). Such parties form the bulk of the 4% observed dots on the map.

Starlings are able to fully take advantage of the islands in the Forth with probable and confirmed breeding records in the *Atlas* from Cramond Island, Inchmickery, Inchkeith and the Bass Rock and possible records on Fidra, where breeding has occurred in the past. Breeding is also regular on Inchcolm and the Isle of May. Such a widespread range on the islands is unusual amongst passerines and reflects the Starling's adaptability.

With 100% of 10-km squares occupied in both 1968-72 and 1988-94, no worthwhile information can be obtained through comparison of the two maps, although it is possible that some contraction from the upper valleys may have taken place within 10-km squares since the *Old Atlas,* in common with other species

that exploit arable land (see Yellowhammer, Rook, Linnet). The *New Atlas* abundance map shows that much of Lothian north of the hills, from West Lothian eastwards to Dunbar, as well as the Merse and the Eye valley hold the highest abundances of Starlings. Moderate numbers surround these areas, mostly into the hill fringes, and there is a large area of moderate abundance in the middle Tweed and Teviot. The hills generally show low numbers, while the highest hills are empty.

Nationally Starling numbers are dropping (*Trends*), possibly due to the conversion of grasslands to cereals that hold fewer invertebrates (*New Atlas*). There is little or no evidence that this is happening in SE Scotland and it is possible that the national statistics may be biased due to the concentration of CBC plots in southern England where such farmland alterations have been widespread (*Trends*).

Fortunately some work has been done on Starlings in SE Scotland. In a survey of birds in the urban edge at Balerno (NT16) (Hurley & Hurley 1990), 169 nests were found in 50km^2, half of a 10-km square. However, 137 of the nests were in just four 1km squares, where the birds nested in modern houses and fed in the surrounding countryside. Even higher numbers have come to light at Eddleston village (NT24N) where 56-70 nests were found in 1995-97 in an area of less than 40 hectares but feeding over a wider area in *c.*4km^2 of the surrounding countryside (Murray *in prep.*). This colonial-type nesting in modern housing nowadays might hold the bulk of breeding Starlings in our area. In Edinburgh *c.*40ha of woodland at the Hermitage of Braid (NT27K) held 53-70 nests between 1986-88, mostly birds nesting in natural sites within the woodland and feeding in the surrounding grassland, parks and gardens. Other loose colonies noted in the *Bird Reports* include 13-19 pairs in Roslin Glen (NT26R) and 18 pairs in Newbattle Abbey (NT36I), while 38 pairs have bred on Inchkeith island. About 10-11 pairs breed at St. Abb's Head (5prs/km^2), a value close to da Prato's study in arable farmland (1985) which did not, however, include houses and gardens. A later study by da Prato (1989) in urban habitats at the Royal Botanic Garden in Edinburgh and in Tranent town found densities of 7-9prs/km^2. Local BBS returns suggest 11-17prs/km^2, very close to the farmland CBC value quoted in the *Old Atlas* of 11-19prs/km^2. The semi-colonial nature of Starling breeding creates difficulties in any calculation but a value of 10-12prs/km^2 would produce a local population of about 51,000-62,000 pairs in SE Scotland.   ***D.J.Kelly & R.D.Murray***

Starling

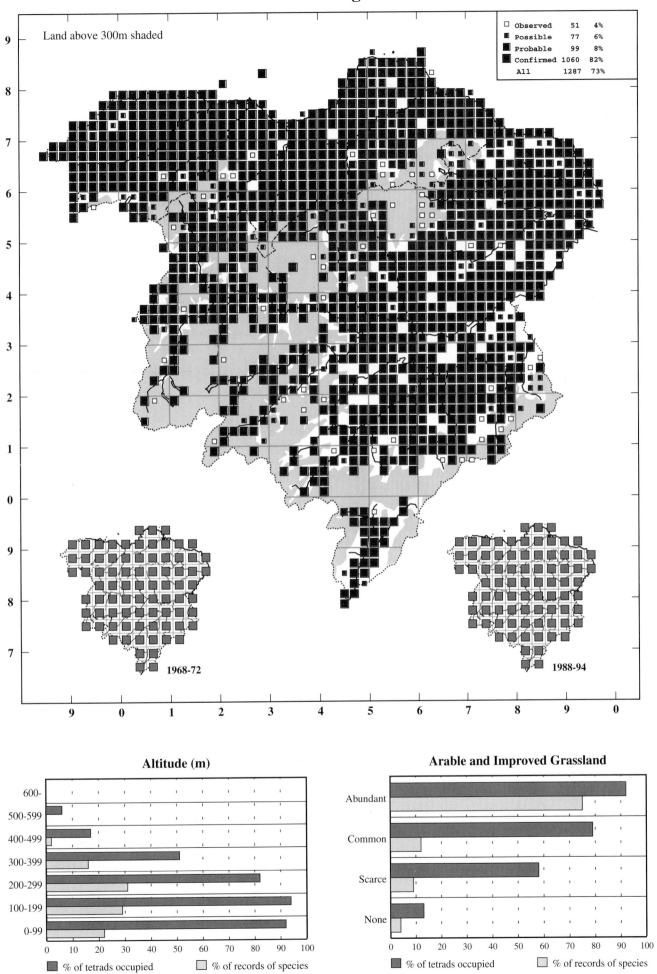

Land above 300m shaded

	Observed	51	4%
	Possible	77	6%
	Probable	99	8%
	Confirmed	1060	82%
	All	1287	73%

1968-72

1988-94

Altitude (m)

% of tetrads occupied % of records of species

Arable and Improved Grassland

Abundant

Common

Scarce

None

% of tetrads occupied % of records of species

House Sparrow
Passer domesticus

Considered 'ordinary' by many bird-watchers and non-birders alike, the House Sparrow is in fact full of interest. House Sparrows have reached and survived in amazingly varied environments across the world. They spread and increased through England in the 18th century and and reached remoter parts of the Scottish highlands by the late 19th century. They are absent from mountains, moors, large woods and plantations. Young House Sparrows require insect food, and so densities are higher in suburbs with gardens than in built-up city centres.

Fieldwork produced confirmed and probable records in 96% of all tetrads with House Sparrows. Half the confirmed records were of occupied nests and a third were of young seen, while probable were mostly of territory and pairs seen. House Sparrows remain close to their nesting locations except in late summer when some stray further out into grain fields (*BWP*). As the *Atlas* fieldwork was done before this time, the map opposite should be a good record of the breeding distribution.

The map shows a solid spread of House Sparrows over the low ground with fingers extending higher by way of river glens. There are a few low-ground tetrads showing no House Sparrows. In some of these birds may have been overlooked, but in tetrads with no buildings or only a few small exposed farms (e.g. NT48X,67J &R,72J,76Z) House Sparrows may truely be absent. Although Sparrow tetrads look continuous through the lowlands, in reality it is only the spots of human settlement within these tetrads that actually have breeding House Sparrows. There are birds at some isolated settlements quite far up most of the river glens, although between these there are farms with none. House Sparrows are present in the upper Liddel and Hermitage Waters (NY49,59) where farming is amost exclusively stock-grazing, and where this *Atlas* finds other arable-liking species such as Yellowhammer, Tree Sparrow and Linnet to be absent or very scarce. The hills, moorlands and large conifer forests stand out as gaps with no House Sparrows.

The graphs bear out the map interpretations. The first graph shows a pronounced association with human settlement: 100% of large settlements have House Sparrows, 96% of of tetrads with villages up to 0.5km^2 have them, dropping to 68% of tetrads with 1-3 farmsteads having House Sparrows. The minute number of Sparrows apparently with no settlements will be an artefact of small buildings being present but not seen on maps. The second graph reveals that 85% of all tetrads with House Sparrows are where arable or improved grassland is abundant. The mere 1% with birds and no arable or grassland must account for all urban House Sparrows, apart from those in tetrads on the margins of settlements next to arable land. Altitude records show that almost 90% of all tetrads up to 200m have House Sparrows, quickly declining from 300m to seven tetrads occupied at 400-450m. House Sparrows can live higher if habitat factors allow; they have lived in Scottish villages at over 1,000m (*B&R*) and at 3,750m in the Andes – probably the highest resident House Sparrows in the world (Dott 1986).

The number of House Sparrows in Britain is thought to have peaked about the early 1970s but has since been declining. The decrease is occurring in rural and urban areas, and range has decreased in northern and western Britain, and in England, on a scale finer than the 10-km grid shows (Summers-Smith 1988, *New Atlas*). The BTO Garden Bird Feeding Survey indicates a 15-20% drop in House Sparrows visiting suburban gardens in the period 1977-88 (*Trends*).

In SE Scotland evidence points to considerable decreases in House Sparrows. In the centre of Edinburgh approximately a ten-fold decrease has occurred from the 1980s-90s (Dott & Brown *in prep.*).

In the suburbs of southern Edinburgh there has been an unmeasured decrease since the 1960s or 1970s, and at farms around the Pentland and Moorfoot Hills House Sparrows have declined or disappeared (this author, R.W.J. Smith, G.L. Sandeman *pers.comm.*, Munro 1988). The 10-km maps reveal no significant change; the SW marginal squares with House Sparrows in the earlier map would have been birds over the boundary in lower areas. Square NT56 must have held overlooked birds in 1968-72. However, the disappearance noted from margins of the Pentland and Moorfoot Hills is probably part of a wider shrinkage from upper farmland generally in SE Scotland as these farms have changed from mixed farming to pure stock farming, with loss of corn stacks from fields and yards and reduced winter stubble. Lower down increased pesticides in farms and gardens, and in towns the disappearance of horses and change from bins with misfitting or unplaced lids to sealed refuse sacks, may all have affected House Sparrows. Decreases may not apply equally over SE Scotland. Towns with two-storey housing next to farmland, such as Tranent and Livingston, appear to hold better numbers than the sparse colonial distribution in Edinburgh (*pers.obs.*), and grain-growing areas with thicker field hedges in parts of Berwickshire and East Lothian have better abundance than other farmland. The *New Atlas* abundance map shows small spots of high abundance at Edinburgh, Dunbar and towards Berwick-upon-Tweed. Counts in the *Bird Reports* of summer flocks are unrevealing on breeding trends. In 1988-94 one Forth island, the Bass Rock, had House Sparrows until 1993. Formerly Inchkeith, Inchcolm, Fidra and Isle of May had breeding House Sparrows until after the lighthouse keepers left (*Andrews*).

The estimate of 2.6-4.6 million pairs in Britain (*New Atlas*) is based on 10-20prs/km^2 as in the *Old Atlas*, less 15% to allow for decrease since then. Summers-Smith (1963, 1988) gives density ranges of 25-62prs/km^2 for rural habitat and 300-500prs/km^2 for towns and villages. These would be too high to apply to SE Scotland as the figures he gives for English habitat indicate. In the town of Tranent da Prato (1989) found *c*.360 terr/km^2, and far less than this in the Royal Botanic Garden and in high-rise housing in Edinburgh. The mean figure for all Edinburgh would be lower than for Tranent (this author). Local BBS plots suggest *c*.10-15prs/km^2 in rural habitats. Examination of OS maps shows that of the 968 tetrads with House Sparrows, 787 contain less than 0.25km^2 of urban/ suburban habitat, and 181 tetrads contain more than 0.25km^2 of this habitat but only *c*.50% of the total area of these 181 tetrads is actually occupied by this habitat. Taking a guessed mean of 15 and 100prs/km^2 for these "rural" and "urban/suburban" tetrads respectively, suggests that SE Scotland has *c*.83,000 pairs of House Sparrows, over half in rural habitat and less than half in urban/ suburban habitat. An alternative approach is to divide the British population in proportion of SE Scotland's area of Britain, which suggests 65,000-115,000 pairs for our area. However, the *New Atlas* abundance map shows that the bulk of high abundance of House Sparrows is heavily weighted to southern Britain. A realistic estimate for House Sparrows in SE Scotland is 80,000-90,000 pairs.

H.E.M.Dott

House Sparrow

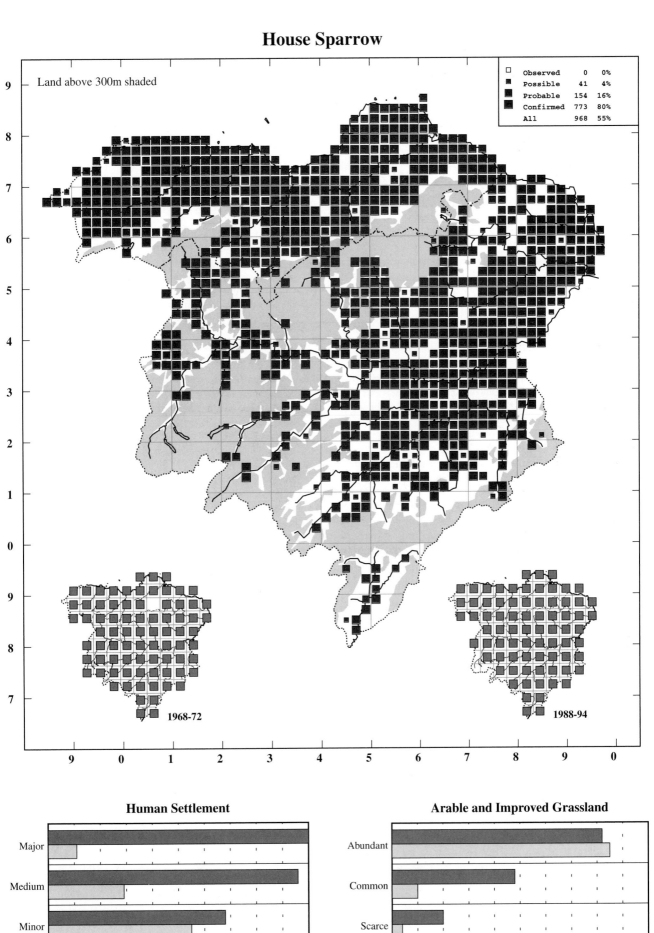

Land above 300m shaded

☐	Observed	0	0%
◼	Possible	41	4%
◼	Probable	154	16%
◼	Confirmed	773	80%
	All	968	55%

1968-72

1988-94

Human Settlement

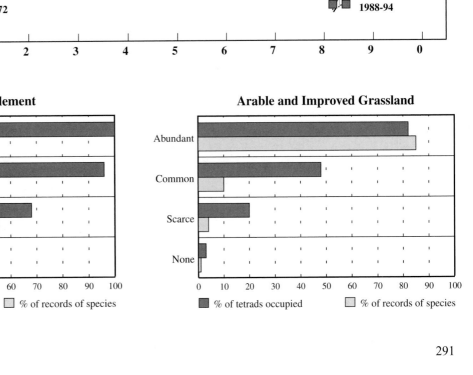

Major

Medium

Minor

None

◼ % of tetrads occupied   ☐ % of records of species

Arable and Improved Grassland

Abundant

Common

Scarce

None

◼ % of tetrads occupied   ☐ % of records of species

Tree Sparrow
Passer montanus

The Tree Sparrow is no longer the common and familiar bird of farmland that it once was. However, it is an unobtrusive bird and is frequently overlooked and so under-recorded. Tree Sparrows are associated with lowland farmland with scattered mature trees with holes which are used for nesting, and occur mainly in the drier east of Britain. They are not found in urban areas or dense woodland. In winter they may form flocks with other seed-eating passerines, but in the breeding season they are more secretive.

Tree Sparrows were recorded in 14% of the area, with a healthy 40% of records providing confirmed breeding. In the main breeding range, likely trees were checked for Tree Sparrow colonies where they were accessible, and as a result almost half of the confirmed records related to occupied nests, mainly from sightings of birds entering holes in colonies in trees. The remaining confirmed records were split between records of recently fledged young and of adults carrying food. Most probable breeding records related to sightings of pairs. The quiet but characteristic 'chip' and 'teck' calls helped locate these pairs or single birds.

The distribution of Tree Sparrows in SE Scotland shows three distinct clusters with large areas unoccupied or with just a few registrations. The main area extends from south central Midlothian (from Roslin and Middleton) through most of East Lothian to south of Dunbar and comprises about 40% of all records. Even in this area there are gaps, especially around Haddington in NT57. West Lothian provides another centre, but the population is split into two, separated by a broad area from Livingston to Linlithgow (NT06-NT07). There is a scattered western population around Linlithgow and south to Bathgate. A more continuous block on the map runs from Queensferry (NT17) south to Balerno (NT16), which stops abruptly on the western edge of Edinburgh. In Borders, the main centre of population lies in the Berwickshire Merse, especially downstream of Kelso in NT73 and north to the Blackadder Water at Greenlaw (NT74). There are also birds in the lower lying areas nearer the coast between Duns, Reston and Paxton (NT85,86&95). Far in the west there is a small pocket near Biggar (NT03), an outlier of a larger population in Clydesdale (A. Wood *pers. comm.*), but otherwise breeding season records are scattered and quite isolated. Almost all sites lie below 200m and only nine occupied tetrads lie above 250m. This discontinuous distribution corresponds well with the occurrence of arable farmland, interupted by the City of Edinburgh and the hills along the Southern Upland fault. However, these factors do not explain the gaps in both West and East Lothian, and the sparse nature of the distribution in Berwickshire. It is possible that the distribution relates to more local habitat features such as the presence of suitable trees with holes for nesting or mixed farmland with a variety of trees, hedges

and fields with winter stubbles, although there are many places with apparently suitable habitat with no Tree Sparrows. This is confirmed by the habitat graph which shows that almost all Tree Sparrows are found in just a quarter of all tetrads where arable and improved grassland is abundant.

There has been much written recently about the nationwide decline of the Tree Sparrow, although historical evidence points to numbers fluctuating over longer periods. Recent BTO statistics show that the species has apparently declined by 92% between 1969 and 1994 (BTO News 207:8-9). The latest population estimate, from the *New Atlas*, is 110,000 territories, which compares to 250,000 for 1968-72 in the *Old Atlas*. Summers-Smith (1989) summarises the different estimates this century and shows that the population has fluctuated, being at a maximum at the turn of the century, then declining during the period 1930-55. The 1950 estimate for the British and Irish population was 130,000 pairs, but there followed a large increase to over 850,000 pairs in the mid-1960s, and a decline since. Much of the fluctuation is attributed by Summers-Smith to irruptions from continental Europe. The Scottish population and changes in distribution mirror these fluctuations (*Thom*).

Though there is little substantiated evidence, there are many pointers to a continued recent decline locally. The notes of G.L. Sandeman for the Queensferry to Cramond area suggest fluctuations similar to those described for Britain. R.W.J. Smith (*pers. comm.*) recalls larger colonies and a wider distribution in Midlothian in the 1960s than before or after. *Andrews* states that the species used to be common in Lothian, although the position in Borders was less clear (*Murray*). This *Atlas*, by comparison with the 10-km maps in the *Old Atlas*, shows that the distribution has shrunk back from the higher western areas of Borders with gaps appearing in the Pentlands, Moorfoots, Lammermuirs and in the upper Tweed, mid Yarrow, upper Ettrick and upper Teviot. There are now no longer Tree Sparrows in Liddesdale. Personal observations indicate that some of the more isolated sites in central Borders now no longer hold Tree Sparrows. This loss from the uplands may be connected to the intensification of grazing in these areas and the loss of a mixed farming economy. It may be that as the national population declines, less well favoured areas are deserted, and the population concentrates into drier lowland areas. A. Wood (*pers. comm.*) states that Tree Sparrows are now much scarcer in the Clyde area since the fieldwork for the Clyde Atlas was completed in 1991.

The species was censused in Lothian in 1982 and a total of *c.*250 pairs was located (*Thom*). This was thought to be an underestimate due to under-recording, and seems low compared to the total of 251 tetrads in Lothian containing Tree Sparrows during this survey. Winter maxima in both regions for the period 1980 to 1994 fluctuate between 30 and 200 (Lothian) and 40 and 216 (Borders) and do not show evidence of a long term decline, although there have been no counts above 80 in Lothian since 1990. Colony sizes locally are not usually reported, but da Prato (1985) quotes densities which equate to between 2.0-2.75prs/km². Taking the lower figure, this *Atlas* records 198 tetrads with at least probable breeding, and about 40 of these are peripheral to the main range and may contain only one pair. Taking a density of 2.0prs/km² for the main range, this would suggest a SE Scotland population of 1,300 pairs. Data from CBC figures used to calculate populations in Summers-Smith (1989) and the *New Atlas* give higher densities, and at 3.42 prs/km² (per Summers-Smith) would give a local population of 2,708 but this seems too high. 1,300 equates to around 1% of the British population.

With a restricted population and a national decline, this species is a clear candidate for a local census, and a survey is planned for 1998 which will aim to include counts of colony size as well as distribution. ***M.Holling***

Tree Sparrow

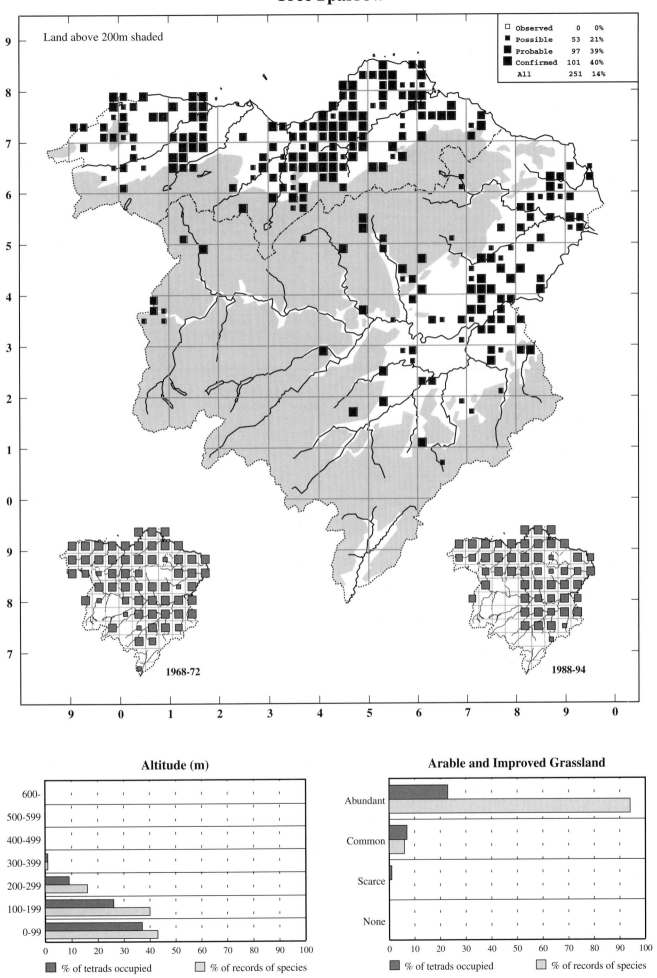

Land above 200m shaded

	Observed	0	0%
	Possible	53	21%
	Probable	97	39%
	Confirmed	101	40%
	All	251	14%

1968-72

1988-94

Altitude (m)

600-	
500-599	
400-499	
300-399	
200-299	
100-199	
0-99	

0 10 20 30 40 50 60 70 80 90 100

■ % of tetrads occupied   ☐ % of records of species

Arable and Improved Grassland

Abundant	
Common	
Scarce	
None	

0 10 20 30 40 50 60 70 80 90 100

■ % of tetrads occupied   ☐ % of records of species

Chaffinch
Fringilla coelebs

The distinctive rattling song and the loud 'pink' contact call of the Chaffinch are familiar sounds in woodlands throughout Britain but Chaffinches will also breed in hedges, parkland, gardens and scrub. Scrubby areas do not have to be large to attract breeding Chaffinches and they are one of the few birds that will nest in isolated patches of birch in remote upland glens. They will exploit a variety of food sources depending on season and habitat. During the breeding season invertebrates are the major food source utilised by Chaffinches. The adaptability of the species has allowed it to become one of the most abundant songbirds in its wide range that covers Europe, North Africa, the Middle East and Central Asia. Chaffinches in Britain, while sedentary, are not particularly distinct from their more migratory continental neighbours which flood into the milder climate of the British Isles to overwinter.

Male Chaffinches are colourful birds with a distinctive song and territorial behaviour that make them relatively easy to detect. The drabber females are harder to find and are wholly responsible for building the nests, which are cryptically camouflaged with mosses and lichens, as well as incubating the eggs and feeding the young. Probable records were mostly of pairs and territorial behaviour, often males singing against one another. The high percentage of confirmed records were shared by fledged young and adults carrying food to feed their young.

The Chaffinch proved to be the third most widespread breeding bird in SE Scotland, the map showing a near ubiquitous species occurring throughout the area, other than on the barest hills where no suitable habitat exists. The few gaps mark the most open parts of the Pentland, Moorfoot, Lammermuir and Tweedsmuir Hills. Note also the fringe of vacant tetrads on the southern edge of the area along the Cheviots. This degree of penetration of the hills is remarkable and a single Rowan in an otherwise bare cleugh is often sufficient habitat for the species. At lower altitudes the coverage is virtually complete, the two vacant tetrads almost certainly being oversights. Only one island, Fidra, apparently holds Chaffinches. As the island is treeless, the birds perhaps use the Tree Mallow as a substitute. Cramond Island shows as vacant, despite having a small wood, again a case of birds probably being overlooked.

The altitude data confirm the ubiquity of the Chaffinch, birds being present in over 90% of tetrads up to 400m and more than 70% of those at the 400-500m level. Only above 500m does representation really fall. No birds were present in the few tetrads above 600m. The habitat data show the association with all types of woodland, over 95% of all wooded tetrads being occupied, irrespective of the amount of woodland in the tetrad.

The very ubiquity of the Chaffinch means that comparison with the *Old Atlas* yields no new data, 100% of squares being occupied in both periods. The *New Atlas* abundance map shows that almost all lowland areas in SE Scotland below the 250m contour hold Chaffinches at the highest abundance level, the only exceptions being Edinburgh and Coldingham Moor which have moderate levels. There is a small area to the northwest of Kelso, as well as the large conifer forests in Craik and Wauchope, which are shown to have low abundance levels, very unlikely circumstances that may have more to do with shortcomings in the fieldwork that produced the figures than any real shortage of Chaffinches in these areas.

The *New Atlas* uses values equivalent to 21.6prs/km^2 in its calculation of the British population, while saying that good deciduous woodlands might have between 50-145prs/km^2 and conifer woodlands 12-100prs/km^2. This compares with 8.5prs/km^2 found in mainly arable farmland by da Prato (1985) in the Tranent area, and 17prs/km^2 in all types of habitat in SE Scotland's BBS plots. Only a few sites in Lothian have any census data but these include 78 territories at Straiton (NT26T), 59 at Roslin Glen (NT26R), 35 at the Hermitage of Braid (NT27K) and 43 at Bavelaw/Threipmuir (NT16R). As most of these sites are of less than 1km^2, the figures per km^2 will be higher than the totals given above, perhaps as much as 120-150prs/km^2. While these are mainly lowland sites, Petty *et al.* (1995), in a study of bird populations in the Sitka Spruce plots in Kielder Forest, produced figures that suggest densities of 400prs/km^2 for continuous spruce habitat, a large area of which exists in the neighbouring parts of Borders.

Using the *New Atlas* mean value, a local population of 140,000 pairs would be indicated for SE Scotland. However, as the *New Atlas* abundance map shows better than average numbers in the area, this total should be somewhat higher and should take into acount the figures seen in conifer habitats, of which there are around 600km^2 in the area, and so a higher figure is needed. Chaffinch densities will clearly vary with the amount of woodland in any tetrad. Accordingly some manipulation of the density figures in relation to the amount of woodland in a tetrad will provide better population estimates than simply multiplying the general average density by the total number of occupied tetrads. Using values of 50prs/km^2 for tetrads with abundant woodland, 30prs/km^2 where woodland is common, 10prs/km^2 where woodlands are scarce and 2prs/km^2 where woodlands are absent, gives SE Scotland a total of 200,000 pairs, making it the commonest species in the area, and comprising 3.7% of the British population.   **D.Kelly**

Chaffinch

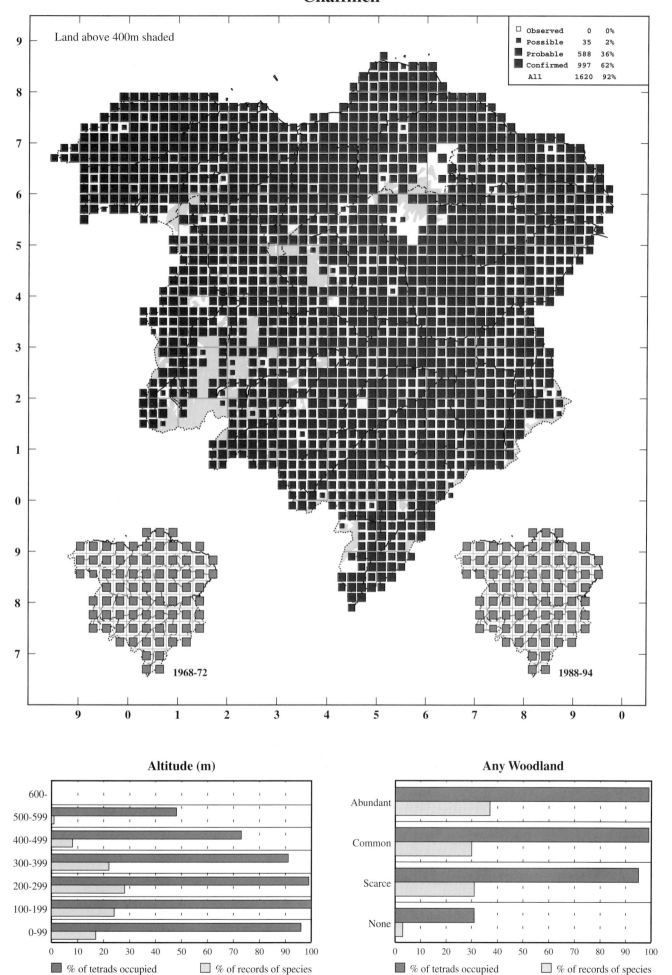

Land above 400m shaded

☐ Observed	0	0%
■ Possible	35	2%
■ Probable	588	36%
■ Confirmed	997	62%
All	1620	92%

1968-72

1988-94

Altitude (m)

Any Woodland

■ % of tetrads occupied   ☐ % of records of species

■ % of tetrads occupied   ☐ % of records of species

Greenfinch
Carduelis chloris

One of the most obvious members of the bird community in towns and villages through its colourful appearance and wheezing call, Greenfinches are recent additions to the birds that regularly haunt parks and gardens. They first moved into such habitats in the middle of the 20th century from arable farmland and woodland edges, where they exploit spilt grain and weed seeds as a source of food. Bird tables and peanut feeders have helped lure them into gardens.

Display flights, a distinctive song and a habit of nesting in loose colonies, made recording of song, display and territorial behaviour easy. These formed many of possible and probable records, along with sightings of pairs. Confirmed breeding was mostly through fledged young and adults carrying food. Studies of Greenfinch behaviour have shown that they possess complex and exotic mating patterns, both sexes being promiscuous within loose colonies.

While the altitude data show a few tetrads above 400m, over 90% of records came from below 300m, being widespread below 200m, where over 80% of all tetrads held birds. This proportion drops to 60% of all tetrads between 200-300m, then falls away rapidly above 300m. There are a number of strong habitat relationships that reveal its adaptability. The strongest is with arable and improved grassland, 85% of all records being where such farmland is abundant. Although not shown, there are also strong correlations with mixed and deciduous woodland, Greenfinches occupying over 80% of all tetrads where such woods are common and abundant, and with human settlement where birds were found in 95-98% of all tetrads with villages, towns and city landscapes. However, in each case a large proportion of the bird records came from tetrads where both woodland (42%) and settlement (53%) were scarce, implying that arable farmland is the key habitat.

The map is typical of a species of arable and improved grassland in SE Scotland, showing a fairly good coverage of the Lothian coastal areas and much of the lower and middle Tweed. Again, typical of species such as Yellowhammer, Whitethroat, House Sparrow, Goldfinch and Linnet, the 300m contour closely defines the range limit in the hill areas, birds filtering up the valley bottoms towards the headwaters of the river system wherever a little arable and improved grassland exists. A few appear to have managed to reach almost all the headwaters, other than that of the Tweed itself where the lack of any large areas of arable farmland has defeated colonisation. The density of tetrads shows some thinning below the 300m contour along the upland margins of the Tweed basin. This is less clearly seen in Lothian, although careful scrutiny shows that this thinning occurs there also, especially in the Howgate-Rosebery area (NT25&35). A common factor could be that stock-rearing is dominant there and that the balance of arable land to improved grassland will favour grass and be less suitable for the seed-eating Greenfinch. The reduced suitability of grass-dominated areas perhaps explains the gaps below 300m in the eastern Lammermuirs (NT65,75&76) and on Coldingham Moor (NT86). A few birds hang on in Liddesdale, an area where birds that favour arable land appear to have difficulties. With the movement of Greenfinches into urban areas it should come as no surprise that Edinburgh is fully occupied, gardens and parks providing suitable habitats. The Greenfinch map is remarkably similar to that of the House Sparrow, a species with which it shares a need for arable fields and human habitations. Agricultural changes during the 20th century have removed much of the wild seed supply that was previously available to Greenfinches, through the development of highly effective weedkillers. Combine harvesters now leave little spilt grain, while autumn ploughing of stubbles has removed valuable feeding areas. Farm specialisation has reduced the amount of arable land in stock-rearing areas. The once huge winter finch flocks have vanished with

the winter stubbles, parties of over 100 birds being unusual in recent years. Yet these changes may have been partially compensated for by the shift into urban areas and adaptation to new crops such as oil-seed rape. This has resulted in little overall change to both Greenfinch numbers and range in Britain (*Trends* and *New Atlas*).

This finding is supported by comparing the current *Atlas* and the *Old Atlas*, showing that birds have disappeared from five squares in the south of the area since 1968-72. These losses, and a significant reduction (one in six) in the number of squares with confirmed breeding, are where stock-rearing is dominant and where most traces of arable cereals have gone or are disappearing in the face of increasing farm specialisation. The headwaters of the Tweed and Ettrick and much of Liddesdale seem to have suffered most in this respect and Greenfinches may be in danger of vanishing wholly from these areas in the near future, judging from the low density of tetrads and the poorer level of breeding evidence that was found in the few tetrads where birds are still present. This pattern is also visible in some of the other arable-liking species (see p.19).

The *New Atlas* abundance map indicates that the Lothian coastlands between Edinburgh and Dunbar may be the stronghold of Greenfinches in the area. Much of the rest of the range, where there are good densities of tetrads, shows moderate to good levels of abundance, excepting an area immediately west of Kelso.

Estimates of Greenfinch numbers are subject to considerable problems related to their mobility and their habit of nesting in gardens inaccessible to fieldworkers. The *New Atlas* uses a cautious estimate of 2.3prs/km² for the occupied 10-km squares in Britain. In his arable study area around Tranent, da Prato (1985) found a value of 3.1prs/km² in a cereal-growing area in the heart of the area where the *New Atlas* abundance map shows good numbers. In urban environments in Lothian, densities varied between 3prs/km² in Edinburgh housing schemes to 8prs/km² in Tranent and 56prs/km² at the Royal Botanic Garden in Edinburgh (da Prato 1989). Local BBS results suggest about 3-4prs/km² in a variety of habitats across the area. Few other counts exist, records in the *Bird Reports* refer to totals of just 1-6 pairs at those sites with counts. The altitude and habitat data indicate no great fall-off in occupation levels with altitude in occupied tetrads, as long as arable farmland is abundant in the tetrad. This suggests that up to 300m overall densities are likely to be fairly uniform, irrespective of altitude. Above that, a sharp reduction may be expected. If a value of 3prs/km² is used for tetrads up to 300m and 1.0prs/km² above that level, a local population of 10,700 pairs can be calculated, 2% of the British total. **D.Kelly**

Greenfinch

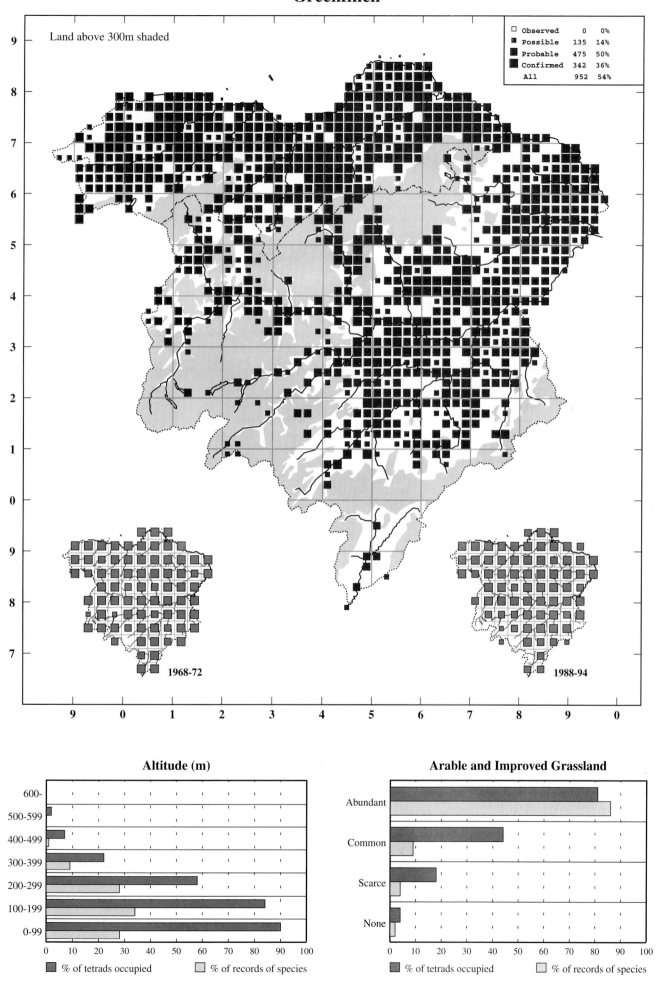

Land above 300m shaded

		Observed	0	0%
		Possible	135	14%
		Probable	475	50%
		Confirmed	342	36%
		All	952	54%

1968-72

1988-94

Altitude (m)

600-
500-599
400-499
300-399
200-299
100-199
0-99

0 10 20 30 40 50 60 70 80 90 100

■ % of tetrads occupied   □ % of records of species

Arable and Improved Grassland

Abundant
Common
Scarce
None

0 10 20 30 40 50 60 70 80 90 100

■ % of tetrads occupied   □ % of records of species

Goldfinch
Carduelis carduelis

The Goldfinch is associated with scrub and tall herbs such as thistles, teasels and ragworts. Its main range is in temperate Europe between the Mediterranean and the Baltic. In Britain they were a favourite quarry of bird trappers and the population was at a low ebb until the Second World War. Legal protection has enabled them to re-establish their range over much of lowland Britain. During the breeding season the unripe, milky seeds of plants such as thistles, teasels, ragworts and groundsels are important food sources, as are tree seeds such as birch and alder. Invertebrates are important high protein food for the chicks. They are sociable birds and often nest in loose colonies. The main food sources are often distributed in patches, causing birds to disperse widely to forage and so birds are often absent from the nest area for long periods of the day.

Goldfinches were seen in almost half of all tetrads in the area. The low level of confirmed breeding may be partly due to birds being absent from the nest area, but more probably due to the relatively late breeding season, few broods appearing in SE Scotland before late June. This lateness, timed to take advantage of ripening seeds, meant that much of the *Atlas* fieldwork period had passed before fledged young were visible. Singing from high perches and eye-catching display flighting made up most of the probable records.

The Goldfinch map shows a striking resemblance to the extent of arable and improved grassland in SE Scotland, with an altitudinal cut-off at about 300m. The altitude and habitat data support this, 90% of the bird records being below 300m, while 83% of records come from tetrads where arable and improved grassland is abundant. Again, typical of arable birds, there is a difference in the density of occupied tetrads between the Tweed basin and the Lothian lowlands, the latter showing a much higher density than the more sparsely occupied middle and lower Tweed. A large part of lowland West Lothian between Edinburgh, Linlithgow and Whitburn, and parts of East Lothian between East Linton, Gifford and Cockburnspath, show better than 90% occupancy. This compares to about 50% occupancy rates in much of the Merse and Lothian between Edinburgh, Penicuik and Haddington. What governs these differences in tetrad density is not known. Goldfinches show considerable penetration in the hill valleys with isolated records at the headwaters of most tributaries, but note the lack of birds in the watershed of the northern hills between the valleys of the Leader and Gala Waters and the South Esk in Lothian. Liddesdale is also occupied, albeit only in the lower parts around Newcastleton. Vacant tetrads in the low ground are most conspicuous immediately around Haddington and in parts of the Merse north of Coldstream. These are areas where arable cultivation is especially intense and, through spraying, this may have resulted in a loss of the weed species that Goldfinches are dependent upon. The gaps in NT65,75,76&86 are where unimproved grassland and heather extend below 300m. The absence of birds above 300m may also be related to a lack of suitable weed species, but here the lack of suitable food sources is more natural, probably being related to climatic limits for the plants.

In SE Scotland there has been a 4% increase in occupied squares since the *Old Atlas*, with gains in five squares compared to losses in just two. However, other than in NT61, the gains involve just a few tetrads in each square and indicate that the spread is purely marginal, mostly occurring at higher altitudes on the southern edge of the range. Of greater interest is the striking improvement in the levels of evidence for breeding. Squares with possible and probable breeding are much reduced, and squares with confirmed records increase by 36% from 44 in 1968-72 to 60 in the present *Atlas*. The obvious inference is that Goldfinches were easier to find due to a higher population level. The number of tetrads in some of these squares supports this view, especially in NT52 which shows birds in 21 of the 25 tetrads, where fieldworkers could only get possible evidence of breeding in 1968-72. Other squares, especially NT16,17,37&77, with only probable breeding then, also now have high occupancy rates.

This implies a significant population rise since 1972, with much infilling of the range and a little marginal expansion. The *New Atlas* attributes some of the national increase to the virtual disappearance of trapping for the cage-bird trade, through legislation enacted in the 1930s and 1950s. However, much of the recovery must pre-date the *Old Atlas* and so the expansion and increase since may have other underlying causes, as must the concentration of new squares in the Moray Firth area in the *New Atlas*, hardly a hot-bed of bird-trapping in times past. Nationally Goldfinch population indices have shown that there has been some decline since the 1980s (*Trends*), possibly as a result of chemical weed control. These contradictions, as far as the local area is concerned, may be resolved when the differences in chemical weed control in arable and stock-rearing areas are considered. Arable farmers are very much more ruthless in controlling weeds, ploughing aiding the weedkillers in reducing cover. In stock-rearing areas, weed infestation in fields devoted primarily to grazing is more tolerated and fields with docks, thistles and ragworts are more commonplace. As cattle and sheep avoid eating these plants, which are also resistant to all but the most powerful weedkillers, good food resources exist in such areas for seed-eating Goldfinches. There is some correspondence between the 10-km squares where birds show some evidence of increase and this lower intensity type of farming where weeds may be more common, especially as weed-controlled cereal cultivation is now less common in stock-rearing areas. The greater incidence of weedy winter-fodder fields may also be of importance in these areas.

The *New Atlas* abundance map shows mostly low-to-moderate numbers in the area, with only the Tranent and East Linton areas showing high abundance. Around Tranent da Prato (1985) found densities of 1.1prs/km^2. Local BBS returns suggest 1.5-2.5prs/km^2, although some caution is required here as Goldfinch flocks could easily bias the returns. The national population estimate is based on a figure of about 1.0prs/km^2, which again should be treated with caution and is likely to underestimate the population. The *Old Atlas* quoted figures of 2.2prs/km^2 on farmland. Using a simple value of 1.0prs/km^2, a population of 3,300 pairs is suggested, some 1.6% of the British population.
                                                                    D.Kelly

Goldfinch

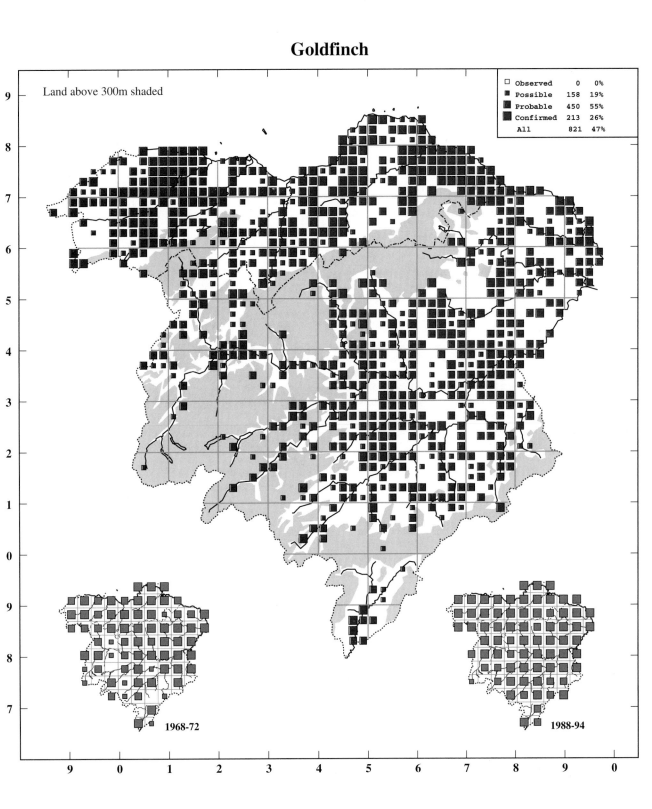

Land above 300m shaded

□ Observed	0	0%
■ Possible	158	19%
■ Probable	450	55%
■ Confirmed	213	26%
All	821	47%

1968-72

1988-94

Altitude (m)

Arable and Improved Grassland

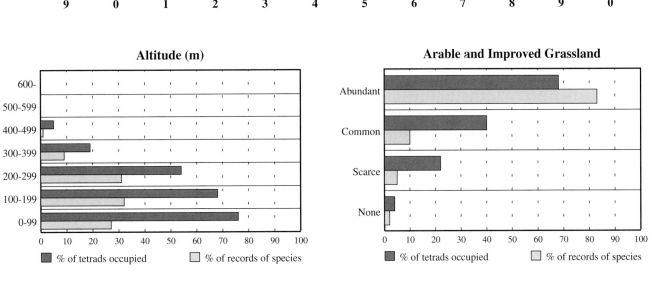

% of tetrads occupied   % of records of species

% of tetrads occupied   % of records of species

Siskin
Carduelis spinus

Siskins are strongly associated with coniferous trees, especially in the breeding season when they feed mainly on the seeds of spruces and pines. Increased afforestation of the uplands since the Second World War has provided much new habitat and in SE Scotland the Siskin is now more widespread than ever before. More recently, there has also been some spread into gardens and parks. Nests are built high in coniferous trees, with April and May being the main nesting season. Siskins are now regular visitors to garden peanut feeders in winter and spring in many areas and this additional food source has probably increased winter survival.

Siskins tend to be conspicuous where they occur in reasonable numbers, but can be overlooked in less typical habitats if the observer is not familiar with the far-carrying shrill flight calls. In March and April, singing males can be obvious as they perform their dancing song flight above the tree tops. Over half of all records were of probable breeding, mainly noted as pairs or territory. Areas surveyed in late June or July would often reveal family parties with recently fledged juveniles still begging for food. Care has to be taken with slightly older families which can wander some distance from the nesting areas, taking advantage of trees in seed. The high numbers of observed records are largely outside the main range where the species is scarce, and perhaps represent areas which may be colonised over the next few years.

The map very clearly shows a correlation with the more extensive coniferous plantations. The Borders forests of the Cloich Hills (NT24&25), the Tweed valley from the source down to Galashiels, Craik (NT20,21,30&31), and the Wauchope and Newcastleton Forests (NT50&60 and NY58&59) particularly stand out on the map. Most of these centres of population were mentioned in *Murray* but the distribution has expanded since then with these populations now spreading out into gardens and parkland habitats. This was demonstrated by displaying birds at Galashiels (NT43) and Peebles (NT24) during the survey period. Breeding has now been proved in Berwickshire, with concentrations around the relatively recently planted Monynut Forest (NT66&76) and also at Longformacus (NT65) and Duns Castle (NT75). In Lothian, plantations in southern West Lothian (NS95&NT05) form the main concentration with less extensive centres around Balerno (NT16), the woods along the South Esk (NT35) and plantations around Soutra Hill (NT45). The first confirmed breeding in East Lothian was only proved during the *Atlas* period, at Spott (NT67S) and Woodhall (NT67W).

Siskins occur in over half of all tetrads between 200 and 400m, but this apparent relationship with altitude is more likely to be associated with the dominance of conifer habitats at these heights. Where plantations occur on low ground (as in NT62 north of Jedburgh) or at higher levels (Craik Forest, NT30), Siskins are present. The habitat graph shows Siskins to be more frequent in tetrads with a large cover of conifers, the frequency increasing with the extent of coniferous woodland. However, over half of all records were from tetrads where coniferous woodland was only common or scarce, reflecting the recent spread of birds into smaller plantations, parks and gardens. Siskins are absent from lower lying areas where the main land use is intensive arable agriculture with few trees, as seen in East Lothian and the Merse, and are absent from hilltops, notably the Tweedsmuirs, Moorfoots and Lammermuirs.

The huge spread since the *Old Atlas* is demonstrated by comparing the 10-km square maps. In the earlier survey, only 27 squares were occupied, but now the species occurs in all squares but five. At the time of the *Old Atlas*, many of Britain's conifer plantations were only recently planted and had not reached cone-bearing age, but by 1990 these had matured and the area of plantation had doubled

(*New Atlas,* Jardine 1993). The *New Atlas* abundance map shows the highest densities of Siskins in the large plantations of Scotland, including the Border Forest area in southern Roxburghshire and the Tweed valley forests. The Siskin is one of the species to have benefited most clearly from large scale afforestation, and the new plantations of the 1980s will provide further habitat in years to come. *Thom* described the recent Scottish expansion of range since the early 1970s, coinciding with the maturation of spruce plantations planted earlier. East Lothian was one of three Scottish counties where breeding had not been proven at that time, and the Siskin was described as scarce or uncommon in West Lothian and Berwickshire. In the present survey the species seems well established in the West Lothian plantations but is still local in Berwickshire.

Numbers of Siskins vary annually with the cone crop, and the winter population is boosted by immigration from the northern coniferous forests of Scandinavia. Thus in 1991, following a particularly heavy cone crop, Siskin flocks appeared to be "everywhere" in the larger Borders forests. In other years, although not scarce, such flocks were less obvious. An estimate of 400 for the Scotch Kershope tetrad (NY58H) in Newcastleton Forest in June 1991 was made by *Atlas* fieldworkers (*Bird Reports*). Because of the very good cone crop, breeding in 1991 was very early and this would have been a post-breeding flock including juveniles (D.C. Jardine *pers. comm.*).

The *New Atlas* suggests densities equivalent to 20 prs/km^2 in prime habitat. However, Petty *et al.* (1995) recorded a mean of 1,406 birds/km^2 in Kielder Forest in spring 1991 when populations were high, reducing to 178 birds/km^2 in 1992 a year after the peak in cone production. Even taking the lower figure and assuming only half of the 600km^2 of coniferous forest in SE Scotland is of cone bearing age, a population of 26,700 pairs is indicated for these forests alone (involving about 270 tetrads). If the tetrads with only possible breeding are taken to represent just one pair (175), and the remainder hold Siskins at 20 prs/km^2, then there may be at least 45,500 pairs in SE Scotland during average cone years. This phenomenal total shows how important the commercial forests have become for some species. In a bumper seed year such as in 1990-91, this number might be 5-6 times, exceeding 200,000 pairs in the area! If these figures are valid, then the British population of 300,000 estimated at the time of the *New Atlas* is now clearly out of date.

M.Holling

Siskin

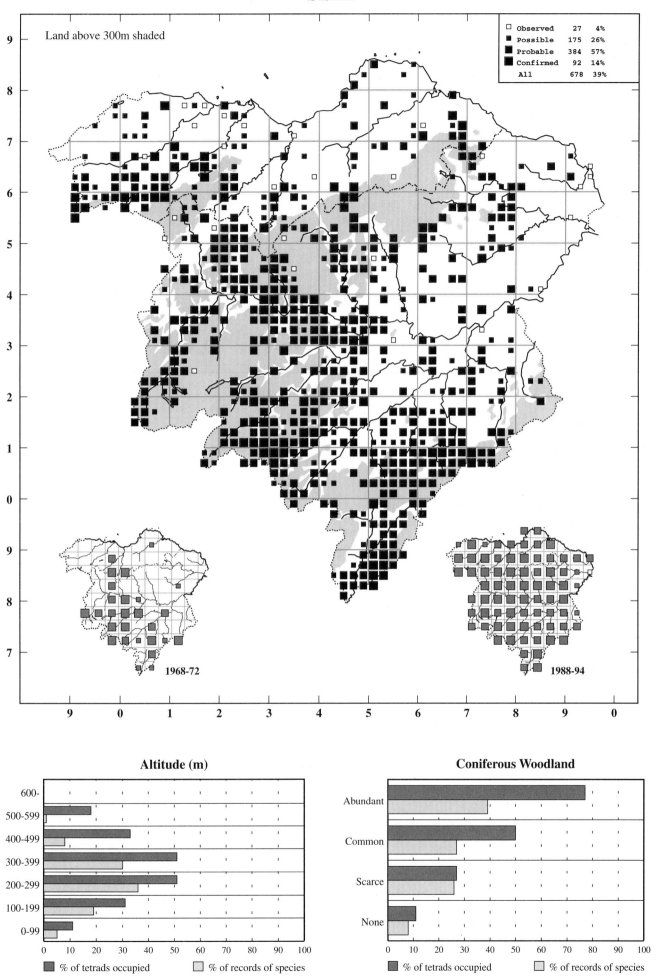

Land above 300m shaded

	Observed	27	4%
	Possible	175	26%
	Probable	384	57%
	Confirmed	92	14%
	All	678	39%

1968-72

1988-94

Altitude (m)

% of tetrads occupied   % of records of species

Coniferous Woodland

% of tetrads occupied   % of records of species

Linnet
Carduelis cannabina

The commonest finch in open countryside, the Linnet is a bird of farmland, hedges, gorse, rough scrub and the edges of woods where weeds are abundant. The Linnet uses the open areas to feed and the cover for nesting. Young forestry offers short-term habitat for Linnets, the birds being excluded as the woodland matures.

No other finch is as dependent on the seeds of weed species, hence the association of Linnets with areas of disturbed ground. As ploughing disturbs the ground annually, farmland used to provide the greatest scope for Linnets, feeding on the weeds that sprang up with the crop. However, the advent of herbicides has greatly reduced the amount of weed seed available, especially in cereals, and so Linnet numbers have suffered accordingly. Turnip fields that are not sprayed and fields of rape, whose seeds are edible, have mitigated these losses somewhat in recent years (*Trends*).

The Linnet is a semi-colonial nester, groups of 2-10 pairs nesting in close proximity with the adults often feeding in small parties. These flocks swell in summer as the juveniles join in the foraging parties. Pairs, usually birds seen within the flocks, dominated the evidence of Linnet breeding. Confirmed records were mostly of adults carrying beakfuls of insect food for their chicks, or juveniles flying with the flock later in the summer.

The map is typical of a species with a widespread distribution in lowland farmland, exhibiting a definite scarcity in upland areas, and generally only penetrating the hills along the river valleys. In common with many species associated with arable farmland there is a difference in the density of tetrads between the low-lying ground of the Lothians and Borders, occupied tetrads being denser in Lothian. This may be related to differences in the intensity of the fieldwork effort or may be genuine. Most birds occur below the 300m contour and the altitude graph shows a real fall in representation above that level. Indeed, 85% of all Linnet registrations were below 300m. Again, the correlation with arable farmland shows that nearly 80% of Linnet records were in tetrads where arable land is abundant. Penetration into the high ground is most marked across the major routeways through the northern hills in the Leadburn-West Linton area (NT14,15,24&25) and at Middleton-Soutra (NT45) where arable and improved pasture extends across the watersheds.

Despite being so widespread below 300m there is a surprising number of gaps within the range of the Linnet, even at these lower levels. One gap is evident in southern Roxburghshire (NT30,31,41,50 &60 and NY49,58&59) where forestry dominates the landscape, and also in the south-eastern Lammermuirs (NT65,75&76) where a combination of low-lying heather moorland and some forestry occurs. The factors causing the lack of birds in East Lothian (NT46,56&57), immediately southwest of Edinburgh (NT16) and east of Linlithgow (NT07) are not obvious but may be related to relatively weed-free stock farming, the major factor behind the scarcity of Linnets in Liddesdale (NY48,49,58&59).

Contrary to the downward trend in Linnet numbers in Britain according to the BTO census data (*Trends*), comparison of the 10-km square maps shows no great change since 1968-72 in SE Scotland. Indeed there is one fewer vacant 10-km square in the current survey and fewer possible squares which suggests some marginal spread. Any changes seem to have affected the upper Tweed, the western Lammermuirs and the Cheviot fringe, all areas where the tetrad map shows Linnets to be at the upper limit of their range. While small-scale fluctuations might be expected here, the Linnet shows less evidence of withdrawal from the upland margins of cultivation than other birds of arable farmland.

The *New Atlas* abundance map shows a radically different picture to the pattern that the density of occupied tetrads might suggest. Birds are shown as most numerous along the coastal lowlands eastwards from Edinburgh to Dunbar, in the Eye Water in Berwickshire, and inland in West Lothian around Bathgate. A zone of moderate numbers surrounds these areas but also extends southwards across the hills in the Leadburn-West Linton area and across Soutra to Jedburgh. Most of the Tweed valley and the northern fringes of the Pentlands and Lammermuirs, however, are shown to hold very low numbers of birds, while the hills between Selkirk, Peebles and Broughton, which are mostly vacant on the map opposite, are shown to hold low numbers of birds in the *New Atlas* abundance map. It is difficult to account for these differences.

Linnet density of 6prs/km^2 is recorded from arable land in the Tranent area (da Prato 1985), while census data on nature reserves at St. Abb's Head and Aberlady yield 13prs/km^2 and 9.5prs/km^2 respectively (*Bird Reports*). All three sites are in areas where the *New Atlas* abundance map shows Linnets to be numerous. Local BBS data, where Linnets are present on a third of plots, suggest an average of 6-8prs/km^2. While no figures are given in the *New Atlas* on how the British population was calculated, the estimate of 520,000 pairs appears to be based on 2.3prs/km^2, a much lower figure when compared to those that have been obtained locally. While the national figure must also account for areas where birds occur at low densities, SE Scotland resembles a microcosm of Britain in that it too has considerable areas of both high and low numbers according to the abundance map. With 5prs/km^2 used to calculate the local population, a total of 20,000 pairs is indicated, 3.9% of the British population. This figure runs ahead of our percentage share of the British mainland, and the local density figures do hint that good numbers of birds are present in SE Scotland.

J.G.Mattocks

Linnet

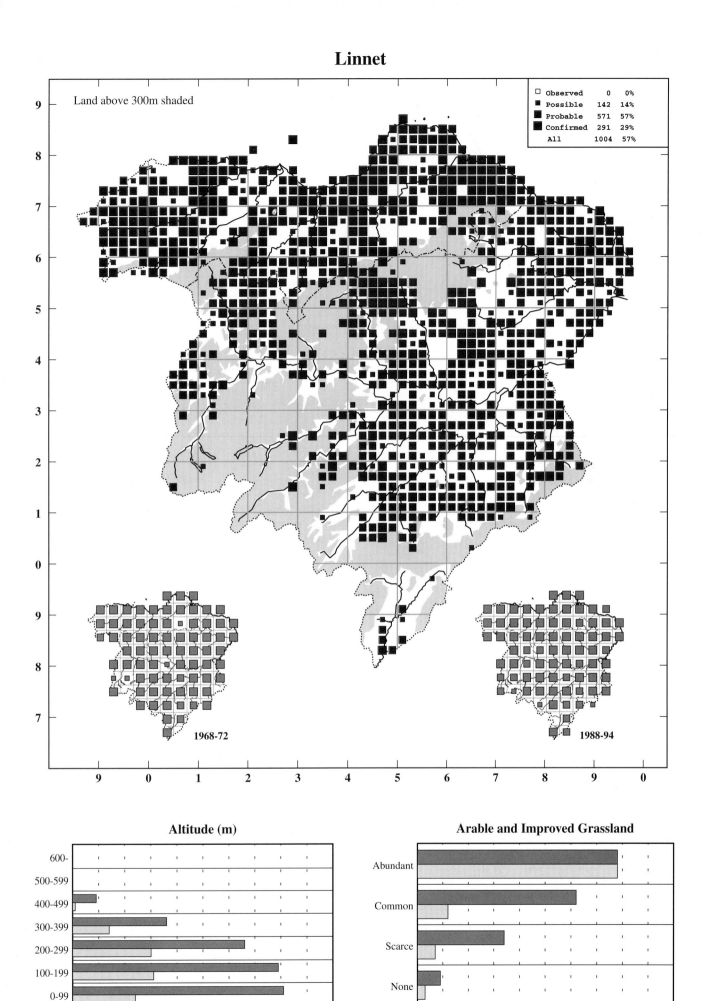

Land above 300m shaded

☐ Observed	0	0%
■ Possible	142	14%
■ Probable	571	57%
■ Confirmed	291	29%
All	1004	57%

1968-72

1988-94

Altitude (m)

■ % of tetrads occupied   ☐ % of records of species

Arable and Improved Grassland

■ % of tetrads occupied   ☐ % of records of species

Twite
Carduelis flavirostris

Twites breed on heather moorland, upland pasture and, in the north of Scotland, on coastal grasslands. This choice of nest habitat explains its alternative English name of Mountain Linnet. The Twite has an unusual distribution, a relict of a larger range that it must have had during the cold phases of the Ice Ages. The European populations occurring in the British Isles, Scandinavia and Finland are now disjunct, being separated from the Central Asian mountain populations by 2,500km of unsuitable habitat. The distribution is also disjunct in Britain, with the northern Scotland birds well separated from outliers in southern Scotland, the Pennines and north Wales.

Twites nest under cover in bracken or heather and fly to nearby areas of pasture to feed. All of the tetrads where breeding was confirmed or probable were characterised by extensive areas of rough grazing and heather moor. In areas where they are common elsewhere in Britain, Twites nest in loose colonies and are social throughout the breeding period, but in areas where they are scarce they are found as widely separated single pairs, making breeding hard to detect or confirm. Any Twites nesting in SE Scotland would be scattered single pairs, and as female Twites can sit very tight, incubating or brooding females would be very hard to detect, even when observers were nearby. Breeding is easier to confirm later in the season when family parties and fledged young are seen. Unfortunately this is mostly in July, towards the end of the fieldwork effort, and so some birds may well have been overlooked. However, the presence of Raptor Study Group members monitoring Merlin, Peregrine and Hen Harrier sites does mean a considerable area of hills is walked each year. The absence of records therefore may mean that birds are genuinely absent in these areas at least.

In southern Scotland the Twite is very localised with two discrete populations in Galloway and along the northern edge of the Southern Uplands in Lanarkshire. The map suggests the occasional breeding record in SE Scotland may be an eastward extension of the birds in Lanarkshire, as most of the records seem to be located near the Southern Upland Fault that marks the boundary between the Southern Uplands and the Central Lowlands of Scotland. Twites are definitely rare with just ten registrations over a seven-year period. Breeding was confirmed by sightings of juveniles in just three tetrads in the Pentlands and Moorfoots. There are two records of pairs in the Lammermuir and Tweedsmuir hills. The remaining records, are of single birds. The two possible records are from areas of heather and grassy moor near Gladhouse and Liddesdale respectively. The other records are of birds seen in farmland. It is possible that these may

have been adults feeding away from nest areas, although this only seems conceivable for the record at Charterhall (NT74T), about 6km away from the nearest moors at Hule Moss.

The Twite is reputed to have bred in the Pentlands, Lammermuirs and Cheviots during the 19th century and indeed Evans (1911) said that breeding sites were too numerous to mention. This is unfortunate as the only quoted historical instance of breeding anywhere in SE Scotland was from Auchencorth Moss (NT15X&25C) in 1887 (*R&B, B&R*). This supposedly large population apparently vanished in the early part of the 20th century. In the more recent past Twites were recorded as definitely breeding in the *Old Atlas* at Coldingham Moor (NT86) in 1972 and as possibly breeding in the high Tweedsmuir Hills in the Broad Law-Manor area (NT12&23). The only other record from this period was a pair seen just south of Peebles (NT23) in July 1979.

There may be some connection between the return of the few breeding pairs during the *Atlas* period and the reappearance of Twites as a wintering species in SE Scotland in reasonable numbers. Flock sizes in Lothian fell during the 1970s and early 1980s but more recently have picked up. These flocks, like the breeding records, are mostly along the northern edge of the hills and it is possibly significant that it is near Gladhouse, where breeding has been confirmed, that the largest winter flocks of up to 175 birds have been recorded. The origin of these wintering birds is not known but is more likely to be further north in Scotland, where the main part of the British breeding population lives, rather than locally.

The Twites of the Southern Uplands hardly register on the *New Atlas* abundance map, indicating that they are present at extremely low densities. The change map also shows that there are hardly any 10-km squares where birds were found in both surveys. This may mean that individual pairs shift breeding areas, a sign of an unstable population on the periphery of the range.

The Twite population of SE Scotland is tiny and in any year in the *Atlas* period varied from nil to a handful of pairs. It seems reasonable to suppose, with such an inconspicuous bird breeding in extensive areas of potential habitat, that a few other pairs might have been overlooked. Even then it is likely that fewer than 10 pairs may be present in any year.
D.Kelly

Twite

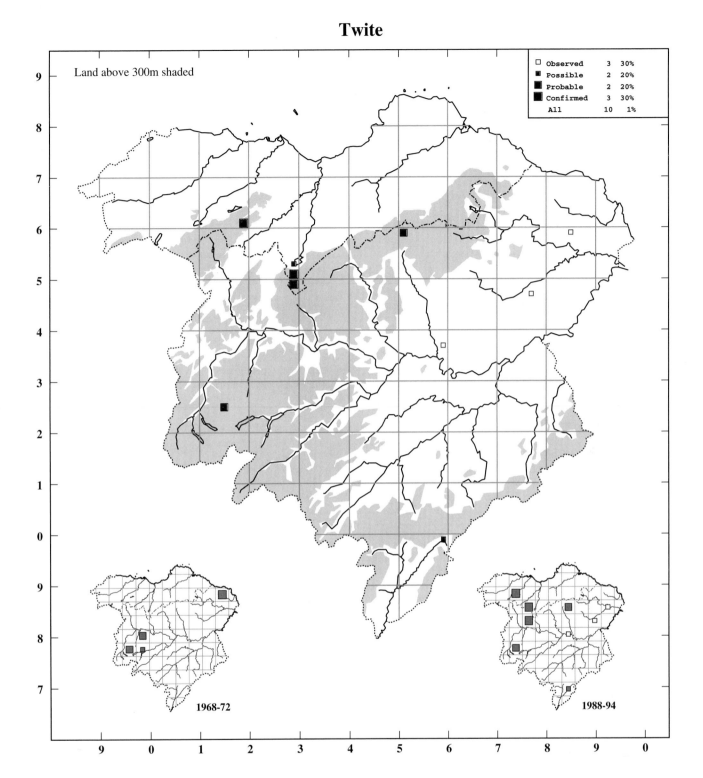

Land above 300m shaded

	Observed	3	30%
■	Possible	2	20%
■	Probable	2	20%
■	Confirmed	3	30%
	All	10	1%

1968-72

1988-94

Redpoll
Carduelis flammea

The lively but elusive Redpoll is a specialist of young woodlands, favouring areas of natural regeneration and the plantation stage of forestry. This specialism is related to their need for small seeds, preferably birch and alder, both of which flourish in young woodlands. Redpolls expanded their range greatly in Britain during the 20th century as large areas were planted with conifers, the seeds of spruce providing an alternative food source. As these forests mature and the smaller birches are shaded out, such habitat becomes less suitable for them although spruce seeds are still available. In commercial forestry the clear-fell stage can allow a second burst of birch growth which benefits Redpolls. The Redpoll is a circumpolar species living in the boreal forest zone. The British birds are very distinctive and were formerly known as the Lesser Redpoll, *C.f. cabaret*.

Breeding Redpolls would be rather unobtrusive birds but for the display flights of males, who advertise themselves, sometimes in small parties, by flying repeatedly to and fro over suitable habitats. The high percentage of probable records is a testament to this display, most probable records being of displaying males. Sightings of presumed pairs, typically in flight, were also of importance for probable records. Confirmed records were relatively rare, probably due to the difficulties of finding nests and the impossibility of distinguishing immatures amongst flying flocks.

Redpolls have dense concentrations of tetrads in the mostly younger-aged forests in southern West Lothian between Cobbinshaw and Harperrig Reservoirs (NT05&15), the upper Tweed (NT01,02&03), Craik (NT20,30&31) and the Border Forest Park (NY48 north-eastwards to NT82). The density falls a little in the older forests along the middle Tweed between Peebles and Galashiels (NT24,33,34&43), presumably because of birch being excluded as the canopy closes. While there is a strong relationship with areas of commercial forestry, Redpolls are able to use fairly small areas of woodland planted as shelterbelts. The habitat data show a strong association with coniferous woodland where 40-70% of all tetrads with such woodlands were occupied. The percentage occupation of tetrads with conifers increases with the size of the woodland cover within the tetrad. However, the figures show that roughly equal proportions of the bird records occurred in each size category. This

suggests that Redpolls are equally at home in any patch of conifers, regardless of size, but that you are more likely to encounter birds when large areas of conifers are present.

The altitudinal data show that two-thirds of all records occur between 200-400m, the zone where conifer woodland is most widespread. Conversely, the lowest altitude band below 100m holds just 8% of bird records and this is evident on the map with birds extremely localised in Lothian lowlands and the lower Tweed. In such areas Redpolls can be found in scrub growing on regenerating old industrial workings near Musselburgh (NT37F&R), along abandoned railways near Tranent (NT47F&S), along the coast at Aberlady (NT48Q&R) and along the Tyne (NT57Y).

Comparisons between the 10-km square maps show no great change in the overall spread of records since the *Old Atlas* with just a few gains and losses on the coast and in the high hills on the margins of the range. There has been a change in the ease with which Redpolls were proved to breed. There are 25% fewer squares with confirmed records in the current *Atlas* and more probable records. This may be an artifact of the recording process. Many squares with probable records, such as NT50,60 & 72, have so many occupied tetrads that there can be little doubt that breeding must actually occur. In such squares fieldworkers may have been happy with whatever standard of evidence they came upon without trying to confirm breeding. In the *Old Atlas*, where a single case of proved breeding was necessary to upgrade a square to confirmed breeding, fieldworkers were often more focused, actively searching for confirmation. One possible cause of an increase in the difficulty of obtaining proof might be associated with the older stage of conifer woodland in several of these squares, confirmations perhaps being easier to obtain in 1968-72 when the forests were younger and Redpolls more abundant. The *New Atlas* abundance map shows Redpolls as moderately abundant across much of SE Scotland with high numbers shown in forests in southern West Lothian and at Craik and Wauchope (NT60).

While Redpoll numbers peaked in the 1970s and early 1980s and have declined since (*Trends*), both *Thom* and Jardine (*New Atlas*) comment that these data give poor coverage of Scotland and in conifer woodland where Redpolls are most abundant, and that any drop in the national index may be more likely to reflect changes in southern and central England where coverage is strongest. Indeed *Thom* doubted that any decline had occurred at all in Scotland. Little support is available from the *Bird Reports* where Redpolls are rather poorly recorded, receiving little attention from birders.

Breeding density data are relatively sparse, da Prato (1985) finding good numbers in the scrub and derelict ground in his arable survey area near Tranent, averaging 4prs/km^2. Local BBS data suggest similar values, perhaps 3prs/km^2. In Kielder in 1991-92, Petty *et al.* (1995) found huge numbers of Redpolls, varying between 55-418 birds/km^2. As the higher figures must have included large flocks in spring 1991, when seed production was exceptionally high, the lower value of the following spring may provide a better figure of 80prs/km^2 to use for areas that the *New Atlas* abundance map shows to be of the highest abundance. The *New Atlas* uses very much lower numbers of 1prs/km^2 to assess the national population.

The BBS estimate and da Prato's data suggest that 3prs/km^2 might be deemed to provide a figure for the low density habitats in lowland and arable areas. However, if the Kielder numbers give a realistic value for the extensive areas of forestry in the southern and western parts of SE Scotland, an overall figure of 5prs/km^2 might be more appropriate for the higher density conifer woodlands, treating the Kielder figures as exceptionally high. As the habitat data show Redpolls were found in 425 tetrads where conifer woodland was common and abundant, a local population of 8,400 pairs is suggested for these woodlands alone, with the other tetrads providing an additional 3,800 pairs, a total of 12,200 pairs.   *D.Kelly*

Redpoll

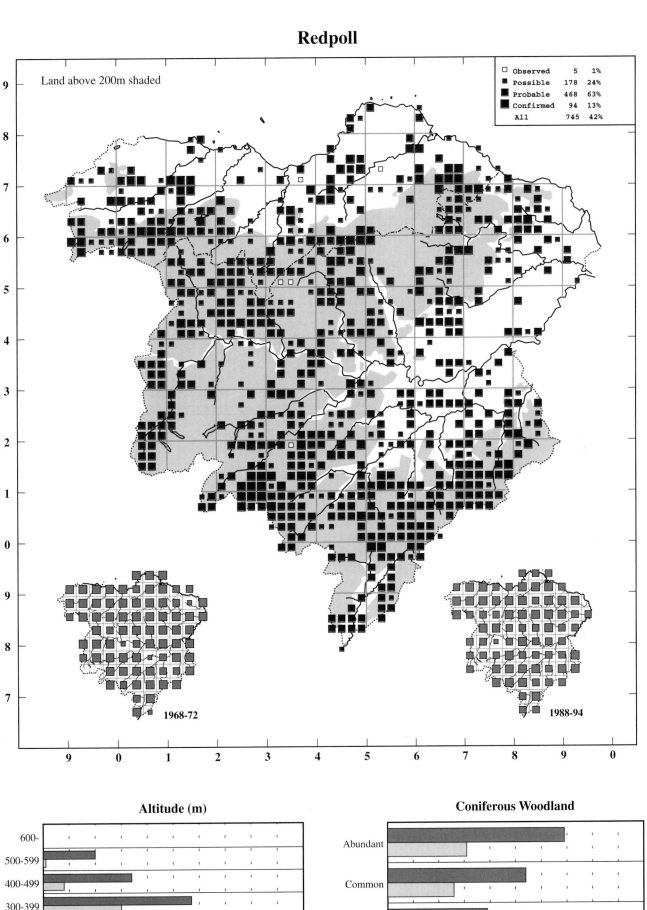

Land above 200m shaded

	Observed	5	1%
	Possible	178	24%
	Probable	468	63%
	Confirmed	94	13%
	All	745	42%

1968-72

1988-94

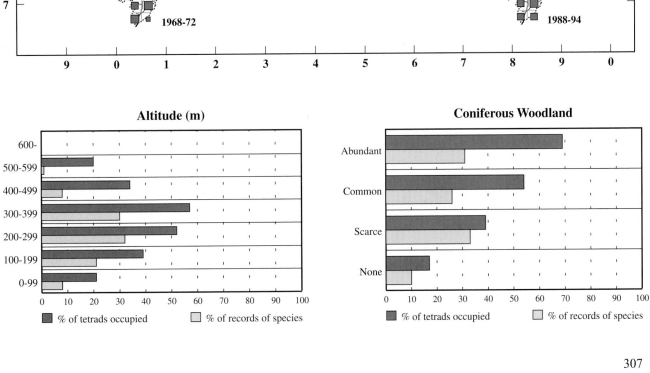

Altitude (m)

% of tetrads occupied   % of records of species

Coniferous Woodland

Abundant

Common

Scarce

None

% of tetrads occupied   % of records of species

Common Crossbill
Loxia curvirostra

Few birds are as dependent on a single food source as Crossbills. They eat the seeds of conifers and little else. Common Crossbills specialise in eating the seeds of spruce and have bills adapted to coping with spruce cones. However, they are adaptable enough to tackle the cones of other conifers such as pine and larch. This diet restricts Crossbills to areas of coniferous woodland but due to the vagaries of cone production each year they can be forced to lead a nomadic existence wandering in search of new areas where cones are ripening. Shelterbelt strips suffice when birds are on the move.

Common Crossbills are not difficult to find when they are on the move in a forest, their 'chipping' call typically being heard long before the small parties hove into view over the treetops. The easily recognisable calls produced a significant number of observed records from outwith areas where fieldworkers might expect birds to breed, presumably mostly parties of birds on the move over unsuitable habitat. Almost 80% of probable records were of pairs, often within flocks, seen flying over suitable habitat. Confirmed records were dominated by sightings of fledged young. One major difficulty with this species is that breeding occurs in winter, mostly outwith the period when *Atlas* records were normally collected. However, a special effort was made to collect records from all sources and in some years additional efforts were made to survey Crossbills during the winter months in the more accessible forests.

Crossbills are subject to large-scale population changes, their breeding success being dependent on the success of the cone crop and the extent that birds immigrate into the area from elsewhere. Birds typically disperse between June and August (see graph) and linger only if an area provides a ready supply of food. This certainly occurred in summer 1990 when numbers shot up as birds poured into SE Scotland. Records from the Northern Isles and Grampian suggest that birds from the continent were involved. Numbers built up through the autumn and remained high until summer 1991 when there was an abrupt departure as the food resources were used up and not replenished by sufficient ripening cones. With the ever-changing population levels, the map, which covers seven breeding seasons, exaggerates the local distribution of the species.

The map, not unexpectedly, shows that Crossbills were most frequently found in areas where conifer plantations are widespread. This is confirmed by the habitat data showing that Crossbills were present in about half the tetrads where such plantations were abundant. However, both the season and the year when particular forests were surveyed may have been of importance too, those surveyed during the peak years having records while comparable forests may lack birds if surveyed in lean years. Crossbills were not found across all areas of commercial forestry as the category 'coniferous woodland' fails to distinguish the age of the plantations and birds would not be present in areas where the trees were too young to bear a significant crop of cones. Indeed this differentiation is clear on the map with Crossbills widespread in the plantations along the Forth-Harperrig area (NS95&NT05), Tweedsmuir (NT01), Glentress to Yair (NT23,33&43), Craik (NT20,30&31), Newcastleton (NY48,58&59), and Leithope (NT70&71), all extensive areas of mature woodland planted in the 1950s and 1960s. In contrast the forests at Cloich (NT14&24), the Leithen valley (NT34), Berrybush-St. Mary's Loch (NT21&22) and the northern Lammermuirs (NT66) are all younger, mostly planted in the 1970s and 1980s. The more scattered tetrads, especially those in the north and east of the map in Lothian and Berwickshire, mostly relate to records in 1990-91 when Crossbill numbers were particularly high. The *New Atlas* noted that registrations were ten times more frequent in 1991 than in 1989.

Comparison with the *Old Atlas* shows a huge increase in the number of occupied 10-km squares where birds were present, from ten in 1968-72 to 66 squares in 1988-94. Similar increases were common across Britain. Most of this expansion is the result of the extensive conifer woodlands that have matured throughout the area since then. The 1990-91 'Crossbill-year' must also have had an effect.

The *New Atlas* abundance map under-recorded Crossbills in SE Scotland mainly because *New Atlas* records were almost wholly collected for that survey in summer when fewer birds are present and in years when birds were not especially common. Few records were collected of 1990-91. Only the West Lothian, Craik and Newcastleton concentrations are shown, with the latter areas showing moderate numbers on the edge of the Kielder area of maximum abundance. Few were recorded elsewhere for the *New Atlas*.

With numbers varying to such an extent, any calculation of the numbers of Crossbills present is problematical. As they live in areas that are not often visited by birders, the number of *Bird Report* records will tend to underestimate the real numbers. However, it is clear that in some years there are very few birds in the area. The graph opposite strongly suggests that few birds (<25 records) were present in 1989, 1992 and 1993 and that there are few years with more than 40 reports. Estimates of birds present during the influx, using timed point counts, varied between 110 birds/km^2 and 1,360 birds/km^2 in Kielder (Patterson & Ollason 1991). A more *ad hoc* survey in Scotland and Kielder (Jardine 1991, 1993) produced mean figures of 105 birds/km^2 and led Jardine (in *Day*) to suggest that in 1990-91 as many as 100,000 pairs might have been present in Northumberland alone! However, in poor cone years the Northumberland population of breeding Common Crossbills might then drop to less than 100 pairs, mostly dependent on the pine and larch that cone more regularly. Some of Jardine's lower density calculations included data collected within Borders and as the forests in SE Scotland and Northumberland are essentially similar in age, the minimum value of 105 birds/km^2 could be used to calculate the local population during the influx. This produces a value of around 63,000 pairs for the 300km^2 of suitably mature conifer woodland in SE Scotland out of the total of 600km^2 of all ages and species. Additional numbers would occur elsewhere. The similarity of species, age-structure and area between Northumberland and SE Scotland may mean that Jardine's estimate of 100,000 pairs for Northumberland would equally apply to SE Scotland. However, as the *Bird Reports* graph shows, numbers can be variable ranging from as little as 100-500 pairs in poor years to as many as 100,000 pairs in the rare exceptional years. Although 'average' years are impossible to quantify, 5,000-10,000 pairs might be present most years.

R.D.Murray

Common Crossbill

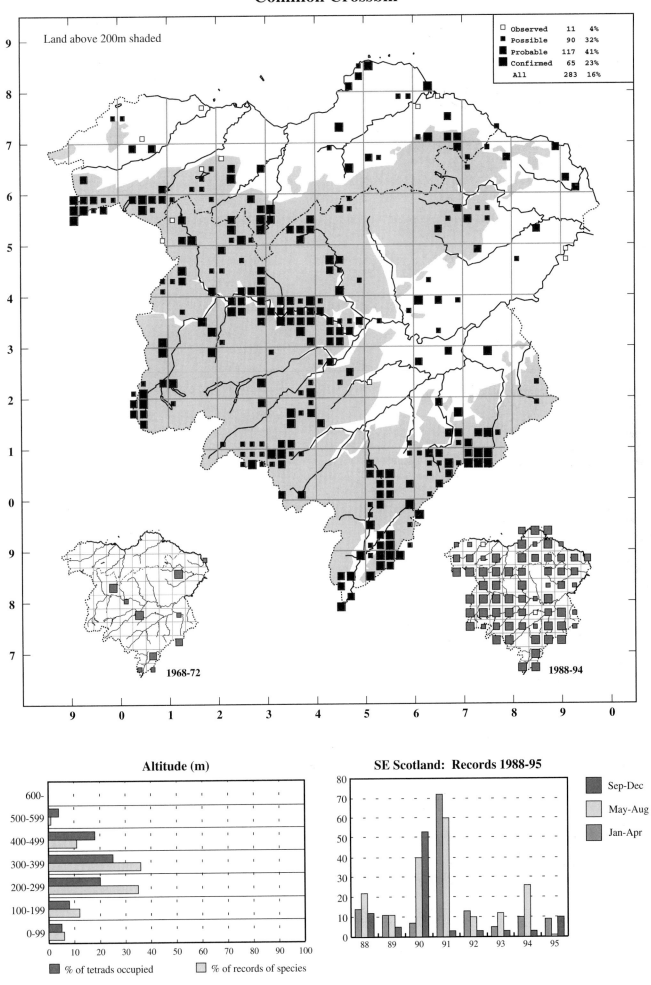

Land above 200m shaded

□ Observed	11	4%
■ Possible	90	32%
■ Probable	117	41%
■ Confirmed	65	23%
All	283	16%

1968-72

1988-94

Altitude (m)

■ % of tetrads occupied   □ % of records of species

SE Scotland: Records 1988-95

■ Sep-Dec
□ May-Aug
■ Jan-Apr

Bullfinch
Pyrrhula pyrrhula

Despite the bright colours of the male and the striking white rump patch of both sexes, Bullfinches are less familiar birds than their field-guide portraits might suggest. Bullfinches are not especially shy but their unobtrusive habits, quiet song and calls, and the relative difficulty in locating them in areas of thick cover, mean that they are more familiar to the general public through artwork in books and on cards than as birds that they have actually seen in the field. Wandering autumn and winter flocks also make them more familiar at that time of year rather than as breeding birds.

These problems with locating birds may have reduced the number of tetrads where Bullfinches were recorded. While their soft piping calls, that typically carry only 20-30m, are diagnostic to birders who are familiar with the species, less experienced fieldworkers could easily have overlooked birds in the thickly-vegetated woodland habitats many Bullfinches prefer. Such difficulties may have contributed to Bullfinches being recorded as the least widespread of the common finches in SE Scotland. They are often seen in pairs, the pair-bond being especially strong in the species, with the sexes only being separated during incubation and the earliest stages of feeding young. Almost all of the probable registrations were of pairs and numerically formed about half of all records of Bullfinch. This bond continues once the young leave the nest and confirmed records were dominated by sightings of family parties.

Bullfinches are quite widespread in SE Scotland, despite only being found in about a third of all tetrads. This suggests that the most suitable habitat may be quite thinly spread throughout the area. However, comparisons with the maps of both coniferous and mixed and deciduous woodland fail to show a precise match which hints that Bullfinches are more catholic in their preferences, and the best match is with the 'all woodlands' map, although again, there are many areas where Bullfinches are not represented. The Bullfinch shows significant differences between Lothian and Borders in the details of the range. In Lothian it is a bird of lowland mixed and deciduous woodland, being widespread in West Lothian, Edinburgh and Midlothian. While large areas of East Lothian are also occupied it is absent where arable farming dominates. In Borders it seems to

be mostly a bird of the valleys, being common in the mixed and deciduous valley woodlands of the middle Tweed drainage and also in the large conifer plantations of the middle and upper Tweed and at Craik (NT21&30) and Wauchope Forests (NT60). The habitat data lend some support to these conclusions. Altitudinal data show a distinct preference for lower altitudes with 80% of records occurring in tetrads below 300m. The data on woodland type show a definite preference for mixed and deciduous woodland but significant numbers of tetrads where conifer woodland is present are also occupied. Tetrads with large areas of woodland, of both types, are preferred to tetrads where such habitats are scarce.

The *New Atlas* abundance map indicates that Bullfinches are rather thinly distributed in SE Scotland with just a few areas of moderate abundance shown in the Lothian lowlands from western Edinburgh to Dunbar and around Eyemouth, in Broughton (NT13), the central Borders and in Craik. Much of the remainder of the area holds few birds. This pattern corresponds to the varying density of tetrads on the map opposite, except in West Lothian where the large number of occupied tetrads in the Almond drainage is shown in the *New Atlas* as holding few Bullfinches.

While Bullfinches occur in most 10-km squares across SE Scotland in both the *Old Atlas* and the current *Atlas*, there are hints that the birds may be slightly more widespread now than in 1968-72. A handful of squares that were formerly vacant are now occupied and generally the quality of proof of breeding has improved since the *Old Atlas* with 12% more squares having confirmed breeding. These changes are mostly in the south and on the hill fringes in places where forestry has become widespread since 1968-72. *Trends* and the *New Atlas* state that Bullfinch population levels are currently declining, citing the drop in the CBC and other monitoring surveys as evidence, and the removal of hedges as the possible cause. The *New Atlas* also shows a shrinkage on the northern and western margins of the range in Scotland. However, neither the *New Atlas* nor *Trends* mention commercial forestry as being of any importance to Bullfinches and overlook the *New Atlas* expansions that have occurred in Scotland in Sutherland and Kintyre in areas where commercial forestry has made great inroads in recent years. There has been a recent adaptation to conifers in west Northumberland just across the watershed from Craik and Wauchope forests (*Day*) while Patterson *et al.* (1995) noted Bullfinches present in 7-8% of study plots in conifer forests in Kielder and Argyll. These findings strongly suggest that Bullfinches may be moving into a new habitat, one that has been mostly overlooked thus far by the ornithological authorities.

Population estimates for a species that is as unobtrusive as the Bullfinch are difficult as it is more likely to have been overlooked than most other species. A Dutch study (Bijlsma 1982) found that about a third of pairs were overlooked by conventional census methods and so it is possible that the map may understate the local range a little, especially on the fringes of the range where population densities will be lower. The only local data on Bullfinch densities are from da Prato (1985) who found 1.2prs/km² in the Tranent area. Local BBS data suggest contacts with Bullfinches are hit-or-miss with a blank in one year and small flocks in other years. Omitting these flocks, however, local densities may be of the order of 1-2prs/km² across the whole area. *Andrews* mentions small sites in Lothian where densities of 16-30prs/km² occur but these densities will have been extrapolated upwards from population figures for quite small areas. The *New Atlas* provides a national figure equivalent to 0.9prs/km² which includes many areas, according to the abundance map, that hold very few Bullfinches. SE Scotland should hold better numbers and accordingly the local population estimate is based on 1.0-1.5prs/km². This would give a local population of 2,240-3,360 pairs, 1.5% of the British population, a reasonable proportion bearing in mind the only moderate numbers suggested by the *New Atlas* abundance map.   **R.D.Murray**

Bullfinch

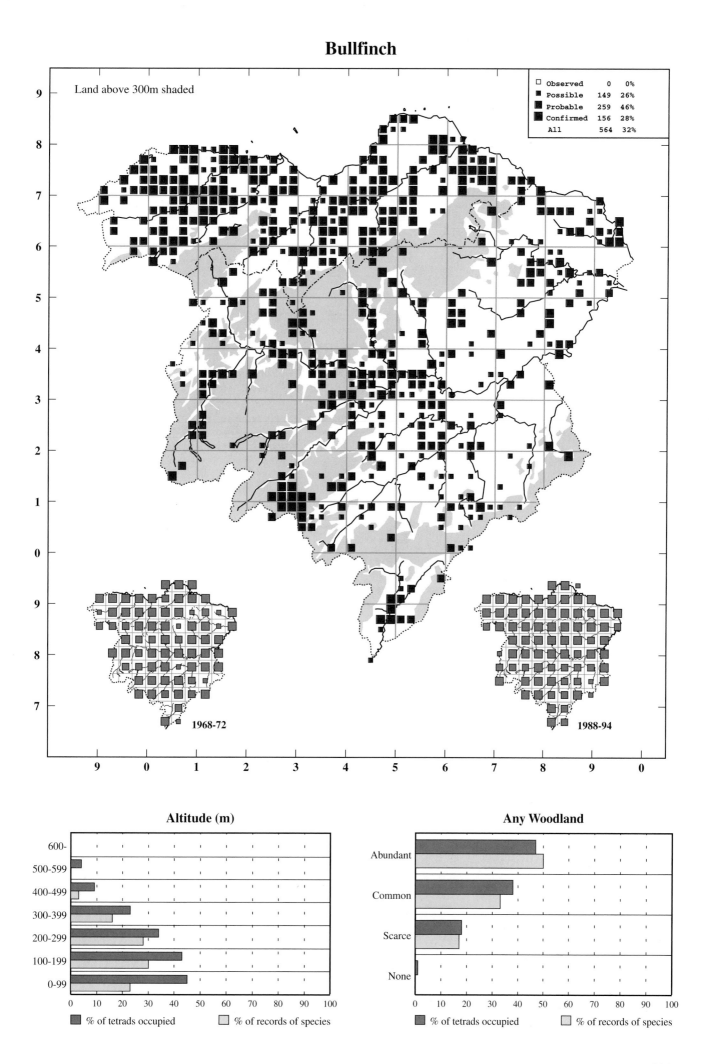

Land above 300m shaded

☐ Observed	0	0%
■ Possible	149	26%
■ Probable	259	46%
■ Confirmed	156	28%
All	564	32%

1968-72

1988-94

Altitude (m)

600-
500-599
400-499
300-399
200-299
100-199
0-99

0 10 20 30 40 50 60 70 80 90 100

■ % of tetrads occupied   ☐ % of records of species

Any Woodland

Abundant
Common
Scarce
None

0 10 20 30 40 50 60 70 80 90 100

■ % of tetrads occupied   ☐ % of records of species

Hawfinch
Coccothraustes coccothraustes

This bulky, elusive pimpernel of a finch is essentially a bird of the deciduous mixed woodlands and cherry and apple orchards of SE England. Ringers fortunate enough to have handled the species will testify ruefully to the power of a beak that can crack cherry stones with ease. In Scotland, as in England, Hawfinches are found predominantly in the low-lying southeast of the country, although they can occur as far north as Aberdeenshire. Probably the largest number of Hawfinches ever observed together in Scotland was a party of 40 at Scone, near Perth, in February 1991 (*Scottish Bird Report*) while in SE Scotland ten at the Hirsel in February 1988 is the local record. The best known localities for most birders in our area are at the Royal Botanic Gardens (NT27M) where up to eight birds have been seen (in 1974 the present writer (A.B.) found a nest in nearby Fettes College) and the Hirsel at Coldstream. Although birds are almost certainly present all year, the majority of records are from the spring and early summer.

Despite a distinctive but thin and easily overlooked call, it is a truism that the Hawfinch, with its secretive behaviour and its penchant for private estates, is generally grossly under-recorded. Hence there is little reason to doubt that in what is already a marginal area for the species, birds will have escaped detection during the course of the *Atlas*. Hawfinches were recorded in just 17 tetrads, comprising only 1% of the area of SE Scotland.

Befitting a bird of the sylvan lowlands, all the current records occur well away from the treeless heights. Although there is no evidence of the loose breeding colonies reported in both the *Old* and *New Atlases*, the distribution map suggests that the species is confined mainly to three general areas within our region: well-wooded gardens in Edinburgh and Midlothian, coastal woods along the outer Forth and the mature parkland of the Teviot and middle Tweed valleys. Breeding was confirmed in just three tetrads during the *Atlas* period: at Tyninghame (NT68F), Hawick (NT41X) and Minto (NT52Q). Probable records were more widespread, coming from the Royal Botanic Gardens in Edinburgh, Dalkeith Palace (NT36I), Ormiston Hall (NT46D), Monteviot (NT62M), Floors Castle (NT73C), Hendersyde Park (NT73M), the Hirsel and Duns

Castle (NT75S). Birds have been regular at some of these sites over the years while at others pairs or small parties have been seen on just a single occasion. Elsewhere, single birds have been found in suitable habitat at Torwoodlee (NT43U), Butterdean (NT47Q), Elvingston (NT47S) and Longformacus (NT65Y). There are reservations about spring birds in coastal areas where passage migrants may appear and while birds at North Berwick and St. Abb's Head were thought to be migrants and are not shown on the map, a record from Pease Dean (NT77V) was considered to be potentially a local bird.

Following an increase in England in the 19th century, the Hawfinch population in Scotland is known to have risen from very low levels since the start of the 20th century (*Thom*). In the 1930s *R&B* considered it a scarce and erratic breeder known at only a very few sites across the Lothians and Borders. Breeding records from the period before the *Atlas* have occurred at Lauder (NT54) in 1910, Jedburgh (NT62) in 1915, Dawyck (NT13S) in the 1930s and 1982, Humbie (NT46R) in 1935-43, Bowhill (NT42D&I) in 1947-55, Peebles (NT23&24) in 1947 & 1956, the Hirsel in the 1950s & 1985, Luffness (NT48Q) in 1959, Floors Castle (NT73C) in 1962, Tyninghame in 1976, the Royal Botanic Gardens (NT27M) in 1974 and 1977-78 and Cousland (NT36U) in 1980-81. The *Old Atlas* shows proved breeding in NT48, NT84 and NT73, presumably Luffness, the Hirsel and Floors/Hendersyde, but also in NT72 where Sunlaws (NT72E), near Kelso, seems the most probable location, despite a lack of documentation about the record. With Hawfinches now found in an additional six 10-km squares compared to the *Old Atlas* it could be that there has been some improvement in the local population. However, it is more likely that its true status is now better known and any increase is more apparent than real. This fits the scanty information about the status of the British Hawfinch population, and both *Trends* and the *New Atlas* regard it as being stable, in the absence of evidence to the contrary.

Estimating the size of the local population is fraught with problems as birds can apparently disappear from a site for years on end before suddenly showing up again. Indeed no Hawfinch records have been forthcoming from Lothian since 1991, but it would be extremely unlikely that they have disappeared completely. In such circumstances any site that has held birds in the last 20 years could be regarded as a potential breeding area for Hawfinch, even those with records from outwith the breeding season. With about two to three pairs being the most recorded at any site, and there being just six regular sites, it is unlikely that the Hawfinch population exceeds 20 pairs.

A.Barker & R.D.Murray

Hawfinch

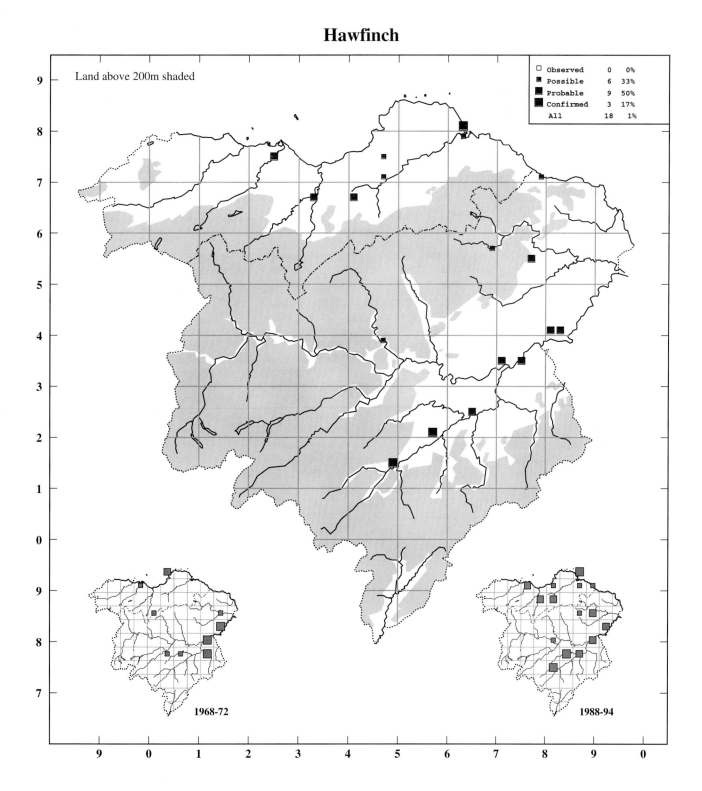

Land above 200m shaded

□	Observed	0	0%
◼	Possible	6	33%
◼	Probable	9	50%
◼	Confirmed	3	17%
	All	18	1%

1968-72

1988-94

Yellowhammer
Emberiza citrinella

The Yellowhammer lives in open country, from woodland edge to moorland fringes across much of lowland Britain. It is most common on arable land in eastern Britain living in intensively cultivated cereal crops, pastures of all types including silage grasses, young plantations, and the immediate vicinity of farms. It rarely penetrates into towns, except where weed-covered open ground is present. Essential requirements in all of these habitats are suitable song-posts and nest-sites, typically in hedgerows, gorse or scrub. Yellowhammers often nest close to the ground where the nest is hidden by the low vegetation growing up into the scrub. They are granivorous and exploit a range of weed and grass seeds including cereal crops. Invertebrates are taken in summer and fruits are eaten when available. The ability to take cereals has ensured the relative success of the Yellowhammer and it is most common in cereal growing areas with hedges.

The habitat analysis shows that Yellowhammers prefer extensive areas of arable land with about 90% of all such areas being occupied in SE Scotland (see graph). As the extent of arable land drops, there is a rapid drop in the representation of birds with almost no birds where there are only limited areas of arable ground.

Yellowhammers proved easy to record, with their distinctive far-reaching song. Half the registrations were of probable breeding, mostly birds singing against one another. Confirmed breeding records were mostly of birds with beakfuls of insects for their young.

The map shows a range largely limited to the lower ground. Yellowhammers are virtually universal between the Firth of Forth and the foothills of the hill ranges to the south, and up much of the lower ground of the Tweed drainage. The range limit follows the 300m contour faithfully and this is particularly true where birds penetrate up the Tweed, Gala, Yarrow, Ettrick and Teviot valleys. Penetration is more general between the Lammermuirs and the Moorfoots in the Leader valley (NT45&54) where the wide valleys offer suitable habitat. There is a sizeable area of occupied ground between the Pentlands and the Tweedsmuir Hills in Peeblesshire (NT03,04,13,14&24). Cereals fields are sparse in this area, and most Yellowhammers are found on farms that grow seed-rich winter fodder crops such as turnips, rape and kale. Birds are more thinly distributed there, as the density of dots indicates.

Altitudinal data show that 91% of records are below 300m and 76% below 250m. This impression is confirmed by the altitude graph that shows around 90% occupation of the ground below 200m with slightly lower occupancy below 100m, the shortfall being largely accounted for by urban areas. The fall-off above 300m is marked, with less than a quarter of possible tetrads occupied. The altitudinal range is doubtless related to the extent of arable ground.

Penetration into Edinburgh is minimal, mostly around the Braid Hills, Arthur's Seat and Corstorphine Hill. Birds reported from temporary 'waste' ground, earmarked at the time of the survey for building on the outskirts of Edinburgh, Livingston (NT06) and the fringes of other urban areas may mean losses in the next decade or so.

The 10-km square maps reveal a clear withdrawal from the high ground to the south and west since 1968-72. This is also true for the only significant area of low ground in the south, Liddesdale, where only a single Yellowhammer record was obtained (NY59T), a marked change from 1968-72 when it bred in three out of the four 10-km squares. The *Winter Atlas* map suggests few birds in Liddesdale in the early 1980s. The withdrawal from high ground in the west fits what is known of regional variation within Britain, of reducing density from east to west (*Trends*). Much of the contraction since the *Old Atlas* was in the west, particularly in Ireland where there have been huge reductions in both range and numbers (*New Atlas*). The switch from mixed farming with some cereal production to specialist livestock grazing appears to be the prime reason for these declines. This is also true in the southwest of our area where cereal crops have largely disappeared. The expansion of forestry in the 1960s may also have created short-term habitats for the birds reported in 1968-72, which has since vanished as the forest canopy closed. The expansion of forestry itself has doubtless meant that stock-rearing farms have disappeared and thus will have reduced the numbers of fields of barley and root crops intended for winter fodder for animals.

Andrews described coastal gorse and other scrub as the main stronghold for Yellowhammers in Lothian. Farmland surveys by da Prato (1985) near Tranent produced an average density of 10prs/km^2 on farmland, with higher densities of up to 115prs/km^2 in scrub. Our few CBCs, such as at St. Abb's Head (0.5 km^2), where 10-12 pairs are present, confirm the higher densities in lowland and coastal scrub. The *New Atlas* abundance map shows three areas of great abundance, a large area on the Berwickshire coast and the Merse, around Jedburgh-Yetholm and near East Linton (NT57). Equally large areas of low abundance are shown centred on the areas where our study indicates that birds are in fact almost absent.

In estimating the British Yellowhammer population, the *Old Atlas* used a very conservative figure of the equivalent of 4prs/km^2 although the 1972 CBC figures indicated 9.5prs/km^2. This compares with da Prato's figure for arable farmland of 10prs/km^2, with pockets of much higher density elsewhere. On the *New Atlas* abundance map the Tranent area has only moderately high densities so the Berwickshire coast may hold higher numbers. The *New Atlas* national figures are calculated on a value of 5.25prs/km^2.

As densities appear to decline with altitude, a breakdown of the altitudinal distribution of the species in SE Scotland, combined with declining density figures for altitude, (10prs/km^2 for 0-100m, 7.5prs/km^2 for 100-200m, 4prs/km^2 for 200-300m and 1.25prs/km^2 for >300m) produces at total of 32,400 pairs. This equates to 2.6% of the British population, what might be expected on a basis of SE Scotland's percentage area of the country.   ***R.D.Murray***

Yellowhammer

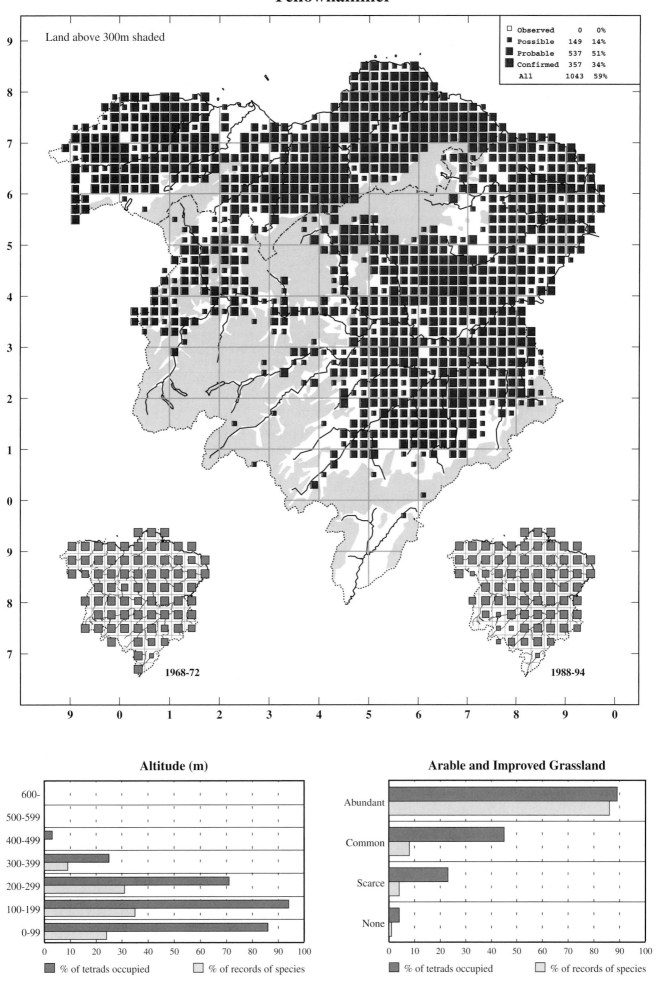

Land above 300m shaded

☐ Observed	0	0%
Possible	149	14%
Probable	537	51%
Confirmed	357	34%
All	1043	59%

1968-72

1988-94

Altitude (m)

■ % of tetrads occupied   ▢ % of records of species

Arable and Improved Grassland

■ % of tetrads occupied   ▢ % of records of species

315

Reed Bunting
Emberiza schoeniclus

No spring walk across the saltings at Aberlady Bay would be complete without the sight of a Reed Bunting proclaiming his territory to the world from the top of a small hawthorn. The Reed Bunting is far from being confined to areas where *Phragmites* thrive, but while being found in arable farmland, scrub and semi-derelict ground, it is most reliably observed in damper habitats. The nest is usually well concealed on the ground but on occasion may be up to 4m high in hawthorns and small conifers.

Reed Buntings advertise their presence through the use of prominent song posts and so are usually not difficult to locate, although the inexperienced might miss their rather weak song. The quality of proof of breeding for Reed Buntings was relatively low, with higher numbers of possible and probable registrations and lower numbers of proved breeding records than most other passerines. This may be partly related to the relatively late breeding season of seed-eating birds in general, extending into the period of lower observer effort in July, but also because of the difficulties of access to many Reed Bunting habitats. Probable records were mostly of territorial song or of pairs, while confirmed records were dominated by adults carrying food for young. Fledged young were also significant.

The map shows that the Reed Bunting is fairly well scattered, being more common in Lothian, where it is present in 40% of tetrads, compared with Borders where it is only present in 21% of tetrads. Within Lothian there is a concentration in western West Lothian. This uneven, scattered distribution is typical of a species whose wetland habitat is scarce and local in the area. Pockets of marshy areas that match concentrations of Reed Buntings occur in West Lothian (NS96), the upper Esk drainage (NT25), between the Leader and Gala valleys (NT44,45&55), around Gordon (NT64) and at the Ettrick Forest lochs (NT41,42&52).

The habitat graph shows a fairly good correlation between occupied tetrads and those where wetlands are common and abundant. Reed Buntings occur in 45-72% of all tetrads where such habitats exist but in only 22% of tetrads where such habitats are absent. The correlation with river habitats is weaker but nevertheless Reed Buntings occur in about a quarter of all tetrads with river features. As Reed Buntings are not tied exclusively to wetland it is to be expected that the range should be wider. In West Lothian the mosaic of less intensive agriculture, mostly rolling fields of livestock farms and grain fields with rough pasture, criss-crossed with old mine workings, abandoned railways, ditches and other rough margins in addition to groups of basin mosses, seems ideal for Reed Buntings. Similar pockets of abundance exist on the hill fringes between West Linton, Penicuik and Middleton (NT14,15,25,35&45). The expanses of the highest ground above 350m, predominantly heather moorland or sheepwalk in the Pentland, Moorfoot, Lammermuir, Cheviot and Tweedsmuir hills are avoided. Where Reed Buntings do penetrate the hills their occurrence can be tied to water bodies such as Gladhouse Reservoir (NT25W&X, 35B&C) or the Ettrick Forest lochs and mosses (NT31,41,42&52). Large gaps also exist in the low-lying intensive grain-growing region of the Merse with smaller gaps in arable East Lothian (NT46,66&67).

The *New Atlas* abundance map shows Reed Buntings are most numerous in a wide swathe in the west extending to both sides of the Pentlands east to Edinburgh and Penicuik, and in East Lothian north of the A1 road. Areas of moderate abundance occur along the lower and middle Tweed and into the Ettrick Forest. As a whole, however, much of SE Scotland holds birds at lower densities than much of England and has large areas at the lowest densities of all.

Comparison with the *Old Atlas* map shows net Reed Bunting losses of four 10-km squares since 1968-72, and closer inspection shows that breeding was very much easier to confirm then than in 1988-94. Breeding was confirmed in 67 squares in 1968-72, as opposed to just 45 squares in 1988-94, indicating that Reed Buntings are both harder to locate and harder to confirm as breeding now, despite the more intensive and longer period of fieldwork. It seems likely that numbers are lower today compared with 25 years ago.

Over Britain, Reed Bunting numbers are in decline, along with populations of other seed-eaters such as the Linnet and Tree Sparrow. Things were very different in the 1950s and 1960s when Reed Buntings moved into the type of agricultural land more normally associated with Yellowhammers due to high population levels in their favoured wetland habitats. It is thought that the high population was a response to a run of mild winters, the species suffering considerable losses in harsh winters when snow cover makes seeds hard to find. The population, measured by the CBC and WBS, remained high until about 1980. It has since declined in farmland, probably due to efficient herbicides eliminating weeds, and nest losses are now 50% higher than occurred in the 1970s. Reed Buntings are now in the "High Alert" category of the BTO's Nest Record Scheme (*BTO News*). Losses have been greatest on farmland and most birds are now found in the core habitats associated with wetlands (*Trends*).

Locally there are several sites that hold high numbers of Reed Buntings, namely Aberlady (maximum 50 prs 1988-94), Bavelaw-Threipmuir (31prs), Tailend Moss (NT06D, 10prs), Gladhouse (9prs) and Bawsinch (NT27W, 7prs), all in Lothian. In Borders the best counts were at Adderston Lee (NT51F&G, 11prs) and Whitmuirhill Loch (NT42Y, 5prs). 18 territories have been counted along the Tweed between Kelso and Coldstream (11km in NT73).

The *New Atlas* used 100prs/10-km square, or 1.0prs/km², to calculate the British population, about half the figure used in the *Old Atlas*. Densities of 1.5prs/km² were found on arable farmland with some scrub around Tranent (da Prato 1985) while local BBS returns equate to 1.0-1.5prs/km². Calculating the local population on the basis of just 1.0prs/km² in occupied tetrads, produces a figure of 1,900 pairs. However, many tetrads possess only a single site that often holds just a single pair and although the seven sites listed above hold over 100 pairs, a slightly lower total figure of around 1,700 pairs may be more likely. This is just 0.7% of the British population, a reasonable figure considering that the *New Atlas* shows large areas of SE Scotland to hold rather low numbers.

A.Barker

Reed Bunting

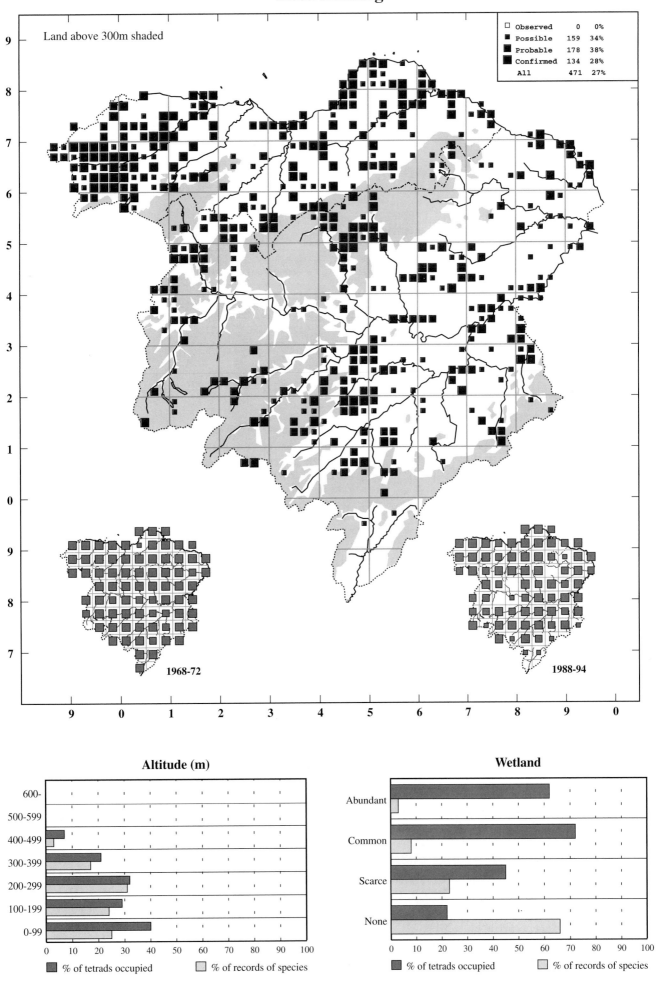

Land above 300m shaded

☐ Observed	0	0%
■ Possible	159	34%
■ Probable	178	38%
■ Confirmed	134	28%
All	471	27%

1968-72

1988-94

Altitude (m)

■ % of tetrads occupied ☐ % of records of species

Wetland

■ % of tetrads occupied ☐ % of records of species

317

Corn Bunting
Miliaria calandra

A mere twenty years ago most birders in the agricultural lowlands of SE Scotland would have been familiar with the dangly-legged flight and jangling song of this dumpy brown bird. Scotland being at the northern extremity of its breeding range, however, the Corn Bunting was even then in serious decline. This trend has continued unabated ever since. The *New Atlas* describes the ongoing population collapse succinctly as catastrophic, a major factor being the changes in farm practices which have seen the virtual disappearance of the winter stack-yard and with it the characteristic flocks of finches and buntings which provided the breeding stock for the next season. Within Scotland, the recent strongholds of the species have been in east Fife, Buchan and on the Hebridean islands of Harris, the Uists and Tiree, where it is also declining.

With a distinctive song Corn Buntings were fairly easy to record once they were located. Probable records were mostly of territorial singing, either birds at one site in consecutive years or two males singing against each other in a single year. The few confirmed records were all of fledged young. Corn Bunting young appear rather late in the summer and it is possible that several broods may have been missed through *Atlas* work being somewhat reduced in July.

As might be expected from such a quintessential bird of open arable farmland, the records for the species in Lothian and Borders come almost exclusively from low-lying arable areas near to the coast. The map shows Corn Buntings were seen in four main clusters between 1988-94: along the Almond between East Calder and Broxburn (NT06&07); in the Esk drainage between Dalkeith, Musselburgh and Tranent (NT36,37&47); in the middle Tyne drainage between Aberlady and East Linton (NT47,48,57&58); and in the Reston-Eyemouth-Lamberton area on the Berwickshire coast (NT86,95&96). There were just three records well away from the coast at the Hirsel (NT84F) in 1989, near Lauder (NT54S) in 1992 and near Ancrum (NT62G) in 1994. It is an obvious indication of the declining fortunes of the Corn Bunting that despite the intensive fieldwork associated with the *Atlas* it was observed in just 40 tetrads over a period of seven years. The map therefore exaggerates the range in SE Scotland through accumulating records spread over a number of years. Within that already limited area breeding was confirmed in just four tetrads at Cousland (NT36Y), Inveresk (NT37K), Laverocklaw (NT47S) and near Eyemouth (NT96L) although it is likely that breeding has occurred regularly in some other tetrads later than the main fieldwork season.

The habitat and altitude graphs confirm that almost all records are from low-lying areas, mostly below 100m, where arable farmland is important, typically dominated by cereal growing. However, as such habitat occurs across a much larger area of the lowlands of SE Scotland other factors must be controlling the precise distribution of Corn Buntings in the area. Farm practices are known to affect Corn Buntings and it seems likely that features such as the length of time that stubble is left prior to ploughing, the presence of seed-rich winter fodder crops such as turnips or kale, and the use of cattle-courts or insecticides, may have an impact on whether or not Corn Buntings can survive in any particular area.

There is very little information about the history of Corn Buntings in the Borders from inland areas, but Evans (1911) mentioned that it was scarce in the Ettrick Valley at the end of the 19th century and had recently vanished from the Duns area. It has probably long been absent as a breeding species from the old counties of Peeblesshire and Selkirkshire where it was at best a very scarce breeding species, being at the altitudinal limit of its range, as well as lacking the essential arable habitats. Corn Buntings may never have been common except in arable lowland areas near the coast (*R&B*). While birds may have declined at the limits of the range at the start of the century, *Andrews* indicates that the population decline in Lothian started in the 1950s. That they were still locally common along the coast and around Edinburgh in the 1960s and 1970s is well remembered by local birders today, and in the 1950s winter roosts in the Duddingston reedbeds could regularly attract up to 300 birds (*Andrews*).

By the time of the *Old Atlas* Corn Buntings were still widespread across most of lowland Lothian and were present on the fringes of the northern hills. Indeed even the former part of Midlothian around Stow in the Gala valley apparently held birds. In the Borders birds occupied the Kelso-Coldstream area and the middle Whiteadder as well as the Berwickshire coast. Since then there has been a massive decline with birds disappearing from over half of the 10-km squares. Concern for the plight of the Corn Bunting was expressed in the 1982 Lothians census (Brown *et al.* 1984) which turned up only 37 birds in just ten 10-km squares, compared to 36 squares during the *Old Atlas*. Brown *et al.* noted concentrations of birds around the East Calder-Ratho area (NT07-17), around Tranent (NT47B), Drem (NT57E) and Fala (NT46F). Local populations seem to have disappeared piecemeal, vanishing from Hoselaw and Yetholm in the 1960s, Grantshouse (NT86C) by 1981, and the last records at Fala were recorded in the 1982 survey.

With Corn Buntings locally on the edge of extinction they seem peculiarly difficult to survey. A survey by the BTO in 1993 could only trace nine singing males in Lothian and one in Borders (*Bird Reports*). Yet, despite finding no Corn Buntings at some well-known sites, birds have been traced at these sites in the years since. It may be that sites must be visited over a period of years to see whether Corn Buntings are present or not, ensuring that *all* surrounding areas are also surveyed.

The status during the *Atlas* period suggests 3-6 birds in the Almond area, 6-7 in the Inveresk-Tranent area, 3-5 males between Drem and East Linton and 5-6 males on the Berwickshire coast, in total some 18-24 singing males. Since 1994 the Eyemouth Corn Buntings have been lost in the creation of a new golf course, while both Reston and Lamberton have been reduced to two males apiece, the Lamberton site losing habitat to the dualling of the A1 road. No birds have been seen at Inveresk since hedges were removed in 1995, while the populations at Drem and the Almond may have halved to only two males in each area. Thus by 1997 the Corn Bunting population of SE Scotland has dropped to less than 10 pairs. Survival into the 21st century is very much in doubt.   *A.Barker*

Corn Bunting

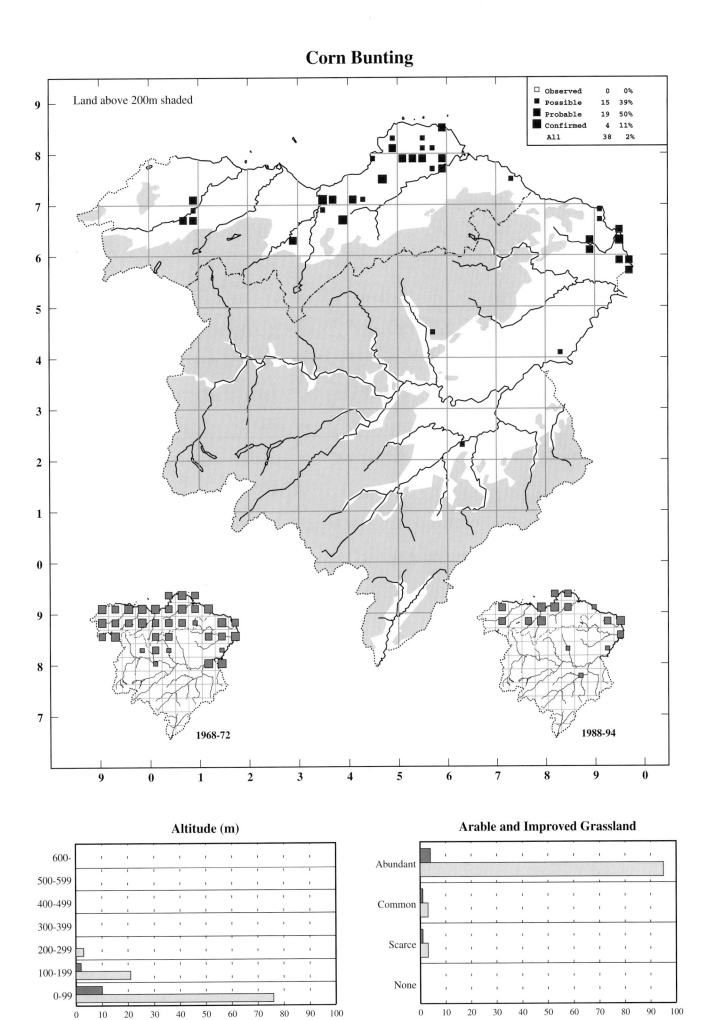

Land above 200m shaded

☐ Observed	0	0%
◼ Possible	15	39%
◼ Probable	19	50%
◼ Confirmed	4	11%
All	38	2%

1968-72

1988-94

Altitude (m)

Arable and Improved Grassland

■ % of tetrads occupied   ☐ % of records of species

319

Additional Species Accounts
Former, New, Occasional, Introduced and Potential Breeding Birds

In addition to the species in the Main Species Accounts that were proved to breed or recorded as possibly breeding in SE Scotland during 1988-94, there are a number of species that have bred outwith the survey period, both before 1988 and after 1994. These include species that nested regularly in the area hundreds of years ago, but have since become extinct. Others may represent attempts at colonisation, while others were just one-off breeding records. Other records of birds submitted to the *Atlas* which were not thought to represent breeding attempts are also noted here.

There is relatively little documented about SE Scotland's bird life before the 20th century, but some of Scotland's oldest ornithological literature (e.g. Turnbull 1867 and Muirhead 1889) provides a tantalising glimpse into the past. It reveals a picture of marshes with Bittern, Marsh Harrier and probably Spotted Crake, the open Merse with Great Bustard, a rocky coastline with White-tailed Eagle, Chough and Black Guillemot, hills with Ptarmigan and a countryside with Honey Buzzard, Red Kite and Nightjar.

The scope of this chapter is SE Scotland except for seabirds, for which summering records in the Forth area are considered. The species below fall into five categories:

a) potential breeding species, which have shown signs of territorial behaviour or remained into the summer (e.g. Golden Oriole, Red-backed Shrike, Black Redstart and Brambling),

b) vagrants that have temporarily sung or shown signs of breeding, but which are unlikely (or extremely unlikely) ever to breed (e.g. Marmora's Warbler),

c) failed introductions, e.g. Golden Pheasant and Capercaillie,

d) feral breeding of escapes, e.g. Black Swan and Night Heron, and

e) summering of injured wildfowl, e.g. Whooper Swan and Pink-footed Goose

In the accounts below, the source of records, unless otherwise specified, is material held by the local recorders and published in *Andrews*, *Murray*, LBR and BBR.

Black-browed Albatross *Diomedea melanophris*

An adult summered with Gannets on the Bass Rock between 1967 and 1969. On one occasion it indulged in an incomplete form of courtship display directed at a Gannet (Waterston 1968). It is possible that the Bass Rock bird was the same individual that visited the Hermaness gannetry in Shetland between 1972-97.

Manx Shearwater *Puffinus puffinus*

In 1996 and 1997 on the Isle of May on nights in late July and early August, a few Manx Shearwaters were heard calling overhead and from burrows and seen on the ground in suitable nesting habitat (Forth Islands Bird Reports). This is in the Forth area though not in SE Scotland.

For some decades Manx Shearwaters have been regular in feeding groups of tens or a few hundreds in summer as far into the Forth as Hound Point, with sometimes over 1,000 in late summer or autumn (*Andrews*, LBR).

Storm Petrel *Hydrobates pelagicus*

There is just one record of Storm Petrels nesting in the Firth of Forth. On 19 June 1904, an adult and one egg were found in a burrow on the Bass Rock (Clarke 1905). Two seen close to Inchkeith through the summer of 1913 were also assumed to be nesting in the area (*R&B*). The only recent summer records in the Firth of Forth concern corpses: one on the Bass Rock in June 1983 and two on Craigleith in June 1986 (LBR). Ringers have successfully tape-lured birds, mostly immatures and non-breeders, on the North Sea coast and on the Isle of May in summer, and breeding is not suspected.

Bittern *Botaurus stellaris*

Historical avifaunas describe the Bull o' the Bog or Mire-Drum, as it was locally known, as a local breeding species in SE Scotland prior to *c.*1830. When the Merse was covered with bogs and marshes, the Bittern was undoubtedly widespread in Berwickshire. Billie Mire, a huge marsh 8km across between Reston and Chirnside, was a prime haunt until it was drained about 1830-35 (Muirhead 1889). Around that period, land improvements resulted in many wet areas being drained, and the Bittern was soon lost as a breeding species. The statement that King James IV flew his falcons at Bitterns at Bathgate Bog in the 15th century (see Muirhead 1889) also paints a fascinating picture.

The lack of suitable habitat presumably precludes any recolonisation, although a male was heard booming at Yetholm Loch on 9 June 1980 (*Murray*). Unfortunately, the birds (up to two) wintering at Duddingston Loch in the 1990s have never stayed beyond 26 March (LBR).

Night Heron *Nycticorax nycticorax*

Night Herons of the North American race *N. n. hoactli* have been at liberty at Edinburgh Zoo since 1950, when several birds escaped from their damaged aviary. In 1957 there were about 30 free-flying birds (Doward 1957), and by 1968 the colony had reached its peak of 60 birds. Since 1980, the population has stabilised at 20-40 birds, some of which are colour-ringed (Young and Duffy 1985, LBR). The small breeding colony is located in coniferous trees in the zoo grounds, and 16 nests were counted in 1984 when 10+ chicks fledged (Young and Duffy 1985). There is no evidence to suggest that Night Herons have ever nested outside the zoo. Indeed, it is doubtful if the birds could survive without the food supplied by the zoo. There are irregular sightings of Night Herons from Edinburgh's rivers and ponds, but relatively few wander east of Musselburgh or into West Lothian.

White Stork *Ciconia ciconia*

In the early 15th century, Walter Bower, the then Abbot of Inchcolm, wrote in his chronicles that in 1416 a pair of storks nested and reared young on St. Giles' Cathedral in Edinburgh (Clarke 1919). This is the only breeding record for Britain and represents the earliest documented breeding record in the *Atlas*. It is, however, an event that is unlikely to be repeated.

Whooper Swan *Cygnus cygnus*

Injured Whooper Swans occasionally remain through the summer. In Borders, the lower Teviot and middle Tweed are noted as regular sites for injured birds (*Murray*). No breeding attempt is known. Two records were submitted to this *Atlas*, an anxious pair in NT42 in 1989, and a late-staying individual in NT63 in 1993.

Pink-footed Goose *Anser brachyrhynchus*

As with other wildfowl, injured Pink-footed Geese are known to summer in SE Scotland. A few feral birds also frequent the Edinburgh lochs, and in 1997 a bird nested at Duddingston Loch. Records of over-staying or feral birds in nine tetrads were reported to the *Atlas*.

White-fronted Goose *Anser albifrons*

A small flock of feral birds was resident at Duddingston Loch for some time in the early 1990s, but breeding is not known to have occurred.

Black Swan *Cygnus atratus*

A feral pair successfully nested on the Union Canal at Ratho in 1997.

Wood Duck *Aix sponsa*

A free-flying pair reported from the Leithen Water in the Moorfoots (NT34G) in April 1993 was not seen subsequently (BBR, *Atlas*).

American Black Duck *Anas rubripes*

A female American Black Duck remained on the River Tyne and adjacent estuary for much of 1985 and 1986 (LBR). It was paired with a male Mallard with which it displayed and mated, but no hybrid young was ever seen.

King Eider *Somateria spectabilis*

A female appeared at Aberlady Bay in July 1988 and then in three successive summers (1995-97) (LBR). It is not known where it (or they) spent the breeding seasons, but it may just have moved from the nearby islands with the post-breeding Eiders, and where it could have attempted to pair.

Honey Buzzard *Pernis apivorus*

The former status of the Honey Buzzard in SE Scotland is difficult to assess. Despite a statement claiming it was once one of the commonest of the larger raptors in the Borders (Evans 1911), it was undoubtedly only an irregular breeding species even then. Evans (1911) implied it nested (or had nested) in Borders, despite intense persecution. He failed to document any details of nesting, apart from a female shot from a pair at Dawyck on 26 June 1907, which may have been prospecting. Similarly, there are no historical breeding records for Lothian, although Turnbull (1867), for example, lists many that had been shot in East Lothian.

A single modern record is significant: a fatally injured juvenile found in East Lothian on 2 September 1991 (LBR) still bore some down feathers and is presumed to have been reared locally.

Red Kite *Milvus milvus*

Historically the Red Kite was a common bird in SE Scotland and its extinction was doubtless caused by improvements in sanitation and increased persecution (*R&B*). There is, however, some difficulty in disentangling the old records of kites and harriers as both were called gleds. There is little published information for Lothian, and no documented breeding records. They were still common in the late 18th century, but by 1845-50 they had become very rare in East Lothian, although still being seen almost annually at one site, Gladsmuir (Turnbull 1867). In the Borders, it used, no doubt, to be a very common and widespread breeding species in the 18th century (Evans 1911). Numbers declined rapidly at the end of that century, and it had ceased to be resident by 1841. The last record was one trapped in Lauderdale *c*.1890 (*R&B*).

The success of recent re-introduction schemes in Britain gives hope that one day these elegant birds will once again grace their ancient Lothian and Borders breeding haunts.

White-tailed Eagle *Haliaeetus albicilla*

It is documented that the White-tailed Eagle used to breed in small numbers in SE Scotland in the 18th century. On the coast, there were eyries on the Bass Rock and on several of the Berwickshire coastal cliffs (*R&B*). Inland haunts were noted on several cliffs in the upper Tweed area, such as around Talla Linnfoots and at the head of the Manor Water (Evans 1911). It is not known for certain when this magnificent raptor last nested in SE Scotland, but stray individuals were still being seen into the mid 1800s.

The old name, Erne, appears in several local place names e.g. Ernesheugh near Fast Castle, and Ernscleugh in the Lammermuirs north-east of Lauder, and these may well indicate where the species formerly bred.

Marsh Harrier *Circus aeruginosus*

This species was seemingly once widespread and common in the marshes and wet moorlands of the Borders, but the population began a downward trend in the mid 1800s. By the 1870s it had ceased to be seen in the area, and Evans (1911) could quote no breeding records. Drainage of the many mires and bogs during the first half of the 19th century was probably initially responsible for the demise of the Marsh Harrier, and persecution and egg-collection only finished it off (*Murray*). There are no old records of breeding in Lothian (*R&B*).

More recently, up to three birds summered in coastal East Lothian in 1976-78 (*Andrews*), and one summered inland in 1996. The re-colonisation of northern Britain has yet to reach SE Scotland, although migrants are being seen with increasing frequency on passage to breeding areas elsewhere in Scotland. During the *Atlas*, Marsh Harriers were reported from a total of seven tetrads, mainly in Berwickshire and all in 1992 and 1994. Although most were single sightings which probably represent passage birds, one individual was recorded in two adjacent tetrads near Duns (NT75) in 1992.

Red-tailed Hawk *Buteo jamaicensis*

An escaped falconer's bird bred unsuccessfully with a Buzzard in Midlothian in 1969 (*Thom*).

Marsh Harrier

Hobby *Falco subbuteo*

The *Atlas* records Hobbies in three tetrads, one each in 1990, 1991 and 1994 in NT44, NT65 and NT86 respectively.

Ptarmigan *Lagopus mutus*

B&R records that Ptarmigans were known around Hart Fell on the border of Peeblesshire and Dumfriesshire in the 17-19th centuries. The entire south-west Scottish population, of which this small outlier formed a part, became extinct about 1820-30.

An attempt was made to reintroduce them in the Leadhills area in adjacent Lanarkshire in the late 1960s and mid 1970s, using eggs collected near Braemar (*Thom*). A few birds moved east into the Tweedsmuir Hills and bred there in the late 1970s. Twenty were seen in the winter of 1977-78, but almost all were shot in 1978. Stragglers were seen in 1980 and 1984.

Capercaillie *Tetrao urogallus*

The natural range of this game bird has never reached SE Scotland, but four attempts to introduce it took place in the Borders between 1870 and 1950. These were at Dolphinton (1870-1904), Dawyck (1930-47), Glentress (1948-50) and near Galashiels. Populations failed to become established due to over-exploitation, poaching and habitat destruction (*Murray*). Although there are 14 records from Lothian between 1849 and 1909 and one in 1946 (*Andrews*), there is no record of birds being released or pairs having bred. It is assumed that, in the main, these originated from stock released into Fife. The last record in SE Scotland was at Portmore in 1959.

Golden Pheasant *Chrysolophus pictus*

Small feral populations became established in the Borders forests at Glentress and Cardrona in the 1960s and 1970s (*Murray*). The population reached 50 birds, but none was seen after 1977 or 1978, almost certainly due to the stock being poached out. There are few subsequent records, and none has bred since the 1970s. A pair was seen in West Lothian near Bathgate (NS96Y) in 1991 (*Atlas*).

Spotted Crake *Porzana porzana*

Muirhead (1895) writes that Spotted Crakes doubtless bred at Billie Mire before it was drained (see Bittern), and surmised that they still awaited discovery in the few (then) remaining Berwickshire bogs. The only proof of breeding in SE Scotland, however, refers to several young found by a small loch in Roxburghshire on 7 May 1912 (*B&R*).

Calling birds were heard at Duddingston Loch on 25-27 April 1991 and 22 April 1992 (LBR, *Atlas*).

There is no documented evidence of the possible breeding record in NT84 shown in the *Old Atlas*.

Great Bustard *Otis tarda*

Some 300-400 years ago Great Bustards are said to have bred in the Merse of Berwickshire. Hector Boece (in 1526) and Sir Robert Sibbald (in 1684) both wrote of its occurrence there; the latter adding that he had been informed that one had been seen in East Lothian not long before.

It is likely that the Great Bustard became extinct in SE Scotland soon after the start of the Agricultural Revolution of the 1700s (*Murray*).

Little Ringed Plover *Charadrius dubius*

Single migrants of this species occur with some regularity on the Lothian coast, but no evidence of breeding has yet been observed. One was seen on a gravel island in the lower Tweed in April 1995 (BBR) and five were together there in April 1996. Although paired in 1996, no birds lingered for more than ten days.

Broad-billed Sandpiper *Limicola falcinellus*

The series of records at Aberlady Bay in 1983-84 included a pair on 8-15 June 1983 (LBR). The male was frequently seen song-flighting, and on one occasion one settled into a depression in short turf, making shuffling movements as though creating a scrape. A single bird was seen intermittently until 4 July. This species has never nested in Britain.

Ruff *Philomachus pugnax*

Ruffs occur in SE Scotland mainly on passage and to a lesser extent in winter. However, occasionally a few birds (usually single adult males) are recorded at Musselburgh and Aberlady Bay in the late May to June period. No breeding behaviour has yet been recorded. *Atlas* records were received of single birds at Bavelaw in 1989, 1990 and 1992. Two breeding plumaged males visited Folly Loch for a week or so in spring 1997.

Black-tailed Godwit *Limosa limosa*

This increasingly common migrant to SE Scotland has only rarely shown signs of settling to breed. At Tailend Moss, two were present during 23-29 April 1992 (with four on 30th) and on one occasion a single bird was seen in display flight (LBR). Also in 1992, three were seen at Whitrig in April and five in May (BBR). One record, at Bavelaw on 12-14 April 1992, was submitted to the *Atlas*.

Greenshank *Tringa nebularia*

A pair of Greenshank was reported to have bred unsuccessfully near a stream in the Lammermuirs ten miles from Lauder in 1925 and 1926 (and probably in 1924) (Ritchie and Grimshaw 1925, McConacie 1930). Two eggs from the 1925 clutch are preserved in the National Museum of Scotland, but these have subsequently been re-identified as being Golden Plover eggs (D. Nethersole-Thompson and Dr. H. Blair *in litt.*). The 1925 record, at least, must therefore be considered unsubstantiated.

Records of single birds in four tetrads were received in this *Atlas*, including one in 1994 in suitable nesting habitat in the Ettrick Forest (NT31).

Green Sandpiper *Tringa ochropus*

What were probably passage birds were reported from four tetrads, but an individual displaying to a Common Sandpiper on the Liddel Water (NY59Z) in 1994 was more interesting (*Atlas*). However, the bird could not be relocated.

Wood Sandpiper *Tringa glareola*

A record of three at Gladhouse Reservoir on 6 June 1955 included one display-flighting over the reservoir (*Andrews*). Breeding is not considered likely in SE Scotland.

Black Guillemot *Cepphus grylle*

Small numbers of this seabird formerly nested on the Bass Rock, at St. Abb's Head and Brander Cove and also on the Isle of May (*R&B*). It last bred at St. Abbs in 1859, and several were still in the area of the Bass Rock (although it was not specified if they were breeding) up to 1880 (Nash 1935). One was seen at St. Abbs in May 1933, but there were no further summer records until 1969.

In the 1970s at least one bird frequented the Forth islands over six summers (*Andrews*). Individuals were seen at Inchkeith (1969 and 1974), Fidra (1976-1980) and Craigleith (1977). Although the Fidra bird was occasionally seen ashore in suitable breeding habitat, no confirmation of nesting was ever obtained. A series of records at St. Abbs and Coldingham since 1986 also suggests that one or two birds are remaining all year at another former haunt. Three tetrads along this coast (NT96) registered in the *Atlas* in 1993.

With Black Guillemots averaging six records annually in Lothian and Borders between 1988 and 1994, and the nearest North Sea breeding site over 100 km to the north, the regularity of the presence of birds allied to the sedentary nature of the species suggests that breeding may occur, overlooked, on one of the islands or even the Berwickshire coast.

Turtle Dove *Streptopelia turtur*

Following two old records of pairs seen in June (at Dunbar in 1877 and Gogar in 1889, *R&B*), Turtle Doves first bred in SE Scotland at the Hirsel in 1946 (*B&R*). Subsequently a few pairs regularly bred in the Borders in the 1950s and early 1960s (*Murray*), and at Longniddry in 1955-66 and during the *Old Atlas* (*Andrews*). There have been no subsequent records of confirmed breeding. Although pairs were infrequently seen in the Aberlady and Tyninghame areas up to 1983, the Turtle Dove is now rarely seen in Lothian even as a migrant. A pair last summered in the Borders at Reston in 1988 (BBR, *New Atlas*) and one was seen there again in 1992 (*Atlas*). Two near Eyemouth on 12 July 1989 may have summered. Judging by the decline of its numbers in England, it is unlikely that the Turtle Doves will recolonise SE Scotland in the near future.

Ring-necked Parakeet *Psittacula krameri*

A group of records of this species, which is established as a feral breeding bird in southern England (*New Atlas*), occurred in SE Scotland between 1976 and 1991 inclusive, in lowland and coastal Lothian and one at Selkirk in Borders. All records but one were of single birds, and no bird was known to remain locally except one which was seen for two to three weeks (*Andrews*, LBR, BBR).

Nightjar *Caprimulgus europaeus*

Historical documents reveal that the Nightjar was once a widespread and locally common breeding species in SE Scotland (*R&B*).

West Lothian records are restricted to Bathgate where breeding was reported in 1845 and 1862 (*B&R*) and for several years prior to 1937. In Midlothian a juvenile was shot at Dalhousie in July 1892 and it was said to have been "common" at Roslin Glen in 1871; one was also heard churring at Colinton after 1920 (*R&B*).

The species' stronghold was evidently in Berwickshire and East Lothian. Muirhead (1889) lists Abbey St. Bathans and Penmanshiel among its favoured haunts. Evans (1911) also stresses the importance of that area, but describes a widespread and stable population through much of the Tweed basin. In 1935 a few still bred at Pease Dean and locally in East Lothian (*R&B*), but the species declined slowly and had virtually disappeared by the 1950s (*B&R*). The fact that it was persecuted by gamekeepers, under the misbelief that it was a bird of prey, only accelerated the species' decline.

There were a few records in Borders in the 1970s and late 1980s, the last being at Eildon in 1989. In Lothian, churring birds have been recorded at Saltoun (two in 1964) and Rosewell (1982). It is conceivable that the odd elusive pair is waiting to be discovered, perhaps on the fringes of afforested land, but unfortunately none was seen or heard during the *New Atlas* or the current fieldwork. The nearest breeding site in Northumberland is less than 15km from the border (*Day*).

Bee-eater *Merops apiaster*

Remarkably, a pair attempted to nest along the River Esk at Musselburgh in 1920 (Clarke 1920) in what must be one of the most unexpected breeding records in recent times. They excavated a nest hole in a sand bank, but the egg-bearing female was captured before the breeding attempt could be completed. A local gardener put it into a greenhouse and supplied it with breadcrumbs, but it died within two days. The male was also caught and entirely destroyed by a cat a few days later (Nash 1935).

Wryneck *Jynx torquilla*

Wrynecks have not been recorded breeding in SE Scotland, although three Borders records are intriguing and raise the possibility that birds have at least summered. Inland records from Swinton (August 1971) and Duns (August 1976) were followed by a recently dead bird found at the Hirsel in early August 1984 (*Murray*).

Thrush Nightingale *Luscinia luscinia*

A male in song was reported at Gullane on 25-26 May 1994.

Black Redstart *Phoenicurus ochruros*

SE Scotland lies well north of this species' normal breeding range, although a pair did nest successfully on the Isle of May in 1994. The following records in Lothian are significant: a pair in Edinburgh on 1 May 1924, with a singing male in the city in April 1951 (*Andrews*). One bird was seen near Penicuik in 1989 (*Atlas*). A male at Gladhouse on 13 July 1990 and a single there on 20 September were considered suspicious in that at least a bird had over-summered (LBR, *Atlas, New Atlas*). A wintering bird at Cockenzie Power Station sang on at least two occasions in February 1995, and on 4 August 1996 a juvenile was seen in a garden in Musselburgh. There are no summer records from the Borders with any suggestion of breeding.

Redwing *Turdus iliacus*

There are three records of single Redwings summering in Lothian: at the Royal Botanic Garden (Edinburgh) in 1928 and 1963, and at Gifford in 1982 (*Andrews*). These records are thought to relate to birds that were injured in some way. More interesting is the pair seen at Houndwood (NT86M) on 18 May 1989 (*Atlas, New Atlas*). The male was heard singing, and the pair also alarmed, but no further indication of breeding was observed. Wintering Redwings can be heard singing from February onwards, and a pair, including a male in sub-song, was reported to the *Atlas* from Dalmeny Estate (NT17T) in April 1988.

Marsh Warbler *Acrocephalus palustris*

Migrants briefly set up territories at Aberlady on 31 May 1985 and St. Abb's Head on 2-3 June 1994.

Reed Warbler *Acrocephalus scirpaceus*

Singing male Reed Warblers have been recorded in the reed bed at the Mire Loch, St. Abb's Head in several recent springs (1977 and 1992-95). At the time these were considered to be migrants. In 1997, however, two pairs were proved to have bred at this site. Two females with brood patches were trapped in August, followed by

two separate juveniles soon after. A singing male at Figgate Pond, Edinburgh on 12 June 1988 (*New Atlas*) is the only relevant Lothian record.

Great Reed Warbler *Acrocephalus arundinaceus*

Migrants sang at St. Abb's Head on 29-30 May 1979, Aberlady on 17 May 1990 and St. Abb's Head on 1-6 June 1997.

Icterine Warbler *Hippolais icterina*

The only vaguely relevant record refers to a migrant which sang at St. Abb's Head on 7 June 1994.

Marmora's Warbler *Sylvia sarda*

A male at St. Abb's Head sang from 23-27 May 1993, although it is of little significance that this vagrant decided to sing.

Dartford Warbler *Sylvia undata*

A male sang at St. Abb's Head on 18 May 1983. This remains the only Scottish record of this southern warbler.

Subalpine Warbler *Sylvia cantillans*

A male sang at St. Abb's Head on 26-27 June 1981.

Golden Oriole *Oriolus oriolus*

In Lothian, birds sang at Aberlady on 7 June 1975, Bawsinch (Duddingston) on 30 May 1978, Muirfield on 24 May 1990, Spott on 3 June 1990 (*Atlas*) and near East Linton on 7-9 June 1996. Only the last individual was heard on more than one day, and most are presumed to have been migrants. In Borders, one remained near Duns in June and July 1980 (*Murray*).

Red-backed Shrike *Lanius collurio*

R&B give two old records of probable breeding in Lothian. A pair summered at Dunbar in 1856 (the female was shot), and a pair probably nested at Blackshiels near Fala in 1932 - a nest with skeletons of birds impaled on thorns below it was subsequently seen by Baxter and Rintoul (1934). More recently a few stray birds have been recorded inland in spring and others have appeared in July which raises the possibility that one day this species may nest in SE Scotland. In 1985, after an exceptional spring passage, possible summering was suggested at Scoughall where a male was seen on 31 July and a female stayed from 2-9 August. Two records were submitted to the *Atlas*, a male at Samuelston in East Lothian (NT47V) in 1988 and a male in song at Gordon Moss (NT64G) in June 1994.

Chough *Pyrrhocorax pyrrhocorax*

Although generally considered a west coast speciality, a small number of Choughs formerly bred on the Berwickshire coast between Redheugh and St. Abbs (Muirhead 1889, Evans 1911). Choughs were "often seen" and "not uncommon" there until *c.*1840, after which there was a sudden decline. The species last bred at Fast Castle in 1846 and possibly 1851 (Muirhead 1889). A series of records between 1895-1903 was regarded as inconclusive by *R&B*. One Chough seen at Dunglass in June 1995 was quite unexpected, and whether a true vagrant or an escaped bird can only be conjecture (BBR).

Brambling *Fringilla montifringilla*

Late spring and summer records of Brambling in SE Scotland are few. Although most records can be attributed to reluctant migrants, breeding must be considered a possibility. A male was seen at Elibank on 10 June 1969 and a singing bird was seen in Lothian on 9 May 1982. On 3 May 1983 two sang at Tyninghame, and there were three records (of ten birds) in coastal Berwickshire in July-August 1984. In 1985, a male in summer plumage sang briefly at Eyemouth on 12 June and the following year a male was at St. Abbs on 2 August. The concentration of summer records along the Berwickshire and East Lothian coast in 1982-86 suggests that breeding may have taken place nearby. Ten widespread tetrads recorded this species in the *Atlas* in 1988, 1992, 1993 and 1994.

Common Rosefinch *Carpodacus erythrinus*

In view of the recent colonisation of northern Scotland and the east coast of Britain, all singing birds are of note. The only such record in SE Scotland is of a first-summer male singing at Seacliff on 9 June 1995 (LBR).

Other species recorded in *Atlas* fieldwork

The following 16 species were also noted by *Atlas* fieldworkers, but were all considered to be passage birds:

Red-throated Diver	*Gavia stellata*
Barnacle Goose	*Branta leucopsis*
American Wigeon	*Anas americana*
Scaup	*Aythya marila*
Common Scoter	*Melanitta nigra*
Red-footed Falcon	*Falco vespertinus*
Grey Plover	*Pluvialis squatarola*
Knot	*Calidris canutus*
Jack Snipe	*Lymnocryptes minimus*
Bar-tailed Godwit	*Limosa lapponica*
Whimbrel	*Numenius phaeopus*
Turnstone	*Arenaria interpres*
Black Tern	*Chlidonias niger*
Bluethroat	*Luscinia svecica*
Woodchat Shrike	*Lanius senator*
Snow Bunting	*Plectrophenax nivalis*

Appendices

The appendices give in full various data which are referred to in the main text above together with some altitude and habitat maps (and associated graphs) which are not included in the chapter South-east Scotland and its Habitats for Breeding Birds.

Population Estimates for all species breeding in SE Scotland 1988-94

Species	ESTIMATE	Year	Notes	Species	ESTIMATE	Year	Notes
Little Grebe	170			Puffin*	26,100	1995	
Great Crested Grebe	25-35 #			Feral Pigeon	6,500-10,000		
Red-necked Grebe	1			Stock Dove	3,900		
Slavonian Grebe	0			Woodpigeon	61,500		
Black-necked Grebe	1		2 in 1997	Collared Dove	2,200-3,300		
Fulmar*	4,165	1995		Cuckoo	350-500		
Gannet	39,751	1994		Barn Owl	125-200		
Cormorant*	320			Little Owl	0-1		
Shag*	1,277	1996		Tawny Owl	1,600		
Grey Heron	450			Long-eared Owl	100-300		
Mute Swan	141	1991	165 in 1995	Short-eared Owl	20-200 #		
Greylag Goose	100		Also 450 non-breeders	Swift	1,500-1,800		
Canada Goose	2-5			Kingfisher	45-60		
Shelduck	150			Green Woodpecker	150-200		
Mandarin	5-10			G. Spotted Woodpecker	1,200		
Wigeon	30-40			Skylark	54,400		
Gadwall	1-2			Sand Martin	7,000		
Teal	180-230			Swallow	6,000-8,500		
Mallard	3,100			House Martin	2,800-4,200		
Pintail	0-1 #			Tree Pipit	1,600		
Garganey	0-1 #			Meadow Pipit	127,000		
Shoveler	10-15 #			Rock Pipit	295-325		
Pochard	5-15 #			Yellow Wagtail	40-50		
Tufted Duck	380			Grey Wagtail	1,000		
Eider*	2,500			Pied Wagtail	14,000		
Goldeneye	0-1 #			Dipper	1,500		
Red-breasted Merg	1-2 #			Wren	134,000-167,000 #		
Goosander	220			Dunnock	63,000		
Ruddy Duck	20		26 in 1997	Robin	92,000		
Hen Harrier	3-7			Redstart	1,000		
Goshawk	45-60			Whinchat	3,100		
Sparrowhawk	1,400			Stonechat	30-50		
Buzzard	560			Wheatear	5,000		
Golden Eagle	2			Ring Ouzel	300		
Osprey	0			Blackbird	64,000		
Kestrel	1,200			Fieldfare	0-5 #		
Merlin	50-60			Song Thrush	29,000		
Peregrine	35	1994	40 in 1997	Mistle Thrush	10,500		
Red Grouse	18,400			Grasshopper Warbler	250		
Black Grouse	500-600			Sedge Warbler	6,750		
Red-leg Partridge/Chukar	40			Lesser Whitethroat	180-200		
Grey Partridge	10,750			Whitethroat	6,200		
Quail	10-60 #		c.250 in 1989	Garden Warbler	2,400		
Pheasant	65,000-70,000			Blackcap	6,750		
Water Rail	25			Wood Warbler	170-190		
Corncrake	0-2			Chiffchaff	2,000		
Moorhen	900			Willow Warbler	112,000		
Coot	600			Goldcrest	105,000-150,000 #		
Oystercatcher	7,000			Spotted Flycatcher	3,500-7,500		
Ringed Plover	125			Pied Flycatcher	30-50		
Dotterel	0-1 #			Long-tailed Tit	800-1,600		
Golden Plover	1,600			Marsh Tit	80-100		
Lapwing	12,500			Willow Tit	5-10		
Dunlin	50-60			Coal Tit	98,000		
Snipe	1,740-2,320			Blue Tit	75,000		
Woodcock	1,400-1,500			Great Tit	30,000		
Curlew	11,450			Nuthatch	10	1994	29 in 1997
Redshank	660			Treecreeper	1,100-2,200		
Common Sandpiper	1,000			Jay	80-100		
Black-headed Gull	19,713			Magpie	1,870		
Common Gull	30-35	1994	75 in 1997	Jackdaw	19,000		
Lesser B-b Gull*	7,850	1996		Rook	55,000		
Herring Gull*	15,650	1996		Carrion/Hybrid Crow	10,500		
Great B-b Gull*	18	1994	25 in 1997	Raven	4-16		
Kittiwake*	35,000	1995		Starling	51,000-62,000		
Sandwich Tern*	0-500 #		None in 1997	House Sparrow	80,000-90,000		
Roseate Tern*	0-20 #		7 in 1997	Tree Sparrow	1,300		
Common Tern*	341-1,029 #		939 in 1997	Chaffinch	200,000		
Arctic Tern*	308-560 #		636 in 1997	Greenfinch	10,700		
Little Tern*	7-47 #		None in 1997	Goldfinch	3,300		
Guillemot*	46,600	1996		Siskin	45,500		
Razorbill*	4,450	1996		Linnet	20,000		
				Twite	0-10 #		

328

Species	ESTIMATE	Year	Notes
Redpoll	12,200		
Crossbill	5,000-10,000		Probably 100,000 in 1990
Bullfinch	2,240-3,360		
Hawfinch	20		
Yellowhammer	32,400		
Reed Bunting	1,700		
Corn Bunting	18-24		8 in 1997

Notes.

Unless stated, all figures are averages or calculated estimates for the period 1988-94. Where the figure relates to a count or estimate in a specific year, this is shown in the Year column.

Figures are for the estimated number of pairs, or equivalent. The unit of estimate for some species is different, thus for some seabirds the total represents Apparently Occupied Nests or Apparently Occupied Sites, and for Black Grouse the unit is lekking males. Refer to the individual species texts for full details.

All totals represent the population in SE Scotland, except for the seabirds and Eider where a significant number also nest on other islands in the Forth. These species are indicated by an asterisk against the species name. For these species, the total covers the whole Forth population, as discussed in the individual species texts.

In some species, a population range is given. This is usually because the estimating method does not allow a more precise figure to be calculated. However, for those species marked with '#', the range represents annual variations. Thus for Short-eared Owl the number of nesting pairs varies from 20 to 200 depending on the availability of food and the success of the previous season. For Goldcrest, the numbers are reduced by a hard winter to around 105,000, but after a series of mild winters the population recovers to a maximum of around 150,000.

Probable and Confirmed Breeding categories in detail, percentage distributions from *Atlas*

This table gives details of the distribution of records *within* the probable and confirmed breeding categories, according to the behaviour recorded. Results are given for each species for which at least 15 records were received. The first column gives the total number of records for the species. The remaining columns correspond to one of the sub-categories of probable or confirmed breeding, indicated by the code in the heading (see p. 24 for description). The entries in the table are the number of records in that sub-category expressed as a percentage of the total number of records within the appropriate category of either probable or confirmed breeding. Sub-categories L and CB are used when no more specific information was given. A dash (-) means there were no records in the category.

Species	Total no. of records	Probable Breeding							Confirmed Breeding							
		L	P	T	D	N	A	B	CB	DD	UN	FL	ON	FY	NE	NY
Little Grebe	132	10	60	27	3	0	0	0	1	0	0	77	11	0	4	6
Great Crested Grebe	47	0	82	18	0	0	0	0	0	0	0	50	15	10	25	0
Fulmar	55	-	-	-	-	-	-	-	10	0	0	0	61	0	16	13
Cormorant	78	-	-	-	-	-	-	-	0	0	0	0	0	0	67	33
Shag	40	0	100	0	0	0	0	0	8	0	0	0	38	0	38	15
Grey Heron	692	-	-	-	-	-	-	-	2	0	5	15	54	2	5	18
Mute Swan	198	0	79	18	0	0	0	3	1	0	1	45	39	0	7	6
Greylag Goose	53	0	100	0	0	0	0	0	0	0	0	79	0	4	4	13
Canada Goose	23	9	91	0	0	0	0	0	0	0	0	67	0	0	33	0
Shelduck	61	0	83	0	14	3	0	0	7	0	0	80	7	0	0	7
Mandarin	17	11	78	11	0	0	0	0	0	0	0	100	0	0	0	0
Wigeon	37	0	91	9	0	0	0	0	0	20	0	80	0	0	0	0
Gadwall	18	0	100	0	0	0	0	0	0	0	0	100	0	0	0	0
Teal	218	2	86	6	1	1	4	0	0	16	0	76	0	0	6	2
Mallard	1119	1	88	7	1	1	3	0	4	2	1	80	4	2	4	2
Shoveler	31	0	100	0	0	0	0	0	0	0	0	100	0	0	0	0
Pochard	32	0	88	13	0	0	0	0	0	0	0	100	0	0	0	0
Tufted Duck	211	3	93	2	2	0	0	0	2	2	0	89	1	0	1	4
Eider	74	0	100	0	0	0	0	0	3	0	3	55	6	3	24	6
Goldeneye	36	0	81	13	6	0	0	0	-	-	-	-	-	-	-	-
Red-breasted Merganser	16	0	80	0	0	0	20	0	-	-	-	-	-	-	-	-
Goosander	260	0	77	10	1	3	10	0	1	3	0	84	9	0	1	1
Ruddy Duck	15	0	83	0	17	0	0	0	0	0	0	100	0	0	0	0
Hen Harrier	54	0	44	11	22	0	11	11	22	0	0	22	0	0	33	22
Goshawk	69	0	39	22	33	0	6	0	0	0	6	6	41	6	0	41
Sparrowhawk	650	9	23	34	25	4	4	1	12	0	12	15	20	28	4	10
Buzzard	444	0	58	31	11	0	0	0	7	0	9	26	14	13	4	26
Kestrel	1156	5	39	41	7	4	4	0	3	1	1	29	19	34	3	10
Merlin	156	0	50	18	14	0	18	0	9	2	2	13	6	4	28	37
Peregrine	144	6	38	19	25	0	13	0	7	0	0	7	43	0	35	9
Red Grouse	469	2	31	30	22	0	15	0	9	5	4	62	7	1	9	2
Black Grouse	227	2	16	23	56	1	2	0	8	17	0	58	8	0	8	0
Red-legged Partridge	71	13	79	8	0	0	0	0	0	0	0	90	0	0	10	0
Grey Partridge	788	2	84	6	1	0	6	0	11	3	4	73	1	1	7	1
Quail	146	5	7	87	2	0	0	0	25	0	0	25	0	0	25	25
Pheasant	1352	1	28	31	34	0	5	0	9	2	7	60	4	1	15	1
Water Rail	29	0	25	75	0	0	0	0	0	0	0	100	0	0	0	0
Moorhen	574	2	69	21	1	3	4	0	5	0	2	71	9	2	9	3
Coot	253	0	80	16	0	0	4	0	2	0	1	61	22	4	7	3
Oystercatcher	1044	1	50	10	11	0	28	0	5	13	1	31	36	1	12	1
Ringed Plover	104	0	78	8	3	0	13	0	2	21	0	48	5	2	19	2
Dotterel	21	0	100	0	0	0	0	0	0	0	0	0	0	0	100	0
Golden Plover	253	2	28	22	8	1	40	0	4	45	4	29	6	0	12	0
Lapwing	1154	2	28	8	24	0	37	0	6	14	0	49	20	0	9	2
Dunlin	51	5	24	19	29	5	19	0	0	67	0	22	11	0	0	0
Snipe	584	1	7	14	72	0	5	0	0	45	2	28	10	0	10	5
Woodcock	300	1	7	23	68	0	0	0	35	6	0	45	6	0	6	0
Curlew	1203	1	18	16	32	0	32	0	5	32	3	38	7	1	10	3
Redshank	450	2	35	13	13	0	37	0	1	33	0	46	5	3	8	4
Common Sandpiper	520	2	46	13	4	0	36	0	2	33	0	53	3	0	8	1
Black-headed Gull	1075	4	22	0	17	9	43	4	6	0	2	19	42	0	24	6
Common Gull	279	0	100	0	0	0	0	0	0	0	0	20	50	0	30	0
Lesser Black-backed Gull	596	0	100	0	0	0	0	0	6	0	0	12	35	6	24	18
Herring Gull	537	0	0	0	50	0	50	0	6	0	0	8	47	0	19	19
Great Black-backed Gull	59	0	100	0	0	0	0	0	0	0	0	0	25	0	50	25
Kittiwake	38	0	100	0	0	0	0	0	7	0	0	7	36	0	29	21
Sandwich Tern	40	0	0	0	100	0	0	0	0	0	0	0	50	0	0	50
Common Tern	50	0	50	0	33	0	17	0	0	0	0	25	38	13	13	13
Arctic Tern	23	0	80	0	20	0	0	0	0	0	0	25	25	0	50	0
Guillemot	20	-	-	-	-	-	-	-	9	0	0	0	27	0	55	9
Razorbill	18	-	-	-	-	-	-	-	8	0	0	0	31	0	38	23
Feral Pigeon	815	1	73	10	6	10	1	0	9	0	3	10	62	1	6	9
Stock Dove	489	0	76	16	3	3	0	2	17	0	1	9	39	1	19	14
Woodpigeon	1534	2	57	23	12	3	1	1	5	0	31	6	37	0	15	5

Species	Total no of records	Probable Breeding							Confirmed Breeding							
		L	P	T	D	N	A	B	CB	DD	UN	FL	ON	FY	NE	NY
Collared Dove	550	2	66	22	7	2	0	1	17	0	3	41	30	3	3	4
Cuckoo	506	4	22	65	9	1	0	0	19	0	0	81	0	0	0	0
Barn Owl	198	2	25	70	0	3	0	0	14	0	4	21	29	11	7	14
Little Owl	17	0	0	80	20	0	0	0	0	0	0	100	0	0	0	0
Tawny Owl	696	5	15	76	0	2	2	0	7	0	1	77	7	2	4	4
Long-eared Owl	91	0	0	80	0	10	10	0	5	0	0	64	3	5	0	23
Short-eared Owl	298	0	36	38	16	1	9	0	3	4	1	27	3	46	4	10
Swift	778	4	49	7	27	13	0	0	7	0	1	8	73	6	1	3
Kingfisher	106	5	23	59	0	5	0	9	4	0	0	22	48	22	0	4
Green Woodpecker	216	3	17	65	1	1	13	1	4	8	8	46	21	0	0	13
Great Spotted Woodpecker	505	4	14	39	9	5	29	1	5	3	23	28	27	4	1	10
Skylark	1510	2	8	36	50	1	4	0	9	4	1	18	8	51	6	4
Sand Martin	362	3	68	16	0	3	0	10	3	0	4	2	82	3	3	3
Swallow	1419	2	70	4	0	19	2	2	5	0	7	12	59	3	4	10
House Martin	875	3	66	6	0	14	1	9	6	0	5	7	69	3	1	10
Tree Pipit	237	5	17	25	46	1	6	1	0	0	0	18	5	75	2	0
Meadow Pipit	1313	1	28	25	30	4	11	1	5	1	0	19	5	57	9	3
Rock Pipit	41	7	60	13	13	7	0	0	15	0	0	35	0	45	0	5
Yellow Wagtail	57	0	67	33	0	0	0	0	4	0	0	63	4	25	4	0
Grey Wagtail	806	1	59	24	1	2	11	2	2	1	0	50	5	34	3	4
Pied Wagtail	1401	4	55	31	2	2	5	1	3	0	0	48	4	38	3	3
Dipper	645	3	42	36	2	2	14	1	2	0	6	37	17	17	8	12
Wren	1672	1	5	59	0	1	33	1	7	2	1	52	8	23	3	5
Dunnock	1282	2	22	62	2	2	10	1	8	0	1	38	3	38	6	5
Robin	1527	2	7	57	1	0	33	1	5	0	0	58	1	29	2	3
Redstart	394	1	16	51	1	1	30	0	3	3	0	47	3	36	3	6
Whinchat	607	1	40	31	4	1	22	1	4	2	0	43	1	41	3	5
Stonechat	41	0	88	13	0	0	0	0	4	0	0	68	4	12	0	12
Wheatear	637	2	56	15	4	2	21	0	3	1	0	57	7	22	2	8
Ring Ouzel	196	3	26	25	0	0	40	5	0	1	4	36	13	16	14	16
Blackbird	1456	1	16	44	0	1	36	2	5	0	2	40	4	39	6	5
Fieldfare	39	0	0	14	0	0	86	0	0	0	0	0	0	100	0	0
Song Thrush	1456	1	12	72	1	1	12	1	5	0	2	37	2	46	4	3
Mistle Thrush	1059	1	34	21	1	2	40	1	4	1	1	50	3	37	2	3
Grasshopper Warbler	194	4	4	88	4	0	0	0	33	0	0	25	0	42	0	0
Sedge Warbler	570	5	7	65	6	1	16	0	9	2	1	17	5	57	1	7
Lesser Whitethroat	92	3	6	70	3	0	18	0	27	0	0	47	7	20	0	0
Whitethroat	617	3	12	46	9	3	26	0	16	3	0	21	4	51	2	2
Garden Warbler	477	2	8	74	1	0	15	1	24	3	0	17	4	44	4	4
Blackcap	604	4	14	72	0	1	8	0	16	6	1	27	4	40	1	5
Wood Warbler	150	6	14	70	5	2	3	0	20	0	0	30	0	50	0	0
Chiffchaff	375	5	5	84	1	2	3	0	28	0	0	19	3	38	3	9
Willow Warbler	1554	1	7	72	2	1	15	1	7	0	0	29	2	55	3	3
Goldcrest	1173	2	22	64	3	1	9	0	6	0	0	58	2	31	0	2
Spotted Flycatcher	879	2	40	43	4	2	12	1	8	0	0	25	8	49	4	7
Pied Flycatcher	81	0	46	36	0	4	11	4	0	0	0	17	17	22	22	22
Long-tailed Tit	404	3	66	13	1	3	7	7	8	0	2	63	7	14	2	4
Marsh Tit	65	8	40	24	4	0	24	0	5	0	0	36	9	50	0	0
Coal Tit	1208	2	28	50	1	2	17	0	3	0	0	56	4	34	1	2
Blue Tit	1174	3	36	28	2	3	28	1	4	0	0	53	9	27	1	5
Great Tit	947	3	40	30	1	1	24	1	6	0	0	50	6	32	1	5
Treecreeper	466	4	34	47	4	4	4	4	7	1	1	37	14	35	1	4
Jay	87	0	46	41	0	3	11	0	0	0	0	80	0	20	0	0
Magpie	360	1	66	18	3	0	13	0	3	0	23	43	23	2	4	4
Jackdaw	1181	2	76	11	1	6	2	4	5	0	1	24	47	17	1	6
Rook	1246	-	-	-	-	-	-	-	5	0	3	3	81	2	1	5
Carrion Crow	1620	2	74	18	1	2	3	1	4	0	19	32	33	5	3	5
Carrion x Hooded Hybrid	38	40	40	20	0	0	0	0	8	0	0	33	17	17	17	8
Raven	73	0	100	0	0	0	0	0	25	0	50	0	0	0	0	25
Starling	1287	4	68	14	2	5	4	3	4	0	1	30	23	33	0	9
House Sparrow	968	3	72	11	2	8	0	5	6	0	1	30	46	12	1	5
Tree Sparrow	251	7	62	16	0	4	7	3	12	0	0	24	42	21	0	2
Chaffinch	1620	1	45	40	1	0	11	1	5	0	1	37	4	45	4	3
Greenfinch	952	1	50	28	17	1	2	1	12	0	1	50	3	21	6	7
Goldfinch	821	2	74	14	5	1	2	2	9	0	0	60	4	15	6	6
Siskin	678	0	43	21	32	0	3	0	0	0	0	64	0	30	0	5
Linnet	1004	2	77	15	4	0	1	2	11	0	0	40	2	31	13	3
Redpoll	745	2	25	13	54	1	5	0	9	0	1	48	1	30	7	4
Crossbill	283	1	78	15	4	0	1	2	0	0	0	91	0	9	0	0
Bullfinch	564	2	76	14	2	0	4	1	11	0	1	58	1	19	5	4
Hawfinch	18	0	100	0	0	0	0	0	0	0	0	67	0	33	0	0
Yellowhammer	1043	1	32	58	2	1	4	1	14	DD	0	22	5	52	4	3
Reed Bunting	471	1	40	51	2	1	5	1	5	0	1	21	1	64	6	1
Corn Bunting	38	5	16	74	5	0	0	0	50	0	0	25	25	0	0	0

Fulmar colonies in the Firth of Forth 1914-1996, AOS

	Inch-garvie	Inch-colm	Inch-mickery	Inch-keith	Hanging Rocks	Fidra	The Lamb	Craig-leith	Bass Rock	Tant-allon	Dunbar	Bils-dean	Dun-glass	Fast Castle	St Abb's Head	Eye-mouth	Fan-cove	Lam-berton	Isle of May
First year prospect	-	1959	-	1942	-	-	-	1938	1923	1929	-	-	-	1920	1914	-	-	1933	1921
bred	1962	1974	1976	1948	-	1938	1963	1953	1937	1930	-	-	1928	1921	1920	-	1934	1936	1930
1933	-	-	-	-	-	-	-	-	-	24	-	-	45	-	-	-	-	+	-
1934	-	-	-	-	-	-	-	-	-	-	-	-	-	-	-	-	*	-	-
1936	-	-	-	0	-	-	-	-	-	-	-	-	-	-	-	-	-	*	4
1937	-	-	-	-	-	-	-	-	*	-	-	-	-	-	-	-	-	-	-
1938	-	-	-	-	-	*1	-	+	-	39	-	-	-	-	-	-	-	-	-
1942	-	-	-	+	-	-	-	-	-	-	-	-	-	-	-	-	-	-	-
1945	-	-	-	-	-	-	-	-	-	-	-	-	-	-	130	-	-	-	-
1946	-	-	-	-	-	-	-	-	-	-	-	-	-	-	-	-	-	-	7
1948	-	0	-	*30	-	-	-	-	-	51	-	-	-	-	-	-	-	-	-
1951	0	-	-	35	-	-	0	4	-	-	-	-	-	-	-	-	-	-	-
1952	-	-	-	-	-	-	-	-	-	-	-	-	-	-	-	-	-	-	19
1953	0	-	-	-	-	0	0	*	-	-	-	-	-	-	-	-	-	-	-
1954	0	-	-	-	-	1	-	-	-	-	-	-	-	-	-	-	-	-	26
1955	-	-	-	20	-	-	-	-	-	-	-	-	-	-	-	-	-	-	37
1957	-	-	-	-	-	-	-	-	-	-	-	-	-	-	150	-	-	-	34
1958	-	-	-	-	-	-	-	-	-	-	-	-	104	259	124	5	51	47	-
1959	-	+1	0	103	-	7	0	23	7	-	-	-	-	-	-	-	-	-	37
1960	-	-	0	145	-	-	0	-	-	-	-	-	-	-	-	-	-	-	-
1961	11	-	+	142	-	6	0	36	-	-	-	-	-	-	-	-	-	-	-
1962	*13	-	0	134	-	9	0	35	25	-	-	-	-	-	-	-	-	-	-
1963	-	-	0	136	-	10	*1	54	-	-	-	-	-	-	-	-	-	-	-
1964	-	-	0	119	-	14	1	-	-	-	-	-	-	-	-	-	-	-	-
1965	25	-	0	167	0	18	1	34	-	252	-	-	-	-	151	-	-	-	-
1966	-	-	0	233	-	14	1	48	-	-	-	-	-	-	-	-	-	-	35
1967	-	-	0	270	-	24	1	40	31	-	-	-	-	-	-	-	-	-	40
1968	-	-	0	-	-	28	1	40	-	-	-	-	-	-	-	-	-	-	-
1969-70	-	-	0	317	0	31	1	22	34	252	-	-	157	146	151	23	125	147	53
1971	-	-	0	431	-	46	2	47	-	-	-	-	-	-	-	-	-	-	-
1972	-	-	0	449	-	50	2	53	-	-	-	-	-	-	-	-	-	-	50
1973	35	-	0	400	-	38	3	60	-	-	-	-	-	-	-	-	-	-	68
1974	38	*8	0	405	-	64	2	90	-	-	-	-	-	-	-	-	-	-	91
1975	48	10	0	396	-	70	0	45	-	-	-	-	-	-	-	-	-	-	72
1976	55	8	*1	446	-	71	2	70	20	-	-	-	-	-	247	-	-	-	57
1977	-	43	0	445	-	54	3	60	65	368	-	-	-	-	187	-	-	-	62
1978	-	38	0	410	-	77	1	52	60	406	-	-	311	501	181	48	108	122	94
1979	-	-	0	523	-	101	2	57	70	-	-	-	-	-	-	-	-	-	108
1980	-	-	0	451	-	88	1	53	81	-	-	-	-	-	-	-	-	-	131
1981	-	60	2	491	-	83	3	77	67	-	-	-	-	-	-	-	-	-	144
1982	-	-	3	634	10	107	1	95	74	507	-	-	264	335	224	21	165	121	-
1983	-	-	6	562	-	119	0	94	75	510	14	16	-	-	-	-	231	-	-
1984	-	-	3	563	12	130	3	77	122	498	8	-	288	-	-	-	-	-	175
1985	-	-	-	-	-	100	2	113	59	498	14	-	-	-	233	-	-	-	-
1986	86	-	9	656	16	160	2	140	75	569	10	-	-	-	320	-	-	-	-
1987	68	138	12	500	10	91	4	111	91	522	9	-	232	373	338	26	175	108	-
1988	86	-	14	473	-	140	4	124	-	-	-	4	-	-	334	-	-	-	-
1989	-	-	10	476	6	168	4	172	102	-	11	-	-	-	307	-	-	-	212
1990	-	-	7	443	-	171	3	138	-	426	10	-	-	-	292	-	-	-	198
1991	82	-	15	575	12	177	2	162	-	-	-	-	-	-	362	-	-	-	221
1992	115	163	24	564	-	191	5	141	-	-	20	-	-	-	361	-	-	-	266
1993	130	129	30	522	-	267	6	182	-	-	-	16	-	-	346	-	-	-	266
1994	159	177	25	473	-	243	2	165	84	653	-	-	337+	-	393	-	-	157	279
1995	184	218	34	514	-	303	8	203	-	665	-	-	203+	-	391	-	-	-	296
1996	188	237	32	429	-	331	14	184	166	574	-	-	-	-	364	-	-	-	308

Inland Colonies

Year	Arthur's Seat birds	Arthur's Seat AOS	Torphin Quarry birds	Torphin Quarry AOS	Traprain Law AOS
1949	-	+	-	-	-
1970	-	-	-	+	-
1971	3	-	-	-	-
1976	4	-	4	-	-
1978	-	-	-	*5	-
1979	34	-	-	-	-
1980	38	-	-	14	+

Year	Arthur's Seat birds	Arthur's Seat AOS	Torphin Quarry birds	Torphin Quarry AOS	Traprain Law AOS
1981	37	*	-	14	8
1982	-	8	-	16	-
1983	-	27	-	21	16
Mean	AOS		AOS		AOS
1984-89	33.5		20.0		18.0
1988-96	30.5		19.0		13.5

+ = first prospecting, * = first breeding. On the Berwickshire coast, Dunglass = Dunglass to Fast Castle Head; Fast Castle = Fast Castle Head to Pettico Wick; Eyemouth = St. Abb's to Eyemouth; Burnmouth = Eyemouth to Burnmouth; Lamberton = Burnmouth to English border.
Sources: R&B, Fisher (1952), Eggeling (1960 and 1974), Harris and Galbraith (1983), da Prato (1986), ENHS, BBR, LBR, IMBOR, FIBR, SAHSR and unpublished diaries.

Cormorant colonies in the Firth of Forth 1972-1996, nests

	Haystack	Car Craig	Cow & Calves	Inchkeith	Eyebroughy	The Lamb	Craigleith	Fast Castle	Fancove	Approx. Totals
1972	-	-	-	0	0	245	6	-	-	251
1973	-	-	-	0	0	228	12	-	-	240
1974	-	-	-	0	0	206	22	-	-	228
1975	-	-	-	0	0	225	0	-	-	225
1976	-	-	-	0	0	150	0	31	-	181
1977	-	-	11	0	0	157	38	37	-	243
1978	-	-	18	0	8	129	80	33	-	268
1979	-	-	32	0	40	65	98	-	-	>235
1980	-	-	32	0	37	64	98	-	-	>231
1981	-	-	0	0	30	102	42	36	-	210
1982	-	-	34	0	28	90	60	-	-	>212
1983	-	-	20	0	55	115	49	47	-	286
1984	-	-	0	4	43	129	35	44	-	255
1985	-	30	0	0	17	134	46	-	-	>227
1986	-	36	0	0	33	104	94	22	-	289
1987	-	137	0	0	20	83	109	41	-	390
1988	-	158	0	0	73	57	83	32	-	403
1989	-	113	0	0	52	91	131	59	6	452
1990	-	182	0	0	49	80	116	-	-	>427
1991	-	220	0	0	1	207	83	21	0	531
1992	-	187	0	14	0	186	89	51	0	529
1993	44	135	0	24	0	52	45	37	-	337
1994	133	4	0	58	0	131	108	44	0	478
1995	-	0	0	112	0	179	82	60	-	433
1996	60	40	0	84	0	137	78	35	-	434

In years after 1976 when no count was made at Fast Castle, the total figure is given as greater than (>) the total of the available counts.
Sources: ENHS, BBR, LBR, FIBR, Lloyd *et al.* (1991), Smith (1969) and the unpublished diaries of R.W.J. Smith and others.

Shag colonies in the Firth of Forth 1970-1996, nests

	Cow & Calves	Hay-stack	Inchcolm	Car Craig	Inch-mickery	Inch-keith	Fidra	The Lamb	Craig-leith	Bass Rock	Dunbar	St. Abb's Head	Rest of Berw.	Isle of May
1970	0	0	0	0	0	0	0	194	104	-	0	49[1]	-	880[2]
1971	0	0	0	0	0	0	*1	196	94	-	0	-	-	-
1972	0	0	0	0	0	0	7	225	99	-	0	-	-	1000
1973	0	0	0	*1	0	0	17	244	164	-	0	-	-	1130
1974	0	0	0	4	0	1	27	255	225	-	0	-	-	978
1975	0	0	0	13	0	3	25	233	214	180	0	-	-	676
1976	*2	*1	0	15	*6	3	20	210	201	213	0	161[3]	-	365
1977	5	4	0	25	7	6	18	156	186	201	0	146[3]	-	816
1978	1	3	0	29	12	3	23	143	208	202	0	134	147	807
1979	-	-	0	-	14	4	25	160	215	188	0	-	-	978
1980	-	-	0	-	-	3	25	143	193	191	0	-	-	1041
1981	-	3	0	-	14	6	43	220	252	154	0	209	-	1163
1982	-	-	0	-	22	6	59	230	344	194	*1	-	177	1425
1983	-	-	0	-	42	5	66	283	356	170	1	-	-	1567
1984	-	-	0	-	22	4	64	284	379	193	1	0	-	1639
1985	-	-	0	0	29	-	55	303	345	101	-	268	-	1524
1986	-	-	0	0	24	20	67	301	382	75	-	364	-	1310
1987	-	0	0	28	24	>10	64	246	465	162	1	396	-	1916
1988	-	0	-	24	24	9	86	250	435	93	1	318	-	1290
1989	-	-	-	25	29	18	124	286	544	111	2	366	-	1703
1990	-	-	-	23	28	19	166	290	522	121	-	338	-	1386
1991	-	2	-	23	33	30	242	305	646	-	-	463	-	1487
1992	-	3	21	23	36	23	255	318	665	-	1	450	-	1634
1993	-	1	12	12	28	11	88	65	155	20	0	300	-	715
1994	-	1	2	0	10	10	73	36	106	13	0	115	-	403
1995	-	1	4	4	20	18	84	81	171	-	0	173	-	503
1996	-	2	3	5	18	16	81	77	159	47	0	175	-	512

*= first breeding. Note 1 = 1969-70 count for St. Abb's Head. Note 2 = 1969 count for the Isle of May. Note 3 = Mean counts for St. Abb's Head.
Despite there being only two counts for the 'rest of the Berwickshire coast', the estimates used for the species account graphs have been calculated from the existing counts. Comparison with the most contemporaneous counts at St. Abb's Head suggests that the values for the uncounted area are likely to be around 94% of the St. Abb's Head figure for the same date, and this estimate has been used.
Sources: ENHS, BBR, LBR, IMBOR, FIBR, SAHSR, Harris and Galbraith (1983), Lloyd *et al.* (1991), and the unpublished diaries of R.W.J. Smith and others.

Grey Heron colonies in SE Scotland 1982-1996, numbers of occupied nests

Lothian

Site	Tetrad	Tree	82	83	84	85	86	87	88	89	90	91	92	93	94	95	96
Aberlady	NT48Q	C							1	x	x	x	x	x	x	x	-
Bangour R.	NT07B	C									0	5	5	6	?	7	-
Bara L.	NT56U	C			3	2	2	1	0	1	0	-	-	-	-	-	-
Beecraigs	NT07C	U	-	-	1	1	0	x	x	x	x	x	x	x	x	x	-
Broxmouth	NT67Y	C							7	8	13	14	12	11	?	5	-
Buteland	NT16G	C											18	17	15	17	
Cauldhall	NT25U	C							2	4	1	0	0	0	x	x	
Cornton B.	NT15Z	C			5	4	3	4	3	x	x	x	x	x	x	x	
Dalmeny	NT17U	U					1	x	x	x	x	x	x	x	x	x	
Duddingston	NT27W	D	2	2	2	1	1	2	4	5	10	12	10	12	12	14	
Dunglass	NT77Q	M											2	2	-	3	
Edgelaw	NT25Z	U	8	4	-	-	-	-	-	-	-	-	-	-	-	-	
Glencorse	NT26B	U				1	x	x	x	x	x	x	x	x	x	x	
Gosford	NT47P	C	2	-	2	1	0	-	1	0	0	0	x	x	x	x	-
Hare Moss	NS96H	U										2	-	-	-	-	-
Middleton	NT35U	U	-	-	-	-	-	-	-	3	-	-	-	-	-	-	
Redside	NT35E	C		3	-	2	1	1	1	1	1	0	1	1	-	1	
Rosebury	NT35D	C				10	8	3	0	0	6	6	5	5	-	-	
Selm Muir	NT06X	U			5	-	-	-	-	-	-	-	3	3	-	5	
Tyninghame 1	NT67J	M	} 13	13	7	11	6	6	4	5	5	5	2	5	-	-	
Tyninghame 2	NT67E	M					5	5	5	6	4	4	4	4	-	-	
Whitekirk	NT58V	C		4	1	5	4	4	4	4	5	5	6	8		6	

Borders

Site	Tetrad	Tree	82	83	84	85	86	87	88	89	90	91	92	93	94	95	96
Abbotsford	NT53B	C	-	-	6	3	-	2	4	3	-	-	-	-	-	-	-
Addinston	NT55C	U	-	-	-	-	-	-	-	-	1	-	-	-	-	-	-
Ayton	NT96F	D	5	-	-	-	4	-	-	-	-	-	2	2	-	x	x
Aytonlaw	NT96A	C	-	-	-	-	-	2	5	5	-	-	-	4	5	7	5
Cavers Carre	NT52N	C	-	-	-	7	-	6	6	9	-	-	-	-	-	-	-
Caverton	NT72M	C	-	-	-	-	-	-	-	-	-	-	-	-	-	7	
Cringletie	NT24H	C									8	7	4	-	5	7	5
Crookhouse	NT72N	C	-	-	15	17	-	10	8	4	4	-	-	-	-	-	-
Crookston	NT45F	C							1	2	4	1	1	1	1	0	
Dalgliesh	NT20P	C				1	-	-	-	-	1	-	-	-	-	-	-
Dawyck	NT13S	C	-	-	20	15	-	-	11	-	-	-	-	-	-	x	x
Dingleton	NT53G	D	-	-	12	18	15	20	37	0	x	x	x	x	x	x	x
Dodburn	NT40Y	C	-	-	-	8	4	-	4	-	-	-	-	-	-	-	-
East Reston	NT96A	C	-	-	-	-	-	-	4	-	-	-	-	-	-	-	-
Fishwick	NT95A/F	D	-	-	-	-	-	-	43	-	-	34	-	-	-	-	-
Friarshaugh	NT53M	U	-	-	-	-	-	-	-	-	6	8	5	3	16	5	-
Gray Hill	NT40N	C						1	4	-	-	5	7	4	7	-	7
Houndwood	NT86L	D							2	x	x	x	x	x	x	x	x
Larriston	NY59S	U	-	-	-	-	6	-	-	-	-	-	-	-	-	-	-
Lintlawburn	NT85P	C						1	-	2	-	-	-	-	-	-	-
Kirkburn	NT23Z	M								1	2	5	6	-	-	6	5
Mellerstain	NT63P	U	-	-	2	-	-	-	-	-	-	-	-	-	-	-	-
Oakwood	NT85R	C										4	-	-	-	9	10
Paxton	NT95H	M	-	-	-	-	-	2	-	-	-	-	-	-	-	-	-
Plenderleith	NT71K	C	-	-	-	-	-	-	-	12	14	-	-	-	-	-	-
Quixwood 1	NT76S	C	-	-	-	-	12	-	2	9	-	-	-	-	-	-	-
Quixwood 2	NT76S	C	-	-	-	-	-	-	-	3	-	-	-	-	-	-	-
Rachan 1 & 2	NT13H	C	-	-		10	14	10	15	10	5	10	x	x	x	x	3
Redmoss	NY48S	C	-	-	-	-	-	-	13	-	25	-	-	-	-	19	16
Sneep	NT63U	C	-	-	3	-	-	-	3	-	-	-	5	x	x	x	
Stobs Loch	NT40Y	C											7	-	-	-	
Stotfield	NT71B	C	-	-	-	-	-	-	-	1	-	-	-	-	-	-	
Traquair	NT33H	C	-	-	-	5	-	-	-	-	-	6	5	-	-	8	
Tushielaw	NT31E	C	-	-	-	5	3	4	6	-	9	6	-	-	x	x	x
Union Bridge	NT95F	U													2	-	
Venchen	NT82J	C									5	-	-	-	-		
Yarrow 1	NT32T	C	-	-	-	-	5	5	-	-	-	-	x	x	x	x	x
Yarrow 2	NT32T	C	-	-	-	-	5	5	2	4	-	-	-	-	-	-	-

Tree types: C=conifer, M=mixed, D=deciduous, U=unknown.
Counts: x = extinct, dash (-) = no count available, no symbol indicates that the colony was not known at that date.
Sources: BBR, LBR, BTO, I.J. Andrews and R.D. Murray.

Greylag Goose confirmed breeding records in SE Scotland 1963-1994

Year of first breeding	Site	Tetrad(s)	Max nests/broods for any year
1963	Duddingston Loch	NT27W	7
1980	Inchkeith	NT28W	3
1982	Penicuik House Pond	NT25E	4
1983	Aberlady Bay	NT48Q	1
1983	Redside Pond	NT35E	3
1985	Beecraigs Loch	NT07C	4
1985	Threipmuir Reservoir	NT16R	4
1985	Gosford Pond	NT47P	7
1986	Gladhouse Reservoir	NT25W&X,35B	15
1986	Glencorse Reservoir	NT26B&G	2
1989	Harperrig Reservoir	NT06V	1
1989	Figgate Pond	NT27W	1
1989	Fidra	NT58D	1
1989-90	Harburnhead	NT06K	12
1990	Baddinsgill Reservoir	NT15H&I	3
1991	West Water Reservoir	NT15B	1
1991	Lochend Loch	NT27S	1
1992	Loganlea Reservoir	NT16W	1
1992	East Fortune Ponds	NT58K	3
1994	Glendevon Pond	NT07S	1
1994	Tweedbank Pond	NT53C	2

Sources: *Andrews* and *Bird Reports*.

Shoveler spring-summer records in SE Scotland 1979-1995

Counts of males/females

Lothian

Year	79	80	81	82	83	84	85	86	87	88	89	90	91	92	93	94	95
Aberlady	-	-	-	-	7/0	-	-	**2/2**	1/1	-	-	-	-	2/0	2/0	3/1	1/0
Almond Pools	-	-	-	-	-	-	-	-	-	-	-	0/2	-	-	-	-	-
Auldhame	-	-	-	-	-	-	-	-	-	-	1/1	-	-	-	-	-	-
Bavelaw	-	-	-	-	3/1	2/1	-	1/1	1/1	**1/1**	3/3	1/1	2/1	**2/2**	**3/3**	4/4	4/4
Belhaven	-	-	-	-	-	-	-	-	-	-	-	-	-	1/0	2/0	1/0	-
Cobbinshaw	-	-	-	-	-	-	-	-	-	-	-	-	-	-	2/0	-	-
Dalmahoy Marsh	-	-	-	-	-	-	-	-	-	-	-	-	-	1/1	-	-	-
Drem	-	-	-	-	-	1/1	-	-	-	-	-	-	-	-	1/0	-	-
Duddingston	-	-	1/1	-	-	-	1/1	-	-	-	-	1/0	-	2/1	2/1	-	-
East Fortune	-	-	-	-	-	-	-	-	-	-	-	-	1/0	-	**1/1**	-	-
Esperston	-	-	-	-	-	-	-	1/1	-	-	-	-	-	-	-	-	-
Gladhouse	-	-	-	3/0	-	-	-	-	1/1	-	-	-	-	1/0	1/0	-	-
Linlithgow	-	-	-	-	-	-	-	-	-	-	-	-	-	1/1	-	-	-
Longyester	-	-	-	-	-	-	-	-	0/1	-	-	-	-	-	-	-	-
Tailend Moss	-	-	-	-	-	-	-	1/1	1/1	1/1	1/1	1/1	1/1	1/0	-	-	-

Borders

Year	79	80	81	82	83	84	85	86	87	88	89	90	91	92	93	94	95
Bemersyde	-	-	-	-	-	2/2	5/2	**2/2**	6/2	-	5/1	4/1	5/3	5/1	2/0	-	2/1
Cauldshiels	-	-	-	-	-	1/0	-	-	-	-	-	-	-	-	-	-	-
Folly L.	-	-	-	-	-	-	-	-	-	-	-	-	-	-	-	-	3/2
Hen Poo	-	-	-	-	-	-	-	-	-	-	-	-	-	-	1/1	1/1	-
Hirsel	-	4/0	3/0	6/0	2/2	7/2	7/1	4/4	**5/2**	3/2	5/3	8/3	12/3	**4/2**	7/2	8/2	**2/2**
Hoselaw	-	0/1	-	-	3/3	1/0	-	-	4/3	-	-	-	-	1/0	-	-	-
Hule Moss	-	-	-	1/1	-	-	2/0	-	0/1	-	-	-	-	**1/1**	10/2	5/5	2/1
Kaeside	-	-	-	-	-	-	-	-	-	-	-	-	-	-	-	1/0	-
Millar's Moss	-	-	-	-	-	-	-	-	-	1/1	1/1	-	-	1/0	-	-	-
Ploughlands	-	-	-	-	1/1	-	-	-	-	-	-	-	-	-	1/1	1/1	-
Slipperfield	-	-	-	-	-	-	-	-	-	-	-	1/0	-	-	-	-	-
Smailholm	-	-	-	-	-	-	-	-	1/1	-	-	-	-	-	-	-	-
Whitrig	-	-	-	-	1/1	1/1	3/0	-	-	-	-	-	-	1/0	2/2	-	-
Yetholm L.	-	-	-	-	-	1/0	-	**1/1**	2/1	-	-	-	-	-	1/0	-	2/0

Totals

	79	80	81	82	83	84	85	86	87	88	89	90	91	92	93	94	95
males	-	4	4	10	17	16	18	12	22	6	16	16	22	24	37	24	16
females	-	1	1	1	8	7	4	12	15	5	10	8	8	11	11	14	10

Figures in bold indicate confirmed breeding.
Sources: BBR and LBR.

Garganey spring-summer records in SE Scotland 1979-1995

Counts of males/females

Year	79	80	81	82	83	84	85	86	87	88	89	90	91	92	93	94	95
Aberlady	-	1/1	1/0	-	-	1/1	-	1/0	2/0	-	1/0	-	-	-	2/1	2/0	1/0
Bavelaw	-	-	-	-	-	-	-	-	-	-	-	-	-	-	1/0	-	-
Cobbinshaw	-	1/0	-	-	-	-	-	-	-	-	-	-	-	-	-	-	-
Drem	-	-	-	1/0	-	-	-	-	-	-	-	-	-	-	-	-	-
Gala Water	-	-	-	-	-	-	-	-	-	-	-	-	-	1/1	-	-	-
Hirsel	-	-	-	-	-	-	-	-	-	-	-	-	1/0	-	-	-	-
Livingston	-	-	-	-	-	-	-	-	-	-	-	1/1	-	-	-	-	-
Mire Loch	-	-	-	-	-	-	-	-	-	-	-	-	1/0	-	1/1	-	-
Musselburgh	-	-	-	-	-	-	-	-	-	-	-	-	2/1	-	-	-	1/0
Newhall L.	-	-	-	-	-	-	-	-	-	-	-	1/1	-	-	-	-	-
Secret site	-	-	-	1/1	-	-	-	-	-	-	-	-	-	-	-	-	-
Tyninghame	-	-	-	-	-	-	1/1	-	-	-	-	-	-	-	-	-	-
West Barns	-	-	-	-	1/1	-	-	-	-	-	-	-	-	-	-	-	-
Williestruther	-	-	-	-	5	-	-	-	-	-	-	-	-	-	-	-	-
Totals	**0**	**3**	**1**	**3**	**7**	**2**	**2**	**1**	**2**	**0**	**1**	**4**	**5**	**2**	**6**	**2**	**2**

Sources: BBR and LBR

Pochard breeding records in SE Scotland 1979-1995

Pochard at potential breeding sites in summer: males/females

Lothian	Tetrad	79	80	81	82	83	84	85	86	87	88	89	90	91	92	93	94	95
Bara Loch	NT56U	-	-	-	-	-	-	-	-	-	-	-	-	-	-	1/1	1/1	0/1
Bavelaw	NT16L/R	-	1/1	-	-	1/0	-	-	-	-	-	-	-	-	-	-	-	-
Duddingston	NT27W	3/3	-	-	(12)	1/1	(6)	1/1	(3)	(2)	7/0	(4)	1/0	(1)	-	(1)	-	-
Dunsapie	NT27W	-	-	-	-	-	-	-	-	-	(2)	-	-	-	-	-	-	-
Gladhouse	NT25W	-	-	-	-	-	1/0	-	-	-	-	1/1	1/1	-	2/0	(1)	-	-
Linlithgow	NT07D	-	-	-	-	-	-	(1)	-	-	-	-	-	-	-	-	-	-
Lochend	NT27S	-	-	-	-	1/0	-	-	-	-	-	-	-	-	-	-	-	-
Rosslynlee	NT25U	-	-	-	-	7/0	-	-	-	-	-	-	-	-	-	-	-	-
Seafield	NT67P	-	-	-	-	-	-	-	(2)	-	-	-	-	-	-	-	-	-
Scoughall	NT68B	-	-	-	-	-	-	-	-	-	-	1/1	-	-	-	-	-	-
Tailend Moss	NT06D	-	-	-	-	-	-	-	1/1	-	-	-	-	-	-	-	-	-
Threipmuir	NT16R	-	-	2/0	-	-	1/0	-	-	2/0	1/0	1/1	-	(1)	-	1/1	-	-
Totals		3/3	1/1	2/0	(12)	10/1	(8)	(3)	(7)	(4)	(10)	(10)	2/1	(2)	2/0	(6)	1/1	0/1

Borders	Tetrad	79	80	81	82	83	84	85	86	87	88	89	90	91	92	93	94	95
Bemersyde	NT63B/C/H	-	-	-	-	1/1	-	?/1	1/0	-	3/1	3/2	6/0	6/4	3/2	5/2	-	3/3
Folly L.	NT62I	-	-	-	-	-	-	-	-	-	-	-	-	-	-	-	-	4/2
Harelaw	NT52G	-	-	-	-	-	-	-	-	-	-	-	-	-	1/1	-	-	-
Green Diamonds	NT42S	-	-	-	-	-	-	-	1/1	2/2	-	-	-	-	-	-	-	-
Hirsel	NT84F	-	-	-	4/4	1/1	-	2/2	2/2	20/5	13/2	8/2	6/2	11/3	8/3	2/0	4/2	3/2
Hoselaw	NT83A/B	-	-	-	-	-	-	-	-	-	-	7/2	7/1	3/0	9/0	-	-	-
Hule Moss	NT74E	-	-	-	-	-	-	-	-	-	-	-	-	6/0	-	-	-	1/0
Millar's Moss	NT96E	-	-	-	-	-	-	-	1/0	-	-	-	1/1	-	-	-	-	-
West Water	NT15B	-	-	-	-	4/0	-	-	-	-	-	-	-	1/0	-	-	-	-
Yetholm L.	NT82D/E	-	-	-	-	-	-	-	2/2	-	1/1	2/1	-	-	-	-	1/1	0/2
Yetholm Marsh	NT82I	-	-	-	-	-	-	-	-	-	-	2/1	1/1	1/2	1/1	-	1/1	1/1
Totals		-	-	-	4/4	6/2	-	3/3	7/5	22/7	17/4	22/8	20/4	29/10	22/7	7/2	6/4	12/10

Pochard production: numbers of broods/numbers of young

SE Scotland	79	80	81	82	83	84	85	86	87	88	89	90	91	92	93	94	95
Bara L.	-	-	-	-	-	-	-	-	-	-	-	-	-	-	1/7	1/6	-
Bavelaw	-	1/?	-	-	-	-	-	-	-	-	-	-	-	-	-	-	-
Bemersyde	-	-	-	-	-	-	1/6	-	-	-	2/7	-	7/25	1/2	-	-	2/7
Duddingston	3/?	-	-	-	-	-	-	-	-	-	-	-	-	-	-	-	-
Folly L.	-	-	-	-	-	-	-	-	-	-	-	-	-	-	-	-	1/5
Hirsel	-	-	-	-	1/7	-	-	2/4	3/15	1/2	1/2	-	2/5	2/6	-	-	-
Tailend Moss	-	-	-	-	-	-	-	1/6	-	-	-	-	-	-	-	-	-
Yetholm L.	-	-	-	-	-	-	-	-	-	-	-	-	-	-	-	1/5	-
Yetholm Marsh	-	-	-	-	-	-	-	-	-	-	1/4	1/2	2/13	-	-	1/2	1/4
Totals	3/?	1/?	-	-	1/7	-	1/6	3/10	3/15	1/2	4/13	1/2	11/43	3/8	1/7	3/13	4/16

Brackets indicate that sexes totals are not known.
Sources: BBR and LBR.

Ruddy Duck colonisation of SE Scotland 1983-1996

Breeding season maximum counts : males/females

	83	84	85	86	87	88	89	90	91	92	93	94	95	96
Linlithgow L.	1/0	-	-	-	-	-	-	-	-	-	-	-	0/1	-
Hirsel L.	1/0	-	-	-	-	-	1/0	0/1	3/1	2/2	1/1	5/2	1/0	2/1
Hoselaw L.	-	2/0	-	-	-	-	-	-	-	-	-	-	3/2	1/1
Ploughlands P.	-	3/0	-	-	-	-	-	-	-	-	-	-	-	1/0
Faldonside L.	-	1/0	-	-	-	-	-	-	-	-	-	-	-	-
Duddingston L.	-	-	0/1	1/0	-	-	-	3/0	1/0	1/0	1/0	-	0/1	-
Gladhouse R.	-	-	-	-	-	1/0	-	-	-	-	-	1/1	1/0	-
Bavelaw	-	-	-	-	-	1/1	1/0	3/1	-	1/0	1/0	2/1	-	-
Bemersyde Moss	-	-	-	-	-	-	1/1	1/1	2/1	3/1	3/1	4/2	5/2	6/4
Gordon Quarry	-	-	-	-	-	-	-	1/0	-	-	-	-	-	-
Nisbet P.	-	-	-	-	-	-	-	1/1	-	-	-	-	-	-
Yetholm L.	-	-	-	-	-	-	-	1/1	-	-	1/0	-	-	1/0
Wooden L.	-	-	-	-	-	-	-	-	2/1	-	-	-	1/1	2/2
Hule Moss	-	-	-	-	-	-	-	-	-	2/3	4/4	5/4	4/3	7/4
Whitrig P.	-	-	-	-	-	-	-	-	-	2/0	-	-	-	-
Musselburgh	-	-	-	-	-	-	-	-	-	1/0	-	-	-	-
Cramond	-	-	-	-	-	-	-	-	-	0/1	-	-	-	-
Folly L.	-	-	-	-	-	-	-	-	-	-	-	-	1/1	9/3
Yetholm Marsh	-	-	-	-	-	-	-	-	-	-	-	-	1/1	2/2
Cobbinshaw R.	-	-	-	-	-	-	-	-	-	-	-	-	2/1	-
Totals	2/0	6/0	0/1	1/0	0/0	2/1	3/1	10/5	8/3	12/7	11/6	17/10	19/13	31/17

Broods

	83	84	85	86	87	88	89	90	91	92	93	94	95	96
Bemersyde Moss	-	-	-	-	-	-	br1	-	br3	-	br3	br3	-	-
Hule Moss	-	-	-	-	-	-	-	-	-	2br9	2br5	-	2br9	2br5
Wooden L.	-	-	-	-	-	-	-	-	br4	-	-	-	-	br6
Hoselaw L.	-	-	-	-	-	-	-	-	-	-	-	-	-	br3
Folly L.	-	-	-	-	-	-	-	-	-	-	-	-	-	3br13
Yetholm Marsh	-	-	-	-	-	-	-	-	-	-	-	-	-	br5
Totals	-	-	-	-	-	-	br1	-	2br7	2br9	3br8	br3	2br9	8br32

Autumn flocks maximum counts

	83	84	85	86	87	88	89	90	91	92	93	94	95	96
Linlithgow L.	1	-	-	-	-	-	-	-	-	-	1	2	1	-
Duddingston	-	2	-	-	-	1	1	1	-	3	1	-	1	-
Gladhouse R.	-	-	-	-	-	-	1	1	-	-	2	2	-	-
Portmore L.	-	-	-	-	-	-	1	-	-	-	-	-	-	-
Hule Moss	-	-	-	-	-	-	1	1	1	6	4	1	12	14
Bemersyde Moss	-	-	-	-	-	-	-	2	-	-	2	5	-	8
Wooden L.	-	-	-	-	-	-	-	2	3	2	5	-	6	10
Yetholm Loch	-	-	-	-	-	-	-	2	-	-	7	6	5	-
Hirsel L.	-	-	-	-	-	-	-	-	4	-	2	-	1	-
Sprouston	-	-	-	-	-	-	-	-	-	1	-	-	-	-
Hoselaw L.	-	-	-	-	-	-	-	-	-	8	10	1	12	10
Lady Moss	-	-	-	-	-	-	-	-	1	1	-	-	-	-
Bavelaw	-	-	-	-	-	-	-	-	-	-	1	1	-	-
Musselburgh	-	-	-	-	-	-	-	-	1	-	-	-	-	-
Whitrig P.	-	-	-	-	-	-	-	-	-	-	-	-	1	-
Folly L.	-	-	-	-	-	-	-	-	-	-	-	-	7	25
Yetholm Marsh	-	-	-	-	-	-	-	-	-	-	-	-	-	3
Ploughlands P.	-	-	-	-	-	-	-	-	-	-	-	-	-	1
Totals	1	2	0	0	0	1	4	9	10	21	35	18	46	71

Sources: BBR and LBR.

Water Rails in SE Scotland 1979-1995, numbers of calling birds, and broods

Lothian

Birds present	Tetrad	79	80	81	82	83	84	85	86	87	88	89	90	91	92	93	94	95
Aberlady	NT48Q	1	-	1	1	-	1	-	1	-	1	br1	1	pr	-	1	-	-
Almond Pools	NT06I	-	-	-	-	-	-	-	-	-	-	-	-	br3	-	-	-	-
Bara L.	NT56U	-	-	-	-	-	-	1	-	-	-	-	-	-	-	-	-	-
Bavelaw	NT16R	-	-	1	-	-	-	-	-	-	-	br1	br1	br1	1	pr	2br3	6br?
Dalmahoy	NT16I	-	-	-	-	-	-	-	-	-	-	-	-	-	-	pr	-	-
Danskine	NT56T	-	-	-	-	-	-	-	-	-	-	-	-	-	1	-	-	-
Duddingston	NT27W	-	-	-	-	1	br2	1	1	2	br5	-	-	-	1	1	pr	br1
Gladhouse	NT25W	-	-	-	-	-	1	-	-	1	-	-	1	-	1	-	-	-
Newlandrig	NT36R	1	-	-	-	-	-	-	-	-	-	-	-	-	-	-	-	-
North Berwick Law	NT58M	-	-	-	-	-	-	-	-	-	-	-	1	-	-	-	-	-
Tailend Moss	NT06D	-	-	-	-	-	-	-	-	-	-	pr	1	1	br1	1	-	-
Threipmuir	NT16R	-	-	-	-	-	-	-	-	-	-	-	-	-	-	-	-	2pr

Borders

Birds present	Tetrad	79	80	81	82	83	84	85	86	87	88	89	90	91	92	93	94	95
Alemoor Res.	NT31X	-	-	-	-	-	1	-	-	-	-	-	-	-	-	-	-	-
Beanrig Moss	NT52E	-	-	-	+	-	-	-	-	-	-	-	-	-	-	-	-	-
Bemersyde Moss	NT63B	-	-	-	-	-	-	-	1	-	-	-	-	-	-	-	-	1
Blackpool Moss	NT52E	-	+	3	+	+	+	+	+	+	+	-	-	-	-	-	-	-
Branxholme W. L.	NT41F	-	-	-	-	-	-	-	-	1	-	1	-	-	-	-	-	-
Borthwickshiels L.	NT41H	-	-	-	-	-	-	-	-	-	-	1	-	-	-	-	-	-
Groundistone Mire	NT41Z	-	-	-	-	1	-	-	-	-	-	-	-	-	-	-	-	-
Haremoss	NT42S	-	-	-	-	-	-	-	-	-	1	br	-	-	-	-	-	1
Hirsel Lake	NT84F	-	-	-	-	-	-	-	1	1	1	-	1	-	-	1	-	1
Hoselaw L.	NT83B	-	-	-	-	-	-	-	1	-	1	-	-	-	-	-	-	-
Hule Moss	NT74E	-	-	-	-	-	-	-	-	-	-	-	-	-	-	1	-	-
Hummelknowes	NT51B	-	-	-	-	-	-	-	-	-	-	-	-	-	1	-	-	-
Lilliesleaf Moss	NT52M	-	-	-	-	-	-	-	-	-	-	-	-	-	-	1	-	-
Lindean Res.	NT42Z	-	-	-	-	2	-	-	-	-	-	-	-	-	-	-	-	-
Linton Bog	NT72X	-	-	-	-	-	-	-	1	-	1	-	1	-	-	-	-	1
Loch Tima	NT20N	-	-	-	-	-	-	-	-	-	-	-	2	-	-	-	-	-
Minto Kaimes	NT52K	-	-	-	-	-	-	-	-	-	-	1	-	-	-	-	-	-
Murder Moss	NT52E	-	+	-	+	+	+	+	+	+	+	-	-	-	-	-	-	-
Nether Whitlaw	NT52E	-	+	-	+	-	+	+	+	+	-	+	+	3	-	-	1	-
Pot Loch	NT42U	-	-	2	+	+	+	+	+	+	-	-	-	-	-	-	-	-
Tandlaw	NT41Y	-	-	-	-	-	-	-	-	-	-	-	-	-	2	-	-	-
Sheilswood L.	NT41P	-	-	-	-	-	-	-	-	-	-	-	-	-	-	-	-	-
Whitmuir Moss	NT52D	-	-	3	-	+	+	+	-	+	-	+	+	-	-	-	-	-
Whitmuirhill L.	NT42Y	-	-	-	-	-	-	-	1	-	-	-	-	-	-	1	-	1
Yetholm Marsh	NT82D	-	-	-	-	-	-	-	-	-	-	-	-	1	-	-	-	1

+ known to be present, no specific counts. br = brood; pr = pair.
Sources: LBR and BBR.

Black-headed Gull breeding sites in SE Scotland 1979-1995, number of nests or pairs

Lothian

Site	Tetrad	79	80	81	82	83	84	85	86	87	88	89	90	91	92	93	94	95	1988-95 estim.
Bavelaw	NT16L/R	-	30	60	100	250	1000	1770	1150	1350	1530	2020	1800	830	440	800	900	800	1090
Black Springs	NT16X	-	-	-	-	-	-	5	-	-	-	-	-	-	-	-	-	-	x
Cobbinshaw	NT05D	-	-	-	-	-	15	180	571	-	-	500	-	-	-	90	300	0	300
Crosswood	NT05N	-	-	2	-	-	-	-	-	-	-	-	-	-	-	+	-	-	x
Esperston	NT35I	-	-	-	30	40	40	140	200	200	-	-	-	-	-	-	-	-	200
Fala Moor	NT45J	-	-	15	-	-	-	-	-	-	3	-	-	-	-	-	8	-	5
Fullarton Burn	NT25Y	-	-	-	-	-	-	-	-	55	-	-	-	-	-	-	-	-	x
Harperrig	NT06V	200	-	+	10	20	30	-	-	20	-	100	-	70	-	+	0	-	80
Kepscaith	NS96L	-	-	-	-	-	-	-	-	-	-	-	-	-	12	-	-	-	12
Morton R.	NT06R	-	-	1	-	-	-	-	-	-	-	-	-	-	-	-	-	-	x
N.Esk Res.	NT15P	0	150	1100	1200	1425	1100	1525	920	414	916	950	-	-	-	-	800	1170	959
Quarryford	NT56M	-	-	20	-	30	10	15	25	75	100	-	0	-	60	-	-	-	80
Rosebery	NT35D	-	-	-	20	125	100	75	75	70	30	-	-	-	-	-	-	-	30
Tailend Moss	NT06D	-	-	-	-	?	-	-	50	70	200	300	200	150	150	175	-	-	195
Toxsidehill M.	NT25X	-	-	-	-	-	-	-	60	60	60	-	-	-	-	-	-	-	60
Wanside Rig	NT66C	-	-	-	-	-	-	-	-	-	-	30	34	40	59	-	-	-	40

Borders

Site	Tetrad	79	80	81	82	83	84	85	86	87	88	89	90	91	92	93	94	95	1988-95 estim.
Acreknowe	NT41V	-	-	-	-	-	-	-	-	-	-	2	-	-	-	-	-	-	2
Akermoor	NT42A	-	-	-	8	-	25	-	-	20	-	-	-	-	-	-	-	-	20
Bellitaw P.	NT64W	-	-	-	-	-	-	-	-	-	-	-	-	-	-	40	-	-	40
Bemersyde	NT63B	-	-	1100	2500	9000	9050	-	10375	11600	-	-	-	14320	-	-	-	-	14320
Blackhope B.	NT35K	-	-	-	-	-	-	-	1	-	-	-	-	-	-	-	-	-	x
Borth'kshiels L.	NT41H	-	-	-	-	-	-	-	-	-	-	-	15	-	-	-	-	3	9
Chapelhill	NT41L	-	-	-	-	-	-	15	35	43	-	-	50	-	10	-	-	-	30
Coldingham L.	NT86Z	-	-	-	1	-	-	-	-	-	-	-	-	-	-	-	-	-	x
Craig Douglas	NT22X	-	-	-	-	-	-	-	-	-	-	40	-	-	-	-	-	-	40
Cralaw P.	NT65L	-	-	-	-	-	-	-	-	-	-	-	-	-	-	10	-	40	25
Crooked L.	NT31L	-	-	-	-	-	-	-	-	-	-	-	-	-	-	-	100	-	100
Dowlaw	NT86P	-	-	-	-	30	1	3	0	-	-	-	-	-	-	-	-	-	x
Dun Law	NT34Z	-	-	-	-	-	-	12	10	-	-	-	-	-	-	-	-	-	x
Folly L.	NT62I	-	-	-	-	-	-	-	-	-	-	-	-	-	-	7	-	150	77
Fruid	NT11E	-	-	-	-	-	-	-	-	2	1	-	-	-	-	-	-	-	1
Gamescleugh	NT21S	-	-	40	-	-	-	-	-	-	-	-	-	-	-	-	-	-	x
Garvald 1	NT15A	-	-	33	25	65	38	-	-	-	-	-	-	-	-	-	-	-	x
Garvald 2	NT15A	-	-	39	22	21	3	d	-	-	-	-	3	-	-	-	-	-	3
Gilston	NT45N	-	-	-	-	-	-	-	-	-	-	-	-	-	4	-	-	-	4
Girnwood L.	NT31R	-	-	-	-	-	-	-	-	20	-	-	-	46	-	-	-	-	46
Glenbreck	NT02K	-	-	2	5	-	-	-	8	-	-	-	-	-	-	-	-	-	x
Gr'n Diamonds	NT42S	-	-	20	9	-	-	-	-	3	-	-	-	-	-	-	-	-	x
Greenside	NT86E	-	-	-	-	-	-	-	157	208	260	-	-	-	-	-	-	-	260
Harden Moss	NT41N	-	-	-	-	-	-	-	-	-	-	-	-	50	-	-	-	-	50
Harehope P.	NT24B	-	-	-	-	3	25	-	1	4	-	-	-	-	-	-	-	-	x
Haremoss	NT42S	-	-	35	-	-	-	-	-	-	-	-	-	-	-	-	-	-	x
Hartwoodmyres	NT42H	-	-	-	-	-	-	-	-	-	5	-	15	-	-	-	-	1	1
Hoselaw	NT83A	-	-	-	-	-	-	-	-	-	-	-	20	50	-	500	800	1250	524
Hule Moss	NT74E	-	-	-	-	-	-	-	-	-	-	20	-	-	-	-	-	-	20
Hutlerburn	NT42B	-	-	-	-	-	-	-	-	-	-	20	-	-	-	-	-	-	4
Kingside	NT31L	-	-	-	7	-	-	-	-	-	-	-	4	-	-	-	-	-	2
Kirkhouse P.	NT33G	-	-	-	-	-	-	-	-	-	-	-	2	-	-	-	-	-	12
Lilliesleaf M.	NT52H	-	-	-	-	-	-	-	-	-	12	-	-	-	-	-	-	-	2
Longf'macus P.	NT65Y	-	-	-	-	-	-	-	-	-	-	-	-	-	-	2	-	-	12
Long Moss	NT86P	-	-	-	-	24	2	-	20	-	4	-	-	-	-	-	-	-	45
Medwyn Mains	NT14J	-	60	-	-	-	7	34	48	50	45	48	125	44	50	40	0	0	x
Megget Res.	NT22B	-	-	-	9	-	-	-	-	-	-	-	-	-	-	-	-	-	88
Mount Bog	NT14B	350	-	-	-	3	-	-	29	6	7	70	230	150	-	20	5	35	x
Muirburn	NT14A	-	-	-	-	-	-	-	2	-	-	-	-	-	-	-	-	-	10
Penmanshiel	NT86D	-	-	-	-	-	-	-	-	-	10	-	-	-	-	-	-	-	x
Pilmuir	NT41V	-	-	-	-	-	-	-	1	-	-	-	-	-	-	-	-	-	40
Rawburn	NT65S	-	-	-	-	-	-	-	-	-	-	-	-	30	-	50	-	-	6
Redmoss	NY48S	-	-	-	-	-	-	-	-	-	-	-	-	-	-	-	-	6	220
St. Mary's L.	NT22L	-	-	-	-	-	-	-	-	99	154	-	-	360	-	-	180	188	1
Shielswood L.	NT41P	-	-	-	-	-	-	-	-	-	-	-	-	-	1	-	-	-	2
Shiphorns	NT24J	-	-	2	108	131	9	d	-	-	-	-	2	-	-	-	-	-	2
Loch Sike	NT42L	-	-	-	-	-	-	-	-	-	4	-	-	-	-	-	-	-	x
Slipperfield M.	NT14J	-	-	-	-	-	-	-	-	-	-	-	-	20	-	-	-	-	20
Stobie Slack	NT32W	-	-	-	-	-	-	-	-	-	3	-	-	-	-	-	-	-	3
Talla Res.	NT12F	-	-	2	-	-	-	-	-	-	-	-	-	-	-	-	-	-	x
Tweedsmuir	NT12C	-	-	2	-	-	-	-	-	-	-	-	-	-	-	-	-	-	767
West Water	NT15B	1000	1200	1500	1870	1400	650	815	800	1630	1200	1000	850	-	-	-	270	506	x
Whitmuirhill L.	NT42Y	-	-	-	-	10	-	-	-	-	-	-	-	-	-	-	-	-	4
Whitrig P.	NT63H	-	-	-	-	3	-	-	-	-	-	-	-	4	-	-	-	-	1
Whitton L.	NT71P	-	-	-	-	-	-	-	-	-	-	-	-	1	-	-	-	-	1
Williestruther	NT41V	-	-	-	-	-	2	-	2	2	-	1	-	-	-	-	-	-	1
Wooden L.	NT72C	-	-	-	-	-	-	-	-	-	-	1	-	-	-	-	-	-	

+ = breeding noted but no count. ? = possibly bred. d = disturbed. x = site deserted or no estimate practicable.
Sources: BBR and LBR.

Lesser Black-backed Gull counts on the Forth islands 1951-1996, pairs or nests

	Inch-garvie	Hay-stack	Inch-colm	Car Craig	Inch-mickery	Inch-keith	Fidra	The Lamb	Craig-leith	Bass Rock	Isle of May	Approx. Totals
1951	0	0	0	0	0	0	0	12	100	+	100	250
1955	0	0	0	0	0	-	0	+	+	+	200	350
1966	0	0	0	0	0	+	0	>10	+	+	+	-
1969-70	2	0	0	0	5	300	0	5	275	50	2000	2640
1971	-	0	-	0	2	>100	5	4	400	+	+	-
1973	-	0	-	0	0	+	10	2	350	+	1000	1650
1975	5	0	15	0	-	250	+	10	+	+	+	-
1976	2	0	20	0	5	+	20	5	+	+	250	1050
1978	-	0	+	0	10	>500	40	4	380	+	250	1300
1981	+	0	0	0	-	+	+	5	250	20	+	2200
1985-87	10	0	730	0	60	1750	140	10	930	30	520	4200
1992	6	1	+	0	54	+	201	50	+	+	751	5700
1994	11	0	669	1	108	2607	492	55	934	60	1270	7200
1995	>6	0	+	3	141	+	+	+	+	+	1635	-
1996	11	1	+	3	196	+	467	140	+	60	1641	7700

Symbols: + = present but no count, - = not counted.
Sources: ENHS, LBR, IMBOR, FIBR, Lloyd et al. (1991), and the unpublished diaries of R.W.J. Smith and others.

Herring Gull counts in the Firth of Forth 1951-1996, pairs or nests

Forth islands

	Inch-garvie	Hay-stack	Inch-colm	Car Craig	Inch-mickery	Inch-keith	Eye-broughy	Fidra	The Lamb	Craig-leith	Bass Rock	Isle of May	Approx. Totals
1951	0	0	few	+	0	+	-	-	150	many	+	1100	-
1955	0	-	-	100	-	-	-	-	+	+	+	3000	5000
1966	-	-	-	-	45	+	180	+	+	+	+	+	-
1969-70	10	+	5	+	30	750	140	100	550	5500	1050	15000	23150
1971	+	+	+	+	100	500	162	60	250	+	+	+	-
1973	+	+	+	+	1	+	+	250	400	5000	+	9000	18350
1975	100	+	500	+	-	4000	+	+	350	+	+	+	-
1976	100	60	400	75	100	+	+	160	300	+	+	2500	12100
1978	+	50	+	100	80	2400	+	450	-	3000	+	2500	10100
1981	+	+	+	+	+	+	150	+	220	2000	250	2900	11100
1985-87	110	+	1040	+	50	4900	170	410	220	2280	325	2100	11700
1992	140	23	+	45	54	+	55	806	200	+	+	1462	11550
1994	210	16	1615	38	108	4977	45	1149	130	2385	230	2122	13050
1995	280	12	+	49	141	+	6	+	+	+	+	2554	-
1996	195	18	+	54	196	+	11	1401	140	+	240	2969	14450

Symbols: + = present but no count, - = not counted.
Sources: ENHS, FIBR, IMBOR, LBR, Lloyd et al. (1991) and the unpublished diaries of R.W.J. Smith and others.

Berwickshire Coast

	A Siccar Point to Pettico Wick NT87A-96E	B St. Abb's Head NT96E-96D	C St. Abb's to Eyemouth NT96D-96M	D Eyemouth to English border NT96M-95T	Totals from Lloyd et al.	Totals A+B+C+D
1957	-	1084	-	-	-	-
1958	1112	-	61	411	-	-
1969-70	262	921	45	70	1516	1298
1976	-	653	-	-	-	-
1977	-	914	-	-	-	-
1978	727	907	148	180	-	1962
1982	201	721	182	213	-	1317
1985	-	782	-	-	-	-
1986	-	718	-	-	-	-
1987	413	697	143	176	1831	1514
1988	-	722	-	-	-	-
1989	-	387	-	-	-	-
1990	-	362	-	-	-	-
1991	-	398	-	-	-	-
1992	-	301	-	-	-	-
1993	-	380	-	-	-	-
1994	-	296	-	-	-	-
1995	-	398	-	-	-	-
1996	-	358	-	-	-	-

Sources: BBR, SAHSR, da Prato (1986) and Lloyd et al. (1991). The reason for the differences between area counts and the global count of Lloyd et al. is not known.

Great Black-backed Gulls in the Firth of Forth 1985-1996, breeding pairs

	Inchcolm	Inchmickery	Fidra	The Lamb	Craigleith	Bass Rock	Isle of May	Total
1985	0	0	0	2	4	-	1	7
1986	0	0	0	1	3	1	3	8
1987	0	0	0	0	3	-	1	4
1988	0	0	3	1	5	-	3	12
1989	0	0	2	1	5	-	3	11
1990	0	0	1	0	6	0	3	10
1991	0	0	1	0	3	-	4	8
1992	0	0	1	1	3	-	8	13
1993	0	0	1	0	3	1	7	12
1994	0	0	3	1	7	1	6	18
1995	1	0	2	2	3	-	7	15
1996	2	1	4	3	6	1	7	24

Sources: LBR, IMBOR, FIBR.

Kittiwake colonies in the Firth of Forth 1970-1996, AON

	Inchcolm	Inchkeith	Fidra	The Lamb	Craigleith	Bass Rock	Dunbar	St. Abb's	Rest of Berwickshire	Isle of May
1970	0	342	104	116	-	-	-	7293	3527	-
1971	0	407	164	125	-	-	-	-	-	3436
1972	0	391	186	121	-	-	-	-	-	3450
1973	0	407	218	116	326	-	-	-	-	-
1974	0	421	272	141	450	-	-	-	-	-
1975	0	404	262	93	350	-	-	-	-	3870
1976	0	351	275	94	351	-	-	8293	>3883[1]	-
1977	0	338	227	95	490	2500	-	9069	>6154[2]	-
1978	0	291	243	55	450	2200	-	10227	7874	-
1979	0	236	258	68	510	2150	-	-	-	4940
1980	0	207	354	57	670	2400	-	-	-	-
1981	0	195	456	96	>136	>900	-	-	-	6100
1982	0	240	483	116	670	1900	282	11951	7049	-
1983	0	254	497	91	610	2300	286	-	-	-
1984	0	257	506	101	>610	2450	292	-	-	6012
1985	0	-	494	125	-	>1950	289	11997	-	-
1986	0	369	532	167	725	-	344	13940	-	4802
1987	0	483	726	199	-	2400	479	15182	-	6765
1988	0	490	622	175	770	-	460	16208	-	7683
1989	0	593	705	250	840	-	559	19066	-	7567
1990	0	556	598	187	850	-	516	17642	-	8129
1991	20	612	494	106	>225	-	671	16183	-	6535
1992	38	678	489	223	-	-	850	16533	-	6916
1993	49	656	452	84	1028	-	479	15268	-	7009
1994	62	440	326	160	564	-	413	13007	-	3751
1995	190	551	435	210	951	-	-	13670	-	7542
1996	144	426	314	143	509	2142	-	13437	-	6269

1: coast to west of Siccar Pt. and east of St. Abb's not counted.
2: coast to west of Pease Bay and east of St. Abb's not counted.

Kittiwake population of the Firth of Forth 1970-1995, estimated breeding pairs

	------- Inner Forth --------		--------------------------------- Outer Forth ----------------------					Berwickshire		May
	Inchcolm	Inchkeith	Fidra	The Lamb	Craigleith	Bass Rock	Dunbar	St. Abb's	Rest of Berwickshire	Isle of May
1970	0	342	104	116	*326*	*1500*	200	7293	3527	3436
1975	0	404	262	93	350	*2000*	*200*	8293	*4729*	3870
1980	0	207	354	57	670	2400	252	*11951*	7049	6100
1985	0	369	494	125	725	2450	289	11997	*7942*	4802
1990	0	556	598	187	850	*2400*	516	17642	*11608*	8129
1995	190	551	435	210	951	2142	413	13670	*9049*	7542

Where no count is available for the year specified or within 2 years of the specified year, an estimate has been made of the likely population (shown in italics). In the case of the Berwickshire coast, a value of 56% of the corresponding St. Abb's figure has been made for the cliffs to the west of St. Abb's and 10.2% for those to the east of St. Abb's. These percentages are based on the relationship between counts at St. Abb's and the rest of the coast when they were counted in a single year.

Sources: ENHS, BBR, LBR, IMBOR, FIBR, SAHSR, Coulson (1983), Lloyd *et al.* (1991), and the unpublished diaries of R.W.J. Smith and others.

Terns in the Firth of Forth 1988-1997, nests or pairs attempting to breed

Sandwich Tern

Year	Lothian coast	islands	Fife islands	Forth total
1988	0	383	-	383
1989	0	272	-	272
1990	0	418	1	419
1991	0	475	-	475
1992	0	122	41	163
1993	0	9	250	259
1994	1	98	31	130
1995	0	1	4	5
1996	1	0	2	3
1997	0	0	0	0

Roseate Tern

Year	Lothian coast	islands	Fife islands	Forth total
1988	0	21	+	21+
1989	1	5	+	6+
1990	0	0	5	5
1991	0	0	+	+
1992	0	0	17	17
1993	0	0	17	17
1994	0	2	7	9
1995	0	1	13	14
1996	0	1	5	6
1997	0	0	7	7

Common Tern

Year	Lothian coast	islands	Fife islands	Forth total
1988	194	146	50+	390+
1989	336	182	60+	578+
1990	+	141	200+	341+
1991	108	126	195+	429+
1992	187	101	204	492
1993	715	91	223	1029
1994	509	105	196	810
1995	443	11	257	711
1996	508	19	328	855
1997	526	5	408	939

Arctic Tern

Year	Lothian coast	islands	Fife islands	Forth total
1988	82	0	200	282
1989	65	0	250	315
1990	8	0	300	308
1991	80	0	415	495
1992	40	0	491	531
1993	21	0	538	559
1994	20	0	540	560
1995	11	0	608	619
1996	13	0	531	544
1997	6	0	630	636

Little Tern

Year	Lothian coast	islands	Fife islands	Forth total
1988	24	0	0	24
1989	47	0	0	47
1990	11	0	0	11
1991	9	0	0	9
1992	13	0	0	13
1993	7	0	0	7
1994	12	0	0	12
1995	1	0	0	1
1996	1	0	0	1
1997	0	0	0	0

- = no information on breeding available. + = birds bred but counts are not available or are not complete.
Fife islands data for 1988-91 are complete for the Isle of May but not for all islands.
Sources: East Scotland Tern Conservation Group, LBR.

Guillemots breeding in the Firth of Forth 1921-1996, birds on cliffs and AOS

	Inchkeith	Fidra	The Lamb	Craigleith	Bass Rock	Dunglass	Fast Castle	St. Abb's Head	Burnmouth	Isle of May
1921	-	-	-	-	-	-	-	-	-	*2596*
1924	-	-	-	-	-	-	-	-	-	*1664*
1928	-	-	-	-	250	-	-	-	-	-
1936	-	-	-	-	-	-	-	-	-	*2080*
1946	-	-	-	-	-	-	-	-	-	*2000*
1954	-	-	-	-	-	-	-	-	-	*2000*
1955	-	-	0	-	-	-	-	-	-	*2000*
1957	-	-	-	-	-	-	-	5111	-	-
1958	-	-	-	-	-	8	376	4728	13	-
1959	-	-	-	-	-	-	-	-	-	*2000*
1960	-	-	-	240	-	-	-	-	-	-
1962	-	-	-	365	1350	-	-	-	-	-
1963	-	-	1	430	-	-	-	-	-	-
1964	-	-	10	245	-	-	-	-	-	-
1965	-	-	24	488	-	-	-	-	-	-
1966	0	0	*64*	350	-	-	-	-	-	-
1967	0	0	*89*	650	-	-	-	-	-	-
1968	0	0	*90*	900	-	-	-	-	-	-
1969	0	0	*97*	620	-	-	-	-	-	9000
1970#	0	0	*135*	650	-	130	544	6042	15	-
1971	0	0	*200*	700	-	-	-	-	-	-
1972	0	3	*210*	900	-	-	-	-	-	*3500*
1973	0	8	*340*	560	-	-	-	-	-	7394
1974	6	21	*400*	1000	-	-	-	-	-	8630
1975	0	27	*500*	1100	-	-	-	-	-	8528
1976	5	28	*500*	1700	2100	-	-	10852	-	8340
1977	3	35	*600*	1500	3000	-	-	10879	-	-
1978	*6*	*14*	*750*	1900	2950	126	1356	13178	130	-
1979	5	25	*860*	1480	1800	-	-	-	-	-
1980	5	38	840	1550	2800	-	-	-	-	-
1981	*6*	*73*	*1060*	-	-	-	-	17000	-	16920
1982	*8*	65	1500	1800	*2250*	261	1556	16925	245	-
1983	16	113	1540	1700	2850	-	-	-	301	-
1984	31	159	2300	1300	4090	-	-	-	-	12972
1985	-	142	2200	-	>2500	-	-	17815	-	-
1986	35	176	2750	2000	-	-	-	22986	-	17585
1987	49	79	860	-	2700	360	1761	26700	373	-
1988	*24*	131	2400	1300	-	-	-	27982	-	-
1989	44	145	3600	1700	-	-	-	30788	-	-
1990	70	89	2400	1550	-	-	-	28942	-	-
1991	48	197	2400	-	-	-	-	-	-	16834
1992	52	245	3250	-	-	-	-	-	-	17512
1993	44	220	3300	1416	-	-	-	28911	-	12418
1994	59	304	3200	1940	-	-	-	-	-	19186
1995	48	289	3170	2122	-	-	-	-	-	-
1996	81	*173*	3650	1877	3225	-	-	**33235**	-	24468

Normal type = birds on cliffs; italics = 'pairs' or apparently occupied sites; bold = 1996 St. Abb's Head estimate.
\#   data from Berwickshire referenced in the archives as '1969-70' has been allocated in this table to 1970.
On the Berwickshire coast: Dunglass = Dunglass to Fast Castle Head ; Fast Castle = Fast Castle Head to Pettico Wick; St. Abb's Head = Pettico Wick to St. Abbs; Burnmouth = Eyemouth to Burnmouth.
Sources: ENHS, IMBOR, LBR, BBR, SAHSR, Eggeling (1960 and 1974), *Andrews*, da Prato (1986), Lloyd *et al.* (1991).

Razorbills breeding in the Firth of Forth 1921-1996, AOS and birds on cliffs

	Inch-colm	Inch-mickery	Inch-keith	Fidra	Lamb	Craigleith	Bass Rock	Dunglass	Fast Castle	St. Abb's Head	Burn-mouth	Isle of May
1921	-	-	-	-	-	-	-	-	-	-	-	*360*
1924	-	-	-	-	-	-	-	-	-	-	-	*160*
1928	-	-	-	-	-	-	*200*	-	-	-	-	-
1936	-	-	-	-	-	-	-	-	-	-	-	*500*
1946	-	-	-	-	-	-	-	-	-	-	-	*400*
1952	-	-	-	-	-	*	-	-	-	-	-	*375*
1955	-	-	-	-	*0*	-	-	-	-	-	-	*375*
1957	-	-	-	-	-	-	-	-	-	225	-	-
1958	-	-	-	-	-	-	-	*5*	84	*192*	6	-
1959	-	-	-	-	-	-	-	-	-	-	-	*300*
1960	-	-	*1	-	-	20	-	-	-	-	-	-
1961	-	-	-	-	*1	-	-	-	-	-	-	-
1962	-	-	-	-	2	55	*100*	-	-	-	-	-
1963	-	-	-	-	1	20	-	-	-	-	-	-
1964	-	-	-	-	4	10	-	-	-	-	-	-
1965	-	-	-	-	4	0	-	-	-	-	-	-
1966	-	*0*	*0*	*0*	2	52	-	-	-	-	-	-
1967	-	*0*	*0*	*0*	5	30	-	-	-	-	-	-
1968	-	*0*	*0*	*0*	10	29	-	-	-	-	-	-
1969	-	*0*	*1*	*0*	16	28	-	-	-	*170*	-	-
1970#	-	*0*	*2*	*0*	10	34	*20*	*14*	*53*	*170*	*20*	*350*
1971	-	*0*	*4*	*0*	6	28	-	-	-	-	-	-
1972	-	*0*	*5*	*1*	6	36	-	-	-	-	-	*600*
1973	-	*0*	*7*	*0*	8	34	-	-	-	-	-	*482*
1974	-	*0*	*12*	*1	*11*	46	-	-	-	-	-	*451*
1975	-	*0*	*14*	*4*	*12*	49	-	-	-	-	-	*525*
1976	*0*	*0*	*15*	*10*	*12*	64	*50*	-	-	*366*	-	*412*
1977	-	*0*	*20*	>5	*18*	65	*45*	-	-	*327*	-	-
1978	*0*	*0*	*18*	*19*	>9	51	*60*	*41*	*168*	*438*	*55*	-
1979	*0*	*0*	*23*	*17*	*20*	64	*67*	-	-	-	-	-
1980	-	*0*	*29*	*13*	-	40	-	-	-	-	-	*c500*
1981	-	*0*	*26*	*28*	*18*		-	-	-	-	-	*1010*
1982	-	*0*	*25*	*32*	-	57	*74*	*69*	*227*	*590*	*99*	-
1983	-	*0*	*30*	*33*	-	44	>54	-	-	-	-	-
1984	-	*0*	*30*	*44*	*21*	42	*110*	-	-	-	-	*1260*
1985	-	*0*	-	*49*	*24*	57	-	-	-	-	-	-
1986	-	*0*	*23*	*48*	*21*	40	*36*	-	*769*	-	-	-
1987	-	*0*	*32*	*38*	*34*	52	*91*	*77*	*198*	*784*	*109*	*1200*
1988	-	*0*	*40*	*53*	*29*	62	-	-	-	*1046*	-	*2000*
1989	-	*0*	*46*	*72*	*41*	57	-	-	-	*785*	-	*2075*
1990	-	*0*	*60*	*75*	*33*	60	-	-	-	*723*	-	*1508*
1991	-	-	*42*	*91*	*32*	80	-	-	-	-	-	*1425*
1992	-	*1	*38*	*72*	*40*	46	-	-	-	-	-	*1909*
1993	-	-	*64*	*65*	*13*	61	-	-	-	*1082*	-	*2052*
1994	*1*	*0*	*55*	*85*	*36*	76	-	-	-	-	-	*2227*
1995	*2	*0*	*56*	*80*	*47*	108	--	-	--	-	-	*4160*
1996	*3*	*0*	*68*	*74*	*73*	73	*188*	-	-	**1100**	-	*3405*

The above table is mostly of apparently occupied sites (AOS) with some counts of birds on cliffs at Craigleith, Bass Rock and Isle of May.

Normal type = birds on cliffs; italics = 'pairs' or apparently occupied sites; bold = 1996 St. Abb's Head estimate. * = first recorded breeding.

\# = data from Berwickshire referenced in the archives as '1969-70' has been allocated in this table to 1970.

On the Berwickshire coast: Dunglass = Dunglass to Fast Castle Head; Fast Castle = Fast Castle Head to Pettico Wick; St. Abb's Head = Pettico Wick to St. Abb's; Burnmouth = Eyemouth to Burnmouth.

Counts of birds on cliffs made in years when counts of AOS were also made

	St. Abb's Head	Isle of May			St. Abb's Head	Isle of May
1978	687	-		1990	1684	-
1982	1072	-		1991	-	1633
1985	1197	-		1992	-	2582
1986	1383	-		1993	1748	3022
1987	-	-		1994	-	3034
1988	1502	-		1995	-	-
1989	1761	2613		1996	-	-

Sources: ENHS, IMBOR, LBR, BBR, SAHSR, Eggeling (1960 and 1974), *Andrews*, da Prato (1986), Lloyd *et al.* (1991).

Puffins in the Firth of Forth 1921-1996, birds and apparently occupied burrows

Year	Inch-garvie	Inch-colm	Inch-mickery	Inchkeith	Fidra	Lamb	Craigleith	Bass Rock	Fast Castle Head	St. Abb's Head	Eyemouth to Fancove	Isle of May
1921	-	-	-	-	-	-	-	-	-	50-100	-	-
1921	-	-	-	-	-	-	-	-	-	-	-	*12*
1924	-	-	-	-	-	-	-	-	-	-	-	*6*
1928	-	-	-	-	-	-	-	*50*	-	-	-	-
1933		-	-	-	-	-	-	-	-	v.few	-	-
1934	-	-	-	0	-	-	-	-	-	-	-	*8-10*
1936	-	-	-	0	-	-	-	-	-	-	-	*50*
1946	-	-	-	-	-	-	-	-	-	*10*	-	*10*
1950	-	0	-	-	-	-	-	-	-	-	-	*5*
1951	0	-	-	-	-	-	50	-	-	-	-	*<10*
1954	0	-	-	-	0	-	-	-	-	-	-	*7-8*
1955	-	-	-	0	0	0	0	-	-	-	-	*5*
1956	-	-	-	-	-	-	-	-	-	-	-	*4*
1957	-	-	-	0	-	-	-	-	-	24	-	*5-10*
1958	-	-	-	-	-	-	-	-	-	-	-	*5-10*
1959	-	0	0	0	0	0	70	-	-	-	-	*5-6*
1960	-	0	0	1	-	0	-	-	-	16	-	-
1961	0	-	0	6	-	0	110	25	-	-	-	*250*
1962	-	-	0	0	0	0	680	-	-	-	-	-
1963	-	-	0	-	0	-	450	-	-	-	-	-
1964	-	0	0	0	-	0	168	-	-	-	-	*500*
1965	-	-	0	*10	0	0	550	-	-	-	-	-
1966	-	-	0	40	11	0	182	-	-	-	-	-
1967	-	-	0	62	*4	1	400	-	-	-	-	-
1968	-	-	0	43	15	1	400	-	-	-	-	-
1969	-	-	0	80	4	3	410	3	-	-	-	-
1970	-	-	0	80	0	0	800	0	-	-	-	*2500*
1971	-	-	0	110	0	0	600	-	-	-	-	-
1972	-	-	0	350	0	0	325	-	-	-	-	*3500*
1973	0	0	3	450	5	0	1400	-	-	-	-	-
1974	0	0	0	490	1	0	1170	-	-	-	-	-
1975	0	0	-	610	12	0	1100	-	-	-	-	-
1976	-	0	8	750	40	0	1350	10	-	45	-	*>6000*
1977	-	-	0	450	57	1	950	12	-	22	-	*6000*
1978	0	0	0	1000	100	0	2000	40	-	8	-	-
1979	-	-	0	660	100	0	1150	15	-	-	-	-
1980	-	-	0	440	100	0	2000	25	-	4	-	*8500*
1981	-	0	0	630	175	0	1400	30	17	-	-	*10000*
1982	-	-	0	650	125	0	2500	12	-	64	-	-
1983	-	-	0	435	80	0	1900	>10	9	6	4	-
1984	-	-	0	775	325	20	700	7	9	10	22	*12000*
1985	-	-	0	-	260	*8*	2450	20	-	52	66	-
1986	-	-	0	1452	300	-	1350	20	-	70	89	*12000*
1987	0	0	0	860	-	-	1165	11	-	88	-	-
1988	0	-	0	1850	350	*10*	1200	-	-	*61	15	-
1989	-	-	0	2350	220	50	3000	10	25	104	66	*18600*
1990	-	-	0	700	150	5	550	17	1	77	67	-
1991	0	-	14	3000	600	>5	1550	-	9	58	12	-
1992	0	50	6	1600	-	15	-	-	3	77	-	*20106*
1993	*1	*35	*7	650	*325*	100	1000	-	2	59	14	-
1994	0	75	*10*	376	*370*	30	550	-	12	81	3	-
1995	-	45	*13*	1200	*370*	*150*	>4000	-	6	106	6	-
1996	-	42	*13*	609	*410*	*148*	148	20	74	-	-	-

Totals in normal type refer to birds counted on land or nearby on the sea. Italicised totals refer to apparently occupied burrows.

Dashes indicate no count in that year, asterisks (*) the first known confirmed breeding.

Sources: ENHS, IMBOR, LBR, BBR, FIBR, SAHSR, Eggeling (1960 and 1974), *Thom*, da Prato (1986), Lloyd *et al.* (1991) and unpublished data held by the Forth Islands Seabird Group, courtesy of Ian Andrews.

Nuthatch colonisation of SE Scotland 1989-1997

Site	Tetrad	Breeding Status	1989	1990	1991	1992	1993	1994	1995	1996	1997
Floors	NT73C	ON	1pr	1pr	1pr	-	2pr	5pr	6pr	6pr	8pr
Hirsel	NT84A&F	ON	1pr	1pr	1pr	2pr	3pr	5pr	6pr	6pr	8pr
Benrig	NT63A	S	-	-	-	1m	-	-	-	-	-
Longformacus	NT65N	H	-	-	-	-	1m	-	-	-	-
Lennel	NT84K	H	-	-	-	-	-	1m	-	1m	-
Ashkirk	NT42R	H	-	-	-	-	-	-	1	1	-
Minto	NT52Q	H	-	-	-	-	-	-	1	-	-
Kershopefoot	NY48W	ON	-	-	-	-	-	-	1pr	-	-
St. Abb's	NT96D&E	T	-	-	-	-	-	-	1-2	1	-
Langlee Wood	NT53C	ON	-	-	-	-	-	-	1pr	2pr	-
Mellerstain	NT63P	ON	-	-	-	-	-	-	2pr	-	-
Newton Don	NT73D	S	-	-	-	-	-	-	1m	-	-
Monteviot	NT62M	FL	-	-	-	-	-	-	1pr	2pr	-
Lees	NT83P	T	-	-	-	-	-	-	-	1m	1pr
Coldstream Hosp.	NT83J	T	-	-	-	-	-	-	-	1pr	
Pirn Lodge	NT44N	S	-	-	-	-	-	-	-	1m	
Lauder	NT54J	H	-	-	-	-	-	-	-	1	-
Abbotsford	NT53B	H	-	-	-	-	-	-	-	1m	-
Denholm Bridge	NT51U	S	-	-	-	-	-	-	-	1m	-
Duns Castle	NT75S	H	-	-	-	-	-	-	-	1	-
Gala Policies	NT43X	P	-	-	-	-	-	-	-	1pr	-
Paxton House	NT95G	T	-	-	-	-	-	-	-	-	3pr
Silverwells	NT86Y	T	-	-	-	-	-	-	-	-	1m
Totals			2pr	2pr	2pr	2pr+1	5pr+1	10pr+1	17pr+4	18pr+9	20pr+1

Non-breeding season

Site	Tetrad		1989	1990	1991	1992	1993	1994	1995	1996	1997
Peebles	NT23P		-	-	1	-	-	-	-	-	-
Gattonside	NT53M		-	-	-	1	-	-	-	-	-
Wells	NT51Y		-	-	-	-	-	1	-	-	-
Dawyck	NT13S		-	-	-	-	-	-	1	-	-
Birgham Wood	NT74V		-	-	-	-	-	-	-	1	-

Note: Breeding status column as of 1997. Breeding status codes are defined on p. 24. m = male; pr = pair. Source: BBR.

Hawfinch Status in SE Scotland 1979-1996

Site	Tetrad or 10-km	Max count 1979-96	Breeding status	No. of years recorded	Last record
Carberry Tower	NT36U	2	H	2	1988
Castlecraig	NT14H	1	winter	1	1986
Cousland	NT36U	2	FL	2	1982
Dalkeith	NT36I	6	P	3	1988
Dawyck	NT13S	2	FL	1	1982
Duddingston	NT27W	1	winter	1	1986
Duns Castle	NT75S	3	P	1	1988
East Calder	NT06Y	1	winter	1	1991
Hawick	NT41X	1	FL	1	1992
Hirsel	NT84A&F	10	FL	12	1996
Glencorse	NT26L	1	winter	1	1989
Gosford	NT47P	3	P	3	1985
Grange, Edinburgh	NT27Q	1	winter	1	1987
Jedburgh	NT62	1	winter	1	1986
Kelso/Floors	NT73C,H&M	5	FL	9	1996
Longformacus	NT65Y	1	H	3	1993
Luffness	NT48Q	1	P	1	1994
Merchiston	NT27L	1	H	1	1981
Minto	NT52Q	1	FL	2	1991
Monteviot	NT62M	5	P	5	1996
Newbyth	NT58V	1	winter	1	1989
Ormiston Hall	NT46D	4	FL	4	1988
Oxenford	NT36X	1	P	1	1986
Pease Dean	NT77V	1	H	1	1992
Peebles	NT23/24	1	H	3	1987
Pencaitland	NT46J	1	P	1	1982
Royal Botanic Gdns.	NT27M	8	N	9	1989
Shank Bridge	NT36F	1	H	1	1982
Spylaw	Not known	1	winter	1	1989
Torwoodlee	NT43U	1	H	1	1992
Tyninghame	NT68F	3	FL	4	1990

Breeding status codes are defined on p. 24. Sources : LBR and BBR.

Maximum Altitude (m)

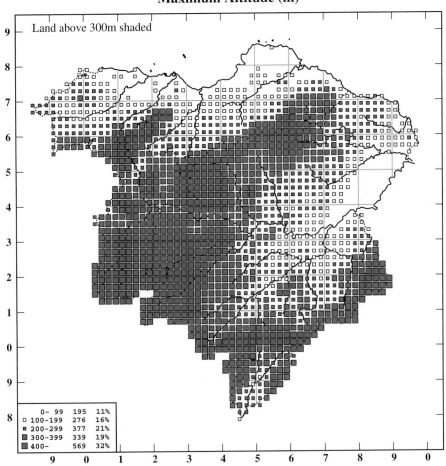

Land above 300m shaded

□	0- 99	195	11%
□	100-199	276	16%
▪	200-299	377	21%
▨	300-399	339	19%
■	400-	569	32%

Minimum Altitude (m)

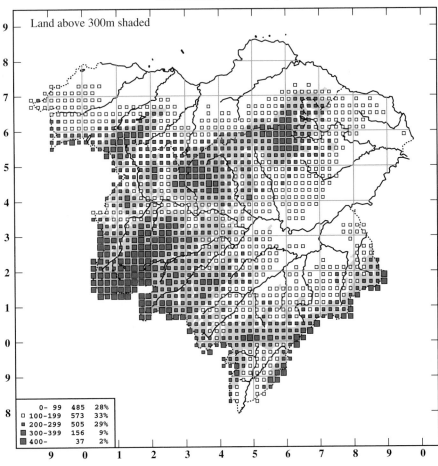

Land above 300m shaded

	0- 99	485	28%
□	100-199	573	33%
▪	200-299	505	29%
▨	300-399	156	9%
■	400-	37	2%

Average Altitude (m)

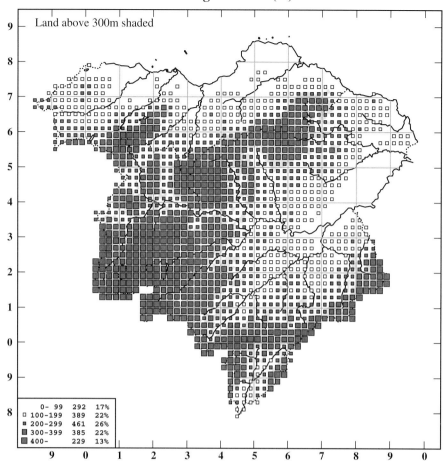

Land above 300m shaded

0- 99	292	17%
100-199	389	22%
200-299	461	26%
300-399	385	22%
400-	229	13%

SE Scotland: any woodland - status by altitude

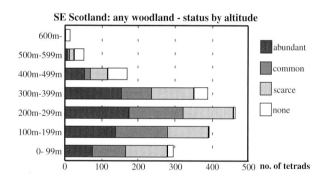

abundant
common
scarce
none

no. of tetrads

SE Scotland: wetland - status by altitude

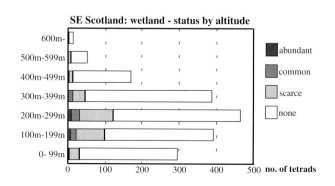

abundant
common
scarce
none

no. of tetrads

Any Woodland

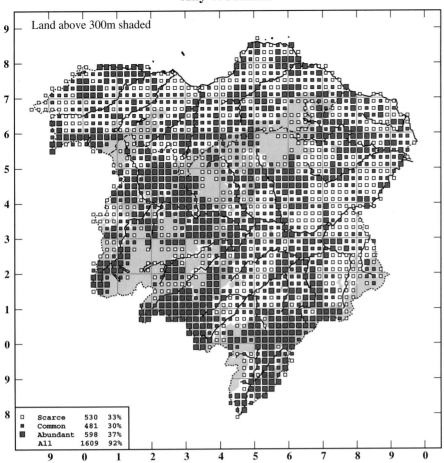

Land above 300m shaded

☐ Scarce	530	33%
▪ Common	481	30%
◼ Abundant	598	37%
All	1609	92%

Wetland

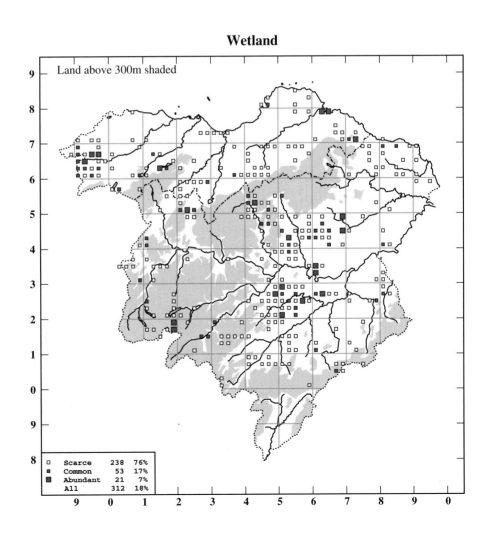

Land above 300m shaded

☐ Scarce	238	76%
▪ Common	53	17%
◼ Abundant	21	7%
All	312	18%

Scientific names of species other than birds mentioned in the text

Animals

Caddis Fly	*Trichoptera*
Common Shrew	*Sorex araneus*
Crane-fly	*Tipulidae*
Fox	*Vulpes vulpes*
Hedgehog	*Erinaceus europaeus*
Herring	*Clupea harengus*
Mayfly	*Ephemeroptera*
Mink (American)	*Mustela vison*
Mussel	*Mytilus edulis*
Rabbit	*Oryctolagus cuniculus*
Rat	*Rattus* spp.
Salmon	*Salmo salar*
Sandeel	*Ammodytes* spp.
Short-tailed Field Vole	*Microtus agrestis*
Sprat	*Sprattus sprattus*
Stoat	*Mustela erminea*
Stonefly	*Plecoptera*
Trout	*Salmo trutta*
Vole	*Microtus agrestis, Clethrionomys glareolus*
Weasel	*Mustela nivalis*

Plants

Ash	*Fraxinus excelsior*
Beech	*Fagus sylvatica*
Birch	*Betula* spp.
Blackthorn (=Sloe)	*Prunus spinosa*
Bottle Sedge	*Carex rostrata*
Bracken	*Pteridium aquilinum*
Buttercup	*Ranunculus* spp.
Chestnut, Horse	*Aesculus hippocastanum*
Cloudberry	*Rubus chamaemorus*
Cotton Grass	*Eriophorum* spp.
Dock	*Rumex* spp.
Douglas Fir	*Pseudotsuga menziesii*
Elm	*Ulmus* spp.
Gorse	*Ulex europaeus*
Groundsel	*Senecio vulgaris*

Hawthorn	*Crataegus monogyna*
Hazel	*Corylus avellana*
Holly	*Ilex aquifolium*
Heather	*Calluna vulgaris*
Juniper	*Juniperus communis*
Larch	*Larix* spp.
Ling	*Calluna vulgaris*
Monkey Puzzle	*Araucaria araucana*
Nettle, Common	*Urtica dioica*
Oak	*Quercus* spp.
Pine, Lodgepole	*Pinus contorta*
Pine, Scots	*Pinus sylvestris*
Ragwort, Common	*Senecio jacobaea*
Rhododendron	*Rhododendron* spp.
Rose	*Rosa* spp.
Rowan	*Sorbus aucuparia*
Rush	*Juncus* spp.
Sea Buckthorn	*Hippophae rhamnoides*
Spruce, Norway	*Picea abies*
Spruce, Sitka	*Picea sitchensis*
Sycamore	*Acer pseudoplatanus*
Teasel	*Dipsacus fullonum*
Thistle	*Cirsium* spp.
Tree Mallow	*Lavatera arborea*
Water Crowfoot	*Ranunculus* spp.
Western Hemlock	*Tsuga heterophylla*
Willow	*Salix* spp.
Yew	*Taxus baccata*

References

Anderson, D.R. and Waterston, G. 1961. Check-list of the birds of Duddingston Loch. *Scott. Birds* **1**: supplement 400-416.

Andrews, I.J. 1986. *The Birds of the Lothians.* SOC, Edinburgh.

Andrews, I.J. 1989. Checklist of the birds of Musselburgh Lagoons. *Lothian Bird Report* **1988**: 93-99.

Andrews, I.J. 1993. The Wildfowl and Wetlands Trust Shelduck Survey 1992: the Lothians. *Lothian Bird Report* **1992**: 87-95.

Andrews, J. and Carter, S.P. 1993. *Britain's Birds in 1990-91: the conservation and monitoring review.* BTO/JNCC, Thetford.

Anon. 1989. Red-necked Grebe breeding in Scotland. *Scott. Birds* **15**: 133.

Armstrong, I.H., Coulson, J.C., Hawkey, P. and Hudson, M.J. 1978. Further mass seabird deaths from paralytic shellfish poisoning. *Brit. Birds* **71**: 58-68.

Baines, D. and Hudson, P.J. 1995. The decline of Black Grouse in Scotland and northern England. *Bird Study* **42**: 122-131.

Ballantyne, J.H. and Vick, L.L.J. 1980. Breeding Dippers in 1980 on River South Esk system in Midlothian. *Edinburgh Ringing Group Report* **8**: 39-40.

Baxter, E.V. and Rintoul, L.J. 1934. Possible nesting of the Red-backed Shrike in Midlothian. *Scottish Naturalist* 70.

Baxter, E.V. and Rintoul, L.J. 1953. *The Birds of Scotland.* Oliver and Boyd, Edinburgh. 2 vols.

Bennie, J.G. 1984. West Lothian Rookeries 1983. *Lothian Bird Report* **1983**: 94.

Bennie, J.G. 1985. A survey of rookeries in ten kilometre square NT07 (West Lothian) in 1983 and 1984. *Lothian Bird Report* **1984**: 84.

Betts, M.M. 1955. The food of titmice in oak woodland. *J. Anim. Ecol.* **24**: 282-323.

Bibby, C.J. 1989. A survey of breeding Wood Warblers *Phylloscopus sibilatrix* in Britain, 1984-1985. *Bird Study* **36**: 56-72.

Bibby, C.J. and Etheridge, B. 1993. Status of the Hen Harrier *Circus cyaneus* in Scotland in 1988-89. *Bird Study* **40**: 1-11.

Bijlsma, R.G. 1982. Breeding season, clutch size and breeding success in the Bullfinch *Pyrrhula pyrrhula*. *Ardea* **70**: 25-30.

Birkhead, T.R. 1991. *The Magpies.* Poyser, London.

Brown, A.W. 1986. BTO Wood Warbler Survey 1984-85. *Lothian Bird Report* **1985**: 97-101.

Brown, A.W. 1987. Breeding Census of Little Grebe, Great Crested Grebe and Tufted Duck in the Lothians 1986. *Lothian Bird Report* **1986**: 61-68.

Brown, A.W. and Brown, L.M. 1978. *The Birds of West Water Reservoir.* Unpublished manuscript.

Brown, A.W. and Brown, L.M. 1984a. Sand Martin breeding survey 1983. *Lothian Bird Report* **1983**: 101-103.

Brown, A.W. and Brown, L.M. 1984b. The status of the Mute Swan in the Lothians. *Scott. Birds* **13**: 8-15.

Brown, A.W. and Brown, L.M. 1985. BTO Ringed Plover Survey 1984. *Lothian Bird Report* **1984**: 77-83.

Brown, A.W. and Brown, L.M. 1993. The Scottish Mute Swan Census 1990. *Scott. Birds* **17**: 93-102.

Brown, A.W. and Brown, L.M. 1997. Mute Swan Breeding Census 1995. *Lothian Bird Report* **1995**: 93-98.

Brown, A.W. and Dick, G. 1992. Distribution and number of feral Greylag Geese in Scotland. *Scott. Birds* **16**: 184-191.

Brown, A.W., Leven, M.R. and da Prato, S.R.D. 1984. The status of the Corn Bunting in the Lothians. *Scott. Birds* **13**: 107-111.

Bryant, D.M. 1978. Moulting Shelducks on the Forth Estuary. *Bird Study* **25**: 103-108.

Buckland, S.T., Bell, M.V. and Picozzi, N. 1990. *The Birds of North-East Scotland.* North-east Scotland Bird Club, Aberdeen.

Buckton, S.T. and Ormerod, S.J. 1997. Use of a new standardized habitat survey for assessing the habitat preferences and distribution of upland river birds. *Bird Study* **44**: 327-337.

Byars, T., Curtis, D.J. and McDonald, I. 1991. Breeding distribution and habitat requirements of Lesser Whitethroats in Strathclyde. *Scott. Birds* **16**: 66-76.

Calladine, J., Harris, M.P., Taylor, S. and Wanless, S. 1995. The status of the Eider on the Isle of May and other Forth Islands. *Scott. Birds* **18**: 1-10.

Campbell, L.H. 1978. Notes on the breeding biology of the Golden Plover in southern Scotland. *Edinburgh Ringing Group Report* **6**: 34-38.

Carter, S. 1995. *Britain's Birds in 1991-92: the conservation and monitoring review.* BTO/JNCC, Thetford.

Castle, M.E. 1977. Rookeries in Scotland. *Scott. Birds* **9**: 327-334.

Chapman, A. 1889. *Bird-life of the Borders.* Spredden Northern Classics, Stocksfield.

Clark, J.M. and Eyre, J.A. 1993. *Birds of Hampshire.* Hampshire Ornithological Society.

Clarke, W.E. 1905. Breeding of the Storm Petrel on the Bass Rock. *Annals of Scottish Natural History* 55-56.

Clarke, W.E. 1919. An old-time record of the breeding of the White Stork in Scotland. *Scottish Naturalist* 25-26.

Clarke, W.E. 1920. The attempted breeding of the Bee-eater (*Merops apiaster*) in Midlothian. *Scottish Naturalist* 151-153.

Clunas, A.J. 1982. Common Tern attacking Little Tern chick. *Scott. Birds* **12**: 119.

Coulson, J.C. 1983. The changing status of the Kittiwake *Rissa tridactyla* in the British Isles 1969-1979. *Bird Study* **30**: 8-16.

Coulson, J.C. and Thomas, C.S. 1985. Changes in the biology of the Kittiwake *Rissa tridactyla*: a 31-year study of a breeding colony. *J. Anim. Ecol.* **54**: 9-26.

Cowper, C.N.L. 1973. Breeding distribution of Grey Wagtails, Dippers and Common Sandpipers on the Midlothian Esk. *Scott. Birds* **7**: 302-306.

Cramp, S. (ed.). 1977-94. *Handbook of the Birds of Europe, the Middle East, and North Africa. The Birds of the Western Palearctic.* Oxford University Press, Oxford. 9 vols.

Crick, H.Q.P. 1993. Studies of moorland birds: Merlin and Golden Plover. In: *Britain's Birds in 1990-91*, J. Andrews and S.P. Carter. (eds.). BTO and JNCC, 121-123.

Crick, H.Q.P. and Ratcliffe, D.A. 1995. The Peregrine *Falco peregrinus* breeding population of the United Kingdom in 1991. *Bird Study* **42**: 1-19.

da Prato, S. 1980. How many Lesser Whitethroats breed in the Lothians? *Scott. Birds* **11**: 108-112.

da Prato, S.R.D. 1985. The breeding birds of agricultural land in south-east Scotland. *Scott. Birds* **13**: 203-216.

da Prato, S.R.D. 1986. The breeding birds of St. Abb's Head. *Borders Bird Report* **1985**: 53-59.

da Prato, S.R.D. 1989. The breeding birds of some built up areas in S.E. Scotland. *Scott. Birds* **15**: 170-177.

Davies, A.K. 1988. The distribution and status of the Mandarin Duck *Aix galericulata* in Britain. *Bird Study* **35**: 203-207.

Day, J.C., Hodgson, M.S. and Rossiter, N. 1995. *The Atlas of Breeding Birds in Northumbria.* Northumberland and Tyneside Bird Club, Newcastle upon Tyne.

Dean, T. 1987. The Nuthatch in Cumbria – its status and distribution. *Birds in Cumbria* **1987**: 55-64.

Delany, S., Greenwood, J.J.D. and Kirby, J. 1992. *National Mute Swan Survey 1990.* Report to JNCC.

Dennis, R.H. 1987. Boxes for Goldeneyes: a success story. *RSPB Conserv. Rev.* **1**: 85-87.

Dott, H.E.M. 1986. The spread of the House Sparrow *Passer domesticus* in Bolivia. *Ibis* **128**: 132-137.

Dott, H.E.M. 1994a. The spread of roof-nesting by gulls in Lothian Region to 1993. *Lothian Bird Report* **1993**: 110-114.

Dott, H.E.M. 1994b. Densities of breeding Magpies and Carrion Crows in south-east Scotland in 1992-93. *Scott. Birds* **17**: 205-211.

Dott, H.E.M. 1996. Roof-nesting gulls in Lothian, 1994. *Lothian Bird Report* **1994**: 113-115.

Dougall, T.W. 1978. *Census of breeding Wigeon (*Anas penelope*) in part of Ettrick Forest.* NCC Report.

Doward, D.F. 1957. The Night-heron colony in the Edinburgh Zoo. *Scottish Naturalist* **69**: 32-36.

Dunnet, G.M. 1992. A forty-three year study on the Fulmars on Eynhallow, Orkney. *Scott. Birds* **16**: 155-159.

Earnst, S.L. 1991. The Third International Swan Symposium: a Synthesis: in J. Sear and P.J. Bacon (eds) 1991. Proc. 3rd International Swan Symposium, Oxford 1989. *Wildfowl,* Supplement **1**: 7-14.

Easterbee, N. and Pitkin, P.H. 1984. *Survey of breeding birds on moorland in south Scotland and north England.* SFSU Report S13, SNH, unpubl.

Eggeling, W.J. 1960. *The Isle of May: a Scottish nature reserve.* Oliver and Boyd, Edinburgh.

Eggeling, W.J. 1974. The birds of the Isle of May. *Scott. Birds* **8**: supplement 93-148.

Etheridge, B., Summers, R.W. and Green, R.E. 1997. The effects of illegal killing and destruction of nests by humans on the population of Hen Harrier *Circus cyaneus* in Scotland. *J. Appl. Ecol.* **34**: 1081-1105.

Evans, A.D. 1988. *Individual differences in foraging behaviour, habitat selection and bill morphology of wintering Curlew,* Numenius arquata. PhD thesis, University of Edinburgh, unpubl.

Evans, A.H. 1911. *A Fauna of the Tweed Area.* David Douglas, Edinburgh.

Fisher, J. 1952. *The Fulmar.* Collins, London.

Fox, A.D. 1988. Breeding status of the Gadwall in Britain and Ireland. *Brit. Birds* **81**: 51-65.

Fox, A.D. 1991. History of Pochard breeding in Britain. *Brit. Birds* **84**: 83-98.

Galbraith, H., Furness, R.W. and Fuller, R.J. 1984. Habitats and distribution of waders breeding on Scottish agricultural land. *Scott. Birds* **13**: 98-107.

Galloway, B. and Meek, E.R. 1983. Northumberland's Birds. *Trans. Nat. Hist. Soc. of Northumbria*: **44**(3).

Gantlett, S. 1993. The status and separation of White-headed Duck and Ruddy Duck. *Birding World* **6**: 273-281.

Garden, E.A. 1958. The national census of heronries in Scotland 1954, with a summary of the 1928/29 census. *Bird Study* **5**: 90-109.

Gardner, M., McGuigan, C. and Porteous, M. 1984. Young Ornithologists' Club (Edinburgh Group) Water of Leith survey 1978 and 1983. *Lothian Bird Report* **1983**: 65-71.

Gibb, J. 1954. Feeding ecology of tits, with notes on Treecreeper and Goldcrest. *Ibis* **96**: 513-543.

Gibbons, D.W., Avery, M.I. and Brown, A.F. 1996. Population trends of breeding birds in the United Kingdom since 1800. *Brit. Birds* **89**: 291-305.

Gibbons, D.W., Reid, J.B. and Chapman, R.A. 1993. *The New Atlas of Breeding Birds in Britain and Ireland: 1988-1991.* Poyser, London.

Giles, N. 1990. Effects of increasing larval chironomid densities on the underwater feeding success of downy Tufted ducklings *Aythya fuligula. Wildfowl* **41**: 99-106.

Gill, D.J.D. 1993. Quail activity at Gowanhill. *North-east Scotland Bird Report* **1992**: 19-20.

Gooch, S., Baillie, S.R. and Birkhead, T.R. 1991. Magpie *Pica pica* and songbird populations. Retrospective investigation of trends in population density and breeding success. *J. Appl. Ecol.* **28**: 1068-1086.

Gordon, P.R. 1991. Cliff-nesting House Martins in East Lothian. *Lothian Bird Report* **1990**: 89.

Gregory, R.D., Carter, S.P. and Baillie, S.R. 1997. Abundance, distribution and habitat use of breeding Goosanders *Mergus merganser* and Red-breasted Mergansers *Mergus serrator* on British rivers. *Bird Study* **44**: 1-12.

Gregory, R.D. and Marchant, J.H. 1996. Population trends of Jays, Magpies, Jackdaws and Carrion Crows in the United Kingdom. *Bird Study* **43**: 28-37.

Groom, D.W. 1993. Magpie *Pica pica* predation on Blackbird *Turdus merula* nests in urban areas. *Bird Study* **40**: 55-62.

Guest, J.P., Elphick, D., Hunter, J.S.A. and Norman, D. 1992. *The Breeding Bird Atlas of Cheshire and Wirral.* Cheshire and Wirral Ornithological Society, Chester.

Hamilton, F.D. and Macgregor, K.S. 1960. The Birds of Aberlady Bay Nature Reserve. *Trans. of the East Lothian Antiquarian and Field Naturalists Society* **8**: 1-33.

Hancock, M., Baines, D., Gibbons, D., Etheridge, B. and Shepherd, M. (in press). The status of Black Grouse (*Tetrao tetrix*) in Britain 1995-96. *Bird Study*.

Harding, B.D. 1979. *Bedfordshire Bird Atlas: an atlas of the breeding birds in the county of Bedford from 1968 to 1977.* Bedfordshire Natural History Society, Luton.

Harris, M.P. 1984. *The Puffin.* Poyser, Calton.

Harris, M.P. and Galbraith, H. 1983. Seabird populations of the Isle of May. *Scott. Birds* **12**: 174-180.

Harris, M.P., Halley, D.J. and Wanless, S. 1996. Philopatry in the Common Guillemot *Uria aalge. Bird Study* **43**: 134-137.

Harris, M.P. and Murray, S. 1981. Monitoring of Puffin numbers at Scottish colonies. *Bird Study* **28**: 15-20.

Harris, M.P. and Wanless, S. 1990. Breeding success of British Kittiwakes *Rissa tridactyla* in 1986-88: evidence for changing conditions in the northern North Sea. *J. Appl. Ecol.* **27**: 172-187.

Harris, M.P. and Wanless, S. 1996. Differential responses of Guillemot *Uria aalge* and Shag *Phalacrocorax aristotelis* to a late winter wreck. *Bird Study* **43**: 220-230.

Harris, M.P., Wanless, S. and Smith, R.W.J. 1987. The breeding seabirds of the Firth of Forth, Scotland. *Proc. Royal Soc. Edinburgh* **93B**: 521-533.

Henderson, F. 1996. Surveys and Studies (Partridge and Grouse Survey 1994/1996). *West Lothian Bird Club Report* **1995**.

Holland, P.K., Robson, J.E. and Yalden, D.W. 1982. The status and distribution of the Common Sandpiper *Actitus hypoleucos* in the Peak District. *Naturalist* **107**: 77-86.

Holling, M. 1991. Roof-nesting gulls in Lothian. *Lothian Bird Report* **1990**: 99-100.

Holling, M. 1997. Are there any Marsh Tits left in Lothian? *Lothian Bird Report* **1995**: 109-110.

Holling, M. and McGarry, O. 1994. A review of the changing status of Buzzard in the Borders. *Borders Bird Report* **14**: 76-82.

Hoodless, A. 1995. Studies of West Palearctic Birds 195: Eurasian Woodcock *Scolopax rusticola. Brit. Birds* **88**: 578-591.

Hornbuckle, J. and Herringshaw, D. 1985. *Birds of the Sheffield Area including the North-east Peak District.* Sheffield Bird Study Group and Sheffield City Libraries.

Home, H.Douglas. 1950. Little Owls in Berwickshire. *Scott. Naturalist* **62**: 125-126.

Hurley, B. and Hurley, C. 1990. 1989 Nesting Starling Survey – Balerno area. *Lothian Bird Report* **1989**: 76-81.

James, P. 1996. *Birds of Sussex*. Sussex Ornithological Society.

Jardine, D.C. 1991. 1990 - the year of the Crossbill. *Birds in Northumbria* **1990**: 103-106.

Jardine, D.C. 1993. Crossbills in Scotland in 1990/91 – an invasion year. *Scott. Bird Report 1990*, **23**: 65-69.

Jenkins, D. 1971. Eiders nesting inland in East Lothian. *Scott. Birds*. **6**: 251-255.

Jenkins, D., Murray, M.G. and Hall, P. 1975. Structure and regulation of a Shelduck (*Tadorna tadorna* (L.)) population. *J. Anim. Ecol.* **44**: 201-231.

Kaiser, E. 1997. Sexual recognition of Common Swifts. *Brit. Birds* **90**: 167-174.

Kelly, G. 1986. *The Norfolk Bird Atlas*. Norfolk and Norwich Naturalists' Society, Hunstanton.

Keymer, R. 1980. The breeding birds of Red Moss nature reserve. *Edinburgh Ringing Group Report* **8**: 10-17.

Lack, P. 1986. *The Atlas of Wintering Birds in Britain and Ireland*. Poyser, Calton.

Little, B. and Davison, M. 1992. Merlins *Falco columbarius* using crow nests in Kielder Forest, Northumberland. *Bird Study* **39**: 13-16.

Little, B. and Furness, R.W. 1985. Long distance moult migration by British Goosanders *Mergus merganser*. *Ringing and Migration* **6**: 77-82.

Lloyd, C., Tasker, M.L. and Partridge, K. 1991. *The Status of Seabirds in Britain and Ireland*. Poyser, London.

Lockie, J.D. 1955. The breeding habits and food of Short-eared Owls after a vole plague. *Bird Study* **2**: 53-69.

McConachie, W. 1930. *The Glamour of the Glen*. Oliver and Boyd, Edinburgh.

McGinn, D. 1977. The alphabetical list of farms in NT51 having Swallows nesting in the summer of 1974. *Borders Biological Records Centre Bulletin* **1977**: 18.

McGrady, M.J. 1990. Sparrowhawk breeding within the City of Edinburgh. *Lothian Bird Report* **1989**: 82-86.

Madge, S. and Burn , H. 1988. *Wildfowl: an identification guide to the ducks, geese and swans of the world.*. Christopher Helm, London.

Marchant, J. 1997. Rooks rally. *BTO News* **209**: 6.

Marchant, J.H., Hudson, R., Carter, S.P. and Whittington, P.A. 1990. *Population Trends in British Breeding Birds*. BTO/NCC, Tring.

Marchant, J.H. and Hyde, P.A. 1980. Aspects of the distribution of riparian birds on waterways in Britain and Ireland. *Bird Study* **27**: 183-202.

Marquiss, M. 1989. Grey Herons *Ardea cinerea* breeding in Scotland: numbers, distribution, and census techniques. *Bird Study* **36**: 181-191.

Marquiss, M. and Duncan, K. 1994. Seasonal switching between habitats and changes in abundance of Goosanders *Mergus merganser* within a Scottish river system. *Wildfowl* **45**: 198-208.

Marquiss, M., Feltham, M.J. and Duncan, K. 1991. *Sawbill Ducks and Salmon*. ITE, Banchory.

Mearns, R. 1983. The status of the Raven in southern Scotland and Northumbria. *Scott. Birds* **12**: 211-218.

Meek, E.R. and Little, B. 1977. The spread of the Goosander in Britain and Ireland. *Brit. Birds* **70**: 229-237.

Meiklejohn, M.F.M., Andrew, D.G. and Macmillan, A.T. (eds). 1960. Current Notes. *Scott. Birds* **1**: 280-281.

Mikkola, H. 1983. *Owls of Europe*. Poyser, Calton.

Miller, A. and Porteous, M. 1989. Y.O.C. Edinburgh Group Water of Leith Survey 1988. *Lothian Bird Report* **1988**: 100-105.

Minot, E.O. and Perrins, C.M. 1986. Interspecific interference competition - nest sites for Blue and Great Tits. *J. Anim. Ecol.* **55**: 331-350.

Montier, D. 1977. *Atlas of Breeding Birds of the London Area*. Batsford, London.

Moore, N.P., Kelly, P.F., Lang, F.A, Lynch, J.M. and Langton, S.D. 1997. The Peregrine *Falco peregrinus* in quarries: current status and factors influencing occupancy in the Republic of Ireland. *Bird Study* **44**: 176-181.

Moss, D. and Moss, G.M. 1993. Breeding biology of the Little Grebe *Tachybaptus ruficollis* in Britain and Ireland. *Bird Study* **40**: 107-114.

Muirhead, G. 1889 and 1895. *The Birds of Berwickshire*. David Douglas, Edinburgh. 2 vols.

Munro, I. 1988. *Birds of the Pentland Hills*. Scottish Academic Press, Edinburgh.

Munro, J.H.B. 1970 Notes on the rookeries in the City of Edinburgh in 1970. *Scott. Birds* **6**: 169-170.

Murray, R. 1988. The 1987 Sawbill and River Birds Census. *Borders Bird Report* **1987**: 62-80.

Murray, R.D. 1985. The 1984 BTO Wood Warbler Survey. *Borders Bird Report* **1984**: 60-61.

Murray, R.D. 1986. *The Birds of the Borders*. SOC, Edinburgh.

Murray, R.D. 1991a. A survey of Tweeddale rookeries 1990. *Borders Bird Report* **12**: 72-76.

Murray, R.D. 1991b. Quail in Scotland 1989. *Scott. Bird Report 1989* **22**: 45-50.

Murray, R.D. 1991c. The first successful breeding of Nuthatch in Scotland. *Scott. Bird Report 1989* **22**: 51-55.

Murray, R.D. 1992. Goosanders in the Borders 1991. *Borders Bird Report* **13**: 65-77.

Murray, R.D., Bramhall, A.T. and Coleman, J. 1996. Breeding success of Mute Swan in the Scottish Borders. *Borders Bird Report* **16**: 70-72.

Murray, S. and Wanless, S. 1986. The status of the Gannet in Scotland 1984-85. *Scott. Birds* **14**: 74-85.

Murray, S. and Wanless, S. 1997. The status of the Gannet in Scotland in 1994-95. *Scott. Birds* **19**:10-27.

Nash, J.K. 1935. *The Birds of Midlothian*. Witherby, London.

Nelson, B. 1978. *The Gannet*. Poyser, Berkhamstead.

Nethersole-Thompson, D. and Nethersole-Thompson, M. 1986. *Waders, their Breeding Haunts and Watchers*. Poyser, Calton.

Newton, I. 1986. *The Sparrowhawk*. Poyser, Calton.

Northumberland Wildlife Trust. 1995. *Facts about Goshawks, including the Population in the English/Scottish Borders*. Northumberland Wildlife Trust.

O'Brien, M. 1994. *Survey of breeding waders on Scottish lowlands*. Interim report, RSPB, unpubl.

O'Brien, M. 1996. The numbers of breeding waders in lowland Scotland. *Scott. Birds* 18: 231-241.

O'Connor, R.J. and Shrubb, M. 1986. *Farming and Birds*. Cambridge University Press, Cambridge.

Ogilvie, M. and the Rare Breeding Birds Panel. 1996. Rare Breeding Birds in the United Kingdom in 1994. *Brit. Birds*. **89**: 387-417.

Ogilvie, M.A. 1986. The Mute Swan *Cygnus olor* in Britain1983. *Bird Study* **33**: 121-137.

Orchel, J. 1994. Forest nesting Merlins. *Scott. Wildlife* **22**: 18-21.

Ormerod, S.J., Allinson, N., Hudson, D. and Tyler, S.J. 1986. The distribution of breeding Dippers (*Cinclus cinclus* (L) Aves) in relation to stream acidity in upland Wales. *Freshwat. Biol.* **16**: 501-507.

Owen, M., Atkinson-Willes, G.L. and Salmon, D.G. 1986. *Wildfowl in Great Britain*. 2nd. edn. Cambridge University Press, Cambridge.

Parr, R. 1979. Sequential breeding by Golden Plovers. *Brit. Birds* **72**: 499-503.

Parr, S.J. 1994. Changes in the population size and nest sites of Merlins *Falco columbarius* in Wales between 1970 and 1991. *Bird Study* **41**: 42-47.

Parslow, J. 1973. *Breeding Birds of Britain and Ireland: a historical survey*. Poyser, Berkhamsted.

Patterson, I.J., and Ollason, J.G. 1991. *Modelling bird/habitat relationships in spruce forests in the northern uplands of Britain.* Report to the Forestry Commission.

Patterson, I.J., Ollason, J.G. and Doyle, P. 1995. Bird populations in upland spruce plantations in northern Britain. *Forest Ecology and Management* **79**: 107-131.

Petty, S.J., Patterson, I.J., Anderson, D.I.K., Little, B. and Davison, M. 1995. Numbers, breeding performance, and diet of the Sparrowhawk *Accipiter nisus* and Merlin *Falco columbarius* in relation to cone crops and seed-eating finches. *Forest Ecology and Management* **79**: 133-146.

Pienkowski, M.W. and Evans, P.R. 1982. Clutch parasitism and nesting interference between Shelducks at Aberlady Bay. *Wildfowl* **33**: 159-163.

Potts, G.R. 1969. The influence of eruptive movements, age, population size and other factors in the survival of the Shag (*Phalacrocorax aristotelis* (L.)). *J. Anim. Ecol.* **38**: 53-102.

Poxton, I.R. 1986. Breeding Ring Ouzels in the Pentland Hills. *Scott. Birds* **14**: 44-48.

Poxton, I.R. 1987. Breeding status of the Ring Ouzel in S.E. Scotland 1985-86. *Scott. Birds* **14**: 205-208.

Prestt, I. and Mills, D.H. 1966. A census of the Great Crested Grebe in Britain, 1965. *Bird Study* **13**: 163-203.

Ratcliffe, D. 1997. *The Raven: A Natural History in Britain and Ireland.* Poyser, London.

Ratcliffe, D.A. 1976. Observations on the breeding of the Golden Plover in Great Britain. *Bird Study* **23**: 63-116.

Ratcliffe, D.A. 1984. Tree nesting by Peregrines in Britain and Ireland. *Bird Study* **31**: 232-233.

Ratcliffe, D.A. 1990. *Bird Life of Mountain and Upland.* Cambridge University Press, Cambridge.

Raven, S.J. and Coulson, J.C. 1997. The distribution and abundance of *Larus* gulls nesting on buildings in Britain and Ireland. *Bird Study* **44**: 13-34.

Rawcliffe, C.P. 1958. The Scottish Mute Swan Census, 1955-56. *Bird Study* **5**: 45-55.

Rebecca, G.W. 1992. Merlins breeding in mature conifer plantation. *North-east Scotland Bird Report* **1991**: 61-62.

Rebecca, G.W. and Bainbridge, I. (in press). The status of breeding Merlin *Falco columbarius* in Britain in 1993-94. *Bird Study.*

Redpath, S.M. and Thirgood, S.J. 1997. *Birds of Prey and Red Grouse.* Stationery Office, London.

Riddle, G.S. 1979. The Kestrel in Ayrshire 1970-78. *Scott. Birds* **10**: 201-216.

Rintoul, L.J. and Baxter, E.V. 1935. *A Vertebrate Fauna of Forth.* Oliver and Boyd, Edinburgh.

Ritchie, J. and Grimshaw, P.H. 1925. Greenshank nesting in Scottish Lowlands. *Scottish Naturalist* 107.

Rossiter, B.N. 1988. A survey of breeding Lapwings and other waders 1987. *Birds in Northumbria* **1987**: 89-91.

Sage, B. and Whittington, P.A. 1985. The 1980 sample survey of rookeries. *Bird Study* **32**: 77-81.

Sage, B.L. and Vernon, J.D.R. 1978. The 1975 National Survey of Rookeries. *Bird Study* **25**: 64-86.

Sandeman, G.L. 1963. Roseate and Sandwich Tern colonies in the Forth and neighbouring areas. *Scott. Birds* **2**: 286-293.

Scott, G. 1992. Preliminary results of the Edinburgh University Blue Tit study. *Lothian Bird Report* **1991**: 89-90.

Scottish Raptor Study Groups. 1997. The illegal persecution of raptors in Scotland. *Scott. Birds* **19**: 65-85.

Sharrock, J.T.R. 1976. *The Atlas of Breeding Birds in Britain and Ireland.* BTO, Tring.

Shawyer, C.R. 1987. *The Barn Owl in the British Isles.* The Hawk Trust, London.

Simms, E. 1978. *British Thrushes.* Collins, London.

Sitters, H.P. 1988. *Tetrad Atlas of the Breeding Birds of Devon.* Devon Birdwatching and Preservation Society, Yelverton, Devon.

Smith, G.D. 1994. Buzzards in Lothian – A Success Story. *Lothian Bird Report* **1993**: 108-110.

Smith, K.W., Dee, C.W., Fearnside, J.D., *et al.* 1993. *The Breeding Birds of Hertfordshire.* Hertfordshire Natural History Society.

Smith, R.W.J. 1966. The Forth Island bird counts. *Edinburgh Nat. Hist. Soc. Newsletter* **1965**:12-14.

Smith, R.W.J. 1969. Scottish Cormorant colonies. *Scott. Birds* **5**: 363-378.

Smith, R.W.J. 1974. SOC Great Crested Grebe enquiry 1973. *Scott. Birds* **8**: 151-159.

Smout, A-M. 1986. *The Birds of Fife.* John Donald, Edinburgh.

Snow, B.K. and Snow, D.W. 1982. Territory and social organisation of Dunnocks *Prunella modularis. J. Yamashina Inst. Orn.* **14**: 281-292.

Speak, P.W. 1994. Sand Martins in Lothian, 1993. *Lothian Bird Report* **1993**: 115-118.

Stone, B.H., Sears, J., Cranswick, P.A., Gregory, R.D., Gibbons, D.W., Rehfisch, M.M., Aebischer, N.J. and Reid, J.B. 1997. Population estimates of birds in Britain and in the United Kingdom. *Brit. Birds* **90**: 1-22.

Stroud, D.A., Reed, T.M. and Harding, N.J. 1990. Do moorland breeding waders avoid plantation edges? *Bird Study* **37**: 177-186.

Summers-Smith, D. 1963. *The House Sparrow.* Collins, London.

Summers-Smith, J.D. 1988. *The Sparrows.* Poyser, Calton.

Summers-Smith, J.D. 1989. A history of the status of the Tree Sparrow *Passer montanus* in the British Isles. *Bird Study* **36**: 23-31.

Tasker, M.L., Jones, P.H., Blake, B.F. and Dixon, T.J. 1985. The marine distribution of the Gannet *Sula bassana* in the North Sea. *Bird Study* **32**: 82-90.

Tatner, P. 1978. A review of House Martins *Delichon urbica* in part of south Manchester, 1975. *Naturalist* **103**: 59-68.

Taylor, D.W., Davenport, D.L. and Flegg, J.J.M. 1981. *The Birds of Kent: a review of their status and distribution.* Kent Ornithological Society, Meophan.

Taylor, I.R. 1993. *Barn Owls: An action plan and practical guide for their conservation in Scotland.* University of Edinburgh, Edinburgh.

Taylor, K., Hudson, R. and Horne, G. 1988. Buzzard breeding distribution and abundance in Britain and Northern Ireland in 1983. *Bird Study* **35**: 109-118.

Thom, V.M. 1986. *Birds in Scotland.* Poyser, Calton.

Thompson, K.R., Brindley, E. and Heubeck, M. 1996. *Seabird numbers and breeding success in Britain and Ireland, 1995.* JNCC UK Nature Conservation No. 19, Peterborough.

Thompson, K.R., Brindley, E. and Heubeck, M. 1997. *Seabird numbers and breeding success in Britain and Ireland, 1996.* JNCC UK Nature Conservation No. 20, Peterborough.

Thomson, D.L. and Dougall, T.W. 1988. The status of Wigeon in Ettrick Forest. *Scott. Birds* **15**: 61-64.

Thomson, D.L., Douglas-Home, H., Furness, R.W. and Monaghan, P. 1996. Breeding success and survival in the common swift *Apus apus*: a long-term study on the effects of weather. *J. Zool., Lond.* **239**: 29-38.

Tucker, G.M., Heath, M.F., Tomsalojc, L. and Grimmett, R.F.A. 1994. *Birds in Europe: their conservation status.* Bird Life International, Cambridge.

Turnbull, W.P., 1867. *The Birds of East Lothian.* Privately published, Glasgow.

Tyler, S.J., Lewis, J., Venables, A.J. and Walton, J. 1987. *The Gwent Atlas of Breeding Birds.* Gwent Ornithological Society.

Village, A. 1990. *The Kestrel.* Poyser, London.

Voous, K.H. 1960. *Atlas of European Birds.* Nelson, Elsevier.

Walsh, P.M., Brindley, E. and Heubeck, M. 1995. *Seabird numbers and breeding success in Britain and Ireland, 1994.* JNCC UK Nature Conservation No.18, Peterborough.

Wanless, S. 1988. The recolonisation of the Isle of May by Common and Arctic Terns. *Scott. Birds* **15**: 1-8.

Wanless S., Harris, M.P. and Morris, J.A. 1991. Foraging range and feeding locations of Shags *Phalacrocorax aristotelis* during chick rearing. *Ibis* **133**: 30-36.

Waterston, G. 1968. Black-browed Albatross summering on the Bass Rock. *Scott. Birds* **5**: 20-23.

Williamson, K. 1974. Breeding birds in the deciduous woodlands of Mid-Argyll, Scotland. *Bird Study* **21**: 29-44.

Wilson, J.D. 1996. The breeding biology and population history of the Dipper *Cinclus cinclus* on a Scottish river system. *Bird Study* **43**: 108-118.

Wood, A.D. 1990. The 1987/88 survey of rookeries in the Clyde area. *Clyde Birds* **2**: 74-77.

Yalden, D.W. and Pearce-Higgins, J.W. 1997. Density – dependence and winter weather as factors affecting the size of a population of Golden Plovers *Pluvialis apricaria*. *Bird Study* **44**: 227-234.

Yalden, D.W. and Yalden, P.E. 1989. The sensitivity of breeding Golden Plovers *Pluvialis apricaria* to human intruders. *Bird Study* **36**: 49-55.

Yalden, D.W. and Yalden, P.E. 1991. Efficiency of censusing Golden Plovers. *Wader Study Group Bull.* **62**: 32-36.

Young, G. and Duffy, K. 1985. Night Herons in Scotland. *Royal Society of Scotland. Annual Report 1984*, 40-46.